PRIVATE CAPITAL

Volume I: Funds

Eli Talmor   Florin Vasvari

www.privatecapitalbook.com

Private Capital:
Volume I: Funds
Copyright © 2020 by Eli Talmor and Florin Vasvari
Edited by Kontent360
Printed in the United Kingdom

ISBN 978-1-9162110-4-9

About the Authors

Eli Talmor is professor at London Business School and founder of its Institute of Private Equity. He practices venture capital and is a serial cornerstone investor with multiple exits. He also served on the advisory board of the African Venture Capital Association. Professor Talmor is a prominent speaker to business executives worldwide. He was asked by the UK Parliament to provide a leading testimony on private equity and to advise the UK Prime Minister office. Professor Talmor was previously on the finance faculty at the University of California (UCLA and Irvine) and the Wharton School. He holds a Ph.D. from the University of North Carolina at Chapel Hill and a B.Sc. (Cum Laude) from the Technion – Israel Institute of Technology.

Florin Vasvari is professor at London Business School and head of its Accounting faculty department. He is also the Academic Director of the Private Equity Institute. His research and consulting covers private equity and debt markets, and he has published extensively in top tier academic journals. Professor Vasvari is regularly invited to present his research at major business schools in the United States and serves on the board of top academic journals. Professor Vasvari also sits on the advisory boards and investment committees of private equity firms. He holds a Ph.D. from the University of Toronto, Rotman School of Management and an M.A. from University of Toronto, Department of Economics.

To Dahlia, Yael, Lauren and my grandchildren

Eli Talmor

To Bianca, Albert and Mirela

Florin Vasvari

Contents

PREFACE TO VOLUME I

By all measures, the continuous growth and expansion of the private capital asset class has been astounding. The industry has grown over 200 times in a quarter of a century, and is estimated to triple further over the next ten years. Once regarded as a small blip at the margin of alternative investments, private equity has become an asset class of its own and moved to the centre stage of capital markets. With its long-term record of successful performance, the private equity investment model has benefited from an unprecedented increase in the capital allocation by pensions, endowments and sovereign wealth funds around the world. Furthermore, the success of private equity's corporate governance model, which aligns investors with fund managers very well, has led to an expansion to other types of assets in private markets such as infrastructure, real estate and private credit, and subsequently to the rebranding of the industry as *private capital*. This expansion has allowed institutional investors to gain exposure to private assets on a massive scale.

From a pedagogical perspective, we continue to be amazed by the wide range of issues that are covered by the private capital asset class. Nearly all business aspects are at the heart of its matter – valuation, corporate governance, strategy, operations, financial structuring, asset allocation, risk management, entrepreneurship, reporting, tax, regulation and government policy.

The two-volume book provides a comprehensive overview of the main topics in private capital that are relevant to graduate students, investors, regulators and other professionals seeking to understand the many facets of the asset class, as well as private equity practitioners who wish to have a broader analysis of the sector. The book has grown out of our teaching the popular Private Equity and Venture Capital course and the senior executive education program at London Business School. Over the years, our focus has broadened considerably as the industry matured. Working closely with the global professional private capital community proved particularly valuable in generating up-to-date knowledge and expertise on the industry trends and best practice.

Expanding on our previous textbook *International Private Equity* published in 2011, the current book is arranged in two volumes which provide a comprehensive overview of the main topics in private capital. This volume is devoted to fund level aspects: private capital as an asset class, fund structuring and types, performance measurement, fundraising, fund due diligence, accounting and reporting, governance, fund administration, fund taxation, risk management and ESG. Special chapters are devoted to cover important specializations of the private capital industry such as secondaries, private debt, infrastructure, natural resources and real estate funds.

Volume II is devoted to an analysis at the investment level. It covers valuation of private equity companies, deal screening and due diligence, acquisition finance, LBO transactions and modelling, post deal execution, harvesting of private equity investments, operation in emerging markets and more. A major part of Volume II is dedicated to early-stage investing: angel investing, venture capital, incubators and accelerators, university technology transfers, and alternative sources of funding such as governmental support initiatives, crowdfunding, corporate venture capital and venture lending.

For each chapter we have asked a leading professional who is expert in that specific field to write a text box, commenting on practical aspects and current trends. We are thankful to all the distinguished contributors.

Our thanks go to our students, private equity partners, lawyers, scientists and other professionals who reviewed, commented and helped with research on the chapters: Fiona Agha, Gus Black, Anthony Cecil, Heloisa Chaney, Amanda Das, Robert Gaut, Sam Gautam, Marian Gheorghe, Giri Girisanthan, Edward Gera,

Hanna Grahn, Lemy Gresh, Raul Gutierrez, Brenlen Jinkens, Johan Johansson, Haim Kedar-Levy, Therése Lennehag, Kevin Lester, Sarah Lobbardi, Ravi Longia, Arnold May, Chris McDermott, Christophe Michotte, Martin Milev, Eduard Motta, Jörg Mugrauer, Joseph Newton, Mark O'Hare, Justin Patrick, Dwight Poler, Quentin Python, Paurnakrishna Radhakrishnan, Sandra Reich, Marine Richard, Carlos Sanchez, Michael Schad, Francois Scheepers, Stephen Severo, Ira Shaw, Jim Strang, Alan Synnott, Joe Topley, Avi Turetsky and Ron Yachini.

The project was most effectively and professionally directed by our managing editor Michal Bohanes. Catie Phares provided exceptional editorial services. We owe them both a great deal of thanks.

Eli Talmor and Florin Vasvari, August 2020

1 Private Capital Overview

I am a better investor because I am a businessman and a better businessman because I am an investor.
Warren Buffett

INTRODUCTION

In November 2004, private equity hit the front lines of the financial media in a major way: on the cover of the *Economist* and being the subject of the leading article titled: *The new kings of capitalism*. The subtitle was more skeptical: "In two decades, private-equity firms have moved from the outer fringe to the centre of the capitalist system. But can they keep it up?" In the years that have passed since then, the industry has quintupled. This figure becomes all the more impressive when considering the ongoing massive distributions to investors and the additional fire powder we will later refer to as shadow capital.[1]

The nature of private equity funds was not understood well in the past, leading to times instances where their public image was somewhat controversial. This was particularly the case with buyout funds during the 1980s as well as the mid-2000s whereby many mega public-to-private buyouts took place. The change came during the latest global financial crisis when private equity was appreciated for its resilience, as well as the subsequent years where its modus operandi has proven both powerful and successful.

Private equity is the name given to that part of the asset management industry where investments are made into companies which are usually not quoted in the public markets. Private equity funds act as intermediaries between institutional and other long-term investors and private companies seeking capital. The capital is provided to a wide array of companies, ranging from business start-ups to very large and mature companies. The funds provide transitional capital that fits companies in need for growth capital or for turning around. The style of investing is active with engagements in the corporate governance of the companies that receive capital and striving to add value by providing relevant advice.

Investments in these companies are typically made through special purpose fund structures with finite life (typically ten years), which are managed by a team of professionals, called the *general partner (GP)*. The GPs deploy the capital and mange it according to predefined investment strategies that are accepted by fund investors. The investors do not take part in the day-to-day management of the investments, and their liability is limited to their capital commitment to the fund. Thereby they are referred to as *limited partners (LP)*. The LPs are mainly institutional investors, typically pension funds, insurance companies, endowments and sovereign wealth funds. These investors either make their investments into the asset class directly or via a specialist private equity investment manager (a so-called "fund of funds"). Investments by individual investors are typically limited to family offices and ultra-high-net-worth individuals. Given that investors in private equity funds need to qualify as accredited investors, the asset class is subject to less regulation than publicly listed companies, adding more flexibility into their operation.[2] Exhibit 1 portrays in a most crude way the

---

[1] For every year since 2010, the aggregate distributions to investors have outpaced fund draw downs (known as capital calls), leading to positive net cash flows to investors. Since 2013, the ratio of distribution to contributions exceeded 2 annually.

[2] Retail investors can only invest in the asset class through listed private equity funds.

structure of a private equity type fund although similar structured are used for private debt, real estate or infrastructure funds.

Exhibit 1: Schematic structure of a private equity investment vehicle

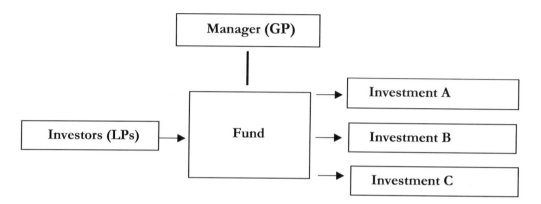

The funds are structured as long-term investment vehicles to which LPs commit their capital for the entirety of the fund's life. Unlike asset classes where money is drawn down in one tranche, private equity commitments are called at the discretion of the GPs once concrete investment opportunities need to be funded and is returned as soon as a liquidity event is attained. It prevents cash from sitting idle, boosts the rate of return and instils a mind-set of discipline and timeliness. Having access to undrawn capital commitments, the so-called *dry powder*, proves most effective in situations where the ability to transact fast can seize highly attractive opportunities particularly during financial droughts and accompanying recession periods.

At its highest level, the private equity industry is subdivided into buyout and venture capital funds. Both buyout funds and venture capital funds share similar organizational structures in terms of management fee structure and longevity. However, they are quite different in their investment strategy. Buyout funds usually focus on established and mature companies rather than young businesses and the use of debt to complement equity financing. They also tend to be larger in size than the venture funds. Venture capital funds focus on young high-growth companies, typically technology enabled or science based. In both cases the general partners play an active role in the ongoing lives of their portfolio companies, appoint management, control the board, set a strategic plan and closely monitor its delivery. A successful investment would see the execution of the strategy and an outright exit within several years, five years on average, aiming not to exceed the remaining term of the fund's ten-year life. Both buyout and venture funds follow a predefined investment thesis. This applies to the target company size such as large buyouts vs. a mid-market strategy; the geographical mandate (global vs. regional such as CEE vs. a specific country); the stage of the target companies (e.g., early stage venture vs. growth and late stage); sector specializations (technology, healthcare, luxury goods, to name a few); and investment strategy (e.g., cross border such western venture capital funds dedicated to investment in China).[3]

---

[3] A more technical distinction between venture capital and buyouts is that the latter which invest in mature companies buy the share of the current owners and hence the majority of its investment is as a secondary share transaction. In contrast, venture capital injects cash into the company through the issuance of new shares, where the entrepreneur is not bought out but should remain committed to the business.

Private equity funds differ significantly from mutual funds and other vehicles dedicated to the public markets. For instance, buyout funds need to limit the number of portfolio companies to 10-15 per fund to allow the GPs ample resources and attention to work with companies' management and influence the destiny of these companies. Prior to investing they conduct extensive due diligence and gain significant access to the views of the management of these companies, industry professionals as well as their own domain expertise. On occasions it takes years to track a company and groom the relationships before investing in it. With a focus on strategic and operational aspects alongside financial engineering, buyout funds act with more sound information and stronger controls over their portfolio companies than funds investing in the stock market.

The success of its corporate governance model has led to a massive expansion of private equity beyond its traditional domains of buyouts and growth capital to new types of assets. In particular, with the increasing limitations on loans by banks, the industry has strongly expanded into private debt instruments. Other lucrative sectors of great interest for deploying capital are real estate, infrastructure and natural resources. Exhibits 2 and 3 portray the growth in asset under management for private equity and private debt funds. The overall growth into new sectors has reached such a magnitude that the industry has now commonly rebranded itself from private equity to *private capital* to encapsulate its broader domain.[4]

Exhibit 2: Private equity funds: assets under management ($bn), 2000-2018

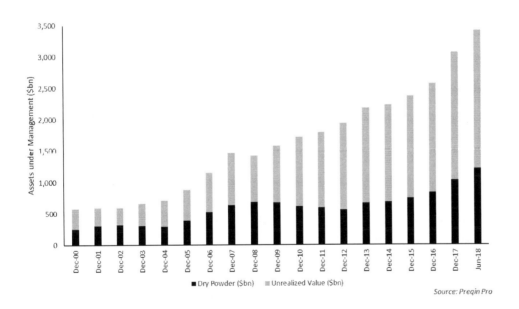

Source: Preqin Pro

---

[4] All the data in this chapter is based on Preqin (2019) unless otherwise specified.

Exhibit 3: Private debt funds: assets under management ($bn), 2009-2019

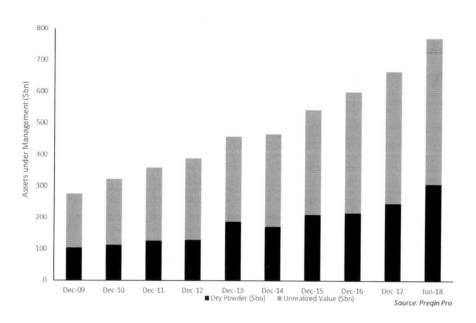

Source: Preqin Pro

HISTORICAL BACKGROUND

The origins of private equity funds

Private equity as a vehicle for institutional investment in private companies started in venture capital. The American Research & Development Corporation (ARD) was founded in Boston in 1946 by General Georges Doriot to encourage private sector investments in small firms. It was the first early stage investment vehicle that did not depend on wealthy individuals and families. ARD is also credited for formalizing the model of due diligence and post investment monitoring. The second firm that is associated with the birth of venture capital is J.H. Whitney & Co., also formed in 1946 by John Hay Whitney together with Benno Schmidt who coined the phrase venture capital to distinguish their activity from investment banking.

However, the big boost for venture capital in the U.S. came in the 1970s; first with the reduction of the capital gains tax, followed by the enacting of the Employee Retirement Income Security Act (ERISA), a set of pension reforms designed to help U.S. pension managers into more balanced custodianship. This act was clarified in 1979 to explicitly permit pension funds to invest in alternative assets such as private equity funds. Consequently, in the late 1970s and early 1980s pension funds started to add a small amount of venture capital to their portfolio and a few university endowments joined in.

Across the Atlantic, the first venture capital fund in Britain was the International and Commercial Financial Corporation (later rebranded as 3i), established in 1945 to fund small and medium sized businesses. Funding was exclusively provided by large banks to rebuild the British industry following the Second World War. Whilst having limited partners, this lacked today's key finite fund structure element and was not aimed at new companies.

As for the buyout sector, the original leverage buyout transactions (LBOs) took place in the 1950s and 1960s, but were performed by publicly traded holding companies, notably by Warren Buffett (Berkshire Hathaway) and Saul Steinberg (Reliance) amongst others. These investment vehicles targeted the same type of companies and utilized similar acquisition tactics. Thus, they could be considered the forerunners of the later private equity firms.

The first of today's leading private equity firms, Warburg Pincus, was formed in 1966 and had to raise money from investors one deal at a time. TA Associates followed in 1968 with an early focus on venture and growth capital. Certain other premier private equity firms today were established in the 1970s including Thomas Lee Partners in 1974 which was amongst the earliest independent firms that focused on the acquisition of companies with leverage financing, followed by Clayton, Dubilier & Rice and KKR (Kohlberg Kravis Roberts) both in 1978. In Europe, Cinven was founded in 1977 and was financed by three UK pension funds (British Coal, the Railway Industry and Barclays Bank).

The rise and fall of corporate raiding and junk bonds

During the 1980s, the private equity industry capitalized on the acquisition of poorly run public companies and corporate divestitures. There was a wave of highly leveraged buyouts of large and well-known corporations. These acquisitions were most often viewed as hostile by the management of the targeted companies, leading the naming of the acquirers as corporate raiders. Funding of the hostile takeovers were mostly provided by the investment banking firm of Drexel Burnham Lambert which has pioneered and stretched to the limit the concept of high-yield debt financing, known as junk bonds. For example, when KKR bought America's Safeway supermarket chain in 1986, it borrowed 97% of the USD 4.8 billion the deal cost. The practice of junk bond financing was extremely controversial in the media and within the business community. The highly leveraged transactions often resulted in major layoffs or a variety of other corporate restructuring activities. It popularized the non-glamorous term of asset stripping, tattooing the private equity industry for decades long after the orientation and practices have radically changed to business growth and an operational focus.

One of the final major buyouts of the 1980s proved to be its most ambitious and set both a high-water mark and the beginning of its end. In 1989, KKR completed a $31.1 billion takeover of RJR Nabisco, infamously chronicled in the movie *Barbarians at the Gate*. It was by far the largest leveraged buyout deal in history and remained as such till the present time in real terms. The deal put the leveraged buyout form of investment at the forefront of the public and regulatory scrutiny with a particular attention to the practice of junk bonds. The boom and bust of leverage buyout in their original form of asset stripping was culminated by the rise and fall of Drexel Burnham Lambert under the leadership of Michael Milliken, leading to his indictment. The sudden collapse of the high-yield bond market was followed by a recession (1990–1992) due to a crisis triggered by savings-and-loan institutions in the U.S. The bond market recovered very slowly after this episode, resulting in a very low level of activity in the private equity industry for almost five years.

The foundation of today's form of private equity

In parallel to the junk bonds cycle, the 1980s also witnessed the birth of most of today's other private equity global leaders. Apax Partners, one of Europe's leading private equity firms, has its origin in venture capital on both sides of the Atlantic. It pioneered the American venture capital style across Europe, raising its first European fund in 1981 before moving exclusively upstream to buyouts. Other Pan European leaders were also formed during that era. CVC Capital Partners was founded in 1981 originally as the European arm of Citicorp Venture Capital focusing on both early stage ventures and buyouts. Similarly, many other leading

European private equity firms originated as arms of financial institutions; notably Permira in 1985 originally branded Schroder Ventures and BC Partners a year later as Baring Capital Investors.[5] At the same time in the U.S., General Atlantic was founded in New York in 1980 by billionaire and philanthropist Charles F. Feeney to focus on growth capital. Bain Capital and Advent International were formed in Boston in 1984 followed by Carlyle in Washington DC in 1987. The growth of private equity can be illustrated by comparing Advent's first fund of $14 million in 1985 to their latest $17.5 billion fund raised in June 2019. Similarly, the first funds of Apax in 1981 consisted of £10 million for European ventures and $25 million for US buyouts, compared to Apax $9 billion hard-cap on Fund IX of which $7.9 billion first-close has been secured in June 2016.

It is worth nothing that in both Europe and U.S. the background of the early founders was in corporate finance, primarily from investment banks such as Bear Stearns and Lehman Brothers. Other founding partners were lawyers. Exceptionally for that time, the background of Bain Capital's founders was in consulting, where Bill Bain proposed to Mitt Romney to invest in companies and apply Bain's consulting techniques to improve operations.

Riding the tides of the market cycles: 1990-2007

Throughout the 1990s, debt financing played a less prominent role. First, the Telecommunications Act of 1996, a major overhaul of the U.S. telecommunications law, fostered competition and fueled private equity investments in the sector. Second, the private equity industry was driven by the accelerated economic expansion. This period saw the emergence of more institutionalized private equity firms and a maturing of the investor base. In particular, venture capital firms benefited from a huge surge of interest in the new internet and computer technologies being developed in the late 1990s. These firms started raising greater pools of capital to finance larger deals at higher valuations. This boom ended, however, when the dotcom technology bubble burst in 2000. Over the next two years, many venture capital firms were forced to significantly write off their fund investments. Meanwhile, the leveraged buyout market also declined dramatically. Many buyout funds invested heavily in the telecommunications sector which suffered from the waning of the technology sector in the years following the dotcom bust and also from the corporate sector overbidding on the 3G mobile phone licenses.

The private equity industry recovered relatively quickly from the slump. By 2003 deal activity had exceeded the peak prior to the two-year recession, Throughout the next several years, private equity rode a credit bubble to record deal values. The buyout boom was not limited to the U.S. but also spread in Europe and the Asia–Pacific region and was driven primarily by the availability of syndicated bank debt. Leveraged lending grew larger and more complex than ever before, and investor demand for structured finance vehicles such as collateralized loan obligations (CLOs) powered the market for leveraged loans to new heights.

The combination of decreasing interest rates, relaxing lending standards and regulatory changes for publicly traded companies (specifically the Sarbanes-Oxley Act) would set the stage for large publicly traded companies taken private by syndications of private equity firms, in a process known as club deals.

The global financial crisis in 2008 and its aftermath

---

[5] Among the earlier private equity firms in the continent Chequers in France was founded in 1984, Quadriga in Germany in 1988 (originally part of Citicorp Venture Capital) and Nordic Capital and IK Investment Partners were both formed in 1989 in the Nordic region.

The global financial crisis following the burst of the credit bubble in 2008 had a direct impact on the private equity industry. This was a result of the abrupt economic slowdown, extreme uncertainty in the financial markets and the virtual evaporation of liquidity in the debt markets. Whereas the drop was most dramatic in the buyout industry's traditionally strong North American and European market, also deals in the fast-growing Asia–Pacific markets perceived a certain slowdown. Venture capital deals were also in decline.

Fundraising also decreased significantly, initially coming almost to a halt and then new funds being smaller and taking longer to close. Cash was king after the crisis and the sentiment to make long term investments was repressed. One factor that inhibited new commitments to the asset class was the portfolio constraint of many LPs. Given that private equity investments were valued at historical costs which were not changing, the de facto percentage allocation to private equity as a percentage of total assets under management rose sharply as the value of publicly traded securities fell (the so-called *denominator* effect). A cash flow imbalance between continuing capital calls and the stop in distributions further contributed to the investors lukewarm and greatly reduced appetite to commit to new funds. However, as a whole, private equity was able to make investments on a massive scale when few others were able to do so. This helped spin again the wheels of the economy and demonstrated the role of private equity in critical times, improving its image in the eyes of policy makers and the media.

An added consequence of the global financial crisis was the tightening of regulation. Regulatory oversight of alternative investments has increased, mainly due to the perception that it has contributed to the severity of the credit crisis. In 2010, lawmakers in the U.S. passed the Dodd–Frank Wall Street Reform and Consumer Protection Act which requires private equity funds to register with the Securities and Exchange Commission. Within the European Union, the Alternative Investment Fund Managers Directive 2011 (AIFMD) imposed a regulatory framework which requires funds to obtain authorization and make various disclosures as a condition of operating anywhere within the EU (the so-called *passport*).

But as a whole, the operation of the private equity asset class emerged strongly. Very few of the deals made at the peak of the market prior to the crisis (i.e., deals highly leveraged and at high entry multiples) actually ended up with loses. Despite some predictions, for the vast majority of the cases, a sharp focus on the operation and governance of the portfolio companies proved to be relatively effective in roaring out of the recession unscathed.

The last decade experienced a recovery of the world economy post many rounds of monetary easing and overall strong capital markets. Alongside the revival of funding there has been downward pressure on returns globally. This, combined with high volatility in many parts of the global market, forced investors to look for alternative investments that can deliver better risk-adjusted returns. Consequently, investors' asset allocation started to focus more on the private capital market leading to (i) a rising allocation to alternative funds, (ii) longer-term investments, and (iii) a greater emphasis on post-investment management. All three strategies were aligned with whatever private capital markets could offer, explaining why the private markets became increasingly popular during the post-crisis years.

To summarize, from a $30 billion allocation in the early 90s, the private equity industry grew over 200 times in less than a quarter of a century. Once regarded as a small blip at the margin of alternative investments, private equity moved to the centre stage of capital markets with a long-term record of success and experiencing an unprecedented increase in the capital allocations made by institutional investors.

The Covid-19 pandemic crisis in 2020

As the COVID-19 started to conquer the world in January 2020, governments tried to save lives by restricting travel and locking down economic activities, plunging the world economy into a massive recession. Nationwide lockdowns caused an unprecedented spike in joblessness around the world. Various institutions forecasted that the drop in real global GDP in 2020 will surpass the declines seen at the peak of global financial crisis in 2008-2009. The economy will truly be in uncharted waters. With so much uncertainty, LPs are justifiably very concerned about the pontential impact of this crisis on their portfolios.

Most private capital funds tend to exhibit high levels of cyclicality, calling down more capital in the years leading up to a crisis but less during the crisis. However, a survey of the market provided by Campbell Lutyens, a well known placement agent, found that many funds started to call more capital in 2020 to pay off their bank borrowings (often called subscription lines), to support portfolio companies under stress because of the crisis and to invest in new deals at lower valuations. However, the clearing of subscription lines and capital infusions or investments may put off capital calls in 2021, giving LPs some breathing room and allowing them more time to prepare for these liquidity needs. Based on previous crises, capital call sizes will fall in the coming quarters as deal activity slows down.

The Covid-19 crisis is likely to lead to a steep drop in the frequency and magnitude of distributions in the near term. Not only are GPs unlikely to sell when prices of portfolio companies are down at least 20% to 30% from their 2019 year-end marks, but with credit markets freezing up, dividend recaps will also become less frequent. Since many LPs recycle cash distributions into capital calls for privat capital funds they committed to recently, they will need to tap into their portfolios for additional liquidity. While in normal times, about 50% to 60% of funds that are four years and older have distributions in a given quarter, in a recession, that percentage can drop below 40%. For the funds that do distribute capital back to LPs, the distribution sizes fall sharply being a fraction of the typical amount. Therefore, LPs should be ready for capital calls to far outstrip distributions and be ready to fund regular levels of calls during the coming quarters without much assistance from distributions.

Looking ahead, the LPs should be planning for another period in which buyout funds become net cash flow negative in their portfolios. This swing to net cash flow negative territory will probably be more severe than in past crises because of subscription credit lines. Also, it may not be isolated to buyout funds but will affect also other private capital funds such as real assets and venture funds. For institutional investors with predefined liabilities, such as an endowments or pension plans, the need to fund capital calls from exiting other investments at depressed prices may wreak further havoc on their portfolios. Alternatively, this crisis may present new investment opportunities for the LPs that can act quickly and take advantage of the situation. Some very large LPs has already confirmed they have cash to invest especially in funds that can exploit the market dislocations such as distressed and special situations funds. The history tells us that funds that did the bulk of their investing at lower prices in past downturns were able to record significantly higher returns. This is likely one of the best times in recent history to allocate capital to private funds because fund managers can invest at depressed prices.

Anecdotally, many fund managers have been more aggressive in this crisis than they were following the great financial crisis in 2008-2009 when moving too slowly proved detrimental to eventual fund performance. Large fund managers are sitting on billions in committed capital and reportedly are eyeing deals in the sectors most negatively affected by the crisis such as energy, transportation, leisure or hospitality. Meanwhile, healthcare, communication-centric companies or online businesses have experienced a boon from the need of remote healthcare and the flood of online traffic as people work from home and offices go virtual.

With any crisis comes opportunity, though, and the eventual recovery will likely generate significant returns for the institutional investors that are able to strike at the right time and invest in the right assets. Distressed assets may remain that way only temporarily, opening the door for opportunistic managers that have dry powder at their disposal.

WHY PRIVATE CAPITAL?

The private capital market

Alternative investments consist of assets other than financial securities that are traded over public markets, with underlying assets covering private equity companies, real estate, infrastructure, natural resources, etc. These assets have certain characteristics that are different to publicly traded assets. The two key differences of Private Equity are the engaged-ownership governance model and that being untraded provides more a long term outlook, patience and stability. Investing in alternative assets can therefore improve the returns and reduce the volatility for the overall portfolio of an institutional investor, which has led to the increased popularity of private capital with these investors. The outcomes of the predominant factors above are:

- Private equity assets produced more attractive long-term average returns. According to one of the most reputable sources, Cambridge Associates, the 10-year and 20-year average annual compound return for private equity funds around the world were 12% and 15%, respectively. The 10-year and 20-year average annual compounded return for the leading indices around the world were 6% and 7%, only half the returns for the private equity funds. Exhibit 4 depicts the performance of private equity strategies vs. public markets for 2000-2017. For the private equity composite, the cumulative return over the period was 50% higher than the S&P 500 (4.5X vs. 3X).

Exhibit 4: Performance of private equity strategies vs. public markets 2000-2017

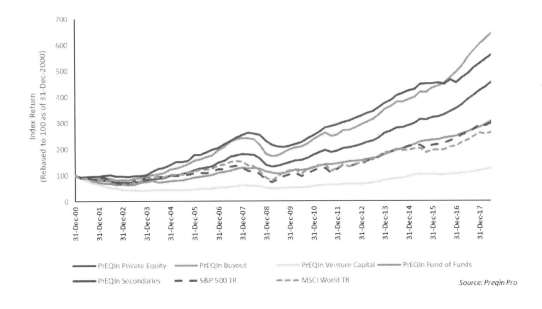

- Private equity assets are less impacted by extreme market volatility and therefore can experience less value loss. This is partly driven by the method in which private equity assets are reported but also because asset managers do not have the pressure to sell the assets when markets are down given that they are able to lock investors' capital for ten years or longer.

Private capital versus public markets

In sharp contrast with this exuberance, stock markets are languishing (if not in active decline), with the number of US listed firms halving in the 20 years between 1996 and 2017. As shown in Exhibit 5, the retreat of the publicly listed company is not unique to the U.S., but persists in other major economies, and is the mirror image of the rise of private equity-backed companies. In addition, the universe of public companies is not just smaller but its structure has shifted towards businesses that tend to be substantially older, larger, and more mature than was the case 20 years ago. The implication is that institutional investors seeking a more diverse spread of equity investment have to look beyond the stock market.

Exhibit 5: The decline in publicly listed companies by country

	Peak	End of 2017*	Decline
Netherlands	392	102	-74%
Mexico	390	141	-64%
South Africa	754	294	-61%
France	1,185	465	-61%
US	7,322	3,436	-53%
Brazil	592	335	-43%
UK	2,913	1858	-36%
Israel	664	431	-35%
Germany	761	450	-41%
Switzerland	289	228	-21%

*Four-year Average

Source: Carlyle (2019)

Exhibit 6 shows that since 2007 the number of companies backed by private equity exceeds the number of listed companies and that this gap continues to widen further. The two contrasting trends of a shrinking stock market and the strong growth in allocation to private equity are not independent phenomena; both stem from the fact that private equity and publicly-listed companies offer competing governance models. It is fair to say that the major strength of private equity over publicly listed firms is in the form of corporate governance it offers.

Exhibit 6: The growth of private equity owned companies

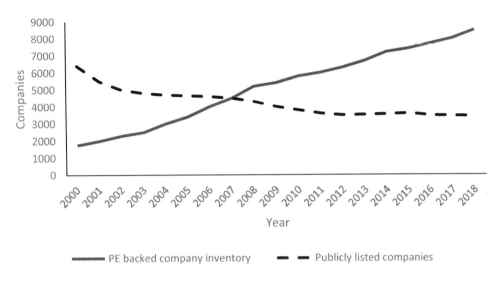

Source: Carlyle (2019)

The separation of ownership and control is a key pillar characteristic of the stock market (and an axiom of modern financial theory more broadly). Yet, the corporate governance and shareholders' control of diffusely owned public companies have been recognized for years to be imperfect, giving rise to all sorts of unsound managerial incentives and a misalignment of interests between shareholders and management — known as agency problems. However, despite the elaborate regulatory mesh, the degree of effectiveness in listed companies has been demonstrated in the academic literature to be very partial.[6] There is a criticism on the functionality of boards of listed companies which are often too large in size and lacking staff members or other resources that limits their style of engagement to be responsive rather than with proactive governance. Shareholders engagement is also very limited in a public company. This is particularly problematic when it comes to the appointment of the board of directors who are often proposed by the management itself. With regard to management incentives, studies have overall failed to agree that there is a linkage between executive pay and corporate performance. Performance-based compensation in the form of granted stock options plans for management has a greatly differing impact than buying shares with one's own money (i.e., a genuine "skin in the game"). Criticism is also around the practice to retain access to cash by multinationals in contrast with the private equity model of an immediate distribution to investors upon realizations. Possibly most troublesome, operational decisions in public companies are highly influenced by the expectations of stock analysts, leading to situations such as the deferral of needed investments to gain short term accounting cosmetics and where earnings management overrides business decisions.

---

[6] For the academic evidence, see Talmor (2018).

Private equity provides a rival governance structure for making large scale investments by institutions. Contrary to the separation of ownership and control, its premise is for an engaged ownership, with a value-add and hands-on orientation. One where the mind-set of seeking an outright exit provides a timely and disciplined code of action indoctrinated all the way down to the plant floor; where performance can actually be measured and GP reputation is critical for the next fund raising.

THE PARTNERS IN A PRIVATE FUND

General Partners (GPs)

The main role of the private equity firm is to provide investment advice to the private equity or debt fund created in a joint partnership with the limited partner investors. The firm, which acts as a general partner of the fund: executes the investment decisions, oversees the fund's investments, and receives fees for these services.

The typical private equity firm is itself organized as a partnership or limited liability corporation. Advent International, Apollo, Bain Capital, Blackstone, BC Partners, Carlyle, CVC Capital, EQT, KKR, Kleiner Perkins and TPG are some of the largest and most prominent private equity firms. In the late 1980s, private equity firms used to be lean, decentralized, and with relatively few investment professionals and employees.[7] Today, the largest private equity firms are substantial businesses, although they are still small relative to the firms in which they invest. All but the very largest private equity firms tend to have fewer than 200 private equity investment professionals. These professionals have a wide variety of skills and experience. Senior team members in private equity funds typically have various backgrounds with investment partners coming from the worlds of industry, finance, accounting, and strategic consulting. Generally, investors view an element of diversity in the makeup of the investment team as a positive.

Investment teams come together for the purpose of raising funds, making investments, and, ultimately, returning profits to investors. To raise funds successfully, teams have to present a cogent and deliverable investment strategy, appropriate investment credentials, and, fundamentally, evidence of prior success in executing a similar investment strategy.

The management team of private equity firms (i.e., the GP) needs to demonstrate that it is able to turn business plans into reality. Their members should be experienced in complementary areas, such as management strategy, finance, and marketing and their roles should be well defined. In the case of technology companies, there will be a combination of technological and business skills that will be relevant.

GPs' experience is key given that the typical manager may receive hundreds of investment proposals each year. Of these proposals, only a very small percentage are chosen for fund investment. Success depends upon GPs' ability to select these proposals efficiently. Efficient selection is properly regarded as a key differentiator and depends on the acumen of the GPs acquired through operational domain expertise, as well as a general experience in the private equity field. That said, having a rigorous and efficient formal process for screening opportunities as they arise is also vital.

[7] See Jensen, M. (1989) which surveyed seven large leveraged buyout partnerships and found an average of 13 investment professionals who tended to come from an investment-banking background.

Investment proposals are first screened to eliminate those that are unpromising or that fail to meet the fund's investment criteria. Private equity firms typically specialize by the type of investment and by industry and location of the investment although very large private equity funds take a generalist investment approach. Specialization reduces the number of investment opportunities considered and reflects the degree of specific knowledge required to make successful investment decisions.

Based on their investment specialization, private equity funds are classified as buyout, venture capital, credit (or debt), real estate, infrastructure or natural resources. Funds vary in their strategies and there are multiple subcategories within each fund type. We discuss these types in some more detail below.

Limited Partners (LPs)

Investors in private equity funds are entities or persons that provide the equity capital to the private fund. They provide a pool of capital which is governed by strict legal rules (established in the Limited Partnership Agreement or LPA) and task the private equity manager (the GP) with executing the prescribed investment strategy of the fund and delivering attractive risk-adjusted returns. The LPs are effectively passive investors with no influence on the investment matters of the fund once it is established. However, it is normal for funds to establish an investors' advisory board. This board is typically formed by the larger and more experienced LPs in the fund. The advisory board normally meets twice per year and its role is to provide guidance and support in matters relating to the running of the partnership and to deal with any potential conflict of interest issues that arise. LPs who are not members of the advisory board rely on the annual meeting of the fund and the quarterly reporting provided by the manager as the formal means by which they are informed of the progress of their investments.

There are several types of investors in private equity funds:

- Public and private pension funds.

- Sovereign wealth funds.

- Endowments, foundations, and other not-for-profit organizations (colleges and universities, medical institutions, professional and research organizations, religious and cultural institutions).

- Family offices and wealthy individuals.

- Funds of funds (funds that invest solely in other private equity funds).

- Government funds.

- Financial institutions (insurance companies, banks, etc.).

- Corporations.

The principal sources of capital for private equity funds are institutional investors (e.g., pension funds, endowments, foundations, and funds of funds), accounting for the large portion of total investment in private equity funds, but also sovereign government wealth funds and wealthy individuals, often through family offices or investment vehicles.[8] In addition, the GPs also contribute to the total investment pool (known as GP Commit) an amount that varies from a minimum of 1% of the total committed capital to up above 20% in extreme cases).

Most LPs invest in private equity for strictly financial reasons. Some of the financial benefits that are expected from private equity investments are:

- Attractive risk-adjusted returns (from the best performing funds)

- Lower correlation to the returns of other asset classes

- Benefits of active ownership

- Diversification away from the public markets.

By investing through a fund partnership rather than directly in the firms in which these funds buy stakes, the investors also gain access to highly skilled investment professionals (i.e., GPs) with demonstrated abilities. Investors delegate to these professionals the responsibilities of selecting, structuring, managing, and eventually liquidating the private equity investments.

Having said that, in recent years many of the larger institutional investors have begun to invest directly in the portfolio companies side by side and at the same time as the private equity fund. Known as co-investment or shadow capital, by bypassing the commingled fund investing it lowers the aggregate fee burden to the LP and also allows for an element of investment timing (as the capital is immediately committed and drawn). These direct investments are implemented by co-investing alongside private equity partnerships managed by private equity firms with whom these investors have close relations and, in most cases, have invested. Effectively, the co- investing LP becomes a small minority investor in the transaction led by the GP in whose fund a major commitment has been made. GPs offer co-investment opportunities to those significant and experienced investors that have contributed a significant amount of capital to the fund especially when the private equity fund cannot invest the full amount due to concentration or diversification restrictions. Besides providing savings in terms of lower fees and, thus, potentially enhancing the returns, co-investments allow the investor to gain experience in structuring, monitoring, and exiting private equity transactions.[9]

A bolder version of shadow capital is a pure direct investing by the LP. This form of investment was traditionally performed by wealthy families, especially for real estate investments. However, it was not prevailing among pure institutional investors since it requires operational managerial skills which rarely fall in the mandate of a financial institutions. The prime exceptions are the Canadian pensions who pioneered the strategy thereby taken the private equity investment model to a new league. Equally, many of the very large Sovereign Wealth Funds also invest directly.[10]

[8] Pension funds are the largest US investors in private equity. Notable names include CalPERS – the California Public Employees' Retirement System, CalSTERS – California State Teachers' Retirement System and the Washington State Investment Board. The university endowments are also prime investors in the asset class (prominently the Yale Endowment under the foresight leadership of David Swensen). In Europe, the composition of LPs is more balanced between financial institutions, fund of funds, endowments and family offices.

[9] Investors that co-invest with a fund pay lower fees or no fees.

[10] Notably, among the Canadian public pensions: Canada Pension Plan (CPP), The Caisse–Québec, Ontario Teachers, OMERS and Alberta Investment Management. As for the sovereign wealth funds, ADIA (Abu Dhabi) and GIC and Temasek (Singapore).

Private equity funds or limited partnerships

Legally, private equity funds are normally organized as limited partnerships in which the GPs manage the fund and the LPs provide most of the capital. U.S. private equity funds are usually structured as partnerships registered in Delaware although some are registered in the Cayman Islands or Bermuda. The U.K.-based and European-based funds are usually registered in Jersey or Guernsey which are offshore jurisdictions within the U.K.

The private equity funds are established as a "blind pool" of capital. Consequently, once LPs commit their investment to the fund only the GPs have discretion on how to invest the money and when to invest it or return it. Most private equity funds are "closed-ended" funds with a finite life. Basically, the funds have a fixed amount of capital that is obtained by issuing a fixed number of non-redeemable shares to investors when they are raised. In a closed-end fund, investors cannot withdraw their funds until the fund is terminated which is usually after ten years. This contrasts with mutual funds (e.g., where investors can withdraw their funds anytime).

It is important to note that private equity funds have several important characteristics that distinguish them from other alternative investment funds such as hedge funds:

- **Life of the fund:** Each private equity fund or partnership has a contractually fixed lifetime, generally 10 years, with provisions to extend the partnership, usually in 1-year or 2-year increments, up to a maximum of 4 years.

- **Committed capital:** Upon launch, only a fraction of the investors' committed capital is payable. The balance is drawn down when investments are identified by the GP. As a result, the capital calls are irregular. This drawdown feature acts to reduce the holding period of the investor's capital.

- **Investment characteristics:** The fund's investments are mainly in private (i.e., unlisted) companies which are highly illiquid.

- **Investment cycle:** During the first 3 to 5 years (normally 5 years from the date of the final closing of the fund), the partnership's capital is invested into companies. Thereafter, the investments are managed and gradually liquidated. As the investments are liquidated, distributions are made to the limited partners in the form of cash (or securities sometimes, such as in the event of an IPO). When all investments are fully divested, the limited partnership can be terminated or "wound up".

Because of the limited life of a private equity fund, the GPs must regularly raise new funds. The legal rules concerning the raising of subsequent funds are usually contained within the LPA. Typically, GPs cannot embark on the raising of successor vehicles until either 75% of the committed capital of the current fund has been called, or the investment period of the current fund has ended. The fundraising process is time consuming and costly, especially if a fundraising adviser (placing agent) is used to facilitate the process. Typically, GPs turn to their existing investors in the first instance and look to them to provide the necessary commitments for a "first closing" of the fund. On aggregate, the fundraising process can take anything from several months to as many as 18 months.

The life of a typical private equity fund is divided into three main periods:

1. **The fundraising period:** This is the period during which the investors pledge capital to the fund. Pledges of capital to the private equity fund are known as committed capital. It can take up 18 months

or more for the investment manager (prospective GP) to raise a new fund. The actual timing depends on the stage in the business cycle, the nature of the investment strategy being proposed, and the credentials of the investment manager (e.g., whether the fund is a "first time" fund or forms part of a well-established fund series). Normally, funds will have a series of "closings" as increasingly more limited partners have their commitments accepted into the partnership. At the final closing, the last of the LPs will be admitted and the fund will be closed for new capital.

2. **The investment period:** During the investment period the GP is tasked with sourcing, evaluating, and executing investments consistent with the investment strategy of the fund. This period normally lasts between 3 and 5 years from the year of the final closing (vintage year). At the end of the investment period the GP cannot draw down further capital to fund further primary investments (new deals).[11]

3. **The harvesting period**: This is the period during which the GPs exit the investments of the fund and distribute the proceeds net of fees to investors. The distribution is based on the "waterfall" provisions in the fund partnership agreement. These provisions indicate how the distributed funds will flow to the investors.

TYPES OF PRIVATE CAPITAL FUNDS

Private equity firms began to specialize in various segments and niches in the mid-1980s. Private equity firms are typically segmented by the types of companies or instruments that they invest in. Common labels for categorizations of private capital funds are buyout, venture capital, debt, infrastructure, real estate or natural resources funds.

Buyout (or leverage buyout) funds

Buyout is the strategy of making investments in which a company or a unit of a company is acquired from its existing shareholders typically with the use of significant financial leverage. In buyouts, funds usually buy significant equity stakes in target companies and then borrow the rest of the acquisition consideration from credit institutions whether banks (leveraged loans), public markets (non-investment grade or junk bonds), and mezzanine investors.

The pure form of buyout transactions is an outright acquisition from a previous owner, be it a family business, a financial investor, a divisional carve-out from a large corporation or a public to private acquisition. Over time, the model of full ownership has expanded and there are many transactions now where the percentage of ownership is partial – whether a majority or a significant but influential minority. This is the case particularly in emerging markets where private equity investments are often growth capital minority deals which are structured with control rights similarly to venture capital investments.

The amount of debt as a percentage of the total consideration varies considerably depending on the specific circumstances (ranging between 40% to 70%). The target companies that are being bought out are typically mature businesses of scale and, thus, can generate operating cash flows that can support the leverage structure. From the way the funds are structured and compensation is computed, the GP seeks to exit the

---

[11] A one-time reinvestment (known as recycling) is typically allowed of proceeds from a portfolio company if received within a defined period —usually one or mostly 24 months—of the time of the investment. This is limited to invested capital (i.e., does not apply to profits) and only during the fund's investment period.

investment within a few years, and therefore to account for an increasingly large fraction of corporate finance. Buyouts are the largest category of private equity, with total funds under management about three times largest as for venture capital.[12] Despite the publicity generated by buyouts of very large companies such as Dell in the U.S.A. and Boots plc in the U.K., most buyout firms are involved in the purchase of mid-market companies of enterprise values up to $500 million. Such companies often respond well to the tools and approach utilized by buyout firms.

Venture capital funds

Venture capital is a broad subcategory of private equity that refers to investments typically made in companies in the very early stages of their development. Venture capital is also typically associated with investments in innovative technology companies that have potential for high growth (hi-tech companies). The industry has expanded significantly and it now targets high growth companies in many sectors: biomedicine (bio-tech), finance (fin-tech), clean energy (clean-tech), agriculture (agri tech), food (food tech), property (prop tech), etc. These young companies have significant information asymmetries due to the fact that they have a very short history and their value lies mainly in hard-to-value intangible assets.

Unlike buyout investing, venture capital funds normally take a minority stake in their portfolio companies. Moreover, venture capitalists usually invest in syndicate with other venture capital investors. Although the venture capital funds take minority stakes, they receive significant rights that protect their investment such as veto rights on major decisions or board seats. These funds invest in different stages, each stage representing a different milestone in a company's evolution. The venture capital firms not only supply the necessary capital through the funds they manage but also significant knowledge to the firms they invest in by providing financial, administrative, and strategic advice or by facilitating network opportunities.

Private Debt (Credit) funds

Credit funds first appeared in the mid-1980s under the form of mezzanine funds. At the time, investors began to use subordinated debt with some equity participation (in the form of warrants) to provide another layer of debt financing for highly leveraged buyout (LBO) transactions. Most private equity firms with "mezzanine" in their title are involved in this type of investing. In the 1990s the funds started to focus on special situations—mainly financially troubled companies. These distressed investing funds often focus on "loan-to-own" strategies where the fund acquires debt securities of a troubled company in the secondary market in the hope of emerging from a corporate restructuring in control of the company's equity. There are also credit funds that focus on "special situations" or "turnaround" strategies where the fund provides debt and equity investments (i.e., "rescue financing") to companies undergoing operational or financial challenges. Following the recent credit crisis, the market has seen a surge of direct lending funds which provide a range of debt products to small and medium size companies, predominantly loans. These loans are repaid with interest, along with any agreed fees and charges, over a set period and they are comparable in functionality to bank loans.

---

[12] In 2018 the aggregate capital raised globally by buyout funds was 235 billion vs. 79 billion for venture funds. Interestingly, the magnitude is reversed with respect to the number of funds in that vintage that year (215 and 605 respectively), making the average buyout fund $1 billion and the average venture fund $130 million. Growth funds are accounted separately and their average 2018 vintage size was $300 million. Source: Preqin Global Private Equity and Venture Capital Report.

Private equity strongly expanded into credit following the global financial crisis of 2007-2008. The new regulatory environment after the crisis, particularly the Dodd-Frank Act and the Volcker rule in the US and Basel III in Europe impose new requirements on lending banks in terms of capital adequacy, stress testing and market liquidity risk. As a result of these legislative measures, banks have been unable to extend much of the corporate and transactional credits they used to serve. The huge void is being replaced with non-bank credit in which private equity firms play a key role.[13]

As of 2018 there were 1,500 credit funds globally, with over $600 billion in asset under management which account for 13% of all private capital. Each private credit fund has its own investment strategy to attain a desired sliver of risk profile. Common types include direct lending; Senior debt (acquisition); Senior debt (origination); Distressed debt; Unitranche; Subordinated / Mezz (acquisition vs. origination); Collateral loan obligations (CLO); Asset-backed financing; Funds of funds; Venture debt and even the more esoteric ones such as Royalty financing.

Real estate funds

Real estate funds make debt and equity investments in the property markets, allowing therefore the GPs must have a dedicated expertise in the real estate sector. Returns are achieved through several means, such as capital appreciation on properties and land, rental yields, and fees and interest from financing activities. Real estate private equity funds employ widely divergent investment strategies. One strategy is to acquire high-quality real estate at basically market yields and achieve the target returns on equity through structured financing. Another strategy is to acquire large portfolios of non-performing real estate loans at wholesale with the purpose of reselling the individual loans separately. Or, these funds might finance the development of real estate via either a "greenfield" land development or the construction of new buildings. In the parlance of private capital, the list of typical strategies includes: Core; Core-plus; Value added; Opportunistic; Distressed; Real estate debt; Real estate mezz; Fund of funds, and Secondaries real estate funds.

Infrastructure and Natural Resources Funds

Infrastructure assets are the facilities essential for the orderly operation of an economy, such as transportation networks, healthcare, social care, waste management, and telecommunications towers. While investment in infrastructure and its continuous maintenance is principally the role of the government, private capital is increasingly involved in both financing and operating such projects. It allows risk-shifting to the private sector, does not require government borrowing and it alleviates the budgetary burden. In essence, private sector funding provides off-balance-sheet financing to government infrastructure projects. The economic model for the private sector is structured such that the governments often provide guaranteed, contracted revenues, known as Public Private Partnerships (PPPs) to ensure a certain return for delivering and operating an individual asset (e.g., a road, school or hospital). In other cases, while the revenues are not guaranteed they are nevertheless regulated (most notably regulated utilities).

Natural resources include sectors such as energy, mines and agriculture, which have a shared characteristic since that even if governments do not own the assets or have a principal responsibility, investments still

---

[13] Expansion both generalist firms such as TPG, GS, Apollo and Permira diverse debt funds alongside debt specialists (e.g. Ares Capital and ICG) dramatically expanded as well as new comers such as Paris based Tikehau who in a short period raised several billion euros funds.

require licensing and regulation. The risk-return investment profile of natural resources is different from infrastructure due to the exposure to commodity prices fluctuations.

Commonality exists with other classes of private capital. As in real estate risk profiles change significantly as the project moves both within and between planning, construction, and operational phases. In addition, as in real estate, location is critical in both infrastructure and natural resources projects. Infrastructure assets and natural resources also resemble buyouts in that the projects are typically large and gravitate to platform investments such as cellular towers, wind farms, and healthcare facilities. Many of these projects share traits with venture capital in cases where the investment is staggered in stages with a strong dependency on early milestones before further and more significant capital is committed.

In terms of private capital funds, three sectors have seen the most investment in recent years: power generation, transportation and energy. In particular, conventional and renewable power account for 40–50% of total new infrastructure investment, depending on the specific continent. In transportation, revamping and operating airports can prove very successful for private capital funds. The energy sector consists of gas pipelines and storage, including upstream and midstream infrastructure, as well as consumer-facing gas distribution networks.

THE PRIVATE CAPITAL ECOSYSTEM

While fund managers and investors are the prime players of the industry attention, there is a wide array of professional companies and organizations which provide services to the general and limited partners. This section will briefly outline the major functions.

Gatekeepers

Gatekeepers are professional advisors operating in the private equity market on behalf of their clients. Smaller or newer investors in the private equity asset class lack experience or scale to retain on board an in-house expertise. Gatekeepers first emerged in the 1970s in the United States, when they developed close relationships particularly with public pension plans that were operating under strict rules which often made the use of investments consultants obligatory. They focus on helping clients develop allocation strategies across asset classes, private equity portfolio construction, fund due diligence, fund selection and access where relationships are built over time. Institutional investors such as the insurance companies, pension funds and the larger foundations often even use several gatekeepers in parallel, for different investment strategies and geographies.

Fund of funds is probably the most common type of vehicle in this context. A fund of funds pools a group of investors and uses the capital to assemble a diversified portfolio of private equity funds. Fund of funds operate on a fully discretionary basis where it is given the authority to make investment decisions without first notifying its clients.

Consultants are another type of gatekeepers that offer non-discretionary services, where investment decisions require the client's consent who thus keeps control over the investment process. Non-discretionary services are often preferred by larger and more sophisticated investors who want to retain control of the investment decisions when placing larger orders. Consultants focus on the needs of institutional investors and offer a wide range of services. They help with research and assist in the assessment of investment proposals, however they leave the final investment decision to their clients. Account managers are increasingly assuming complete responsibility for negotiating the partnership terms and conditions and in managing allocations.

Agents and advisors

With a growing level of sophistication of the private equity market, various groups of intermediaries have developed, aiming to support and assist market participants. Their formation has helped to raise the efficiency and transparency of the market. These are the agents and advisers who facilitate the search by private companies for equity capital, place private equity capital, raise funds for private equity partnerships, and evaluate partnerships for potential investors. These intermediaries overall reduce the costs associated with information problems that arise in private equity investing.

The types of agents and advisers for main market participants are discussed below.

- **Investment banks:** Investment banks and M&A boutique advisory firms are agents for potential issuers of private equity but also advise on the structure, timing, and pricing of private equity issues and assist in negotiations. First, they provide search, valuation, and advisory services by identifying firms that are potential candidates for a private equity investment, accumulating information and data about these firms, and distributing it to potential investors. Second, investment banks offer assistance to companies in the assessment of contractual terms and conditions. Their knowledge of current market conditions can help with obtaining better terms in negotiations. They can also support institutional investors that evaluate investments in various limited partnerships.

- **Fundraising agents:** Fundraising (or "placement") agents assist private equity firms to raise funds. They are a relatively pervasive feature of the market. It is rare to see a fund successfully raised without the involvement of a placement agent in some form. The possible exception to the rule would be the GPs who have successfully raised several funds, have deep and long-lasting relationships with investors and substantial dedicated in-house investor relations teams. GPs that are attempting to raise very large sums, that look to expand their client base of investors, that have limited track record or a track record "with hair on the deal" and a more complicated story to be told to justify, and that specialize in investments which are less known to institutional investors, frequently approach agents for help. These agents add credibility and recognition to the fund being raised, make the process more efficient for the managers and accelerate the fundraising process. Their role is also to educate investors and expand the potential investor universe by addressing relevant queries during the fund due diligence process. A competent placement agent should have the ability to help the investor to resolve specific regulatory compliance, jurisdiction and additional matters that arise in the technically cumbersome paperwork and approval process. This function is paramount to ensure that the investment transaction gets completed in a timely manner not to miss a hard deadline for the fund close. Other roles such agents may play are project management of the fund-raising process, strategic advice to managers on terms, positioning and appetite among investors, and on occasions assistance in internal negotiation among partners.

- **Other advisors:** Advisors cover a large array of services to the private equity fund, from legal aspects to accounting and communication issues. Most GPs still retain the services of outside advisors, regardless of how much in-house resources they may already have put in place. Law firms counsel on legal aspects of private equity transactions and the structuring of the private equity fund. For instance, they deal with the legal issues of the acquisition agreement with the vendor in a buyout transaction, with the investment documentation of a venture-financing deal, the portfolio company's arrangements with its bankers, the general partners' positions as directors or employees of the portfolio company, etc. The accountants act as financial advisors to the general partners and the management of the portfolio companies. They may carry out feasibility studies at an early stage of an investment opportunity. They also advise in detail on management business plans and on negotiations with the owners of the companies in which the fund invests.

More on the GP side, fund administrators can handle the booking and compliance of the fund; whereas custodian manage the cash movements of investments, management fees and distributions based on the rigid waterfall specified in the LPA. Accountants serve funds and their portfolio companies, and tax experts advises on relevant aspects of the portfolio companies. Some executive search companies (HR head-hunters) are dedicated to private equity, whether to recruit for the fund or to their portfolio companies. On the investors side, there has been a recent surge of experts who provide analytical tools for performance measurement, back office tracking and management of the investment portfolio, data and analytics.

The outer circle

At the outer of the ecosystem, there is a vast media and publications, database aggregators, conferences and events organizations that are dedicated to the industry. Also, there are membership associations such as BVCA (UK), AVCA (Africa) and NVCA (US venture capital), etc. that play an important role not only in meetings and conferences but also in training. Last but not least, ILPA (the Institute of Limited Partners Association) has been playing an increasingly powerful role in assuring more transparency in the industry and in leading the drive towards more uniformity in fund terms.

While fund managers and investors are the prime players of the industry attention, there is a wide array of professional companies and organizations which provide services to the general and limited partners. This section will briefly outline the major functions.

GENERAL STATISTICS AND PERFORMANCE[14]

Private equity and venture capital funds have historically outperformed the rest of the private capital market sub categories, with an average return of 13% across 2006-2015 vintages. Real estate funds with vintages 2009 and 2011 are the exception and performed better than the buyout funds. However, the real estate funds' performance has declined over the past three consecutive vintages. Private debt funds have been the most stable of all private capital asset classes over the 2006-2015 vintage period whereby an average return varies between 9% and 12% across vintage years.

Private equity funds (including venture capital) are the largest asset class in terms of capitalization and also offers the highest risk and return profile. The net average return for these funds was about 12% with a standard deviation of returns of 17%. This is largely influenced by the volatile venture capital funds. Real estate funds have a similar but lower risk/return profile than private equity funds, with a net average return of 11% and a standard deviation of returns of 15%. The private debt funds represent the more neutral risk/return profile with both average return and standard deviation of 10%. The natural resources funds

---

[14] All performance data is from Preqin Pro, 2019.

represented the worst risk/return relation with a net average return of 7% and a standard deviation of returns of 16%.

Private equity and venture funds

Breaking down the private equity and venture capital funds to specific asset classes, buyout funds outperformed the rest in overall returns with a median net IRR of 17%. Secondary funds performed better on recent vintages and had the second highest average returns of 14%. Venture capital funds are among the most volatile in terms of returns, followed closely by growth funds, reporting an average net return of nearly 14%. The average median net IRR for all private equity funds was 14.5%.

The risk/return profile and capitalization size of the different fund types differs significantly. Buyout funds represent the largest in terms of capitalization and are the most neutral in terms of risk/return profile. Buyout funds for vintages 2005-2015 reported an average return of 13% with a standard deviation of net IRR of 14%. The second most important group of funds in terms of capitalization are the fund of funds. Fund of funds provide more diversification opportunities, and for that reason they have reported an average return of 11% with a standard deviation of net IRR of 7%. The riskiest fund profile belongs to the early stage funds, which have delivered average returns of 11% but with a standard deviation of returns of 34%, which is significantly riskier.

Private debt funds

Private debt is a steady asset class for investors, offering downside protection amid turbulent market volatility. Assets under management continue to grow, reaching record levels once again as investors are drawn to the asset class for its diversification and favorable risk-adjusted returns. Within private debt, there are multiple strategies offering different risk/return profiles. Direct lending funds have the lowest average median net IRR of 9% for the 2015 vintage funds, however they also have the lowest associated risk with a standard deviation of returns of almost 5%.

On the other side, distressed debt funds have an average return of 13% for the 2015 vintage, but the standard deviation of returns is significantly higher at 15%, which is indicative of a higher risk/return profile. In the vintage years from 2005 to 2015, direct lending funds have consistently posted median net IRRs of between 9.0% and 11.7%. Mezzanine funds are even more consistent, returning a median of between 9.0% and 11.4% across all vintage years. Median net IRRs for distressed debt funds, though, range from 8.6% to 12.9% – in every vintage year but two (2008 and 2009) they have either the highest or the lowest median IRR of the three strategies.

Private equity real estate funds

The band of net returns of real estate funds is narrower, as expected given the underlying risk associated with each strategy. Each of the major private real estate strategies operated by funds with vintages 2010-2015 have largely returned median net IRRs above 10. Using the most up-to-date data, the average median net IRRs of funds of these vintages are as follows:

- Debt: 10%

- Core/Core-Plus: 12%

- Distressed: 13%

- Value Added: 14%

- Opportunistic: 14%

Debt investments are typically the least volatile and report the lowest median net IRR. The higher-quality property investments of core/core-plus real estate are the next in the spectrum, with equity exposure to low-yielding property delivering higher returns than those of debt investments. Value-added strategies represent higher-risk property assets than those of debt and core/core-plus, with extra return expected given the risk associated with development and property improvement.

Infrastructure private equity funds

Infrastructure as an asset class promises moderate returns with relatively low risk compared with other areas of alternatives. The nature of the underlying investments is that investors can usually expect a steady income stream. Comparing between infrastructure investment strategies, core strategies have displayed relatively little fluctuation in median net IRRs over the past 10 years compared to non-core funds, reflective of the low-volatility and low-risk nature of the strategy. Over a longer period (vintages 2004 to latest available), value-added funds have also demonstrated attractive risk and return with median net IRR of 12% and standard deviation of 12.6%.

Natural resources private equity funds

The performance of natural resources funds over the past 15 years has been disappointing: it has averaged just under 7% per annum over this period, as compared with 10-12% for the other asset classes. Meanwhile, the risks entailed in investing in natural resources funds — as measured by the standard deviation between fund returns — place it on a par with real estate and private equity. Within natural resources funds, energy is by far the dominant strategy. Over the period 2007-2018, natural resources funds have delivered net returns that compare favorably with the public indices.

RECENT TRENDS AND CONCLUSION

The private capital industry has gone through an astounding growth and expansion over the past twenty years. The number of new funds has dramatically increased and the amount of capital raised by new and existing funds is at all-time high. More capital has been raised, invested and distributed back to investors than in any other period in the industry's history. With its long term record of performance and unprecedented increase in allocation by institutional investors, the private equity governance model has been expanded to other types of alternatives: in particular, real estate, credit, infrastructure and natural resources.

Venture capital has regained its pre dot-com era luster with a rebounded venture activity and eye popping exit home runs. There has been a proliferation of unicorns, and importantly, one third was founded outside the US, peaking with the NYSE listing of Alibaba -- the world's largest-ever stock market flotation. Today, venture dominates the big charts with five out of six top US companies by market capitalization are venture originated founded in 1975 onward.

There were many other signs for the maturing of the asset class. The regulatory environment has become more stringent and further disclosure requirements were put in place around the globe, and also a more synchronized pressure from the institutional investors associations for term transparency and increased uniformity. Liquidity has sizably increased and secondary transactions became common, practically eliminating the entire discount over NAV in secondary transactions. A more recent innovation is the so-called GP-led secondary which effectively allows investors to choose whether to stay in the fund beyond its mandated end of life or to exit. Furthermore, at the fund level, innovation in fund finance, through the introduction of capital call facilities (subscription lines), NAV facilities and other forms of funding against fund underlying assets.

Investors face now a much wider spectrum of possibility in which form to invest. Specifically, co-investment, direct investing and separate management account has become standard for the larger and more mature institutional investors. Together these alternatives to investment in the commingled fund are known as shadow capital. Whilst exact figures are not available, it is estimated that the magnitude of shadow capital account for an additional 25%-30% on top of the reported figures for the asset class.

At the portfolio company level, investment strategies have become more sophisticated including cooperation with strategic buyers through minority stake investments and in providing capital to finance add-on acquisitions for their portfolio companies. There are also embryonic measures to quantify and control risk exposure at the deal level.

Of concern is the fact that capital concentration has increased in the past years, with the majority of the capital raised in 2018 committed to the 50 largest funds closed during that year. Returns were still strong relative to other asset classes in 2019 but a trend of a slow decline toward public market averages is noticeable. Moreover, persistent high prices, volatile capital markets, political and economic disputes between countries, and the threat of a recession have injected a sense of uncertainty that deal makers in the private capital industry dislike. More dramatically, there is a resurgence of populistic rhetoric by politicians, often falsely accusing the industry of market and systemic failures, job losses and other claims, as a reincarnation of the industry's early days when it was first described as "barbarians" and "vultures" in the 80s and 90s, and then labelled as "locust" in Europe a decade later.[15]

Amid the increasingly competitive environment and the slowdown in capital flow, GPs are expanding their menu of offerings as part of a differentiation strategy. Consequently, the number of funds per firm has increased over the past 5 years as GPs have been carefully stretching beyond their core. Menu expansions have been specifically popular in four areas: credit funds especially with a sector focus, specialized funds, long-term duration funds, and growth equity funds. Specialized funds have become increasingly important as the market for deals has become more competitive. These allow GPs to double down on areas in which the firm has deep experience and extensive network to source attractive targets. Several longer duration funds were introduced by the largest fund managers, as yet another way to broaden their offerings. Attractive new targets

[15] "The private equity firms are like vampires -- bleeding the company dry and walking away enriched even as the company succumbs," Elizabeth Warren, US Democratic presidential contender, July 18, 2019.

are becoming harder to find and GPs are seeing the value of holding onto high-quality companies for as long as they continue in generating value.

Recognizing the increased importance of client relationships, the giants of the private equity industry, notably Blackstone and KKR, have strategically migrated to be asset managers, offering far broader types of assets to their clients. This was built on the reporting and back office capabilities that were developed once they become publicly listed. Another strategic innovation is by private capital funds management firms with a dedicated strategy of acquiring minority stakes in other private capital GPs.[16]

As the Private Equity industry continues to grow and further develop, so too does the universe of investors. North America remains the primary source of capital for the industry, housing almost half of all private capital fund investors. However, as globalization of the industry continues, more emerging markets-based institutions look to invest new wealth, consequently, the sources of capital for the industry are ever changing. Europe and Asia have increased their share in the industry, with Asia experiencing the greatest growth.

The challenge for the private equity industry going forward is to assess how best to put record amounts of raised capital to work productively amid heavy competition for assets and soaring purchase price multiples. In order to face this challenge, fund managers must get better and smarter. Many of them started to use advanced analytics to shed light on both value and risks in ways never possible before and to focus on adjacent investment strategies which take advantage of existing capabilities, whilst resisting the temptation to stray too far afield.

Going forward there are major unresolved matters and opportunities to advance the industry; among which:

- From an academic standpoint, there are no well-defined tools for on optimal portfolio construction. The common practice is to split the asset allocation to listed vs. private equity buckets of capital. Indeed, the governance model is different, as is the ability to handle extreme market volatility as discussed above. However, for asset allocation, risk exposure and correlations among underlying assets are primarily around industries and other company specific operational fundamentals, not whether the company is listed or held privately.

- Another direction which requires more sophistication in the industry is the use of derivatives and other synthetic securities. Practically all other major types of assets: listed equity, fixed income, foreign currency equities, and commodities have an abundant use of options, futures, swaps and other types of derivatives. None of it exists in private equity or private capital more broadly.

- Lastly, attempts should continue towards the holy grail of accessing private capital to retail investors. With the giants of private equity firms being themselves listed companies, there is a greater experience in valuation credibly assessed and disclosed in a timely matter; however the distance till daily marking to market is still far away.

---

[16] Most notably, Dyal Capital Partners (a part of Neuberger Berman) acquired 38 minority equity stakes in GPs between 2012-2019; among which in Vista Equity Partners, Providence, HGGC and Silver Lake. Other leading private equity firms who employ a similar strategy are Goldman Sachs AIMS Group and Blackstone.

REFERENCES

Jensen, M. C. (1989), "Eclipse of the public corporation," Harvard Business Review, 67, pp. 60–70.

Talmor, E. (2018), "Private Equity: Rethinking the Neoclassical Axioms of Capital Markets," Journal of Alternative Investments 21, Fall 2018, pp. 10-15.

In his own words: Mark O'Hare, Founder and Ceo, Preqin

Private capital asset classes have grown beyond all recognition over the past decade. Global assets under management (AUM) have surged from $1.6 trillion in 2008 to $5.2 trillion in 2018, and are forecast to expand further to $9.3 trillion by 2023[1]. Moreover, the industry has an increasingly complex ecosystem: it now features wider participation from institutional investors, a deeper bench of skilled fund managers, ever more finely segmented and targeted strategies, and a supporting cast of agents, advisors and service providers.

This prompts several questions: how and why has this growth occurred, how far is this growth likely to continue, and how insulated will it be against economic shocks?

Factors Underlying Private Capital Growth

The phrase 'Follow the Money', made popular by the 1976 movie *All The President's Men*, sums it up. Whichever data source you care to use – bottom-up fund-level performance benchmarks from Cambridge Associates or Preqin, or top-down analysis of pension fund returns – you arrive at an inescapable conclusion: private capital investment has delivered excellent net returns (i.e. after fees and carry) to its investors. This pattern has persisted through good times and bad – and in particular through the Global Financial Crisis. Meanwhile, expected returns in public markets are declining, and it is becoming increasingly difficult for investors' portfolios to outperform the market. Investors understand this, and Preqin's regular surveys confirm that institutional investors intend to allocate increasing proportions of their total AUM to private capital.

But how does private capital deliver these superior returns? What are the mechanisms? Judicious use of debt certainly plays a role, but that only gets you so far. After all, listed companies raise debt too, and sophisticated institutional investors can always leverage their portfolios of listed stocks, so debt alone isn't the answer. Rather, the biggest difference comes from private capital's fully aligned governance model. In private equity-owned businesses, the motivations and rewards of all players are closely aligned around a common set of objectives – from the limited partners investing in the fund, through the general partners managing the fund, to the managers and employees in the companies owned by the fund. This model may not be perfect, but it has proven to be far more effective than the poorly aligned model of listed company ownership, with all its 'principal/agent' problems and other drawbacks.

How Far Can the Growth Continue?

As large as private capital is today, it still comprises only 5-10% of most investors' portfolios and of the global investable asset universe. Preqin is predicting continued rapid AUM growth – 12% compound per annum – to 2023. Thereafter, how far can the growth go?

We can be certain of the following: a) the trend of private capital gaining share from listed assets is being driven by powerful economic forces that are long term in nature and are more likely to become stronger rather than weaker, e.g. data technology; b) empirically, there is no evidence of any slowdown in institutional investor appetite for alternative assets, or in the ingenuity and innovation of alternative asset managers in finding creative solutions to meet investment needs; and c) private capital has been proven to deliver through both good and bad economic times.

In summary, private capital will continue growing in importance for investors, and those of us in the industry – including data and service providers like Preqin – will continue to work to evolve and improve the opportunities for investors and fund managers, and through them, benefit the wider economy.

(1) Source: Preqin, *The Future of Alternatives* report

2 Private Capital Fund Economics

Everything has a pattern and a partner.
African proverb

LIMITED PARTNERSHIP FUNDS

Most private e.quity funds are organized as limited partnerships, with private equity firms serving as general partners(GPs) of the funds, and large institutional investors and wealthy individuals providing the bulk of the capital as limited partners (LPs). A prime virtue of the limited partnership over a corporate structure is that it is tax transparent to investors. Over the years, this investment vehicle has become the norm in private equity: it offers limited liabilities protection to investors and is relatively simple to understand and implement.

The commercial and legal terms of such funds are typically contained within the limited partnership agreement (LPA). The private equity funds are established as a *blind pool* of capital: once commitments to the fund are made, only the GPs generally have discretion on how and when to invest the capital as long as this is done in accordance with the investment policy, strategy, and restrictions contained in the LPA. GPs also have discretion on the realization of investments within the fund life, and proceeds should then be distributed to investors at periodic intervals that are specified in the LPA. Most private equity funds are *closed-ended* with a finite life; investors cannot voluntarily withdraw their invested capital or change their minds on undrawn capital commitments that they have undertaken.[1]

Private equity funds have several important characteristics that distinguish them from other alternative investment funds such as hedge funds:

- **Life of the fund**. Each private equity fund or partnership has a contractually fixed lifetime, generally 10 years. This time frame makes investment in private equity relatively illiquid, in contrast to listed and other money management vehicles like mutual funds, which offer flexibility on withdrawals.

- **Committed capital**. Upon launch, only a fraction of the investors' committed capital will be payable to fund an initial investment and/or to pay the establishment costs of the fund. The balance is called when investments are identified by the GP, and to pay, at periodic intervals, the GP's management fee and operating expenses of the fund. Such capital calls are referred to as "drawdowns" (or "takedowns"), and their nature of being spread over several years reduces the average holding period by the fund of the investor's capital.

- **Investment characteristics**. The fund's investments are mainly in private (i.e., unlisted) companies which are highly illiquid and therefore match the illiquid nature of the fund capital.

- **Investment cycle**. There is a defined period (typically five years, commonly referred to as the "investment period" or "commitment period") during which the partnership's capital can be invested

---

[1] With the exception that some LPAs or side letters may provide investors with the right to be excused from certain investments on pre-specified grounds.

into companies. Thereafter, the investments are managed and gradually harvested.[2] As they are liquidated, distributions are made to the LPs in the form of cash or securities in the realized companies. When all investments are fully divested, the limited partnership can be terminated or "wound up."

Because of the finite life of a private equity fund, GPs regularly raise new funds. There are contractual rules concerning raising other funds alongside the current fund, which are contained in the LPA. They address both the raising of subsequent or "successor" funds (which have substantially the same investment objective or strategy as the current fund), and the managing or raising of non-competing funds (which do not have an objective or strategy similar to that of the current fund). In general, GPs cannot embark on the raising of successor funds until the earlier of (1) the time when 75%[3] of the committed capital of the current fund has been called and/or reserved for investments, management fees, and partnership expenses, or (2) the investment period of the current fund has ended. Raising other types of funds (which would have to be non-competing/have differing investment strategies) is also restricted where stipulated constraints mostly pertain to the levels of personal time and effort that the GP team may commit.

As a rule, all of the fund's LPs are subject to the same terms and conditions. While some investors may be afforded preferential rights in a *side letter* (discussed in greater detail below), all investors are otherwise subject to the same terms found in the LPA. In particular, preferential informational and/or economic terms may be offered to LPs who make a particularly large capital commitment, or to investors who are part of what is defined below as the first close.

A number of documents govern the terms of the fund by laying out many different parameters:[4]

- The fund's duration period is set with rules for extending the period (typically up to two years) for the remaining unrealized positions;

- LPs are passive investors whose limited liability is capped at their commitment amount;

- Rules are set on the procedures for capital calls and remedies in case of a default on drawdown commitments;

- Broad investment parameters and restrictions are outlined regarding the size, type, and concentration of investments and reinvestments that can be made and limitations on fund borrowings;

- Agreements are made on management fee charges, profit sharing principles, organizational expenses and other such arrangements.

- Information and other rights granted to LPs are set out as well as reporting and accounting obligations of the partnership.

- Key person rules are written, and cause and no-cause rights are granted to the LPs to remove the GP, dissolve the fund, or stop investment activity.

---

[2] Many funds also permit a limited ability to make "follow-on" investments after the fund's investment period into portfolio companies for the purposes of enhancing or preserving their value. For VC funds and platform private equity investments, such as in developing renewable energy projects, the business model of the fund is deliberately based on staged investments, which could continue until year 10. In fact, follow-on investments by VC could be larger in terms of deployed capital than the original investment in the start-up company.

[3] While 75% is the most common figure, market practice can vary from 70% to 85%.

[4] Key legal fund documents other than the LPA and side letters include a private placement memorandum, subscription agreement or booklet, and legal opinions.

As noted, private equity funds are commonly structured as a limited partnership. This choice of structure is mainly motivated by the tax transparent nature of limited partnership vehicles: there is no "double charge" to tax on the capital gains and income from the fund's underlying investments or portfolio companies distributed to investors. In other words, no charge to taxation should arise on the fund itself, as capital gains and income from the fund's underlying investments or portfolio companies are treated as arising directly to investors (as if the investors had directly invested in the portfolio companies themselves; the existence or imposition of the limited partnership vehicle between the underlying investments and the fund's investors is ignored).

This structure contrasts with a fund structured as a company or similar corporate vehicle, where a double charge to tax would apply to capital gains and income from such fund's underlying investments—first, at the level of the fund (at the applicable rate of corporation tax) when it receives distributions (whether capital gains or income) from its underlying investments, and second, at the level of the investors when they receive distributions from the fund (usually in form of dividends, which are typically subject to higher rates of income tax applicable to investors) in respect of those distributions received by the fund from the underlying investments. This double tier of tax arises because corporate vehicles are considered to be "tax opaque" (as opposed to being tax transparent). The obvious effect of this treatment is to reduce the quantum of distributions that a corporate-structured fund makes to its investors relative to a similarly performing fund taking the form of a limited partnership, thereby reducing the net returns achieved by investors from that fund. Having explained this, it is worth noting that U.S. private equity funds are often structured and registered in Delaware, although some are registered in the Cayman Islands or Bermuda. U.K.-based and European-based funds are typically registered in England, Scotland, Jersey, Guernsey, or Luxembourg.

FUND LIFE CYCLE

The life cycle of a private equity fund spans three partially overlapping periods: (1) *fundraising*, which lasts one to two years on average; (2) *investing* (aka the *investment period*), which generally lasts up to five years and which, depending on the fund in question, starts from either the beginning of the fundraising period (known as "first close") or the end of the fundraising period (known as "final close"); and (3) a period commonly referred to as the *harvesting* (or *divestment*) phase of a private equity fund, which generally lasts from four to five years commencing after the end of the investment period, during which time the underlying investments within the private equity fund are managed and exited.

The fundraising period

During this phase, fund terms are agreed and investors pledge their capital. It can take between a few months and two years for the GP to raise a fund. The actual length of the period depends on the overall market sentiment and business cycle, the wider economy, the appetite for the specific investment strategy being proposed, and the credentials and track record of the management team. A key consideration is whether the fund is a *first-time* fund or whether the fund forms part of a well-established fund series with a strong track record. Normally, funds will have a series of *closings* spread across the fundraising period as more LPs make their commitments to the partnership. The first close is particularly important since a fund may seek a certain amount of capital at this initial stage so that the GP can begin making investments by closing deals while new investors can still join for a limited time (e.g., one year from first close). Furthermore, it is often the case that most of the economic terms of the partnership are established through negotiations leading to the first close. "Final close" means that once a certain threshold of capital has been reached, the fund is closed to new capital. Though the manager has some flexibility regarding the final size of the fund, investors expect the fund documents to provide for (1) a "target size" for the fund or the aggregate total commitments expected to be raised from investors by the final close, and (2) an absolute maximal capital that could be raised and known as a "hard cap."

Investors' requirement for a clear statement in the fund documents as to its minimal target size is motivated by a desire to confirm that they are investing in a fund that has economies of scale. Concerns about a fund's hard cap arise since if the fund is too large, not only will investors' participation in the fund be diluted but the fund may have excess "dry powder" without the corresponding deal opportunities in which to put that capital to work, in which case, the fund may be tempted to pursue too large or too many investments.

Fundraising is a very time-consuming and costly process, even for seasoned private fund houses. Often a fundraising adviser (i.e., placement agent) is used to facilitate the process. Where a successor fund is being raised, GPs turn first to their existing investors and look to them to provide the necessary commitments for a first closing of the fund, a process known as a "re-up" from existing investors. In the case of both first-time funds and successor funds, the fund managers also invest their own money alongside the passive investors, which is known as the "GP commit." Although 1–3% of the fund is the current market norm for GP participation, this figure could be higher (in some cases, significantly higher, e.g., 10–15%). The GP commit is considered an important part of demonstrating the alignment of interests between the LPs and GP, and is referred to in market parlance as having "skin in the game."

During the fundraising process, GPs may present to prospective LPs a term sheet with key economic terms relating to management fees, profit sharing, and other investment terms, including establishment and operating expenses, investment strategy and restrictions, key persons, and cause/no-cause rights for LPs to remove the GP. Investors often try to influence the terms of the LPA with varying degrees of success. However, GPs usually have the upper hand and are quite persistent with preserving their economic and other investment terms. For instance, when a fund is oversubscribed, a GP can be selective as to which prospective investors to admit and this can often allow the GP to dictate terms to investors. In other cases, the investor base may be predominately composed of investors lacking the "firepower" to push more LP-friendly terms. Yet, exceptions to the rule exist, such as "ultra large" investors (e.g., certain sovereign wealth funds and public pension plans) whose large investment tickets mean that, in some instances, they are able to push for substantial changes in LPA terms and obtain significant bespoke side letter rights.

Another reason why terms may be difficult to negotiate is the "divide and conquer" practice employed by GPs, whereby terms are first agreed with some more receptive investors, enabling the GP to reach a first close while leaving the other investors with a nearly binary choice of whether to get in the fund or stay out. Moreover, collaboration among existing LPs takes substantial time and effort, and there are also concerns with anti-trust violations which discourage communication and negotiation collusion. For all of these reasons, investors find it more advantageous to negotiate minor special terms through a side letter than to fundamentally influence the fund terms.

With that said, certain legal terms have evolved to become ever more protective and beneficial for investors. These developments have stemmed mostly from the efforts of institutions such as the Institutional Limited Partners Association (ILPA) and regulators that look to help develop *best practice* among LPs.

The investment period

During the investment phase, the GP is tasked with sourcing, screening, and executing deals that are consistent with the investment strategy of the fund. This period lasts up to five years from the date of either the first or final closing, and may be extended by the GP with LP approval. Depending on the investment policy and strategy of the fund, the investments may take one of several forms: acquiring an entire business (i.e., a buyout deal); investing in an existing business while existing shareholders remain (e.g., in venture capital or growth capital into a family-owned business); or investing in a long-term development project (e.g., certain infrastructure assets). The investment can be done solo or alongside another private equity firm, another investment firm, or the existing management of the company. In some cases, the investment may be made together with existing LPs and/or third parties, referred to as "co-investing." In all cases, the investments become what are known as "portfolio companies."

As the GP sources deals, it calls money from its investors pro rata to their respective capital commitments. At this stage, the capital commitment translates into an actual funding obligation, which is then drawn down in an uneven manner over time until, as noted above, either the committed capital is exhausted or the fund investment period reaches its end. Investors take the lion's share of both the risk and the economic payoff from companies in which the fund invests, but have no active involvement in the governance of the portfolio companies.

As long as part of the committed capital has not been called, the outstanding balance is referred to as the remaining "unfunded" or "undrawn" commitment. LPs maintain their contractual obligation to inject capital up to the unfunded amount; it is their responsibility to ensure that they have sufficient cash when it is called by the GP.

Once the investment period has elapsed, the fund managers cannot make further primary investments (i.e., new deals). However, funds retain some "reserve" capital that can be called after the investment period to complete prospective investments in the process of being finalized immediately before the end of the investment period, to make investments subject to a binding agreement entered into by the fund immediately before the end of the investment period, and/or for follow-on investments in existing portfolio companies. The ratio between primary and follow-on capital for investment varies greatly based on investment strategy. Buyouts may make as little as no follow-on investments and as much as 100% of the primary investment amount, typically to finance bolt-on acquisitions. Venture capital (VC) investments (especially when investing in early stages) can expect several multiples of the primary investment to be required in subsequent rounds to avoid the fund's share in the portfolio company from being diluted.

The divestment period

This is the harvesting phase during which the fund managers manage the portfolio companies with a view to realizing them at a gain, and distribute the resulting net proceeds to investors. From the time of investment, the GP's aim is to add value to the portfolio companies and improve their economic performance. The expected holding period for an individual portfolio company is most commonly kept to within the life of the fund to allow proper time to enhance the business and to sell it in a desirable manner. Returns take place in one of several forms, including by means of

- an initial public offering,

- an exit through a trade sale (i.e., a sale to a third-party buyer operating in the same industry as the portfolio company),

- a secondary buyout (i.e., a sale to another private equity fund),

- a leveraged recapitalization whereby the fund is able to extract cash from the portfolio company without actually selling it (achieved by re-leveraging the company, i.e., substituting some of the company's equity with additional debt, usually by borrowing from a bank or issuing bonds, which amount is then used to repurchase the company's own shares from the fund), and

- return through asset disposal of a portfolio company.

The GP distributes the proceeds to the LPs either in cash when investments are liquidated or in kind (i.e., shares or other securities in the company).[5] Extensions to the life of the fund might be necessary to ensure successful exits. The distribution to investors is based on the *waterfall* provisions in the fund partnership agreement, which stipulate how the distribution will flow to the investors. As will be detailed below, the first priority is to return to the investors the principal of their funds invested, referred to as "paid-in capital." The next priority is then to pay the investors a "preferential (or preferred) return" on that capital, also known as a "hurdle." Once the paid-in capital and the preferential return have been distributed, the GP starts sharing the profit, known as "carried interest"; in the first instance, this can be via a "catch-up" mechanism and then pari passu with the LPs based on the agreed profit share, or, where there is no such catch-up, pari passu with the LPs.

MANAGEMENT FEES, ORGANIZATIONAL EXPENSES, AND OPERATING EXPENSES

Management fees

Broadly set as a percentage of the fund size, management fees should cover the ongoing day-to-day expenses of managing the fund: salaries, offices, travel, due diligence, broken deals, on-going engagement with the portfolio companies, investor relations, and other back office functions. Yet the reality from an LP perspective is more complicated in computation, disclosure, and even in the fundamental fee economics. The headline figures are straightforward where the vast majority of funds charge 2% per year on committed capital throughout the investment period. Multibillion-sized funds, secondaries funds, and certain other strategies would charge less—anywhere from 1% per year—and there are smaller funds, venture funds, and emerging market firms that can charge premium levels of 2.5%. Some funds may charge management fees based on invested capital rather than committed (this is more common among direct lending funds). The topic of whether management fees should be based on commitment or invested capital is frequently debated in the industry, with GPs wanting to maintain the higher levels through committed capital calculations arguing that this better aligns their interests with LPs as it avoids an agency problem of incentivizing GPs to rush into potentially underperforming deals to deploy the capital as quickly as possible to start earning fees.

---

[5] LPAs only permit a GP to make in kind distributions to investors during the term of the fund if the shares or other securities proposed to be distributed can be easily disposed (e.g., listed shares).

Following the investment period, most fund terms include a *step-down* or reduction in the annual management fees. An important part of the step-down is that after the investment period and through the end of the life of the fund, the management fee is no longer calculated based on level of commitment to the fund, but rather, a much lower figure that is a function of either carrying value (i.e., net asset value (NAV)) or unrealized investment amount (cost of investments less any write-offs and realized investments). The management fees therefore continuously decline over the harvesting phase as the fund liquidates its investments. As noted, extensions to the life of the fund might be necessary to ensure successful exits. Whether management fees will be charged during any such extension period can be a matter of negotiation between the GP and the LPs.

Less common methods for setting management fees are having a fixed fee for the whole life of the fund or an annual budget. These approaches are most likely to be encountered among micro funds, single-LP funds, incubated funds, corporate VC funds, and other niches.

The economic consequences of bearing this management fee to investors are not negligible; as they can often form a significant portion of an investor's commitment, management fees can materially reduce net returns to investors. Further, since the fees are paid to fund the GP, there is a natural suspicion about the justification for such large fees to allow a GP to fund its own day-to-day overheads (i.e., that they are being used as a profit center, particularly in the case of large private equity houses receiving management fees across a host of predecessor and successor funds, and not solely for their intended purpose). For these reasons, management fees can be one of the most hotly contested areas between LPs and GPs, and a topic that draws substantial attention from some regulators, politicians, and the media. To illustrate the contentious nature of these fees in absolute terms, consider a typical case of 1.5% management fees on a $7 billion fund, which comes to $105 million in annual fees for a total of $550 million by the end of the investment period. It is difficult to ignore such a high fixed fee figure given that the number of investments per fund rarely exceeds 15 over the entire course of its life, and in view of the multiple additional fees and charges that will be discussed below.[6]

Management fees are paid in regular intervals—usually on a quarterly or, less commonly, semi-annual basis and typically in advance. Terminology-wise, for fund administrators and in LPs' internal accounts, capital calls that are used to cover fees are tabulated as part of the lifetime fees, whereas the part of the paid-in capital that is used to make investments in portfolio companies is marked as invested capital.

In practice, the effective management fees are much lower. A survey by Preqin (2016) confirms the overall decline in management fees charged by private equity GPs. Average annual fees during the investment period declined from nearly 2% in 2007, to 1.9% in 2014, to 1.78% in 2016. The survey also provides a breakdown based on fund type and size. VC funds have an average annual management fee of 2%, similar to mezzanine funds (presumably compensated for the shorter term of such funds). On the other side of the spectrum, funds of funds and secondaries funds only charge an average of 0.9% and 0.92%, respectively, which is consistent with their business model as more of an asset manager than building operational companies. Infrastructure and real estate funds lie in the middle with fees of 1.5%. As for fund size, funds smaller than $250 million charge 2% on average, whereas the management fee of funds above $2 billion averages 1.53%.[7]

---

[6] CalPERS, the largest U.S. pension fund and one of the most respected opinion leaders in the institutional investors industry, explicitly goes on record to describe management fees as a profit center for GPs, not budget based.

[7] For a comprehensive study of fund fees, factors affecting variances from common norms, and implications, see Jacobides and Umana, (2017).

In practice, however, the effective management fees are much lower. A study by StepStone (2016) analyzed a large sample of funds with vintage years ranging from 2001 to 2015 and representing a variety of different private equity strategies. This study found that the effective management fee paid by LPs is only half of the standard 2% annual management fee on committed capital. Three reasons are mentioned for this result: large funds charging far less than 2%; fee offsets; and management fees after the investment period are significantly lower as described above. In addition, the increasing popularity of co-investments and separately managed accounts strongly reduce the average fees on the private equity portfolio, as fees are reduced and co-investments may sometimes bear no fees at all. Not surprisingly, fees and the mechanics of offsets play a very large role in the discussions between GPs and cornerstone investors.

When excessive, high management fees may lead GPs to make unwise decisions. In circumstances of poor or mediocre fund performance where the GPs are neither likely to receive carried interest nor to raise another fund, the annual income from management fees could provide a wrong incentive to delay the realization of portfolio companies. Instead of realizing portfolio companies when the right exit opportunity presents itself, managers may be tempted to delay realizing such investments toward the end of the fund's life in order to prolong the receipt of fee revenues.

With respect to U.S.-based funds, U.S. managers sometimes elect to waive a portion of management fees in exchange for an equal amount of share of profits that is taxed at a lower capital gains rate. This arrangement is made through a special priority allocation and bears no cash consequences to investors. In July 2015, the U.S. Treasury and the Internal Revenue Service issued proposed regulations that address the tax aspects of fee waiver in return for the receipt of a profit interest in the partnership.[8]

Organizational expenses

In addition to management fees, there are also organizational expenses. These include the legal, accounting, and other expenses of fund formation: structuring the various legal entities such as the GP, the management company, and other related vehicles, as well as regulatory filings and compliance. These expenses have risen significantly in recent years due to increasingly complex fund structures and the escalating costs of preparing marketing and regulatory documents and negotiation of fund terms, documentation, and side letters with investors. It is usual for a fund to bear a certain capped percentage of the organizational costs. Further, investors tend to specifically carve out the set-up, regulatory, and compliance costs of the manager from the fund's organizational and ongoing expenses charged to the LPs.

Operating expenses

Along with the initial fund formation costs, there are ongoing fund expenses, including auditors, administrators, custodians, insurance, risk compliance, and the costs of LP advisory committees (LPACs), annual general meetings, taxes, and other governmental fees that may be levied against the fund. Investors are expected to pay for the fees and expenses that are related to the establishment and operation of the fund.

---

[8] Also see Polsky (2009).

CARRIED INTEREST

Carried interest (or "carry") is the performance-based return earned by fund managers. It specifies their share in the profit after the paid-in capital (invested and fees together) is returned to the investors. The precise mechanism by which carried interest is computed and paid varies from one situation to another; however, the basic premise is straightforward. Normally, GPs charge a fixed carry of 20% of the profits of the fund. The other 80% of the profit is distributed to the investors pro rata according to their share in the fund. While a carry of 20% is the market standard, some GPs (particularly of VC funds) have successfully set a higher figure or a *ratchet* mechanism where increasingly higher percentages of carry are paid for exceptional investment performance.[9]

To account for the LPs' opportunity cost of funding, most distribution waterfalls employ a *hurdle rate* (also known as "preferred return"), typically set at 6–8% per annum. The hurdle rate means that carry only becomes payable after the investment principal has been returned plus the preferred return on a compounded basis.[10] Under these terms, LPs are entitled to all of the realized proceeds from exits until they have received back their entire invested committed capital (the case in European funds aka the "fund-as-a-whole" model, discussed in more detail below alongside its contrasting U.S. "deal-by-deal" counterpart) plus the preferred return, after which the managers share 20 cents of every additional dollar, with investors simultaneously receiving the remaining 80 cents of every such additional dollar (colloquially referred to as an "20/80 split"). It is also worth noting that before distributions are made in the form of the 20/80 split, the GP will usually be entitled to 100% of all distributions (known as the "catch-up") after the preferred return is paid until the GP has received an amount equal to 25% of the preferred return. Aggregated together, the catch-up distribution and the GP's share of the 20/80 split allow the GP to receive carry equal to 20% of the overall profits of the fund.

The following simplistic case illustrates the profit split between the investors and the fund managers. A fund made a single investment of $100 which was sold a year later. There are no management or other fees except for a 20% carry subject to an 8% preferred return with full catch-up (i.e., 100% of all distributions to the GP after investors receive their paid-in capital of $100 plus preferred return until the GP has received an amount equal to 25% of the preferred return). In this numerical illustration, if the net proceeds of the realization were $140, then the hurdle rate has been comfortably surpassed, and the preferred return is $8. Therefore, investors receive the first $108 (i.e., the paid-in capital of $100 plus the preferred return), and then the GP receives the catch-up distribution of $2. The remaining $30 is distributed to the GP and the LPs along the lines of the 20/80 split. The aggregate effect of the full catch-up and the 20% share of the $30 ensures that the GP receives 20% of the net profits (i.e., $(2+6)/$40 = 20%). Without the catch-up, the GP would have only received $6.40 (i.e., 20% of $32) or 16% of the net proceeds (i.e., $6.40/$40 = 16%).

Next, consider the scenario where the net proceeds at exit are only $110 and under alternative catch-up mechanisms. In this case, the first $108 go to the LPs. The remaining $2 should be distributed entirely to the

[9] As an example of a carried interest with a ratchet, Vista Foundation Fund III raised $2.5 billion in 2016 for small cap technology-focused buyout deals. Carried interest was set at 20% if LP returns are up to 2.5x multiple; 25% if they are between 2.5x to 3x multiple; and 30% if they exceed 3x. Interestingly, Vista Equity Partners (the sponsors of Vista Foundation Fund III) have been raising a larger $10 billion buyout fund in parallel where the carry is fixed at 20%.

[10] A hurdle rate is less likely to be encountered with a venture fund. Recently, a couple private equity funds have also dropped the hurdle rate, most notably Advent International, whose $13 billion buyout fund closed in 2016 when the hurdle was dropped from 8% to zero, thereby permitting the GP to share the profit from the first dollar. The lack of a hurdle did not deter investors as it took Advent only six months to close the fund, which was heavily oversubscribed with (reportedly) $20 billion of demand. However, for the vast majority of private equity funds, the hurdle rate remains a standard feature.

GP if a 100% or full catch-up has been agreed. Alternatively, if the catch-up mechanism is partial, the amount above the preferred return is allocated at a more modest pace until the GP has caught up. For instance, if the catch-up pace is on a 50/50 basis (i.e., the GP and the LPs will each receive 50% of all subsequent distributions until the GP has received an amount equal to 25% of the preferred return to the extent there are sufficient distributions), then carried interest to the GP is only $1. If there were no catch-up, the GP would receive carried interest of only $0.40 (20% of $2).

The presence of an accumulating hurdle rate in the partnership agreement aims both to motivate the GP to exit the investments early, and to provide investors with a meaningful preferred return. However, there can also be a negative side to a hurdle. Setting an excessive hurdle increases the chance of not meeting the threshold and thus, the likelihood of misalignment of interests: managers are financially better off when they do not exit their current investment portfolio since it enables them to keep receiving the fixed management fees.[11]

It is more straightforward to calculate the profit after the original capital has been paid back to the investors. This *fund-as-a-whole* approach requires that all capital contributions of investors, including fees and expenses, are returned before the GP begins to receive any carry. Being the prevailing structure in Europe, this approach is commonly known as the "European waterfall." The more prevalent arrangement in the United States is for carried interest to be distributed on a *deal-by-deal* basis, which is therefore known as an "American waterfall." While a pure deal-by-deal approach is rare nowadays, a deal-by-deal with a loss carry forward is common in the U.S. market.[12] This model requires the use of escrow and clawback provisions, which are triggered if the fund has subsequently underperformed and, on calculating the funds aggregate returns, the managers are deemed to have received more than their contractual share.

Recently, there have been pioneering alternative carry waterfalls offered by top-end funds, aimed to further incentivize top young talent to prevent their departure. Mid- and junior-level fund managers have different cash flow needs than senior partners, and prefer to take carry earlier in the life of a fund. To achieve this arrangement, investors are offered the flexibility to choose their preferred carry model between a fund-as-a-whole or a deal-by-deal structure.[13] In order to lure LPs toward the more GP-favorable deal-by-deal option, a "sweetener" is often offered, usually in the form of a reduction in management fees. A potential problem with two different waterfalls in the same fund is the situation of falling back on one carry structure but not on the other; this gives rise to knock-on complexities, such as the question of whether the proceeds from one clawback could be used on the one that has not performed. These considerations add to an already complex fund structure, both in terms of subscription documentation and fund administration.

Escrow, clawback, and guarantee provisions can be hotly negotiated between LPs and GPs. Previously distributed carried interest would need to be refunded if realizations bring the overall fund performance either below the preferred return or to a level of carry below the one already distributed.[14] In all configurations, there

---

[11] This is particularly acute in the current low interest rate (and hence risk-adjusted rate of return) environment in capital markets. Keeping the hurdle at its historical level of 8% ensures that a larger proportion of funds will be performing below the hurdle, and even if they are producing an adequate return in terms of public market benchmarking, managers are induced to act sub-optimally since they are compensated more when passing the hurdle, thereby postponing realization of investments that are arguably ripe for exit.

[12] For VC funds, the fund-as-a-whole approach is also more common in the United States.

[13] In other cases, investors are offered the ability to split their commitments between the two waterfall structures into any desired proportion. Another model offers a fixed ratio for all investors with a percentage of each LP's contribution going to one carry model, and the rest going to another.

[14] Clawback is negotiation dependent—it may only cover where the GP has received excess carry or it may also cover where investors have not received their contributions back with preferred return, even where the GP has not hit carry.

is a counterparty risk in enforcing clawbacks. Carry recipients may have left the firm, used the money for consumption, or invested in real estate or other illiquid assets. Repayment of previously distributed carried interest is partial also because it is capped to the amount received by management, net of their personal taxes.

Carried interest charges are usually not contested like fixed management fees are. By being linked to performance, they are a fair, success-based compensation mechanism to share profit, especially in the presence of the stiff preferred return required before carry is entitled.[15]

PORTFOLIO COMPANIES' FEES

In addition to management and carry fees that are charged to investors, GPs and their affiliates may also charge the fund's portfolio companies an array of transactional, monitoring, and other fees. Although LPs are not charged directly, these fees affect the portfolio companies; hence, the economic consequences are borne by the fund investors. Typically, LPs believe that such fees paid to the GP and/or its affiliates from portfolio companies create a misalignment of GP and LP interests, and an avoidable inflation of the management fee paid to the GP. LPs generally prefer that the GP be motivated by the profits derived from the carried interest distributions.

In light of the above, LPs increasingly expect to share all the portfolio company fees received by the GP by having them netted, or offset, against the management fees. Accordingly, most LPAs contain management fee offset provisions which provide for reductions of management fees if the investment manager (or its affiliates) receives transactional fees directly from the fund's portfolio companies. While in the past, management fees were typically reduced by 50%, the current trend is to reach a 100% fee offset.[16]

Recently, expenses charged to portfolio companies have come under intense regulatory scrutiny. The first important development was the investigation of the U.S. Securities and Exchange Commission (SEC) into the matter of private equity hidden fees. On May 6, 2014, Andrew J. Bowden, Director of the SEC's Office of Compliance Inspections and Examinations delivered a speech in New York City with the unambiguous title, "Spreading Sunshine in Private Equity."[17] The speech summarized a long investigation by the SEC on deficiencies and wrongdoings regarding hidden fees. Lack of transparency and strict violations with respect to fees and expenses were found to be common. In particular, Bowden pointed out the widespread use of GPs' own operating partners as consultants charging full fees and expenses. Another fee that received considerable criticism was the accelerated monitoring fee (also known as the "termination fee") collected from portfolio companies at the time of exit.

In a subsequent development, in August 2015, one of the world's largest private equity investors, PGGM (a Dutch pension fund with over €180 billion in assets under management), announced that it would stop investing in outside money managers, including private equity firms, which do not fully disclose all of their fees. A few months later, the SEC announced that it "will continue taking action against advisers that do not adequately disclose their fees and expenses" following a settlement with Blackstone over accelerated

---

[15] However, some LPs dislike the automatic assumption of a 20% carried interest fee as being market standard. In particular, there is a downward pressure for first-time managers on reducing their carry fees.

[16] Large fee offsets can present tax issues because the investors may be viewed as sharing an income for services performed by the management company (which are taxed at ordinary income rates), rather than investment income (taxed at preferential, long-term capital gains rates).

[17] https://www.sec.gov/news/speech/2014--spch05062014ab.html.

monitoring fees. In December 2017, a settlement was also reached with TPG on similar claims of non-disclosure to investors of accelerated fees.

CalPERS lists the following types of fees that GPs or their affiliates receive from the portfolio companies:

- **Transaction fees:** For transactions that are consummated by the fund with respect to the portfolio company.

- **Monitoring fees:** Fees received in consideration for general ongoing advisory services provided.

- **Directors' fees:** Cash and non-cash directors' fees received in connection with serving as directors on the board of the portfolio companies.

- **Commitment fees:** Fees received for making available equity or debt commitments in respect of fund investments, regardless of whether such commitments are actually utilized (e.g., a fee on unused amounts in a revolving credit facility).

- **Break-up and topping fees:** Fees relating to transactions not completed and, in the case of topping fees, to the extent the transaction is not consummated as a result of another bidder.

- **Capital markets and financial advisory fees:** Fees for underwriting services and financial advisory services to the underwriting syndicate, and in respect of fund investments.[18]

To gauge the frequency and magnitude of portfolio company fees, Phalippou et al. (2016) gathered comprehensive data on 454 private equity-backed companies that went public between 1981 and 2013. Portfolio company fees were reported to represent over 6% of the invested capital, of which transaction fees represented nearly half of all fees. Interestingly, the most criticized accelerated monitoring fee was typically not found. When applied to CalPERS data, portfolio company fees were estimated in the study at $2.6 billion. Compared to $4.1 billion of management fees paid by CalPERS during the same period, portfolio company fees do not seem negligible.

In January 2016, ILPA released a fee reporting template and guidelines on how GPs should report fees and expenses to LPs. The new fee disclosure template seeks to revolutionize how private equity firms report fees, and to drive uniformity and clarity in reporting practices across the industry. The spreadsheet contains two parts: a section detailing the direct costs of participating in a given private equity fund, and a second section for a breakdown of fees, incentives, and reimbursements received by the GP. Many of the largest U.S. GPs have recently committed to use this standardized reporting template. With the buy-in of the industry trendsetters, the latest ILPA initiative may well see widespread uptake by both LPs and GPs.[19]

---

[18] Source: CalPERS Private equity workshop presentation November 2015. Some of these charges are labelled differently in other sources. Other common labels are exit fees, closing fees, placement fees, origination fees, consulting fees, acquisition and disposition fees, excess fees, and affiliate services fees. However, the CalPERS list is comprehensive and refers to the same items.

[19] In another development, as of mid-2016, the SEC has further intensified its enforcement of transparency into the disclosure of how fees and expenses are charged to portfolio companies or the funds. The SEC's enforcement division set up a unit specifically dedicated to investigating potential securities-law violations by asset managers, including private equity firms.

DISTRIBUTION WATERFALLS

The fund distribution waterfall sets the order and tiered priority for the payment of proceeds from investments. The layering of waterfall tiers can be a matter of negotiation, and a wide variety of practices exist. The foremost choice is whether the distribution is on a deal-by-deal basis or on a fund-as-a-whole basis (i.e., the American and European structures discussed earlier). The general distribution rules are as follows:

- First priority is the return of capital contribution to investors with respect to the investment giving rise to the distribution, unreturned capital contribution of previously disposed investments, and write-downs of current unrealized investments. Proceeds are apportioned to all partners pro rata to their investment percentage; this includes the investment by the GP side by side with the LPs.

- Second in the waterfall is to return to investors the organizational expenses and management fees.[20]

- Next priority is to pay the promised preferred return hurdle to investors, calculated either on the capital contribution made toward the specific investment or on the total amount of the drawn-down contribution.

- Next priority is a profit participation catch-up to the GP until the GP has received a 20% share of distributed profits (i.e., the preferred return hurdle plus the amount of the catch-up). Usually, 100% of the incremental cash goes to the GP until it is fully caught up with the investors.

- Finally, any remaining cash is split between the GP and the investors 20/80, or any other split that has been agreed, including sliding scales.

It is instructive to review costs to the LPs in aggregate, and to benchmark private equity to other alternative asset classes. Exhibit 1 displays the total fees to fund managers which are reported by the Texas Retirement System, one of the most prominent U.S. pensions (with a total of $25 billion under management). Fixed annual fees and performance-based carry paid in 2015 are shown for each of the main classes of alternative investments. The table also includes the size of assets under management in each category and the annual returns.

Management fees in private equity and in almost all other groups amount to about 2% (with the exception of opportunistic credit). Note that the ratio of performance-based carry to fixed fees in private equity is remarkably higher than in any other asset class, especially when judged together with the corresponding performance that forms the basis for the carried interest.

---

[20] More precisely, this stage is only for a deal-by-deal model. For a fund-as-a-whole model, organizational and operating expenses plus management fees would be included in the return of drawn-down capital that constitutes stage one.

Exhibit 1: Texas Retirement System average annual fees to alternative asset managers in 2015–2016 (in US$ millions)

Alternative Investments	Management Fees	GP Carried Interest	Fair Value at Dec. 31, 2016	Average 2015–2016 Annual Return
Private Equity	55	70	3,100	11.6%
Private Real Estate Partnerships	12	11	572	9.8%
Hedge Funds	97	46	6,158	1.2%
Opportunistic Credit	22	18	1,630	6.7%
Distressed Debt	11	17	575	5.6%

Source: Texas Retirement System annual financial reports for December 31, 2015 and December 31, 2016.

LP LIQUIDITY MANAGEMENT

Drawdown of capital commitment occurs on an as-needed basis to fund investments, partnership expenses, and management fees. However, the timing of capital calls to fund investments cannot be anticipated in advance, and once announced, payments must be promptly met on a short notice of 5–10 business days. To address the LP liquidity need, a drawdown reserve could be set through a special purpose account which holds assets that can be liquidated at short notice. In practice, such accounts are rarely set up and some LPs simply sell liquid financial assets such as stocks and bonds to meet the required capital calls.[21] Similarly, there is no fixed schedule of distribution that can be relied upon. Overall, the LPs' cash flow from investing in the fund is a step function that has a J-curve property. Exhibit 2 portrays a realistic cash flow pattern (J-curve) that reflects drawdowns and distributions netted out over the entire fund's life.

However, from an LP viewpoint, it is more relevant to consider the entire portfolio of positions rather than examine a single private equity fund. Whereas the cash flow from a single fund demonstrates a J-curve, the aggregated cash flows of a portfolio of funds across multiple vintage years can be drastically flattened. In effect, distributions from earlier funds that are deep in the harvesting period and drawdowns of unfunded commitments from later (younger) funds that are in the investment period partially offset each other.

Although a portfolio of private equity positions is very beneficial to manage liquidity, the offsetting process cannot be made precise. There is an inherent uncertainty in the timing of when GPs make their investments and when they sell them, so perfect foresight in the cash planning is impossible. Some years are net cash flow positive for LPs and others are net cash flow negative, a good indication of overall market sentiment. These patterns are correlated with the overall market conditions. It is more difficult to exit during periods of negative market sentiments; IPOs rarely take place and valuations as a whole are considered to be low, which often makes it difficult to find a trade buyer. These trends tend to affect all of the funds in the LP portfolio in a similar way, making the funding deficit bigger.

---

[21] Fund-of-funds LPs will have to draw capital from their own investors to meet their capital call obligations.

Exhibit 2: The J-Curve, simulated cash flow pattern of a fund since date of launch

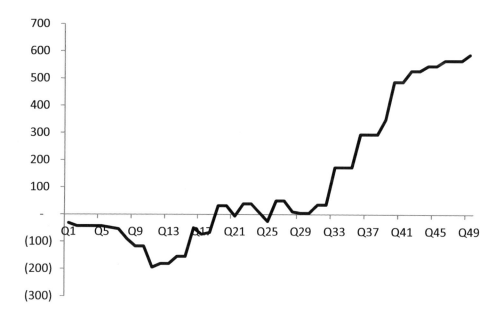

BORROWINGS AND FINANCIAL MANAGEMENT

Financial management policies at the fund level are evolving in terms of both sophistication and prevalence. Generally, fund agreements have policies and restrictions relating to fund borrowings, use of hedging instruments (in particular, currency hedging), and other derivatives. Whereas in the past, some would argue that funds should not be utilizing such instruments as it is not their core competency or part of their intended investment strategy, as the industry matures, funds cannot afford to miss taking advantage of the benefits of financial management.

There are three types of fund borrowings that are worth noting.[22] The first is cross-collateralization between portfolio investments—a policy that is restricted by most funds as it introduces substantial contagion risk within the investment in the fund. The second is the use of leverage at the fund level as part of the intended investment strategy. This type of borrowing is most commonly found among funds with investment strategies that have a yield component, such as private credit, infrastructure, and real estate. The third type is known as "capital call facilities," "subscription lines," or "drawdown facilities," which were originally used to overcome constraints of completing deals around holiday periods, to overcome short-term cover of an LPs default on a capital call, or to aggregate multiple drawdowns within a short period of time. Over time, these latter facilities were extended so that funds could make quarterly or periodic drawdowns at pre-determined dates (though the amount would still only be determined at the time of drawdown), which made the LP's management of the investment more efficient and less administratively onerous. These borrowing facilities

---

[22] A fourth, and much less common, form of fund borrowing is a *distribution facility* or *NAV facility*, by which secondary funds borrow against their matured asset in order to accelerate distributions.

are secured by the undrawn commitments of LPs to the fund, and are therefore extremely cheap as the risk of default is the risk of all LPs defaulting, which is quite low.[23]

In recent years, a clear trend has emerged. There has been a proliferation of cases where drawdown facilities were extended by up to a year, thus effectively financing the equity with inexpensive debt for part of the duration of the investment; this defers the calling of LP capital and simplifies the capital calls by enabling the GP to make investments and pay fund fees and expenses without frequent capital calls. The benefits to the LPs are double: predictability in planning cash flow drawdowns and substantially improved return on investment (by shortening the time over which investor capital is used). The use of borrowed money can flatten the J-curve of early returns. Since management fees are charged on total committed capital, their impact on NAV is drastic during the early period in the fund life where a relatively small percentage of capital has been put to work.

Unlike leverage on a fund, drawdown facilities do not provide incremental capital to invest and are simply a temporary loan against LP capital call commitments. Hence, they do not impose an additional leverage to the investment. Nevertheless, the use of capital call facilities has negative aspects as well. First, interest payments on borrowed capital reduce the fund's dollar lifetime gains and its multiple of capital. Second, some LPs investing in U.S. funds seek to avoid having so-called "unrelated business taxable income" (UBTI). The use of capital call facilities increases the risk of UBTI to these LPs. Third, the existence of borrowing facilities could complicate the process of selling an LP interest in a secondary transaction in cases where the buyer is less creditworthy than the seller. Fourth, as the use of fund-level borrowing increases, banks are requiring more intrusive financial information from LPs, which is often met with an increasing resistance. Some LPs are expressly demanding to be excluded from borrowing against their drawdown commitments, which can lead to a negative dynamic between the LPs and GP. Fifth, since the use of borrowing instruments results in there being fewer but larger capital calls, the magnitude of potential defaults by LPs is increased, along with the potential consequences.[24]

Borrowing through capital call facilities significantly complicates the fund performance analysis that must be performed by the LPs as part of their due diligence. Now there is a need to disaggregate the performance of the portfolio companies from the boosting effect of fund borrowing, which requires a computation of the detailed loan facility cash inflows and outflows.

Various hedging strategies may also be incorporated into a fund's investment structure or risk management practice. Whereas there has always been a level of treasury and corporate finance activity that incorporated hedging strategies within portfolio companies, now GPs also consider it at the fund level. For instance, a common goal is to mitigate currency risk and other risks that could have an impact on performance, or to address concerns of LPs whose base currency for investment differs from that of the fund.

Some LPs view financial management positively since the ultimate outcome is delivering a better performance and an ability to demonstrate fund management skills which go beyond deal-making skills. Yet, the flip side is that financial management can be viewed as a manipulation of performance results—in particular, it can push the performance above the hurdle threshold at which fund managers start earning their carried interest. Another negative aspect is that credit facilities are secured against a fund's LP base and its ability to honor capital calls. If lenders earmark certain large, blue-chip institutional investors against which to lend, this may limit the ability of these investors to liquidate their position through a secondaries sale. Such a

---

[23] Bank loans against future capital calls are limited as a percentage of the LP's capital commitments. Commitments from the most creditworthy LPs earn 90% advance rate, whereas commitments from lesser credits earn lower advance rates.

[24] The analysis of capital calls facilities has largely benefited from the April 2017 letter of Howard Marks to Oaktree Capital clients.

transfer may be blocked until the GP is able to negotiate an alternative assurance with the credit provider. Finally, financial management of a fund can threaten to change its risk profile in the eyes of the regulator, and thus expose it to greater oversight. For instance, in Europe, using leverage at the fund level increases the regulatory burden under the AIFMD.

Terms relating to financial management have become quite prevalent in fund agreements. GPs will inevitably have to embrace the use of these instruments in a savvy way to remain competitive, while LPs should command a deep understanding of these strategies and analyze the effect of their implementation on the drivers of fund performance.

OTHER ISSUES

Side letters

Side letters have long been used by fund managers to allow an investor to make its investment in a fund on terms that are different from the main fund legal agreements. Originally, this customization of terms by a side letter was confined to matters like promising the investor a seat on the investor committee, enhanced information rights, or preapproved transfers. Although these are important concessions from an investor's perspective, they are not fundamental to the operational terms of the fund. Historically, it was common for funds to include a *most favored nation* (MFN) clause. The MFN provision obliges fund managers to disclose all side letter terms to their investors generally and, in most cases, allows investors elect to receive the benefits of side letter terms.

Recently, however, the customization sought (and, in many cases, achieved) by big investors has accelerated and broadened in scope. GPs continue to facilitate these requests by entering into side letters with the investors, although it would be more appropriate to describe them as "special deal" letters, as they effectively make significant changes to the terms of the particular investor. Alongside this development, more and more funds are excluding MFN clauses (the elective rights in particular, and more rarely, the right to receive disclosure of the terms of other side letters too) or, if one is included, peppering them with exceptions and eligibility criteria, generally weakening the protection that they provide to investors. For instance, funds might state that the right to elect to receive the same terms as other investors does not extend to provisions relating to economics.

A high proportion of buyout funds now invoke the concept of tiering investors for the MFN clause, which limits an investor's ability to receive the benefit of side letter terms based on the size of its fund commitment. For example, an investor that commits €100 million may be confined to choosing terms in side letters signed by investors making commitments of €100 million or less. Some GPs have also been creating tiers for their MFN rights to deny disclosure of the terms of any side letter to LPs who do not commit at least as much as the ones who were granted the side letter; this makes it very difficult for investors to understand how good or bad their terms are in comparison to others' terms, and may also make it difficult for them to oversee the GP effectively.

LP default

The obligation on the part of LPs to meet capital calls is a contractual one: they are legally bound to meet calls when requested by the GP, after which, they have between a week and two weeks to wire funds. There is no discretion on the matter (although an LP may have negotiated a right to opt out of certain investments in the side letter, for reasons such as being bound by ethical investment guidelines), and a failure to meet this obligation is unacceptable to both the fund manager and the other LPs. Defaulting on a capital call is extremely rare and would entail penalties, the severity of which depends on the policies adopted by the GP and the terms agreed in the LPA. Penalties range from a punitive interest until a payment is made, forcing the LP to sell its position in the fund to other investors (potentially at a steep discount to fair value), or being forced to give up its entire stake in the fund (which is then split among the other LPs). An LP defaulting is also likely to result in exclusion from participation in future investments or even future funds raised by that GP or by others.

Investors could face an acute liquidity constraint which does not enable them to meet their undrawn obligation. In such a case, they may opt to sell their stake in the secondary market even at a discount. This scenario is particularly relevant at the earlier stage of the fund life when the outstanding commitments are large and the absolute cost in terms of discount to NAV is relatively small. At the extreme, LPs may even be willing to pay other investors to step into their shoes just to preserve their clean record, thereby avoiding being excluded from future investment participation. Such a situation occurred during the height of the global financial crisis in 2009, when fund vintages were only one or two years old, with the vast majority of commitments still to be honored. At that time, many investors lacked the liquidity or were constrained by allocation restrictions that were out of sync due to the denominator effect of the fallen valuations in equities and other asset classes.

Recycling of capital commitments

Once investments are realized, it is generally obligatory to distribute the proceeds to the investors. A few exceptions in the fund operating agreement may allow the fund to *recycle* capital (i.e., to reinvest the proceeds rather than distribute them). These exceptions include investments yielding a quick return (typically when realized within one year after the investment is made) and returns on investments during the investment period.

While recycling is an esoteric consideration for buyout, growth, and venture funds, it is quite important in other segments of private equity where the average holding period is shorter. One-time recycling is very common in secondaries funds and private credit, and quite justifiable given the high fund set-up costs. Recycling allows these costs to be spread over more investments as long as they fall within the fund life. Finally, private equity vehicles that are structured as closed-end funds obviously practice recycling as their core business.

Key person

As in many other situations where the existing management is key to the decision to invest, a key person clause is standard in the LPA. Track record and skills are associated with key investment professionals, who are literally handed a blank cheque to invest and operate with for 10 years. Investors seek downside protection by preventing key persons from departing in order to keep the team together. Similarly, investors look to guarantee that the key persons are truly committing their time and efforts to the benefit of the fund rather than to other enterprises.[25] Should a key partner cease to work on the fund, certain LPA-stipulated events occur, usually triggering an immediate end to the investment period.

An unusual twist in private equity is when the GP firm avoids listing partners as key persons, so as not to give these individuals undue power within the partnership (in that their departure would trigger the key person clause). Conversely, founders could insist to be listed as a key person as an anti-takeover device, so that they could not be forced out by their peers. Indeed, it has become more common to see these key person events being triggered when a certain portion or majority of listed partners leave.

Co-investments

Co-investments are a solution to allow GPs to make deals that were larger than their investment strategy and concentration restrictions. When investment size restrictions apply, acquisitions are structured by augmenting the fund's capital with funding injected directly to the deal by the LPs, known as "co-investment." The economics of the co-investment could be structured to be the same as the fund's capital, though in most cases, investors' expectation is that their additional capital would be invested on preferential economic terms relative to the investment in the deal through the fund.[26] Thus, co-investing has grown in importance for LPs as it offers a way to reduce the total cost of investing with the GP on a capital-weighted average basis.

Fund agreements mostly grant the GP full discretion regarding how to manage the allocation and economics of co-investments. Side letters may be used to grant specific co-investment rights to certain investors; however, this is a problematic arrangement as it results in certain LPs potentially getting preferential treatment at the expense of others. Furthermore, the allocation of expenses relating, in particular, to broken deals where co-investors were involved has come under the scrutiny of regulators. Given the prevalence of co-investing and the potential conflicts arising from current structures, better governance methods will need to be adopted. One example of a cleaner solution is the use of a pre-determined co-investment fund vehicle, sometimes referred to as an "overflow fund" or "top-up fund," that is raised alongside the main fund and used for co-investments. Raising such a vehicle at the outset of the funds life clarifies to all LPs how co-investments will be allocated, to whom, and at what economics.

CONCLUSION

The last two decades have seen a prodigious expansion of private equity into new asset types and geographies. As the industry has matured and gained experience, the economic principles that govern the relationships between investors and fund managers have become more complex. More structures have been designed, offering an elaborate web of variations to accommodate the growing needs of investors. An additional driver of change may have been legislation that set the asset class under far more regulation. Led in parallel by the European Union, the U.S. Treasury, and ILPA, this legislation has resulted in greater transparency, risk

---

[25] Managers define business time in different ways. Some exclude time given over to charitable, civic, or political activities, or to managing private investment portfolios. In addition, time committed is often defined as relating to the manager as a whole (i.e., all funds managed by that manager) rather than the particular fund in question. Stipulation of the minimal time commitments also decreases following the end of the investment period.

[26] It is quite common to have the co-investment capital invest with no fee and no carry to the GP.

compliance, and, to some degree, a change in terms. Finally, as in all other corners of capital markets, macroeconomic and political forces filter their way into the rules affecting the industry.

REFERENCES

Jacobides, M. and M. Umana (2017), "What you pay and what you get... The evolution of fund terms, fundraising and returns in private equity," Adveq Applied Research Series, London Business School.

Phalippou, L. et al (2016), "Private equity portfolio company fees," Oxford University working paper, April.

Polsky, G. D. (2009), "Private Equity Management Fee Conversions," Tax Notes, Vol. 122, No. 7, 2009.

Stepstone (2016). "Uncovering the costs and benefits of private equity," April

In his own words: Dr. Jim Strang, Head of Europe, Hamilton Lane

Most private equity funds adopt the tried-and-tested structure of the LPA. While the industry has evolved a great deal over the last 20 years, the LPA nevertheless has remained the most prevalent structure by which most private equity vehicles are managed. In principle, such a structure allows the vehicle to have an individual legal identity and to afford the LPs a relatively simple and tax-efficient mechanism within which to hold their assets. The relationships between the investments, the investors, and the manager of the fund (i.e., the GP) are all clearly enshrined in this simple structure.

One of the reasons why the limited partnership has persisted as the vehicle of choice for managing private equity investments is that it has proven to be an ideal platform for the prevailing economic model of the industry, the classic "2 and 20." The fundamental mechanics of fund economics have for the most part remained unchanged since the inception of the industry, and are ingrained in basic principles. The GP receives an annual, typically all-encompassing management fee as a percentage of the aggregate commitments made to the fund. In addition, the fund manager has the ability to earn a performance fee or "carried interest" of typically 20% of the profits generated by the vehicle. This latter carried interest is nearly always subject to the returns of the fund beating a compounding hurdle, which has historically been set at 8% per annum. As the industry has developed, there has been some moderation in management fees charged, notably by larger funds, but the notion of sharing 20% of the funds profits with the GP, subject to beating an 8% hurdle rate, has remained very much in place thus far.

Insofar as GPs market their products through one comingled structure, investors do seek to negotiate the key terms of the documents. Often, these negotiations center on the investment mandate of the vehicle, the governance of the vehicle, the key economic levers, and the provisions for the rights and responsibilities of the parties should something deviate from the agreed-upon plan. The success of these negotiations largely depends upon the relative negotiating power of the investor, how large a commitment is being envisaged, and, to some extent, the point in the financial cycle at which negotiations are taking place. Instances in which the balance of power to make material changes rests more with the GPs than with the investors are relatively low. In the case of a first-time fundraising in a weaker fundraising environment, the ability to make substantive changes is far greater. Typically, each investor will at least have an agenda of points to negotiate in the main documents and will seek to do so. Often, the most challenging area for negotiation is—perhaps unsurprisingly—around the economic levers, with the quantum of fees and the operation of carry waterfalls representing the most sensitive items.

In addition to the standard negotiations, some investors also enter into specific bilateral negotiations through "side letter" agreements. These are adjunct to the main partnership agreements and relate to particular requests and needs of individual LPs.

Notably, these side letters can outline any co-investment relationship the investor seeks to have with the GP. The operation of co-investment, the means by which the opportunities are allocated, and the manner in which deal-related expenses are apportioned are all relevant points and subject to increasing scrutiny and review. Side letters add a further layer of complexity to the overall negotiations and are frequently responsible for delaying the closing of a vehicle. Nonetheless, they appear set to remain a feature of the operation of the agreements, at least for now.

As investors have sought (successfully) to manage down the fee leakage of the asset class over time, a number of different areas have been targeted, notably transaction fees, offset provisions, and GP clawbacks. Recently, investors have increasingly looked to co investments and separately managed accounts (SMAs, or "funds of one") as ways to drive down the marginal costs of investment and to fit specific constraints. Often structured as a partnership themselves, SMAs are simply tailor-made vehicles that allow bilateral deals to be done between GPs and specific investors. The key differentiator here is that each SMA is unique, meaning there are no predefined terms as would be the case in a co-mingled fund. Each is effectively a negotiation with no anchoring of key terms. The dynamic here tends to be good for the fee-conscious LP and less so for the GP. A key point in negotiating and assessing such agreements has to do with the precise manner in which any SMA will operate by being fully transparent to any relevant fund LPs, particularly as these agreements relate to deal and cost allocations.

In summary, as long as private equity managers continue to deliver the level of net performance to investors that they have achieved historically, it seems likely that the economic structures, at least as they pertain to funds, will remain in place for the foreseeable future. Evolution has occurred but, thus far, there has been no major revolution in the way the various structures operate. It is difficult to see what might cause this to change in the future; however, if there was one likely catalyst on the horizon, it would be the imperative to open up the asset class to a wider investor universe through the establishment of liquid vehicles. That would be a game changer for the industry.

3 Types of Private Capital Funds

Strength lies in differences, not in similarities.
Stephen R. Covey

INTRODUCTION

Various types of private equity funds have evolved over time. This evolution has led to funds that differ significantly in terms of their specialization and organization; their diverse characteristics affect their investment focus and pace, the necessary skills of their managers, the structure of the investments made, and the management of those investments. The real lifespan of a private equity fund may stretch to as long as 15 years. This period usually involves four stages that often overlap, regardless of the type of private equity fund:

1. **Fundraising period** (1–2+ years): During fundraising, fund managers aim to convince investors to provide capital to finance the strategy of the fund. During the interval between the first capital raising (i.e., initial closing) and the final funding round (i.e., final closing), the fund manager may make some investments thus starting the investment sourcing period.

2. **Investment sourcing period** (2–5+ years): During this stage, a dedicated team spends a substantial amount of time and effort identifying investments that fit the strategy of the fund. Depending on the type of the fund, fund managers can create significant value at this point by paying the right price for investments.

3. **Managing and improving the portfolio period** (3–7+ years per investment): Once investments are made, the fund's managers must work to monitor them and improve their value. Managers might sell some investments early, leading to an overlap of the liquidation and portfolio management periods.

4. **Liquidation period** (varied time frame): Exits may occur as quickly as six months after an investment if the right buyers and economic conditions are present. However, if the investment underperforms/develops slowly, the economic conditions are not favorable, or buyers are not present, the exit of an investment may drag out for eight years or more.

Most private equity funds receive capital from third-party investors, such that no single investor holds a majority stake in the fund (i.e., independent funds). Yet, there is a set of funds where one shareholder provides the majority of the capital, known as *captive funds* (if the main shareholder provides all of the fund's capital) or *semi-captive funds* (if the main shareholder contributes capital together with third-party investors). Captive funds are often subsidiaries or departments of a larger parent organization, such as a financial institution, technology or industrial company, or a local/central government.

Generally, private equity funds can be classified across two sets of criteria (see Exhibit 1):

1. **Life cycle of the firm:** Funds under this classification focus on investing in early stage, growing, mature, or declining companies.

2. **Type of investment:** Funds of this type focus on specific assets such as debt securities, infrastructure, real estate, other private equity funds, and so on.

Exhibit 1: Company life cycle and form of funding in the private capital market

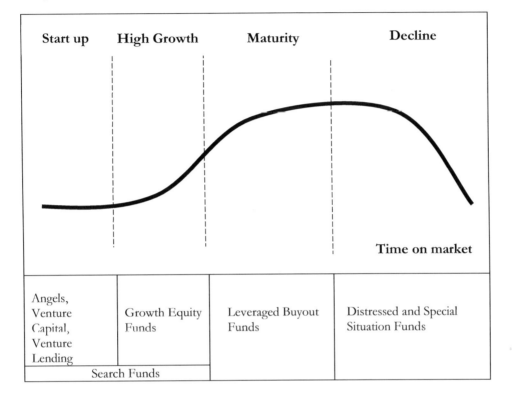

This introductory chapter aims to provide an overview of the different types of funds in the private equity space, along with a summary of the primary rationale and value proposition that each fund offers. We discuss the structures, strategies, and operations that are unique to each type of fund in greater detail in later chapters.

ANGEL INVESTING

One of the most important considerations that new and small firms face in the transformation from entrepreneurial ideas to revenue-generating companies is how to secure capital. Because traditional avenues of finance, such as debt, are often unavailable, many young firms seek risk capital from business angels and venture capital (VC) funds. Angels tend to invest in smaller amounts and at earlier stages of development than VC funds do. Therefore, they place capital at risk in young companies that have a high degree of uncertainty and entrepreneurs with limited track records.

Angels tend to be high-net-worth individuals who invest their own funds in start-ups operated by entrepreneurs who are neither friends nor family members.[1] Given that they invest their own capital, these

---

[1] The term "angel investor" originates from the financiers of Broadway shows in the early 1900s. These wealthy individuals provided capital to help launch new theatrical productions. As patrons of the arts, these investors were considered "angels" by theatre professionals.

investors are accountable only to themselves, and have no need to refer decisions to others for approval. Typically, this type of investment is carried out either through close friends (by introducing entrepreneurs to potential investors through relatives, friends, colleagues, or professors) or through angel networks when one angel investor can get others interested in investing. Because of time and financial constraints, angels rarely undertake extensive due diligence.

Business angels are motivated by financial returns on their investments but they also have alternative reasons to invest. For instance, some angels may want to work at the companies they invest in; others might simply enjoy helping another entrepreneur build a business; and still others may seek to benefit from tax incentives.[2] Hence, beyond financing, angels can provide value-added services to entrepreneurs in the form of seasoned advice or business networks. Angels usually participate informally, although sometimes they may enter into a formal employment or consulting relationship with the start-up.

At present, however, an increasing number of angels are abandoning informal operations in favor of *business angel networks* that facilitate the pooling of their investments. These networks can be local, regional, national, based on direct contact, or purely online. The advantages of working in a network include gaining easier access to pre-qualified deal flow, leveraging the intellectual capital and expertise of individual members, and learning from each other with respect to deal evaluation skills, interactions with VC fund managers, and so on. Angel networks not only facilitate funding for larger deals through the pooling of member angels' resources, but also enable greater due diligence, provide consulting services to young entrepreneurs, develop codes of conduct for angels to promote best practices, and engage in regular dialogue with governments to help shape policies.

VENTURE CAPITAL AND VENTURE LENDING FUNDS

VC funds provide early stage equity funding to potentially high-growth private companies. Their capital generally follows a founder's self-funding and seed funding stages from business angels, and is used to facilitate the company's growth and increase its scale. VC fund managers are often heavily involved with their portfolio companies, both in daily operations and as strategic advisers.

The typical investment approach of a VC fund is to acquire a *non-controlling* stake in the private company via preferred shares, and to provide the *capital in tranches*. This approach minimizes investment risk and allows the VC fund manager to learn more about the entrepreneur and the prospects of the business before deploying the full capital amount. For instance, a VC fund might contractually commit to provide equity capital to a company if specific financial and non-financial hurdles (e.g., revenue targets, clinical test approvals, licensing agreements, etc.) are met over time.

Another approach involves *staging the capital*, whereby a discrete and smaller pool of capital is provided by the VC fund for a specific stage or round of financing. The entrepreneur must raise subsequent capital after the capital from a particular round has been exhausted. Even within round financing the capital is provided gradually on a contingent basis, subject to specific milestones. The multiple rounds of finance can be broadly split into *pre-revenue* and *post-revenue rounds*, and then more specifically into *start-up, seed, early, mid-*, and *late stage* financing. The start-up, seed, and early stages are typically pre-revenue, while the mid- and late stages apply to post-revenue firms. Each round of financing involves at least two VC funds, with one being the lead

---

[2] In many countries, governments offer tax relief on the amount invested in early stage ventures, which has an immediate effect on the annual income tax of the angel investor.

investor. The presence of multiple VC fund managers offers different perspectives and increased industry contacts while providing incrementally more capital, distributing the risk, and validating the valuation of the company.

Like many of the other private equity funds discussed below, VC funds are usually structured as partnerships, wherein a set of passive LPs supplies the capital and the GP invests and manages the fund. The primary difference between buyout funds and VC funds is the amount of the fund: a VC fund will rarely exceed $500 million due to smaller deal sizes and extensive post-investment involvement in the portfolio companies.

Most VC funds have a fixed 10-year lifetime, with potential extensions to liquidate investments. A GP may spend one year fundraising (depending on investor interest), with investors committing a fixed amount to the GP for a specific VC fund.[3] After the fundraising period ends, VC fund managers spend the next five years, on average, sourcing and completing investments. Years five through eight are spent managing the investments and improving value in portfolio companies. The last two years of the fund's life reflect the exiting phase, during which the fund monetizes its investments through a variety of methods, including a trade sale or merger, IPO, or stock buyback. These time frames are subject to many factors, including the GP's track record, the team of venture professionals and its stability, market conditions, and types of investment strategies.

Many established corporations set aside capital into funds with the purpose of investing in independent early stage entities that operate in related sectors. These *corporate venture capital* (CVC) funds can serve as another available source of capital for early stage companies. CVC funds invest both for strategic as well as financial reasons and, like traditional VC fund managers, professionals running CVC funds may offer strategic advice and other support services to start-ups to help foster their development. In many cases, CVC funds operate alongside traditional VC funds as an additional source of finance for early stage companies.

One of the primary factors driving CVC investments is corporations' need to gain competitive advantage via early access to a new concept or product. By becoming an investor in a promising young entity, a large corporate can monitor developments on new concepts or products and gain a first-mover advantage for any joint venture or licensing schemes. CVC also avoids costly and uncertain M&A transactions, although a corporation may subsequently acquire developed entities that it encountered through previous CVC investment activities.

Finally, early stage companies can receive capital from *venture lending funds*. Venture lending is defined as debt offered by a fund to a company that is still reliant on VC. Venture debt can be secured by the future cash flows expected to be generated by the start-up or collateral (e.g., receivables, inventories, intellectual property, etc.). This debt could offer bridge financing between various equity rounds, or provide funding to sustain the company through product development and testing, marketing campaigns, and other similar phases that are necessary to expand the company.

Venture lending funds often receive equity warrants in addition to interest payments and fees as consideration. These warrants add an equity component that compensates for the risk undertaken, thus resulting in a debt-equity hybrid investment instrument. While the returns required by venture lending funds are lower than those of pure equity investors, the all-in rate from interest, fees, and warrants makes the venture debt considerably more expensive than the debt offered by commercial banks. Further, venture loans come with strict financial and operational covenants that may restrict the activities of the early stage company.

---

[3] Exceptions include most funds raised by the top VC firms, which have historically been many times oversubscribed.

However, the right use of venture lending can help the entrepreneur optimize dilution while still raising enough capital for the business.

GROWTH EQUITY FUNDS

Growth equity (or *growth capital*) *funds* follow an investment strategy that falls between those of VC and control leveraged buyouts. Growth equity funds facilitate the target company's accelerated growth through expanding operations, entering new markets, or consummating strategic acquisitions.

While definitions of growth equity strategies can differ between funds, a growth equity investment is usually characterized by (1) a minority position in the target; (2) a target company without prior institutional investors that is founder-owned; (3) no (or minimal) leverage; (4) a target company with an established product or service, existing customers, and an established business model; and (5) a growth inflection point where capital can drive organic growth in excess of 10% per annum. Therefore, the key trait of the investment strategy of these funds is entering a target company at an inflection point where growth capital can fuel substantial revenue and profitability progression. The capital provided serves as a launching pad for the next stage of development, or can contribute to changing some part of the company's business model.

The above investment traits generally serve to keep the risk profile low by avoiding companies with technology or adoption risks and isolating the execution risk. In addition, the capital provided by growth equity funds is typically more senior than common equity, and often comes with negotiated control provisions (such as veto rights on certain reserved matters), board representation, and approval rights to mitigate the risks associated with owning a minority position in a growth stage private company. Overall, these terms inherently create a portfolio with less risk.

Unlike VC managers, growth equity fund managers need to convince entrepreneurs of the merit and potential behind the capital injection and partnership upside as many target firms do not need to raise any capital. Many growth equity managers use a "cold calling" approach with team members reaching out to management teams of potential target companies to build a relationship and better understand the company's operations and receptivity to taking institutional capital.

Growth equity funds appeal to investors for three main reasons:

- **Lower risk profile:** By making minority investments with little or no leverage, a growth equity fund is able to maintain a lower risk profile relative to traditional buyouts and VC funds. Growth equity funds also target companies that have lower technology and adoption risk than VC targets. Typically, target companies are already profitable and have achieved product-market fit. The senior equity position and protective shareholder and governance provisions common in growth investments further mitigate downside risk compared to other common strategies.

- **Good investment performance:** Growth equity fund returns are in line with those of leveraged buyouts and exceed those of VC funds. Additionally, these returns have been distributed across the fund universe, prompting both leveraged buyout and late stage VC funds to infringe into the space when the environment fluctuates in their main line of business.

- **Secular growth:** Growth equity funds seek out targets that are concentrated in sectors that facilitate consistent organic growth. This approach has resonated strongly with investors during periods of low-growth macroeconomic conditions.

Given that growth equity funds usually take a minority interest in their target companies, they are vulnerable to management teams that might have misaligned incentives. In order to address this issue, *redemption rights* have become an important factor that affects the success of the growth equity strategy. These rights allow the growth equity fund manager to compel the issuer to redeem its stock at pre-negotiated redemption values. The three most common triggers for these rights are: (1) *time*, typically set at 60–66 months from the date of the original growth equity investment; (2) *performance milestones*, benchmarked against the investment thesis or management case, defined revenue targets or profitability growth, customer wins, and so on; and (3) *covenant defaults*, based on the issuers' failure to satisfy defined financial covenants of debt financings.

Redemption values differ from one investment to another, but common levels include the original issuance level plus interest, a set multiple (or IRR) on the original issuance level, or the fair market value of the equity. The company must then repay to the investor the redemption value and/or undertake a liquidity generating process to raise sufficient capital for the redemption. If the company is not able to pay the redemption value, it may enter into default. Thus, negotiating redemption default remedies has become a key aspect of the growth equity investment strategy.

LEVERAGED BUYOUT FUNDS

Leveraged buyout funds acquire controlling stakes in mature private companies using a mixture of third-party debt and the funds' own resources. The amount of debt used is typically around 50% of the target's purchase price, but this figure rose to as high as 90% on some deals during the peak transaction years before the credit crisis. The debt is usually either unsecured, or secured against the target's assets. The target's free cash flows are used to service and repay the debt.

The acquisition debt used by buyout funds almost always includes a loan portion that is senior and secured, and is arranged by a commercial or investment bank. Very often, the bank transfers this debt to institutional investors (e.g., hedge funds, debt funds, or collateralized loan obligations). The debt in leveraged buyouts also includes a junior, unsecured portion that is financed by either high-yield bonds or "mezzanine debt" (that is, debt that is subordinated to the senior debt).

Because of the use of debt, buyout funds mostly invest in companies that have unused debt capacity. Potential targets should also have predictable and strong cash flows as well. High levels of acquisition debt with acceptable interest rates are only possible if the company can reliably service the interest and principal repayments. In addition, companies need to have a strong asset base (i.e., a large amount of tangible assets) that can be used as collateral to secure the debt.

Buyout funds hold target companies for between four to seven years on average, and then sell them to realize a return that is expected to be at least 20% per annum. The buyout fund managers use a combination of three principal mechanisms to achieve this objective: (1) implement operational improvements to boost the target's revenues and earnings; (2) pay down the debt raised to acquire the target using the target's free cash flows from operations, thereby increasing the equity portion in the capital structure of the company; and (3) sell the target company at a higher multiple.

Like VC funds, buyout funds are typically structured as limited partnerships with a fixed (usually 10-year) life which can be extended in increments of two years. They are managed by managers (the GPs) on behalf of their investors (the LPs) who commit capital that is drawn down over the fund's life when the managers wish to buy a target company.

DISTRESSED AND SPECIAL SITUATIONS FUNDS

Distressed private equity funds are vehicles investing in securities of companies facing financial distress or bankruptcy. While the returns of more traditional private equity fund types (such as buyout and VC) are generally positively correlated to economic growth, the reverse is true for distressed private equity funds. Contractions in credit markets and slowdowns in economic growth provide great investment opportunities for these funds.

Distressed funds follow several investment strategies:

- **Trading** involves purchasing debt obligations trading significantly below par value and reselling them over a relatively short period at a higher value to generate a trading profit.

- **Active/non-control** strategies involve the accumulation of significant positions in debt issued by companies that are likely to go through, or are in, a bankruptcy restructuring process. The goal is to gain a position of influence in the negotiations over the restructuring process to maximize returns. This strategy can also involve purchasing pooled assets from banks or other financial institutions at a steep discount from their par value, and holding the assets until maturity or restructuring them; these assets are typically *non-performing loans*. By pooling the assets, the funds can diversify credit risks.

- **Control** strategy means the fund manager builds a controlling position in a debt security issued by a company that is close to, or in, a bankruptcy proceeding in order to effectively obtain control of the target company through the bankruptcy process. With this strategy, the distressed debt position is, in many respects, the start of a much longer process. After winning control of the target, the fund manager acts very much as a buyout fund manager would, controlling the company and turning it around (or restructuring it) to maximize profitability.

Hedge funds provide strong competition in the distressed debt sector, especially to funds pursuing trading strategies. However, in most distressed debt and restructuring funds, deep knowledge and experience in bankruptcy law and its processes are key. Bankruptcy regulations can differ tremendously from country to country; success in one legal environment under a specific set of regulations does not set a template that can be automatically duplicated in another jurisdiction.

Funds that pursue control type investment strategies are also called *restructuring* or *turnaround* or *special situations* funds (the terminology is not widely accepted). Generally, *special situation funds* follow the mantra of investing at the time of maximum pessimism. Managers of these funds prefer companies with particular circumstances that compel investors to trade the security based on the special situation, rather than the underlying fundamentals or some other investment rationale. Essentially, an investment made due to a special situation is often an attempt to profit from a change in valuation as a result of the special situation. Therefore, these funds might invest in a restructuring, turnaround, or any other unusual circumstances that a company can face. Investments are structured both as equity and debt instruments.

Institutional investors find these special situation funds compelling for many reasons. First, these funds have lower fees than other private equity funds (e.g., the management fees might be significantly lower than

2% while performance fees are below 20%). Since special situations funds play off the strengths and expertise of their fund managers by pursuing investments or themes that are already implemented in another fund run by the same manager, the costs necessary to explore these investments are much lower.

Second, while both buyout funds and special situation funds take commitments up front, buyout fund managers collect fees throughout the period when they are identifying investment opportunities, whereas special situation fund managers collect fees only once a specific investment opportunity is identified.[4] In certain isolated cases where a concept never fully materializes, a manager may wind down the special situations fund without ever calling capital or charging fees; this is a unique investor-friendly attribute.

SEARCH FUNDS

A search fund is an investment fund in which investors provide financial support to an entrepreneur (or group of entrepreneurs) who seeks to identify and acquire a small privately held company with stable cash flows and profits. An initial amount of *search capital* is first raised to finance the search stage, which involves identifying and evaluating the target company as well as negotiating the acquisition. To raise this initial search capital, entrepreneurs (also called *searchers* in this setting) often need to tap a wide network of potential investors, including friends and family.

Once a target is identified, the investors that provided the search capital are given the right of first refusal on their pro rata share of capital that will be raised to acquire the target company (i.e., the *acquisition capital*). The initial search capital is commonly rolled over at a stepped-up rate (e.g., 1.5x in the acquisition capital round, regardless of whether the investors that provided the search capital decide to participate in the acquisition or not. In addition to the follow-on investment provided by investors, the searchers often use capital from a combination of other sources (e.g., seller's debt, bank loans, or equity financing from new investors). Investor debt, usually in the form of subordinated debt, may also be added to the capital structure of the acquired company.

Searchers receive equity in the acquired company according to a vesting schedule and typically run the company themselves. Unlike in a traditional private equity fund model, management fees are minimal, if they exist at all. Instead, searchers receive a market rate salary in their post-acquisition managerial role. Because the searchers are generally less experienced with the operations of the company, in most cases, some investors take advisory roles to support them. Accordingly, it is important that search funders collaborate with a good mix of investors with different skills, such as operations experience or industry expertise.

For investors, a search fund represents an attractive investment for several reasons. First, the search fund is a staged investment. The purchase of a unit in a search fund does not create a commitment to contribute additional capital in the acquired company. The investor has the opportunity to become more familiar with the searchers during the process, and to analyze the investment opportunity provided in the second round with far more information. Moreover, the initial investors often gain preferential rights in the acquisition round. Second, some investors are partly motivated by their interest in helping a young team succeed. Of course, the financial aspect of the deal needs to be appealing, but this secondary motivation can forge a strong bond between investors and the searching entrepreneurs.

---

[4] This arrangement helps avoid the dreaded J-curve return profile (i.e., drawdowns at the start and returns appearing in later years).

DEBT AND MEZZANINE FUNDS

Debt funds are investment vehicles focusing on various debt securities issued by private companies. Managers of these funds have a dedicated expertise to originate loans by screening and selecting suitable borrowers and their projects (i.e., *direct lending*). Hence, debt funds address segments of the market that are often neglected by the banking sector (e.g., bespoke transactions, complex refinancing, lending based on operational cash flow patterns or intellectual property, etc.). Debt fund managers usually follow a flexible approach to structuring and pricing the loans, adapting the terms of the loan contract to the investee company's needs and activities. While debt funds are active in the primary lending market, they are also operating in the secondary loan market by purchasing loans originated by banks or other institutional investors.

Private debt funds have been increasing in size since the credit crisis, as banks can no longer sustain the same level of lending due to weak balance sheets and strict regulations. The funds appeal to investors who search for good return investments with diversification potential in a low-interest-rate environment. The funds' returns are achieved by investing in three distinct types of debt products: senior debt (first-ranking, secured loans used to finance buyout transactions and growth investing), mezzanine debt (debt that ranks between senior debt and equity in a company's capital structure), and distressed debt (debt trading significantly below par value). The typical investment strategy is to buy and hold these debt securities until maturity.

Funds investing in mezzanine debt have been well established for over 10 years, given that such debt plays an important part in the financing of acquisitions and leveraged buyouts. Managers of mezzanine funds usually structure the debt as an unsecured or subordinated note that is senior only to equity in the capital structure. They also demand an equity stake in the borrowing private company that takes the form of attached warrants or conversion features.

In contrast to senior debt, which generates returns mainly via interest payments, mezzanine funds aim to generate a certain rate of return which can come from five sources:

- **Cash interest:** This is the interest that is paid in cash regularly by the borrower, as agreed in the lending contract.

- **Payment-in-kind interest:** A periodic form of payment in which the interest payment is not paid in cash but rather, by increasing the principal amount of the security in the amount of the interest.

- **Equity ownership:** Along with the typical interest payment associated with debt, mezzanine capital will often include an equity stake in the form of attached warrants or a conversion feature, similar to that of a convertible bond.

- **Participation payout:** Instead of equity, the mezzanine fund manager may take an equity-like return in the form of a percentage of the company's performance, as measured by total sales, or EBITDA as a measure of cash flow, or profits.

- **Fees:** Mezzanine lenders often charge an arrangement fee, payable up front at the closing of the transaction. Arrangement fees contribute the least return and are primarily intended to cover administrative costs, and serve as an incentive to complete the transaction.

LISTED PRIVATE EQUITY FUNDS

Listed private equity (LPE) funds are funds listed on a stock exchange, offering investors the opportunity to participate either directly or indirectly in private equity investments. Managers of LPE funds tend to focus on different industrial sectors, geographies, and investment strategies (e.g., buyout, VC, or growth). They offer investors regular, easy-to-digest information, which is supplemented by ongoing research from an increasing number of brokers. The information provided includes details about the portfolio; lead indicators of portfolio performance; the vehicle's share rating, trading performance, and gearing levels; the progression of the net asset value of the fund; and the structure of the balance sheet.

Although LPE funds utilize the same structure and investing strategies as other private equity funds, they differ from traditional unlisted private equity funds in a number of ways:

- First, shares in LPE funds are listed and hence, relatively liquid. In contrast, transactions with shares in a private equity fund are more difficult and time consuming as share exchanges between LPs go through an auction house, requiring both due diligence and approval by the GP.

- Second, while traditional private equity funds have fairly high minimum investment requirements (usually millions of dollars), LPE funds have no minimum investment requirement or other requirements, such as a proven track record as an investor. As a result, LPE funds are accessible by smaller retail investors.

- Third, LPE funds are typically small, have an unlimited life ("evergreen"), and often retain and reinvest realized proceeds; by comparison, private equity funds are often large, have a limited life, return realized proceeds to investors, and liquidate once all investments are sold.

- Fourth, LPE funds do not offer co-investment opportunities to their investors.

While traditional private equity funds are virtually always structured as limited partnerships, the picture is much more heterogeneous for LPE funds. These vehicles may be structured as corporations, closed-end investment trusts, publicly traded partnerships, unit trusts, or other structures that charge significantly lower fees than many traditional private equity funds.

The majority of LPE companies are organized as *listed direct* private capital investment companies. In this context, the term "direct" indicates that the company is invested directly in the underlying companies, and not via limited partnerships. Thus, by purchasing shares traded on an exchange, an investor can gain exposure to a diversified portfolio of private companies directly held by the listed company. This organizational structure offers the investor not only direct exposure to a diversified portfolio of private companies, but also the change to participate in GP's revenues generated by the additional fund management business.

LPE funds may also invest in funds managed by others (i.e., they can act as funds of funds). These vehicles generally aim to offer a more broadly diversified exposure across private equity investments and vintage years to minimize the J-curve effect and reduce specific risks.

REAL ESTATE PRIVATE EQUITY FUNDS

Real estate private equity is an investable asset class that consists of debt and equity investments in the property markets, allowing multiple investors to pool their funds. Fund managers must have a dedicated expertise in the real estate sector. Returns are achieved through several means, such as capital appreciation on properties and land, rental yields, and fees and interest from financing activities.

Real estate private equity funds employ widely divergent investment strategies. One basic strategy is to acquire high-quality real estate at market yields and achieve the target returns on equity through structured financing. This *non-opportunistic* strategy is essentially the leveraged buyout model applied to real estate. It is a proven strategy if (1) the property performs as expected, (2) the spread between the property yield and the borrowing rate is large, and (3) a high proportion of the investment can be debt financed.

Many funds employ a variety of *value-enhancing* strategies, one of which is the acquisition of large portfolios of distressed assets (typically non-performing real estate loans) at wholesale with the purpose of reselling the individual loans separately. Another value-enhancing strategy is to finance the development of real estate via either raw land development or the construction of new buildings. When appropriately underwritten and leveraged, development generates pro forma equity returns in excess of 20%.

Management fees of real estate private equity funds are similar to those of buyout or venture funds. However, direct real estate private equity funds may charge additional real estate development fees or acquisitions/structuring fees. While the exact fee levels vary between funds and strategies, funds that follow non-opportunistic strategies generally charge lower fees.

INFRASTRUCTURE FUNDS

Infrastructure funds build portfolios of infrastructure assets into pooled vehicles that offer longer-term, high-yielding, defensive, risk-adjusted returns. A portfolio of defensive infrastructure assets is characterized by its low correlation to other asset classes, its relatively high inflation-linked cash yield, and its low overall volatility. Assessing the long-term profile of investment target assets is critical to successful infrastructure investing; to do so, managers should focus on sustainability of earnings, growth rates, risk factors, barriers to entry, and the competitive landscape. It is this combination of characteristics that supports the argument that infrastructure warrants its own allocation within an investment portfolio. These funds are well suited to pension funds and other long-term-oriented investors seeking steady, reliable, low-risk returns.

Due to the nature of the investments, private infrastructure funds can have life cycles of 25 years or more, with most falling between 10 and 15 years. Many investors struggle to produce management incentive plans, which combine incentives for short-term success and long-term stewardship. Creating an appropriate incentives environment can be the difference between deal success and failure. In most infrastructure funds, LPs receive the basic bond-related return free and clear (i.e., the GP does not participate in the base level of return, which can often be compared to a bond of comparable duration to which is added, in certain circumstances, a further margin).

Infrastructure funds typically fall into one of the following four structures: traditional 10- to 15-year maturity, hybrid, evergreen, and alternative.

- **Traditional 10- to 15-year maturity funds** have the most common structure among infrastructure funds, with a slightly longer maturity than the average private equity fund to account for the long-term nature of the underlying assets. More mature investors often seek to hold or enjoy exposure to contractually well-defined and stable assets for as long as possible.

- **Hybrid funds** are designed to invest across the infrastructure risk/return spectrum, aggregating investments with both shorter and longer maturities. Greenfield investments may be sold once they are completed and stabilized (generating higher IRRs than if the intent was to hold them to ultimate maturity), while other projects with naturally longer maturities may be either transferred in some way at the end of their life to LPs focused on long-tailed returns, or sold to other investors.

- **Evergreen funds** are designed to focus on longer-term holding periods, often with a greater emphasis on yield generation. Realized investment returns are recycled back into a fund rather than being distributed to LPs. Investments that potentially fall into this category include secondary infrastructure assets, core real estate assets, and any other asset class with a significant income component, longer-term hold, and lower risk profile than private equity or opportunistic strategies.

- **Alternative** forms of investment require larger capital commitments and substantial human resources to carry out the due diligence and portfolio monitoring that accompany investment in separate accounts and co-investments.

Infrastructure fund managers are usually value investors with a focus on the cash generative potential of targeted assets (majority of investments have current dividend yields). The infrastructure fund manager is responsible for the sourcing of deals, the execution of transactions (both acquisitions and, later in the life of the fund, divestments) on behalf of the fund, and the ongoing management of those assets held by the fund. Infrastructure managers employ execution and asset management teams that are comparable to private equity investment teams, albeit with specific skills and experience in relation to the regulatory and market considerations that affect the value of infrastructure assets.

SECONDARIES FUNDS

A secondaries fund focuses on buying out commitments of existing LPs in funds. The purchaser in the secondary transaction not only takes over the seller's existing stake in the fund but also the unfunded capital commitments. This is a specialized strategy which has been experiencing consistent strong growth recently. The main reasons for secondaries transactions can either be LP-led (where an existing LP wishes to liquidate the stake in a private equity fund sooner than the end of the fund life) or be GP-led (where the GP is perhaps looking to extend the fund life by bringing in new investors and providing existing investors to exit the fund and generate cash). The former is the more traditional transaction structure and accounts for about 70-75% of total secondaries volume while the latter is increasingly gaining more traction in the industry with several innovative transaction structures and uses.

There are dedicated secondaries funds who only conduct secondary transactions as well as large LPs or funds of funds that have secondaries teams focusing on such transactions. Secondaries investments can often mitigate the J-curve as well as reduce the investment risk since the underlying companies are already known and can be diligenced by the fund buying the existing LP stake. Most secondary transactions also specialized advisors who are market experts. Secondaries advisory firms help with pricing the transaction, and connect relevant parties interested in buying or selling fund commitments. There are instances where a secondary transaction allows a buyer to get preferential treatment for the next fund raised by the GP. Such transactions are called *stapled transactions* and are a good way of obtaining access to the most popular and oversubscribed funds raised by top quartile fund managers.

Secondaries funds also generally mirror the typical private equity fund structure and are set up as limited partnerships. The manager must perform due diligence on both the underlying portfolio that is being purchased as well as on the GP whose fund is involved in the secondary transaction. GPs will often help with due diligence process to give additional comfort to the secondaries fund that is purchasing the stake.

The main benefits of secondaries funds are:

- **No J-curve effect:** Since fund stakes are often purchased after the investment period of the fund, the buyer of the stake can expect returns to be generated soon and doesn't have to go through the initial period of the J-curve where returns are negative due to fund expenses and fees.

- **Diversification:** Secondaries stakes are often diversified across companies, markets and sectors such that the buyer can purchase a lower risk stake across several portfolio companies.

- **Access to top GPs:** Via stapled transactions, access to the most popular GPs can be obtained which would otherwise either not be possible or be very tough.

- **Good source of returns:** In certain scenarios, the secondary stakes are priced at discounts to NAVs and so the buyer has a good chance of making superior risk-adjusted returns.

- **Lower risk:** As compared to direct investments in blind pools of capital managed by GPs, secondary transactions often involve a portfolio of investments where the underlying companies are known and can be subjected to relevant due diligence.

FUNDS OF FUNDS

A fund of funds (FoF) raises a pool of capital from investors and invests it in a portfolio of private equity funds, which in turn make direct private equity investments. Thus, an FoF is an additional step in the intermediation between investors and the target investment. Fund managers are private equity experts with a broad network across the private equity sector.

If they are unfamiliar with the space and funds available, asset managers and institutional investors looking to allocate meaningful amounts of capital into the private equity asset class usually start by allocating capital to an FoF that will broadly track the returns of the private equity asset class minus management fees.

FoFs generally mirror the direct private equity fund structure and are set up as limited partnerships. Similar to direct private equity investing, FoFs follow an underlying strategy wherein LPs provide capital in a blind pool, and the FoF manager sources, screens, and executes the investments. In addition to investing in private equity funds, FoFs may also co-invest in private companies alongside direct private equity funds. They rely on investment strategies developed by their management teams, their portfolio diversification mechanisms, their risk management strategies, and their due diligence and monitoring procedures to deliver good returns.

FoF teams must raise funds on a regular basis from their LPs so that they always have fresh capital to invest. There are various approaches to fundraising, including raising a large fund every three to five years, or raising capital annually for investment that year. Managers of FoFs face some important capital allocation and risk management decisions. For example, first they must choose an approach to portfolio design; common approaches include the bottom-up, top-down, and mixed techniques. Further, FoF managers must develop a diversification strategy by (1) manager, (2) sub-asset class (e.g., buyouts, venture, debt funds, etc.), (3) geography, (4) industry, and (5) vintage year.

At the same time, FoFs present several crucial advantages:

- **Jumpstart allocation:** FoFs provide investors with a sound introduction to private equity before they have to seriously commit resources to develop fund screening capabilities in-house.

- **Outsourcing:** Investors who lack the resources or general knowledge choose to avoid the challenges of managing multiple GPs by outsourcing this task to FoFs.

- **Economies of scale:** FoFs leverage their multiple investments across markets and geographies to gain deeper insight into the industry.

- **Diversification:** FoFs provide investors with significant diversification, which reduces risk.

- **Scaling of investments:** Small LPs take advantage of FoF pooling to get diversification and risk management benefits that they would not have in a concentrated allocation.

- **Deal flow availability:** FoF managers leverage their networks and reputations to source deals, which allows them to benefit from larger and more consistent deal flow.

- **Access to top GPs:** Accessing top-performing GPs is difficult as their funds are often oversubscribed; however, they are usually willing to deal with FoFs that allocate large amounts of stable capital.

Criticism of FoFs typically focuses on the relative value offered to investors versus other private equity subsectors. The main disadvantage of this type of vehicle is the additional layer of fees that must be paid for the above services. As with direct private equity funds, FoF managers' incentives are closely aligned with those of the fund's LPs: pure FoFs charge around a 1% management fee and a carry of 10–20% only on the capital co-invested with private equity funds. The variability of terms depends on factors such as the management team's track record, the fund size, and the strategy followed. A management team with a proven track record of exceptional performance may be able to charge higher fees, whereas a first-time fund may have to limit fees to attract more investors. Similarly, a large fund may be able to cover expenses with a reduced management fee as a percentage of committed capital.

4 The Fundraising Ecosystem in the Private Capital Industry

It always seems impossible, until it's done.
Nelson Mandela

INTRODUCTION

Though it may not generate the same level of public attention as headline-grabbing portfolio company acquisitions or exits, fundraising is a vital activity for any firm that manages private capital funds. The fundraising process is all about fund managers looking for capital from potential investors. Traditionally, fundraising was handled by dedicated individuals whose main job was to raise money from existing or new investors every few years. However, the distinction between "fundraising" and "investor relations" has become more blurred over time as the interaction between fund managers and their investors turned into a partnership running on a continuous path (rather than being a cyclical exercise).

The investors or limited partners (LPs) contribute capital to a private fund managed by a firm or a general partner (GP) and as a result, they benefit only from the investments made by that fund. The contribution of capital takes the form of commitments, whereby investors do not transfer the capital to the fund immediately but rather, when the fund starts making investments or management fees need to be paid. Since private capital funds are closed-ended, investors decide to commit their capital at the outset of the fund's life and do not have the right to forego investments that the GPs subsequently decide upon. When fund managers identify investment opportunities, they draw down (or "call") the capital from the investors who provided commitments to the fund through the fundraising process. These capital calls might spread over three to five years, which is the typical investment period of most private capital funds.

The fundraising stage is critical in the life cycle of a private capital fund because it validates the fund managers' investment theses against the current realities and expectations of the market, given the historical performance and/or experience that the manager provides. Thus, similar to any initial or secondary public equity offering, private capital fund managers are basically selling stakes in their funds in exchange for capital that is used to exploit potentially profitable investment opportunities. Persuading investors is always a challenge in the context of a competitive market, regardless of whether the economic environment is troubled or booming.

Fundraising is a regulated process in most jurisdictions across the world. It requires both careful and articulate management, strategy, legal planning, and a healthy dose of salesmanship. For a successful fundraising period, there must be the right match between LPs' demand for the specific investment thesis offered by the fund and the experience of the GP (mostly established through a track record of relevant past performance). This match has to come at the right time and with an agreement on commercial terms within the context of a competitive environment. Thereafter, in order to reach the final execution stage, fund managers must comply with ever-expanding regulatory and legal set of requirements and an in-depth LP driven due diligence process.

Managing all of these aspects requires expertise. Some fund managers, especially those growing and introducing multiple parallel product offerings, employ in-house talent through investor relations (IR) and legal teams that may manage part or all of the fundraising process. Alternatively, fund managers may decide to outsource certain activities and engage the services of a placement agent and/or a legal firm. In certain jurisdictions, such as Korea, regulation requires the use of a duly authorized and licensed agent or adviser. Legal firms are typically engaged for fund formation that includes preparation and negotiation of all legal documentation, regulatory registration and licensing, and formation of different legal entities in the structure. Placement agents and advisers may be used to write marketing materials, advise on the strategic and commercial positioning of the fund, introduce new pockets of capital from various geographies or segments of investors (for example endowments of universities), and/or manage the entire process. Even the most sought after funds (whose managers know that they will be many times oversubscribed) often engage third-party placement agents to help manage the relationships with LPs as they compete for their fund allocations. When considering to what extent they should engage third-party advisers or in-house teams to manage the fundraising process, fund managers make decisions in the context of their market position—just as they would when considering whether to outsource any other quasi-core function with a cost-benefit analysis.

Regardless of whether the process is managed internally or outsourced, the GP's investment and management teams, and in particular the most senior partners, are often highly engaged with the LPs and become involved in the sales process. Similarly, the fundraising due diligence process typically requires the involvement of a broader team in the management firm, including junior and mid-level professionals that fulfill specific functional roles within the firm, managers of portfolio companies, advisers, and senior operating partners.

The outlook for the private capital industry is bright, but there are always significant challenges to raising a fund. Due to a regulatory environment that is becoming increasingly cumbersome (especially in the United States and in Europe) and the rising level of sophistication within the LP community, fund managers are expected to provide more in-depth disclosures and meet ever higher due diligence standards. In addition, the growing overhang of capital committed to private capital funds but not invested (i.e., "dry powder") coupled with an increase in portfolio companies' market pricing for several years is raising investors' concerns about the availability of attractive investment opportunities and the future level of expected returns. Furthermore, the market has become extremely competitive as the number of fund managers in the market competing for LPs' capital has steadily increased year-on-year for the last two decades.

Fundraising for a first-time fund continues to present challenges to GPs, especially if they are a new team. Whereas first- and second-time funds have generally performed statistically better than later-generation funds due to stronger motivation and alignment of interests, it can be difficult to convince investors to commit to first-time funds, given the lack of an easily assessable track record. Moreover, because regulations and greater demands from investors have substantially increased the cost of setting up a fund, first-time managers with limited resources face greater barriers to entry.

Finally, another challenge facing the industry is the growing preference of some investors to invest directly in private companies themselves. Some examples are the very large Canadian pension funds and certain sovereign wealth funds, as well as other large investors. This trend could potentially lead to fewer commitments in the primary fundraising market.

OVERVIEW OF FUNDRAISING ACTIVITY

Market statistics

The sustained growth in assets under management (AUM) over the last two decades demonstrates that private capital funds have become an increasingly important asset class. According to a fundraising update from Preqin, a London-based private equity research and data firm, 2018 was the sixth consecutive year in which private capital fundraising surpassed the $500 billion mark, reaching levels close to those seen just before the credit crisis. As the graph below indicates, over the 10-year period ending in January 2019, the number of funds fundraising in the market increased by a factor of three, while the amount of capital targeted doubled. In terms of the type of private capital funds raised, private equity funds (buyout, growth, venture capital, funds of funds and secondaries) still target the largest portion of investors' capital (51%). Other fund categories raise smaller proportions (credit funds - 14%, infrastructure funds - 10%, natural resource funds - 11% and real estate funds -14%). North America has the largest number of funds in the market followed by Europe in the second place and Asia in the third place.

Exhibit 1: Private Capital Funds in Market over Time, Jan. 2009 to Jan. 2019

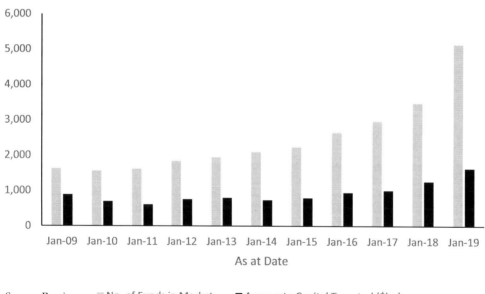

Source: Preqin   No. of Funds in Market   Aggregate Capital Targeted ($bn)

The strong fundraising environment in the private capital fund market can be attributed to increasing levels of portfolio target allocations to the asset class by the large institutional investors. The larger allocations are likely to be influenced by the good returns provided by private capital funds. For instance, since 2011, the aggregate cash distributions by private equity funds surpassed capital calls, meaning positive net cash flows to LPs from the these funds for several years. Thus, LPs have the challenge of maintaining levels of over-committed capital relative to target capital allocations in order to have exposure to increasing levels of private equity allocations.

While investors committed more money to new private capital funds as a result of significant cash distributions, they channeled increasingly larger amounts of money via alternative routes beyond the traditional fund structure. Some large investors started to allocate additional capital to existing separate account mandates while also pushing for more co-investments with the private equity funds. In addition, "pledge and search" private equity funds started to gain prominence among emerging private capital fund managers.[1] These alternative routes to market equip investors with a platform that allows them to negotiate better fund terms and gain greater control over their investments.

The global financial crisis affected a great number of private equity managers. According to a report by Bain & Company (2016), close to 26% of the 4,019 buyout firms that raised a fund between 2002 and 2008 went quiet after the crisis, not raising another fund since 2009, and appearing unlikely to ever do so again. However, by one crucial measure—the proportion of total AUM controlled by firms that struggled to raise new funds —the effects of the credit crisis were far milder than they were during the burst of the dotcom bubble in 2001. The AUM held by the firms that did not raise new funds after the dotcom bubble was 20% of the industry's total raised in the prior period. In sharp contrast, firms that failed to raise a new fund after 2009 represented just 6% of the total buyout fund AUM raised between 2002 and 2008. The main reason that the effects of the crisis were so limited is that most of the private equity firms that could not raise money after 2008 were small firms, with more than half of them having raised just one fund prior to their demise. Thus, the credit downturn culled the young and weak firms while barely putting a dent in the health of the overall private capital industry.

Among the types of investors, pension funds remain the biggest and most committed providers of capital to private capital funds. Fund managers prefer pension fund commitments as they are perceived to be "sticky money" and pose minimal hassle. The increasing capital contribution of pension funds is particularly prevalent in Europe. Sovereign wealth funds have also been providing more capital to private equity funds due to their increasing size and their larger allocations to private equity. In terms of geographic distribution, investors in North America continue to provide more than 50% of the capital raised in private funds globally.

The regulatory environment in Europe and the United States

Regulatory changes in response to the financial crisis have greatly affected the private capital fundraising environment. Of particular relevance is the Alternative Investment Fund Managers Directive (AIFMD), which seeks to regulate the marketing and management of alternative investment funds (AIFs) throughout Europe. The directive came into force in 2011, but started being adopted by European Union (EU) member states in 2013. Besides mandating disclosure requirements for private capital funds operating in Europe, one of the primary aims of the directive was to streamline the fundraising process by giving authorized fund managers a so called "*marketing passport*" that enables them to freely market European AIFs to institutional European investors.

When enacted, the directive envisaged that the pan-EU marketing passport may be extended at a later date to cover both EU and non-EU fund managers in respect to both EU AIFs and non-EU AIFs. However, the process of evaluating non-EU countries' equivalence has, so far, been extremely slow, with the Europe-wide regulator, ESMA, adopting a jurisdiction-by-jurisdiction approach. Consequently, many fund managers that are not domiciled in the EU market AIFs to European investors under the *national private placement regimes*

---

[1] Unlike traditional committed private equity funds, in the case of pledge and search funds, investors provide capital on a deal-by-deal basis. Essentially, the investors provide a loose commitment of capital to the manager of the fund to make investments within a certain set of parameters. Thereafter, investors decide whether to pursue each transaction provided by the manager independently.

(NPPRs) of each relevant country. Because NPPR rules vary significantly between countries, non-EU managers can experience several complications:

- What is considered "marketing" (and therefore subject to the relevant NPPR) depends on the individual EU country. Accordingly, what one can and cannot say in relation to an investor depends on the investor's country.

- While certain EU countries with more mature private capital markets can be accessed with relative ease, others require considerable time, cost, and effort to access.

- Reliance on the NPPR of an EU country requires supervisory cooperation agreements in place between the regulator of the EU country where the fund is marketed and the regulators in the countries in which the fund and its manager are located. A lack of cooperation may lead to constraints in marketing a fund in certain countries.

Hence, before considering fundraising in Europe, non-EU fund managers must identify target countries and conduct proper due diligence on each fundraising market to understand what each NPPR requires, what level of pre-marketing may be undertaken, the timing and cost of the approval processes, and whether the appropriate supervisory cooperation agreements are in place. While there has been growing interest in the likely introduction of an EU-wide passport for non-EU managers, uncertainty about the implementation and timing of such measures continues to persist.

Among the most significant recent legal developments in the United States for the private capital industry is the enactment of the *Dodd-Frank Wall Street Reform and Consumer Protection Act* (known as the Dodd-Frank Act), especially its investment adviser registration provisions. The Dodd-Frank Act requires that the majority of U.S. (and many non-U.S.) advisers to private capital funds register with the U.S. Securities and Exchange Commission (SEC). This registration obligation became effective on July 21, 2011. As a result, new private capital firms that raise funds must implement fairly complex and robust compliance systems and spend more resources on law firms and regulatory compliance consulting firms with expertise in this area. Another important aspect of the Dodd-Frank Act for the private capital industry is the *Volcker Rule*, which requires that banking entities invest in no more than 3% of a private capital fund and its aggregate investments. In addition, the overall investments in alternative assets (including private capital) should not exceed 3% of a bank's capital. Consequently, a meaningful amount of capital that historically came from banks can no longer be deployed to the private capital asset class.

Finally, the *Foreign Account Tax Compliance Act* (FATCA), enacted in 2010 by the United States Congress with the purpose of detecting and deterring tax evasion, also forced private capital fund managers to enhance their transparency and processes. Managers had to strengthen operations, processes, and technology systems to collect, analyze, and report investor information. For instance, during fundraising, GPs are now expected to take steps to ensure that subscription documents capture the information necessary to comply with FATCA. Further, they require tax advisers' opinions to assess the implications of various fund structures for their American investors. Penalties for non-compliance are quite high, so managers need to treat these issues very seriously.

Overall, these regulations have contributed to a more challenging fundraising environment and increased difficulties in the fundraising process. Private capital fundraisings are taking considerably longer, with a series of rolling closings being very much the norm (typically extending a year or more beyond the date of first closing). Certainly, the cost to comply with all the regulatory burden has increased and far more attention is given to compliance in general.

THE FUNDRAISING PROCESS

Fundraising involves the fund managers convincing the investors to commit money to be invested over a specified period, usually up to 10 years. Given the long term of the commitments, investors engage in careful due diligence and negotiations of the investment terms. As most investors are institutions, this process is subject to strict requirements of transparency and fiduciary duties of care, making fundraising more complex, lengthy and iterative. A capital commitment may include multiple hierarchal layers of approval, including one or two iterations by the institutions' investment committees.

Detailed, advanced planning of the fundraising process by the fund manager is therefore critical to the successful launch of a private capital fund. Such planning deals with many moving parts and uncertainties that should be minimized over the (sometimes very long) fundraising period. According to a report by Preqin (2019), the private equity funds closed took an average of 16 months to reach a final close.

Key Players

The fundraising activity periodically reconnects the GPs with their existing investors as well as with prospective new investors. Since private capital funds are not open to retail investors, the LPs are all institutional investors or sophisticated high-net-worth individuals. Both GPs and LPs often engage and benefit from the wide presence of intermediaries and advisers. On the institutional investors' side, LPs rely on the advisory services of gatekeepers and consultants when investing, while most private capital funds have engaged placement agents or advisers in some capacity to assist and guide the marketing and fundraising process.

General partners

In a private capital fund, a GP controls the fund and has unlimited liability. The GP sets up the fund as a limited partnership or a limited liability company (LLC) so that investors in the fund benefit from limited liability. Their obligations to contribute capital or make other payments to the fund are limited to their respective capital commitment. The legal framework for limited partnerships and LLCs primarily provides flexibility, allowing the partners or members to structure a wide variety of economic and governing arrangements. In addition, these entities are termed "pass-throughs" for income tax purposes and thus, are not usually subject to corporate income tax. Instead, the fund's income, gains, losses, deductions, and credits are passed through to the partners/members and taxed only once at the partner level (both GPs and LPs).

Each time a fund is raised, a new management (or GP) entity is created. This arrangement is principally to limit the liability exposure from one fund to the next and to address the fact that the principals of the next fund may not overlap exactly with the principals of the prior fund. The management company provides management, advisory, and administrative services to the fund.

Limited partners

Investors in private capital funds are formally known as limited liability partners or LPs. There is a vast range of institutional investors given that private capital funds offer diversification, the prospect for attractive returns, and investment opportunities that may not be otherwise available, such as investing in young and fast-growing firms or providing loans to mid-market private companies.

The most prominent investors participating in the fundraising process are pension funds, government agencies (including sovereign wealth funds), endowment funds, financial institutions (banks and insurance companies where and as permitted by regulators), family offices, foundations, funds of funds, asset management firms, and high-net-worth individuals. Different types of investors have different needs when investing in private capital funds. For example, public pension funds have significant capital at their disposal, but generally require more rights and impose more oversight of GPs' day-to-day operational fund activities than other types of investors; meanwhile, certain insurance companies may put more emphasis on the yield generated by the fund and thus, relative to other investors, have a greater appetite for private credit or infrastructure funds.

It is worth noting that the LP's size and operational organization determines part of its investment strategy. Only LPs that are able to have appropriate investment teams can adequately participate in co-investments with the private capital funds or allocate money with first-time private capital fund managers.

LP consultants and gatekeepers

Finalizing a fundraising almost inevitably involves lengthy interactions with the consultants that sit beside the major pension funds, insurers, and other LPs acting as gatekeepers for their investments, as well as the funds of funds, which often take a leading or anchor LP role. Consultants can provide a wealth of knowledge and experience for the benefit of LPs in terms of strategies, processes, and negotiations.

Consultants employ different business models, ranging from a boutique approach to a broad client base; specializing in a specific asset class or even sub-asset class (e.g., venture capital); or advising on holistic asset management and investing. Some consultants look to advise on a discretionary basis, some require investments through their own funds (co-mingled funds and funds of funds), and still others offer only opinions and information. In addition, some consultants provide fund administration and other services, whereas others may just help with terms and negotiations, or with gaining access to GPs that are in high demand. Consultants' views of a private capital fund manager can make or break a fundraising process. These advisers have the ability to greenlight capital commitments of large LPs and can carry several investors along with them.

It is important to note that not all investors come with consultants on their side. LPs may choose to engage consultants on a partial mandate to advise on a particular portion of their portfolio. In light of the competitive environment and the relationship basis of such engagements, LPs often benefit from extensive information and other services far beyond the remit of the consultants' engagement. Objectivity and alignment of interests between consultants and their clients is key; thus, it is critical to ascertain the full range of the consultant's activities and determine the LP's relative position as a client.

Placement agents and GP advisers

While LPs use third-party advice, GPs also engage the services of advisers in some capacity. GPs with limited previous fundraising experience (especially first-time and emerging managers), may engage a placement agent with a broad mandate to advise on everything from marketing material preparation in the early stages to the negotiation of investment terms in the last stage. GPs with an exceptional track record and great demand from LPs may still ask an adviser to help manage the process of allocation—as well as LPs' expectations—to help foster a more efficient and satisfactory fundraising process. GPs with an established investor relations team may engage niche placement agents in certain territories where required for regulatory reasons (e.g., in Korea) or for accessing new pockets of LP capital.

A placement agent is an intermediary that specializes in finding institutional investors who are able to invest in a private capital fund. These intermediaries are informed agents that contribute to the resource allocation and welfare of private capital fund investors. Reputable placement agents bring significant market knowledge that has been gained over multiple fundraising experiences with various clients in various market conditions and geographies. Placement agents may be independent boutiques (with a local focus or a global reach), the placement arms of large investment banks, or even individuals with personal investor relationships.

There are thousands of private capital fund managers in the market, most of which are too small to afford marketing staff and are therefore totally dependent on placement agents. Sometimes, fund managers hire a placement agent so they can focus on fund management issues rather than on raising capital. However, even if the bulk of the fundraising activity can be managed internally, the placement agent still adds value through access to new potential investors. According to an analysis by Preqin, close to 50% of the funds that raised capital over the period overt the last ten years engaged placement agents.

Placement agents seek to raise capital from a variety of institutional investors (e.g., pension funds, insurance companies, endowments, funds of funds, sovereign wealth funds, etc.), as well as family offices and high-net-worth individuals. Some focus on a particular type of institutional investor (e.g., American Pension Advisors for corporate and public pension funds). The services provided by placement agents can be invaluable, especially to smaller and emerging market managers. Given their periodic interactions with investors, placement agents can provide important insight on how investors might react to a package of economic and governance provisions, thus increasing a fund's probability of successfully securing investments from potential LPs.

While placement agents' main responsibility is to introduce and secure suitable investors to the fund, they also provide other financial services. They offer advice to GPs on how to approach investors, assist with pre-marketing preparation through rigorous due diligence (i.e., shape GPs' business plans), manage the fundraising process, negotiate major terms with investors, and provide insight on market conditions. Moreover, their market insights can reduce the GPs' costs of collecting and analyzing market information. Depending on a fund's needs, placement agents may support the fund from the concept development phase until it is finally closed. Thereafter, certain placement agents provide outsourcing solutions for investment relation functions that allow GPs to manage their ongoing relationships with their investors.

Placement agents are most often compensated through fee arrangements based on the amount of money raised and the services provided. Their fees are supported by the fund or the manager they are representing, and are usually paid over one or two years.[2] A placement agent's agreement with a GP sets out basic terms relating to the engagement, including compensation and the scope of the engagement that specifies whether the placement agent is retained on an exclusive basis or for certain specific jurisdictions or types of investors. Most placement agents prefer to operate as the sole marketing representative of a fund, and many like to be involved early in a process so that they can help craft the strategy. However, placement agents can be asked to participate in different ways.

---

[2] Some agents prefer to roll over part of their cash compensation into to the fund. Investors view placement agents' cash commitments to the fund positively as they signal that the placement agents truly believe in the manager they are supporting.

- **"Top-offs"**: Well-known fund managers raising follow-on vehicles with strong investor support may bring in a placement agent solely for its relationships with a certain type of investor or experience in a specific geography, usually for a very minor portion of the capital being raised. In effect, the placement agent is brought in as part of a split mandate in which the fund manager acts as the primary agent, directing everything except the small portion of capital carved out for the external agent.

- **Restarts**: At times, fund managers may decide to launch a fund without a placement agent. However, when market conditions prove challenging, they look for the assistance of a placement agent in an attempt to "restart" the fundraising process. The constraint in such a situation is that there is only one chance to make an impression, and a fund manager who has already approached the market with its story has lost the chance to "re-do" that impression. Placement agents are usually reluctant to participate in a restart which, almost by definition, has limited momentum in the investor community.

As the private capital market has matured, secondary sales of partnership positions have become more commonplace. Prudent fund managers, aware of investors looking to sell positions in their funds, have sought to take a more proactive role in using the sale of such positions to build relationships with targeted investors whom they would like to attract to their next fund. Placement agents with a strong background in both the primary and secondary markets can use the secondary sales process to kick-start the process of raising a fund through a *"primary secondary"* or *"staple secondary."* In a "primary secondary," a potential seller and the fund manager make an arrangement such that a buyer of the secondary position not only commits to its purchase but also agrees to commit a specified amount to a new fund that the fund manager is about to raise. Such an arrangement is most effective early in the process of raising a fund, where commitments secured can be used to boost the size of a fund's first close and bring momentum to fundraising. The buyers of "primary-secondaries" are most often funds of funds, which have active primary and secondary investment programs, but also certain primary market players looking to establish strategic relationships with the fund managers.

In summary, while the fund manager selects and retains a placement agent and is the party contractually responsible for paying the fee, placement agents that enjoy trusting relationships with investors, built over long periods of time, must maintain a balance between the needs of both investors and fund managers. Integrity and transparency are the foundations for developing a strong reputation in the fundraising market. By serving as a bridge between GPs and LPs, placement agents perform a critical capital formation role for private capital funds.

Investor relations (IR) professionals

Larger and more established private capital fund managers, especially those with multiple products, are likely to have a dedicated IR professional (or even a team), sometimes at the partner level. The IR professional's role is to develop deep and long-lasting relationships with current investors, as well as with institutions that are targeted to become future investors. Strong relationships allow GPs to have a base of loyal investors who can support them during volatile fundraising periods. Fundraising for many of these firms has thus become a permanent, ongoing process where activities like dissemination of financial reports, deal updates, and hosting annual and other investor meetings are seen as pre-marketing events for the next fundraising period. The internal IR team may choose to handle several of the functions of a placement agent or outsource any part of the process and management.

IR professionals should form a core part of the fund manager. They will have important responsibilities such as meeting the information needs of the investors, facilitating the firm's growth through fundraisings, and ensuring smooth communication between deal partners and investors. LPs expect IR professionals to have some transaction and investing experience, and the ability to provide tailored information to meet specific needs.

A broad investor base is necessary as most fund managers want to maintain a diversified capital base and identify investors from a wide range of geographies, institution types, and industries that are unlikely to be simultaneously impacted by negative economic forces. Hence, many fund managers look to broaden their investor base and introduce new LPs in every fundraising period, and they often consider using a placement agent to do so. Only a few of the very largest private capital fund managers who oversee a portfolio of funds with different private capital strategies have full-scale internal fundraising teams.

Managing the fundraising process

The private capital fundraising process is highly detailed. It consists of evaluating and developing a conceptual strategic growth plan or information memorandum around the GP's management team.

The Institutional Limited Partners Association (ILPA), a trade association that represents the interests of large institutional investors in private capital funds, developed principles to establish a best practices guide regarding fund relationships between GPs and LPs. ILPA identifies three main guiding principles for an effective fund partnership (see Exhibit below): (1) the alignment of interest, (2) good governance, and (3) high transparency. Under these three principles, various partner interests and concerns are addressed in a "best practice" manner; the principles are not laws or industry standards. Thus, to ensure a successful fundraising process, fund managers should be prepared to address investors' questions on how these principles are implemented with respect to the organization of the GP and the management of the fund.

Exhibit 2: ILPA principles

Alignment of Interest	Governance	Transparency
Waterfall structure	Team	GP related disclosures
Carried interest	Investment strategy	Risk management
Management fee	Fiduciary duty	Financial fund information
Fee offsets	Fund changes	LP information

LPs have become stricter with their screening process during fundraising periods. Given the cost and time associated with screening, they focus on fewer funds in the formal due diligence process. As a result, GPs that have long and established relationships with LPs are likely to be prioritized over new and emerging GPs.

Preliminary preparations

Before any preparation for a new private capital fund's fundraising process begins, the GP designates the key internal staff who will kick-start and be responsible for fundraising. This team will usually have major responsibilities during the fundraising period, such as contacting and meeting investors, complying with applicable marketing laws, collecting fund information that needs to be provided to potential investors, verifying the origin of the capital committed, and so on. Some GPs find it beneficial early in the process to engage with a legal counsel that has fund formation expertise, knowledge of prevailing market trends, and insight into the needs and preferences of the target investors. GPs can also consult knowledgeable advisers to understand the market dynamics for the type of fund they are proposing to raise, and how non-market terms they would like to obtain could affect the success of fundraising. Finally, tax planning is crucial when deciding to form a new private capital fund. Appropriate tax planning and structuring must be implemented for both GPs and different investor categories.

At this early stage, GPs should be prepared to pledge their own contributions to the new fund. Those who enjoyed success during their careers will likely be expected to provide at least 2–3% of their money to the fund's total capital commitments, while new managers with less capital should consider commitments of 1–2% for their first fund. Fundraising comes at a high cost, so GPs must also be prepared to cover legal and travel expenses incurred in the process.

The internal fundraising team often needs to balance its time (fundraising vs. fund investments), so GPs must determine how much of the fundraising process can be managed in house, and how much by placement agents. The fundraising period is important for both GPs and investors: market terms typically dictate that the fund's final close should take place within 12–18 months from the first close, unless the LPs consent to prolong the process.

Finally, at this early stage, the GP should also consider how to structure the fund. Fund structuring has become an intrinsically international and multi-disciplinary exercise, for reasons linked with the GP, the target investors, the investments targeted, and the expertise required. U.S.-based GPs typically have a preference for limited partnerships based in Delaware or Cayman Islands, while U.K.-based GPs tend to default to limited partnerships based in England or Channel Islands. Many European GPs set up their private capital funds as Luxembourg specialized investment funds. Regulatory compliance requires expertise, both in structuring and running the fund. If the proposed structure does not provide everything that investors want, parallel funds combining an onshore regulated vehicle (e.g., a Luxembourg special limited partnership) with an offshore unregulated vehicle (e.g., a Cayman partnership) can be another option for GPs.

Setting the investment strategy

The next step is for GPs to outline the investment strategy and differentiate their financial goals from those of their competitors. Establishing the strategy requires significant research into a defined market or individual sector. For instance, a fund may focus on sectors such as healthcare, energy, or hospitality, while others are generalist funds (i.e., they are "sector agnostic"). Ultimately, investors want to know more about the fund's goals. As GPs articulate the investment strategy, they should consider whether the fund will have a geographic focus or a focus on a certain industry or country. Alternatively, the fund may emphasize a specific strategy in similar emerging markets. The strategy should also specify how value will be created. Will the fund aim to improve portfolio companies' operational and strategic direction, or will it focus entirely on cleaning up the balance sheet? Placement agents can act as strategic advisers to help the GPs correctly position the fund in the market.

Documentation and logistics

The main private capital fund document used in the fundraising process is the *private placement memorandum* (or PPM). This document should be prepared early, ideally with the assistance of a placement agent, and made available to prospective LPs sufficiently in advance to allow the investors to start their due diligence process and negotiate the fund terms. The PPM is the first written communication that LPs receive in the sales process, and is expected to provide a convincing case to LPs that commit to the fund. It should stand out among the many PPMs that institutional investors receive. In addition to the PPM, other appropriate documents should also be circulated, such as (1) *a subscription agreement*, (2) *a confirmation of fund participation*, (3) *partnership terms*, and (4) *a due diligence questionnaire*. At this point, the legal entity that will manage the fund might not be established yet, and the structure of the fund may not be finalized. However, these documents describe the offer and its essential characteristics. The ongoing negotiations throughout the fundraising process mean that, until the final closing of the fund, some of these documents will be continually revised to reflect feedback collected from discussions with the LPs. In the context of continuous amendments, it is vital that all LPs receive the *same* information about the fund before they make an investment.

The PPM should cover several important matters that are relevant to potential investors, including (1) the investment philosophy of the fund, (2) the relevant track record and biographical information of the fund managers, and (3) a summary of the economic and other key terms of the fund, such as the length of the investment period, the overall term of the fund, and so on. GPs often prepare a *flip book* (or slide demonstration) that they use, along with the PPM, to make presentations to potential investors. The fund presentation should address the following specific topics:

- **Investment strategy:** The fund investment strategy description should include the investment scope of the fund (e.g., target firms, geographies, sectors, etc.), the investment policy, investment criteria, investment restrictions, and the investment period of the fund. Information on applicable investments in the pipeline, lending and borrowing guidelines, responsible investment policies, and the procedures for ensuring compliance with such policies is also necessary.

- **Team:** Investors should receive a description of the management structure and the management team that identifies the key executives of the team, and the regulation of key man events.[3] The GP must decide on the roles and titles that the firm's leaders will assume (e.g., the role of partner, portfolio manager, investment manager, etc.). The management team, including the CEO, CFO, chief information security officer, and/or the chief compliance officer of the fund, should be established if such positions are necessary. In addition, a description of the team's skills and experience should be provided, along with details on team continuity, dynamics, decision-making processes, and member succession. The success or failure of a fundraising process often rests on the quality and reputation of the fund management team. High-quality, experienced key executives are one of the main reasons why investors choose to invest with a particular GP.

- **Track record:** The track record of prior investments made by the management team of the fund should be thoroughly explained. The track record should discuss realized, unrealized, partially realized, and total investments made in the past. If a manager was involved in several generations of funds, each fund generation (i.e., Fund I, Fund II, etc.) should be listed with its performance broken down by each

---

[3] Key man provisions are contractual clauses which typically state that, if a specified number of key named principals cease to devote a specified amount of time to the private equity fund partnership, the manager of the fund is prohibited from making any further new investments until new replacements are appointed.

type of investment, as stated above.[4] Principals who cite their track record information from their time as a prior fund manager or other type of employer may need to obtain disclosure consent to divulge such information and to use the logos or other proprietary marks from these firms. When analyzing a track record, investors attach great importance to continuity between track records, team stability, and a consistent investment strategy.

- **Alignment of interests:** This segment should describe the expected compensation of the GPs, how the compensation is spread across professionals in the firm, and GPs' own capital contributions to the fund. GPs with significant "skin in the game" (i.e., high commitments to the fund relative to their own wealth) and fair distributions of the carried interest are considered to be highly aligned with investors. On the other hand, if compensation of the GPs is heavily reliant on fee income (e.g., management fees, transaction fees, portfolio company monitoring and advisory fees, etc.), GPs are perceived by investors to be less aligned.

- **Structure and powers:** This section includes the legal structure of the fund, a summary of the GP's powers, resolution procedures for conflicts of interest, remit and composition of the LP advisory committee, and the GP's reporting obligations to the LPs.

- **Financials:** The description of the fund's financials should discuss the cost and fee structure (including expenses borne by the fund), how any transaction fees and directors' fees received by the GP will be treated, the GP's commitment, and carried interest arrangements. More detailed information can be presented as well, such as the procedures for commitment drawdowns, events of LPs' default on drawdowns, portfolio valuations, pricing of LP interests, distributions to LPs, and so on.

- **Co-investments and follow-on investments:** This part should provide details on investors' co-investment rights, the policy on co-investments with other funds managed by the GP or any of its associates, and the level of provisions that the GP will set aside for follow-on investments. Co-investments have emerged as a huge area of LP interest over the past few years.[5]

- **Term, exits, and new funds:** This section should include the term of the fund (e.g., 10 years for a private equity fund), the process for extending the fund's term, termination and liquidation procedures for the fund, investment exit strategies, and the circumstances in which investments may be purchased from or sold to other funds managed by the GP or its associates. To provide more flexibility, GPs may create *parallel funds* during the fundraising process to address individual investors' requirements. Some GPs may also create *executive funds* to allow employees and other persons affiliated with the GP to invest. Very often, GPs also mention the circumstances under which the fundraising team or the GP can establish another fund with a similar investment strategy.

- **Risk factors:** This section provides a summary of any risk factors relevant to the investments made with the fund's capital, and how these risks will be mitigated. GPs usually include a general warning to LPs on the risks that are inherent when investing in the fund. They might also discuss particular risk factors that may adversely affect the fund's ability to carry out the investment policy or to meet any projections or forecasts made.

---

[4] Calculation of the fund's IRR is the backbone of a track record and plays an important role in the assessment of a fund's underlying investments. Correctly calculating and interpreting the IRR is crucial, as several different ways of calculating it can lead to different interpretations and conclusions (please see the chapter on performance measurement in private equity).

[5] Co-investments alongside the fund are typically offered with "no fee, no carry" to make LPs' investments in the fund more attractive. Co-investing can also provide valuable experience for LPs looking to build direct investment programs.

The fundraising process is extremely costly, and organizational/legal expenses are normally reimbursed by the fund once it is raised. The GP should ensure there is sufficient capital to carry the management team through at least the initial closing of the fund. If such capital is not available, the management team could obtain seed money from various investors. Seed money is provided in exchange for a portion of the carried interest and/or the management fees generated by the newly formed fund.

Once the preparatory steps outlined above have been completed, fundraising can begin. The GPs can schedule meetings with investors, prepare formal presentations with rehearsals/role play, prepare data rooms, and brief the top management of portfolio companies (if they already manage existing funds).

Road show

The real work of fundraising starts by getting the PPM to dozens or even hundreds of potential investors and meeting with as many as possible. This process is known as a *road show*. The road show commences with a list of potential investors (that can be made available by a placement agent if one is engaged), a timeline for the initial closing on committed capital, a schedule of meetings with targeted investors, and the specific goals for each meeting. The period from the early investors' initial evaluation of the PPM to the receipt of the first tranche of committed capital can last from one month to one year but typically takes three to six months. The time frame depends on the quality of information provided and made available by the GP, and the extent to which the investors are familiar with the GP.

Any placement agents that are engaged tap into their networks of investors, gauge initial interest, and arrange meetings with interested parties. These agents often visit investors and present the fund together with the GP. Potential LPs must be made aware of any changes to information provided to them at any point during the fundraising process to make an informed decision.[6] Interested investors may also visit the GP's office and a few of the selected portfolio companies. The goal of the GP is to "close the deal." Four to six meetings will typically be required with each potential LP before its counsel and advisers begin reviewing the proposed limited partnership agreement and other governing documents in detail.

LPs who remain interested after seeing the fund presentation, reading the PPM, and conducting due diligence will request copies of the fund's governing documents. These include a proposed *limited partnership agreement* (a key document which sets out in detail the legally binding relations between investors and the GP), a *subscription agreement* (an agreement between the fund and the investors documenting the number of shares sold to each investor), and a *management agreement* (a document that outlines the services the management company will provide as well as the management fees that the management company will receive).

During the road show, the best practice is not to communicate with the media regarding the fund or its offering, and not to address any of this communication to a general audience. These kinds of communications may be regarded as general solicitations even if it is reasonable to believe that all documents are qualified under the relevant securities laws (e.g., the Securities Exchange Act of 1934 in the United States).

Due diligence

Due diligence is a comprehensive investigation by LPs of the viability of a new private capital fund. The due diligence undertaken on an individual fund can take anywhere from 2 to 10 weeks, depending in part on the

---

[6] In some circumstances, these presentations may be made to potential LPs at an early stage, even though they have not yet been given any formal fund documents. Information provided by the fundraising team that may influence investor decisions is often subject to regulations in various countries.

availability of information and how far the fund is into the fundraising process. The increased influence of LPs in private capital funds has led to greater transparency from the funds and an increasing number of independent due diligence procedures performed by LPs. Most GPs understand that being very transparent with investors at this stage on everything—from how the investments in the portfolio are valued to how the carry is split between investment managers—is important as it creates trust. To deal effectively with increasing information demands from investors, some GPs utilize software tools (e.g., secure web-based interfaces) to provide the information as quickly as possible and to comply with regulatory requirements.

GPs must be well prepared for close scrutiny and ready to justify the basic premises and assumptions underlying their fund. Their prior transactions and returns (or track records) are of primary importance in attracting investor commitments.[7] The fundraising team will normally also assemble a comprehensive data pack or virtual data room as well as documents about the fund and its investment strategy, collectively comprising the due diligence materials. In turn, interested investors often ask GPs to fill out detailed *due diligence questionnaires* about the fund and the principals that will be running it.

These due diligence questionnaires have grown in number and scale over the past few years, even though the vast majority of the questions they contain might have already been covered elsewhere in the GP's marketing materials. The questions vary depending on whether they come from LPs who invest extremely widely or those who know the asset class very well. Often, these supplementary questions are heavily focused on the internal workings of a manager, covering processes that may not be outlined in detail in the PPM (e.g., how investment decisions are made). Other issues that attract closer examination may include the team's track record, the ownership structure of the management company, the accuracy of the track record using different forms of analysis, the stability of the team, the longevity of working relationships, and so on.[8] It is therefore prudent for the GP to prepare for these questionnaires in advance by organizing materials such as

- CVs for each principal;

- spreadsheets outlining the proposed economic arrangements between principals and investors;

- detailed financial performance information for each fund managed by the principals;

- detailed investment strategy information, including breakdowns of prior investments by stage, industry, geography, and so on;

- information about litigation or investigations involving the principals or a prior fund;

- summaries of all the material terms of the operative documents of the fund;

- backup materials such as excerpts from third-party publications or articles to substantiate statements made by the principals in the PPM about their background, track record, and so on;

- forward visibility on the deal pipeline;

- draft responses to common due diligence questions related to the foregoing materials; and

- materials (or software) that demonstrate back office capabilities.

---

[7] LPs are expected to verify the performance claims made by fund managers. This often involves checking not only the data provided but also discussing with third parties that are used as references.

[8] The GP's answers will be similar across the questionnaires provided by various investors but they usually need to be put into different types of questions using different formats.

Because fundraising is a continuous process, GPs often maintain an up-to-date biography for each management team member, the financial performance of each fund they manage, a summary of terms of the limited partnership agreement for the most recent fund, and a current investment strategy so that they can respond in a timely manner to due diligence questionnaires and save time preparing the PPM.

It is very easy for materials covering the GP's track record to be misread or be designed to mislead potential LPs, particularly in view of changing circumstances, such as a selective presentation of the fund. Gross and net track record information should be calculated and compiled in accordance with the valuation and accounting standards appropriate for the fund's jurisdiction. The fundraising team may also wish to make forecasts regarding likely performance in the fund's chosen sectors, a target internal rate of return (IRR), and money multiples.

LPs are also increasingly inquiring about funds' third-party service providers, and in some instances, meeting with them and conducting their own reviews. As LPs are becoming more aware of management fees and the calculations behind them, they expect management fees to be used to cover operating expenses rather than being a revenue source for the management team.

Due diligence should be a two-way process: while LPs will learn more about the fund, GPs must learn whose money they are receiving. The fundraising team should maintain a record of all persons to whom it markets the fund, and a record of all information provided to them. The existing LPs are the most important in terms of reputation building; they will be followed by others who might replace some of the existing LPs. Verifying the quality and reliability of new potential LPs involves: (1) checking the origin of their capital, and (2) assessing the ability to honor capital calls promptly.

In the case of the first issue, the GP should check not only on the investing entity but also the "ultimate beneficiary" to prevent people from attempting to launder money through the new fund. Subscription documents should include suitable warranties from LPs in the fund regarding the origin of money invested. With respect to the second issue, failure to meet capital calls can lead to lost deals. As drawdowns are made throughout the life of the fund, if one LP defaults, even when suitable sanctions are applied, other LPs are likely to be disadvantaged, especially when the fund cannot honor its investment commitments. Managing LP default situations requires GPs' time, and may well reflect negatively on their reputations. Thus, if proper checks on the credit quality of the LPs are not made during the fundraising period, the management team may find it difficult to secure additional financing at short notice.

When compiling a list of potential LPs, their investment strategies and restrictions should be closely evaluated for fund compatibility. Their characteristics, as well as the advantages and disadvantages of different types of investors, should be determined before selecting investors. A fund's ideal investor base should be diverse so that issues affecting a particular class of investors do not unduly affect the fund during its operations. In many areas, there are restrictions on the types of LPs to whom it is permissible to promote funds. Tests for determining investor suitability vary too, such as the potential LP's net worth or the minimum size of investment. Another consideration is the long-term nature of the relationship with a prospective LP, and whether the LP is likely to invest over multiple fund cycles.

Negotiation process

The negotiation of investors' capital commitments is a fine balancing act. A fund's terms need to be commercially attractive to the fund manager while simultaneously addressing key investor concerns around transparency, alignment of interest, and governance.

GPs should expect potential investors, along with their advisers and counselors, to have questions about and comments on the proposed limited partnership agreement. Most potential investors request changes or additions to the proposed limited partnership agreement before they commit to invest in the fund. Some may also request a *side letter*, which is a separate and confidential agreement between the investor and the fund to address non-economic regulatory or legal issues particular to that investor, or to set more favorable fund terms. As the fundraising process unfolds and prospective investors commit to invest, the GPs negotiate with investors regarding the terms in the limited partnership agreement, the subscription agreement, and side letters. Funds with repeat investors may not face such negotiations if they can justifiably cite the prior fund's terms as precedent, subject to appropriate updating, especially if the previous fund was successful.

With respect to side letter negotiations, some LPs will request a *most favored nation provision* in their side letter that requires the fund to offer the investor the benefit of any favorable term offered to any other investor in a side letter. For example, if the fund offers one investor a right to co-invest in portfolio companies alongside the fund, then another investor who has asked for and received a most favored nation provision in its side letter would be entitled to the same right. Other typical side letter provisions include the right of fund of funds investors or public pension fund investors to disclose specified fund information that would otherwise be confidential to the fund of funds investors. For successor funds, the side letters from the prior fund are usually used and updated as necessary for repeat investors.

GPs should try to minimize the number of side letters and additional rights they grant to the fund's LPs. The more side letters and additional rights the GPs grant, the more confusing it will be to operate the fund on a day-to-day basis without violating one or more of these individual rights. The best way to minimize side letters and additional rights is to establish a strategy for targeting and negotiating with likely investors. GPs must give careful thought to any side letter provisions, including understanding how burdensome these provisions will be to comply with, and the likelihood of inadvertent failures to comply with them.

The placement agent often plays the "middleman" role in the negotiation process between LPs and GPs. Simultaneously negotiating with multiple investors is time-consuming and requires close attention to each investor's requests. It is quite common for investors' comments to conflict with each other and/or with the principals' preferred terms. As the negotiation process evolves, the economic or other terms of the fund often change in a manner that differs from the terms initially outlined in the fund's PPM. In this case, a supplement to the PPM may be issued to keep all investors informed of the latest terms. Similarly, if new information comes to light (e.g., a prior fund disposes of a portfolio company for a high return or a principal leaves the fund), the PPM may need to be amended or restated. Any such documentation should also be distributed. It is good practice to obtain an acknowledgement of receipt of the update.

The main terms of the fund investment that result from negotiations are stated in *a term sheet*. LPs may want certain preferential rights or economic advantages such as positions on the LP advisory committee, preferential co-investment rights, reduced management fees, or a participation in carried interest. Trade and strategic investors have different investment priorities from those of financial investors. For instance, some LPs may require specific *opt-outs* or *excuse clauses* that will allow them to avoid participating in certain investments. Any preferential treatment should be clearly disclosed to *all* other LPs, as most LPs consider very carefully the extent to which any individual LP is granted influence over the fund's management. If such influence alters the management structure of the fund, it can compromise the limited liability of the LPs. Moreover, substantial influence on the management of a fund (in particular, the decisions to invest or divest) can subject the fund to merger regulations and notification requirements with undesirable consequences for both the fund and its LPs.

The economic arrangements between the GPs and the LPs in the fund are important. When deciding to form a private capital fund, GPs should take care not to become too aggressive with the economic terms of their proposed fund, or they will risk losing investors. The GP (usually through a management company they control) typically earns an annual management fee of 1.5–2.5% of the total committed capital of the fund. This fee adjusts down after a certain period, such as when the active investment phase of the fund winds down and/or when the principals raise another investment fund.[9]

The investors also negotiate *key executive clauses*. These clauses give a level of investor protection by providing for certain contractual consequences in the event that a specified number of "key executives" cease to devote a specified amount of time to the fund. For example, the investors might have the ability to terminate the investment period of the fund early if key professionals cease to be actively involved in the fund. In negotiating key executive provisions, the need for investor protection has to be balanced with the practical reality that individuals do sometimes leave their employer, for various extraneous and personal reasons. It is not in any party's interests for the proper functioning of the management team to be hampered by impractical key executive provisions when such situations arise.

In addition to the economic terms between LPs and GPs, there are also complex tax issues, voting rights, and separation issues to consider. Knowledgeable fund counsels can help the GPs move this potentially issue-laden process forward and provide critical tax advice.

Capital commitments

Funds often receive capital commitments over several closings with a period of 9 to 18 months between the first and the final close. A capital commitment involves signing a *letter of intent* (i.e., a written agreement with LPs to commit funds subject to any required regulatory hurdles), the completion of the final documentation, and the receipt of the committed capital.

An investor generally becomes an LP in a private capital fund by subscribing to a capital commitment. In most cases, the commitment is not funded at subscription or even all at once, but in separate installments, which the sponsor designates by making "capital calls" on an as-needed basis to make investments and pay fees and expenses over the life of the fund. Investors typically like to see GPs demonstrate "skin in the game" by making their own commitments to the fund. A substantial commitment by the GPs is an attractive marketing element because fund investors believe it better aligns the interests of the manager with those of the investors, since managers who make significant commitments share in losses as well as profits. Because GPs receive a disproportionate share of profits, such commitments mitigate the incentives for GPs to take excessive (or unwarranted) risks.

An *initial closing* of the fund occurs when the GP identifies the first set of investors who are ready to commit capital to the fund. Often, a fund is only permitted to hold an initial closing after a minimum amount of capital has been raised. After the initial closing, subsequent closings may be held throughout the fundraising period, which often ends either 9 to 18 months after the initial closing, or once the fund has reached its fundraising cap on capital commitments (as set forth in the fund's operating agreement). If potential investors assume

---

[9] The management fee is intended to cover the day-to-day operating expenses of the fund, such as finding and vetting potential investments, office leases, employee salaries, computer equipment, and other normal overhead expenses. It is generally negotiated on the higher side of the range for smaller funds and first-time funds. First-time funds require a higher percentage management fee, as most such funds have high start-up costs and do not receive fees from prior funds to offset those costs.

there is a lack of interest in the fund because the amount raised at the initial closing is not significant, the fund will have a difficult time raising the entire targeted amount at subsequent closings.

The initial closing is an important fundraising milestone, one that requires proper planning and preparation. The subscription agreements with each investor participating in the initial closing contain a list of conditions that must be satisfied by the management team and the fund before the initial closing can be completed. After these conditions are satisfied, the subscription agreements and limited partnership agreement are formally signed at the initial closing by the GP and each LP participating in the initial closing. At that point, those investors become LPs of the fund. Some GPs that experience very strong demand for the fund use the first funding round investments as a way to guarantee that LPs get their preferred allocation to the fund. Unless LPs invest in the first close, they are not guaranteed their allocation to the fund in subsequent closings.

The initial closing may occur as a *wet closing* (with each LP contributing capital) or a *dry closing* (with no capital contributions). Most funds undertake a dry closing, because it is administratively easier to deal with collecting signatures without also having to collect checks or wire transfers. In addition, deferring the capital contribution until the first portfolio company investment improves the fund's IRR, the most important metric of a fund's success. Issuing a press release or making any other public statement (including on the fund's website or at an industry conference) regarding the initial closing of the fund (or any closing of the fund prior to the final closing) could be a violation of local securities laws. Therefore, the GPs should delay all public statements regarding fundraising activities until after the final closing of the fund.

At the final closing, the GPs, with the help of their advisers, draft a *memorandum* and create a chart summarizing the fund's investment restrictions contained in the limited partnership agreement, subscription agreements, and any side letters entered with the LPs. This memorandum is distributed to all parties involved in the fundraising process.

Private capital funds are structured as closed-end investment vehicles. Once the fund receives enough capital commitments to reach the maximum fundraising target (i.e., the hard cap), the fund may not accept additional investor subscriptions. The hard cap should reflect the likely appetite of investors for a fund, and a maximum size that can be sensibly invested during the fund's investment period. The size of the fund targeted is usually significantly lower than the hard cap with the purpose of insuring that a minimum amount will be raised to be able to close the fund. However, in buoyant fundraising environments, the best managers receive so much investor interest that in some cases, investors want to commit much more capital than even the hard cap. In these situations, it is tempting for GPs to relax the fundraising discipline and accept more cash, even if it means changing the "immovable" hard cap. To do so, GPs require consent from the majority of the fund's LPs, and must rewrite the limited partnership agreement. Taking these steps can raise questions from LPs as a fund that is vastly larger in size to what was originally pitched can struggle with the rate of capital deployment, provides fewer co-investment opportunities and, crucially, might impair the GP's ability to follow the investment strategy. A solution to this issue is to start fundraising without setting a hard cap initially. Setting the hard cap later, once the fundraising process is well underway, can allow GPs to assess the market interest for their fund. The time frame for a private capital fund is shown in Exhibit 3.

It must be noted that, historically, the measurement of private capital fund performance has been based on the capital actually called up and invested by the GP. However, this approach does not consider the fact that LPs have no control over when the GP will call up their committed capital; thus, LPs must have capital available to fulfill a capital call. LPs with large and long-established alternative investment programs can make educated estimates regarding the timings of aggregate cash flows in their portfolios, and can therefore employ an "over-commitment" strategy to maintain a stable allocation to the asset class.[10]

Planning for the next fund

The timing of the next fundraising is contingent upon market conditions and restrictions in the current fund's limited partnership agreement. GPs are not permitted to start raising a new fund until a certain percentage of their most recent fund has been invested. They should keep close track of this percentage considering the timetable for fundraising: if they start too early, they will conflict with this restriction; if they start too late, they may run out of money to pursue good investment opportunities.

GPs commence planning for their next fund as soon as they close their current fund. LPs like to receive frequent updates about the current fund's investment activities, plans, and prospects. During the life of the fund, and prior to beginning active fundraising for a new fund, GPs regularly meet with major LPs and potential new LPs. When it is time to raise a new fund, the principals should inform the LPs that they are contemplating raising a new fund as soon as they are aware of the timetable for the fundraising process. The LPs can then plan to allocate some of their investable capital in the next fund.

Marketing between funds is a necessity, both to nurture existing LP relationships and advance discussions with potential new LPs. This activity is especially important for some smaller funds, as they may have a less prominent position in the investor's portfolio. To the extent that the GPs have had any successful exits in their current fund, this will provide a good track record for the next fund. However, if the current fund has not had any exits, or has had exits that have not been very successful, the GPs will need to explain why.

DETERMINANTS OF FUNDRAISING

Fundraising is determined by both supply and demand factors. The supply of capital reflects the desire of investors to allocate their funds to private capital, while the demand is driven

by the number of companies looking for this type of finance. The success of any fundraising process and the time it takes to raise a fund depend on a variety of factors, with most key factors falling into one of two categories: macroeconomic developments (LPs' top-down analysis) and GP-specific factors (LPs' bottom-up analysis).

---

[10] An alternative (and less explored) view of private capital fund performance is to observe it in the context of total capital committed by LPs at the fundraising stage. The Preqin Private Equity Committed Capital Index (Preqin PECC Index) captures the net performance of buyout funds on a committed capital basis. The Preqin PECC Index aims to represent the returns on committed capital by including the actual amount of money invested in private equity partnerships, as well as returns that the dry powder will generate if invested on a risk-free basis.

Exhibit 3: The fundraising process

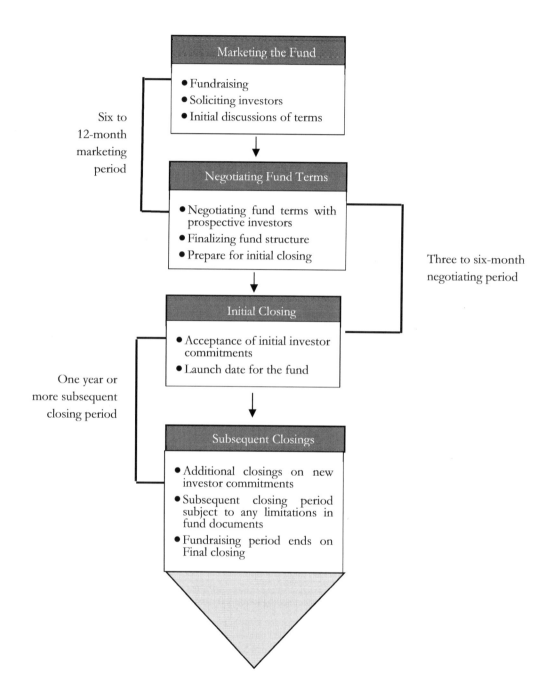

Macroeconomic factors

LPs' availability of capital and their willingness to spend it on private capital investments is driven by current macroeconomic factors, among other things. As a result, the general state of the economy (global, regional, national, sectorial, etc.) and the regulatory environment are thoroughly analyzed "top down" by the LPs during the fundraising process. The following factors are associated with an increase in fundraising activity:

- **Economic growth:** When GDP growth is positive and the economy grows, investors have more capital available and are more willing to commit to private capital funds. Moreover, a growing economy provides good investment opportunities for private capital funds.

- **Interest rates:** Higher long-term interest rates suggest that there are alternative investments to private capital funds. Thus, the volume of private capital funds raised might decrease.

- **Equity market capitalization:** A strengthening of public equity markets increases the amount that can be committed to private equity funds given that most institutional investors' allocations to private equity are set as a fixed percentage of the overall AUM. Further, the equity market capitalization proxies for the degree of development of the capital market, which may be viewed as a general reference of liquidity for private equity funds' investments. If the size of the capital market is large, it creates a favorable environment for investment and the possibility for fund managers to exit investments.

- **Labor market flexibility:** More labor market flexibility encourages an entrepreneurial culture that can lead to more start-ups.

- **More efficient bankruptcy and accounting procedures:** Efficient bankruptcy and accounting procedures enhance the transparency of private capital funds' investments, increasing their appeal to large institutional investors.

- **AUM in pension funds:** When pension funds receive greater contributions from their stakeholders (either due to regulatory changes or to a growing base), the additional capital is more likely to be invested in alternative diversifying investments such as private capital funds.

- **Regulatory changes:** Given that many investors in private capital are regulated (e.g., pension funds, financial institutions), regulatory changes that allow these investors to allocate more capital to alternative assets have a positive effect on the supply of capital to private capital funds.

- **Decreases in capital gains tax rates:** Lower rates increase the desire of taxable investors to make new commitments to funds and incentivize workers to become entrepreneurs.

- **Policies that promote technological innovation:** Government policies that encourage innovation contribute to an entrepreneurial culture and help new private entities grow, creating a large set of potential investment opportunities for private capital funds that will likely trigger more fundraising.

GP-specific factors

LPs engage in a thorough bottom-up analysis to assess the quality of the fund managers in light of the competition for their capital. LPs expect an underlying solid GP track record that demonstrates successful execution, the presentation of a well-articulated specialized investment strategy, the use of placement agents, success of the initial closing, and effective communications:

- **Track record:** To raise a fund, fund managers need to find investors willing to trust them to invest capital. Therefore, unsurprisingly, a demonstrable track record is the key attribute that GPs must exhibit in order to successfully attract LP commitments. While new managers or those with a less established track record find it challenging to attract investor capital, managers with a proven track record are oversubscribed.[11] GPs' track records are analyzed in terms of the volume of investments and the divestments made, as well as the level of past returns generated. Higher recent returns lead to greater capital commitments to new funds. Reputation, in the form of firm age and size, also positively impacts the ability to raise new capital. Thus, older and larger organizations typically attract more capital. The decision to invest is clearly predicated on the expectation of good future returns, and both past performance and reputation are indicators of expected future returns. Without a track record, GPs should find some other connection with LPs to assure them that the investment strategy will be successful. That connection usually comes from the manager's existing relationships.

- **Specialization:** Specialized fund managers tend to be more successful at raising new funds, likely because of the expertise accumulated by the GPs over time. For instance, stage specialization (measured as investing in companies that are at an early stage versus a later, more mature stage) includes very different types of transaction and monitoring skills. Buyout transactions require significant participation by banks, as acquisitions are done with a large portion of debt, next to the fund's capital. In contrast, venture capital deals involve no debt. Buyout transactions lead to majority equity positions with full control of the target, while venture investments lead to minority positions with contract-based control rights. Specialization can also occur at the industry level. Some fund managers specialize in certain industries to gain greater insights and capabilities into the sourcing and execution of deals in those industries. Industry-specific knowledge is beneficial to the development of target companies.

- **Use of placement agents:** Placement agents support a more successful fundraising process by helping managers with the definition of the fund concept and selling the concept to investors. These agents are often wary of backing fund managers without a proven track record. When it comes to recommending selected funds, placement agents consider the amount of capital available in the market and the fund manager's reputation. Investors expect placement agents to certify funds with a quality above a certain threshold.

- **The initial closing:** Momentum is widely understood as a prerequisite for a successful fundraising period. A strong initial closing is critical to establish the fund's viability and signal to other potential LPs that they should commit in subsequent closings. Importantly, commitments from the prior fund's large investors serve as a good signal to the marketplace about the new fund's viability. Based on the results of detailed interviews with over 100 institutional investors, Preqin (2013) finds that 35% of investors do not commit to a fund until it has reached a first close. Many of these investors will not consider committing to a fund until they see which managers are able to secure initial capital.

- **Continuous communication:** GPs must keep their LPs informed with respect to the status of their funds and the portfolio's performance. This task can be accomplished through quarterly updates, annual meetings, and individual meetings with major LPs. LPs that are kept up-to-date on the performance of prior funds require less due diligence when they contemplate investments in the next fund. Regular fund updates are also effective marketing tools and help keep LPs appraised on when to expect a new fundraising. The most important mechanism driving a successful fundraising (outside of

---

[11] Fund managers must also demonstrate historical consistency as well as effective retention programs for the top professionals in the firm.

these prerequisites) is giving LPs a reason to act. Whether that reason is preferred economics for committing early in a fundraising or access to co-investments on a reduced or no-fee basis, offering motivation beyond the typical fundraising tools will generate necessary momentum to drive successful closes.

Notably, for first-time managers in emerging markets who lack a track record, the presence a *development finance institution* (DFI) among the investors is a critical determinant of fundraising. First-time fund managers benefit from the "halo effect" of having their due diligence completed by DFIs, which are typically long-standing, well-connected, and sophisticated investors in riskier emerging markets. DFIs come in all shapes and sizes, but share an investment mandate focused on economic development by providing private capital in growth markets where private investors who are focused purely on financial returns may be more reluctant to invest. DFIs have a goal of sustainable, long-term investing aimed at encouraging growth in smaller and medium-sized enterprises.

DFIs often require managers to include a restriction on the percentage of capital raised from DFIs to oblige managers to seek other sources of capital. Thus, as anchor investors in emerging markets funds, DFIs pave the way for participation by more commercially driven investors. It is important to note that DFIs are often subject to internal policy restrictions on investments in certain sectors or geographies. Managers usually accommodate such restrictions by way of excuse provisions in the fund documentation or inclusion in the fund's investment criteria.

DEAL-BY-DEAL FUNDRAISING FOR PRIVATE EQUITY INVESTMENTS

Operating on a deal-by-deal basis is an alternative option to a traditional 10-year private equity fund when the fundraising environment is difficult or when new fund managers want to prove themselves. Once viewed with skepticism, the deal-by-deal approach to private equity investing has become commonplace in recent years, alongside traditional fundraising.

GPs operating via a deal-by-deal fund create a dedicated vehicle for the purpose of making an investment in a single target opportunity (or single portfolio of target opportunities). Unlike the traditional private equity fund model, where investors commit capital to the fund on a "blind-pool basis" and depend on the fund's investment team to identify and execute investment opportunities going forward, investors considering an investment in a deal-by-deal fund have full transparency on the underlying investment and are able to perform "M&A-style" diligence prior to deciding whether to commit to the deal-by-deal fund. Pursuing a deal-by-deal strategy relieves the GP of marketing a traditional fund offering, a process which has become increasingly expensive and time consuming.[12] Deal-by-deal funds can be easier to market than traditional private equity funds because they help to allay prospective investors' concerns about committing to managers with unproven or imperfect track records.

Investors usually make *soft commitments* to the deal-by-deal fund prior to its investments being identified. However, unlike with traditional private equity funds, investors are given the right to *opt out* of (or *opt in* to) each investment opportunity that the manager of the pledge fund presents to investors. In this way, each of the investors is able to make an individual decision about whether or not to participate in each investment

---

[12] Charterhouse Equity Partners, Duke Street, and AAC Nordic are examples of private equity firms that abandoned their fundraising efforts amid harsh fundraising conditions to switch to a deal-by-deal approach.

opportunity (instead of being required to participate in each investment, as is the case in traditional private equity funds). Each time the manager finds a deal, he/she presents the investors with a due diligence memorandum describing the opportunity, and investors have a set number of days to opt in. This period allows investors to conduct their own further due diligence. Each investor may opt into a deal for an amount up to the maximum allotment (which is determined based on the size of the investor's soft commitment relative to the overall commitments). If an investor subscribes for less than his/her maximum initial allotment, other investors who opted in are allowed to subscribe for the unsubscribed amount.

Since they have to make an investment decision at the time of the deal, investors should have simultaneous (or as close to simultaneous as possible) and equal access to information. Managers should have an agreed-upon format for deal memoranda and for answering questions received from investors. Fund managers should prioritize the pledges of investors who are able to process information quickly in these situations.

Despite investors' increasing comfort around deal-by-deal investing, deal-by-deal funds have some significant disadvantages:

- **Fundraising to close the deal:** The need to raise equity for each deal can easily derail the deal in a competitive process. Due to the need for investors to conduct due diligence on and approve an investment opportunity prior to participating in such an investment, deal-by-deal funds can face a degree of uncertainty and delay. These problems can place such funds at a disadvantage in a competitive acquisition process, as a seller may be reluctant to engage and progress the sale process with a buyer that has limited control over its ultimate ability to fund the acquisition. These sellers might prefer investors who can potentially close the deal immediately. However, this is mitigated by deal-by-deal funds who: (a) consciously originate their deals outside of a competitive process and/or (b) have a solid track record of raising funds comfortably in a competitive auction process context.

- **Deal costs:** A deal-by-deal model requires the manager to front the costs of identifying, investigating, and negotiating the investment opportunity prior to prospective investors' consideration. Deal-by-deal funds do not pay a management fee at all, although the manager may charge a one-off transaction fee from investors upon successful completion of the underlying investment. To the extent that a management fee is charged, that fee tends to be based purely on invested capital, and to be a lower percentage than the 2% typical for traditional small and mid-sized private equity funds. When managers have more leverage with investors, they may be able to charge a "commitment fee" for the obligation to show deals.

- **Recruitment:** Another disadvantage of the deal-by-deal model is that the private equity firm cannot recruit staff in a stable environment, given the uncertainty about the capital that will be managed under this approach.

- **Complexity:** The management, administration, and documentation associated with a deal-by-deal (or pledge) fund is more complicated because the exercising of opt-out/opt-in rights by different investors changes the composition of the investor group for each portfolio investment; this raises issues regarding the tracking and allocation of expenses (e.g., broken deal expenses) and other liabilities.

- **Investor protection:** Investors in deal-by-deal funds are more likely to view their participation as that of an active co-investor rather than a passive fund investor. As a result, these investors may seek a range of investor protections, including exit conditions, anti-dilution rights (including pre-emption rights in connection with the funding of any follow-on investments), and consent rights over certain key decisions regarding the underlying investment. They might also want to appoint a representative to the board of directors of the relevant company. Such protections are not typically given when traditional funds are being raised.

Yet, while deal-by-deal models have disadvantages, they also have distinctive advantages:

- **Deal-by-deal carried interest:**[13] Deal-by-deal models allow private equity professionals to earn carried interest on a deal-by-deal basis, thus potentially providing another motivational factor. Being paid out when the deal is exited (e.g., after three to four years) and not having it offset the gains on the deal by the returns on lower-performing deals in the fund can provide a considerable advantage to fund managers. In a 10-year fund structure, fund managers will likely have to wait eight years or more to receive their carried interest.

- **Strategic flexibility:** A deal-by-deal model allows GPs to be very flexible in terms of the investment strategy, as they can go outside of the typical investment parameters if they source a good deal that can make adequate returns. A deal-by-deal GP can also adopt a flexible approach to match fundraising market circumstances.

- **The ability to "cherry-pick":** LPs are able to cherry-pick the deals that balance their overall portfolios. They can also get closer to the underlying company and deploy money from their co-investment funds, which are increasingly raising more capital. GPs are more able to tailor their investment to meet these individual LPs' needs. In addition, LPs are more conscious of fee reduction strategies provided by the GP.

- **Suitability to family offices:** Family offices tend to prefer deal-by-deal GPs as they generally have little interest in investing into funds. Some family offices have a solid background in specific industries (especially if their family wealth originates from these sectors) and are able to add considerable strategic value when they are involved at the deal level.

- **Limited pressure to exit:** A fund in carry may incentivize GPs to sell their investments prematurely (i.e., before these investments have reached their maximum value) in order to pay out the carried interest earlier. In a deal-by-deal fund, all interests are aligned, in that the GP wants to maximize the value of each individual investment.

Deal-by-deal funds can be a stepping stone for emerging managers to enter into private equity or bridge periods between committed funds. Nevertheless, some very successful GPs adopt the deal-by-deal model consciously, given the advantages mentioned above.

THE "PAY-TO-PLAY" SCANDAL

As noted, placement agents are essentially intermediaries or middlemen paid by fund managers to help gain access to capital from institutional investors. They range from specialized divisions of large brokerage firms to small and mid-sized independent firms. In the United States, placement agents are regulated by the SEC,

---

[13] Carried interest is usually charged to investors on a deal-by-deal basis, and 20% is the starting point. In certain cases, a manager may earn more than 20% depending on the performance targets of individual investments. Thus, while deal-by-deal investing offers GPs lower management fees than a regular fund, it allows access to carry interest at a faster rate than a 10-year fund structure.

the Financial Industry Regulatory Authority (FINRA), and/or other federal, state, and international agencies and authorities. In the United Kingdom, they are regulated by the Financial Conduct Authority.

The placement agent industry has been under increasing scrutiny in the United States following several large scandals involving interactions between U.S. state government retirement plans and fund managers or those raising money for them (i.e., their placement agents). This scrutiny has focused on allegations of wrongdoing tied to "pay-to-play" contributions. The most common variant of these scandals involves the hiring of a politically connected placement agent by a fund sponsor to ensure that a public retirement plan invests in the sponsor's fund. Fees paid to this placement agent subsequently flow back to the public official in charge of managing fund investments. In a different scenario, fund managers and placement agents make campaign contributions to public officials to gain access to government retirement plans and secure an affirmative investment decision by the public official in charge of the government's investments. These activities were allegedly tied to prominent investors, including the New York State Common Retirement Fund (the second-largest government retirement plan in the country), the Illinois State Retirement Systems/Boards, and the state of New Mexico's retirement plan.

The CalPERS story

The experience of the California Public Employees' Retirement System (CalPERS), the largest state-run pension fund in the United States, is similar that of a number of other public pension funds. Since 1985, the assets in CalPERS' investment portfolio have grown from about $29 billion to over $375 billion.[14] The portfolio is held for the benefit of over 1.9 million California public employees, retirees, and their families.

Given that external money management fees constitute its largest recurring expense, CalPERS wanted to gain deeper insight into how external managers use the fees they receive. During the summer of 2009, it sought and obtained information from all of its external money managers regarding their use of placement agents, including the details of those arrangements and the fees the external managers had paid. CalPERS learned that some placement agents had been paid tens of millions of dollars in placement fees by some of its external managers, and none more than Alfred Villalobos and his firm, Arvco Capital Research, which were reportedly paid more than $60 million. According to media reports, Villalobos was a former CalPERS board member who had since become a placement agent for private equity funds.

CalPERS further discovered that its former chief executive, Fred Buenrostro, had signed documents purporting to be on behalf of CalPERS, dated both during his tenure as the CEO of CalPERS and shortly after it ended, stating that CalPERS was aware of millions of dollars in payments that were made to Villalobos. The documents signed by Buenrostro were necessary for Villalobos to obtain payments of over $20 million dollars in expected placement agent fees from Apollo Global Management, LLC. Apparently, these documents made a series of representations to firms like Apollo, among others, that became the subject of law enforcement actions and investigations.[15]

[14] CalPERS has over 2,8750 employees, all of whom are state civil servants. The pension fund is governed and overseen by a 13-member board of administration.

[15] Villalobos, who had denied wrongdoing, committed suicide on January 13, 2015, several weeks before his trial was to start on federal bribery charges. The Attorney General of California has agreed to a $20 million payment to settle a civil lawsuit accusing Villalobos of bribing officials. The settlement indicated that the bankruptcy estate of Villalobos' defunct firm, Arvco Capital Research, had to pay $10 million in penalties and another $10 million to cover the state's legal fees.

The excessive nature of some of the fees paid by CalPERS created an environment in which external managers were willing and able to pay placement agent fees at a level that bore little or no relationship to the services they provided. Moreover, the involvement of placement agents apparently led to pressure to accept external management fees that may have been higher than they should have been; the millions of dollars in fees managers were paying were, in turn, corrupting internal processes at CalPERS.

External managers seeking investments from CalPERS mainly enlisted two types of placement agent firms. The first type of firm was small, often "local" (based in or near California), and had close connections with CalPERS. This type of firm was hired primarily because of its contacts, and was paid specifically or principally for CalPERS investments. Of the approximately $180 million that external managers evidently paid to placement agent firms in connection with CalPERS' investments, over $120 million was paid to placement agent firms of this type.

The second type of placement agent firm tended to be hired because of its broader relationships with institutional investors. These firms were often affiliated with large financial institutions and firms typically placed no more than 15% of a total fund with CalPERS. Unlike the first type of placement agent firm, these firms could generally move on to other institutional investors and still obtain fees even if an investment could not be placed with CalPERS. Some of these firms made millions of dollars by placing a large number of investments across a broad range of external managers.

CalPERS has now taken significant steps to address the fees and other issues related to its business practices. The organization should continue its efforts in this regard, including improved access for external manager investment proposals, so that no firm feels that it must hire a placement agent to succeed. Further, the investment office staff of the pension fund continued its efforts in realigning the interests of external money managers with those of the institution, including ensuring that management and incidental fees (as distinct from incentive fees) are not profit centers for its external managers.

Lessons learned

The fund managers learned not to deal with unregistered agents, unfamiliar with the relevant private placement regulations and policy requirements in a market. This practice led to greater transparency when soliciting government pension plans.

Under U.S. federal securities laws, entities engaged in brokering the purchase or sale of securities for issuers, such as placement agents, are required to register as broker-dealers under the U.S. Securities Exchange Act of 1934. There are four factors the SEC considers in determining whether someone is a broker-dealer or a finder:

- **Receipt of transaction-based compensation:** A person who receives transaction-based compensation in connection with a securities transaction is almost always deemed to be a broker-dealer.

- **Involved in negotiation or advice:** A financial intermediary who is involved in negotiations or who provides detailed information or advice to a buyer or seller of securities is likely to be deemed a broker-dealer.

- **Solicitation of investors:** Solicitation is a factor that weighs in favor of finding a person to be a broker-dealer.

- **Previous securities sales experience or disciplinary action:** Experience selling securities and/or discipline for violations of securities laws indicate that regulators will consider a person a broker-dealer.

New policies require disclosure of placement agents used in relations with state government retirement plans. Responding to the pay-to-play schemes, the SEC proposed a rule curtailing, among other activities, the use of placement agents who have made campaign contributions. The rule would apply to both registered and unregistered advisers exempt from registration under the U.S. Investment Advisers Act of 1940. Another aspect of the proposal prohibits third-party solicitations of government retirement plans, including engaging firms that have arranged or solicited contributions to an elected official or candidate with respect to the proposed investment. Finally, the rule requires additional recordkeeping and disclosure to the SEC of campaign contributions to elected officials, candidates, and political action committees by the placement agent and its employees. If information about a fund sponsor's (or its placement agent's) political contributions is not properly disclosed, a government retirement plan investor may have the right to rescind its commitment to the fund.

These new rules significantly affect placement agents. In the U.S., public pension and municipal plans make up the majority of capital raised, as the public sector accounts for more than 50% of the aggregate capital committed to North American private capital investment funds. When engaging a placement agent, GPs should address the issue of whether public pension plans will be a target in the fundraising, whether a placement agent will be involved, and whether the placement agent or any of its affiliates have any relationships with the plan trustees or other government officials (e.g., familial relationships, political donations, etc.) that would preclude the agent from participating in any solicitation.

CONCLUSION

While fundraising might not be one of the core functions of a firm that manages private capital funds, it is nonetheless an extremely necessary activity. The fundraising market has matured at an ever-increasing rate, and processes are becoming more complex and regulated. Accordingly, managers embarking on the fundraising journey should bear the following advice in mind:

- **Be organized:** To raise capital in a newly competitive era, fund managers must be able not only to point to a track record of success, but also to articulate how that track record was achieved and, even more critically, how it will be maintained and repeated. As such, they must provide a detailed representation of their past performance and be able to describe its fundamental underpinnings—in particular, the skills, team, focus, and other capabilities that the firm brings to its deals. Managers also need to explain how these capabilities are evolving to allow them to keep ahead in a competitive market. As LPs look for differentiated strategies with relevant and proven capabilities, GPs need to be ready with clear answers.

- **Stay on top of the rules:** With the introduction of regulations like AIFMD or the Dodd-Frank Act, compliance requirements have intensified. While such measures can be burdensome for smaller managers, they still require compliance.

- **Invest in relationships:** As the balance of power between GPs and LPs shifts, and the environment and governing terms evolve (whether to the benefit of LPs or GPs), both sides must adapt and stay abreast of market conditions. Both sides need to appreciate the fact that the fund is a partnership, and invest in strengthening this partnership to better achieve their goals.

5 Fund Due Diligence

Diligence is the mother of good luck.
Benjamin Franklin

INTRODUCTION

Fund due diligence is a process that allows investors in the private equity asset class (i.e., limited partners (LPs)) to investigate and evaluate the investment premise of specific private equity funds. The main objective of this diligence is to arrive at better investment decisions by following a rigorous stepwise investigation of the fund managers (general partners (GPs)) and the strategies they aim to employ. Given that (a) LPs essentially give GPs a free hand to manage the private equity funds, (b) these funds are lightly regulated, and (c) there is significant variation in the performance of the best versus that of the worst GPs, undertaking comprehensive due diligence when selecting managers can be the difference between poor and great investment returns for investors. [1]

As the private equity asset class has matured, the breadth and volume of potential investment opportunities that LPs can pursue has widened. The asset class now encompasses a wide variety of investment styles that include buyouts, growth capital, venture capital, distressed debt, direct lending, mezzanine financing, turnarounds, infrastructure, real estate, and natural resources spanning many geographies. An examination of these different strategies across the world requires a diverse skill set and expertise, as well as access to extensive data. As a result, LPs need to allocate significant resources to conduct a rigorous examination of private equity fund managers. Of particular focus is the way that LPs deploy staff capable of handling this challenge, with some investors preferring to outsource the expertise (i.e., by engaging outside advisers and funds of funds) while others opt to hire staff internally and build in-house teams. The decision to outsource the fund diligence and investment process might be based on a lack of internal resources or expertise, although some more sophisticated investors continue to use consultants as a second opinion.[2] The decision is also driven by the scale or amount of capital allocated to private equity – an LP with a large amount of capital deployed would typically have an in-house team as the go-to option which may be supported by outsourced consultants or advisers.

Diligence activities are both quantitative and qualitative: they involve data analysis as well as extensive qualitative research. The evaluation of private equity funds is a challenging process for three reasons. First, the fact that these funds are typically structured as private partnerships means that publicly available information is very limited. Unlike managers of registered investment companies such as mutual funds, private equity fund managers are not usually forced to pass detailed information on their investments and activities into the public domain, which makes it difficult to compare different GPs that raise funds simultaneously. Second, GPs are normally reluctant to disclose commercially sensitive information that would confer an advantage if it fell into the hands of their competitors. Third, critical GP skills—such as deal sourcing

---

[1] LPs typically find comfort in the regulatory oversight of the investment adviser (or management company) rather than a specific fund. Most GPs/investment advisers are, in fact, regulated.

[2] External advisers not only carry out fund due diligence, but also recommend the appropriate asset allocation mix and propose investments in specific private equity funds.

capability, the ability to add value post investments, or the ability to exit deals successfully—are not readily observable even when LPs have full access to pertinent information.

Potential investors are therefore reliant on GPs, their prior LPs, or their portfolio company managers to provide a suite of information that will enable the evaluation of the fund investment opportunity. This disclosure process is often managed by the GP with the help of an adviser known as a "placement agent," who will take responsibility for preparing the information and handling any follow-up inquiries. While this information is valuable, it is generally considered insufficient to complete a full and rigorous diligence process. Thus, LPs need to structure their own quantitative and qualitative diligence processes so that they can move from plain analysis to insightful conclusions. In particular, LPs with a global investment program must have local professionals in key international markets to be able to understand local market dynamics and gain access to the best investment opportunities.

Unlike the investment decisions that investors in the public markets are required to make, an investment in a private equity fund does not allow investors to form a view on the assets they are being asked to invest in. The investment decision that an LP makes is actually a commitment to participate, alongside other LPs in the fund, in a series of future investments that the GP will make over the investment period of the fund in question (typically 4–5 years). At the time of the commitment, none of these investments have yet been made, so the fund is also known as a "blind pool." In this respect, the evaluation methods used to assess investments in public equity markets are not really relevant to private equity assets.

Due diligence of private equity funds has evolved significantly over recent years as this class of assets has become a larger part of institutional investors' asset allocations. This evolution has been helped in part by the increasing involvement of industry bodies such as the Institutional Limited Partners Association (ILPA), which has been driving best-practice standards on diligence processes and fund terms and conditions. While diligence practices still exhibit a wide degree of variability, depending on the skills and experience of the LPs, the investment process focuses on five broad areas:

- The investment strategy that the private equity fund will pursue;

- The organization of the private equity firm that manages the fund;

- Specific skills and attributes of the team that makes the investments in the fund;

- Prior investment performance of this investment team; and

- Legal terms and conditions associated with the fund.

Beyond the commercial aspects of the investment opportunity, LPs focus on other aspects that indirectly affect the success of the fund and that are often covered during the so-called "operational due diligence process."[3] Some of the topics investigated include (1) *litigation risks* (for the private equity firm managing the fund or its employees); (2) *operational and back-office procedures and systems* (e.g., quality of the IT system, reporting quality, cash flow management, tax and audit procedures, fund administrators and their procedures and systems etc.); (3) *public relations* (e.g., how GPs manage public interactions with a wide set of stakeholders); (4) *conflicts of interest* (e.g., whether GPs have other business interests or activities that might conflict with the activities of the private equity fund); and (5) *environmental, social, and governance* (ESG) aspects.[4] By including

---

[3] This could be done by the investment team of an LP, a dedicated operational due diligence team within the LP organization which conducts an independent underwriting, or a third-party consultant appointed by the LP.

[4] We discuss some of these issues in separate chapters that cover fund administration, fundraising, and ESG.

these other aspects in the due diligence process, LPs acknowledge that private equity firms may fail not only due to poor investment performance, but also because of non-investment-related reasons, such as weak internal operations and systems, failings arising from the GP's service providers, public scrutiny of their deals, compliance gaps, or poor risk management.

Before we discuss the due diligence process in greater detail, first it is important to understand, via an overview of the overall LP investment process, how portfolio allocation potentially influences due diligence activities.

LPS' INVESTMENT PROCESS

LPs typically engage in three major activities when planning and making investments: (1) strategic asset allocation, (2) portfolio construction, and (3) individual fund selection. The due diligence process (which we examine in detail later) is part of the individual fund selection process.

Strategic asset allocation

The first step in the investment process requires the investor to form a clear view of the role that the private equity program will play in the broader asset allocation. Although this step is a straightforward analysis for investors whose sole activity is to invest in private equity, for most institutional investors, the process is more complex, given that private equity will typically represent only a small part (up to, say, 5%) of a global asset allocation.

Note that private equity is both an asset class and an investment strategy. LPs' asset allocation decisions should be based on the risk and return characteristics of the private equity asset class; however, in practice, most portfolio allocations are based on the perceived risk and return characteristics of private equity funds. On the one hand, the public equity asset class includes all publicly listed companies. Investors can gain exposure to the public equity asset class by purchasing shares of publicly traded companies or shares of investment vehicles (e.g., mutual funds) that purchase shares issued by public companies. On the other hand, the private equity asset class is formed by all non-public (or private) companies. Purchasing shares directly in privately held companies or investing in private equity funds that buy these companies' shares can achieve exposure to this asset class. While LPs could, in theory, passively invest in a basket of all private corporations, this is not possible given the large number of private companies, the inability to acquire minority stakes, and the fact that the true value of private companies is rarely observable. Therefore, when investors make an allocation to private equity, it is not a passive investment in the basket of most private companies that form the private equity asset class, but rather, an investment in a skill-based active strategy with two primary sub-strategies: leveraged buyouts and venture capital.[5]

To develop a point of view on the high-level allocation to the private equity asset class, investors need a clear idea of how the expected risks and returns from the asset class will impact a broader portfolio construction. At this stage, investors must consider not only the effects of private equity style risks and returns

---

[5] It is important to note that the standard deviation of the private equity asset class returns is lower than the standard deviation of private equity fund returns. One reason for this difference is that individual private equity funds are not fully diversified, and thus face high levels of idiosyncratic risks.

on the overall portfolio, but also cash flow planning and liquidity management for what is inherently a long-term and illiquid asset class.

Once LPs have determined the aggregate allocation to the asset class in terms of the amount of capital required, the proportion of the total investment program, and the investment time horizon, they then need to consider the sub-allocation within the private equity asset class with reference to geography, investment strategy (e.g., leveraged buyouts, growth equity, venture capital, turnaround, or private debt) and underlying asset diversification. This process also has to reflect the amount of capital LPs are seeking to invest because some strategies, such as investing very substantial capital in small and emerging private equity markets, may not be deliverable.

It can be extremely challenging to form a view on the above allocation given the vast array of options which are now available to investors. For example, the number of secondary funds (i.e., funds investing in previously established vehicles and buying over fund stakes from original LPs who are seeking liquidity from their positions) coming to market has rapidly increased over the past decade, as has the number of funds targeting investments in private debt instruments (as opposed to equity). Geographic allocation is also complicated by the emergence of regional and, in some cases, global funds.

LPs (and, where relevant, their advisers) need a structured approach to navigate this complex picture. One possible such framework involves forming a view on opportunities across six different dimensions:

- Strengths of the underlying macroeconomic environment;

- Structural drivers for private equity returns;

- Relative valuation metrics for private equity assets;

- Cultural acceptance of private equity (in specific geographies, where applicable);

- Standards of governance that are in force (once again, in specific geographies); and

- Appreciation of foreign exchange risk.

This analysis is challenging, but its final product is an asset allocation decision that can help as an investment roadmap. In addition, the analytical process will help investors to fully understand their institution's tolerance for risk.

Underlying macroeconomic environment

Private equity is an inherently cyclical asset class. When forming a view on its attractiveness, an obvious starting point is to consider the current and likely future economic environment in which investments will be made. The general economic environment can be analyzed from various perspectives to determine how conducive it will be to successful private equity investment. Legitimate indicators are, for example, metrics such as GDP per capita (and, importantly, recent changes to GDP growth), the state of the labor markets, and the current and prospective inflation, interest (particularly relevant for buyout strategies), and exchange rates. The analysis should also consider the impact of any structural imbalances present within the economy, such as excessive levels of consumer indebtedness (at the time of writing, these factors are particularly significant). The economic analysis should be structured in a way that allows it to be used both across asset classes and over time.

Developing an accurate view of the current position in the economic cycle is vital, because different asset classes will have differing degrees of attractiveness. For instance, primary investments into buyout funds tend to be countercyclical in terms of investment timing. All things being equal, the best time for new investment is in a period of declining economic growth, and the best time for divesting is in a period of economic expansion.

Structural drivers for private equity returns

In addition to the state of the economic environment, the strength of the structural drivers of the asset class is another key to determining market attractiveness. A good starting point for this analysis is to understand the penetration of private equity in any given country market. A useful metric is annual private equity investment as a percentage of GDP, because it is freely available for many markets and over several years. Countries such as Sweden have a higher penetration than countries in Asia and Latin America, for example.

Other useful metrics are the breadth and depth of the mergers and acquisitions market and IPO activity in a specific geography and the share of total activity of each accounted for by private equity transactions. Again, these data points are generally available but are also cyclical due to the size and distribution of large-cap private equity transactions.

Another fundamental driver of any given market is its industrial structure, specifically, the number of corporate entities of different sizes within the economy. For example, certain economies, such as Germany, Italy, and Spain are dominated by small and medium-sized private enterprises (SMEs), which represent a large universe of potential targets for private equity funds. A logical further step in this analysis is to review the gradual trajectory of both the volume and value of private equity transactions completed in specific markets.

Valuation metrics

A key driver of value creation in any transaction is the difference between the multiple at the time of entry and at the time of exit. Hence, any analysis of a local market must take into account the typical acquisition multiples paid for businesses. This analysis needs to be interpreted with care, because structural differences across markets can affect average entry multiples. For example, multiples have historically been lower in Germany than in the Nordic markets—a result driven partly by the typical transactions completed in these markets. The analysis can also be complicated by the nature of the GPs operating in a local market. For instance, in the United Kingdom, where many of the larger pan-European GPs are based, the statistics can be affected by the very large transactions that these groups complete, which are generally completed at higher multiples than those exhibited by small transactions. Any review of transaction multiples can also include a very useful analysis of the typical debt structure and debt multiples in use across different markets, because the availability (or lack) of credit can have a major impact on multiples paid. This information can be readily obtained from credit rating agencies (e.g., Standard & Poor's), which collate statistics for the syndicated loan markets.

In forming a view of the attractiveness of a specific private equity market and the likelihood of high multiples being paid, a further key variable to consider is the amount of committed but uninvested capital available. This metric is known as "dry powder." As private equity funds are often raised with a five-year investment period, arithmetically, there should always be an element of capital "overhang," which can be measured in terms of the number of years' worth of transactions it reflects and how this has changed over time. For instance, in the aftermath of the 2008 financial crisis, dry powder was at a historically high level.

Finally, no analysis would be complete without reviewing the historical valuation metrics in the private equity market and comparing them with their public equity market benchmarks.

Cultural acceptance of private equity

Private equity has developed considerably in recent years, but despite the global growth of this asset class, markets can vary significantly in terms of their cultural acceptance of private equity as a mechanism for securing a change in corporate control. The degree to which private equity is understood and accepted in a particular market will depend on a range of factors, such as the level of government support for free market practices, the entrepreneurial climate within the country, how private businesses are dealing with succession, the size of the pool of professional managers, and the types of agency relationships between shareholders and managers at play in the economy.

Standards of governance

Yet another important stage in the process of strategic asset allocation is forming a view on the quality of corporate governance. This step focuses on understanding the unique systems for corporate control operating in each specific country. In particular, it involves evaluating the legal and accounting frameworks in operation and understanding the political agenda of the incumbent government and its likely impact on such frameworks. One way to develop an understanding of the conditions that prevail in a specific market is to engage with local legal and accounting firms.

Foreign exchange risk

LPs must carefully consider two main related foreign exchange (FX) risks. The first arises from the potential mismatch between the LP's base currency and the currency of denomination of the private equity fund. In this case, an FX risk is created at the time of the original commitment to the underlying private equity fund (and crystallized with any subsequent cash flow movements) as the size of this commitment in the LP's own currency will vary with spot rates.

The second risk arises from the potential currency mismatch between the private equity fund's base currency and the currency of any underlying company investments. This type of foreign currency risk will remain unrealized until such underlying investments are sold and the proceeds are distributed to LPs.

While it is important for LPs to appreciate the impact of foreign exchange movements on the performance of the private equity funds they are investing in, the long-term investment horizon involved makes hedging such a risk prohibitively expensive for practical purposes. Thus, most LPs will monitor currency exposure at an aggregate investment portfolio level and hedge any significant FX risk at this level.

The strategic asset allocation process allows LPs to develop a strong view on the attractiveness of each geography and asset class for private equity investing, both in absolute and—critically—in relative terms, both to other private equity markets and to other asset classes. As a result of completing this process, LPs should be able to articulate the anticipated risk and return trade-off for each private equity market, and to design a coherent asset allocation that is consistent with their investment objectives.

Portfolio construction

Following the strategic asset allocation process, the next stage in the investment process is portfolio construction. Here the LP develops a high-level map of the prospective portfolio to articulate a recommended GP diversification strategy within the context of the broader strategic asset allocation. Like the strategic framework, the GP diversification strategy is also driven by the projected time frame of the investment activity and by the list of attractive and addressable GPs likely to be open for investment in the various markets and asset classes throughout the investment period.

So far we have focused on the LP's role as an investor in private equity vehicles managed by third-party managers. However, recently, many LPs have expanded their investment activity to include direct co-investment, which sees these LPs invest directly in specific transactions that are normally (but not exclusively) sourced by funds in which the LPs have invested. There are several benefits to LPs from doing this: (1) LPs can more accurately "time" their investments, as each co-investment relates to an actual transaction as opposed to a commitment; (2) they can gain deeper insight into the operations and investment process of the GP concerned; and (3) such co-investments are usually offered to LPs on a fee-free basis, thereby helping to lower the overall fee burden across their private equity portfolio. Therefore, in the portfolio construction phase, an LP may wish to set aside some of the capital to be allocated to a direct co-investment program.

Individual fund selection

Today, LPs face a vast universe of private equity funds operating in different geographies and pursuing different strategies. With several thousand managers operating worldwide, LPs must adopt a robust process for mapping, filtering, and analyzing prospective investment opportunities. This process starts with the development of a comprehensive list of potential investments. It can be a time-consuming task to establish all the "qualified" groups that fall within the mandate of the investment program, but this has been made easier by the increased number of private equity data providers (e.g., Thompson Venture Economics, Preqin, PitchBook) and the many local market trade associations that now exist such as the British Private Equity and Venture Capital Association (BVCA). In addition, relationships with placement agents will help to provide market intelligence on the fundraising calendar (i.e., who is raising and when) for each market.

The central premise of the process is to start with the broadest possible list of potential investments in each geographic area and asset class, and to work from this broad list to a set of qualified fund investment opportunities. Having ensured that any attractive fund investment identified is suitable, both technically and legally, the next step is to progress—as rapidly and efficiently as possible—to a list of actual investment targets. Exhibit 1 provides a high-level representation of this process.

LPs must also develop a perspective on the addressability of specific investment opportunities. Depending on the circumstances, it may be very difficult for new investors to gain access to investment funds that are highly attractive as the demand for these funds may exceed the capacity available (referred to as "oversubscription"). Traditionally, some of the most renowned U.S. venture capital groups have fallen into this category.

Therefore, as LPs go through the fund selection process, they need to be mindful of whether they will be able to execute all the investments they would seek (i.e., commit their target amount of capital to a given fund). This fund selection process is shown in Exhibit 2.

LPs use several different decision forums to progress opportunities through the investment process, and a decision of whether or not to continue must be made at each stage of the process. At the end of the process (after the due diligence phase), the outcome will be whether the opportunity is approved for investment or not. Only if the opportunity is approved will it be considered for the portfolio, taking into account the overall portfolio construction (which has already been set). In the early stages, the investment team usually meets informally to manage opportunities through the process, but at the analysis and due diligence stages, "go/no-go" decisions are likely to be made by the fund manager's formally appointed investment committee.

Exhibit 1: An overview of the fund investment process

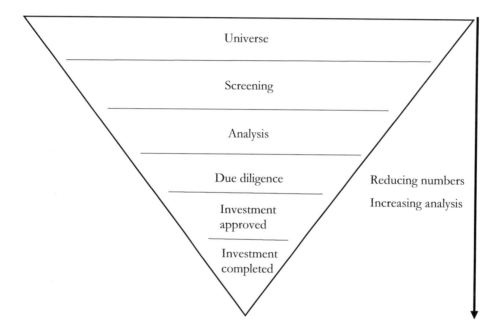

Investment sourcing

Once LPs have developed an understanding of the universe of different GPs operating in the market, they must then ensure that they log the maximum number of new investment opportunities. The aim is to identify as many opportunities as possible that have the potential to produce attractive, risk-adjusted returns at the very highest level of the evaluation process. As LPs identify individual opportunities, they form a preliminary view of their quality; if an opportunity qualifies, they pass it through to the next step of the process.

New fund opportunities are identified through various sources. To achieve the best position, LPs require strong local market knowledge, which they typically have gained either through accumulated investment experience or through a local network of advisers. However, LPs are often also introduced to opportunities through placement agents, who match them with appropriate well-funded investors. While such intermediaries are motivated to bring investors the best possible investment opportunities, it must be remembered that placement agents are paid by the fund manager, so investors need to conduct their own analysis and due diligence rather than rely on the agent.

Exhibit 2: Fund selection process

	Investment sourcing	Investment screening	Investment analysis	Investment due diligence
Objective	Maximize investment opportunity set	Eliminate non-investment grade opportunities	Filter out highest potential investment opportunities	Recommend opportunities for investment approval
Actions	Identify widest possible set of investment opportunities	Develop high-level understanding of manager group and fund strategy	Validate strategic attractiveness of the fund and capability of the manager	Complete detailed validation of investment opportunity
Timing	Ongoing	2–3 hours	2–3 days	30 days
Responsibility	All members of the investment team	One member of the investment team	One member of the investment team	Two members of the investment team

Investment screening

At the investment screening stage, LPs complete some preliminary analysis to understand the nature of the opportunity. High-level screening often involves desk analysis and the application of existing knowledge; actual face-to-face time with staff from the GP concerned is usually limited. At this stage, the LP seeks to identify any "deal-breaking" characteristics of the opportunity, and to develop a high-level hypothesis for the opportunity. Deal breakers may be issues specific to the opportunity or may relate to the LP's internal criteria, such as portfolio concentration limits or governance structures. The key output from this stage is a short one-page summary that articulates the merits and risks of the opportunity at a high level and presents a recommendation and rationale for the next steps (i.e., whether to proceed with further analysis or to pass). Exhibit 3 provides an example of such a summary.

Investment analysis

Opportunities that move into the analysis stage see significantly higher levels of diligence performed, and considerably more engagement with the team members of the GP. At this stage, the LP spends time developing a full understanding of the fund's investment premise and a working hypothesis of the GP's ability to deliver attractive risk-adjusted returns. Analysis is both quantitative and qualitative, and involves multiple meetings with the GP team. If it is decided that the opportunity merits full diligence, the LP should develop a full diligence hypothesis that articulates all of the outstanding concerns that must be addressed. The LP should identify not only what those elements are, but the potential mitigating factors.

Exhibit 3: A first-time fund

Spanish Private Equity Firm is seeking to raise its first independent fund after spinning out from a Bank. This team, which has invested together for several years, is seeking to raise a fund of EUR 130 million (hard cap EUR 150 million). The fund is expected to have a first closing around April 2012.

Criteria	Preliminary ranking
Strategy and process	4.0
Organization	3.75
Team	4.0
Track record	4.5

Recommendation: This certainly appears a very interesting fund opportunity. The fund offers many of the attributes of a successful investment: a clear strategy targeting a relatively uncompetitive market segment, an independent organization, a strong and cohesive senior team that has worked together extensively, and a long track record of investment success (52% of realized deals (11/21) returning over 5x investment cost). Key questions for diligence involve fully validating the team's investment credentials and gaining clarity over the role and relationship the team enjoyed with its prior parent organization. First-time fund risks will also need to be considered. Further analysis is recommended.

Investment due diligence

Investment due diligence is the final stage of the diligence process. Its goal is to reach a final decision on whether to approve the opportunity under review for investment (although there may be some iterative steps). This stage sees the LP execute the diligence activities identified in the diligence hypothesis that was established and agreed upon at the analysis stage. Final due diligence is a time-consuming and detailed process that involves extensive qualitative and quantitative analysis, and may also involve the use of external consultants to deal with specific topics.

FUND DUE DILIGENCE IN DETAIL

The previous section discussed the different stages of the multifaceted LP diligence process, and outlined the process and steps within it. The central principle of the process is to form an efficient and effective means to process large numbers of opportunities and develop rigorous data-driven answers. This section will describe the due diligence process further, focusing on the specific elements that need to be addressed at each step.

Due diligence activities should be designed to deliver meaningful insights that lead to better investment decisions, given the significant downsides of choosing a poor-performing fund. Accordingly, LPs require not only a fully developed perspective on the specific opportunity being investigated (an investment hypothesis), but also a clear picture of the pros and cons of the other investment opportunities in the "peer" universe of competing investments. Selecting the "wrong" private equity fund might have severe repercussions for two main reasons: (1) the performance spread between the top and bottom quartile funds is significant (e.g., approximately 20%) and higher than it is in other asset classes as well as persistent over time; and (2) reversing a GP selection decision is difficult and expensive due to the illiquid nature of the investment and the discount involved when selling the fund interest in the secondaries private equity market.

The best way to think of due diligence on a specific fund is as a 2x2 matrix (see Exhibit 4). LPs will want to test two broad areas: the commercial aspects of the investment opportunity and its legal (and taxation) aspects. In so doing, LPs will conduct diligence on certain items as a matter of course (i.e., steps that they would follow for every fund that they conduct diligence on) while also tailoring specific items to the working investment hypothesis for the particular opportunity in question.

Most LPs have developed a checklist of questions that they need answers to in any due diligence process (an example checklist is included in Appendix A). This checklist is known as a due diligence questionnaire (DDQ). The idea is to maintain a list of questions that are universal constants in any diligence process (e.g., have any of the team members of the GP been convicted of a crime?). It is highly unlikely that the answers to any of these standard questions will convey a great deal of insight or improve the quality of a decision, but they may reveal certain deal-breaking pieces of information.

Funds that are attempting to raise capital often provide their own, somewhat biased, DDQ, which is designed to cover many of the standard information-gathering questions that form part of the LP's diligence process but also double up as a marketing document. The diligence process therefore often involves a rather inefficient matching of the investor and GP DDQs.

Exhibit 4: Due diligence as a 2x2 matrix

General diligence items	Opportunity-specific items
Legal issues	
Is the fund structure acceptable from the investors' perspective?	Is the key man clause appropriate?
Etc.	Etc.
Etc.	Etc.
Commercial issues	
Is the full investment track record of the carried proposed team accurately disclosed?	What is the proposed sharing of carried interest within the investment?
Etc.	Etc.
Etc.	Etc.

As the diligence process progresses, LPs will dedicate increasing amounts of time and resources to face-to-face sessions with the GP. To make best use of the GP's and LPs' time and resources, the most effective way to manage these sessions is to use a hypothesis to drive the diligence process.

The LPs develop a hypothesis for the investment that articulates what they need to believe to be true in order to recommend the investment for approval. The most effective way to develop such a hypothesis is to form a logic tree (see Exhibit 5 for an example).

Exhibit 5: Due diligence hypothesis for an investment in ABC LLP

Strategy/Process	Organization	Team	Track record
1. The investment strategy is buyouts with EVs principally < €80 million. The German market is attractive for the specific strategy that this fund is pursuing. 2. The competitive environment that this fund will operate in is not expected to deteriorate over the investment period. No new entrants/GPs dropping down. 3. Any step-up in deal size for this fund will not detract from its overall attractiveness. 4. ABC has strong, maintainable, and attractive deal flow as a function of the longevity of the team in the local market.	1. New management company is likely to be a stable 2. No underlying tensions between the senior partners for decision making is inclusive. 3. Organization is sufficiently large and has the necessary capacity to deliver on the investment strategy. 4. Distribution of carried interest is sufficient to incentivize and retain the investment team. 5. There are no legacy issues involving the separation of the team from its previous parent. The separation arrangements are finalized. We are satisfied with any issues pertaining to the history of the organization in prior ownership.	1. The ABC team has sufficient strength in depth to execute the prescribed investment strategy. The core partner group has a deep and varied network of contacts within the target set of potential investments. 2. The spread of the GP's franchise is sufficiently strong to survive the departure of any one senior partner.	1. Track record of the GP is accurately portrayed and attributed: – ABC's role on each deal is accurately portrayed. – Valuation policies are consistent with IPEV best practice. – The track record is wholly inclusive of all deals done. 2. Most significant overall driver of performance has been EBITDA growth within the portfolio companies. 3. The GP has been able to source transactions at multiples that compare favorably with those paid by competing GPs. 4. Evidence of value creation within the yet unrealized investments coming from a number of different drivers.

Approaches

The LP's task is to cover several key points, asking pertinent questions and seeking answers along the way. These questions can be addressed by exploring the following topics.

Internal quantitative analysis

There are two key areas that investors should analyze: the GP's financials and the track record that the GP is presenting to support the fundraising process. LPs will want to understand the financial flows into the GP's management company, mainly because they need to form a view on alignment of interests. LPs should aim for full and proper alignment with the GP, insofar as the prime investment objective is to deliver significant capital gains. If substantial profits are generated from the day-to-day business of running the management company, then this will weaken the desired alignment. Thus, LPs will analyze the GP's accounts to form a view on appropriate alignment. Broadly speaking, the larger the fund is, the weaker the alignment; however, there is really no objective measure of what constitutes sufficient alignment. LPs will therefore need to make a judgment call on whether the GP team is sufficiently motivated by the promise of carried interest generated from capital gains or whether it is more focused on the shorter-term fee-generating aspects of the business.

GP alignment can also be achieved via GPs having their own investments in the fund; this is a typical way to align GP and LP interests since it is a sort of "hurt money" or "skin in the game" which has to be contributed by the GP (staff) at the start of the fund. This alignment works especially well when a fund is not going to be close to paying carry (i.e., when the alignment from the carry structure is not working). There are various ways to structure GP investments: cash (highly preferred), fee deferrals, or loans (or a combination of these). It is also important to look at the source of a GP's investment in the fund. Ideally, the investment would come from both senior partners as well as from other investment professionals in the firm according to their pro rata share in the carry structure.

However, most of the LP's analytical work will focus on the track record that the GP presents to support the fundraising process. LPs will examine this track record across three dimensions:

- **In absolute terms**—what realized and unrealized returns has the GP generated?

- **In relative terms**—how do these returns compare with other funds that the LP regards as peers?

- **In detail**—what are the key underlying drivers of these returns?

An obvious area of focus for LPs is the GP's aggregate performance in both absolute and relative terms. The mechanics for this process are covered in Chapter 3, which deals with the performance measurement of private equity funds. Interrogating performance data in an insightful way is not a trivial task, as recognizing top funds can be extremely difficult. Many funds could potentially claim a top-quartile performance by manipulating portfolio company valuations and performance metrics (e.g., selection of a different peer group or benchmark can move a fund's average performance into a top-quartile performance on a relative basis). In general, private equity funds should be compared based on fund vintage year, fund type, and primary geographic focus, although peer or benchmark data for some specific markets is sometimes based on samples which are too small to be used. For example, it would be meaningless and potentially misleading to benchmark a German buyout fund against other German buyout funds of the same vintage, given that typically, fewer than five German buyout funds are raised in any one vintage year. Instead, the German buyout fund would be benchmarked against all European buyout funds of the same vintage.

In detailed analyses, the main area of focus will be the disaggregation of realized returns from exited transactions. In any transaction, value can be created in three ways: improving profitability, reducing the leverage between acquisition and exit, and multiple arbitrage (i.e., selling the business for a higher multiple of profits than it was acquired for). Ideally, the investment will benefit from all three of these drivers, but in the LP's eyes, the first aim—growing the profits of the underlying business—is the hardest to achieve (and therefore the most valuable). This analysis would give the LP a sensible perspective on whether the GP's track record is *proprietary* and *repeatable*. Private equity is a long-term investment, and thus, LPs will normally find that a significant number of the portfolio companies managed by the GP are unrealized. These companies are still within the portfolio and under the management of the GP. The challenge for LPs is to form a view on the performance of these companies and, critically, their valuation. Valuation of unrealized investments is a complicated business, because the valuation methods applied are notoriously sensitive to a small number of assumptions, such as selecting the appropriate multiple for valuing the company. The latest set of valuation guidelines (IPEV) go some way to solving this problem, but forming a view on current valuations and future prospects for unrealized portfolio companies remains a real challenge. For such GPs, LPs will typically employ a forward-looking methodology to estimate the exit valuations of the unrealized portfolio in order to evaluate this component of the track record.

Internal qualitative analysis

Given the scarcity of quantitative data on private equity funds, the qualitative assessment of a fund investment opportunity is of paramount importance. This type of assessment mostly involves interviews with GP team members and portfolio company management teams, as well as reference calls with other relevant third parties with a relevant point of view. These interviews can be invaluable in terms of the insight they generate. In addition to these interviews, the continuity and compensation structure of the private equity investment team should be adequately assessed. Funds also require well-thought-out succession plans, as top-heavy funds with executives that are nearing retirement are generally considered to be a red flag. Finally, LPs view a fair distribution of carry between the investment team members as a positive signal, as it provides a strong incentive for the younger team members to stay with the fund. LPs need to consider three elements when undertaking qualitative interviews: what to ask, who to ask, and how to ask?

What to ask

In terms of what to ask, LPs should focus on three areas: (1) How does the GP source its investment opportunities? (2) Once it has completed an investment, how does it create value for investors? (3) How has the GP performed in terms of managing capital for third-party investors?

- **Deal sourcing**: Effective proprietary deal sourcing is key, due to the efficiency of investment bank-led auction processes, which lead to inflated prices and hence, reduced investment returns. A second benefit of "off-market" deal sourcing is that evaluating a deal outside a formal auction process allows the GP to properly diligence the underlying investment.

- **Value creation**: LPs will want to establish exactly how a GP adds value: is it just clever financial engineering or is there an operational value-add component that gives the manager an edge over other funds? Operational improvement skills are now highly valued by LPs in the fund evaluation process as they are evidence of differentiation and repeatability, compared with financial engineering skills, which are more of a commodity.

- **Fund management**: Aside from the pure deal-making side of the business, LPs should also investigate a GP's track record of managing funds for institutional investors. Potential investors will want to know how the GP has performed in terms of overall risk management and portfolio construction, as well as how they have communicated with investors during the life of prior funds. Given the long-term nature of a fund investment, LPs need to be comfortable with the nature of the partner they are taking on.

Who to ask

In terms of who to ask, LPs often need to be creative in their thinking. GPs normally furnish a list of referees, in addition to making their own teams available for interview, but these interviews may not provide the most insightful answers. LPs must make use of their own personal networks to source interviews that can deliver more insight; these might include interviews with prior members of the GP team, as well as bankers, consultants, and prior portfolio company employees.

How to ask

LPs should give careful consideration to how to ask questions, and how they interpret the answers. All respondents will come with a bias of one kind or another, and it is critical to establish at the outset where that bias lies. Few LPs are skilled interviewers, able to structure and conduct interviews to optimal effect. For interviews to be effective, the right people need to be in the room and the right questions need to be asked in the right way. For instance, should the interview be one-on-one or can several people be involved? Should the questions be open-ended or should the interviewer present a thesis for discussion? LPs may seek help from external consultants to address these points. It is worth noting that GPs are increasingly attempting to manage the reference calling process in order to minimize the disruption to referees, who can sometimes receive an unmanageable number of requests for reference calls; this is done by hiring a single service provider (usually a large firm of headhunters) to conduct a reference calling program, the results of which can be made available to all potential investors as part of the diligence process.

External support

No matter how skilled or competent the LP is, at some point, external advisers are likely to be involved in the due diligence process. The most obvious way in which this involvement occurs is through the involvement of legal advisers who assist in negotiating the limited partnership agreement (LPA)—the key document which sets out the legal terms of the fund and the relationship between the investors and the fund manager.

LPs may also call on the services of other business advisers, depending on the circumstances. Usually, the investment hypothesis and diligence logic tree will show whether there are any diligence elements that cannot be addressed through normal means. For instance, the LP may need to do a detailed background check on a GP that operates in a distant country; this is likely to fall outside the LP's core network, and so a third party will need to be involved to do the work.

The diligence process can be viewed as a funnel: as an opportunity passes through each successive stage in the process, fewer issues are investigated, but those that are investigated are investigated in greater detail.

Investment due diligence

Typically, each fund opportunity should be evaluated across three broad dimensions:

1. Fund strategy.

2. Investment process of the fund.

3. Assessment of the GP.

As noted, the best approach to analyzing fund opportunities is to form a working hypothesis on the attractiveness of each opportunity, and then to test this hypothesis fully in the detailed stages of the due diligence process. Exhibit 6 shows a high-level overview of the objectives in analyzing each of the different elements.

Exhibit 6: Objectives when analyzing a general partner

Fund strategy/Investment process	GP assessment
Understand the strategy of the fund	Understand the organization structure of the GP
Develop a point of view on the strength of this strategy in the specific geographic area and asset class	Develop a view of the strength and likely longevity of the organizational structure
Determine the strength of the investment process	Develop a view of the appropriateness of the organization structure with respect to the strategy being followed
Critically assess the ability of the process to deliver against the strategy	Understand the strength and weaknesses of the investment team
	Develop a perspective on the likely stability of the team and its ability to deliver against the chosen strategy given the organizational structure
	Develop a view of the quality of the risk-adjusted returns generated in the past and the likely return profile expected in future funds

Fund strategy

LPs spend a significant amount of time investigating the investment strategy of the fund under consideration. They then consider this strategy in conjunction with the work already completed during the portfolio construction process. When LPs are evaluating the fund's strategy, they consider both the attractiveness of the broader geographic and asset class strategy that the fund will adopt, as well as the GP's approach to value creation and how it differs from those of its major competitors.

LPs should evaluate, in detail, the consistency with which the fund's broader strategy has been adopted in the past. If the GP has let its strategy "drift," this detracts from LPs' confidence in its prior performance as an indicator of its future performance.

Investment process of the fund

GPs' approaches to value creation can vary widely, from a purely "financial" model to one based on significant "hands-on" involvement in the day-to-day operations of investee companies. Different approaches to value creation are more or less attractive in terms of their potential to generate returns, depending on the market conditions prevailing in the geographic market or asset class.

The view formed on the operating model employed, as defined in the fund's strategy, is used in conjunction with the overview of the general attractiveness of the asset class and geography to frame the parameters within which the GP's investment process can be evaluated (see Exhibit 7).

Exhibit 7: Fund investment process

Sourcing	Investment evaluation	Execution	Value creation	Exit
Sourcing executable investment opportunities	Evaluating the attractiveness and potential returns from specific opportunities	Successfully completing transactions, including negotiating with sellers and structuring debt/management packages	Constructing and delivering against a cogent plan for value creation	Successfully exiting the investment and returning capital to LPs

By examining the fund's strategy and investment process, LPs should obtain answers to some key questions:

- How does the fund's specific strategy play against the LP's macro view for the geography/asset class?

- What is the structure of the investment process and what are the key gating decisions and committee members?

- Given the maturity of the market/asset class, what is the relative importance of the different elements of the investment process?

- What are the strengths of the process and its ability to deliver high levels of investment return in the context of the market environment?

- Sources of deal flow by type (e.g., proprietary vs. intermediated).

- Key sourcing initiatives in place.

- Consideration of exit strategy when sourcing a potential investment.

- The current deal pipeline (i.e., potential investment opportunities set).

Exhibit 8 illustrates the differences between constituent elements of the investment process (in terms of their importance), dependent on the market environment. Here, the light-colored boxes represent one possible hypothesis on the more important aspects of value creation. This example shows an understanding of the contributions made by different elements of the GP's investment process to generating high levels of return in different market scenarios.

Exhibit 8: Thinking behind the differences

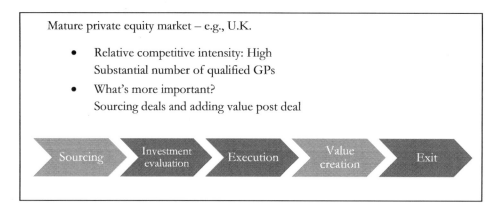

Sourcing

Certain key metrics must be properly understood when evaluating the strength of the GP's deal-sourcing capability: (1) the volume of deal opportunities seen each year by the GP, both in absolute terms and (where applicable) as a percentage of the total deal flow in the segment; and (2) the relevance of the deal flow in terms of the fund's investment objectives.

Investment evaluation

In assessing the GP's investment process, the LP needs to understand the team's ability to evaluate specific deal opportunities. In practice, the LP could evaluate whether the GP

- understands the industry's dynamics and the business's position within it;

- develops an executable business plan;

- creates a transaction structure that introduces appropriate leverage and management incentive, consistent with the strategy contained in the business plan; and

- develops an "edge" in the transaction that gives it an advantage in the competitive bidding processes.

Investors should evaluate both the effectiveness of the GP's internal resources and the effectiveness with which it engages external parties (such as due diligence providers and part-time operating partners). They must also understand whether the GP operates a sector-based investment model and, if so, how long this model has been in place. Managers that follow sector-based strategies generally have a deeper understanding of the specific areas that they focus on, and so may be better positioned to make sound judgments on the attractiveness of investment opportunities in these sectors.

LPs also need to thoroughly understand the GP's attitudes to transaction valuation and structuring. The manager's prior investments should be examined to reveal the typical pricing of past transactions. The LP should consider the types of businesses that the GP has previously acquired (insofar as growth transactions usually change hands at high multiples), and compare the prices paid with historical averages for the market subsector in which the GP operates. The LP should then analyze the levels of indebtedness that the GP loads onto its transactions to understand how this compares with market norms and the individual investment strategies adopted in varying circumstances.

Investors must be cognizant of the macroeconomic cycle when evaluating the GP, as various asset classes will have differing degrees of attractiveness through different stages. Typically, GPs will not be beholden to a single strategy in order to preserve the ability to exercise discretion when approaching investment decisions (i.e., avoid being cornered into a difficult strategy during an unfavorable part of the cycle). It is crucial for the LP to understand and be comfortable with all potential strategies as funds are rarely static and tend to evolve over time, which may alter the risk profile or incentive alignment of the fund.

Finally, investors should also invest heavily in discovering exactly how the GP designs the business plans that its investments follow. Such an analysis should focus on the types of transactions that the GP prefers to make (e.g., a rollup strategy, where multiple small firms in the same market are acquired and merged), the way the GP will seek to deliver value post closing (e.g., via a 100-day plan), the ways in which ongoing value will be created, and the manner of exit that is envisaged.

Execution

The manager's ability to execute transactions needs to be tested. To this end, LPs should assess the manager's ability to negotiate successfully with counterparties to the sale process. Accumulated transaction experience within the GP is an appropriate metric for this analysis. Whether the GP has employed any functional experts (e.g., debt-structuring experts) to help in the execution process is another important factor. The LP should insight into these execution abilities through extensive referencing with intermediaries used by the GP.

Value creation

A critical part of the overall evaluation process is to assess the GP's ability to add value to portfolio companies. The following are some relevant questions that can help in this assessment:

- What kinds of strategies does the GP have experience implementing? For example, is the GP a specialist in executing "rollups" within a market, or is it a specialist in executing international expansion? The LP will try to understand the full scope of the strategic options that the manager may seek to adopt in different circumstances and the manager's relevant credentials with respect to each.

- What model does the GP implement to deliver against the chosen strategy? The answer to this question should illustrate how the GP engages with the investee company. The GP may be a relatively "hands-off" investor, choosing instead to enfranchise a strong management team to deliver against a previously agreed business plan, with the GP monitoring the investment via standardized reporting. Alternatively, the GP may be extremely "hands-on," implanting members of its own investment team in portfolio companies to assist in delivering the plan.

- Operational value creation is naturally one of the most critical (and often, one of the most controllable) components of value creation. Thus, LPs have become quite focused on "operational improvement" funds that are heavily staffed with professionals with operating backgrounds, due to their distinct value creation abilities. However, GPs are finding it increasingly difficult to afford operating partners as a result of downward pressures on management fees. Therefore, most GPs are in a conundrum: they realize the importance of improving returns and meeting LP expectations, but are facing difficulties doing so without negatively impacting their near-term profitability. Consequently, some GPs depict extensive operational value creation capabilities in their LP marketing documentation without really investing in staff resources. Many examples can be found in practice: (1) funds with a couple of operating partners on their payroll, (2) funds with senior operating advisers, and (3) funds that take on a general contractor or outsourcing approach. These tactics create the appearance of extensive in-house operational value creation ability, but are, in practice, barely what an LP requires (i.e., a consistent and repeatable approach to operationally improve their portfolio companies over a 10-year horizon). Reaping these operational value creation rewards often goes beyond the surface and delves deep into the heart of a GP's capability, which calls for a comprehensive due diligence effort by the LP. When done well, operational value creation arises mostly from streamlining/restructuring operations, concentrating on the right strategic initiatives, and providing pragmatic management advice on crucial day-to-day matters.

- What is the GP's record of success? LPs must thoroughly examine the GP's levels of success in terms of value creation enjoyed by each investment. This value should be disaggregated into the three drivers of overall value creation: EBITDA generation, debt reduction, and transaction multiple arbitrage. LPs should also identify any differences in value creation according to transaction size, sector invested, and generic strategies employed. LPs must determine whether past fund success was the result of a meticulously executed, repeatable investment strategy, or the result of large, risky transactions.

- What actions has the GP taken in instances where a transaction has underperformed? In developing an understanding of the GP's ability to add value, it is important to look at the record of turning around "difficult" investment situations where the original investment hypothesis failed, for whatever reason. How quickly did the GP react to the failure of the original plan? How did it manage the downside risk? What was the strategic redirection? What ultimate success was achieved?

- LPs should understand the quantum of exits the GP has achieved, both in terms of the volume and value created. LPs should also assess the GP's breadth of experience with regard to achieving exit through different means (e.g., IPO, trade sale, or secondary purchase).

Assessment of the GP

The GP's organization

The GP's organization can be evaluated using three pertinent questions:

- Is the GP's ownership structure best organized to maximize likely returns to investors? LPs should evaluate the GP's ownership structure to understand whether the alignment of interests between the

GP and investors is optimal. As part of this process, the incentive structures in place should be evaluated.

- Is the GP likely to remain stable? Evaluating the likely stability of the GP involves understanding the GP's ownership structure in detail, including which members of the GP hold significant proportions of the equity in the management company. As part of this evaluation, LPs should understand the succession plans in place at the GP.

- Is the day-to-day running of the management company effective? The way the management company is run provides an indication of the organization's effectiveness. LPs could evaluate the internal processes and committees used to run the company and the way resourcing is managed. It is also relevant to understand the organizational hierarchy, and how this contributes to effective decision making.

The GP's investment team

Each LP should spend considerable time in one-on-one sessions with individual team members and with groups of team members (to assess interpersonal dynamics). The team could be analyzed in separate groups, according to seniority (i.e., senior leadership, mid-level members with experience and execution skills, and junior employees).

The first purpose of the investment team analysis is to understand the team's basic background, according to elements like its size in terms of number of professionals, the ages of team members, their educational backgrounds, professional experience, level of applicable staff private equity experience, staff turnover, and remuneration/incentive structures. Long tenures are quite conventional within a GP, and LPs find comfort in such stability. However, it is also worth noting that like any organization, a GP must bring in new blood in order to refresh its skill set and introduce new ideas. LPs should therefore look for a good balance between team stability and new joiners/promotions.

A second aim is to investigate the intra-team dynamics and determine how effectively the various investment teams work together. This investigation will also provide information on the coaching and mentoring activities within the team, and the career paths open to team members at different levels within the GP.

The GP's track record

Unlike with public equities, where the mantra "past performance is uncorrelated to future performance" is a treasured belief, past performance is very indicative of future results in private equity. Successful GPs are widely known to persist in their high performance. Managers who can demonstrate how they have created value in the past (beyond just benefiting from favorable market developments) and who can make a compelling case for future value creation should be high on an LP's list of potential investments. Before investing in a private equity fund, an LP should have sufficient evidence that the manager stands out from his or her peer group. In other words, LPs should confirm superior past performance by (1) reviewing portfolio reports, (2) inspecting audited financial statements, and (3) authenticating realized IRRs.

However, it is also important to note that the purpose of analyzing the past track record is to provide a proxy for the return potential of the current fund. The LP must decide how much predictive value the prior performance has on the next fund. If the new fund has a completely new team in place or has lost key decision makers, there could be relatively little value in relying on prior performance. If the same team has committed to managing the next fund and strategy has not altered significantly in years, prior performance is often the best indicator for prospective LPs.

Analysis of the track record is absolutely imperative in the due diligence process. It starts with a detailed portfolio analysis of all past investments made by the fund manager to quantify the return generated by each investment measured in terms of the cash multiple of original cost and the associated IRR and loss rate. Historical information on past fund performance is essential, and should be analyzed by fund as well as by individual underlying investment.

Is performance driven by a particular team member, a particular size of transaction, a particular strategy, or by deals completed in a particular sector? Interactions with the fund manager can clarify his or her impact on the value contribution of past and future investments. A key part of this analysis is understanding the key drivers of return, deal by deal; this involves allocating the total return between EBITDA growth, debt paydown, and transaction multiple arbitrage. The LP should evaluate both realized and unrealized transactions, paying particular attention to the valuation approach used to evaluate unrealized deals, and adjusting as necessary.

Once the individual track record of the manager has been analyzed, the results should be compared with the track records of other GPs operating in the same market space (thus, deep industry knowledge is key). This peer group benchmarking allows fund offerings with a good risk–return potential to be identified.

The performance data from prior funds managed by the GP should be measured as of the beginning of the vintage year of the focal fund, as this snapshot is relevant for focal fund due diligence purposes. The final performance of these funds when they reach their liquidation age may differ from this snapshot. If performance data from several prior funds is used, performances should be aggregated by weighting funds by their size and duration; this is the closest possible approximation of the overall performance of the GP.

Various performance measures can be used, including the following:

- IRR of the latest mature fund.

- Incremental IRR of the latest mature fund computed as fund IRR minus weighted-average IRR of same vintage of all prior peer funds.

- Performance quartile relative to the same vintage and similar stage peers of the latest mature fund.

- Weighted-average performance quartile relative to the same vintage and similar stage peers of all prior funds.

Operational due diligence

Operational due diligence (ODD) is often overlooked by investors, but in fact, it is just as important as the investment due diligence. Past studies have shown that over half of fund failures are a result of operational breakdowns. In recent years, more LPs are starting to perform some kind of ODD on GPs and funds as well as often on their service provider network. However, it is frequently light in scope, leaving gaps in the verification and understanding of day-to-day operations.

ODD is about understanding a manager's internal operations to protect investors from losses resulting from operational failures. It allows LPs to improve their portfolio standards and avoid reputational damage and monetary loss. Losses due to operational failures tend to be larger in magnitude than investment-related losses.

Typically, a successful ODD process is conducted by performing interviews with the fund managers, making phone calls, collecting and reviewing information, and making on-site visits. The analysis should cover three main dimensions of the fund:

- Business structure of the fund.

- People (members and roles)

- Investment process of the fund

Sound ODD should reveal the day-to-day operations of the fund, the GP's operational procedures, its employees, the commitment to regulations and industry best practice standards in relation to legal structures and documentation, risk management, compliance, IT, and other processes. An adequate ODD requires significant time and resources; however, it could be done by the investment team of an LP, a dedicated ODD team within the LP organization which does an independent underwriting, or a third-party consultant appointed by the LP. A more detailed description of an ideal ODD process is provided below.

Business structure

The ODD process starts by understanding the general aspects of the GP, like its business structure, investment and growth strategy, financial strength, track record, compliance policies, and third-party suppliers. Analyzing these aspects will give the LP a general overview of the GP's operation on a day-to-day basis. Exhibit 9 displays a high-level overview of each of the different elements.

The people

It is crucial to perform due diligence on the managers and employees who drive the business of a GP as well. This analysis should cover all levels and areas within the GP's personnel structure. Exhibit 10 provides an overview of a high-level diligence recommended in this dimension.

The investment process

The third key dimension of a successful ODD is the investment process. The business structure of the fund and the quality of its employees are evaluated to help determine the repeatability of the investment process. The investment process not only describes the business strategy, but also how the strategy is executed in the real world. A detailed, well documented, and accountable investment process is essential to a successful fund. The main components of an investment process are highlighted in Exhibit 11.

In conclusion, the ODD provides information that will help the LP better understand the business structure, the people and the investment process of a fund. It is useful to understand how the GP and the fund operate in order to identify the aspects that add value and the weaknesses that need to be addressed to create a reliable investment product. Today, the evolution of the private equity industry, the regulatory environment, and the requirements of a more sophisticated investor base all require a GP to be evaluated beyond its relative performance.

Exhibit 9: Business structure diligence

Business structure	Investors want to ensure alignment of interests between the GP and the LP. Therefore, it is important to evaluate the following items: ownership structure of the GP, partnership structure, fee structure, compensation and incentives, redemption and/or distribution policies, other affiliations/business activities, governance, and firm viability, among others.
Investment and growth strategy	This is an area where investors must "buy in" to the strategy and plan for execution. Analysis should include the investment allocation criteria, investment size/mechanism, deal flow/trade flow, valuation policies, risk management, and growth strategy. A fund must have a diversified portfolio to mitigate the risk for the LPs. Funds that attempt to grow too quickly can run short of quality deal flow and/or outsize their advantage in the industry.
Financial strength	The financial strength of the GP is an important factor to assess the perceived stability of the fund in the future. Investors should look into the sources of the fund's assets and ensure the GP has a reputable and solid investor base. Additionally, the GP must have sufficient financial reserves that will allow it to navigate tough times.
Track record	The track record of the GP's managers is a key indicator of the expected performance of the fund. Investors typically require audited returns for a period of three years or more. If the GP is of recent creation, it would be enough for most investors if the managers can demonstrate their previous track record as individuals or as a team unit.
Compliance	Investors must also evaluate the GP's compliance policies to ensure a solid regulatory ground. LPs should verify that the fund policies are well structured and compliant with regulatory requirements, including in terms of anti-money laundering/"know your client," structure and competence of the team, appropriateness of compliance manual/code of ethics, litigation, registration status, investor guidelines, and so on.
Third-party suppliers	Third-party suppliers include (but are not limited to) auditing, fund accounting, legal, brokerage, marketing, and technology providers. The higher the quality of the providers, the higher perceived quality of the firm itself. Institutional investors value managers who can outsource, improve, and grow using high-quality, reputable providers.

Exhibit 10: Overview of the management diligence

Principals and portfolio managers	A detailed overview of who is accountable for which actions within the firm is highly important. Any potential issue should be addressed proactively to diminish the impact of any action or irregularity.
Employee compensation and equity ownership	Investors should ensure that key employees are fairly compensated and invested in the business in order to ensure the alignment of interests between them, the fund, and the fund's investors.
Back-office support staff	It is essential for the GP to build a team of back-office and support staff to ensure the timely and responsible execution of the fund's strategy. The ability to efficiently distribute operational workflow across all levels of the employee structure is a necessary component of a successful fund. Smaller funds tend to rely on "star players," and may not effectively utilize the time and expertise of high-level employees.
Command structure	Identifying who the decision makers are—and in what areas—is extremely important in determining accountability. The investment process should be repeatable as a whole to ensure the fund is not relying on just one or two individuals.
Succession and contingency planning	In addition to knowing the current command structure of the fund, it is crucial to outline a succession and contingency plan. Typically, one or two individuals carry the burden of responsibility and this is often accepted in the short term. However, a long-term and "realistic" contingency plan must be properly documented and communicated to the relevant parties.

Exhibit 11: Overview of the investment process

The repeatability of the process

An investment process needs to be well documented and detailed, but also flexible in order to be applicable in varying market conditions with appropriate risk protection measures and growth projections. It is important for institutional investors that funds have repeatable processes to ensure a proper execution of the investment strategy.

Risk management and metrics

A successful GP should attempt to balance the risk profile of the fund by diversifying its investments across industries, geographies, asset classes, or by the number of investments within the fund. An effective due diligence process identifies where the risk is hiding and requires the development of concrete risk measures for decision-making and monitoring purposes.

Appropriate growth pace

The goal for a fund should be to pursue a "smart" growth pace. As mentioned, funds that seek to grow too quickly may run short of quality deal flow, which may affect the correct implementation of the investment process; this leads to suboptimal decisions that could be detrimental for the fund's performance.

Legal due diligence

The key points of the fund's legal structure are typically disclosed in the term sheet that is made available to LPs at the start of the diligence process. Thus, LPs are normally aware of any deal-breaking legal stipulations very early in the process and can act accordingly. We provide an extensive legal due diligence checklist in Appendix B and a list of items in a typical term sheet in Exhibit 12..

As nearly all funds have their own lawyers advising them on the legal aspects of fund creation, market standard terms are generally well known. Hence, broadly speaking, most new funds conform to this standard. If a GP seeks to raise a fund with a clear deal-breaking legal structure (e.g., demanding deal-by-deal carried interest), the legal adviser is likely to counsel strongly against this in Europe. Thus, most funds are launched with a set of terms that are broadly in line with what is regarded as the market standard. Every fund has its own nuances regarding these terms; typically, GPs' willingness to "stretch" terms depends on how they view the strength of their own franchise and, to some extent, on the conditions prevailing in the fundraising market. For instance, a major fund with a long and successful track record of raising money in a buoyant fundraising market will feel more able to stretch terms at the margin than a first-time fund.

Typically, LPs conduct more detailed legal due diligence toward the end of their own diligence process. At this stage of the process, LPs are seeking comfort around the detailed terms of the LPA and, quite possibly, are negotiating a side letter to this document relevant to their particular circumstances. In these negotiations, the LP's ability to make material changes to the document depends on the strength and scale of the LP and, critically, on where the fund is in the fundraising process. A large and powerful LP looking to make a commitment to a fund in the first closing of the fundraising process has far more power to make changes to the LPA to its favor than a small investor looking to invest at the end of the process. However, investors that do invest at the end of the fundraising process often benefit from what is termed the "most favored nation" clause; this allows LPs to benefit from a range of amendments to the LPA negotiated by earlier investors.

Exhibit 12: Typical term sheet items

Investment objective	Size of partnership
Strategic focus	Legal structure
Manager	Currency
Minimum commitment	GP Commitment by named executives
Drawdown procedure	Actions on default
Investment period of fund	Term of the fund
Actions on subsequent closings	GP's share (management fees)
Treatment of fees and abort costs	Establishment costs
Operating expenses	Carried interest
Escrow provision	Distribution policy
Reinvestment policy	Fund reporting
Advisory committee	Exclusivity
Removal of GP	Named executive
Key man provisions	Borrowing
Transfer provision	Indemnification
Tax considerations	

Legal advisers report in two broad areas: the fund's specific legal terms and its suitability for the investor from a tax perspective. Regarding the specific terms, the legal adviser will report on the key terms of the LPA and give a recommendation on each. Some of the main elements for consideration are

- investment strategy (how specifically defined it is?),

- fund length (investment periods, harvesting periods, and extensions),

- management fees (levels, periods, and step downs),

- carried interest structures (percentages and mechanisms),

- wind-up clauses, and

- key man clauses.

The investor can then form a view on these key terms and negotiate whichever points are important. Any amendments may be incorporated in a revised LPA, or they may be included in a side letter that is specific to the investor concerned.

With respect to taxation, the structures being used by the fund and the LP must be compatible from a tax perspective. Normally, these structures can be designed so that the investment gains are tax transparent, but some jurisdictions (e.g., Japan) have their own national tax complications and LPs need to be assured that the tax structuring of their investment is suitable.

ESG due diligence

GPs have a massive opportunity to create social value (e.g., jobs, renewable energy, health, and wellbeing) and improve the environment while generating financial returns. This concept is generally addressed by an integration of ESG factors into the private equity investment and portfolio management process. Recently, LPs have been attaching increasing importance to GPs that (1) invest while embracing the ESG principles and (2) demonstrate a structured approach to managing ESG risks and opportunities. This trend has induced many GPs to incorporate ESG programs that manage these principles both at the acquisition stage and at the portfolio level. During an investment holding period, a GP can positively impact the ESG performance of a portfolio company by, for example, creating jobs and improving corporate governance in a private company. Currently, very few GPs calculate the value they create from ESG activities (mainly because it is not a straightforward exercise), but standards are being developed to solve the vacuum. In the near future, it will be imperative for GPs to adopt a disciplined approach toward ESG in the context of due diligence by LPs. In other words, GPs that do not have strong ESG practices will find it very difficult raise money from LPs in the future.

PLACEMENT AGENTS, INVESTMENT CONSULTANTS, AND RECENT OBSERVATIONS

Placement agents and investment consultants, which help fund managers to raise capital and investors to allocate capital, face similar challenges to investors during their own due diligence. The LPs, as well as the placement agents, rank key considerations when making an investment decision. One of the major initial filters is the ability of the GP to reach its target fundraising. The potential performance of a fund becomes irrelevant if its fundraising target is unattainable in the first place. Thus, investors must be sure to seek out funds that are likely to reach their fundraising targets. The key success factors for reaching target fundraising are (1) experience/expertise with the fund's strategy, (2) a returning investor base, and (3) a successful performance track record overall and in relation to the proposed team for the new fund.

While track record is often quoted as one of key due diligence items, the correlation between predecessor and successor funds is not straightforward. The overall performance of a fund is only fully realized when it is liquidated, 10–12 years after the launch. If investment professionals have to wait for funds to liquidate before giving meaning to their performance, then predecessor funds would often have to be ruled out of the due diligence process, as fund managers tend to bring new funds within a series to market between four and six years after their immediate predecessor. Reviewing performance track record is a crucially important part of fund selection due diligence; therefore, it is noteworthy that performance data indicates a significant correlation between interim performance in the fourth and sixth years of a fund and its final performance with a strong correlation between the best and worst performing funds.

CONCLUSION

Private equity fund due diligence involves a great deal of hard work and rarely leads to a completely clear-cut conclusion. Its principal aim is to identify and then analyze, in depth, the various merits and risks of a specific investment opportunity so that the investor can make an informed decision about whether to invest or not. In particular, the process must be supported by tools that allow for a structured assessment of a fund, helping to ensure that it is properly evaluated relative to other similar investment opportunities; this is probably the most difficult aspect of fund due diligence, given that no two funds are alike in terms of team and track record, so comparisons must be made on the basis of mostly qualitative (rather than quantitative) factors. Finally, it must be emphasized that the objective of fund diligence is to be forward-looking rather than backward-looking, so investors are advised to approach the exercise in terms of identifying and understanding the key merits and risks behind each opportunity.

REFERENCES

SteelBridge Consulting (2015), The Importance of Operational Due Diligence, White Paper

Rops, M. and D. Bertolet (2017), Practice Analysis of Due Diligence Analysts, Investment Management Due Diligence Association (IMDDA)

APPENDIX A: DUE DILIGENCE QUESTIONNAIRE

1. Strategy

Sector/Geography
- What sectors/geographies will the fund focus on?
- What is the strategy within each sector/geography?
- What are the current trends in each sector/geography, and how do these trends relate to the fund's strategy?

Market environment
- Who are the fund's peers/competitors? What is the fund's comparative advantage?
- How does the fund's strategy/target market compare with that of peers/competitors?
- How does the current environment impact the fund's strategy?

2. Investment process of the fund

Sourcing
- What is the GP's ability to generate deal flow?
- What are the deal-sourcing channels?
- How relevant is the deal flow to the fund's strategy?
- Does the GP have initiatives in place to improve the deal flow?
- How many deals are expected to be completed per year?

Investment evaluation
- What is the GP's ability to evaluate specific opportunities?
- Does the GP have knowledge to structure transactions appropriately?
- How does the GP design the business plans for each investment? Does the fund's strategy differ from the prior strategies of the GP?

Execution
- What is the GP's ability to negotiate with counterparties?
- What is the GP's execution experience?
- Is the GP receiving good references from parties it has interacted with?

Value creation
- What kinds of strategies does the GP have experience implementing?
- What model does the GP implement to deliver against the chosen strategy?
- What is the GP's record of success?
- Is the GP's success driven by EBITDA generation or by debt reduction and multiple arbitrage?
- What actions has the GP taken in instances where the transaction has underperformed?
- What is the GP's approach to deal structuring and risk controls (relating to deal risk, sector risk, country risk, currency risk, etc.)?
- What is the GP's approach to the supervision of investments?
- What is the GP's ability to exit transactions?

3. Assessment of the GP

Organization of the GP
- Is the GP's ownership structure best organized to maximize likely returns to investors?
- How are incentives provided to staff?
- How was the carry split among the GP's staff in previous funds? How is it split with the current fund?
- Is the GP likely to remain stable?
- Does the GP have plans to hire additional staff?
- Is the management company run effectively on a day-to-day basis?

GP's investment team

- What is the background and professional experience of each team member? Are there any gaps in the professional history of key team members?
- How long has each team member held his/her current position?
- What is the performance of each member in terms of working with other members?
- How much capital will each principal commit to the fund? Will this commitment be in the form of cash or other resources?
- What other business interests do the key team members have?
- Has a clear succession plan been articulated?

GP's track record

- Request a summary of the GP's prior investment performance by deal and by fund. This information should include the following:
  - Detailed cash flow information for each deal previously completed by the firm/team, as well as management fees and carried interest cash flows.
  - Realized and unrealized gains/losses for each deal to date.
  - Gross and net IRR for each deal.
  - Multiple earned on capital invested in each deal.
- What role(s) do the GP team members play in identifying, monitoring, and exiting the investments?
- Which particular team members are associated with better performance?
- What are the core drivers of the returns, deal by deal?
- How is the concentration of returns divided among deals (sector/size/geography)?
- What is the GP's approach to valuation of portfolio holdings?

APPENDIX B: LEGAL DUE DILIGENCE CHECKLIST

1. Documents

- Limited partnership agreement (plus side letters to all LPs, etc.).
- Subscription materials.
- Management/advisory agreements.
- Co-investment agreement(s) with parallel vehicles, if any.
- Legal opinions.
- Private placement memorandum.

2. Form and structure of investment vehicle

- Legal form of the fund investment vehicle; governing laws.
- Limitations on the size of the fund: What is the target size? Is there a minimum (critical mass) requirement? Is there a commitment to a maximum size?
- Limitations on marketing period, including the date of closing. Is there a limitation on the period between the first and final closing dates? Are there provisions to extend the marketing period? Do additional LPs pay for their proportionate share of the cost of existing investments, incurred expenses plus interest?
- Formation of parallel vehicles; co-investment agreements between parallel vehicles (pro rata, etc.); are favorable economic terms on offer to subsets of investors ("friends and family," entrepreneurs' side funds, etc.)?

3. Duration and termination

- Initial duration of fund's life; provisions for extension; approvals required to extend (e.g., at GP's discretion, with reference to or consent of advisory committee, majority, or supermajority vote of LPs); limitations, if any, on activity during period of extension.
- Duration of investment period: Under what conditions can funds be invested after the investment period has ended (e.g., existing obligations, follow-on investments, fees, and expenses)? Is the manager permitted to reinvest capital (i.e., proceeds of all or part realizations)? If so, under what conditions, for what time period, and on what

terms (e.g., right to reinvest investment proceeds up to acquisition cost with a time limit of two years after distribution)?
- Are there any means of exiting the fund prior to the expiration of its term?
- Transfer provisions; level of GP control over transfers and acceptance of substitutes (absolute discretion, etc.); is there reference to the types of associated entity (e.g., subsidiaries, beneficiaries, etc.) to which transfers will be permitted?

4. Commercial terms

- What is the GP's capital commitment, and/or that of affiliates? Is it absolute or variable?
- Management fee (or priority profit share, etc.): How will the GP be compensated? Is the compensation to be paid to the GP a fund-level expense, or will the investors bear such amounts directly, and in addition to their capital commitments? What calculation base is used to compute the fee (e.g., committed vs. invested capital), and is there a changeover point between alternative methods (e.g., expiration of investment period)? Is there a right of waiver, with a complementary right to a priority distribution? How often is the management fee payable (e.g., quarterly or semi-annually)?
- Other sources of fee income: List each fee and the terms (e.g., transaction fee, investment banking fee, directors' fees and options, monitoring fees, and all other income). Fee offsets: Is a proportion of any or all such fees offset against the management fee?
- Are fees and expenses charged to portfolio companies by the GP? Are LPs' fees reduced by the fees charged to portfolio companies?
- Establishment/organizational costs. Are these chargeable to the fund LPs? Are they capped? How are placement agents compensated?
- Ongoing costs; treatment of fees/costs incurred, such as consultants' fees, auditors' fees, travel expenses, broken deal costs; are these offset against transaction fee income (as opposed to being charged to the fund's LPs)?
- Treatment and level of other expenses (accounting, legal, printing, and annual general meeting costs, etc.); who bears abort costs?
- Other sources of income and potential conflicts: Will the GP or its affiliates receive management, advisory, or other fees from the partnership or other parties in transactions with the fund?
- Carried interest, or other forms of incentive payments: Is the carried interest calculated on a fund as a whole, or on an investment-by-investment basis? Is there a preferred return? Operation of "waterfall" provisions (GP "catch-up," etc.).
- Clawback provisions: Will the GP be required to return amounts received in payment of its carried interest if the fund incurs subsequent losses? If so, is the amount to be repaid gross or net of tax? Do all the managers guarantee the clawback, and is there a vehicle over which the LPs would have a claim (e.g., escrow account, in which case, what are the terms for early payment from the escrow account)? Is the guarantee joint and several, so that on the death of one manager the liability does not cease?
- Is the fair market value of investments held (or securities/other assets in kind distributed) used in determining the GP's carried interest entitlement? If so, what valuation method is applied, and is there an independent check?
- Are any other forms of incentive arrangements in place (such as employee co-investment schemes)?
- Are there provisions for tax distributions to all partners, and do these have priority over other distributions?
- Are there any safeguards or independent checks over the amounts paid to the GP (e.g., audit review, advisory committee oversight, requirements of notice to the investors, specific annual or other period reports of all compensation to the GP and its affiliates)?
- What is the notice period for calls on contributions? What is the period for which cash may be held by the GP if a proposed investment is not made? Is there a requirement to invest in short-term AAA investments?
- What is the timing of distributions after disposal of a portfolio company?

5. Investment policy and restrictions

- What is the stated investment purpose?
- Restrictions (where appropriate) on investments relating to
  - concentration of the fund's capital invested in a single portfolio company (e.g., 15–25%);
  - geography, or regional concentration;
  - sector, or concentration by sector;
  - public company investment;

- – hostile transactions;
- – investment in other funds or pooled schemes (except for funds of funds);
- – specific industries; and
- – ethical issues.
- Provisions concerning cross-fund investment.
- Distributions: Can the fund distribute securities or other assets in kind as well as in cash? If so, must these be freely marketable?
- Limitations on fund indebtedness.

6. Reporting and communications

- Reporting:
  - – Is there a requirement to produce audited accounts? Is there a provision to ensure that reputable auditors will be used, and that the accounting principles are acceptable? Is there a maximum period between the end of the accounting period and the production of accounts? Are items of information to be included defined (e.g., a list of the fund's investments and the value thereof, capital accounts for individual LPs, balance sheet and income statements, explanation of any revaluation of securities listed therein, etc.)?
  - – Is there also a requirement to produce more frequent (e.g., quarterly or semi-annual) reports? What will these reports contain? Is there a maximum period between the end of the accounting period and the production of this report?
  - – Will reports and valuations conform to applicable guidelines from local associations (e.g., BVCA, EVCA, etc.)?
- Meetings: What types of meeting are planned to inform LPs? How frequently will they be held? Rights of other (non-member) LPs to attend or have access to proceedings (minutes, etc.); frequency of meetings.
- Advisory committee (or similar): Will such a body be constituted, and what will its composition be? Who has rights of appointment and removal? What will the scope of its activity be (e.g., review of valuations, resolution of conflicts of interest such as cross-fund investments, etc.)? How will its authority be limited (e.g., consultative vs. right of review vs. required approval)? Do any members have weighted votes depending on the size of commitments? Indemnification of LP representatives and LP appointers;

7. Other investor protections

- Provisions pertaining to the departure of the GP:
  - – Does the agreement permit the GP (or principals of the GP) to withdraw from the fund?
  - – Provisions for removal of GP, or otherwise suspending or terminating the fund, for cause and without cause "for fault" and "no fault divorce" provisions. What is the period of notice to be given to the GP? What are the voting arrangements in such cases, and requirements for majority and/or supermajority votes? What are the terms of the financial settlement with the departing GP? Are appropriate parties excluded from sensitive votes, such as to remove the GP (e.g., related parties and sponsors)?
  - – Indemnification: Is protection provided (including the exclusions) to the GP/manager reasonable?
  - – Key man provisions: Are the right people included, and is the trigger point sufficiently sensitive? Is there a suspension period if the key man provisions are effective, and are there reinstatement provisions?
- LP protections, and potential conflicts between LPs' interests:
  - – Do the documents contain provisions addressing potential conflicts of interest between the fund and the GP?
  - – Do the documents contain provisions limiting the formation of future funds until after a specified portion of the investors' commitments has been invested?
  - – Are there restrictions on investments in affiliates of the GP, and in the portfolio companies of prior associated funds?
  - – How will investors who default in making their capital contributions be treated (e.g., expulsion)? How will the capital account balances of defaulting partners be allocated?
  - – Counsel to the GP(s) should render an opinion concerning the limited liability of the LPs. In making and managing investments, the GP and manager should take due care to ensure that limited liability is preserved.
  - – Are side letters or other undertakings being given to any LPs? Is there a "most favored nation" clause?
  - – How is demand for co-investment among LPs satisfied?

- Taxation, regulation, and related matters:
  - Does the fund structure permit participation of an LP of a particular type and domicile?
  - Do the documents contain covenants by the GP (e.g., "best efforts" or similar language) to ensure that tax-exempt LPs will not be subject to tax on unrelated business taxable income?
  - Do the documents contain covenants by the GP (e.g., "best efforts" or similar language) to protect against the creation of tax reporting obligations or tax liabilities to non-domiciled investors arising from effectively connected income trade or business income?
- General LP protections:
  - LPs' liability for liabilities, debts, etc. of the partnership should be limited to their stated capital commitment with an exception for recycling (see above).
  - Amendments to the LPA: What is the proportion of LPs required to bind all LPs? No amendment should be made to increase the financial obligations of LPs, or which affects their limited liability.
  - LPs should not participate in management or control (subject to any safe harbor laws of jurisdiction of partnership's incorporation).
  - Are there excuse provisions to enable LPs not to contribute if legal/constitutional/regulatory prohibitions apply?
  - Confidentiality obligations by LPs and the GP relating to information concerning portfolio companies, the GP, and LPs; are there acceptable carve-outs?
  - Time and attention and non-competition restrictions by key men.
  - Warranties by the fund to LPs about its incorporation, powers, and authorities, etc.
  - Warranties by LPs to the fund.
  - Is there an obligation to effect indemnity insurance cover?
  - Calls: What is the minimum period of written notice? Payments to investors be in cash (and not in kind such as shares).
  - Are there monetary limits on total calls per annum?

In his own words: Joe Topley, Managing Director, Ontario Teachers' Pension Plan

I consider team assessment to be far and away the most important aspect of diligence when committing to a new private equity fund. Most fund commitments last longer than the average marriage, and yet we often know relatively little about those to whom we choose to entrust our capital for such a long period of time. LPs will look at many aspects of a GP team and organization but I would highlight the following as critical: (a) the team members' experience—how many deals have they actually done and have they learnt lessons from any with challenged investments? (b) investment capacity—does the team have adequate resources to manage the existing, unrealized portfolio as well as source and execute new deals? (c) ability to originate new deals—are the team members proactive "hunters" or do they simply wait for intermediaries to introduce them to the latest auctions? (d) sharing of economics—do the founders retain an overly large share of the carried interest, which might be demotivating for other members of the team? (e) overall team culture and opportunities for career progression—often, remuneration is less important than the ability to grow professionally and develop one's career, so are those opportunities available to more junior members of the team?

While formal fund diligence can provide superficial answers to many of these questions, the fact is that LPs will really only gain a level of comfort on these points by getting to know the GP as a collection of individuals and by understanding the dynamics between these individuals. Reference calls are helpful and can fill in some of the gaps, but unfortunately, there is still no substitute for spending time with the people involved—much of it informal, away from the boardroom table and PowerPoint presentations. Ultimately, the real questions that LPs need answered are: Who does what within the team? Why are they good at what they do? What motivates them? How well does the team operate? Success in private equity is less about hitting home runs and more about consistently avoiding the bad deals through smart investment decision making. My feeling is that this usually comes from having a well-run and aligned team with generally positive dynamics. Getting to this point is hard and time consuming, but the investment should pay dividends

6 Fund Structuring

Life is really simple, but we insist on making it complicated.
Confucius

INTRODUCTION

As the private equity industry has developed over time, private equity funds have evolved in to various shapes and sizes. They invest in many types of securities issued by non-listed private firms and pursue a wide range of different investment strategies. However, despite these differences, private equity funds share significant similarities with respect to their structuring (or formation), which we discuss in this chapter.

The establishment of a private equity fund is generally preceded by a determination of the optimal structure for both the fund sponsor and potential investors from a tax, regulatory, and practical perspective, balanced against a framework that can offer stakeholders acceptable commercial terms. A common characteristic of private equity funds is that they are structured to minimize, to the greatest extent possible, the amount of regulation that they need to comply with, while simultaneously ensuring that investors in the funds would not be in a worse tax position that if they had invested directly in the assets of the funds. In addition, structuring of the funds aims to create an investment vehicle that is cost effective and minimizes risk and exposure for the investors.

Regarding regulations, fund managers ensure that they do not market their funds to the general public, and that the pools of capital they manage are provided by investors with significant net worth and sophistication. A high degree of contractual flexibility and relative freedom from regulation (historically, at least) has allowed private equity fund structures to be closely tailored to the demands of the fund managers and investors. With respect to tax, it is essential that the fund vehicle, regardless of its legal form, does not pay tax in order to avoid tax being paid by both investors and the fund. Double taxation is usually avoided onshore by the use of fiscally transparent structures such as limited partnerships, or offshore by choosing jurisdictions that allow companies to be exempt from taxes on investment income and gains.

However, the structuring of a fund can be extremely complex given that it takes into account many issues, such as whether the fund is established onshore or offshore, how the fund will be marketed to investors, local compliance regulations, how the proceeds generated by the fund will be distributed to investors and managers,

This chapter has been co-authored with Gus Black, Partner and Global Co-Chair Financial Services Group at Dechert LLP. in London.

what types of investments will be made, the types and domiciles of the investors, managers' compensation arrangements, and so on.

Most private equity fund structures have been developed in common law countries such as the United States and the United Kingdom. U.S. private equity funds are typically structured as Delaware or Cayman Islands limited partnerships, while English limited partnerships have been common in the United Kingdom. In terms of offshore jurisdictions, funds operating from the United Kingdom are typically structured in Jersey and Guernsey.

THE FRAMEWORK

The appeal of the limited partnership model

Limited partnerships are the most common private equity fund vehicle precisely because of their ability to offer a combination of the features that both investors and fund sponsors find important. They are a combination of (1) one or more general partners (GPs)—that is, partners whose liability for the debts and obligations of the limited partnership is unlimited, but who are entitled to participate in the management of the partnership's business, and (2) one or more limited partners (LPs)—partners whose liability for those debts and obligations is limited, but who cannot (with certain limited exceptions, which are discussed below) participate in that management without risking their limited liability. The affairs of these two sets of partners are governed by a limited partnership agreement (LPA), which establishes the parameters of the relationships among the LPs and between the LPs and GPs. LPAs vary significantly in the level of detail they contain depending on the number of investors. Regarding fund structuring, LPAs generally specify that the expenses related to the initial structuring of the fund are the responsibility of the limited partnership.

Limited partnerships provide a series of key advantages that include the following:

- **Tax transparency** in the jurisdiction of establishment (i.e., flow-through tax treatment) so that investors do not incur tax at the level of the fund (i.e., the limited partnership). Some LPs prefer tax transparency because they are tax exempt (e.g., pension funds) or they are not taxpayers in the jurisdiction where the fund is based. GPs prefer tax transparency to increase the chances of incurring capital gains tax treatment on disposals of assets by the limited partnership when carried interest is being generated and allocated. Capital gains tax can offer a lower tax rate when compared with income tax.

- **Flexible remuneration arrangements for GP:** Allows the GP to set up distinct entities which earn management fees and carried interest

- **Flexible internal governance and control:** Allows the limited partnership to be exempt from certain regulations pertaining to companies (such as Companies Act in different jurisdictions) that may often impose a heavier regulatory burden in some cases.

- **A light statutory framework:** Limited partnerships give investors a high degree of flexibility on the terms on which they are able to invest, while preserving private law remedies for breach of contract.

- **The provision of limited liability** to certain partners.

- **"Mechanical" flexibility:** Investment terms can differ among investors in the same fund (i.e., in essence, each investor is, within certain limits, able to vary the terms of its private contract with the fund structure). This variety allows for easy adjustments of an investor's capital account in a way that is specific to that investor with a much greater degree of flexibility than would be the case even if different investment classes were used in a corporate structure.

English limited partnerships are regulated by the Limited Partnerships Act 1907 (the "1907 Act"). The 1907 Act specifies that each partner need not have unlimited liability for the debts or obligations of the firm, and that certain partners can be restricted from taking part in the management of the partnership business. A limited partnership must be registered with the Registrar of Companies, advertise changes in partners, and make public notifications of certain changes to the limited partnership. More recently, the Partnerships (Accounts) Regulations 2008 require "qualifying partnerships" (including all partnerships whose members directly or indirectly have limited liability, including limited partnerships whose GPs are limited liability companies) to make available the accounts of the partnership. The content of the accounts is similar to the standard that would be required were the qualifying partnership a small, medium-sized, or large company. These regulations require the inclusion, for example, of information about auditors' pay and the appointment and removal of auditors. Further, the accounts must be prepared within nine months of the end of the qualifying partnership's financial year.

As noted above, the disclosure regime in relation to most limited partnerships is relatively light. The public disclosure requirements for English limited partnerships are restricted to notifications to be made on admission or changes of partners, and a need for certain limited partnerships to publish accounts. However, even the former disclosure obligation can be a step too far for many investors who prefer not to have to publicize their investment programs, and can be a reason for some sponsors to consider alternative jurisdictions which do not have such requirements.

In many offshore jurisdictions, the main disclosure obligations arise not as a matter of statute but as a matter of contract—under the terms of many limited partnership agreements, LPs have a right to inspect the partnership registers, and may discover who their fellow investors are. Nevertheless, they are bound by strict confidentiality obligations that cover not only the identities of those fellow investors, but also the terms on which they have invested and the returns that they are making (although fund sponsors do, of course, use overall historic returns when marketing new funds). The exercise of the right to inspect the partnership registers may even require recourse to the courts. Other disclosure obligations have been created on the basis of industry-wide initiatives.[1]

The Alternative Investment Fund Managers Directive (AIFMD), discussed in greater detail below, also created a series of disclosure obligations, with private equity fund managers marketing or managing their funds in Europe now being required to make certain prescribed disclosures to regulators, investors, and stakeholders in the portfolio companies in which their funds invest. A number of these disclosure obligations duplicate obligations to which private equity funds would already have been subject to under their partnership agreements, under voluntary industry codes, or as a matter of national company law.

Legislative reform in the United Kingdom

The Legislative Reform (Private Fund Limited Partnerships) Order 2017 ("Reform Order"), which came into force in April 2017, introduced the concept of a *private fund limited partnership* (PFLP) to the United Kingdom for the first time. The purpose of this order was to modernize the partnership structure for use in the private fund context.

An important aspect of investing in a limited partnership is that an LP's liability is limited to its capital contribution. The 1907 Act established this limitation on the liability of an LP on a statutory basis so long as the LP is "not taking part in the management of the partnership business." To provide LPs with guidance as to which activities are permissible with respect to a PFLP, the Reform Order introduces a "white list" of

---

[1] See, for instance, the industry-driven (and voluntary) regulation on disclosure and transparency set out in the Walker Guidelines for Disclosure and Transparency in Private Equity, which is aimed at FSA-authorized private equity firms and U.K. portfolio companies owned by private equity firms that exceed certain size thresholds.

activities that LPs can undertake without losing their limited liability status (provided such activities are allowed under the relevant LPA). The list is non-exhaustive and covers many of the activities commonly undertaken by LPs under an LPA (e.g., serving on an LP advisory committee or taking part in a decision about varying the terms of the LPA). Significantly, the white list introduces a safe harbor for members and employees of a manager who are themselves investing in the fund as part of the GP commitment (or similar arrangement). This approach is consistent with that taken in many of the jurisdictions in which limited partnerships are used in a fund's context.

The 1907 Act requires LPs to make capital contributions to the limited partnership for which the LP is liable until the end of the life of the partnership (even if that LP has withdrawn from the partnership). As a result, the market practice in the private fund industry has been to utilize a "loan capital split," whereby an LP makes a small capital contribution to the partnership, with the bulk of the partner's commitment being advanced as an interest-free loan. This practice is no longer necessary for LPs in funds formed on or after April 6, 2017, as the requirement to return any capital contributions withdrawn prior to the end of the life of the partnership does not apply. It is therefore anticipated that going forward, private equity funds in the United Kingdom may operate with the same all-capital structure as limited partnerships formed in comparable jurisdictions.

The Reform Order also indicates that an LP does not have a duty to render accounts and information to other partners, nor a duty to account for profits made in competing businesses. This indication is a welcome change in the private fund context, where these duties are unlikely to align well for passive LPs who may make investments in multiple funds which may be pursuing similar investment objectives and strategies. In particular, the Reform Order highlights that PFLPs may disclose less information than other limited partnerships, both upon registration and during their life. For instance, PFLPs do not need to register or update details regarding the nature of the partnership's business or, as mentioned above, an LP's capital contribution.

Alternative jurisdictions for limited partnerships

The other jurisdictions have addressed some of the problems of the English limited partnership structure to create alternatives that may be more attractive (with some of the benefits that these jurisdictions offer forming the basis for some of the reform proposals of English partnership law). These include the following:

Scotland

Scottish limited partnerships differ from English limited partnerships in that they have a separate legal personality and are therefore able, in their own name, to own property, hold rights, and assume obligations, as well as to sue and be sued.

Channel Islands

Partnership law in both Guernsey and Jersey provides for LPs to be able to take some role in the management of limited partnerships without losing their limited liability. These "safe harbors" include approving the purchase or sale of assets, the creation of any obligation of the limited partnership, acting as an agent of the limited partnership, and acting as a director of the GP. Because there is no liability on LPs to repay capital distributions unless the partnership is insolvent at the time of the distribution (with a six-month longstop on any repayment obligation), the loan/capital split that is common in English limited partnerships is not necessary for Jersey or Guernsey limited partnerships (more on this subject below). In addition, both Guernsey and Jersey offer limited partnership structures with separate legal personality.

Delaware

Delaware is the destination of choice for U.S. private equity funds. Delaware law provides for very broad safe harbors that allow LPs to have extensive involvement in management without risking the loss of their limited liability. Under Delaware law, no substantive connection with Delaware is required to form a limited partnership in Delaware. Moreover, disclosure of LPs' identities is not required. However, under Delaware law, a GP has unlimited liability for the partnership's debts and liabilities to third parties. GPs have a duty of loyalty to their LPs that is similar to that of a director of a Delaware corporation. For example, GPs cannot use their position to promote their personal interests or to enter into transactions that are not fair to the partnership.

Cayman Islands

In 2009, Cayman Islands limited partnership law was revised to expand the safe harbors that LPs can use, which now include an ability to appoint a person to serve on any board or committee (including an investment committee) and to hold an office or interest in (or enter into contracts with) the GP.

Luxembourg

Although technically "corporate" structures, Luxembourg special partnership vehicles function, in virtually all respects, just like limited partnerships, and have adapted over the years to use terminology and documentation that is extremely close in content and style to that found in Cayman Islands, Delaware, and English limited partnerships. In common with the other jurisdictions above, limited partnerships can be formed without requiring regulation at the structure level, and legal personality for the partnership itself is possible. Interest in and utilization of these structures has increased significantly following AIFMD and the announcement of Brexit.

Ireland

When the 1907 Act was enacted, Ireland was part of the United Kingdom. The legislation remained in force in Ireland and as such, the limited partnership structure is available to be utilized in a private equity fund context. Historically, uptake has been very limited, although we have seen more deployment of the structure of late. The Irish legislation does not benefit from the recent reforms in the United Kingdom. In addition to the 1907 Act limited partnership, Ireland has a special regulated fund structure known as the "investment limited partnership." It is essentially a regulated fund structure and thus, while it shares some of the features of a traditional limited partnership, it is does not offer the same flexibility.

Other jurisdictions

Private equity structures used in the domestic markets of other jurisdictions—in particular, France and Germany—are not true limited partnerships but may be contractual or corporate vehicles. Limited partnerships are available in other jurisdictions, although their use tends to be more associated with particular strategies or investment regions. For example, Mauritius offers a limited partnership structure, but this tends to be more commonly utilized by Africa-focused managers due to favorable tax treaty arrangements between Mauritius and certain investment locations in Africa or the Indian subcontinent. Certain Asian jurisdictions, such as Singapore and Hong Kong, also offer domestic limited partnership legislation, although take-up has been limited, with managers generally preferring to use the more internationally recognized standard of the Cayman Islands limited partnership. As appetite for the Cayman Islands structure wanes in some investor constituencies, and regional investors increase in importance, it is possible that this position will evolve.

It is worth noting that offshore jurisdictions exist to provide an alternative to onshore jurisdictions that prohibit (either through regulation or tax rules) certain structures or transactions. Funds that are set up in offshore jurisdictions are often structured as limited companies that can issue shares. Some offshore jurisdictions may require more information about the fund manager and that certain activities related to the fund occur with the jurisdiction (e.g., advisory board meetings). When selecting a particular offshore jurisdiction for a fund, managers typically ensure that there is a low tax, a low cost to launch and manage the fund, and that the jurisdiction is highly reliable from a regulatory perspective. For instance, while Luxembourg and Ireland provide greater flexibility than many onshore locations, they have extensive approval processes and requirements that might be time consuming. In contrast, the British Virgin Islands and the Cayman Islands are efficient, but they face reputational concerns from certain investor groups.

FUND STRUCTURES

Factors influencing the choice of fund structure

Although there are other relevant factors to fundraising (e.g., economic conditions and track record), a well-thought-out fund structure which provides a tax-efficient vehicle that is familiar to investors, coupled with appropriate fund terms, is likely to result in a more successful fundraise. Private funds, by their nature, have significant constitutional and regulatory flexibility, which allows them to accommodate a wide variety of strategies and investors. Considering the various issues in detail at the structuring stage means that the fund can be tailored to deal with specific legal and regulatory matters and to provide for the likely investor base.

Structuring a fund usually involves a certain measure of judgment and compromise, and the choice of structure will be heavily influenced by the following key issues:

- **A structure to accommodate the chosen strategy:** For example, private equity funds where the portfolio ends up being very concentrated in a small number of large investments, or where it takes many years to fully deploy the capital, do not work well under certain regulated fund regimes that require a greater level of diversification to be achieved more quickly.

- **Investors familiarity** with the proposed type of fund vehicle and the choice of jurisdiction. Managers want to differentiate on the basis of their team, approach, and track record, not their legal vehicle.

- **Legal and underlying financing structure as tax efficient as possible** for investors, the fund, the fund manager, and the key principals. Typically, a tax-transparent or tax-exempt fund entity suitable for the target investors is essential, so that there is no (or minimal) tax leakage at the fund level. The use of structures in different locations needs to be carefully considered from a tax perspective to ensure where possible that the chosen fund vehicle is regarded as tax neutral locally and tax efficient for the fund managers and investors.

- **Fit for target investors from a regulatory perspective,** allowing them to deploy capital favorably relative to other structures. Notably, investors who are regulated themselves may have particular requirements as to structure; this may be in view of the regulatory capital treatment that will be applied to their investment or other regulatory requirements that govern how they allocate capital.

- **Fund and its underlying financing structure is cost effectiveness** to manage on a day-to-day basis, with a manageable and cost-effective regulatory and operational burden.

- **Fund structure to accommodate a wide group of investors:** Fund sponsors should consider who their target investor base is and whether these investors are likely to have any specific commercial or structural requirements, in order to confirm that these can be accommodated. Investors often have specific legal, prudential, and tax requirements or preferences.

- **Whether selected jurisdiction for the fund has suitable service providers:** The sponsor should have existing service provider relationships that are more suited to one particular jurisdiction than another.

- **Impact of the existing operations on the fund:** For example, if the sponsor already has board members, regulated entities, or other "substance" in a certain jurisdiction, that may make that jurisdiction more compelling as a location for the fund structure. There may be a range of efficiencies to be obtained in co-locating the fund structure with other existing operations (e.g., management/advisory entities or downstream investment holding companies), and doing so may also be helpful in showing additional substance, either from a tax or regulatory perspective.

Yet, a private equity fund rarely exists as a single legal entity. While the above factors will be relevant in helping to determine the right location for the primary fund vehicle (the one that will be taken to market first or that the sponsor expects to accommodate the largest amount of commitments), it is normal for the overall fundraise to require one or more additional vehicles to accommodate the divergent needs of different types of investors.

The geographical perspective also matters when it comes to fund structuring. For instance, while both U.S. and U.K. private equity funds are structured as limited partnerships, there are significant differences between the U.S. and U.K. structures:

- U.K. funds use loan advances from LPs in addition to capital commitments, while U.S. structures do not use loan advances.

- U.K. (as well as European) funds pay carried interest on a fund as a whole basis rather than on a deal-by-deal basis, as U.S. funds do.

- U.K. funds typically structure the management fee payments as priority profit shares to the fund managers to secure efficient tax treatment in the United Kingdom.

LPs' commitment to the fund

As noted, a GP in an English limited partnership is responsible for the management of the partnership. The GP is also the legal "face" or personality of the partnership, and has authority to bind the partnership. The scope of this authority will almost invariably be set out in the LPA. In contrast, LPs have no power to bind the partnership and may not take part in management as they run the risk of being treated as a GP if they do so.

Historically, LPs in an English limited partnership have been liable up to the level of capital committed, even if it is returned to them during the continuance of the partnership. For this reason, the majority of an LP's overall commitment to an English limited partnership is structured as loan capital, with only a small proportion (usually in the order of 0.1% or less) classified as "equity capital." In this way, by repayment of their loan capital as investments in the funds that are being harvested, LPs can receive a return of dividends generated by portfolio companies or the proceeds of sale of investments prior to the dissolution of the partnership, without that repayment being at risk of being clawed back.

The loan capital portion of an LP's commitment is typically structured as an interest-free subordinated loan, and is only repayable—as a matter of contract rather than statute—in limited circumstances. The Reform Order allows for a PFLP to adopt an-all capital structure, which would remove the need for this structuring.

Master-feeder structures and parallel funds

Sometimes, different investor requirements simply cannot be accommodated within a single vehicle. For example, U.S. tax-paying investors often want to invest in a fund vehicle that is transparent or disregarded for tax purposes. On the other hand, U.S. tax-exempt investors often want to invest in a fund that is tax opaque. An entity can only be one or the other, so to accommodate both of these investor requirements within a single fundraise, the overall fund structure will need to include both types of vehicles; this is generally accomplished either by structuring a "master fund" into which various different feeder entities invest, or by structuring two or more entities that invest in parallel.

In a master-feeder structure, the master fund can either serve only to aggregate investment by the feeders (i.e., no one invests directly in it) or it can be directly investable. In either case, all capital and investment returns will flow through the master fund entity. With parallel funds, each parallel fund will operate its own "balance sheet" and waterfall, with investor capital only being co-mingled across the entire structure at the investment level, in which each parallel vehicle co-invests.[2] Such co-investment is usually pro rata and on identical terms across the parallel vehicles, and documented in a co-investment or side-by-side agreement.

Differing tax treatments are not the only reason to use master-feeder or parallel fund structures. A wide range of factors can lead to different fund vehicles being required. In simple terms, each of these scenarios involves a situation where the preferences or requirements of all investors cannot be satisfied through a single legal entity. For example, consider the following scenarios:

- Investors may wish to invest in a vehicle denominated in a different currency from that of the main fund. In this case, a feeder or parallel vehicle could be established and denominated in that currency.

---

[2] In practice, this is likely to be at the level of a special purpose vehicle holding company that holds one or more investments.

- A feeder vehicle can be used to aggregate high-net-worth investors, who individually would not invest sufficient capital to clear the master fund's minimum investment criteria. Such a vehicle can also be structured to provide a fee for the intermediary—such as a private bank—organizing such a vehicle.

- Certain investors may wish to invest in a more highly levered variant of the main fund's strategy, in which case a feeder or parallel vehicle can be used to offer a more leveraged option without exposing the main fund to the risks associated with such leverage.

- Some U.S. tax-exempt investors may be sensitive to "unrelated business taxable income" (UBTI) that would arise if they invested directly in the master fund (which is generally tax transparent from a U.S. federal tax perspective). A feeder or parallel fund vehicle that has elected to be taxed as a corporation (albeit one which would usually still be structured as a partnership) can be used to "block" UBTI for these purposes.

- European investors may be sensitive to so-called "effectively connected income" with certain investment strategies; as with U.S. investors, a feeder fund can serve as a "blocker" for these purposes.

Further, as outlined in the examples below, some investors will prefer certain types of fund vehicles over others, whether for reasons of familiarity, tax treatment, legal considerations, or otherwise.

- Many U.S. investors will be unfamiliar with some of the legal vehicles used in structuring European funds; as such, it can be advisable from a commercial perspective to offer them a vehicle with which they have more familiarity or comfort (such as a Delaware limited partnership).

- Conversely, many investors outside the United States will not want to invest in a Delaware limited partnership due to the U.S. tax filings that they would need to make, among other reasons.

- The jurisdiction of the fund will be relevant to the tax position of some investors. For example, certain tax authorities will impose punitive tax treatment on returns from investment vehicles structured in so-called "tax haven" jurisdictions; as such, investors in those countries will most likely prefer to invest in an onshore vehicle domiciled either in their own jurisdiction or one that is not perceived to be a problematic jurisdiction by their own tax authority.

- Some EU-regulated investors may obtain a better regulatory treatment, including a better regulatory cost of capital, if they invest in a fund domiciled within the European Union.

- There may be perception issues around the fund domicile, influenced by anything from previous experiences in that jurisdiction to public opinion or press stories. Investors are often accountable to their own stakeholders or influenced by a range of stakeholders (e.g., workers' representatives, charitable trustees, public authorities, etc.), which can influence where they are prepared to allocate.

In sum, the more diverse the investor base or the more widely targeted the fundraise, the more likely it is that a range of different legal structures will be required in order to meet the needs and wants of each investor constituency. The use of master-feeder and parallel fund structures is illustrated diagrammatically in Exhibits 1 and 2 below via two simple case studies, which also discuss the rationale behind using a master-feeder fund over a parallel fund, and vice versa.

The parallel fund structure

LPs located in different jurisdictions might have preferences for the vehicles in which they want to invest. The fund manager needs to establish vehicles that meet these investors' preferences. These vehicles are then managed on a parallel basis. For instance, assume that the investor group consists of three sub-groups: taxable U.S. investors; U.S. tax-exempt investors; and European investors. The fund structure and investment program gives rise to UBTI concerns. Different preferences emerge:

- The taxable U.S. investors prefer to invest in a fund that is treated as a partnership for federal tax purposes, so they invest through a Delaware limited partnership.

- Given the UBTI concerns, the U.S. tax-exempt investors prefer to invest in a fund that is treated as a corporation for federal tax purposes. They could invest through a Cayman Islands limited partnership that has elected to be taxed as a corporation.

- European investors prefer a parallel fund domiciled in the EU and managed by an EU-authorized alternative investment fund (AIF). In this case, a Luxembourg SCSp could be used.

Exhibit 1: Parallel fund structure

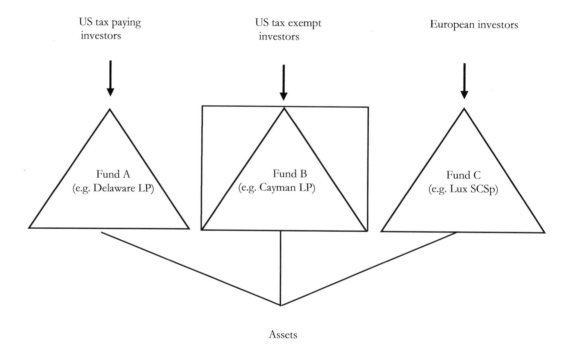

Situations where a parallel fund structure such as this may be more suitable than a master-feeder structure include the following:

- Situations (such as in the case study above) where an EU "passportable" vehicle is required. In order to be eligible for the passport, the EU fund cannot be a feeder fund of a non-EU fund.[3]

- In cases where one of the parallel vehicles will have a different leverage profile than the others (e.g., in some credit fund strategies, it is not uncommon for the sponsor to offer a leveraged variant of the strategy through a parallel fund structure). As the leverage provider may well require security down to the underlying asset level, this will likely require separation down to the underlying asset level, and hence, parallel structuring.

- In cases where parallel funds must exclude certain investments (e.g., non-Sharia investments), as this arrangement would not work in a master-feeder context.

- Many other scenarios where the economic interest in the assets can be relatively easily divided among multiple parallel vehicles and the relative simplicity of separate fund structures is desired.

Exhibit 2: Master-feeder fund structure

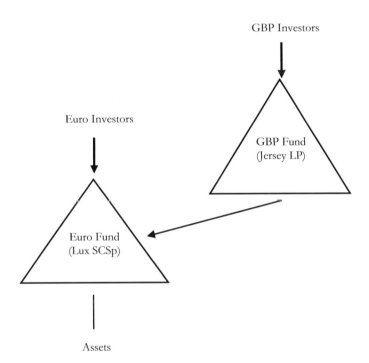

---

[3] On a related note, it is also important in this case to ensure that any underlying special purpose vehicle entity used to aggregate capital and hold assets is structured so that it is not deemed to be a master fund in its own right, especially if it is domiciled outside the EU.

The master-feeder structure

Master-feeder structures rely on multiple tiers of vehicles. The feeder funds are established as legally separate entities to meet the needs of particular investors while the master fund aggregates the capital from all feeder funds and invests it more efficiently. Usually, most of the capital in the feeder funds flows through the master fund. Feeders might be set up in different countries or be denominated in different currencies. The main advantage of this type of structure is that the fund manager oversees a single portfolio without the need to allocate investment decisions across parallel funds. In addition, the feeder fund structure can aggregate subscriptions to meet the minimum investment requirements of the master fund. Further, in some circumstances, the feeder funds preserve the confidentiality of the investors from other parties that invest in other feeder funds.

For instance, assume that a private equity fund structured as a Luxembourg SCSp is denominated in euros. A small group of investors may wish to allocate capital to the fund in British pounds sterling (GBP). Accordingly, a Jersey-domiciled partnership is established which is denominated in GBP.

Situations where a master-feeder structure such as this may be more suitable than the parallel structure include the following:

- When the funds receive capital from U.S.-based tax-exempt investors. These investors prefer to make their capital commitments through an offshore vehicle (e.g., a Cayman Islands or British Virgin Islands entity). The offshore feeder is generally treated as the beneficial owner of the fund. Therefore, this feeder, and not its investors, must provide a tax identification number and report to the Internal Revenue Service.

- Where it is difficult to divide the assets between different investment vehicles; this is rarely the case in private equity, as the portfolio companies will almost invariably be held by a holding entity/special purpose vehicle (SPV) structure, the economic interest in which can be relatively easily apportioned among different investing entities. However, there may be some situations (e.g., in state-controlled or heavily regulated industries) where it is more difficult to divide ownership or economic entitlement in this way.

- If it is desirable to maximize the size of the master fund (e.g., when utilizing the 25% "plan assets" limitation for Employee Retirement Income Security Act (ERISA) purposes).[4]

- Currency situations (such as the one outlined above) where it may be administratively easier to deal with a situation where the euro/GBP rate moves and the GBP investors "run out of money" (as in the above example) in a master-feeder context than it would be in a parallel context.

- In some scenarios, the feeder vehicle will not be under the "control" of the sponsor group; this would be common in the context of, for example, high-net-worth aggregation vehicles set up by some private banks, or "wrap" feeder structures set up by local sponsors to access investments from Chinese investors. In these cases, the sponsor will likely prefer to have such a vehicle invest in the main fund than to be a co-investor in each deal.

---

[4] A discussion of ERISA is beyond the scope of this chapter, but in very broad terms, the 25% exemption referred to is a commonly utilized exception whereby fund sponsors restrict so-called "plan assets" investors to less than 25% of the fund. If the plan assets are higher than 25%, the fund manager becomes a fiduciary under ERISA exposing the manager to potential liabilities and potentially prohibiting some fund transactions. The presence of an ERISA in the fund requires a comprehensive analysis of ERISA issues by the fund manager.

The allocation of costs among parallel and feeder fund entities must be carefully considered by the sponsor. For instance, will the costs of feeder funds be borne by the master fund or only by the particular feeder? Will the costs of parallel funds be borne only by the investors in that entity, or will all costs be aggregated and smoothed pro rata among all investors in a structure? These questions can be argued both ways. On the one hand, if the feeder fund helps increase the size of the overall fundraise and, in so doing, helps to diversify investment risk, then this can be in all of the investors' best interests. On the other hand, if particular costs have been incurred in order to address the needs of only one group of investors, why should the other investors pay these costs? The key here is to determine a position that makes the most sense in the context of that particular manager, fundraise, and investor group, and provide adequate disclosure as to the basis of cost allocation to investors. In doing so, one must also pay particular attention to the regulatory requirements of both the jurisdiction of the fund itself and any manager entities involved in the investment process, as well as those of the key investor jurisdictions.

Regardless of whether all investors invest through the same structure or not, there may be instances where, for tax or regulatory reasons to do with a given investment, a separate structure is created through which investors invest solely for the purpose of that one investment. This entity—commonly called an "alternative investment vehicle" (AIV)—will have a mirrored set of management or advisory arrangements and investment terms that follow, as far as is possible, those of the "master" limited partnership. Usually, the LPAs of the private equity funds have provisions that enable the manager to create an AIV. The AIV may be established in the same jurisdiction as the main fund or a different jurisdiction. For example, unlike a parallel fund co-investing with the main fund in all investments, an AIV may be formed as an alternative vehicle for LPs; in this case, the investment made through the AIV reduces the LP's remaining capital commitments to the main fund. However, the investment results of the AIV are aggregated with those of the main fund when implementing the "cash waterfall" set out in the LPA.

GP STRUCTURES

A universal feature of the limited partnership is that it requires a GP. In common parlance, the GP and the private equity firm are one and the same thing. In legal terms, the GP (not least due to the fact that it generally has unlimited liability for the debts and obligations of the partnership) is typically structured as a stand-alone entity for a particular fundraise, which then delegates the provision of investment advice or the management of the fund's assets to one or more operating entities in the fund manager's group.

There are two common approaches to structuring the GP, which are discussed in turn below. The first approach is to structure the GP itself as a partnership, so that economics (particularly carried interest) can "flow" through it in a tax-efficient way. The second approach is to structure the GP as a corporation, and have the economics (particularly carried interest) allocated to a separate vehicle.

Carried interest allocated through a General Partner Limited Partnership (GPLP)

The GP of the fund may itself be structured as a partnership (see Exhibit 3). This structure, which is common in the United States, allows carried interest to be allocated to the GP and from there to "flow through" to the management team, retaining its tax character. As both the main fund and the GP are partnerships, they are both disregarded for tax purposes and carried interest holders are essentially taxed as if they had participated in the underlying investments directly, which is often crucial to tax-efficient carried interest structuring. In the United States, this structure has historically offered an efficient way of dealing with the private equity firm's economics, as both the management "fee"/priority profit share and carried interest can be allocated to the GP and participated in by the management team. Moreover, in the United States, a management company separate from the GP is established to provide administrative services to the fund following a management contract. The management fee is paid to the manager pursuant to the terms of this contract.

In the context of funds managed from the United Kingdom, the creation of a GP partnership (as in the United States) has historically allowed a priority profit share to be allocated to the manager (instead of a management fee being paid to a third-party management company). This structure is adopted to maximize the deductibility of the management fee for UK based investors and is also efficient from a value-added tax perspective. In addition, to the extent that such allocations may have the character of capital gain, it could be possible for the manager (or individual investment professionals) to be taxed on the basis of capital gains rather than income. Changes in tax laws in the United Kingdom have, in general, reduced the positive effects of this structuring for U.K. tax payers.

Exhibit 3: General Partner Limited Partnership structure

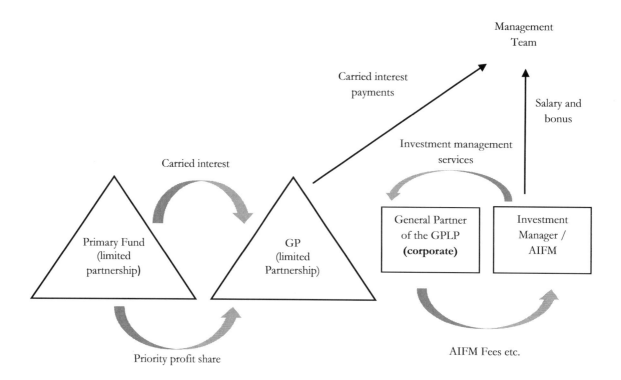

The special limited partnership structure

An alternative, which is more common in European funds, is to structure the management fee as a limited partnership rather than priority profit allocation, on the basis that the tax advantages of the latter approach are likely to be much more limited or non-existent.

European funds also allocate only the management fee to the GP, with carried interest allocated to a special carried interest vehicle, which is commonly known as a "special limited partner" (special LP) or "carried interest partner." As is shown in Exhibit 4, The special LP is itself a partnership, which allows for the same tax transparency with respect to the carried interest flow as the above structure, where this was flowed through a General Partner Limited Partnership (GPLP).

There are several reasons why the special limited partnership is now the default choice for many U.K. sponsors:

- As the GP has unlimited liability with respect to the partnership, many teams prefer to keep this entity firmly away from the carried interest entitlement. There is a direct contractual relationship between the investors and the GP that does not exist with other fund management entities; as such, it is a susceptible target for investor legal action. The special limited partnership is a much less attractive target if it does not have significant economics flowing through it.

Exhibit 4: Special LP structure

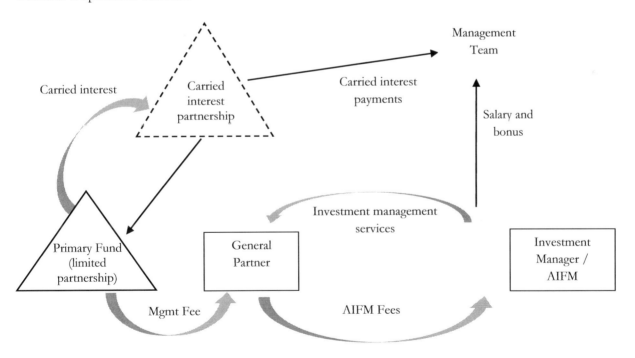

- As the GP is an integral part of the fund structure, investors may request to see its organizational documentation as part of their due diligence. If the fund was a partnership entity, this would include requesting the LPA, which would need to contain various provisions for dealing with carried interest apportionment and entitlement among the management team members. While it should be possible to keep certain items (e.g., carried interest award letters) out of investor due diligence materials, this approach may involve a greater level of disclosure regarding the management team's carried interest arrangements than the team would prefer.[5]

- Having the carried interest arrangements documented in a separate special limited partnership that is not a part of the main fund structure also means that any dispute as to carried interest entitlement among members of the management team should be less visible to (or capable of having an impact on) investors.

- The special LP route makes it easy for carried interest entitlement/awards to be completely separated from the management fee economics.

- For a number of reasons, it is convenient or necessary to form the fund well before a first closing (e.g., to expedite service provider or bank onboarding, to allow the fund to issue documentation prior to regulatory marketing approval processes, etc.). This deadline requires at least one LP to join the fund, but the special LP provides a convenient way of meeting this requirement without having any third-party investors actually join the fund at this stage.

- The same carried interest vehicle can be used by the management team to participate in multiple funds, whereas it would generally not be appropriate to use the same GP across multiple fund vintages or strategies.

- The special LP can be used as a means by which management can co-invest in the fund, and many of the above factors would also be relevant from this perspective. However, given the potential differential between management co-investment amounts and carried interest entitlement (both in terms of the amounts invested and the rights and obligations of the management team in relation to it, particularly with regards to "leaver entitlements"), it may be more straightforward to keep these two functions separate and use separate vehicles: one for the carried interest and one for management co-investment.

It is helpful if the special LP has legal personality, so that it may be entered on the books and records of the main fund as an LP in its own right. Scottish limited partnerships (having the ability to elect for their own legal personality) have traditionally been used for this purpose in the context of U.K. domestic funds. A range of other onshore and offshore fund vehicles have the ability to elect separate legal personality and are equally suitable.

CO-INVESTMENT FUND STRUCTURES

A co-investment scenario is a situation where the whole investment amount is not allocated to the main fund. Instead, the main fund takes a portion of the total investment amount, and the balance is funded by one or

---

[5] However, it is worth noting that the carried interest terms may well be of interest to investors in any event, and so as a commercial matter, the management team may be required to give reasonably full disclosure as to how this will be apportioned.

more co-investors who invest in the deal alongside the main fund. The co-investors are often some subset of the main fund investors who wish to increase their exposure to that particular transaction. A co-investment situation usually arises when the manager is not able to allocate all of a deal to the fund because it would breach a concentration limit or some other investment restriction, or because the fund has insufficient undrawn commitments to invest the total investment amount in full.[6]

While the varied considerations behind the allocation of co-investments are outside the scope of this chapter, the starting premise is generally that co-investing is a way for the fund to keep its allocation of an underlying deal "right sized," rather than a means by which the manager can allocate deal flow away from the fund. This distinction is important, as the manager is a fiduciary, and should not be prioritizing co-investors ahead of the main fund. The fund's correct allocation of a particular transaction should be determined first, with co-investors being offered the remainder.

A co-investment program can be an attractive feature even to those investors who do not wish to take it up directly. First, it allows the manager a way to optimize the fund's exposure to each particular investment in accordance with an asset allocation model. Second, the co-investment "firepower" allows the fund to pursue bigger transactions, which may offer more attractive economics or give the fund a greater choice of opportunities.

Direct co-investment

The simplest way of structuring a co-investment is to bring the co-investors directly into the special purpose vehicle that is used to acquire the company (see Exhibit 5).

Exhibit 5: Direct co-investment: A simple schematic

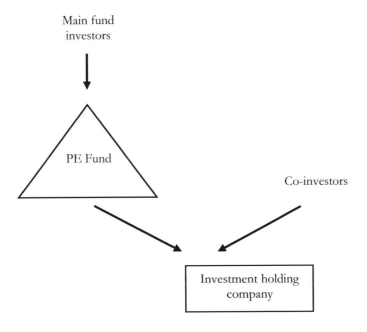

---

[6] Co-investments are increasingly popular because they allow the LPs to pursue a more finely tuned asset allocation model by selecting specific deals in areas they wish to invest in. Co-investments also reduce the fees on the capital allocated to private equity.

Although this can be an attractive structure in some situations—particularly when co-investors intend to be "active" and have greater autonomy over their investment—it requires a shareholder agreement or some other contract between the fund and co-investors. Direct co-investment also necessitates thinking through all of the various scenarios around that investment (including ongoing governance, participation in follow-on rounds, partial disposals, and complete exits) to ensure that these situations—and, in particular, how the fund and co-investors will interact—are agreed upfront. In practice, direct co-investment can be considerably more complicated and time consuming than the alternative structure, indirect co-investment, which is discussed below.

Indirect co-investment through a co-investment vehicle

Indirect co-investment through a co-investment vehicle entails creating a separate structure for each co-investment opportunity, which brings together the various co-investors (see Exhibit 6). That structure is organized and controlled by the fund sponsor, which allows the co-investment to be operated in parallel with the main fund's investment in the underlying deal. This arrangement provides the most straightforward approach for most situations.

That is not to say that the wheel needs to be reinvented each time there is a co-investment deal. If the investors have participated in other co-investments, then it may simply be a matter of agreeing to use the same form of documentation as last time around.

Exhibit 6: Indirect co-investment: A simple schematic

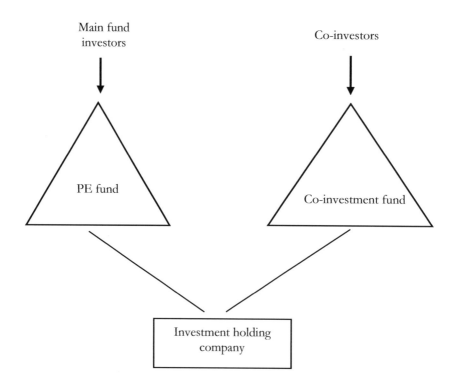

The starting point for a co-investment vehicle is usually the main fund structure. For example, if the primary fund is a Cayman Islands limited partnership, it would be logical to utilize this structure for the co-investment vehicle. There will presumably be some efficiencies regarding service providers, GP directors, and so on in using the same vehicle as the main fund. In addition, the fund agreement from the primary fund will provide the best possible starting point for the co-investment vehicle, requiring only commercial and legal amendments to address the terms of the co-investment structure, rather than any change in domicile or legal structure.

This approach may be re-evaluated if the main fund is in an expensive jurisdiction or is a highly regulated structure (which will likely add extra cost and time). In such situations, it may be more appropriate to locate the co-investment vehicle in a less regulated jurisdiction where the vehicle could be set up more quickly and the terms could be more flexibly changed in due course, if needed.

The co-investment vehicle could, in principle, share a GP with the primary fund; however, this can place additional strain on the conflict of interest inherent in any co-investment scenario. Depending on the jurisdiction and overall corporate governance context within the GP group, it may be preferable to have a different GP for the main fund and any co-investment vehicle, although both would be affiliates with the sponsor group. If the vehicles are managed or advised by the same sponsor, the decision making and governance of the underlying portfolio investment is aligned.

The right time to discuss structuring a co-investment vehicle with the potential co-investors is usually long before the first deal is in sight. This time frame allows structuring considerations to be ironed out and agreed, and documentation to be prepared and legally reviewed, well in advance. Yet, in reality, co-investors often come together and review documentation only in the context of a live deal situation.

Although some structuring flexibility exists (depending on the particular scenario), co-investment vehicles would often be considered AIFs for the purposes of the AIFMD in Europe. This factor can lead to particular challenges within a European context if the vehicle needs to be established and invested quickly in the context of a particular transaction.

Co-investment fund

Where the fund sponsor anticipates a lot of different co-investments, it may consider structuring a co-investment fund (sometimes known as a "sidecar fund" or an "over-allocation fund") alongside the main fund vehicle. The sidecar fund will have "first option" on any portions of deals that the sponsor does not wish to allocate to the main fund. This approach may be useful if there are investors who are very keen to participate in co-investment opportunities, and who are all comfortable with the same legal structure. It can be especially useful for the manager if the speed of capital deployment is an issue, as the structure is set up and ready to go. The sidecar fund may function on a blind pool basis, such that investor approval for a deal would not be required. Alternatively, the investors may need to approve a transaction. However, obtaining approval of the deal alone should be considerably more straightforward than doing this while simultaneously trying to get the investors comfortable with the co-investment documentation.

Consider, for example, a middle market private equity fund sponsor that raises a €500 million fund with a deal concentration limit of 10% (i.e., the fund is limited to deals of €50 million or less after allowing for costs, follow-on capital, etc.). However, if the manager considers that the environment has changed and the most interesting opportunities are deals with a greater value, a solution is needed. The fund sponsor could of course structure deal-by-deal co-investments, but it can be inefficient to do this for every single transaction. The fund sponsor could also propose an amendment of fund terms to raise the concentration limit, but would most likely find that not all investors would be comfortable with this, resulting in a divided investor base. The solution may well be to raise a sidecar fund, allowing the manager to pursue its revised investment program while each group of investors maintains its desired risk profile.

DOWNSTREAM INVESTMENT STRUCTURES

Portfolio assets will ordinarily be held through investment holding company structures established in countries that offer a favorable set of double taxation treaties (e.g., Luxembourg or Ireland) or in offshore jurisdictions (e.g., the Cayman Islands). The location and type of structure will depend on a number of factors, including the location of the asset in question.

Apart from ensuring that the structure offers a tax-efficient route of streaming dividend income and capital gains to investors, a multi-level holding structure also allows different levels of debt—senior, junior, and mezzanine—to be introduced at different levels in the holding structure, and for debt servicing costs to be offset against profits generated by the portfolio company, thereby reducing the tax liability of the underlying portfolio companies. We discuss these structures in more detail in the chapter on acquisition finance.

Many private equity funds prohibit the fund itself from taking on significant levels of debt for the purposes of leveraging the fund's investment program. Any recourse to the LPs (other than a pledge over undrawn commitments) would most likely be commercially unacceptable. A multi-layered holding structure allows debt to be pushed into portfolio companies without creating a risk that LPs will become responsible for this debt.

CONCLUSION

Private equity funds have traditionally enjoyed the advantages of the ability to structure their funds to suit their needs and those of their investors. Limited partnerships continue to be the choice of legal entity structure for fund vehicles since they allow regulatory compliance to be easier and enable the LPs to have limited liabilities for the funds they invest in. The flexibility of structuring their funds and other related entities allows GPs to serve LPs across jurisdictions while meeting various other criteria such as tax efficiency, reducing operational and administration overheads, enabling co-investments for increased exposure to certain underlying investments or optimally allocating profits as per the waterfall.

With changes in regulations and tax codes, it can be expected that fund structuring will continue to evolve to optimize the operations of private equity funds. Although in the past GP limited partnerships (GPLPs) were the norm and to this day, most private equity funds are structured as such, a growing number of publicly listed private equity firms such as Blackstone and KKR have converted their status to a publicly listed corporation from GPLPs. One objective is to become eligible to be included in market indices and investment mandates of more investors. Additionally changes to the US corporate tax code meant that the tax advantages pertaining to limited partnerships over corporations became smaller as compared to those in the past. However given the other distinct advantages, it is likely that most private equity funds (especially unlisted ones) will continue to be structured as limited partnerships and be managed by GP entities that are structured as limited partnerships too.

In his own words: Gus Black, Partner and Global Co-chair Financial Services Group at Dechert LLP

Except in terms of economics, the co-investment partnership will typically have very similar terms to those of the main fund. As noted, the starting point for co-investment vehicle documentation is the primary fund's LPA, which can then be cut down to remove some of the functionality that is not needed in a co-investment scenario. For instance, it is likely that the investor syndicate will be fully settled at the outset, so subsequent closing and equalization mechanics may not be necessary. A number of provisions will need to be carefully reviewed to ensure that they interact properly with the main fund and reflect the agreed commercial deal as well as any regulatory or tax considerations. As the co-investor syndicate will likely be comprised of primary fund investors, the documentation process should be reasonably straightforward.

In addition to these changes, the documentation can also be amended to reflect the economics of the co-investment that the fund sponsor has agreed with the co-investors. The economics of co-investment are outside the scope of this chapter, but suffice it to say that it would be relatively rare for the sponsor to enjoy identical economics in a co-investment as it does in the primary investment. However, there is no "one-size-fits-all" approach to co-investment economics, and the eventual arrangements may be quite specifically tailored to the particular investor syndicate.

This tailor-made aspect will likely include a unique basis for fees. Typically, rather than receiving a "full" management fee and a corresponding transaction fee offset, the co-investment structure has a lower management fee but with certain costs, such as transaction advisory or directors' fees, being chargeable by the fund sponsor. It is important for the fund sponsor to ensure that primary fund investors as well as co-investors are aware of the economics of the co-investment and any indirect effects they could have. For example, if a deal advisory fee in relation to the co-investment is paid by the target portfolio company to the fund sponsor, this effectively reduces the target's balance sheet for everyone—fund and co-investor alike.

7 Performance Measurement in Private Equity

There is something that is much scarcer, something rarer than ability. It is the ability to recognize ability.
Robert Half

INTRODUCTION

The main reason for the explosive growth of the private equity asset class over the past 10 years has been its financial returns, which are substantially higher than those produced by other asset classes. However, investors in private equity have always faced difficulties in measuring private equity funds' performance. First, given the focus on private companies, the investments of private equity funds are illiquid and opaque. In addition, the cash flows generated by the funds are not under the investors' control. Finally, there is a lack of widely accepted benchmarks to assess the relative performance of the private equity asset class. This issue in particular prevents investors from fully understanding the risk, return, and correlation characteristics of private equity investments, and thus the optimal share of private equity investments in a diversified portfolio that covers different asset classes.

The payoff of a private equity fund is similar to that provided by a bond that pays coupons, but there are some critical differences. Bonds involve a cash outflow at the very beginning and generate regular cash inflows whose timing and magnitude can be predicted with relative accuracy based on the terms of the bond contract. In contrast, in the case of private equity funds, fund managers draw down the money whenever they find investment opportunities over the five-year average investment period and distribute proceeds back to investors whenever they decide to sell the investments. As a result, the timing and magnitude of the cash flows are impossible to predict.

These irregular cash flows and their uncertain magnitude make measuring private equity fund performance a challenging task. The industry has devised several performance metrics that deal with these issues, but each have their pros and cons. The most widely used measure of performance is the *internal rate of return* (IRR), which takes into consideration the timing of cash contributions and distributions to and from the fund, and the length of time an investment has been held in the fund. Given that the IRR measure and its derivatives (i.e., modified IRR, public market equivalents, etc.) are somewhat hard to calculate and interpret, the industry also uses an alternative measure of performance, the money multiple. This metric reflects the proceeds received by investors from a fund plus the valuation of any remaining investments in the fund scaled by the investors' capital contributed to the fund. While money multiples are quite straightforward to compute, the simplicity of their interpretation may be an illusion. Multiples can be heavily influenced by fund managers, especially when funds have recycling provisions, as outlined below.

It is important to note that no single metric is perfect when it comes to measuring the performance of private equity funds and their investments. As a consequence, both investors and fund managers use different combinations of these metrics.

MEASURES OF PRIVATE EQUITY FUND PERFORMANCE

As a private equity fund matures, the sale of the investments in the portfolio generates cash and/or stock distributions to investors. Thus, over time, an increasing proportion of a fund's performance will reflect actual distributions to investors, rather than valuation estimates of portfolio companies still held in the fund. Although private equity funds have an agreed fixed life of 10 years, they often show a residual asset value for a considerable time beyond these 10 years before the assets are finally wound up. This amount represents investments that have not yet been realized but still have value. Calculating the rate of return of a private equity fund requires the final and definitive valuation of the residual assets in the fund's portfolio, as well as the exact timing and magnitude of the cash received from or distributed to investors.

As stated, the private equity industry typically computes two sets of measures to determine the performance of a private equity fund: money multiples and IRRs. Both sets of measures are computed during the fund's life using valuation estimates for unrealized investments. We first discuss the multiples before turning our attention to IRRs.

Multiples

Money multiples are a very popular and simple way to assess the performance of a private equity fund. They are computed by dividing the sum of returns generated by the private equity fund by the capital invested in the private equity fund. These ratios of "proceeds over investments" are simple to calculate and easy to interpret: if the fund triples an investor's money, the fund's money multiple is 3. Funds usually report three multiples: distributed value to paid-in ratio (DPI), residual value to paid-in ratio (RVPI), and total value to paid-in ratio (TVPI). Paid-in capital is the portion of committed capital that has been drawn down by the fund manager for investments, fees, carried interest, and/or fund expenses. Private equity investors often compute an additional multiple that does not capture the fund's performance which is called the *paid-in capital* multiple (PIC). This multiple is computed as paid-in capital to committed capital and shows how much of the investors' committed capital has been drawn by the fund manager. The metric reflects the fund's investment pace during its investment period. PIC also indicates when a fund manager might be coming back to market to raise another fund. A high PIC means that the current fund has invested most of the committed capital.

While GPs sometimes use gross and net multiples interchangeably in their conversations with investors and marketing materials, careful investors should always clarify which figures are actually being represented. Gross multiples represent the fund's gross returns and do not account for fund managers' compensation. Net multiples are more representative of the actual returns received by investors because they include the effects of management fees and carried interest. Note that net multiples can vary dramatically between investors in the same fund due to investor-specific factors such as side letters, discounts, co-investments, and exchange rates. We outline the computation of net multiples below, since they are most relevant to investors.

Distributed value to paid-in ratio (DPI)

DPI (also called realized multiple, cash-on-cash, or multiple of invested capital) measures the distributions to LPs scaled by the amount of capital contributed by LPs in the fund:

$$DVPI = \frac{\sum_{t=1}^{t<T} CF_t^{PAST,RECEIVED}}{\sum_{t=1}^{t<T} CF_t^{PAST,PAID-IN}}$$

where CF^{PAST;RECEIVED} are net cash flows distributed by the fund as a result of past investments (including both cash and stock distributions from selling investments, dividends, or interest payments), and CF^{PAST;PAID IN} are all cash flows paid into the fund (e.g., capital invested, capital non-invested, or fees paid). The cash flows are cumulated since the beginning of the fund's life (vintage year) until the year when the performance measure is computed (T).

When DPI is equal to one, the fund has broken even, as capital drawn down for investments or fees is equal to the capital distributed to investors. Any number above one indicates that the fund has generated a profit, as it paid out more than the capital drawn down.

This multiple is often relevant for measuring the performance of the fund towards the end of its life. DPI shows the net performance of the investment relative to all money that has been used either to compensate the management of the fund (fees and carry) or invest in portfolio companies. DPI is not a good measure of fund performance when the fund is at a stage where capital committed has not been fully invested (i.e., at the beginning of the fund's life) since a lot of the value generated by the fund will be in unrealized investments. However, the exclusion of the net asset value (NAV) of unrealized investments makes this ratio a less subjective and more conservative performance measure.

Residual value to paid-in ratio (RVPI)

RVPI (also called the unrealized multiple) measures the NAV of the private equity fund (i.e., the fair value of the unrealized investments) compared with the amount of capital contributed by the LPs to the fund:

$$RVPI = \frac{NAV_T}{\sum_{t=1}^{t<T} CF_t^{PAST,PAID-IN}}$$

where NAV is the fair value of the private equity fund's holdings at the date of RVPI's computation T, adjusted for the expected fees that will be paid to the fund manager, and CF^{PAST;PAID IN} are cash flows transferred to the fund (e.g., capital invested and fees paid).

This ratio is most useful early in the life of a fund before there have been many distributions. RVPI is highly dependent on the quality of the valuation estimates provided by the fund manager and may show a misleadingly low return if the fund is accounting for its investments very conservatively.

Total value to paid-in ratio (TVPI)

TVPI is the ratio of the total value of all distributions to date plus the current value of remaining investments within the fund to the total amount of capital paid into the fund to date. In other words, it is the sum of DPI and RVPI:

$$TVPI = \frac{\sum_{t=1}^{t<T} CF_t^{PAST,RECEIVED} + NAV_T}{\sum_{t=1}^{t<T} CF_t^{PAST,PAID-IN}}$$

where CF^PAST;RECEIVED are net cash flows distributed by the fund as a result of past investments (including both cash and stock distributions from selling investments, dividends, or interest payments), NAV is the fair value of the fund's holdings at the date of TVPI's computation T, adjusted for the expected fees that will be paid to the fund manager, and CF^PAST;PAID IN are cash flows transferred to the fund (e.g., capital invested and fees paid).

TVPI is perhaps the best available measure of performance before the end of a fund's life. Residual asset values should be subject to conservative valuations, and ideally represent the lower limit of capital that will be distributed at a later stage (adjusted for the expected fees that will be paid to fund managers). The ratio of the sum of past distributions and residual value to paid-in capital should therefore represent the minimum multiple that investors can expect from a private equity fund. Still, the subjectivity involved in estimating residual values makes this performance metric prone to measurement errors.

It must be noted that many fund managers, when computing TVPI, include the value of a portfolio company's shares exited via an IPO, which is measured at the time of the shares' distribution to LPs. However, LPs receiving these shares face a lock-up period that restricts their ability to sell the shares in the open market. Thus, it is possible that these investors may receive significantly less at the end of the lock-up period when the shares can be freely traded. As a result, the money multiple reported in this instance is higher because the value of the shares distributed might be higher than the value of the shares when they are actually sold by investors. In addition, the reported IRR (which we discuss below) will also increase because the cash flow is recognized much earlier.

Drawbacks

The money multiple measures have several drawbacks:

- The first drawback is that they do not consider the length of time that the money has been invested in the fund (i.e., they are not time sensitive). To illustrate, a money multiple of three does not capture the difference between an investment that took 10 years to triple investors' money and an investment that achieved the same return in only two years. In the former case, the investor might have been better off with a basic investment such as an emerging market government bond, whereas the performance of the second investment is clearly very good and cannot be easily matched by a lower-risk alternative.

- Second, multiples do not inform the investor about the underlying risks of the fund, and in particular, the level of leverage used. For instance, a fund that achieves a multiple of three by borrowing $1 for each dollar invested is significantly less risky than a fund that achieves a multiple of three with $2 borrowed for each dollar invested.

- Third, multiple measures are heavily distorted when early realizations in the fund can be recycled (i.e., reinvested instead of being distributed to investors). For example, assume that a fund invests $100 at the beginning of year 1, exits the investment at $150 at the beginning at year 2, makes another investment of $150 at the beginning of year 2, and exits the second investment for $300 at the beginning of year 3 (for simplicity, assume that there are no fees). If the fund does not have a recycling option, TVPI will be (150 + 300)/(100+150) = 1.8. If the fund can recycle the value obtained at the beginning of year 2, then TVPI will be 300/100 = 3. As this example illustrates, even though investors receive the same net cash flow, the multiple measure is much higher if the capital is recycled; this provides opportunities to manipulate the reported performance of the fund.[1]

A simple solution to these problems is to provide additional disclosures. Fund prospectuses could report the multiples together with three additional pieces of information such as

- the *duration* of the fund;

- the *extent of leverage* used to achieve the multiple; and

- the *amount of capital reinvested*.

Internal rate of return

IRR is defined mathematically as the discount rate which, when applied to discount a series of cash outflows followed by cash inflows, returns a net present value (NPV) of zero. The most intuitive way of understanding the meaning of IRR is to think of it as the equivalent constant interest rate during the life of the fund at which a given series of capital drawdowns must be invested in order for the private equity investor to earn a given series of cash distributions as income.

Private equity practitioners use IRR because it offers a means of comparing funds with irregular cash flow timings and magnitudes:

- **Timing:** In contrast to money multiples, IRRs consider the time value of money by placing a lower weight on cash flows that arrive later in the fund's life. Because IRR reflects the cash flows' timing, it is calculated and stated not as an annual return of any particular year but as a *compound return* from a certain year (the year of formation of the fund, which is the vintage year) to a specified year.

- **Magnitude:** As private equity funds make investments of different sizes, the assessment of their performance should give higher weight to returns that were realized on a larger capital basis. Unlike alternative return measurements such as the annually compounded return, IRR conveniently accounts for this phenomenon. Therefore, IRR is referred to as a "dollar-weighted" return, while the annually compounded return is referred to as a "time-weighted" return. The time-weighted rate of return measure is commonly used in public markets and does not capture the critical effects of cash flow management within the control of the GP and, thus, is not comparable with the IRR measure used for private equity returns. The time-weighted rate of return eliminates the effects of interim cash flows by revaluing the portfolio at each cash flow date while the IRR gives weight to interim cash flows based on their amounts and timing.

IRR calculation: Interim versus final IRRs

As a result of the issues outlined above, managers report both net and gross IRRs. It is essential that they determine whether IRRs are gross or net of management fees, carried interest, and other compensation to the fund manager, as there can be major differences between the two metrics. These differences are particularly large when the fund has been holding investments for long periods (i.e., there is a significant "management

---

[1] Griffiths (2016) proposes a new multiple called net value divided by net paid which solves the problem of capital recycling.

fee drag") or when the fund has quickly generated a disproportionately large, successful exit. Investors prefer that IRRs are computed net of management fees and carried interest to reflect the net return they receive.[2] Another important issue when computing net IRRs is whether the capital contribution of the manager to the fund is included or not. These capital contributions are provided on a non-fee basis. Accordingly, net IRRs that are computed with large manager capital contributions included are distorted upwards, creating comparability issues with the net IRRs of funds that do not include managerial contributions, or that include only small contributions.

IRR can be measured during the life of the fund, even if the fund is not close to liquidation. This IRR measure is called an *interim* IRR. It reflects the discount rate that equates the present value of all capital drawdowns with the sum of the present value of all cash distributions accruing from it and the present value of the unrealized residual portfolio (i.e., unliquidated holdings), adjusted for managers' expected fees:

$$\sum_{t=1}^{t \leq T} \frac{CF_t^{PAST,RECEIVED}}{(1 + IRR_{interim})^t} + \frac{NAV_T}{(1 + IRR_{interim})^T} = 0$$

where $CF^{PAST,RECEIVED}$ are net of free cash flows distributed by the fund as a result of past investments (including cash from the sales of investments, the value of stock distributions, dividend payments, and interest payments), and NAV is the net asset value net of expected management fees and carry that belong to the fund manager (i.e., value of the private equity fund's holdings at the date of the computation T net of fees).

When the fund is liquidated, the manager can then compute the *final* IRR which is the discount rate that equates the present value of all capital drawdowns to the present value of all cash distributions during the life of the fund. After a fund is liquidated, there is nothing left in the portfolio (i.e., NAV in the formula above is zero or insignificant).

The interim IRRs fluctuate around the final IRR towards the end of the fund's life. Thus, an accurate picture of the performance of an individual private equity fund can only be obtained when the fund is liquidated. This is a crucial fact to remember, given that most of the evidence presented by the industry (or by researchers) on the fund performance relies on interim IRRs of funds that are not liquidated.

Drawbacks

IRR measures have several important drawbacks that investors should be aware of when reading private equity funds' performance reports:

- The IRR formula is rather complex, depending on the timing and variance of the fund's cash flows, making it less intuitive to interpret.

- IRR calculations can be highly sensitive to the timing of cash flows. Two similar private equity fund investments over a 10-year period can produce very different IRRs, although the multiples on investment can be the same: the private equity fund that distributes cash earlier will report a higher IRR. Despite the 10-year life of the fund, the period of time during which the invested capital is returned can be as short as two years. Because of the sensitivity of IRR to the distribution of cash flows,

---

[2] Managers compute average net IRRs because private equity fees are not standard and different investors in the same fund can pay different fees. Investors that commit money early during the fundraising process or make a larger allocation to the fund receive might receive fee breaks.

some managers may have incentives to drive up IRRs by timing the exits in the fund's early years.[3] However, carry compensation should dissuade some managers from exiting investments early at lower valuations, since they will potentially lose 20% of each dollar wasted.

- The IRR does not give any weight to the absolute dollar amounts of gain or value generated from investments. An IRR of 30% does not inform an investor about the scale of the investment – the IRR number would be the same for a $1 million investment and for a $10 billion investment although in the latter case, much more value is being created.

- IRRs implicitly assume that after one portfolio investment is liquidated and cash is distributed to investors, another equally profitable opportunity to place money just received by investors can be found. This so-called *reinvestment hypothesis* is questionable, especially in the private equity sector. There is no guarantee that a private equity investor can identify similarly profitable investment opportunities at little notice. Consequently, the *effective rate of return* received by investors differs from the IRR. They are equal only if investors can reinvest intermediary distributions at the IRR and borrow at the IRR to finance intermediary payments, which is impossible in practice.[4] Therefore, investors prefer a short investment with a high IRR only if the proceeds can be reinvested at attractive returns. If this is not the case, a longer investment with a lower IRR is usually desired.

- Interim IRRs are measured based on the fund's NAV, which captures investments that are not fully realized. The value of these investments is computed using valuation methods applied by the manager which may or may not follow valuation standards set by the industry. Aggressive revaluations of ongoing investments could exaggerate the performance during critical fundraising periods. Alternatively, valuations might also be very conservative or outdated.

- Another shortcoming of the IRR is linked to its mathematical computation. If the private equity fund generates a mix of positive and negative cash flows over time, the iterative algorithm that computes the IRR may not converge, or may generate multiple IRRs that make the NPV of these cash flows equal to zero (i.e., the solution is not unique).

- IRRs cannot be compared with a time-weighted return measure, which is the typical measure that captures the performance of investments in public markets.

- The IRR assumes that all cash flows are invested at the same discount rate. In the real world, these rates will fluctuate, particularly with longer-term investments.

Ultimately, using IRR as a key measure for comparing private equity fund performance might be misleading without understanding what drives the IRR at the portfolio company or investment level. Common IRR components include the following:

- **The baseline return:** This part comes from cash flows that the investment made by the fund is expected to generate without any additional improvements. Strong performance on this dimension highlights a manager's acquisition skills.

---

[3] Limited partnership agreements often allow the reinvestment of capital coming from investments that are shorter than 12–18 months. Such a provision provides an incentive to exit the first few investments early because it offers GPs a chance to reinvest funds. The reinvestment increases the assets under management, thus generating potentially higher fees and carried interest.

[4] There is an incentive to report high IRRs because GPs usually raise money for new funds based on their past performance as measured by IRR.

- **Return due to improvements in performance:** This part is attributed to a manager's operational value creation efforts (e.g., revenue growth, margin improvement, increase of capital efficiency, etc.).

- **Return due to strategic repositioning and market trends:** This part is attributed to improvements in growth opportunities or favorable market trends—both leading to increases in the exit valuation (i.e., EV/EBITDA valuation multiples).

- **Return due to the use of leverage:** This part is generated as a result of using leverage when making the investment.

- **Other return components:** This part is attributable to other drivers, such as currency movements, shareholding restructurings, or industry-wide changes.

The goal of the IRR decomposition is to identify whether the IRR is driven by the GP's active management and contributions, or by uncontrollable factors.

The J-curve effect

Importantly, as noted, a definitive evaluation of an individual private equity fund can only be made once the fund is liquidated. During the early years of a fund, the value of the (interim) IRRs tends to be zero or negative for two reasons:

- **Management fees** and **start-up costs** of a limited fund partnership are usually financed out of the initial drawdowns, meaning that part of the sums drawn down during the first years do not create net book value for the limited partnership.

- **Conservative valuation guidelines** suggested by industry bodies suggest that investments are valued at acquisition cost at the very beginning. Upward adjustments are only made when the portfolio company has substantially increased in value. If early investments do not perform well, they might be immediately written off. Since these losses usually impact fund performance earlier than successful realizations, interim valuations of young funds tend to be lower.

In the final years of the fund, higher valuations of the portfolio businesses are confirmed by the partial or complete sale of the fund's investments, resulting in cash distributions to investors which offset their initial investment. As a result, interim IRRs turn positive (i.e., the private equity fund "breaks even"). This pattern generates the so-called *J-curve* (see Exhibit 1).

The J-curve is generated by plotting the interim IRRs. The first observation represents the interim IRR of the fund for the first year of its life, the second represents the interim IRR of the fund for the first two years of its life, the third represents the interim IRR for the first three years, and so on. Interim returns are typically negative in the early years (the "investment phase"), break even in the middle years (the "maturity phase"), and become positive in later years (the "harvesting phase"). The explanation for this curve is that, in the early years, investors mainly contribute capital to the fund. This capital is often not realized until the second half of the 10-to-12-year life cycle of the fund. After the first five years, assuming returns materialize, fund managers usually begin exiting early investments and making distributions.

Exhibit 1: The J-curve of a private equity fund

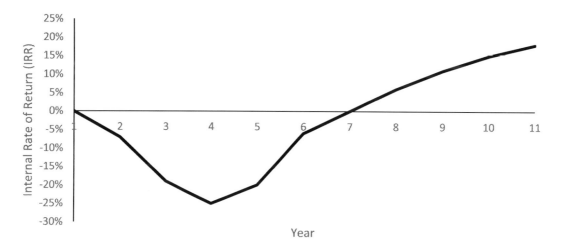

The plot in Exhibit 1 does not indicate that the fund returned -25% in year 3. Rather, it shows that if we map all the cash flows from the beginning of the fund to the end of year 3, an IRR of -25% can be calculated. Similarly, it is not saying that the fund's performance for year 6 was flat; it is saying that from the beginning of the fund to the end of year 6, positive cash flows exactly match negative cash flows, so that the IRR of the first six years is zero.

The J-curve in Exhibit 1 does not represent the J-curve of any real fund, but is a broad generalization of what can be expected. The only difference between this example and any real fund will be in the shape of the curve, which is driven by factors such as the level of capital calls, willingness of the manager to write off bad investments, overall success of the fund, or health of the economy (which is reflected in the valuation of the fund's investments). For example, buyout funds tend to pay back their capital more quickly than venture funds. Yet, even this generalization is enough to show that it is meaningless to look at the performance of a private equity fund in its early years.

Some LPs view the J-curve effect as an annoyance, as they must report negative IRRs to their stakeholders shortly after investing in a private equity fund. Thus, instead of calling capital from LPs to make investments in the first two years, some GPs fund these investments with capital from *subscription lines* (i.e., debt at the fund level).[5] This borrowing, often provided by banks at very attractive rates, is secured not by the fund's assets, but by the unused capital commitments of the LPs. The use of subscription lines delays capital calls and shortens the J-curve, enhancing the IRR early in a fund's life.[6] This arrangement seems to carry advantages for both sides:

- GPs benefit by enhancing the IRR of the fund, which is usually the main focus of investors in the fundraising market, and by lowering a hurdle that must be cleared before they get access to carried interest. IRRs increase because LPs' capital is drawn down later. Subscription lines also give GPs quick access to funding, which allows them to avoid missing out on attractive investments.

[5] The subscription lines do not allow the funds to invest more than their committed capital; in this way, they differ from fund-level debt, which allows more investments than the committed capital.

[6] It should be noted that because subscription lines bear interest rates that lead to additional cash outflows from the fund, the money multiple decreases relative to a situation where subscription lines are not used.

- LPs benefit because they can smooth cash flows and limit the administrative burden of responding to multiple capital calls. LPs also benefit by potentially being able to use the undrawn capital to make investments over the maturity of the subscription lines; the returns on these investments add to their overall profits.

The J-curve effect is different for secondary private equity funds. Secondary funds tend to smooth the J-curve effect because of the rapid deployment and return of capital. In contrast to a primary LP who commits to funds, an LP in a secondaries fund acquires an existing interest in a private equity investment from the original investor who is looking for an exit prior to the fund's termination. These secondary interests may either be partially drawn down or completely funded. The LP acquires the interest at a negotiated price and usually assumes any outstanding undrawn commitments of the seller. As a result, LPs in secondary funds acquire existing private equity investments with immediate NAVs which provide distributions to investors much earlier; this shortens or even removes the J-curve effect. In this way, secondary funds allow investors to bypass the time-intensive investment selection process, early investment write-offs, and early value creation periods. In short, their capital is put to work in a shorter time frame.

Computation of IRRs for a set of private equity funds

LPs often need to benchmark the performance of a private equity fund. Little insight is gained by comparing funds at different points in their life cycle, as IRRs would naturally be expected to differ significantly. Accordingly, funds are frequently compared against other funds which launched in the same year, giving rise to the concept of "vintage year." The assumption is that funds with the same vintage year should have experienced similar economic environments, making comparisons among them more meaningful. Therefore, the computation of the aggregate IRR of a benchmark group of funds is usually appropriate only when the funds in the group have (1) similar investment strategies and (2) the same vintage year. The aggregate performance of the funds that were raised in the same year typically reflects that vintage year's return.

There are several ways of aggregating the return of a group of private equity funds that meet the two above criteria:

- Calculate an **average IRR** across all funds in the group. Yet, this method can be problematic since it attaches an equal weight to all funds irrespective of their size (i.e., the average IRR can be skewed by large returns on relatively small investments).

- Calculate a **capital-weighted IRR** to reflect size differences between the funds. The capital weighted IRR weights each IRR by the capital committed to each fund. However, this approach does not take into account the different time periods that the capital has been under management.

- Calculate a **pooled IRR**. Monthly cash flows from all funds in the group can be pooled, and then the IRR is calculated based on the net cash flows of this "mega" fund. The metric avoids the downsides of the first two solutions. While the pooled return may be appealing theoretically, in practice there is no investable pooled index that represents the average return of a set of private equity funds.

- Calculate a **duration-weighted IRR**. The IRRs are weighted by the duration of each fund in the group.[7] The first step is to calculate the duration of a zero-coupon bond with the same IRR and the same multiple as that private equity fund based on the latest date for which the performance is available.

[7] This approach assumes that an investor would have invested the same amount in each fund in the group.

This calculation basically involves solving for duration in the equation (1+IRR)^(Duration)=Multiple. A duration-weighted IRR is often lower than the simple average IRR because lower-return funds tend to have longer durations.

Following the cash flow pooling approach, many private equity firms that are raising money report the performance of all their past funds by pooling them. The arbitrary grouping of funds to compute a pooled IRR can bias performance dramatically, especially when firms have had some high-performing investments in their early days. By grouping all funds together, the reinvestment assumption of the IRR (i.e., that future payouts can be reinvested and earn the same return as past payouts) will kick in, and effectively hide bad recent investments from potential investors.

Modified IRRs

Investors can overcome issues related to the reinvestment assumption of the IRR by using a modified IRR (MIRR). To compute an MIRR, one can assume that the capital committed to a private equity fund is put into a "savings account" that earns the hurdle rate (usually 8% per year). The capital called by the fund to make investments is taken out of this account (and starts earning the IRR of the fund), and the capital distributed by the fund goes back to the savings account to continue to earn 8% until the end of the fund's life or until the fund is liquidated. When the fund is liquidated, the MIRR is computed by extracting it from the following equation:

$$Capital\ Commited\ to\ the\ Fund = \frac{Balance\ in\ Savings\ Account\ at\ Liquidation}{1 + MIRR^T}$$

where T is the number of years from the vintage year to the year of liquidation. This formula basically boils down to calculating an NPV but gives a per annum return number.

The range of returns obtained for a fund is much more narrow when a measure like MIRR is used because it is closer to the *actual effective rate of return* achieved by investors. Relative to the IRR, an MIRR better captures the extent to which (1) the committed capital has been fully invested and (2) the committed capital remained invested over a longer period. A high IRR can reflect a high return earned on a small amount of capital for a short period of time, which does not really help investors make a good return on their overall allocation to the private equity fund. However, despite the advantages of using MIRR, many practitioners resist using it because it requires that the reinvestment rate be identified.

A worked example below compares the performance of a potential private equity fund on an IRR and MIRR basis under two scenarios (see Exhibit 2). In the first scenario, the fund distributes an additional $100 from an early exit to investors in year 3. In the second scenario, the fund distributes only $10 in year 3 and then holds the investment until year 7, earning a return on the investment of 20% per annum (i.e., $100 goes up in value to $207.36 by the end of year 7). Under the first scenario, the IRR is 26.14%, while in the second scenario the IRR drops to 23.94% because the cash flows are distributed later to investors. For the MIRR computation, we assume a reinvestment and financing rate of 8%, in line with the hurdle rates of most funds. In the first scenario the MIRR is only 17.29%, while in the second it goes up to 20.91%. Thus, most investors would prefer the second scenario (i.e., that the manager keep the $100 and earn a return of 20% on it from years 3 to 7). The MIRR is closer to investors' effective rate of return.

The MIRR provides many of the same advantages as the IRR. It allows investors to compare funds of different sizes and with irregular cash flows, and takes into account the time value of money. At the same time, it avoids two major shortcomings of the IRR:

- The MIRR does not assume that the fund's returns from investments can be reinvested at the same rate of return. Rather, the methodology uses an assumed reinvestment rate, which is usually the hurdle rate of the fund; this is significantly lower than the return of the investment.

- Its computation is not affected by the presence of alternating positive and negative cash flows, which lead to a failure of the IRR algorithm to find a solution or obtain multiple solutions. The MIRR approach always generates only one solution as the computation involves only two cash flows: a negative cash flow at the beginning (the capital committed to the fund) and a positive cash flow at the end (the capital accumulated in the "savings" account).

Exhibit 2: IRRs versus MIRRs

| | Case 1: | | | Case 2: | | |
| | Distribution of capital in year 3 | | | Distribution of capital in year 7 | | |
Year	Cash Flows	Investment Returns (8% reinvestment rate)	Cumulative Returns	Cash Flows	Investment Returns (8% reinvestment rate)	Cumulative Returns
0	-80	0.00	(80.00)	-80	0.00	(80.00)
1	-20	-6.40	(106.40)	-20	-6.40	(106.40)
2	0	-8.51	(114.91)	0	-8.51	(114.91)
3	110	-9.19	(14.10)	10	-9.19	(114.10)
4	50	-1.13	34.77	50	-9.13	(73.23)
5	30	2.78	67.55	30	-5.86	(49.09)
6	40	5.40	112.95	40	-3.93	(13.02)
7	10	9.04	131.99	217.36	-1.04	203.30
IRR	26.14%			23.94%		
MIRR	17.29%			20.91%		

RELATIVE PERFORMANCE MEASURES

The IRR and money multiples are absolute measures of performance and make no attempt to account for the opportunity cost of private equity investments. However, investors must be able to assess whether private equity funds meet specific return/risk targets. This assessment necessarily involves benchmarking the performance of the fund to an investable alternative opportunity. It is difficult to construct a replicable investable index given (1) a lack of a readily available universe of transactions in private markets, (2) a long private equity investment horizon whereby success is measured over many years, (3) unpredictable cash flow timing, and (4) a significant negative performance early in the life of a private equity fund due to the J-curve effect.

The purpose of this section is to outline the key considerations when selecting a benchmark, and how to construct a relative performance measure using a benchmark.

How to pick a benchmark?

Since relative performance measures require a benchmark, first one must understand how to pick benchmark rates of return. To be valid, a benchmark needs to have certain important characteristics (e.g., Bailey et al., 1990):

- **Certainty:** The investor should be certain about the names and weights of all securities in the benchmark portfolio.

- **Investability:** The investor should be able to invest in the benchmark by adopting a totally passive approach.

- **Measurability:** The investor should be able to calculate returns to the benchmark reasonably frequently.

- **Appropriateness:** The chosen benchmark should include securities whose payoffs are similar to those of the private equity fund being assessed.

- **Acceptability:** All investors in the private equity market must have current knowledge of the benchmark.

In light of the above criteria, investors struggle to find appropriate benchmarks when attempting to measure and assess the performance of private equity funds. Generally, they use two sets of benchmarks—neither of which is perfect:

- **Private equity fund peer groups:** Investors may use an average (or median or first-quartile) return of a group of similar private equity funds. This peer group generally includes private equity funds with similar investment strategies, raised in the same geographical location and during the same vintage year as the private equity fund assessed.

- **Public market equivalents:** Investors may compare private equity returns with some index of public equities. The performance of public equity is a natural benchmark given that investments in private equity funds are often funded out of public equities, and are expected to achieve an excess return over public equities.

Benchmarking the performance of private equity funds is particularly important when investors decide to invest in a new fund. Typically, an investor will start by analyzing the historical performance of past funds managed by the manager raising the new fund. This past performance is compared with some established peer group indices published by data providers and/or national industry associations. Potential peer groups can be created across a host of different investment styles (e.g., buyouts, venture capital, distressed, and secondaries) as well as various geographies, allowing comparisons based on common return drivers.

A judgment is then made depending on whether or how often the manager's prior funds fall within the *first-* or *second-best performance quartiles* according to these benchmark statistics. Such a comparison is valuable, as it allows assessment of the performance of the GP's prior funds relative to the population of all funds of the same stage and geographic focus that were raised in the same vintage years. Nevertheless, one must accept the fact that the peer group benchmark is not investable, as investors will not have access to all managers that eventually make up the peer group. Further, a peer group benchmarking is affected by gaps in data, self-reporting (valuation methodologies between managers may not be consistent), and survivorship bias (only the successful managers make it into the datasets).

With respect to the second benchmark, the approach used in most industry statistics is to compare the long-term IRR of private equity investments with the annualized long-term passive ("buy-and-hold") returns from public market indices. However, this approach ignores critical factors, such as the irregularly timed cash flows of private equity fund investments, and the differences in operating and leveraging risk between private equity fund investments and "the market" as captured by these indices. These issues confound attempts to compute standard time-weighted returns typical of publicly traded assets for comparison. The IRR, a cash-flow-weighted return rate, cannot be directly compared with time-weighted public benchmarks. More importantly, since IRR does not measure the opportunity cost of capital, it ignores the benchmarking objective. Given these difficulties, we provide a more detailed discussion of methodologies that use public market benchmarks in the following section.

The public market equivalent

The basic idea behind the comparison of private equity fund investments and public market investments is straightforward: it simply answers the question, "How much performance would a similar investment in the public markets have generated?" The discussion becomes tricky, however, when it comes to the exact definition of "similar" investments. The investments of the "mimicking" public market portfolio need to match the private equity investments in terms of cash flow timing and risk adjustments.

- **Cash flow timing:** The standard approach to the construction of a mimicking portfolio is to calculate the returns to a broad public market index, such as the S&P 500 or the MSCI Europe, such that the pattern of purchases and sales of the index mimic exactly the irregular timing of the private equity fund's cash flows related to investments and distributions. Importantly, the industry convention generally dictates the use of indices with reinvested dividend income to provide the most "like-to-like" comparisons.

- **Risk adjustments:** Comparisons to wide public market indices explicitly assume that the risk pattern of private equity investments is identical to that of the chosen index. Yet, companies that receive venture capital financing are typically much smaller and younger, while those receiving buyout funding typically have much higher financial leverage than the average company in a broad stock market index; both aspects influence the risk pattern substantially. One possible way to correct for the differences in risk between private equity investments and public market investments is to match operating betas and financial leverage between the two. This approach is based on the methodology implemented by Groh and Gottschalg (2009).[8] The exact determination of the risk-adjusted mimicking portfolio requires the following information for each transaction of the private equity fund:

- a peer group of publicly traded companies with the same operating risk;

- the equity betas for each of these "public peers";

- unlevering these beta factors to derive their operating or unlevered betas;

- a market-weighted average of these operating betas for every peer group; and

- relevering of these betas on the level of the private equity fund's investments at closing and exit. The unlevering and relevering procedures require the specification of the risk borne by lenders, the risk of tax shields that the equity investor can benefit from, and an applicable corporate tax rate.

An equal amount of equity for every private investment transaction of the fund is invested in a representative market portfolio, and is levered up with borrowed funds to the same beta factor as the private equity investments at closing. The risk of the public market index investment is then adjusted every year, tracking the risk of the private equity investment in the fund. Therefore, every position is liquidated annually, interest is paid, debt is redeemed, and the residual equity is levered up again with borrowed funds (respectively, funds are lent) to the prevailing beta risk of the private equity investment. This procedure is repeated until the exit date.

The public market equivalent (PME) methodology

The basic premise of the PME approach, originally proposed by Long and Nickels (1995), is to translate time-weighted returns to money-weighted returns, and thus allow a like-to-like comparison of the performance of private equity funds and that of public equity markets. The methodology calculates hypothetical cash returns by buying and selling a public equity index to mirror the cash flows of the private equity investment. It also provides additional insights into the different components of private equity returns. Moreover, this approach avoids the use of betas, which can be unreliable due to data limitations.

The PME methodology can be implemented in four distinct stages:

Stage 1: Compute the IRR of the private equity fund based on the net-of-fees cash inflows and outflows. The residual values of unrealized investments (i.e., the NAVs) can be considered as accurately reflecting the NPV of these investments, and can therefore be treated as a final cash inflow in the IRR calculation. Alternatively, these residual values can be set to zero, especially if the fund is close to the end of its life (this is the most conservative approach). The IRR measure of the fund's net cash flows will be compared with the return on the public benchmark.

Stage 2: Replicate the approach used in standard industry statistics and calculate the compounded annualized passive (buy-and-hold) returns from a public market index over the period from the first cash flow to the last cash flow of the fund. The IRR that results from this computation is the return that could be obtained by an

[8] Ljungqvist and Richardson (2003) and Phalippou and Zollo (2005) consider operating betas in their analysis of private equity investments, while Groh and Gottschalg (2009) benchmark the fully risk-adjusted performance of U.S. buyouts by correcting for differences in operating risk and financial leverage.

investor who makes investments in the amount of the capital committed to the private equity fund at the day of the fund's first cash flow, and liquidates this position at the day of the fund's final NAV.

Stage 3: Consider the particular timing of the cash flows and the operating risk of the private equity funds to compute an industry-matched (unleveraged) PME return. The observed annual net cash flows from the private equity fund can be imposed on a public market index by purchasing the index to represent negative net cash flows and selling the index to represent positive net cash flows (A capital call triggers the buying of the index, while cash distributions trigger the selling of the index.) Since the aim is to capture the operating risk of the underlying investments, the investment should not be in the overall market index but in industry indices that reflect the industry of an individual investment made by the private equity fund as well as the size of that investment (i.e., ideally, industry-specific and size-matched indices).[9] This industry mix should change from one year to another to track any industry changes that occur at the fund level.

To calculate the industry-matched (unleveraged) PME return, the portfolio holdings in sector indices are constructed according to the industry mix at the fund level. The final value of the PME portfolio created is calculated based on the market value of the portfolio on the last day of the fund (i.e., the day on which the NAV of the fund is available, given its financial statements). This value can be thought of as being the additional final cash flow representing the liquidation value of the final public equity market portfolio. The IRR of the industry-matched (unleveraged) PME is calculated by using both the mimicking annual net cash flows and the final cash flow:

- If the final value of the industry-matched (unleveraged) PME portfolio is positive, it implies that the public market has produced a greater return than the private equity funds whose cash flows were superimposed on the public market.

- If the final value of the industry-matched (unleveraged) PME portfolio is negative, it implies that the public market has produced a smaller return than private equity.

The IRR that results from this computation is the return that could be obtained by an investor who makes investments in industry-matched bundles of public securities and exits these securities by mimicking exactly the timing of the private equity investments and exits.

Stage 4 (for buyout funds only): Estimate the performance of the buyout fund had it not been levered up but had the typical degree of leverage of publicly traded firms at the time. This step enables differentiation between the portions of buyout returns attributable to fundamental performance, on the one hand, and the effect of higher leverage, on the other. Assess the difference between the average level of leverage of the portfolio of the buyout fund and the level of leverage of industry-matched public market investments for each year. Then construct an investment vehicle that replicates the level of leverage of industry-matched public market investments for the buyout fund. Finally, compute the IRR of the cash flows that investors in such a vehicle would have achieved.

This four-step approach decomposes the buyout fund's returns into four elements: (a) the portion driven by returns on the broad stock market (the IRR of the vehicle at stage 2); (b) the portion driven by the performance differential between the broad stock market and returns of the industry sectors in which the

---

[9] The indices chosen should be total return indices where dividends are reinvested, as this is the basis on which private equity investments operate.

fund invests after taking into account the timing of these investments (difference between the IRR computed at stage 3 and the IRR computed at stage 2); (c) the effect of buyout-typical leverage on the buyout funds' returns (difference between the IRR at stage 1 and the IRR of the vehicle at stage 4); and (d) the residual intrinsic value generation of the buyout fund (i.e., the private equity alpha (difference between the IRR at stage 4 and the IRR at stage 3)).

Other PME approaches

Kaplan and Schoar (2005) propose a PME measure defined as the ratio of the sum of the fund's discounted distributions to the sum of discounted capital calls. This approach uses the realized total return on the S&P 500 (or it can be any other market index) from the fund's inception (or any arbitrary reference date) to the date of the cash flow as the discount rate. Specifically, the PME equals the NPV of the fund's cash flows scaled by the present value of capital calls, where a realized market index return is used as the discount rate in the computation:

$$\text{PME} = \sum_{t=0}^{T} \frac{D_t}{\prod_{\tau=0}^{t}(1+r_\tau)} \bigg/ \sum_{t=0}^{T} \frac{C_t}{\prod_{\tau=0}^{t}(1+r_\tau)}.$$

In this expression, D_t and C_t are, respectively, distributions and calls occurring at time t, and r_τ is the (time-varying) realized return on the S&P 500 (or any other appropriate index).[10] In terms of interpretation, a PME of 1.30, for instance, implies that at the end of the private equity fund's life, investors ended up with 30% more than they would have if they had invested in the public markets (net of fees).

One can view the PME ratio as reflecting the funding surplus/gap associated with a zero-cost position in private equity formed by shorting a public index to meet capital commitments and then using the subsequent distributions to close out the short positions when the distributions occur. This approach is consistent with industry practice: many pension fund managers meet capital calls in their private equity portfolios by selling positions in liquid public equity indices.

Sørensen and Jagannathan (2013) as well as Korteweg and Nagel (2016) show that if investors have log utility, PME embeds all necessary adjustments for the public equity market risk of the fund. However, even in this case, PME will not account for risks unspanned by public equities (such as the liquidity risk of private equity commitments), nor will it account for public equity risks due to factors unspanned by the market portfolio (such as the Fama-French factors).

Tailored PMEs can be computed the same way as the standard PME but with alternative benchmark indices to help capture non-market factors in public equity returns. Robinson and Sensoy (2016) use the NASDAQ 2000 index for venture capital funds and the Fama-French size tercile indices for buyout funds, according to whether the fund is self-described as a small-cap, mid-cap, or large-cap buyout fund.

A potentially better PME was developed by Capital Dynamics, a fund of funds, to address the problem of short exposure that can be present in the PME calculation.[11] *PME+* does this by fixing the closing NAV of

---

[10] Note that many large LPs in the United States use alternative indices instead of the S&P 500, such as S&P 1500, Russell 3000, or MSCI All Country World Investable Market.

[11] If the private equity investment significantly outperforms the market, it is possible under a standard PME metric that the hypothetical market vehicle will have to sell more shares than it has available to match a private equity distribution to investors. As a result, the market vehicle goes short on the index.

the benchmarking vehicle investing in the public market index to be the same as the closing NAV of the private equity fund. Only total return indices can be used, as measures that ignore dividends render the index invalid and can result in distortions. Essentially, distributions out of the public market index are scaled by a fixed factor until the final valuation of the public market index is equivalent to the private equity NAV. As a result, the private equity fund and the public market fund have the same capital calls and the same final NAV, but different distributions. By selling a fixed proportion of the corresponding private equity cash flows instead of an amount equal to private equity cash distributions, PME+ ensures a positive end balance, preserving the overall cash flow pattern. While PME accumulates the overperformance or underperformance of the public market investment in the final NAV, PME+ spreads it over time across all distributions. Yet, this approach does not guarantee that the exposure to the public market remains positive over the entire investment period.

Cambridge Associates has proposed another PME measure called the mPME which is similar to the PME+ metric discussed earlier. The mPME uses a time-dependent scaling factor instead of using a fixed factor. This scaling factor is a function of the interim IRRs.

EVIDENCE ON THE PERFORMANCE OF PRIVATE EQUITY FUNDS

Most statistics provided by industry associations report superior returns for private equity investments depending on the assumptions made. However, academic evidence regarding the extent to which private equity funds outperform public market replication strategies (such as the one discussed in the prior section) is mixed, for several reasons.

- First, more recent funds include a high proportion of unrealized deals. The final performance of these funds can deviate considerably from that reported when many of the investments are unrealized. Restricting benchmarking exercises only to substantially realized funds circumvents the issue but reduces the sample size considerably, limiting the generalizability of the results.

- Second, consecutive funds by the same GP may contain the same portfolio companies because consecutive funds that are both in their investment phase often have the right (or even the obligation) to invest pari-passu in the same deals.

- Third, although benchmarking performance against funds of the same vintage year is conventional, this approach has various drawbacks. GPs can define a vintage year with a degree of leeway according to the first or final closing of a fund or the year the first company is acquired. One can avoid this issue entirely if the analysis is performed at the deal level (rather than the fund level) as the date of each investment is known.

- Other challenges in using fund-level data to study performance persistence include underlying heterogeneity regarding fund investment strategies, geographies, sectors, or currencies. For example, investment returns may vary substantially between sectors or geographies so that a disproportionate exposure to above- or below-average geographies or sectors could distort the results.

On the one hand, Harris et al (2014) find that average U.S. buyout fund returns have exceeded those of public markets for most vintage years since 1984.[12] By employing the PME method of Kaplan and Schoar (2005), they show that outperformance versus the S&P 500 averages 20% to 27% over the life of the fund,

[12] Higson and Stucke (2013) and Robinson and Sensoy (2013) provide similar inferences.

and more than 3% per year. The buyout fund outperformance remains similar in magnitude when they use other benchmarks (NASDAQ, the small-cap Russell 2000, etc.). These results are consistent with Ljungqvist and Richardson (2003), who evaluate the private equity funds of one large U.S.-based investor from 1981 to 2001 and find that private equity investments of closed funds outperformed the S&P 500 by more than 5%.

On the other hand, Kaplan and Schoar (2005) study the returns to private equity and venture capital funds and observe that private equity fund investors earn slightly less than the S&P 500 index net of fees (they also find that experienced funds and U.S.-based funds offer significantly higher performance). Phalippou and Gottschalg (2008) note that private equity funds underperform the S&P 500 by 3–6% per year net of fees, and show that few adjustments contribute to the discrepancy relative to other studies. First, they show that the estimated performance of private equity funds depends heavily on the valuation of non-exited investments at the end of the sample period. They argue that it is more reasonable to write off non-exited investments when the fund is close to the end of its life, or is beyond 10 years. Second, Phalippou and Gottschalg (2008) claim that academic studies investigating the performance of private equity funds might be subject to selection biases; namely, some of these studies use funds that are larger, more U.S.-focused, and more experienced than others. These characteristics are all found to be positively related to performance. Third, the authors observe that prior papers do not capture the significant variance in the funds' returns. Aggregating IRRs from multiple funds can overstate the historic performance. Phalippou and Gottschalg (2008) find that both the "size-weighted average IRRs" and "pooled IRRs" overstate performance relative to the more accurate method of weighting each fund's IRR by the product of the present value of its investments and its duration. The magnitude of this overstatement is about 3% per annum.

Even without this particular study, there is enough evidence to show that, historically, private equity fund managers have created substantial value: their average gross of fees performance usually exceeds public market indices substantially. However, the fee structure of private equity funds is such that the average fund manager may collect far greater fees than whatever value is created. Thus, the investor in the average private equity fund may be left with returns that are below those of a broad public market index fund. To a certain extent, returns have been driven by capital availability over time: for both venture and buyout funds, returns have been greatest during periods when relatively small amounts of capital were available. Conversely, there is evidence that periods of large capital availability depress future returns. It must be noted that the difference in fund performance measured by the IRR between funds in the 25th and 75th percentiles can be very large. This heterogeneity greatly underscores the importance of identifying top-performing funds, and could possibly explain why investors continue to invest in private equity funds.

Another aspect of private equity fund performance that has garnered increasing attention is its persistence. For a sample including venture capital and buyout funds with vintage years up to the late 1990s, Kaplan and Schoar (2005) find noticeable top-tercile persistence. Phalippou (2010) confirms this pattern and finds a strong relation between the final performance of two subsequent funds by the same manager. However, Braun, Jenkinson, and Stoff (2017) document a much smaller performance persistence for a much larger sample of buyout funds, which includes both early and more recent funds. Their deal-level analyses find that performance persistence has largely disappeared in recent years, consistent with the private equity sector maturing, and with financial engineering and valuation techniques becoming commoditized. Braun, Jenkinson, and Stoff (2017) also sort deals into performance quartiles for each year, and find significant evidence of top quartile performance persistence in low-competition states, but much less so when competition for deals is high. When running a similar analysis for the bottom quartile of deals, they find that managers that do bad deals tend to repeat the behavior, irrespective of the level of competition.

Interestingly, Harris et al (2013) use fund-level data and observe continued performance persistence for the top venture capital funds (but not for buyout funds). On the buyout side, they argue that the lack of persistence is due to the fact that most deals in United States or Europe are auctioned by investment banks and other intermediaries, debt financing is highly competitive, deal structures vary little, and vendors focus on the price paid. Consistent with these findings, Sensoy, Wang, and Weisbach (2014) also find that performance persistence of LPs has disappeared in recent years. Their findings suggest that LPs' established relations with successful GPs that were valuable when the market was developing are now much less valuable, and no longer a source of LP outperformance.

CONCLUSION

Private equity continues to be a rapidly growing asset class as global investors seek new ways to diversify against market volatility and enhance portfolio performance. As with all investments, questions regarding past performance arise when deciding to add private equity within the overall asset allocation of a portfolio, or when deciding to invest in a particular private equity fund manager. Therefore, private equity performance measures serve a crucial purpose by providing quantifiable benchmarks and comparative data. Investors look at different metrics of performance, depending on their individual needs: some are looking for spread above the public markets while others aim to maximize their absolute returns. Unfortunately, both private equity managers and their investors often use diverse (and sometimes inconsistent) approaches when calculating the performance of private equity funds, increasing the ambiguity surrounding private equity performance measurement.

This chapter clarifies some of these ambiguities by introducing the most commonly used metrics and assessing the advantages and limitations of each when evaluating private equity performance. The most important challenge going forward is to refine our collective understanding of what works and what does not work in private equity. Only then can we ensure that the enormous potential of the private equity model to generate great returns and benefit the acquired companies is being fully realized. Giving up the illusion of disproportionately high private equity returns across the board may be the first step in the process.

Constant repetition of the (empirically unwarranted) claim that private equity offers great returns per se is dangerous for the industry. It attracts additional capital at times when fund sizes and deal sizes are at a record high. Most importantly, repeating this claim also attracts capital from less experienced and less sophisticated investors, who may end up backing the wrong GPs based on the belief that even a random fund selection process will lead to supposedly attractive average returns. In fact, these average returns are not necessarily attractive and, more problematic for the industry as a whole, as long as less skilled GPs continue to receive capital, average future returns are less likely to increase than they otherwise would be.

REFERENCES

Bailey, J., Richards, T., and Tierney, D. (1990) "Benchmark portfolios and the manager/plan sponsor relationship," in F. Fabozzi and D. Fabozzi (Eds.), Current Topics in Investment Management, Harper & Row, pp. 71–85.

Braun, R., T. Jenkinson, I. Stoff, (2017) "How persistent is private equity performance? Evidence from deal-level data" Journal of Financial Economics, 123 (2), pp. 273-291

Griffiths, G. (2016), "MaxMult:A New Performance Metric for Private Equity", Landmark Partners report.

Groh, A.P., and Gottschalg, O. (2009) "The opportunity cost of capital of U.S. buyouts," working paper.

Harris, Robert S., T. Jenkinson, and S. Kaplan. (2014) "Private equity performance: What do we know?." The Journal of Finance 69.5: 1851-1882.

Harris, R., Jenkinson, T., Kaplan, S., Stucke, R., 2013. Has persistence per- sisted in private equity? Evidence from buyout and venture capital funds. UAI Foundation and University of Virginia, Research Triangle Park, NC, and Charlottesville, VA Unpublished working paper .

Higson, C., and R. Stucke (2013). "The performance of private equity." SSRN

Kaplan, S.N., and A. Schoar (2005) "Private equity performance: Returns, persistence, and capital flows," Journal of Finance, 60, 1791–1823.

Lerner, J., Schoar, A., and W. Wongsunwai (2007) "Smart institutions, foolish choices: The limited partner performance puzzle," Journal of Finance, 62(2), 731–764.

Ljungqvist, A., and M. Richardson (2003) "The cash flow, return and risk characteristics of private equity," NBER Working Paper 9454.

Long, A.M. and Nickels, C.J. (1995), A Private Investment Benchmark.

Phalippou, L. (2009) "Beware of venturing into private equity," Journal of Economic Perspectives, 23(1), 147–166.

Phalippou, L., 2010. Venture capital funds: flow-performance relation- ship and performance persistence. Journal of Banking and Finance 34, 568–577 .

Phalippou, L., and Gottschalg, O. (2009) "The performance of private equity funds," Review of Financial Studies, 22(4), 1747–1776.

Phalippou, L., and Zollo, M. (2005) "Performance of private equity funds: Another puzzle?" working paper, University of Amsterdam.

Sensoy, B., Wang, Y., Weisbach, M. (2014). Limited partner performance and the maturing of the private equity industry. Journal of Financial Economics 112, 320–343 .

8 Fund Accounting, Governance, and Reporting

Honesty and transparency make you vulnerable. Be honest and transparent anyway.
Mother Teresa

INTRODUCTION

The maturation of the private equity industry has led to greater public accountability with regards to governance and reporting practices. This chapter focuses on the accounting and reporting of private equity funds. Given that private equity funds have a limited life, involve investments in non-listed companies at various stages of their development, and are generally illiquid, the ultimate financial returns on these investments are not known until the fund is liquidated. These unique characteristics of this asset class require specific accounting treatments and reporting standards. The reporting picture is further complicated by the fact that investors in the private equity asset class invest through individual funds, funds of funds, or directly into unquoted companies on a co-investment basis alongside individual funds.

In order for any performance-reporting requirements to be meaningful, the funds' returns must be calculated by using timely valuations for the underlying investments. Since it is difficult to objectively value and report private equity investments, a series of harmonized guidelines have been developed by various private equity associations, such as the International Limited Partners Association (ILPA), the British Venture Capital Association, the European Venture Capital Association (now renamed Invest Europe), and the U.S. Private Equity Industry Guidelines Group, and the International Private Equity and Venture Capital Valuation (IPEV) Guidelines. These guidelines establish a broad foundation for valuing and reporting private equity assets with the main goal of improving comparability between funds and fund managers. This foundation is built on the concept of "fair value," defined as the amount at which an asset could be acquired or sold at arm's length in a current transaction between willing and knowledgeable parties. While fair value estimates provided by fund managers do not assume an intention to sell at the date of valuation, they reflect the likely exchange price between two parties that make subjective judgments based on expectations about fund investments' current and future performance.

In addition to guidance from independent industry bodies, regulators in Europe and the United States have introduced further onerous reporting requirements. These regulations were designed to provide greater protection to those who invest in alternative investment funds (e.g., private equity funds). The Dodd-Frank

We acknowledge the significant input received from Anthony Cecil (partner at KPMG).

Act in the United States spawned a number of risk-related regulatory reporting requirements to the U.S. Securities and Exchange Commission, such as requirements to disclose the financial and risk profile of a fund, the extent of leverage incurred by portfolio companies, the use of bridge financing, and the funds' investments in financial institutions. In Europe, the Alternative Investment Fund Managers Directive (AIFMD) requires most private equity funds to meet certain minimum disclosures in terms of (1) the contents and frequency of fund reports, (2) total remuneration of private equity professionals and how this is split between fixed and variable components, (3) the overall risk profile of the fund, and (4) acquisition and disposal of shares in portfolio companies owned by the funds.

While reporting in accordance with industry standards and regulations can impose significant costs, particularly to smaller managers, the need for additional information by limited partners (LPs) can further increase these costs. LPs often have divergent information requirements that involve information being formatted in a different way, information being provided more frequently or at different times, information on portfolio companies beyond valuation movements, or information about events that affect the general partner (GP). Today, LPs take on substantial reputational risk by investing in private equity; as a result, they expect GPs to communicate problems quickly and transparently to help their investors stay ahead of any potential issues.

Beyond investors' information needs, the accounting and reporting of private equity funds is driven by key factors such as the investment strategy of the fund, the legal form of the fund (and its manager), and the limited partnership agreement (LPA) between LPs and GPs, which stipulates how money generated by the fund is distributed, the frequency of reporting, the accounting standards that should be implemented, and many other arrangements.

The use of fair values for private equity fund reports has resulted in an important shift of responsibilities from GPs to LPs. For an LP to use the valuation of a fund as reported by the GP, it must satisfy itself that the valuation is free from material error. In effect, the GP's reported number becomes the LP's number the moment that the LP includes it in its accounts. Thus, an LP must have processes in place to allow it to assess and challenge the fund's accounts where appropriate.

ACCOUNTING ISSUES

Most private equity funds prepare accounts for investors using International Financial Reporting Standards (IFRS) or the U.S.-based generally accepted accounting principles (GAAP). It has long been suggested that IFRS and U.S. GAAP may converge, but for the time being, many differences exist between these two main accounting standards with respect to several key issues that are faced by private equity funds (see Exhibit 1).[1] We discuss each of these issues in greater detail in the subsections of this chapter.

Exhibit 1: Main differences between IFRS and U.S. GAAP.

Accounting issue	IFRS	U.S. GAAP
Overall framework	Nothing fund specific	AICPA Audit and Accounting Guide: Investment Companies

---

[1] In February 2006 and November 2008, the IASB and FASB agreed on memorandums of understanding that identified short-term and long-term convergence projects and enabled companies that prepared financial statements under IFRS to ensure that their financial statements were accepted by U.S. regulators; PriceWaterhouseCoopers, Accounting for Private Equity Funds Presentation by Mike Byrne and Mary Bruen.

Presentation of financial statements	Driven by the requirements of IAS 1: • Income Statement (Other Comprehensive Income) • Balance Sheet (Statement of Financial Position) • Cash Flow Statement • Statement of Changes in Net Assets Attributable to Partners • Notes to the Financial Statements	Driven by the requirements of Chapter 7 of the Audit and Accounting Guide: • Statement of Assets and Liabilities • Schedule of Investments • Statement of Operations • Cash Flow Statement • Notes to the Financial Statements • Financial Highlights (may be included in the notes)
Consolidation— the fund	Requires consolidation of underlying investments where those structures are controlled.	Does not require consolidation of underlying investments. One exception to this general principle is an investment in an operating company that provides services to the investment company.
Consolidation— GP	Requires consolidation of the fund where the GP controls it unless criteria of investment entity under IFRS 10 is met.	Requires consolidation of the Fund where the GP • is the primary beneficiary of the fund under FIN 46(R); or • controls it under EITF 04-5.
Equity accounting	Requires associates to be recorded using equity accounting except where they have been designated as fair value through profit or loss.	Does not require equity accounting for underlying investments unless those entities are investment companies themselves.
Valuation of investments	Requires investments (designated as "fair value through profit or loss" or "fair value through other comprehensive income") to be stated at fair value.	Requires investments to be stated at fair value. FAS 157 requires, among other things, new disclosures around the inputs used to determine fair value.
Valuation of quoted securities	Requires quoted securities in active markets to be stated at bid price multiplied by the number of shares. Marketability discounts are generally not permitted.	Requires quoted securities in active markets to be stated at end-of-day market prices. Where a legal, contractual, or regulatory restriction exists then the market price should be adjusted for the effect of the restriction (requirement of new Fair Value Standard).
Treatment of partners' capital	Where the fund has a finite life, partners' capital is generally treated as debt under IAS 32.	Partners' capital is generally treated as equity unless there is an obligation to redeem the capital at a specific date at a specific amount.
Functional currency	IFRS and U.S. GAAP requirements are essentially the same: an entity's functional currency is defined as the currency of the primary economic environment in which the entity operates.	
Derecognition of financial assets	De-recognize financial assets based on risks and rewards first; control is secondary test.	Derecognize based on control. Requires legal isolation of assets.

In discussing accounting processes and proposed courses of action to change them in the sections below, we outline many widely used accounting principles. In many instances, the preparer of the accounts must use personal judgment about how to apply these principles. The first rule of accounting for any limited partnership is to read the LPA to thoroughly understand the contractual relationships between the partners.

Consolidation

Consolidation within the fund

Accounting standards have generally been formulated to fit the majority of business models encountered in a corporate environment. Shareholders in a conglomerate will benefit immensely from understanding the overall financial operations of the group as a whole, as well as the group's financial position. However, this is one clear area where the private equity business model is not suited to the developed accounting standards. Private equity entities commonly take controlling positions in underlying businesses to manage these new investments as they see fit.

In a conglomerate, investors can judge the management team and look for their investment return from all the entities that are controlled within the group. The dividends to the investors are paid from profits generated by the group and, indeed, the earnings of the group and the expected dividend stream are important metrics in establishing a price for the shares. In contrast, information on the consolidated operations is largely irrelevant to an investor in a private equity fund. The financial position of the fund is not assessed by adding together all of the individual underlying assets/liabilities, and the performance of the fund is not judged by adding together revenues, costs, and profits/losses of a collection of disparate businesses. Instead, funds are assessed by considering the value of the underlying businesses. Accounting standards generally agree with this assertion, so long as the fund only holds a small equity position—but if the fund owns sufficient equity to control a business, the accounts should reflect a consolidation of all businesses controlled, unless certain specific criteria are met.

For a private equity investor, the value of the investments in the fund (treated in the same way regardless of the size of the equity holding) is highly relevant information; a summation of assets and liabilities is not. This focus toward value also reflects the way that private equity managers run their businesses. Most importantly, portfolio companies in a fund do not have common arrangements regarding the management of cash flows, employees, or investments that are usually present in a group. In fact, usually there is no interaction between portfolio companies, especially if these companies are in very different industries.

These aspects of consolidation suggest that consolidated accounts do not provide relevant information to investors. As a result, fund reporting focuses on being able to provide information on the basis of the *fair value* of each portfolio company rather than consolidation. To understand how to arrive at this value, one must consider the accounting standards and other pieces of legislation that drive the requirement to consolidate.

IFRS 10 ("Consolidated Financial Statements") requires that the fund consolidates the entities it controls. "Control" is defined as power over the entity, exposure to variable returns generated by the entity, and ability to affect the entity's returns. In a situation where a single entity owns more than 50% of the equity in an underlying investment, it is hard to argue that these control conditions are not met. However, with careful fund structuring, it is possible that no single entity might "control" the underlying investment, thus removing the requirement to consolidate at the fund level. If a number of parallel limited partnerships—bound together by a co-investment agreement and ensuring that no single partnership is larger than all the others put together—jointly acquire a controlling interest, then no individual limited partnership can be deemed to control the investment, thereby avoiding consolidation of the investments. While IFRS 10 likely suggests that the fund vehicle needs to consolidate the investments, international accounting standard setters have been formulating guidance so that genuine investment vehicles, such as private equity funds, can avoid consolidation of investments and value them individually on a fair value basis instead.

Typically, the fund's investments are classified as "fair value through the profit and loss account" of the fund. While "fair value through other comprehensive income" may appear to be an accurate description of the fund business model, fund managers frequently use complex capital structures and special terms on realization. If the assets are designated as fair value through other comprehensive income, detailed considerations and possible separations of any embedded derivatives may be required.

U.S. GAAP anticipate the issues arising from consolidated accounts. Once standards have determined that a private equity entity is an "investment company," it may follow the American Institute of Certified Public Accountants (AICPA)'s Investment Company Accounting Rules. In essence, these rules remove the requirement to consolidate, and all investments may be included on the balance sheet of the fund at fair value. Any changes in the fair values reported on the balance sheet flow through the income statement of the fund. IFRS offer a similar approach that is now available for investment entities.

Consolidation within the manager

In a typical fund structure, the limited partnership is a subsidiary of the GP entity set up to run the fund, which is in turn a subsidiary of the private equity firm (i.e., the manager). This structure would suggest that, under IFRS, the manager is the ultimate controller of the limited partnership and, potentially, any controlled underlying portfolio companies. In the extreme situation, where that interest is negligible, the manager's accounts would consolidate the results and financial position of the GP as well as all the limited partnership and portfolio subsidiaries, with all profits and net assets arising from fund activities being included as a minority interest, unless investment entity accounting is applied. Using a set of accounts that were prepared on this basis to decipher the results of the financial operations arising from management activities and the financial position of the manager would be very difficult. Since consolidation issues do not exist under U.S. GAAP, we provide a more detailed discussion of these issues within the manager under IFRS.

When setting up the private equity fund, the fund manager usually sets up another separate entity (often called a GP) that manages the operations of the fund, which is structured as a limited partnership. The GP has the ability to govern the financial and operating policies of the fund, and thus obtain benefits. In the event that the GP's interest in the limited partnership is negligible and is only remunerated (in line with market rates) for management services, the inflows received are clearly from its management activities, and not from "controlling the policies for benefit." In this situation, one can reasonably conclude that the GP entity does not "control" the limited partnership and there is no need to consolidate.

LPs often require managers to invest in the fund. In this case, the GP is acting in a dual role, partly as manager and partly as owner. When considering whether the GP, acting in this dual role, is deriving benefit from its ownership or management activities, one must ascertain for which activity the "benefits" are being received over the expected life of the fund. This question is further complicated when the carried interest is also received by the manager, GP, employees, or partners. Many analysts argue that carried interest is a benefit of management (regardless of how it is structured for taxation purposes). Since carried interest is only available to the management team, it does not carry the full downside risk if the overall performance is negative, and is linked to the profits generated from the management activity.

The whole question of "for benefit" is highly judgmental and each situation must be carefully considered on its own facts. If accountants decide that the manager receives significant benefit from ownership interests, then they might expect that the limited partnership is consolidated by the manager as the owner of the GP. Conversely, if the majority of the inflows are anticipated from management activities, then it might be reasonably held that the GP, while controlling the limited partnership, does not do so for ownership benefits.

The LPA establishes the rights and responsibilities of the individual partners. LPs are excluded from management of the limited partnership since involvement in the same jeopardizes their limited liability protection. LPs can, however, retain rights of removal and appointment over the GP without damaging this status. If LPs reserve the right to remove the GP and appoint a successor—commonly referred to as "kick-out rights"—then it may appear that the GP's powers are restricted. Whether these kick-out rights are sufficient to maintain that the GP does not have control (i.e., "substantive kick-out rights") is a matter of judgment. Typically, to be substantive, these rights must be capable of being exercised; this consideration would include the number or percentage of the LPs that would need to vote for removal, whether specific grounds were required to initiate the process, the overall cost to the LPs by following this course of action, and anything else that might provide a barrier to the rights being exercised.

Where the LPA is structured to ensure that substantive kick-out rights exist, particularly in situations where there is a single LP with a significant interest, the right to eject the GP (and thereby control the limited partnership) may have inadvertently been placed in the hands of a single investor. Should this be the case, the requirement to consolidate the limited partnership has merely moved from the GP to one of the LPs.

Management fees or priority profit shares

In a limited partnership structure, the GP is commonly entitled to receive a priority share of profits in consideration for managing the limited partnership and for having unlimited liability. This share may be referred to as management fee, priority profit share (PPS), or GP's share, and it is usually around 2% of the committed capital or net cost of investments made.

The LPA is structured such that the GP is entitled to this amount, before any profits are allocated to the LPs. To ensure that the GP has sufficient resources to meet its management costs, in the event that there are insufficient profits to cover the PPS, an interest-free loan is made by the fund to the GP. This loan is not repayable. It may only be settled by the future allocation of profits. Therefore, the GP receives an annual amount, which is never repaid.

In substance, this loan is akin to a management fee and it should be recognized in a similar manner in the accounts of the fund. It is shown as a deduction from profits (or losses) in the fund's income statement. In early years, the fund is unlikely to generate profits, and it is important that the PPS is recognized in full in the income statement and allocated fully in the partners' accounts. The rationale for this treatment is that the substance of the transaction is an expense payment rather than a loan. The loan cannot be recognized in the balance sheet as an asset since it does not meet the definition of an asset. Even if it were recognized as an asset, it should be considered as impaired, since it is not repayable.

In the manager's accounts, the receipt is recognized as turnover on the basis that it is in relation to an annual contract and is not repayable.

Carried interest

Usually, fund managers set up a carried interest partner (CIP) (sometimes known as the *founder partner* or *special LP*) as an investor in the fund. Its purpose is to be a vehicle that aligns the interests of investors and managers, rewarding those managers with a share of realized profits in a tax-efficient manner. Carried interest schemes typically operate on the basis of realized profits, and not on the basis of portfolio valuations (as is common in other alternative asset classes). We discuss the structuring of private equity funds and the establishment of the CIP in a separate legal chapter.

Often, the CIP has an investment in the limited partnership capital, but no loan commitment. This capital commitment typically entitles the CIP to 20% of the realized profits generated by the fund (the timing and share of the profits to which the CIP is entitled are set out in the LPA). Some funds might have a different carry of 10% or 25%, depending on their investment strategy and investor interest in the fund. A target rate of return (the "hurdle rate") may also be set for the fund somewhere between 5% and 12%. Hurdle rates vary depending on the type of fund, anticipated market returns in that geography, and the overall carry arrangements.

When considering the accounting treatment of any carry scheme, the exact terms of the LPA must be reviewed in detail. There are three different types of schemes:

- **Deal by deal with no hurdle or clawback** (one end of the range). In this type of scheme, no return levels are required to be met and serviced to LPs prior to the CIP accessing a share of the profits, which prevents the CIP sharing any realized losses. This scheme is rarely seen in Europe since it is generally viewed as being too generous to the CIP at the expense of the investors.

- **Whole fund with hurdle** (the other end of the range). In this scheme, the CIP only shares in realized profits after the investors have received all of their original investment, plus a target rate of return. This scheme is arguably the most common one in the current market as it ensures that the CIP only benefits from its investment after the managers have fulfilled the fund objectives. This arrangement typically results in carry interest only being paid to the CIP about 6–10 years after the fund was raised.

- **Deal by deal with a whole fund calculation and clawback**. This scheme is essentially the same commercial term as "whole fund with hurdle," but it allows payments to be made and subject to reclaim by the fund. Payments may be made to the CIP when profits are realized, as long as (a) the fund remains on course to achieve its objectives and (b) the amounts can be recovered from the CIP in the event that this proves to be false. The obvious advantage of this scheme to the CIP is that payments may be received earlier in the life cycle of the fund.

Between the extremes, there are an infinite number of quirks and variations that may be introduced through the LPA negotiations. Whatever these quirks and variations, the accounting issues arising should all fall within the same principles as the three schemes set out in this section.

In the accounts of the fund

It is important to appreciate the distinction between profits allocated and distributions made when considering the treatment of carried interest in the accounts. Once the fund has been raised, there are two critical trigger points in its life cycle which significantly change the expectations of carry being paid:

- **Trigger Point A** is when the fair value of the fund's investments exceeds a value beyond which, if all the investments were sold at that value, carry would be due to the CIP.

- **Trigger Point B** is when the conditions are met such that carry is actually due to the CIP.

Crucially, when accounting for carry in the common limited partnership structure, carry can never be an expense of the fund. The carried interest mechanism is merely an allocation of profits between the various partners in the fund, which is a limited partnership.

The most common terms of the carried interest arrangement include that the CIP's entitlement to receive carry is only at the point of realization. After Trigger Point A is passed, a useful disclosure to make is a simple statement that discloses the amount that would be allocated to the CIP in the event that the investments were sold at their carrying value. The different types of schemes determine when profits are allocated to the CIP and distributions made to them:

- With a **deal-by-deal scheme**, since the CIP is entitled to a share of the profits at the point of realization, a share of each realized profit together with a transfer of historic fair value movements is allocated to the CIP. On realization, cash is distributed to the partners in accordance with the LPA. The cash will reduce the balance outstanding on the LPs' loan accounts and the income accounts of both the LPs and the CIP.

- Under a **whole fund with hurdle** scheme, proceeds from realization and other realized profits are distributed to the LPs as repayments of their loan capital and any profits allocated. All profits are allocated to the LPs (or the fair value reserve) until Trigger Point B, when the CIP is due to receive its share (commonly 20%) of all future distributions from the fund. This point is reflected in the accounts by transferring an amount equal to the CIP's share of all remaining net assets from the LPs' accounts to the CIP. Future profits are allocated in the profit-sharing ratio, and cash distributions follow the terms of the LPA. The terms of the LPA will determine when Trigger Point B is achieved; this may be when the LPs have received their loan capital back, in cash, from the fund together with the hurdle. If a fund draws more loan capital down from the investors after Trigger Point B (sometimes permitted under the terms of the LPA to provide additional funding to existing investments), the CIP is not entitled to any profits until that further loan and hurdle thereon are repaid. During this period—that is, after the trigger is met and undone and before Trigger Point B is re-achieved—the accounting is less clear-cut and subject to judgment. It may be held that the subsequent drawdown of the loan is of such a size that Trigger Point B will not be reached again, in which case the allocation to the CIP should be reversed. More commonly, it is anticipated that Trigger Point B will be achieved again in a reasonable period of time, and allocations to the CIP are merely ceased until that date.

- **Deal by deal with a whole fund calculation and clawback** represents an amalgam of the above accounting treatments. The terms of these types of agreements vary hugely, but a typical commercial agreement would be that the CIP partners may share in the profits arising on realizations, so long as the valuation of the investments in aggregate exceeds the amount of loans and hurdle outstanding. Any amount distributed is paid into an escrow account, under the control of the CIP, which is available to be clawed back by the limited partnership in the event that the fund does not ultimately meet its objectives (clawback). The CIP may withdraw funds from the escrow account subject to a separate set of rules and conditions. In these situations, calculating Trigger Point B can be very complex, depending on the LPA terms.

Once Point B is passed, the CIP may participate in the next realization, so long as it continues to be passed at that time. On realization of an investment, the appropriate share of the profit is allocated to the CIP and an amount is distributed to the escrow account. At this point, although the fund expects to achieve its objectives, the ultimate outcome remains uncertain. Accordingly, it is unlikely that there will be an allocation of unrealized profits to the CIP from the LPs within the partners' accounts.

So long as the fund continues on track, it is unlikely that the accounts of the limited partnership will reflect any balance held in the escrow account. Typically, the fund is excluded from the LP accounts because the CIP, subject to the escrow rules, has control over the funds. If the performance of the fund declines, the amounts distributed to the CIP may be accessed by the limited partnership to distribute to the LPs. The amount required to restore the LPs' position might then be recognized as a receivable amount in the limited partnership accounts. Whether the full amount of the receivable should be treated as recoverable will depend on the individual circumstances. If the balance resides in the escrow account, recovery is reasonably certain. Once amounts have been distributed to individual managers who participate in the CIP, recovery is likely to be more difficult.

In the accounts of the CIP

When preparing the accounts of the CIP, the main considerations are the recognition of income and the treatment of the investment in the fund. Carried interest vehicles are commonly limited partnerships, as they can preserve the tax nature of receipts from the fund. These have historically been non-qualifying limited partnerships; they may be managed by the GP. Since the potential recipients of the accounts are themselves closely involved in the fund's management, they may believe that they are sufficiently aware of the results and financial position, and do not need audited financial statements. Accordingly, the reporting requirements of the CIP are minimal. It would be extremely unusual for the managers to prescribe a requirement of accounts for the CIP through the LPA.

Carried interest should be recognized by the CIP when it is probable that future economic benefit will flow to the CIP. Under the terms of a typical LPA, this condition is met at the point of realization of an underlying asset in the fund. The contractual receipt of realized gains is relatively straightforward. However, complications arise in the interaction between the carrying value of the CIP's investment in the fund, the realization of gains, and any clawback provisions.

Although it may be suggested that the CIP's interest in the fund is a derivative of sorts, this investment by the CIP in the fund is best regarded as a highly geared investment. Under IAS 39, the investment in the fund is recognized at fair value. In considering the fair value of the CIP's investment in the fund, there is usually no market for that interest and the preparer has to estimate the fair value based on what a hypothetical third party might pay for that interest.

At the establishment of the limited partnership that will become the fund, following the commitments of LPs, the only asset of the limited partnership is the capital introduced. If there are no further assets or agreements, the cost of the capital introduced is likely to be the most reliable indicator of value on the date when it is introduced. Thereafter, the fair value estimate is subject to significant judgments and opinions.

There are no established rules for estimating the value of the CIP's interest in the fund. Ultimately, the fair value will be based on the expected timing and quantum of returns generated from that investment. The following points in the life of the fund might reasonably be expected to change an individual's views regarding the likelihood or quantum of those returns:

- The LPs making commitments to the limited partnership and the fund closing.

- The fund being fully invested.

- Trigger Point A, when carried interest would be paid if the investments were sold at their carrying value.

- Trigger Point B, when the CIP is entitled to a share of future realizations.

- Actual receipts of carried interest.

- Liquidation of the fund.

In the accounts of the manager

The CIP may be consolidated into the accounts of the manager under either GAAP or IFRS. The consideration of whether consolidation is appropriate is similar to that for consolidation of the fund (i.e., is the manager "controlling the CIP for benefit"?). If the carried interest receipts are entirely directed to the individual managers as LPs on the basis of their original personal investment with no carried interest being paid to the manager, it is likely that the CIP will not meet the requirements for consolidation. If the manager receives a significant element of the carried interest in its own right, or is able to distribute the payments among the individuals after the CIP's establishment, then it is likely that the manager would be held to be "controlling for benefit" and the CIP consolidated.

In practice, the situation is generally less clear than these extremes. The preparer of the accounts must consider all the terms by which the individuals invest, including vesting rights and the provisions regarding an individual's rights to the investment on leaving the organization. The more terms that exist putting rights into the hands of the manager over the individuals, the more likely it is that the CIP should be regarded as a vehicle of the manager and consolidated. If the CIP is consolidated, then the receipts by the CIP would be income in the manager's consolidated accounts, and the payments to the carry recipients would be treated as minority interests. When the manager does not consolidate the CIP or the fund, there will be no entries in the primary statements relating to the receipts and subsequent payments.

Partners' capital

In a typical limited partnership, there are two types of "capital." All the partners make an *equity capital* contribution to the CIP, with the LPs providing additional loan capital to the fund. The ratios of the equity capital contribution to the CIP are usually the same as the carried interest participation by the CIP, so for a 20% carry scheme, the LPs will receive four shares for each share received by the manager. The managers will normally only make a nominal contribution to the capital, unless required to make a contribution as a co-investment alongside the LPs. Therefore, the bulk of the "capital" for investment is provided in the form of subordinated loans, since this allows for the simplest legal processes in terms of drawdown and distribution.

The first question is whether the equity capital contribution should be regarded as equity or whether, being of a finite life and due to be repaid at the end of that life, it should be regarded as a liability. The principal feature of this capital contribution is that it entitles the holder to participate in the profits and net assets of the entity on a winding up. The winding-up date is largely predetermined by the LPA. The only feature that would suggest that this is a liability is that it will ultimately be repaid. A reading of the standards indicates that, where an equity instrument is redeemable at the end of the expected life of the vehicle, this factor alone would be insufficient to make the instrument a liability. Accordingly, the equity capital contribution is generally regarded as equity capital.

In a private equity limited partnership, the "loan capital" or "commitment" from the LPs has the following characteristics:

- It is drawn down on demand by the GP.

- It is redeemable when the GP deems it appropriate.

- It is not subject to any repayment schedule.

- It bears no rate of interest.

- It is unsecured.

- It is only repayable to the extent that funds are available to make the repayment.

- To the extent that it has not been redeemed at the conclusion of the limited partnership, it will be written off.

- It ranks below any external creditors.

To many, this commitment would appear to have few of the characteristics or risks associated with a loan, and would be more akin to an equity risk. However, although subordinated, these "loans" do not entitle the holder to participate in the residual net assets of the entity and the capital contribution of the partners ranks lower than these loans. Hence, these loans should properly be shown as a liability of the limited partnership.

FUND GOVERNANCE

In this section, we discuss governance guidelines provided by ILPA, the trade association for institutional limited partners. Founded in the early 1990s, ILPA is a non-profit organization with more than 515 members from pension funds, endowments, and insurance companies. These members collectively represent more than $2 trillion in investments in the private equity world. ILPA's goal is to facilitate greater communication and collaboration among these investors.

In 2009, ILPA released a set of documents known as the ILPA Private Equity Principles (hereafter referred to as the "Principles"). The most up to date version of this publication (Institutional Limited Partners Association, 2019) is used as a benchmark. The objective of the Principles was to provide a common set of guidelines that LPs can use as reference for negotiations with fund managers. The Principles were developed with the goal of improving the private equity industry for the long-term benefit of all of its participants. Since their release, the Principles have been adopted by many LPs in their day-to-day activities, and the response from both LPs and GPs has been very positive. Recently, ILPA sought feedback from LPs and GPs to improve upon the guidelines, and released a new set of Principles. While they retain the same tenor, the new Principles have increased clarity and practicality in the industry.

The ILPA Principles

The three fundamental ILPA Principles are (1) alignment of interest, (2) governance, and (3) transparency. These principles can be applied to virtually any successful private equity partnership, as they form the set of best practices that can be referenced by GPs and LPs during their discussions of partnership agreements and fund management practices. Note that these Principles are not steadfast rules, but are instead a reference set that can be used as benchmark.

Alignment of interest

While many different arrangements are employed by GPs and LPs, the best alignment between LP and GP interest is achieved when the primary source of wealth creation for GPs comes from returns resulting from a substantial equity commitment to the fund, and when GPs receive a percentage of profits *after* LPs' return requirements are met; in this way, the GP has "skin in the game" by having its own capital at risk. In contrast, alignment of LP and GP interest is very weak when GPs' wealth comes from excessive management fees, transaction fees, and other fees.

When it comes to the payment structure, the waterfall practice that entails "all contributions plus preferred return back to LPs first" is perhaps best, although deal-by-deal carry arrangements with escrow accounts and/or clawback mechanisms could also be used. Any of the above-mentioned elements can be combined (depending on the situation) to arrive at the best practices for a partnership. We list the best practices guidelines—including the ideal cash waterfall, management fees/expenses, and other fund terms—that facilitate a closer alignment of interests in Exhibit 2.

An optimal alignment of interest may be achieved through different combinations of the aforementioned best practices. Additionally, new approaches and practices may be identified by both GPs and LPs.

Exhibit 2: Best practices on the alignment of interest

	Carry/waterfall best practices

Waterfall structure	• A standard all-contributions-plus-preferred-return-back-first model must be recognized as a best practice.
	• For the deal-by-deal model, one could improve it by employing one or several of the following:
	  o Return of all realized costs for a given investment with continuous makeup of partial impairments and write-offs, and return of all fees and expenses to date (as opposed to pro rata for the exited deal).
	  o For purposes of waterfall, all unrealized investments must be valued at lower of either cost or fair market value.
	  o Require carry escrow accounts with significant reserves (30% of carry distributions or more) and require additional reserves to cover potential clawback liabilities.
	• The preferred return should be calculated from the day capital is contributed to the point of distribution.

Calculation of carried interest	• Carried interest should be computed on net profit, and usage of gross profits should be discouraged. • Carried interest computation should be based on an after-tax basis. This implies that other taxes as well as foreign taxes should not be considered for distribution. • Until complete investment of the capital, the carry should not be considered

Clawback	<ul><li>A clawback mechanism should be in place and should be paid in full and on time when the need arises.</li><li>Clawback periods should not be limited to the fund's life but should extend well beyond to cover situations such as liquidations and distributions for LPs.</li></ul>

Management fee and expenses best practices

Management fee structure	<ul><li>Excessive management fees should be avoided.</li><li>Whenever the management fee is used, it should be based on a reasonable estimate of the GP's expenses.</li><li>The GP should provide LPs with a fee model. This model can then be used as a benchmark/guidance for setting the fees.</li><li>In case the term of a fund is extended or there is a follow-on fund in place, the management fee should be such that it provisions for lower expenses.</li></ul>
Expenses	<ul><li>When the management fee is used, it should cover normal operations of the GP. This could include, but is not limited to, staff salaries, deal souring expenses, travel costs, administrative expenses, and overheads.</li><li>If there is an arrangement between the GP and placement agents, then this structure should be fully disclosed to prospective LPs during due diligence. The fees that are due to placement agents should be an expense borne by the GP.</li></ul>

Other alignment of interest best practices

Term of fund	<ul><li>The provision for extension of a fund's life should be in one-year increments, and this should be approved by a majority of LPs.</li><li>If this approval is not given, then the GP must liquidate the fund completely within a year after the fund term has completed.</li></ul>
GP fee income offsets	<ul><li>Transaction, monitoring, directory, advisory, and exit fees, and other considerations charged by the GP to portfolio companies should accrue to the benefit of the fund and be shared with the LPs.</li></ul>
GP commitment	<ul><li>The GP should have its own skin in the game by having capital at stake, and this should be through cash commitments rather than waivers (e.g., management fee waivers).</li><li>Rather than being able to pick and choose investments in specific deals, the capital commitment of the GP should be through a pooled fund vehicle.</li></ul>
Standard for GPs that manage different funds	<ul><li>Key persons should devote all their business time to the fund, its predecessors, and successors within a defined strategy.</li><li>The GPs must not close or act as a GP for a fund with substantially equivalent investment objectives and policies until after the investment period ends, or the fund is invested.</li><li>The GP should not invest in opportunities that are appropriate for the fund through other investment vehicles unless such investment is made on a pro rata basis under pre-disclosed co-investment agreements established prior to the close of the fund.</li><li>Fees and carried interest generated by the GP of a fund should be directed predominantly to the professional staff responsible for the success of that fund.</li><li>Any fees generated by an affiliate of the GP, such as an advisory or in-house consultancy, whether charged to the fund or an underlying portfolio company, should be reviewed and approved by a majority of members in the Limited Partner Advisory Committee (LPAC).</li></ul>

Governance

As the second overarching Principle, governance plays a key role in private equity as a vast majority of funds in this space are long term and illiquid in nature. The GP has complete discretion regarding investments, and the LPs commit to them based on their confidence in the GP, the investment professionals, and their understanding of investment strategy and associated parameters. Since every contract is an incomplete contract, it is necessary to have appropriate structures in place to avoid any unforeseen conflicts. Some of the best governance practices in this regard are outlined in Exhibit 3.

Exhibit 3: Best practices on governance

	Governance best practices
Team	• If a key man event or cause (such as fraud, breach of fiduciary duties, etc.) happens, then the LPs should be notified immediately and there should be automatic suspension of the investment period. • If principals find themselves in a situation where their ability to devote required resources (in terms of time and attention) is impacted, then they should immediately discuss this with the LPs. • Key personnel leaving the fund should be disclosed at first knowledge to the LPs.
Investment strategy	• The fund's purpose statement should define the investment strategy as clearly and unambiguously as possible, and there should be specified limits on industry and/or investment concentration. If needed, there could be limits on pace of investments as well. • GPs should honour any investment exclusion policies set by LPs. • Any authority to invest in debt instruments, publicly traded securities, and pooled investment vehicles should be explicitly included in the agreed strategy for the fund.
Fiduciary duty	There should be careful provisions to ensure that GPs are not able to escape from or shirk their fiduciary duties: • All potential and current conflicts should be clearly disclosed to LPs, and the GP should allow LPs to resolve these conflicts. • GPs should strive to provide an equivalent standard of care to all LPs and not have any preferences for particular LPs such that arrangements with these preferred LPs might bring out about advantages at the expense of the rest of the LPs. This is often relevant when allocating co-investment opportunities among LPs. • The high standard of fiduciary duty applicable to the GPs should preclude provisions that allow for them to be exculpated in advance or indemnified for conduct constituting a material breach of the partnership agreement, breach of fiduciary duties, or other "for cause" events. • A majority of LPs must be able to remove the GP or terminate the fund for cause, and there should be specific conditions/mechanisms in place for removal so that the damage is not irreparable or significant. • To the extent that an all-partner clawback is appropriate in order for the fund to indemnify the GP, this should be limited to a reasonable proportion of the committed capital (never more than 25%) and limited to a reasonable period, such as two years following the date of distribution. • GPs' performance should be independently assessed by auditors and third-party observers. While performing the assessment, the auditor should provide an assessment of valuations annually to LPs; and review capital accounts and provide verification of distributions to the GP and LPs. • If a governance issue occurs, then a minority of LPs should be able to take the advice of independent parties at the expense of the fund.

Changes to the fund	<ul><li>There should be sufficient clauses to allow GPs to work in an unrestricted manner.</li><li>LPs should be able to suspend or terminate the fund should there be material breaches of fund policies. ILPA recommends a simple majority of interest for the investment period suspension and a super majority of interest for reinstating the investment period.</li><li>Whenever any amendment has to be made related to the fund, it should be voted for by a majority (and sometimes super-majority) of LPs. ILPA recommends a super majority of interest for LPA amendments.</li><li>No fault rights upon two-thirds in interest vote of LPs for the following: suspension of commitment period and termination of commitment period.</li><li>No fault rights upon three-quarters in interest vote of LPs for the following: removal of the GP and dissolution of the fund.</li></ul>
Responsibilities of the Limited Partners' Advisory Committee (LPAC)	<ul><li>The LPAC generally engages with the GP on discussions related to operations, auditors, compliance, conflicts, expense allocations, GP-led secondary transactions, and new business initiatives. The GP should not actually be a member of the LPAC in any form whatsoever. Where some LPs in the LPAC might own stakes in the GP, this should be disclosed to the LPAC.</li><li>While the LPAC has no defined governance role per se, its role and responsibilities are generally defined by the LPA and involve reviewing and monitoring.</li><li>The LPAC should review and approve the following among other things:<ul><li>– Transactions that pose conflicts of interest, such as cross-fund investments and related party transactions.</li><li>– The methodology used for portfolio company valuations (and in some cases, approving the valuations themselves).</li><li>– Certain other consents or approvals pre-defined in the LPA.</li><li>– Fund term extensions.</li><li>– Use of leverage and any form of fund finance.</li></ul></li><li>The work of the LPAC should be over and above the communications between LPs and GPs.</li><li>The LPAC should work in an environment of high trust and confidentiality, and must take careful measures to ensure that decisions are upheld.</li></ul>

The LPA should not be expected to contain provisions for all possible contingencies that a fund may face over its lifetime, as these can be very specific and numerous. At the minimum, an effective LPA should define the communication mechanisms necessary to successfully address unforeseen conflicts.

Transparency

The third principle is that of transparency, and it forms the core of all communications between GPs and LPs. Since GPs are entrusted with fund management, they must also provide detailed reports on aspects of fund performance (e.g., financial information, risk management information, and operational and transactional information on investments) to LPs in a transparent and timely manner. Such communications allow LPs to make informed decisions regarding the fund and perform their fiduciary duties to the best of their abilities. Exhibit 4 outlines some of the guidelines related to transparency and the best practices suggested by ILPA.

Exhibit 4: Best practices on transparency

	Transparency best practices
Management and other fees	• GPs must faithfully disclose all aspects of fees (such as transactions, monitoring, financing, etc.), and this information should be represented in audited financial statements, along with call and distribution notices. • If any affiliate of the GP or related party is charging to the fund, then such fees should also be disclosed in a similar manner as above. • ILPA recommends that any monitoring or other fees charged to portfolio companies should be offset against the management fees and should accrue to the fund. • The ILPA published a reporting template for fees in 2016.
Capital calls and distribution notices	• Capital calls and distributions should provide information consistent with the ILPA Standardized Reporting Format (discussed in more detail below). • The GP should also provide estimates of quarterly projections on capital calls and distributions.
Disclosure related to the GP	• The following should be immediately disclosed to LPs upon occurrence: – Any inquiries by legal or regulatory bodies in any jurisdiction. – Any material contingency or liability arising during the fund's life. – Any breach of a provision of the LPA or other fund documents. • Other activities related to changes in the actual or beneficial economic ownership, voting control of the GP, or changes or transfers to legal entities who are a party to any related document of the fund should be disclosed in writing to LPs. Such activities include but are not limited to the formation of public listed vehicles, the sale of ownership in the management company to other parties, the public offering of shares in the management company, the formation of other investment vehicles, etc.
Risk management	• The annual fund reports should include portfolio company and fund information on material risks and how they are managed. These should include the following: – Concentration risk at fund level. – Foreign exchange risk at fund level. – Leverage risk at fund and portfolio company levels. – Realization risk (i.e., change in exit environment) at fund and portfolio company levels. – Strategy risk (i.e., change in, or divergence from, investment strategy) at portfolio company level. – Reputation risk at portfolio company level. – Extra-financial risks, including environmental, social, and corporate governance risks, at fund and portfolio company level. • More immediate reporting may be required for material events.
Release of financial information	• Annual reports: Funds should provide information consistent with the ILPA Standardized Reporting Format for portfolio companies and fund information at the end of each year (within 90 days of year-end) to investors. • Quarterly Reports: Funds should provide information consistent with the ILPA Standardized Reporting Format for portfolio companies and fund information at the end of each quarter (within 45 days of the end of the quarter) to investors.
LP information	• A list of LPs, including contact information, excluding those LPs that specifically request to be excluded from the list. • Closing documents for the fund, including the final version of the partnership agreement and side letters. • LPs receiving sensitive information must keep such information confidential. Agreements should clearly state that LPs may discuss the fund and its activities among themselves. LPs should support the GP in taking appropriate sanctions against any LP that breaches this confidentiality.

Appropriate transparency levels in all of these areas will enable effective communication between LPs and GPs. This effective communication, in turn, will help LPs fulfill their own fiduciary duties.

The Limited Partner Advisory Committee (LPAC)

ILPA offers best practices with respect to the LPAC to provide a model for the committee's duties, its role in the partnership, and the protocol for LPAC meetings. The role of the LPAC is not to directly govern, nor to audit, but to provide a sounding board for guidance to the GP and a voice for LPs when appropriate. Common objectives for every board should include

- helping the advisory board fulfill its responsibilities (as specified in the LPA or by mutual agreement), without undue burden to the GP;

- creating an open forum for discussion of matters of interest and concern to the partnership while preserving confidentiality and trust; and

- providing sufficient information to LPs so that they can fulfill their responsibilities.

Exhibit 5: Best practices on LPAC formation

	LPAC best practices

LPAC formation	• The GP should issue a formal invitation to those LPs it has agreed to invite to serve on the LPAC. Such invitations should provide
	  – information about the meeting schedule
	  – expense reimbursement procedures
	  – an outline of LPAC's responsibilities under the LPA
	  – a statement of indemnification.
	• Simultaneously with each closing, the GP should compile a list of LPAC members and their contact information and circulate this list to all LPs, providing an updated list if and when any information is changed.
	• The LPAC should represent a diverse group of LPs that invested in the fund.
	• Any replacements of LPAC members should be determined by the GP with any additional or eliminated seats to be approved by mutual consent of a majority of the LPAC and the GP.
	• A standing LPAC meeting agenda should be developed and a calendar established as far in advance as possible.
	• Clear voting thresholds and protocols should be established, including requiring a quorum of 50% of LPAC members when votes are taken.
	• LPAC members should receive no remuneration, but the partnership should reimburse their reasonable expenses related to their service on the LPAC.

Convening a meeting	• LPAC meetings should be held in person at least twice a year. The GP should convene the LPAC more frequently to discuss time-sensitive matters of importance (e.g., conflicts). • After initially consulting the GP, a minority of three or more LPAC members, using reasonable judgment and discretion, should have the right to call for an LPAC meeting.

Agenda	• Any member of the LPAC may add an agenda item to the LPAC meeting subject to a reasonable notice requirement to the GP. • With any request for consent or approval by a fund's LPAC, the GP should send each LPAC member background information on the matter at least 10 days in advance of the meeting. • The LPAC should have access to partnership auditors to discuss valuations. A representative from the audit firm should attend each year-end LPAC meeting or annual meeting.
Voting	• Any meeting requiring a vote of the LPAC should be held with only the members of that specific fund's LPAC in attendance. • For convenience, LPAC meetings and/or members of other related funds may be pooled when general topics are discussed. • The partnership should indemnify members of the LPAC. • LPAC members should consider whether they have any potential conflicts of interest prior to voting in all circumstances and should disclose those conflicts.
Records	• The GP should take minutes at all LPAC meetings. LPAC meeting minutes should be circulated to LPAC members within 30 days and submitted for approval at the next LPAC meeting. • The GP should record all votes taken during conference calls or at meetings and maintain a copy of consents obtained in writing, by facsimile, or by email.

Clawback best practice considerations

Carry clawback situations represent one of the greatest challenges to the GP-LP relationship. Appropriate processes and remedies must be put in place at the start of the fund, as alignment between the GP and LPs will usually be at a low point when clawbacks occur. Exhibit 6 presents the "building blocks" that could be considered.

Exhibit 6: Best practices on clawbacks

Clawback best practices	
Seek to avoid clawback situations	• Adopt a whole-fund with hurdle cash waterfall as this will minimize excess carry distributions. • If a deal-by-deal carry is adopted, then require (1) an NAV coverage test (generally at least 125%) to ensure a sufficient "margin of error" on valuations, and (2) interim clawbacks, triggered both at defined intervals and upon specific events (e.g., key man clauses triggered, insufficient NAV coverage, etc.)
Ensure GPs backstop themselves	• Require joint liability of individual GP members. If the liability is not provided, a potential substitution can be a creditworthy guarantee of the entire clawback repayment by a parent company, an individual GP member, or a subset of GPs. • Repayment obligations should directly track the carry distributions. • An escrow account (generally of at least 30%) may also provide an effective mechanism for clawback guarantees.

	• LPs should have robust enforcement powers, including the direct ability to enforce the clawback against individual GPs.
	• Actual and potential GP clawback liabilities should be disclosed to all LPs annually along with additional disclosure in the audited financial statements.
Ensure fair treatment of tax burden	• Instead of assuming the highest hypothetical marginal tax rate in a designated location, managers should base the rate on the actual tax situation of the individual GP member and take into account
	– loss of carryforwards and carrybacks,
	– the character of the fund income and deductions attributable to tax payments,
	– any ordinary deduction or loss as a result of any clawback contribution or related capital account shift, and
	– any change in taxation between the date of the LPA and the clawback.
Fix the clawback formula	• The clawback amount should be the lesser of excess carry or total carry paid, net of actual taxes paid. However, there are often errors in the stipulated formulas which have a material impact on fund cash flows:
	– The tax amount should not simply be subtracted from the amount owed under the clawback.
	– The clawback formula should take the preferred return into account.

FUND PERFORMANCE MEASUREMENT AND REPORTING

Reporting of fund performance

The most common measure of performance within the private equity industry is the internal rate of return (IRR). Accurate IRRs can only be computed when all investments have been realized and the cash has been paid back to investors, after the deduction of carried interest, management fees, and other applicable professional and ancillary charges.

Other frequently used measures of performance within the private equity industry are (1) *distributions to paid-in capital (DPI)*; (2) *residual value to paid-in capital (RVPI)*, and (3) *total value to paid-in capital (TVPI)*. We discuss these measures in detail in the chapter on performance measurement in private equity.

The International Private Equity and Venture Capital (IPEV) Investor Reporting Guidelines assert that fund performance should be reported by presenting both gross and net IRRs. The ILPA also recommends that both levered (appropriate when capital call credit facilities are employed) and unlevered IRRs should be disclosed separately. This helps in comparing fund performance across managers.

Gross fund IRR

The gross IRR is computed using investment cash outflows as well as investment related cash inflows (e.g., fair valuation adjustments, divestments, interest and dividends received from investments, repayments of loan principals, etc.). The focus is on transactions between the fund and its investments, regardless of whether these investments are realized or not.

The valuation of the unrealized fund portfolio (consisting of wholly unrealized investments and the unrealized portions of partially realized investments) does not include cash and other assets held by the fund, nor does it include the impact of carried interest or charges of any kind, such as management fees paid to the private equity firm by the investor, fees paid by a portfolio company (either to the fund or the private equity firms), and fees paid or due to lawyers, accountants, and other advisers.

Ideally, the gross IRR should be computed for both realized and unrealized returns:

- For **realized investments**, the return is computed based on all cash outflows (investments) and inflows (divestments, interest, dividends received, etc.) which take place between the fund and its realized investments. Inflows also include the cash flows from partially realized investments. Similarly, in the case of partially realized investments, the investment cash outflows should be allocated between realized and unrealized on a pro rata basis at the dates of each cash outflow.

- For **fully unrealized investments**, the IRR calculation is based on all investment cash outflows and inflows (e.g., interest and dividends) related to unrealized investments. Unrealized investments should be fair valued in accordance with the IPEV Valuation Guidelines.

Net fund IRR

The net IRR is calculated based on the actual cash flows which take place between the fund and the LPs. It takes into account (1) the carried interest paid to the GP, (2) the management fees paid to the GP, and (3) all other applicable professional and ancillary charges paid out by the fund in the course of investing, managing, and divesting from the investment portfolio.

As with the gross IRR, it is advisable to report the net IRR separately by including realized or unrealized investments only. In the case of unrealized investments, the GP needs to estimate the expected fees (management and carried interest). The net IRR computed using unrealized investments allows investors to assess the impact of valuations on the overall net IRR. The valuations may turn out to be poor indicators of the ultimate values extracted when the investments are realized in the future.

Financial statements and other reports

The ILPA has developed a set of reporting guidelines with the aim of achieving standardization in the private equity space. These guidelines are designed to lead to better disclosures and allow LPs to decrease their fund monitoring costs.

The financial statements represent one of the fund's most important sets of documents. Funds should provide annual and quarterly financial statements to investors. While the annual financial reports should be audited and released within 90 days after the year-end, the quarterly reports can be unaudited and should be provided within 45 days after the end of each quarter. The primary purpose of these statements is to keep investors updated about the performance of the fund along multiple dimensions. Disclosures should include (but are not limited to) the following:

- A **summary letter** that discusses the fund performance and activities.

- **Audited financial statements**, along with an independent assessment from the auditor about the reporting quality of the financial statements. The financial statements include the usual *balance sheet*, *income statement*, and *cash flow statement*. (Appendix A provides examples of a balance sheet and an income statement that follow ILPA's reporting guidelines.)

- **Additional statements** which include the *statement of partners' capital*, the *schedule of investments, portfolio company update report*, and a *management report*.

- **Capital calls and distribution notices**, which constitute the GP's announcement of a required transfer of capital between itself and its LPs.

We elaborate on the contents of each of these disclosures in Exhibit 7. ILPA suggests several items for each type of disclosure as guidance; however, this list of items is not intended to be comprehensive. Fund-specific characteristics often require deviations.

Exhibit 7: ILPA's reporting standards

	Summary letter

Summary letter	• A summary letter should include the following components:
	  – Management's discussion of key drivers of fund activity and performance during the fiscal period
	  – Explanations of extraordinary movements in the fund.
	  – Discussions of material events in portfolio companies and/or with the GP firm (e.g., company default, LPA breaches, etc.).
	  – Discussions of any material changes in risk factors at the fund level (e.g., foreign exchange risk, realization risk, leverage risk, etc.).

	Financial statements

Balance sheet	• A balance sheet should include the following components:
	  – Current period end vs. prior audited period end columns.
	  – Receivables and payables to affiliates.
	  – Investments at cost and fair value.
	  Fund-level debt.

Income statement (statement of operations)	• The income statement should include the following components:
	  – Current period, year-to-date, and since inception information.
	  – Breakout of investment income.
	  – Breakout of expenses.
	  – Net operating gains/losses.
	  – Breakout of gains (losses) on investments.

Statement of cash flows	• The cash flow statement should include the following components:
	  – Current period, year-to-date, and since inception information.
	  – Breakout of cash flows from operating activities.
	  – Breakout of cash flows from financing activities.
	  – Cash and cash equivalents.
	  – Supplemental cash flow information.

Footnotes to financial statements	• Footnotes to the statements should include the following components:
	  – Organization/fund details (e.g., key dates, structure, commitment amounts, and other relevant fund details).
	  – Significant accounting policies.
	  – Management fees and other fee breakdowns.
	  – Related party and other transactions.
	  – Carry detail (e.g., fund-level carry paid and/or accrued, amount escrowed if applicable, etc.) and detailed description of carry calculation (waterfall).
	  – List of members on the advisory board.
	  – Subsequent events.

Additional statements

Partners' capital account statement	• The partners' capital account statement should include the necessary components for an LP to assess the value of their investments and reconcile the allocation of cash flows across relevant periods. It should include the following:
	  – Breakout of the total fund by LP, GP, and total.
	  – LP and GP commitments.
	  – Capital drawdowns by LP, GP, and total.
	  – Current period, year-to-date, and since inception information.
	  – A bridge that links the prior net asset value to the current net asset value.
	  – GPs' balances.
	  – Accrued carried interest should the partnership liquidate.

Schedule of investments	• Full detail on realized and unrealized investments. • Debt and equity positions should be reported separately. • Fund ownership (fully diluted). • Initial investment date. • Final exit date for realized investments. • Investment-related data (e.g., total capital committed, total capital invested, current cost, current value, realized proceeds, performance metrics, etc.).

Portfolio company update report	• A page on each investment will give the LPs a qualitative and quantitative synopsis, and should include:
	  – Company overview (e.g., description, acquisition details, current metrics, expectations, etc.).
	  – Financial tables (e.g., investment structure, capitalization table, financial results, calculations, etc.).
	  – Recent events and key initiatives (e.g., staff changes, key developments, achievements, etc.).
	  – Valuation bridges (e.g., how is value being created, and valuation methodology).
	  – Risk assessments (e.g., foreign exchange exposure, leverage, realization, strategy, reputation etc.).

Management report	• The management report should highlight the key firm and fund level information.
	• Executive summary with
	  – Firm data (e.g., AUM, portfolio companies etc.).
	  – Fund-level data (e.g., total commitments, total distributions, etc.).
	  – Portfolio breakdown by industry and region.
	• Fund performance:
	  – Key valuation metrics (RVPI, TVPI, DPI).
	  – Historical fund performance.
	• Capital and fees:
	  – Schedule of carried interest.
	  – Management fees and their breakdown.
	  – Partnership expenses.
	  – Capital calls and distribution notice dates.

Capital calls and distribution notices

For investments	• Name and description of the company/investment. • Deal parameters (e.g., anticipated closing date, total financing amount, etc.). • Notional capital contribution amount.
For management fees and/or fund expenses	• Expenses to be covered. • Calculation of the amount drawn down. • Reductions or offset amounts. • Management fee waivers, including any expenses paid to the GP prior to applying the waiver.
For cash distributions	• Name of company/investment. • Amount and description of distribution. • For a sale, date of transaction, type of purchaser/buyer, proceeds held in escrow, and the fund's potentia portion of the escrow. • For partially exited investments, the amount distributed to date and the cost basis of the remaining investment. • Amount of carry accrued and/or paid to the GP. • Amount of carry held in escrow.
For stock distributions	• Name of company/investment. • Shares distributed, historical cost of shares, current value of shares, and basis for value, as defined in the LP • Shares distributed to the GP in consideration of carried interest distribution and supporting calculations. • Settlement location for shares, and contact information for settlement location. • Restrictions on the sale of shares.

CONCLUSION

Before the financial crisis, the only external reports that private equity fund managers had to provide were investor statements. Today, virtually all private equity managers must periodically report many details about fund operations, investment performance, and risk profile to both regulators and LPs.

On the investor side, private equity managers are seeing more demands, especially from institutional investors, to provide not only performance and expense data, but also very detailed information regarding individual portfolio companies and the fund as a whole that goes beyond financial information. For example, many investors expect information about policies and procedures that ensures that the private equity fund manager is compliant with investors' social and environmental investment guidelines.

Clearly, in this new environment, reporting requirements are not something that private equity fund managers can ignore. Fund managers must ensure that their back-office infrastructure, processes, and controls are solid and efficient enough to address all external reporting needs in a cost-conscious manner. Many fund managers now use qualified and experienced outside advisers to confirm that their reporting approach fully meets the legal and regulatory requirements for proper reporting to regulators and investors.

In today's market, more and more institutional investors place a high premium on transparency from funds and managers (with greater focus on risk-related disclosures) when investing. Thus, managers can better differentiate themselves from competitors by providing the appropriate external reporting.

REFERENCES

Institutional Limited Partners Association. (2019). ILPA Principles 3.0: Fostering Transparency, Governance and Alignment of Interests for General and Limited Partners.

APPENDIX A

Sample Balance Sheet Following ILPA's Best Practices

Private Equity Fund, L.P.

December 31, 2020

	Current Period End 12/31/2020	Current Period End 12/31/2019
ASSETS		
Investments at Cost	$38,000,000.00	$39,000,000.00
Unrealized Gain/Loss on Investments	3,300,000	2,900,000
Investments at Fair Value	41,300,000	41,900,000
Cash and Cash Equivalents	8,000,000	250,000
Other Assets	2,000,000	50,000
Receivable from Affiliates	100,000	25,000
Total Assets	**$51,400,000.00**	**$42,225,000.00**
LIABILITIES AND PARTNERS' CAPITAL		
Liabilities		
Accounts Payable and Accrued Expenses	2,910,000	4,120,000
Notes/Revolver Payable	50,000	75,000
Payable to Affiliates	7,600,000	725,000
Total Liabilities	10,560,000	4,920,000
Partners' Capital		
General Partner	443,400	396,050
Limited Partners	40,396,600	36,908,950
Total Partners' Capital	40,840,000	37,305,000
Total Liabilities and Partners' Capital	$51,400,000.00	$42,225,000.00

Sample Income Statement Following ILPA's Best Practices

Private Equity Fund, L.P.

December 31, 2020

	Current Period	Year-to-Date	Since Inception
	(Oct. 2020–Dec. 2020)	(Jan. 2020–Dec. 2020)	(Feb 2012–Dec. 2020
Income			
Portfolio Interest Income Earned	$16,000	$64,000	$160,000
Portfolio Dividend Income	24,000	96,000	240,000
Other Interest	4,000	16,000	36,000
Total income	44,000	176,000	436,000
Expenses			
Management Fees, Net	250,000	1,000,000	3,000,000
Broken Deal Fees	20,000	100,000	250,000
Interest	2,000	8,000	20,000
Professional Fees	10,000	35,000	50,000
Bank Fees	15,000	35,000	60,000
Advisory Directors' Fees	5,000	30,000	40,000
Insurance	2,000	8,000	20,000
Total Expenses	304,000	1,216,000	3,440,000
Net Operating Income/(Deficit)	-260,000	-1,040,000	-3,004,000
Realized and Unrealized Gain/(Loss) on Investments			
Net Realized Gain/(Loss) on Investments	1,253,152	125,312	2,500,000
Net Change in Unrealized Gain/(Loss) on Investments	75,000	300,000	3,300,000
Net Realized Gain/(Loss) Due to F/X	-	-	-
Net Realized and Unrealized Gain/(Loss) on Investments	1,328,152	425,312	5,800,000
Net Increase/(Decrease) in Partners' Capital Resulting from Operations	1,068,152	511,152	2,696,000

9 Fund Administration

Efficiency is doing things right; effectiveness is doing the right things.
Peter Drucker

INTRODUCTION

The administration of private equity funds is undergoing significant changes, led primarily by two drivers. First, new regulations—most notably, the Dodd-Frank Act in the United States and the Alternative Investment Fund Managers Directive (AIFMD) in the European Union—are prompting expanded disclosures, new reporting requirements, and a fundamental rethink of how and where general partners (GPs) should base their operations, domicile their funds, target their investors and run their investment and operational processes. Second, a shift in the requirements of limited partners (LPs) in the wake of the 2008 financial crisis is reshaping the way capital is allocated to private equity funds. LPs are becoming more selective and sophisticated in their due diligence and monitoring processes. As a result, they are demanding more timely and granular information on everything from managers' track records to hiring practices or succession planning.

Having the right systems in place, together with more flexible fund structures, goes a long way toward building trust with investors. During and beyond fundraising, LPs want to understand the people, processes, and technology that will deliver the key financial information on their investment in the fund. GPs need to explain how key business risks are identified and managed, how regular reports will meet investors' information demands, and how the firm will comply with industry regulations.

Implementing the best operational practices and establishing high-quality reporting and monitoring systems involves GP decisions at both operational and strategic levels. On the operational side, regulations and LP scrutiny introduce new costs in areas such as fund registration, portfolio company valuations, custody, and fund reporting. Changes in accounting standards and increasingly complex fund structures further add to these costs. On the strategic side, GPs must review the viability of their business models and their geographical and industry focus. By instituting a framework to streamline and harmonize fund administration, successful GPs can negotiate these challenges and turn them to their advantage. A common method of achieving these aims is to partner with providers of fund administration services[1]. Service providers not only help shoulder new operational burdens but also deliver the professionalism and best practices that LPs expect. Moreover, fund administrators can provide considerable expertise and guidance on the evolving regulatory processes.

Outsourcing fund administration is likely to become more commonplace. Functions that are typically outsourced include accounting functions like partnership accounting and financial reporting. These include audit coordination and the generation of the annual statutory accounts. Other day-to-day fund operations that can be done by a third-party fund administrator include cash management, vendor payments, reporting of fund performance, generating capital account statements (CAS) or holding statements for LPs and portfolio

---

[1] A particularly interesting case study is that of Permira, a private equity firm based in London, that bought out a leading fund administration company, Alter Domus, in Luxembourg. Following the acquisition, Permira pursued further M&A in the sector to build out a larger fund administration platform

company valuations. Fund administrators can also take over much of the administrative interaction with investors by catering to their tailored information requirements and processing capital calls and cash distributions. Often, administrators can also help liaise with other service providers such as tax advisors and help do the required tax filings.

As an illustration of how the role of an external service provider has become more central, consider the LP's due diligence reviews. In the early 2000s, the majority of LPs performed their due diligence reviews only on the GP. Today, LPs require full due diligence on every regular service provider that supports the GP. Fund administrators are now increasingly expected to complete due diligence questionnaires and respond to formal requests for information or interviews by LPs during the due diligence process. Outsourced fund administration demonstrates a separation of duties and allows for checks and balances that potentially reduce the risk of errors or fraudulent behavior.

THE MAIN FUND ADMINISTRATION ACTIVITIES

We start the discussion by first providing a summary of the main activities that relate to the administration of private equity funds, and the tasks involved for each of these activities (Exhibit 1). Note that some of these activities are serviced by specialist fund administrators hired by the private equity firm. We then provide more detailed discussions on each activity.

Exhibit 1: Summary of the main fund administration activities

Activities	Tasks
Administration of the fund	• Support fund setup support • Coordinate and process payrolls and payroll tax compliance for the GP that manages the fund • Open and maintain bank accounts • Operate bank accounts by monitoring receipts and making disbursements • Calculate capital calls (including management fees), and distribute and prepare notices • Carry modeling • Compile the fund's operational, investment, and financial reports • Perform equalization calculations and update the register of the fund's investors • Compute fund and investment performance (e.g., internal rates of return, cash multiples, etc.) • Make investor capital calls • Reconcile partners' capital • Calculate management fees • Disclose fund diversification

Accounting and valuation support	• Keep accounting records of the fund's investing and operating activities • Advise on accounting matters • Draft the fund's quarterly and annual consolidated financial statements and footnotes • Calculate investors' capital account balances • Prepare bank account reconciliations • Prepare audit related work papers • Liaise with external auditors • Monitor accounting processes • Perform financial due diligence on deals • Reconcile historical profit and loss accounts of portfolio companies • Coordinate subordination, non-disturbance and attornment agreements
Investor services	• Prepare investor-specific reports (e.g., ILPA Fee Reporting template, GAAP reconciliations, IRRs) • Maintain individual investor capital accounts • Distribute investor reports and notices to appointed representatives • Process investor transfers and update the fund's register • Deal with correspondence and queries received from investors (e.g., requests for assistance with supporting documentation for fair value reporting under generally accepted accounting principles or the analysis and monitoring of cash waterfall provisions) • Deliver and maintain secure Internet portals
Regulatory and Tax Reporting	• Complete regulatory reporting and filings (e.g., AIFMD, FATCA, CRS) • Advise on regulatory matters • Offer depository services • Prepare national and local partnership tax returns • Prepare personal property tax returns • Prepare tax projections • Provide tax assistance with structuring acquisitions and dispositions • Monitor investors' tax compliance • Prepare tax exemption certificates • Calculate required withholding of national and local taxes

Compliance	• Craft and monitor documentation on
	   – Mortgages
	   – Credit facilities
	   – Partnership/operating agreements
	   – Lock-box accounts and associated cash waterfalls
	   – Joint venture agreements
	   – Property management agreements
	• Insurance:
	   – Analyze and monitor property insurance policies and premiums
	   – Analyze and monitor insurance provisions in commercial leases
	• Operational compliance audits

Information Technology Services	• Accounting software license and support • Information portals • Reporting software support • Human resources software support • Cybersecurity • Creation and maintenance of databases • Automated emailing service • Disaster recovery and business continuity services
Secretarial Services	• Organize board meetings • Record board meeting decisions • Maintain corporate records • Assist with statutory filing requirements • Maintain statutory registers with registrar • Provide office of company secretary and registered office • Attend to other secretarial services (e.g., incorporation of the company, provision of directorship, and drafting of board resolutions)
Loan Administration (debt funds only)	• Prepare loan documents • Prepare monthly interest, amortization, and escrow invoices • Securities agent • Coordinate tax and insurance premiums payments associated with loans • Oversee escrow disbursements

Administration of the fund

The introduction of new regulations in Europe and the United States has increased the importance of professionals that are familiar with the implementation of these regulations at the early stages. As a result, engaging with fund administrators (either in house or third parties) to provide compliance and regulatory reporting services could contribute significantly to a successful fund launch. Another important area of support when funds are raised is the content of the partnership agreement and side letters signed with LPs. An administrator can provide comments about the feasibility of certain clauses added to such agreements, and whether they might add to the complexity of the fund's operations. Administrators can also suggest alternatives for the GP to consider given their experience with other funds. Administrators can record, monitor, and report the terms of these side letters to the GP, and work together with the GP to ensure that the clauses are adhered to throughout the fund's life, thereby increasing the LP's trust in the GP. As more funds are being raised, GPs need to coordinate closings with a larger set of LPs. This daunting process can be more easily navigated with the support of a fund administrator. Finally, fund administrators play a key role by providing due diligence and know-your-customer (KYC) checks when investor commitments are received. As soon as a GP's investor relations team receives firm interest from an investor, it should involve the fund administrator to make the necessary checks. The earlier administrators get involved, the easier it is for them to discreetly gather information from publicly available sources, thus streamlining the number of requests addressed to the investors. As funds increase in size, new investors are being attracted from all over the world and these investors' capital must be properly reviewed before being accepted. The source of funds—and sometimes the source of wealth (if the investor is a high-net-worth individual)—must be verified and confirmed.

The administrator would also assist with the back-end calculations of capital calls and distributions, management fees, and carried interest in accordance with the fund documents; issue notices to all stakeholders; receive funds; and process the funds accordingly and on a timely basis. When new investor commitments are subscribed to the fund, and once the GP affirms the closing date, the administrator will kick-start the equalization process and rebalance calculations to help the GP work out the right amounts to flow amongst the LPs. The ability to monitor these movements also enables the administrator to compute each investor's capital account.

Other optional services available to a GP would include payroll processing and assistance with opening and operating the fund's bank accounts. Opening a bank account for the fund can be laborious as banks also perform extensive due diligence on their customers. After the bank account is opened, the administrator can assist by providing signatories and additional approval levels in arrangements that are as flexible as the GP prefers.

Administrators can further support the GP by consolidating the various reports required by the LPs into a comprehensive pack that meets their needs as well as the financial reporting requirements.

Accounting and valuation support services

The core accounting and valuation support services provided by fund administrators include (1) maintaining the accounting records of the fund at a sufficient level of detail (e.g., investment spending, partnership expenses, etc.) and ensuring that adequate supporting documentation is archived safely; (2) ensuring that the fund and any investment holding vehicles comply with the applicable financial reporting framework (whether it is IFRS, U.S. GAAP, or others stipulated in the fund agreement); (3) supporting valuations for fund-of-funds reporting by receiving capital statements and calculating movements; (4) conducting management reporting; (5) conducting financial reporting; and (6) drafting quarterly and annual financial statements. Most fund administrators that provide accounting and financial reporting services are also expected to devise audit schedules and coordinate with external auditors during the audit process.

In order to service multi-jurisdiction fund structures, administrators require expert knowledge in different accounting frameworks that are applicable to the private equity industry. Moreover, someone within the organization will have to keep on top of the ever-changing accounting standards; when GPs outsource, they are in fact leaving that responsibility with the administrator, thereby capitalizing on the technical expertise of a qualified and professional pool of accountants.

Reporting asset values at "fair value" by marking-to-market is now standard practice in the private equity world. Accordingly, GPs have been required to report interim valuations at "fair value"—essentially a hypothetical price at which the company could be sold at the time of compiling the financial reports. As a result, some GPs may attempt to value portfolio companies opportunistically (e.g., underestimating the value of portfolio companies so that current investors in the fund do not get any negative surprises, or overestimating the value of portfolio companies when marketing the next fund to potential new investors).[2] However, in Europe, AIFMD requires fund managers to ensure that any internal valuations are conducted independently of the portfolio management function. Thus, the GP needs to ensure no undue influence is exerted on the individuals conducting the internal valuation of the fund's assets. One way to ensure this

[2] According to a Bloomberg News article in 2014, the SEC reached a settlement with the private equity unit of Oppenheimer & Co. Inc. in March 2013, which was accused of marking up the value of its investments in order to help market a new fund. The settlement required Oppenheimer to be censured, to pay penalties, and to return the capital commitments to the investors it had misled.

independence in valuation is to engage fund administrators that are able to provide valuation services. Further, some fund administrators can provide an independent validation of the valuation models or liaise with third-party valuation experts.

Although a large number of private equity investment professionals have extensive deal experience and are former consultants, investment bankers, or investment managers at larger private equity houses, most have rarely been involved in the execution of a deal from start to finish, as this is usually done by in-house finance teams. In contrast, a fund administrator, when involved, can provide an integral link across all deal stages in collaboration with third-party corporate finance, accounting and legal advisers.

Investor services

Another set of activities that fund administrators perform relates to portfolio performance and reporting to investors. Historically, in the absence of widely adopted industry standards, GPs have reported to their LPs based on their internally determined best practices or by borrowing the customized reports offered by fund administrators, leading to fund reports that varied dramatically in terms of form and content. The Institutional Limited Partners Association (ILPA) published a series of reporting templates to help standardize reporting to investors. Invest Europe (formerly the EVCA), another leading industry body, has published investor reporting guidelines containing best-practice disclosure principles with worked examples. These efforts are likely to lead to greater efficiencies, uniformity, and transparency, and should eventually lead to reduced expenses with respect to the administration and monitoring of private equity investments.[3]

The benefits of standardized and more detailed reporting are straightforward. However, implementing a reporting framework with more comprehensive content in a specific format can present challenges to GPs that do not have adequate systems, flexible reporting capabilities, and/or the human resources to manage data aggregation. Fund administrators have both the resources and capabilities to deliver these kinds of reports. Furthermore, administrators have developed processes to keep the data secure and confidential. The financial and reputational risks associated with data security and privacy protection are high, and managers cannot afford to ignore them. A high proportion of managers routinely communicate confidential information to investors via email, which is currently considered a high-risk delivery method. It is safer to provide real-time access to reports that can be downloaded from a secure online portal run by a fund administrator. Fund administrators can also offer virtual data rooms for investors that perform due diligence on the GP. Administrators are able to integrate online web interfaces with their accounting and investor reporting platforms so that reports can be produced directly from core platforms and automatically uploaded to virtual data rooms with no manual intervention.

In addition to the availability of information, the demand for investor relations support has been identified as another key trend. Investors are requesting more information and more frequently, given that there are so many different classes of LPs investing in the industry, each requiring a bespoke set of information for its own purposes. The GP's burden can be eased by assigning this responsibility to the administrator, who can be the first point of contact to filter (and address, where possible) investor-specific queries before passing them on to the GP if necessary. For example, many LPs track the underlying portfolio companies in their own systems and want more specific operating data. Assuming the GP has limited resources, it is imperative to have a process in place to handle these requests in a timely and efficient manner. Fund administrators can

---

[3] Nevertheless, many GPs are reluctant to adopt these standardized approaches.

deal with special LP requests for underlying information on the portfolio companies more effectively because they can potentially manage the disclosure of sensitive information more carefully. The fund administrator needs to first assess whether the information requested by the LP is material non-public information. For instance, if the LP is subject to the Freedom of Information Act in the United States, sensitive information might get out in the public domain and trigger liabilities. Administrators also ask for GPs' consent before sharing information with an individual LP; if the GP believes that the information is sensitive, then the administrator needs to explain the lack of disclosure to the LP. Potentially, the administrator can be an independent disinterested party in such a scenario that can validate the GP's justification to not disclose specific information.

Supporting LPs that come from all over the world can be extremely complex given the different time zones, languages, and/or regulatory requirements involved. For this reason, hiring an outside fund administrator that can provide global coverage and multilingual services to investors is sometimes necessary. Such an administrator can also handle the different time zones of the LPs, providing "follow-the-sun" investor servicing models.

Major issues that involve investor support services relate to capital call notices and the computation of fees. Regarding capital notices, LPs do not just want to see a capital call notice for a certain amount of money. A one-computation-fits-all approach is less relevant now that it is quite common for LPs to negotiate specific terms with the GP; hence, there is a need for the individual LP's calculation, which can be performed by the fund administrator. Additionally, LPs want to understand what portion of that money is for the actual investment, and what portion goes toward things like management, organizational, or partnership expenses. Some influential LPs even refuse to sign on with managers unable to provide a capital call notice in the format they want, meaning a loss of capital for any firm running an antiquated software system that is unable to process the complicated formats requested by some LPs.

With fee calculations, investors want some level of assurance that things are reasonable. Fund administrators can provide improved transparency in this respect, given the conflicts of interest that are faced by the GPs (e.g., with carried interest calculations as it directly affects the GP's profits). Having a third party perform the calculation provides additional assurance to the LPs. Further, scrutiny around private equity fee structures has been on the regulators' agenda for some time.[4] Some U.S. state legislators are introducing laws requiring external money managers to disclose their fee structures to pension trustees. Similarly, the U.K. Financial Conduct Authority is reviewing retail fund practices and their conflicts of interest. A particularly serious problem is the issue of accelerated monitoring fees. Essentially, portfolio companies are required to enter into multi-year contracts to pay annual fees for advisory services that extend for as many as 10 years. If the company is sold before the end of the contract, then a payment is triggered and the GP gets the payments for the remaining years in one lump sum for services that were never provided.[5] Transparency around such arrangements allows LPs to fully understand how much the GP is earning from the fund it is managing, and whether this amount should be deducted from the GP's income.

Fund administrators also act as another pair of watchful eyes for investors in terms of GP expense practices, notably the allocation of expenses in the "operating partner" model (where an operating professional close to the GP is dedicated to a portfolio company and the services are treated as a fund or

---

[4] Andrew Bowden, former director of the Office of Compliance Inspections and Examinations at the Securities and Exchange Commission, said there had been violations of law and weaknesses in controls around fees and expense allocations in over 50% of the private equity houses inspected by the U.S. regulator (https://www.sec.gov/news/speech/2014--spch05062014ab.html).

[5] For instance, Blackstone settled with the U.S. Securities and Exchange Commission (SEC) to the tune of $39 million following charges that it failed to inform investors about the benefits obtained from accelerated monitoring fees and discounts on legal fees.

portfolio company expense). The U.S. Securities and Exchange Commission (SEC) found a trend of GPs shifting their back-office expenses onto the LPs during the fund's life. For example, some private equity firms reclassify operating partners as consultants rather than employees and charge investors for their services. Traditionally, the executives that provided these services were salaried employees of the private equity firm. Therefore, by reclassifying them as consultants paid by portfolio companies, the profits of the private equity firm are higher.

Regulatory and tax reporting

One of the primary requirements of new regulatory directives (particularly the AIFMD in Europe) has enhanced the importance of a particular type of service provider, the *depository*.[6] Regulations now require an independent depository to be responsible for monitoring the asset (i.e., ensuring it is registered in the name of the fund and continues to be held in the name of the fund until disposal). AIFMD harmonizes the function of the depository throughout Europe, sets out its responsibilities, and also determines which providers are allowed to perform this role. Whereas in the past the execution of the depository function required a bank license, private equity funds have the opportunity to appoint a non-bank entity—such as a fund administrator—as a depository. Depository services can be priced based on fixed fees or variable basis point fees. The basis-points-based fees can vary from 50 to 250 basis points with the upper range only applicable to very specific funds with unusual assets and locations. Despite the cost, most investors are happy to have an additional layer of independent and regulated controls over their investments and the way they are managed, given the Madoff investment scandal discovered in late 2008.[7]

The depository's three main responsibilities are (1) to monitor of the fund's assets, (2) to monitor significant cash flows through the fund, and (3) to oversee the main processes related to the operation of the fund (e.g., regular checks on valuations, fund net asset value calculations, income distributions, subscriptions, redemptions, etc.). These responsibilities make the depository the central hub of communication between GPs and their investors. The safe-keeping function relates to the ex-post verification of the deal and the ownership documentation. The depository needs to verify the proof of ownership as well as assess the existence of the target company's assets, thus providing additional comfort to LPs and partially discharging the GP from its liabilities.[8] The cash-flow-monitoring function involves ensuring that cash flows into and out of the fund are properly monitored, that significant cash flows are identified, and that any issues/discrepancies are resolved. It is also necessary to perform daily reconciliations when cash movements occur.[9] As the speed of execution is key to GPs, depositories are expected to have efficient controls embedded into the GP's processes to ensure smooth transactions.

Since fund administrators in private equity funds act as the main coordination hub for accounting, legal documentation, payment processing, and investor servicing, they can be expected to handle as much as 80% of the information and documentation required for the depository to execute its duties effectively; this means

---

[6] The Dodd-Frank Act, signed into law in July 2010, created sweeping changes across the United States' financial markets. As a consequence of fund registration, GPs must comply with the Custody Rule 206(4)-2, which seeks investor protection by formalizing the verification and safekeeping of documentation evidencing investment.

[7] In December 2008, Bernard Madoff, former NASDAQ chairman and founder of the Wall Street firm Bernard L. Madoff Investment Securities LLC, admitted that the wealth management arm of his business was an elaborate Ponzi scheme.

[8] If something goes wrong, an investor can make claims against the GP and, based on the responsibilities conferred by the AIFMD, against the depository as well. Both the GP and the depository can be held accountable before the courts. The depository must then demonstrate that it acted professionally and executed due care and diligence.

[9] Reconciliation generally refers to the process of ensuring that two sets of records agree with each other.

that a strong cooperation between the fund administrator and depository is critical. Unsurprisingly, service providers that are able to provide both fund administration and depository services are best placed to deliver added value to GPs. In such a setup, the GP has a single point of contact with deep knowledge about the business model and processes, and the service provider can better synchronize fund administration and depository processes. This setup also allows all stakeholders to ensure compliance with the regulatory requirements and ensure operational efficiency at the same time.[10]

To facilitate the regulatory and tax reporting process, many GPs leverage the expertise and core competencies of qualified fund administrators, custodians, depositories, and independent valuation agents to fully assess the costs and benefits of outsourcing work on this reporting versus continuing to maintain and build these functions in house. In addition to reporting to both tax authorities and investors, managers must submit several reports to regulators. GPs are subject to various types of regulations under U.S. federal laws, in particular the Dodd-Frank Act, while in Europe they need to follow AIFMD requirements. Fund administrators provide crucial support with these reports.

Most fund administrators provide support regarding the following reporting requirements in the United States:

- **Form ADV:** All U.S. and non-U.S. investment advisers registered with the SEC must file this form with the SEC within 90 days after the end of their fiscal year. In May 2015, the SEC proposed several changes to disclosure and recordkeeping requirements of fund managers that require more detailed information concerning a private equity firm's separately managed accounts and the firm's use of borrowings and derivatives. The SEC also requires managers to disclose if they make use of an "outsourced" chief compliance officer, usually a fund administrator, which is a common practice among smaller private equity firms that may have limited internal resources.

- **Form PF:** Most registered managers who advise one or more private equity funds are required to file an annual update to Form PF, the systemic risk reporting form, within 120 days after the end of their fiscal year. Private fund advisers need to report regulatory assets under management as well as risk exposure data regarding the type and size of assets held by the private fund firm. The implementation of Form PF requires the GPs and their fund administrators to implement new workflows and technological solutions to capture over 80 fields of data to be reported on an annual basis. This situation is prompting GPs to rely more on fund administrators that have the capabilities to deal with this complexity.

- **Annual Compliance Review:** An SEC-registered manager must maintain, adopt, and implement written policies and procedures reasonably designed to prevent violation of the Advisers Act by the adviser and its employees. The adviser must also review, no less frequently than annually, the adequacy of these policies and procedures and the effectiveness of their implementation. A GP should consider focusing its annual compliance review on the following areas: (1) fee and expense allocations, (2) valuation policies, (3) marketing and performance presentations (particularly disclosures with respect to the methodology for calculating internal rates of returns), (4) allocation of investment and co-investment opportunities, and (5) other potential conflicts of interest.

- **FATCA and CRS Compliance:** The Foreign Account Tax Compliance Act (FATCA) went "live" in the United States on July 1, 2014. Many countries have entered into intergovernmental agreements with

---

[10] It is important to note that a complete merger between fund administration and depository services is not recommended. AIFMD imposes oversight duties of the depository over fund administration services. Both services need to be reasonably independent and segregated from an organizational point of view.

the United States that set forth the requirements for FATCA compliance for financial institutions located in each country. From January 2016, fund GPs have also faced similar regulations which implement the OECD's Common Reporting Standard (CRS), an initiative to which over 100 countries have committed. Collectively, the FATCA and CRS agreements on the automatic exchange of information (AEOI) between countries for tax purposes require GPs to collect important information about the tax statuses of their investors. For U.S.-based private equity funds, FATCA compliance means complying with due diligence, withholding, and investor reporting requirements. For non-U.S. funds, AEOI compliance generally means registering with the Internal Revenue Service (IRS) in the United States, performing required due diligence on investors, and reporting information on reportable investors (from the United States and elsewhere) to local tax authorities. If an investor claims non-reportable status, then the GP may need to obtain follow-up information to establish that status. Further, the GPs, with the help of fund administrators, must establish procedures to identify amounts subject to FATCA withholding, and to withhold and pay the IRS as required.

- **CFTC Filings/Exemptions:** Most GPs need to rely on an exemption from registration with the U.S. Commodity Futures Trading Commission (CFTC) if they trade commodity interests (e.g., futures and options on commodities). If GPs qualify for the exemption, the fund must meet some tests each time a commodity position is established. For instance, the sum of the notional amount of each commodity interest position should not exceed the liquidation value of the fund. GPs that rely on these exceptions must file with CFTC within 60 days after the end of each calendar year. GPs that cannot qualify for an exemption may have to register with the CFTC as commodity pool operators or trading advisers, which will result in additional disclosure, recordkeeping, and reporting requirements (e.g., annual reports for each commodity pool operated, quarterly form CPO-PQR, etc.).

In Europe, GPs must comply with AIFMD disclosure rules. Unfortunately, however, AIFMD does not remove the time-consuming idiosyncrasies of different national rules within the European Union.[11] For example, while a fund marketed in Germany needs a depository lite solution, this is not the case in other European markets. Reporting requirements in Europe comprise the following:

- Annual reports for each fund for as long as the fund is marketed in Europe and/or an investor from Europe is invested in the fund. The fund manager must make each report available to the European investors in the fund and the local regulator in each European jurisdiction in which the fund is marketed within six months after the end of the financial year to which the annual report relates. The funds will have to meet certain minimum disclosure requirements in terms of the contents of the annual report. These requirements include a balance sheet, an income and expenditure account, and a report on the activities during the financial year. In addition, AIFMD requires disclosure of the total remuneration and how this is split between fixed and variable components. These figures must be further broken down between those whose actions have a material impact on the risk profile of the fund and those whose actions do not.

- Information that has to be made available to investors at the same time as the annual report (or in some cases more frequently), such as the percentage of assets that are subject to special liquidity arrangements that affect the redemption rights of investors; whether the manager exceeds a specific limit with respect

---

[11] One way to avoid the directive is to not accept Alternative Investment Fund Manager (AIFM) status (i.e., rely on private placements). However, because of various EU-wide restrictions, GPs relying on private placement rules cannot seek investment from insurance companies, pension funds, or family offices in much of Europe.

to market, credit, liquidity, counterparty or operational risks; the total leverage along with the maximum and average levels employed during the reporting period; and so on.

- Information on where the fund, directly or indirectly, acquires control of companies or voting rights in excess of certain thresholds (starting at 10% and continuing in increments up to 75%). Once the fund acquires a controlling interest in a company it must also alert the board of the target company and its shareholders.

- Reports to country regulators that cover information about the manager and the funds it is managing and, where relevant, marketing.

Over the coming years and months, the need for regulatory reporting will place an increasing burden on private equity firms. More data will have to be collected and stored. That data will also have to be analyzed and reported to an increasingly wide range of regulators. Thus, given the way the private equity sector has evolved in recent years, GPs must look beyond their own institutions to deal with fund administration.

Against this background of multiple regulatory challenges, there are opportunities for fund administrators to add significant value and help guide GPs through a complex set of directives and market changes (Appendix A discusses requirements in the AIFMD context). The combination of cutting-edge technology, professional expertise, and the ability to service across multiple jurisdictions and multi-currencies are likely to be the key competitive differentiators for a successful fund administrator. However, while GPs can outsource reporting and regulatory compliance functions to providers with specialist knowledge, they cannot outsource potential liabilities. Paying a fee to a fund administrator is not the same as eliminating the risks.

Compliance

A GP's reputation takes years of strong fund performance to build, but even a stellar reputation—along with scores of investors—can be lost in an instant when compliance breaches are revealed. Establishing a compliance program that meets regulatory standards can enhance a private equity firm's ability to detect and prevent violations of federal and state securities laws or violations of contractual arrangements.

Fund administrators that deal with compliance must monitor and review all regulatory filings, review fund documentation distributed to investors, ensure that deadlines are met, ensure that all relevant ethics codes are followed, and monitor insurance coverage. They can also arrange for employee training programs, decide whether to accept or reject an investor based on the money laundering risks that have been identified, review reports of suspicious activities from the private equity fund personnel, and complete other such tasks.

Information technology services

Private equity firms may view cybersecurity issues as less relevant to their business, as they typically deal with less personal information and fewer transaction processing demands than broker-dealers or retail investment managers. However, private equity managers should not be complacent about cyber-related risks, both to the fund's assets and to a firm's reputation. LPs have recognized the importance of this issue and are conducting greater diligence on cybersecurity in the course of the private equity fundraising process. U.S. and U.K. regulators have been increasingly outspoken about the need to strengthen cybersecurity, not only at private equity firms, but also at portfolio companies and third-party vendors.

Regulators are expecting GPs and their fund administrators to have a strategy to prevent, detect, and respond to cybersecurity threats. Managers should be very concerned about the reputational risks of any data leaks as well as the legal and regulatory implications. While banks have very strong and well-defined processes for cybersecurity since their industry is highly regulated, private equity fund managers only recently started to worry about these issues—particularly after the leaked information from Mossack Fonseca.[12] Fortunately, the industry as a whole did not suffer from the leakage given that Panama is rarely used in the private equity world as GPs prefer other jurisdictions that offer preferential tax treatments, such as the Cayman Islands, Delaware, Guernsey, Jersey, Hong Kong, and Luxembourg.

Fund administrators, by virtue of putting data into information technology (IT) systems, are providing IT support and are expected to conduct periodic assessments of the information maintained, threats and vulnerabilities, existing controls and processes, the impact an incident might have, and the governance structure for management of cybersecurity risks. They are also expected to design strategies that prevent, detect, and respond to cybersecurity threats, and to implement written policies and procedures along with training and monitoring. For instance, fund administrators can design a strategy on the controlled access to systems and data, the use of encryption and monitoring software, data backup and retrieval, and the development of an incident response plan. Fund administrators can also help develop business continuity programs in the event of unforeseen circumstances or disruptions and make sure that the operations of the GP would still be able to run smoothly.

Further, administrators are now developing and promoting more web-based tools that collate information on portfolio companies so it is accessible to GPs on a real-time basis. Traditionally, administrators created graphs for quarterly reports manually; today, these are generated at the push of a button. And because the systems are web-based, high-quality information is readily available wherever an employee is in the world. At the same time, these systems create a need for portfolio companies to be prompt with their reports. If they are not, this delay can be seen by the GP as an early warning system.

A recent survey of fund administrators conducted by Longitude Research found that 89 percent of such firms anticipate making investments in new technology systems before 2020.

---

[12] On 3 April 2016, German newspaper *Süddeutsche Zeitung* announced that 11.5 million confidential documents from Mossack Fonseca had been leaked. These documents, dubbed "the Panama Papers," reveal how clients hid billions of dollars in tax havens.

Secretarial services

Fund administrators can assist GPs with secretarial services that involve statutory reporting and filing, convening boards of directors and shareholder meetings, board pack preparations, minute taking during meetings, or coordinating communications between the board of directors and other stakeholders as required. Some also provide a registered office address for the GP, eliminating the need to establish a presence in jurisdictions that do not make economic sense.

Loan administration (debt funds only)

The increasing prevalence of private debt funds has enhanced the role of service providers catering to this particular asset class of investors, especially in the space of loan administration. Two important responsibilities managed by loan administrators (which can be hired by the GP in house or contracted out) entail functioning as a *facility agent* and as a *calculation agent*.

- The facility agent's role is to manage all administrative aspects of the loan. A major component of the administration function is to facilitate the ongoing communication between the lenders and the borrower. As a facility agent, a loan administrator holds loan documentation and forwards notices, maintains a register of creditors, organizes meetings, coordinates waivers and amendments, monitors compliance and undertakings, and follows up on compliance certificates.

- As a calculation agent, a fund administrator undertakes independent calculations for transactions where the amounts are to be based on underlying factors such as interest rates, indices, or similar. The loan administrator provides daily calculation of interest rates, sends automatic emails with interest adjustments and payment instructions to issuers and investors, and monitors coupon payments.

Another service typically offered by fund administration service providers to a private debt fund is the role of a *security agent*. This responsibility involves holding security on behalf of one or more creditors within different jurisdictions. Having a neutral, independent third party hold the security on behalf of creditors also enables changes of creditors without having to re-register the security, thereby reducing costs. Thus, as a security agent, a service provider can hold debt securities on behalf of investors, control and file security documents, maintain a document archive for each security, file electronically for each security, and release/enforce securities.

WHY OUTSOURCE THE ADMINISTRATION OF PRIVATE EQUITY FUNDS?

A significant number of GPs keep fund administration in house when they raise their first fund, while some first-time GPs prefer to learn from the experience and guidance of an independent third-party fund administrator. When they raise subsequent funds, many GPs realize that having staff "wear multiple hats" may stifle the progress of the private equity firm. Nevertheless, firm size does not always dictate whether a firm should outsource. Sometimes experience that comes with the management of multiple funds drives a GP to keep its back-office functions in house. As some firms continue to grow in size, they build a dedicated in-house staff while still collaborating with a service provider. Many large fund managers prefer to use an administrator to augment their own in-house fund administration team, as a system of checks and balances.

The fund administrator slots into the middle of the workings of the private equity fund, providing an interaction platform between GPs, LPs, and other parties such as regulators, tax authorities, or bankers. Exhibit 2 illustrates the role of the administrator.

Exhibit 2: Summary of the main fund administration activities

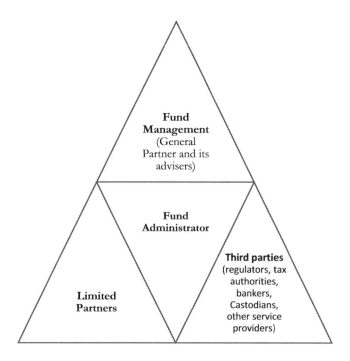

Outsourcing may not be suitable for every private equity firm. GPs must make the decision to use external providers based on the size and complexity of their funds, as well as their in-house talent and experience. In considering whether to outsource any function, two questions are relevant. First, is the function something that requires constant activity and data collection, or is it infrequent and unpredictable? Outsourcing relatively frequent activities such as the preparation of regulatory and financial reports is more common. Second, how sensitive is the activity given the interests of the LPs and the relevant regulatory requirements? For instance, activities that relate to the handling of LPs' personal information can be very sensitive, so GPs may be less likely to outsource them. Regardless of the question, outsourcing functions should make economic sense. GPs scrutinize service providers to ensure that, for a certain level of quality, the cost they incur from these providers is lower than the cost of an in-house team.

Advantages of outsourcing

The main rationale for outsourcing administrative functions is based largely on scalability. Even relatively simple tasks can be labor-intensive for fund managers whose small scale means they do not have specialists with specialist knowledge to deal effectively with each issue that arises.[13] In contrast, for a large third-party administrator, the scale of the team dedicated to a particular issue faced by many GP clients means that it can do the work very efficiently, ensuring a high level of quality. A benefit of external fund administration is the ability to be more efficient and focused. By handing administration responsibilities to a proven fund administrator, GPs are able to concentrate on their core competencies (e.g., sourcing deals, making investments, or advising portfolio companies). Internally, firms that outsource can be more efficient with the people they employ. Front office employees do not have to spend their time on administration when they could be concentrating on deals and investor relations. This benefit is particularly useful for smaller firms that do not have full-time administrative support staff to cater to the information needs of various investors or to meet regulatory and reporting requirements across many jurisdictions.

Second, external service providers and fund administrators allow a GP to leverage the latest technology and best practices. By outsourcing to an administrator, the GP can benefit from its scale and systems, while simultaneously avoiding the expense of building and maintaining costly infrastructure. Since fund administrators have many clients requiring similar services, they develop deep experience over hundreds of funds as well as better software technology than most private equity firms.

Third, outsourcing to an external administrator enables GPs to benefit from specialist expertise in different accounting frameworks/standards and tax reporting requirements, as well as comply with the ever-increasing regulatory requirements. These compliance demands can create difficulties for some GPs that may not be able to deliver the reports their LPs need. Conversely, fund administrators have regulatory knowledge across a whole portfolio of clients and jurisdictions, and are therefore able to provide the best possible solutions to implement any necessary changes. First-time GPs in particular can leverage the standard procedures and templates that fund administrators possess, rather than starting from ground zero. Even if the independent administrator does not have the requisite expertise on a certain issue, it is usually able to introduce the GP to the right legal and tax advisers, to ensure that the most efficient structures are in place.

Finally, another significant advantage of outsourcing is that LPs have the comfort of knowing that their accounting and administration functions are managed independently and professionally by a reputable service provider. Reports prepared by fund administrators are often seen by investors as more objective and free of actual or perceived conflicts of interests; basically, LPs view independent administrators as watchdogs on their assets under management. GPs can also use administrators as evidence to their policy of being transparent, which is a positive signal given that LPs generally do not have substantive control over the fund's activities.

Disadvantages of outsourcing

The main downside of an external fund administration is the risk of mishandling sensitive information. Given that the private equity industry is still very focused on confidentiality and discretion, some GPs may be apprehensive toward outsourcing. Certain fund managers believe that fund administration is not separate from the investment making and investor relations side. The two can be so interconnected that GPs might not want to risk information flows with anyone outside the firm, especially with a fund administrator that might work with competitors.

Outsourcing administrative functions also carries the disadvantage of having to manage the turnaround time/agreed time with the service provider versus having an employee. In addition, external providers are not likely to facilitate the hiring and retention of the relevant employees with administrative responsibilities in the

---

[13] In addition, holidays, sickness, and maternity/paternity leave can all have detrimental effects on the effectiveness of a small team.

private equity firm. In contrast, in-sourcing allows the GP to secure immediate access to dedicated, responsive employees, along with direct supervision of all internal controls. Because the GP can deal with the administrative staff directly, it can judge the quality of the work and make decisions about hiring and firing. When staff is outsourced, the GP can only evaluate the performance of the outsourcing partner.

Outsourcing may also have negative consequences with respect to data integration. A GP that outsources various administrative tasks might have to purchase different systems from different vendors, creating a situation where the information is spread across many platforms.[14] This scenario can lead to difficulties in finding and compiling data reliably and in a timely manner. For instance, the GP could be using an investor portal from one vendor and portfolio management software from another to integrate with the fund administrators' systems. The situation can become more complicated if the GP manages different types of funds (e.g., credit funds and buyout funds) that have different reporting needs. In such a scenario, an ideal solution is an in-house master repository of information, which means creating a standardized data format across all GPs' internal systems and, for firms on the larger end of the spectrum, a proprietary data warehouse. However, most small and medium-sized fund managers do not have the resources to purchase or develop such sophisticated software, so outsourcing might be a more viable option.

An additional downside of outsourcing is the cost involved. The cost largely depends on the service quality of the fund administrator and the complexity and scale of the fund. Pertinent factors in the determination of fees charged by administrators include the type of fund (e.g., management buyout, debt, real estate, or fund of funds), fund structure (e.g., stand-alone versus master-feeder funds), number of LPs in the fund, number of banks used, expected level of activity of the fund, number of special purpose vehicles created, frequency of reports, jurisdiction of the fund, and so on. Naturally, fees are also affected by the types of services provided, which can go beyond fund accounting and processing of investor allocations, fee calculations, capital calls, investor closes, or transfers of commitments. Additional services such as regulatory reporting, customized reports for investors, cash management, and custodial and depository services further increase the costs. This can reduce the initial cost involved, but with increasing and changing compliance burdens and requests from LPs, these solutions can quickly become outdated. For some firms, to outsource even a single fund can cost as much as the price of the entire technology system for all of the funds that a firm might have.

One more reservation that fund managers have when considering an outsourcing partner is their flexibility and responsiveness. In the deal business where there is always something going on, administrators with a rigid structure can hold up the investment process; this is especially important when GPs are expected to conform to the administrators' service level agreement. When GPs keep functions in house they can assign dedicated staff to the firm's transactions, while at a fund administrator the team may have to work on planned deliverables for other clients.

Lastly, another factor to consider may be managing any switches to a new fund administrator. According to Preqin (2017), more than 36% of GPs surveyed had changed their fund administrators within the preceding 12 months whereas this same figure was 20% for placement agents or auditors and 24% for lawyers. The main reasons given for changing administrators were portfolio complexity, insufficient ability to handle regulatory complexity, and poor standards of service quality. Switching fund administrators can add to operational burdens at the end of the GP.

So how can GPs avoid these pitfalls of outsourcing? The first step is to make sure the fund administrator has the right knowledge and capability to handle the account. GPs seek to ask exhaustive questions about the

---

[14] Some managers prefer to buy multiple software solutions for different target areas from the same provider as a way to allow for greater communication between different in-house functions.

team that will work on the functions outsourced and the expertise of that team (the subsequent section will detail how fund administrators are chosen). The ability to understand the nuances of LP agreements is essential, in addition to knowledge of a jurisdiction's accounting framework. Often, GPs will only outsource what they view as low-value parts of their back-office chain. While they are more inclined to hand over certain administrative procedures and bookkeeping to an administrator, they may be reluctant when it comes to managing investor relations or distributing LP notices. This attitude is understandable given the paramount importance of maintaining strong LP relationships in such a competitive market.

A second step is to appoint an individual responsible for collaborating with the administrator. Good communication and collaboration between the GP and the service provider is critical. This dedicated executive should be involved in the due diligence process leading to the selection of the administrator, and in the execution of the actual outsourcing arrangement. The individual can also help with a rigorous oversight of and communication with the administrator, and maintain an understanding of the administrator's systems, service quality, and procedures.

The trend of increased outsourcing is expected to continue as LPs are putting more pressure on management fees. The goal of a GP should ultimately be to minimize costs and maximize efficiency. Unlike hedge funds where nearly 90 percent of firms outsource fund administration, only 30 percent of private equity and real estate firms were using a third party. However, this is expected to increase to more than 45% in the coming years.

CHOOSING AN INDEPENDENT FUND ADMINISTRATOR

When choosing a fund administrator, GPs should consider several factors in the due diligence process to ensure that the administrator is able to meet the demands of various stakeholders, including the LPs. The needs may change over time so GPs must determine the level of service expected and whether it is affordable. Focal areas will include the administrators' capabilities, processes, and people. Given their increasing demands and the competitiveness of the fund administration market, service providers should be prepared to undergo very close scrutiny:

- **Capabilities:** First, before private equity fund managers can even start the process of choosing a fund administrator, they need to figure out which business functions to outsource and what type of firm they are looking for. Once GPs decide what they want to outsource, they must then assess which fund administrators would be a good fit for their needs and analyze their capabilities. For example, while one administrator may be able to handle a "month-end only service," that same administrator may not be able to handle daily cash reconciliations or FATCA reporting services. Of equal importance are the administrator's knowledge of the private equity industry, and whether the firm has the right technology to meet all industry-specific expectations and requirements. GPs can collect information on capabilities by speaking to the administrator's clients; this can provide an indication of how the fund administrator will perform. Another factor could be the geographic locations of the fund administrator and whether or not the fund administrator has offices in relevant locations for the GP – for instance, close to the GP's headquarters and in major cities where the LPs may be located. Additionally, language capabilities and jurisdictional expertise (by being present on the ground in the relevant jurisdiction) could be additional factors to be considered.

- **Processes:** GPs frequently investigate whether the fund administrator has the right certifications in place. They can ask whether the administrators have a Statement on Standards for Attestation

Engagements number 16 (SSAE 16) certification in the United States, which is issued by the American Institute of Certified Public Accountants, or an International Standard on Assurance Engagements No. 3402 (ISAE 3402) outside the United States, which is issued by the International Auditing and Assurance Standards Board. These standards were developed to certify the adequacy of internal controls within a service organization, thereby distinguishing high-quality service providers such as fund administrators. Such certifications provide GPs and their investors with confidence that the fund administrator has adequately devised its processes and internal controls, and that it operates effectively to achieve its specified objectives. In particular, both GPs and their LPs need to understand how the administrator's processes ensure that the work performed is free of errors. Fund administrators should have strict internal quality control departments that operate independently from the operational team that serves as an extra set of eyes to review transactions and reports. Processes are also affected by which technology platform the administrator uses. GPs are expected to assess the reliability of the platform via a number of questions: Is the platform owned by the administrator? Is it scalable? Is it user friendly? Can the platform withstand cyberattacks? Can it be integrated with the GP's in-house systems? Etc.

- **People:** Just as an LP would not commit to a fund without assessing the fund managers, GPs should not commit to a fund administrator without learning more about the team that will service them. This team will be an extension of the fund manager's own staff, so it is crucial that the GP know and trust all team members. GPs should (and are expected to) demand detailed information about the team that will support them, and inquire about the team's experience in private equity fund administration, how long the members have worked together as a team, whether they have any conflicts of interest, etc. The team's experience can be assessed by interviewing key team members and asking about their exposure to other funds and various situations that have prepared them to effectively administer one of the GP's funds. Another area of interest for GPs is the administrator's staff retention rate. Staff turnover is an issue that has the potential to impact fund administrators, so GPs must be confident that their administrator has a competent human resource management team and appropriate incentives in place to ensure that key team members stay with the organization. Team continuity is incredibly important, and GPs should be asking detailed questions about the stability of the team that will be servicing their funds. Finally, since every private equity fund is different, GPs should expect to collaborate with teams that can provide customized services rather than a one-size-fits-all service.

When choosing an administrator, GPs pay close attention to the prices charged by administrators as well as their business strategy. However, the cheapest providers may not provide the service expected. In an effort to submit the lowest bid to win the mandate, some administrators underestimate the level of interaction and responsiveness the GP expects, or the level of transactional activity and reporting required. When it comes to the business strategy, GPs prefer to work with service providers whose core business is fund administration as these providers can be more focused on servicing the GP beyond the current fund rather than having other lines of business affect the service quality. If the GP has plans to diversify into multiple types of investments or geographies over the next set of funds that will be raised, providers whose core activity is fund administration are likely to be able to service those as well. Moreover, these administrators have dedicated compliance teams that can easily provide regulatory review and monitoring services specific to those funds.

Ultimately, what sets a fund administrator apart is its expertise in the private equity industry, flexibility with GPs' and LPs' individual needs, and ability to navigate through all regulatory and accounting changes to administer a fund successfully.

INDEPENDENT FUND ADMINISTRATION AND FUND COMPLEXITY

Historically, independent fund administrators have located their businesses in the domicile of the fund, and have generally been single-domicile businesses; this is still the case for most. Increasingly, however, independent fund administrators must take a more holistic approach as the days of single domiciliary structures are long gone. Often, the main fund will sit in one domicile, fed by investor-specific vehicles domiciled elsewhere, with complex multi-entity (and sometimes multi-domiciliary) vehicles used to purchase investments. A structure using five different domiciles is not uncommon. While professional advisers offer advice based on investor needs and tax planning concepts, unless the administrators involved are able to administer such structures in an economic and efficient manner, much of the economic benefit created by the structure will be wasted.

Independent fund administrators designed to manage and control small local funds are not designed to manage global funds. With multi-domiciliary structures, managers may be forced to use multiple administrators. This situation undoubtedly leads to inefficiencies and increased costs. Multiple parties must be involved, creating additional complexity in what can already be a highly complex transaction. Cash needs to be moved across multiple organizations and multiple bank accounts, raising risk of delays within the international banking system. Finally, with multiple organizations involved (each keeping accounts and financial records for their own part of the transaction), there may be a need to re-key data from one administrator to another, which can only be inefficient, generate unnecessary costs, and open the door to data input errors.

An additional source of fund complexity arises from the increasing regulation that is starting to have a major effect on administrators' businesses. Regulators are creating more legislation that has a global effect (e.g., FATCA, AIFMD, CRS). Administrators must be able to service the regulations no matter where it may originate from.

Therefore, organizational structures based around the concept of small local offices may not be the best model for full global fund administration. To gain maximum efficiency, and to provide the appropriate economic benefits and service efficiencies to clients, the centralization of work and processing must be considered. Individual offices, each replicating numerous tasks, are both inefficient and expensive and are likely to lead to inconsistencies within the organization. GPs do not necessarily want to speak and liaise with multiple parties across multiple local offices of the fund administrator. Instead, they want a single point of contact, with coordinated and efficient processing.

A global independent fund administration business needs a stable, scalable technological infrastructure. But with powerful, consistent technology (providing multi-lingual reporting), new opportunities are available, including the ability to "move" work around time-zones; the ability to maximize the use of resources wherever they may be in the organization; and the ability to provide a consistent level of reporting to GPs, wherever their funds or investors are domiciled in the world.

CONCLUSION

To keep pace with regulation and the due diligence demands of investors, fund administrators need to make investments in new systems and technologies. As demands for data continue to grow, these service providers are also expected to administer not only more complex instruments, but also multi-asset products. As well as managing variety, fund administrators must deliver quickly, as GPs demand faster and more dynamic delivery of management information. Fund administrators must also be prepared to be subject to regular operational due diligence from the LPs as part of the GP's due diligence before a capital commitment is made.

With the possibility of large technology firms entering the market, automation can help incumbent independent fund administrators protect their margins by enabling them to cut costs and increase their scale. In addition, innovative thinking can allow these firms to identify opportunities to add more value to GPs and redefine themselves as business partners. By understanding managers' strategic directions and working closely with them to develop supportive technologies, independent fund administrators can empower their GP clients and help them differentiate or gain a competitive advantage. The most successful firms providing fund administration services understand precisely what their clients want and need and consistently deliver on time. These fund administrators have recognized that their clients are global players (either in terms of their portfolios or their investors), and that to best service their clients they too must be truly global.

APPENDIX A

Which AIFMs need to report to the regulators and which regulators they need to report to?

All authorized or registered AIFMs need to report to the regulators. EU-AIFMs only need to report to their home regulators. Non-EU AIFMs need to report to the regulators of all EU countries where they are marketing their funds.

What is the format of the report?

The ESMA template of the reports that the regulators have used to develop their own versions can be found on ESMA's website.

Put simply, the first tab shows the AIFM report. The second tab is the AIF report applicable to all funds. Third tab is the AIF report only applicable to fund managed by an above-threshold AIFM. The fourth tab is applicable to funds that employ leverage.

When does the reporting need to happen?

Small AIFMs need to report on an annual basis for year-end December 31 each year.

Private equity AIFMs managing unleveraged AIFs that invest in unlisted companies to take control are also only required to report on an annual basis.

Frequency of reporting of other AIFMs can be found in ESMA's guidance.

How much time is provided for the reporting?

All reporting needs to happen within 30 days of the period end. Fund of funds get 45 days.

What is the process of submitting the reports?

Reports in the United Kingdom need to be submitted through the FCA's Gabriel system and can also be manually filled in using the online interface. Reports to most other regulators need to be submitted by generating an XML file.

What if the fund does not have any numbers to report?

AIFMs which have notified the regulators that they will be marketing their funds will need to file a report as per their reporting frequency, even if no close has been made and the fund has not called any money. Such a return is called a nil return and has minimal information to report.

In her own words: Heloisa Chaney, Partner and COO at Blantyre Capital

The pricing and valuation of illiquid portfolio investments bring significant administrative and operational challenges for private capital funds whose investors expect greater transparency, better reporting and tighter accounting processes. In most situations, fund managers can model individual positions on a case-by-case basis, but when funds invest in impaired assets whose values are difficult to assess or when assets in their portfolio become impaired, it is difficult to obtain accurate valuations. Aside from that, warrants and options are sometimes built into some of the investment strategies, increasing the complexity of valuations.

It is important that, in the event of a problem with an individual investment or when investing in distressed and special situations, managers are in a control position. Given that not all investors are aligned, a control position allows managers to convince other stakeholders to coordinate some form of legal action. As the private capital market has matured, a developed infrastructure of service providers, from lawyers to fund administrators, has evolved. Nevertheless, fund managers are expected to have in house capabilities to deal with distressed credit such as specialist credit analysts and valuation experts.

The regulatory environment both in the US and in Europe, where it varies from country to country, brings additional complexities especially because of new rules that are continuously aiming to bridge the gaps between regulated and unregulated lending activities. Compliance with the Alternative Investment Fund Managers Directive in Europe remains a major challenge for fund managers who must ensure that there is independence between risk management and portfolio management activities in the case of complex and illiquid strategies. Challenges are even higher when it comes to reporting as different types of investors are regulated themselves. For instance, pension funds require Solvency II reporting.

Larger private capital fund managers have expertise in-house, but many the mid-range managers must rely on third-party service providers. The burden of greater credit risk capability, due diligence and technology that comes with regulatory pressures and complex investment strategies in illiquid markets force these managers to look to third-party fund administrators for the provision of additional services. Outsourcing administration enables fund managers to focus on creating value in their fund and generating good returns.

10 Tax Considerations in Fund Structuring

You must pay taxes. But there's no law that says you gotta leave a tip.
Morgan Stanley advertisement

INTRODUCTION

The tax consequences to fund managers and investors inevitably play a critical role in the fund structure. In evaluating these tax consequences, an additional consideration must be the investment strategy of the fund. This chapter provides a high level overview of the principal U.S. federal income tax and U.K. tax issues that arise in relation to the formation and operation of private investment funds. Section 1 outlines the U.S. federal income tax considerations that are the key drivers for typical investment funds, fund managers, and fund investors. Section 2 addresses the overriding tax principles in the United Kingdom, in relation to income tax, capital gains tax, and value-added tax (VAT). General terms of the U.S. income tax framework are outlined in Appendix 1, and Appendix 2 contains a glossary of all abbreviations used in this chapter.

U.S. TAX CONSIDERATIONS

An investment fund is usually organized as an entity that is a partnership for U.S. federal income tax purposes. This way, there is no federal income tax imposed on the fund, and instead, the U.S. tax consequences to investors in the fund will be based on each investor's particular status. In addition, when the fund is organized as a partnership for U.S. federal income tax purposes, each partner's share of tax items realized by the fund (e.g., dividend income or long-term capital gains) will generally retain the character those items had at the fund level.

For any one investor, the optimal structure for the fund will be driven based on the expected type of income and gains realized by the fund (which typically will vary based on the investment strategy of the fund) and the investor's particular tax circumstances. Because of the different tax consequences applicable across classes of investors, the final structure of the fund will balance the different considerations of the classes of investor, taking into account their relative investment in the fund. The following is a discussion of the

This chapter was co-authored with Arnold P. May and Robert E. Gaut, Partners, and Stephen Severo, Associate, at Proskauer Rose LLP.

structural considerations for certain classes of investor based on an investment fund's strategy. This discussion is of a general nature only, and there are numerous exceptions and limitations to the rules discussed below. Accordingly, this chapter should be used as a framework to understand the general tax concepts, but not as a substitute for careful tax planning.

General U.S. tax rules for an entity treated as a partnership for U.S. income tax purposes

An entity treated as a corporation for U.S. federal income tax purposes is subject to tax at the entity level on its income and gains (including gains from a distribution in kind, measured as if the distributed property had been sold for fair market value), and distributions (whether in cash or in kind) by the corporation are potentially subject to an additional level of tax, usually as a dividend, at the shareholder level. In addition, shareholders are subject to tax on gains from the sale of stock in a corporation (measured as the excess of the proceeds from sale, less basis).

In contrast to the two levels of tax associated with a corporation, an entity treated as a partnership for U.S. federal income tax purposes typically only gives rise to one level of tax, at the partner level. This single level of tax is effected in two ways: first by causing each partner to take into account in determining its taxable income the partner's share of tax items realized by the partnership, and second, by allowing distributions by a partnership to a partner to be received tax free to the extent of the partner's basis in the partnership. To the extent a partner receives a distribution in excess of basis, however, that excess will be treated as gain from the disposition of an interest in the partnership.

Considerations for U.S. tax-exempt investors

Certain types of entities, such as state and local governmental entities, are exempt from U.S. federal income tax. Other types of tax-exempt entities (such as charities, universities, pension plans, and endowments) are *generally* exempt from U.S. federal income tax, except on income that is "unrelated business taxable income" (UBTI). UBTI is widely defined as income from a trade or business regularly carried on, less deductions attributable to such trade or business, that is not related to the tax-exempt organization's exempt purpose. This exception frequently arises when private investment funds hold an interest in an operating business organized as an entity treated as a partnership for U.S. federal income tax purposes, or when investment funds incur indebtedness.

As an initial matter, due to the breadth of the UBTI rules, investment income could be included as an item of UBTI and therefore taxable. However, under the so-called "modification rules," certain items of income (such as capital gains, dividends, interest, rents, and royalties) do not constitute UBTI. These modification rules are the workhorse provisions that allow for tax-exempt entities to earn income and gains from investment funds in a tax-efficient manner.

Yet, the modification rules generally do not apply with respect to a portion of the income or gains from an asset that has "acquisition indebtedness" any time during the year (in the case of income from the asset) or any time in the prior 12 months (in the case of disposition of an asset). The portion of the income or gain to which the modification rules do not apply (where such portion is determined by reference to certain factors, including the amount of outstanding debt at certain periods of time) is referred to as "unrelated debt-financed income" (UDFI). Acquisition indebtedness is typically the unpaid amount of debt incurred (1) to acquire or improve property, (2) before the property was acquired or improved, but which would not have been incurred "but for" such acquisition or improvement, and (3) after the property was acquired or improved if such debt would not have been incurred but for such acquisition or improvement and such acquisition or improvement was "reasonably foreseeable" at the time the property was acquired or improved. Because of these rules, many tax-exempt entities otherwise subject to the UBTI rules will carefully scrutinize the manner in which a private investment fund intends to use leverage.

In most cases, the realization of UBTI or UDFI will result in a tax return filing obligation and an obligation to pay taxes on the applicable income. Historically, tax-exempt investors had a strong desire to avoid the tax return filing obligation, but most tax-exempt entities with exposure to the private investment fund asset class are no longer concerned about this filing obligation, and instead typically evaluate an investment opportunity based on expected after-tax returns. That said, certain types of tax-exempt entities known as charitable remainder trusts will be subject to a 100% tax on their entire income for any year in which the entity has any UBTI. Accordingly, these investors will seek strong assurances regarding the realization of UBTI, or will otherwise structure the investment to ensure no UBTI is realized.

In the past, private investment funds have at times structured their funds to allow eligible tax-exempt investors (certain pension plans and individual retirement accounts) to hold an interest in the fund through a "group trust." The group trust would pay any taxes on UBTI, and would also file applicable U.S. federal income tax returns, thereby relieving the underlying investors from those obligations. Group trusts are not frequently used today. Instead, for these tax-exempt entities that seek to avoid UBTI, it is more common to structure the applicable tax-exempt entity's interest in the fund (or in a particular investment in the fund) through a "blocker corporation," as discussed in more detail below.

Certain types of tax-exempt entities (generally, those which receive a significant amount of overall donations from a group of "related" persons) are referred to as "private foundations." Private foundations are subject to the UBTI and UDFI rules noted above, and also certain excise taxes. One such excise that is a consideration in structuring private investment funds is the excess business holdings tax. Under this rule, additional taxes (and potential loss of tax-exempt status) will apply if a private foundation owns (directly or indirectly), and when aggregated with the ownership of certain other persons, more than 20% of (1) the voting power of a "business enterprise" that is a corporation or (2) the capital or profits interests of a "business enterprise" that is a partnership. Because of these rules, most private foundations will typically limit their ownership interest in a private investment fund to less than 18% of total commitments.

When applying these rules, there are two other provisions of note. First, the 20% threshold increases to 35% if it can be demonstrated that another person has effective control over the corporation. Second, the tax rules provide that an entity will not be a "business enterprise" if at least 95% of the entity's gross income is from passive sources.

Considerations for non-U.S. persons

Non-U.S. persons are generally taxed in the United States only on income from sources within the United States. The manner of taxation depends on the type of income earned and the activities of the non-U.S. person. If the non-U.S. person is "engaged in a trade or business in the United States," income from that trade or business is referred to as "effectively connected income" (ECI). A non-U.S. person that realizes ECI will be required to file U.S. tax returns, and will be subject to tax on the ECI in the same manner as if the person were a U.S. person. In addition, the realization of ECI may give rise to a withholding tax obligation.

For income that is not ECI, the non-U.S. person will be subject to a 30% withholding tax on the gross amount (i.e., no permitted reduction for expenses related to the production of the income) of certain types of income, such as dividends, interest, rents, and royalties. This rate of withholding tax is subject to reduction (e.g., pursuant to a treaty between the United States and the country in which the non-U.S. person is resident). Further, interest that is "portfolio interest" is not subject to this U.S. withholding tax. Portfolio interest is interest paid (directly or indirectly) by a U.S. person to a non-U.S. person that owns less than 10% of (1) the voting power of the payor, where the payor is a corporation for U.S. federal income tax purposes, or (2) capital or profits of the payor, where the payor is a partnership for U.S. federal income tax purposes. To qualify as portfolio interest, certain other requirements must be met, including that the interest not be determined by reference to (1) the receipts, sales, or other cash flow of, (2) the income or profits of, (3) any change in value of any property of, or (iv) any dividend, distribution, or similar payments made by, the debtor or certain persons related (based on attribution rules) to the debtor. The portfolio interest exception is a significant exemption from the general rules applicable to withholding, and loans by an investment fund to a portfolio company are typically structured to qualify for this exception.

Although interest income earned by a non-U.S. person from a U.S. payor is usually subject to a 30% withholding tax (subject to reductions, as noted above), if the interest income is from a "lending trade or business" within the United States, then that income will be treated as ECI. This rule is a significant impediment to non-U.S. persons holding an interest in an investment fund that originates loans.

An important provision of U.S. tax law is that gains realized by a non-U.S. person from the disposition of stock of a U.S. corporation are not treated as ECI, are not subject to a 30% U.S. withholding tax, and do not give rise to a U.S. tax return filing obligation.

Under the Foreign Investment in Real Property Tax Act (FIRPTA), however, gain from the sale of a "United States real property interest" (USRPI) is treated as ECI. A USRPI includes any interest (other than solely as a creditor) in a corporation that is a "United States real property holding company" (USRPHC). A corporation will be a USRPHC if, at any time within the shorter of the five-year period prior to the sale of the securities or the taxpayer's holding period, more than 50% of the value of such corporation's assets consisted of "United States real property interests" (generally, U.S. real estate and assets permanently affixed to U.S. real estate).

There are several noteworthy exceptions to the USRPI rules that are applicable to a USRPHC. First, a corporation is not a USRPHC if it disposes of all of its USRPIs in a taxable disposition. This "purging" sale may lead to transactions being structured as a sale by the corporation of all of its USRPIs followed by a sale of the stock of the corporation. Second, the FIRPTA rules related to a USRPHC are not applicable if the stock of the corporation is publicly traded and the non-U.S. person did not own more than 5% of the stock of the corporation during the shorter of the five-year period prior to the sale of the securities or the taxpayer's holding period. Due to some technical issues related to how this 5% test is applied when a non-U.S. person holds stock of a corporation through a partnership, private investment funds may structure the ownership of stock of a corporation that is, or expected to become, a USRPHC and the exit is expected to be by way of an IPO through a series of parallel partnerships where non-U.S. persons hold interests in a partnership that does not own more than 5% of the stock of the underlying corporation. Note, however, that where stock of a privately held USRPHC is exchanged for stock of a public company, gain from that exchange may nevertheless be taxable even if the exchange would otherwise be tax free under other provisions of U.S. tax law. Lastly, the rules related to taxation of gain from the sale of a USRPHC were recently relaxed, so that certain non-U.S. pension plans are no longer subject to tax on these gains.

In the private investment fund context, in addition to ECI from an investment by the fund in a USRPHC or from a lending business, ECI may arise from an investment in an operating business organized as an entity treated as a partnership for U.S. federal income tax purposes. For these types of investments, generally, the non-U.S. person's share of the income from activities of the underlying operating partnership will be ECI to the extent attributable to a trade or business conducted in the United States, and a non-U.S. person's share of that income will be subject to U.S. withholding tax. The U.S. tax authorities have issued guidance to the effect that the gain from the sale of such a partnership interest, to the extent attributable to the U.S. business activities of the partnership, will similarly be ECI. This guidance has been heavily criticized (mainly due to questions relating to whether the guidance could only be affected by statute), and a recent court case concluded that under the specific facts of the case, gain of this nature was not subject to U.S. tax. As of the time of writing this chapter, it is not known whether the U.S. government will appeal the court decision or whether any statutes will be enacted to mandate that this type of gain be subject to U.S. tax.

In addition to the treatment of ECI, a non-U.S. person that is a corporation may be subject to a 30% "branch profits tax" (or lower rate if reduced by treaty or otherwise) on certain amounts received by the non-U.S. person with respect to its activities from a U.S. trade or business. The branch profits tax was intended to be equivalent to the 30% withholding tax imposed on dividends paid by a U.S. corporation to a non-U.S. person, but it has much broader potential applications. As a result, a non-U.S. person that is a corporation for U.S. income tax purposes should carefully consider these rules before holding an investment in any entity that is not a corporation for U.S. federal income tax purposes and is engaged in a trade or business within the United States.

Certain non-U.S. persons are entitled to special U.S. tax rules. For example, pursuant to Section 892 of the U.S. Internal Revenue Code, non-U.S. governmental entities (so-called "Section 892 investors") are potentially exempt from U.S. source interest, dividends, and capital gains (including capital gains from the sale of a USRPHC). In addition, certain types of non-U.S. entities that would otherwise be subject to UBTI (generally, an entity that is organized exclusively for specific purposes, such as religious, charitable, or scientific purposes) may be eligible for special U.S. tax status, pursuant to which, the entity will only be subject to U.S. tax on ECI that is also UBTI.

The Foreign Account Tax Compliance Act (FATCA) is a U.S. effort to combat tax evasion by U.S. persons holding accounts and other financial assets outside of the United States. Under FATCA, U.S. taxpayers holding financial assets outside the United States must report those assets. FATCA also requires certain non-U.S. financial institutions to report information about financial accounts held by U.S. taxpayers or by non-U.S. entities in which U.S. taxpayers hold a substantial ownership interest. The disclosure reporting requirements apply to non-U.S. funds as well, or such funds may otherwise be subject to U.S. withholding tax on U.S. source dividends and interest, along with proceeds from sales of U.S. securities.

Considerations for U.S. taxable persons

For U.S. taxable persons, typical U.S. federal income tax planning strategies include deferring the recognition of taxable income or gains, maximizing and accelerating the recognition of deductions and expenses, and managing the character of tax items realized in a transaction. In addition, there are two other sets of rules that should be considered when U.S. persons hold (directly or indirectly) stock of a non-U.S. corporation: the passive foreign investment company (PFIC) rules and the controlled foreign corporation (CFC) rules. These rules generally do not apply to U.S. tax-exempt entities or non-U.S. persons.

The PFIC rules protect against the potential abuse where U.S. persons hold assets generating passive income through a non-U.S. corporation. Absent the PFIC rules, a U.S. person could defer current tax liability on income earned by the non-U.S. corporation, and potentially convert income that otherwise would have been short-term capital gain or ordinary income into long-term capital gain. The PFIC rules eliminate this activity by imposing extremely onerous tax consequences to income or gains realized by a U.S. person from an interest in stock of a non-U.S. corporation that has a significant amount of passive income or uses a significant amount of its assets to generate passive income, unless the taxpayer makes certain elections, such as electing to include currently in income the U.S. person's share of income earned by the non-U.S. corporation. Because the PFIC rules are intended to prevent certain conduct, the planning to address these rules is more in the nature of identifying the issue when it arises and ensuring the transaction is structured so that the appropriate elections can be made.

Under the CFC rules, a U.S. person may be subject to tax currently based on the activities of the non-U.S. corporation, even if no amounts are distributed. Moreover, the CFC rules could cause all or a portion of the gain realized from the sale of the stock of the non-U.S. corporation to be re-characterized as dividend income rather than capital gain. The CFC rules only affect "U.S. shareholders" of a CFC (and if a person is a U.S. shareholder of a CFC, the PFIC rules generally do not apply to that person with respect to the CFC). Although the CFC rules were designed to prevent certain conduct that was perceived as having the potential for abuse, unlike the PFIC rules, the CFC rules and their implications are not generally addressed through the decision to make an election.

A non-U.S. corporation will be a CFC only if "U.S. shareholders" collectively own more than 50% by vote or value of the non-U.S. corporation. For these purposes a "U.S. shareholder" is a U.S. person that owns 10% or more of the voting stock of the non-U.S. corporation. The CFC rules identify U.S. shareholders by reference to the stock ownership of a U.S. person (and the determination of stock ownership is based on actual stock ownership as well as indirect ownership, taking into account certain attribution rules). A U.S. person includes a partnership entity organized under the laws of the United States. As a result, ownership of stock of a non-U.S. corporation through a U.S. partnership could cause a non-U.S. corporation to be treated as a CFC (and thus subject each U.S. person that owns an interest in the U.S. partnership to the CFC tax rules) even if no one partner of the U.S. partnership would be classified as a U.S. shareholder based on that partner's indirect interest in the non-U.S. corporation. For example, if 11 unrelated U.S. persons owned equal interests of a U.S. partnership and that U.S. partnership owned 100% of the stock of a non-U.S. corporation, the non-U.S. corporation would be a CFC and the U.S. partnership would be a U.S. shareholder. If, however, the stock of the non-U.S. corporation were held by each of the partners of the U.S. partnership directly, then no shareholder would be a U.S. shareholder with respect to the non-U.S. corporation.

Because of these CFC rules, an investment fund with an investment strategy focused on investments outside of the United States should consider organizing the fund in a non-U.S. jurisdiction, especially if the fund intends to take larger control positions in the underlying portfolio companies. Alternatively, if the fund documents otherwise permit, a U.S. domiciled fund may be able to eliminate the application of the CFC rules by making non-U.S. investments through an "alternative investment vehicle" (AIV) structure, where the AIV is a non-U.S. entity that is "brother-sister" to the U.S. domiciled fund, and all investors hold a direct interest in the AIV. Through this arrangement, the determination of U.S. shareholder status would be based on each investor's ownership interest in the fund.

Funds that only invest in corporate securities

For a fund that acquires debt or equity securities only in entities treated as a corporation for U.S. federal income tax purposes, and where the fund is not engaged in a lending trade or business, the universe of potential income mainly consists of interest, dividends, and capital gains.

For non-U.S. investors, the investment decision from a U.S. tax perspective will center on the expected amount of income subject to U.S. tax. For example, if the fund is expected to realize significant dividend income from a U.S. payor, then a non-U.S. person's share of that income would be subject to a 30% U.S. withholding tax, unless an exception applies. A special consideration should also be given in cases where the fund's portfolio investments are expected to includes any stakes (other than solely as a creditor) in a USRPHC, and for cases where the fund is expected to realize interest income that is not eligible for the "portfolio interest" exclusion as defined above.

Although interest, dividends, and capital gains are within the "modification" rules and therefore exempt from UBTI as a rule, the use of leverage potentially gives rise to UDFI for investors that are tax exempt and otherwise subject to UDFI.

After the potential sources of U.S. tax leakage are identified, structural revisions should be considered. For example, UDFI could perhaps be eliminated if the tax-exempt investor were to hold its interest in the fund through a "blocker corporation." A U.S. blocker corporation is generally not advisable for this purpose since that corporation would be subject to U.S. tax on all of its income. In contrast, a non-U.S. blocker corporation would only be subject to U.S. tax on certain income (in the same way as any other non-U.S. investor, as discussed above), and if the blocker corporation were organized in a tax haven jurisdiction, no entity-level tax would be imposed in the blocker corporation's home jurisdiction. Thus, for a prospective investor that is tax exempt and considering using a non-U.S. blocker structure, the analysis will turn on the expected amount of income that would otherwise be taxable in the United States (e.g., dividends, interest income not eligible for portfolio interest, and gains from the sale of stock of a USRPHC) at the blocker level, and whether any available exceptions could be applied to reduce that tax, balanced against the expected tax leakage under the UDFI rules if the investor were to participate in the fund directly.

When considering the likelihood of dividend income, the investment strategy of the fund is highly relevant. For example, most venture funds do not expect a portfolio investment to pay dividends. Rather, the typical exit is expected to come from a sale of securities or IPO. For a portfolio company of a buyout fund, a dividend—usually funded through additional leverage at the portfolio company—is a realistic possibility, however.

To address the possibility of withdrawing money from the company in the future, fund managers may consider structuring the initial investment to include a loan to the company. In that case, any repayments of the loan will generally be tax free. This type of loan arrangement has an additional tax benefit in that interest expense on the loan may give rise to a deduction at the company level. A non-U.S. investor's share of the fund's corresponding interest income from such a loan would be subject to a 30% withholding tax, unless an exception applies. As discussed above, the portfolio interest exception is frequently used to eliminate this withholding tax. For a non-U.S. person to be eligible for the exception, that non-U.S. person must hold less than 10% of the voting power of the corporation. The test for voting power is based on the ability to elect directors, and is based on both actual ownership of voting power and indirect ownership (e.g., through a partnership). Where a non-U.S. investor holds a sufficiently large percentage of the fund—such that the non-U.S. investor's percentage ownership of stock through the fund would equal or exceed the 10% voting power threshold—it may be advisable to establish a parallel fund, where the non-U.S. investor is a partner in that parallel fund and the parallel fund's stock ownership in the underlying company has low voting power but otherwise has the same economic value.

If the fund expects to hold interests (other than solely as a creditor) in an entity that is a USRPHC, and a potential exit scenario includes an IPO, then the fund may consider structuring the investment to be made through multiple parallel entities, so that investors who are sensitive to ECI (and do not have the benefit of an exception from the imposition of U.S. income tax on gains from a USRPHC) participate in such investment only through partnership entities that own 5% or less of the stock of the USRPHC. In addition, those non-U.S. investors who are sensitive to the potential U.S. return filing obligation from ECI by reason of ownership of a USRPHC may request that the fund structure the investment so that those non-U.S. persons can participate in the investment through a non-U.S. blocker corporation. Although the non-U.S. blocker corporation does not eliminate any actual tax liability to be borne by the participating investors, the blocker corporation would be the party that has a U.S. tax return filing obligation. Certain non-U.S. investors will find attractive this lack of obligation to file a U.S. tax return.

Funds that invest in a company organized as a partnership

If the fund invests in equity securities of an entity treated as a partnership for U.S. federal income tax purposes, and that partnership conducts a business directly or indirectly through one or more other entities that are transparent for U.S. income tax purposes, then the character of income earned by the fund from that investment is the same as the character of income earned by the underlying partnership, and similarly, each fund partner's share of the fund income will retain that same character. These types of "flow-through" investments are frequently expected to give rise to UBTI and/or ECI.

The typical approach to UBTI and ECI in this case is for the fund to allow electing partners the opportunity to participate in the investment through a blocker corporation. In this way, the blocker corporation will have the obligation to file U.S. tax returns, and the blocker corporation will pay the tax on its income that otherwise would have flowed out to the partners participating in the investment. Historically, the blocker corporation would be a U.S. entity. In light of a recent court case regarding the U.S. tax rules applicable to a non-U.S. person from the sale of an interest in a partnership that conducts a trade or business in the United States, a blocker corporation organized under the laws of a non-U.S. jurisdiction may be advisable. The rationale for this conclusion is discussed in more detail below.

At this juncture, it may be helpful to understand why (from a U.S. income tax perspective) an investment would be structured as a partnership rather than a corporation. Examples of the potential U.S. income tax efficiencies of organizing an operating business as a partnership, rather than a corporation, include the following:

- A partnership entity allows for a sale of the business to be structured in a manner that gives the purchaser a new fair market value basis in its assets without the imposition of any entity-level tax. That "stepped up" basis has value because it gives rise to additional depreciation, and that depreciation will usually reduce taxable income for the buyer going forward. In a competitive transaction, buyers will frequently pay more for a business due to this basis step-up. Note that, although an entity treated as a corporation for U.S. federal income tax purposes is not prohibited from selling its assets, such a sale would be a taxable event at the corporate level, and any gain generally would be taxable at the corporate level. The resulting corporate-level tax liability is typically more than the potential tax benefits to the buyer of a basis step-up, and accordingly, a sale of all or substantially all of the business assets of a corporation is often structured as a sale of the stock of the corporation rather than its assets.

- Where the exit strategy includes a sale of assets to multiple buyers, if the business were conducted through an entity treated as a corporation for U.S. income tax purposes, each sale would potentially give rise to tax liability at the corporate level as well as additional tax when the proceeds are distributed by the corporation. In contrast, in a partnership structure, gains from these sales would be taxable at the partner level and distributions to the partners would be tax free.

- Where the investment strategy will include acquisitions with some equity rollover component, a partnership structure allows for the potential to acquire the assets without the sellers realizing taxable gain with respect to the equity received in the exchange. Although an exchange of property for stock of a corporation could potentially be "tax free," such a tax-free transaction must satisfy certain requirements, and those requirements will not necessarily be met in all cases.

- Distributions by a corporation are potentially treated as a taxable dividend, whereas distributions by a partnership are potentially tax free.

With those efficiencies serving as a background, when evaluating whether to participate in an investment through a blocker corporation, the key economic comparison for an investor to make is between the after-tax returns from investing directly compared to investing through a blocker corporation, assuming the investor is otherwise comfortable with the resulting tax return filing obligations and is not at risk of losing its special U.S. tax status by reason of participating in the investment directly.

With respect to current income from operations of a business, generally, if the investor were to participate in the investment without going through a blocker corporation, income from the investment would be taxable (either as UBTI or ECI). Assuming the investor does not have other tax attributes to offset that taxable income, the tax liability to the investor as a result of being taxed on its share of income from the operations of the business would be approximately equal to the tax liability that would be borne by a blocker corporation. Thus, the amount of current income expected to be generated from the investment is not usually considered in the analysis, unless the income is of a nature that would not otherwise be UBTI or ECI, or the investor has tax attributes that could shelter the income (such as net operating loss carryforwards). However, in some cases, it is possible to reduce blocker corporation tax liability by way of capitalizing the blocker corporation with debt.

Similarly, distributions of excess cash flow (i.e., distributions out of operating income or from borrowings) are typically not a significant consideration for tax-exempt investors, since the excess cash flow would not be UBTI regardless of whether the tax-exempt investor participated in the investment directly or through a blocker corporation. There is, however, at least some question of whether the proceeds to a tax-exempt entity from a leveraged distribution by a partnership would cause the tax-exempt entity's other assets to be treated as having acquisition indebtedness.

Distributions of excess cash flow may be a consideration for non-U.S. investors in that, if the non-U.S. investor were to participate in the investment directly, distributions generally would not be subject to further U.S. tax, other than the potential for a branch profits tax imposed on a non-U.S. investor that is a corporation for U.S. federal income tax purposes. In contrast, a non-U.S. person's share of dividends paid by a U.S. corporation is subject to a 30% U.S. withholding tax, unless an exception applies. Note that if a treaty rate applies to reduce the U.S. withholding tax on dividends, the same reduced rate is generally applicable to reduce the branch profits tax.

The impact of the taxation of current income and distributions of excess cash flow is largely overshadowed by the tax consequences upon a sale of the investment. In this regard, the exit (assuming it is a sale of the entire business) potentially could be structured to include a sale of the blocker corporation securities, rather than a sale of interests in the business held by the blocker corporation. A sale of the securities of a blocker corporation may not be possible in all circumstances, however. For example, certain industries, such as oil and gas, are typically conducted through a partnership and a sale of blocker corporation securities is usually not feasible from a commercial perspective.

Where a sale of blocker corporation securities is possible, the buyer will not be entitled to the same basis step-up that would be available when purchasing interests in a partnership, and accordingly, the buyer may negotiate for a purchase price of blocker corporation securities that is less than the price at which the interests in the company held by the blocker corporation would be sold. As an economic matter, that reduced price may be borne solely by the holders of the blocker corporation or by all sellers (with the result that the purchase price is "equalized" among the holders of securities of the blocker corporation and the other holders of direct interests in the company). If the exit could be structured to include a sale of securities of the blocker corporation, the gain from that sale generally would not be ECI (assuming the blocker corporation is not a USRPHC) or UBTI. Assuming the gain is not ECI or UBTI, tax-exempt investors and non-U.S. investors participating in the investment through the blocker corporation would not bear any U.S. federal income tax on their gain from the sale of the business.

In a sale of a blocker corporation securities, unlike the result of a sale of interests in the underlying company, then for tax-exempt investors, all or a portion of the gain could be UBTI (generally based on the amount of debt at the company level that gives rise to acquisition indebtedness, and also based on the amount of depreciation that was previously used to reduce the income tax liability of the tax-exempt entity). Hence, by participating in an investment through a blocker corporation, a tax-exempt investor must evaluate (1) the benefits of potential tax-free returns from a sale of securities of a blocker corporation, coupled with the potential for lower gross proceeds from such a sale as compared to the gross proceeds from a direct investment; (2) the risk of an exit not including a sale of securities of a blocker corporation; and (3) the expected after-tax returns from an unblocked investment.

The analysis for non-U.S. investors is similar, as it relates to the proceeds from a sale of securities of the blocker corporation compared with an exit that does not include a sale of those securities. However, the amount of gain treated as ECI is slightly different and currently somewhat uncertain. There is no doubt that, at a minimum, ECI will include the amount of gain attributable to appreciation in USRPIs held by the underlying company. As discussed, the U.S. tax authorities have issued guidance to the effect that, in connection with the disposition of an interest in a partnership that conducts a trade or business in the United States, gain attributable to the U.S. trade or business is ECI, but this guidance is now in question due to a recent court case. As a result, assuming the underlying company does not hold any USRPIs that have appreciated in value, if the facts of the court case apply and the result is not otherwise reversed by appeal or by enactment of a new statute, the non U.S. investor may be able to maximize after-tax proceeds from a sale by participating in the investment through a non-U.S. blocker corporation rather than a U.S. blocker corporation.

From a structural standpoint, the manner in which investors elect to be blocked can be made either up front or on a deal-by-deal basis. In some cases, the upfront election structure is implemented by placing all investors who desire to be blocked in a separate parallel fund.

Investments by a fund in a manner that accommodates separate blocker corporations for separate investments are affected in various ways, but typically, the underlying investment is made through an AIV where the blocker corporation is a partner of the AIV and the AIV holds no assets other than the applicable investment. Those partners who wish to participate in the investment through a blocker corporation hold stock of the blocker corporation either directly or indirectly through a "feeder" entity. Using this type of AIV arrangement with a feeder entity is preferable, from a logistics perspective, over structuring an exit that includes a sale of securities of the blocker corporation. Note that the key benefit of a blocker corporation is to effect the exit in a manner that includes a sale of securities of the blocker corporation. For this reason, a separate blocker corporation should be used for each investment. Otherwise, the purchaser of a blocker corporation would acquire (indirectly through its ownership of the blocker corporation) interests in a separate business. Alternatively, prior to a sale of the securities of the blocker corporation, the blocker corporation would have to distribute its interest in the other business and that distribution would be a taxable event at the corporate level, as if the corporation sold the separate business for its fair market value at the time.

Funds engaged in a trade or business

Special structural considerations apply to those investment funds with a strategy that itself would be treated as a trade or business within the United States or otherwise generates taxable income other than from the ownership of securities in a corporation. Examples of these circumstances include real estate investments (which generally use leverage, and therefore may give rise to UDFI, although there are some special exceptions for this); royalty income (the income from which is generally not ECI or UBTI, unless the assets have acquisition indebtedness, but non U.S. investors will be subject to a 30% U.S. withholding tax on the gross amount of the royalty income from U.S. sources unless an exception applies); and loan origination (the income from which is generally ECI but not UBTI, unless the assets have acquisition indebtedness).

In these cases, certain investors may benefit if the fund is structured as (or otherwise holds its investments through) a "real estate investment trust" (REIT), a "regulated investment company" (RIC), or an entity organized under the laws of a jurisdiction that has a favorable treaty with the United States.

Special considerations for fund managers

Investment fund managers typically receive two categories of earnings for their management efforts: (1) a management fee, payable to the management company and determined without regard to the portfolio performance, and (2) a carried interest based on the profits from investments.

"Carried interest" is a return to the investment manager that, broadly speaking, is measured based on the profits from the fund's investments. Importantly, from the fund manager's perspective, adding blocker corporations to the structure in order to address the tax concerns of a particular investor should not adversely impact the fund manager. Based on this rationale, generally, any tax liabilities of the blocker corporation are not taken into account in determining the fund manager's carried interest (so-called "carry below the blocker").

For fund managers, the main aspect of tax planning is to structure the carried interest so that it is an interest in the fund, with the result that any earnings from the carried interest are taxed based on the character of income realized by the fund. For fund managers otherwise taxable in the United States, the benefit of retaining the character of income earned by the fund is the potential to be taxed at preferential rates for long-term capital gains (to the extent such items are realized by the fund). If the fund is not expected to generate any meaningful amount of taxable income that is eligible for these preferential tax rates, then a fund manager may consider structuring the carried interest as a fee. In that case, however, certain rules applicable to deferred compensation should be evaluated. In addition, if the fund were to pay the carried interest as a fee, the ability of the other partners to deduct the fee may be limited.

In recent years, a strategy has evolved where the management fee is reduced and the fund manager earns a share of the profits equal to the amount by which the fee was reduced. Moreover, this fee waiver arrangement could be structured so that the amount by which the fee is reduced is used to satisfy the fund manager's capital contribution obligations. The fee waiver strategy has evolved to include many variations, with each variation creating different levels of tax and business risks.

U.S. tax authorities were concerned that these fee waiver arrangements created an opportunity for fund managers to convert what would otherwise have been classified as ordinary income to long-term capital gain in what they perceived as an abusive arrangement. To address those concerns, the tax authorities released guidance (which has not yet been finalized) to the effect that the fee waiver strategy will not be respected, with the result that the fund manager will be deemed to have management fee income rather than a share of profits from the fund, unless the fund manager bears some meaningful amount of entrepreneurial risk with respect to the fee waiver. Essentially, this guidance requires that any share of profits received by the fund manager by reason of the fee waiver strategy be contingent on the fund having sufficient cumulative net profits.

U.K. TAX CONSIDERATIONS

This section outlines the most common U.K. tax issues that arise in relation to the formation and operation of private equity funds. In some ways, the U.K. model mirrors that in the United States, but there are significant differences.

Although alternative structural models are sometimes used, the main vehicle of choice to act as the fund itself is, as in the United States, the limited partnership. For funds where the manager/sponsor is U.K.-based, this has historically been a U.K. (English or Scottish) limited partnership or one established in the Channel Islands (Jersey or Guernsey). Increasingly, particularly with the U.K.'s departure from the European Union (EU) looming in 2019, sponsors are increasingly using limited partnerships formed in a non-U.K. EU jurisdiction, such as Luxembourg.

This section assumes that the fund is formed as a U.K. limited partnership, that its focus is private equity—namely, the acquisition of shares in trading companies to hold as investments for the medium to long term—and that it does not hold debt or real estate investments. For technical U.K. partnership insolvency reasons, a U.K. limited partnership is generally structured with a 99.99% loan/0.01% capital structure for LPs; this represents a structural difference as compared with a U.S. partnership (e.g., one formed in Delaware) but is economically identical to a 100% capital structure. Since April 2017, it has also been possible to form a specialized form of U.K. partnership known as the "private fund limited partnership" which has the principal advantage of benefiting from a "white list" of actions which, if carried out by LPs, will not prejudice their limited liability.

It is also assumed that the fund is managed by a U.K. manager and that the GP is a U.K. company, which is owned by the U.K. manager. Often the GP is itself a limited partnership or, indeed, a U.K. limited liability partnership. The GP will be entitled under the terms of the fund limited partnership agreement (LPA) to a "priority profit share," out of which the management fee is paid to the manager. In the early years of the fund, when profits and gains are low, the fund is able to advance moneys, funded by capital contributions by the LPs, to the GP to enable it to pay the management fee.[1]

As in other areas of private equity, the LPA will also normally provide for the LPs to receive a priority profit share or "hurdle" rate of return on their capital, typically in the 6–9% range. Once that return has been delivered and all invested moneys returned, the terms of the LPA then generally provide that further profits are divided 80% to the LPs and 20% to the carried interest holder, sometimes with a preliminary "catch-up" allocation of the profit sufficient to give the carried interest holders 20% of the aggregate return to date. The carried interest in a U.K. fund structure is normally held by a further limited partnership (normally Scottish) described as the "founder partner" in which the various participants in the carried interest are themselves LPs.

---

[1] This does leave the GP typically in a U.K. loss-making position in the early years of the fund. Its ability to carry forward those losses may be restricted under corporation tax rules introduced in 2017.

Other structures are possible, and are referred to in passing below, such as having a U.K. adviser to an offshore manager. The comments and tax description in this section, however, relate to the "onshore U.K." structure outlined above.

The main principles when structuring a private equity fund with a U.K. manager are to ensure that

- the fund partnership itself is U.K. tax transparent and is not taxed as an entity in the U.K.;

- where possible, the value-added tax (VAT) costs of the structure are minimized;

- non-U.K. resident LP investors are not liable to pay U.K. tax on their fund profits and gains; and

- the carried interest held by the fund executives and others is structured efficiently.

Taxation of investors (LPs)

A private equity fund with the investment rationale described in the introduction will be regarded as carrying on an investment activity for U.K. tax purposes, rather than a trade.[2] This is an important distinction because a non-U.K. resident LP in a partnership that is carrying on a trade would be liable to U.K. tax on its profits and gains from the partnership to the extent that the trade is carried on through a U.K. branch, agency, or permanent establishment. Clarifying this point is a detailed area of law, and requires consideration of double taxation agreements (DTAs) and the U.K. "investment manager exemption," which are beyond the scope of this section.

The fund partnership will be regarded as transparent for U.K. tax purposes, and each LP will be responsible for its own liabilities to tax on income or chargeable gains arising in relation to the fund and for paying any tax due, and such liabilities will not be assessed on the fund.

Limited partners who are not, never have been, and do not intend to become U.K. residents should generally not be subject to U.K. tax on investment income arising to the fund from non-U.K. sources or capital gains on the disposal of assets held by the fund. However, such LPs may be subject to U.K. withholding tax on certain investment income arising to the fund from U.K. sources; in practice, this is normally limited to U.K. source interest, which is subject to a withholding tax of 20%. Such partners' liability to U.K. tax on their share of any U.K. source interest is effectively limited to their share of such withholding tax. Partners resident in a jurisdiction with which the United Kingdom has a DTA may be able to reclaim all or part of their share of such withholding tax.

There is one exception to this rule which concerns non-U.K. resident LPs who hold their interest in the fund as part of their own trade (e.g., non-U.K. financial traders, such as banks or insurance companies). These investors may be treated as carrying on part of that trade in the United Kingdom through a U.K. permanent establishment or a branch or agency which is their U.K. representative, such as the U.K. GP or the U.K. manager. That permanent establishment, branch, or agency can then be assessed to tax the profits of such a partner to the extent the profits are properly attributable to that permanent establishment, branch, or agency (including capital gains on the disposal or deemed disposal of certain U.K. assets, being, broadly, those used in, by, or for the permanent establishment, branch, or agency of the U.K. trade). Yet, exceptions from this rule may be available under domestic U.K. law or under the terms of a relevant DTA, depending on the facts. If this rule is engaged, the manager and/or the GP will normally be entitled under the LPA to retain an amount

---

[2] Confirmed by U.K. Inland Revenue (now Her Majesty's Revenue and Customs (HMRC)) in a statement to the British Private Equity and Venture Capital Association (BVCA) in 1987.

equal to the LP's liability or estimated liability to U.K. tax, and to account for such amounts to the U.K. tax authority (HMRC).

Non-U.K. resident LPs who are themselves tax exempt in their local jurisdiction, and who are not themselves carrying on a trade, will not be liable to any U.K. tax on their investment in the fund, save for any U.K. source withholding tax in the limited circumstances described. U.K. resident tax-exempt investors, such as U.K. pension schemes, will be exempt from U.K. tax on their investment profits from this type of fund.

The GP's share of profits will be a first charge on income and/or capital gains of the fund. Accordingly, the other LPs should not be subject to tax on any income and/or capital gains which is/are so applied. This exemption is particularly important for U.K. resident investors. If the GP's share was instead structured as a fee payable directly by the fund limited partnership to the manager, it is unlikely that such U.K. resident investors would receive a U.K. tax deduction for their allocable share of such a fee.

VAT issues

A crucial U.K. fund structuring issue that is not a factor for the structuring of U.S. funds is VAT. In the standard structure discussed here, the U.K. manager is considered a provider of VAT taxable supplies of fund management.[3] The fund limited partnership and/or the U.K. GP is viewed as the recipient of those supplies.[4] The receipt by the GP of the priority profit share should be outside the scope of U.K. VAT.

Normal structuring involves making the U.K. manager, the U.K. GP, and the fund partnership (via the GP) members of the same U.K. VAT group. Doing so means that the management fee would attract no U.K. VAT, as it would not be regarded as a supply, being between group members. However, the impact of VAT grouping is that VAT input tax incurred by the VAT group on its expenditure would be irrecoverable—and hence, a cost—to the extent that it is incurred in connection with exempt supplies by the group. Many of the VAT supplies of the group (such as transferring shares and other securities to EU-based recipients) will be VAT exempt, which will also affect the ability of the VAT group to recover all of its input VAT on expenses and overhead costs.

In other structures, the VAT position can be very different. If the fund limited partnership is established outside the EU (e.g., in Jersey) and the GP is then also established there, services from U.K. managers will be outside the scope of U.K. VAT, but the manager should be able to recover its associated input tax VAT. In other structures that use a Luxembourg partnership, such as a "special limited partnership" (SLP) with a Luxembourg GP, the broader scope of the VAT exemption for management services in Luxembourg can lead to low levels of VAT leakage.

Carried interest

The tax treatment of carried interest for U.K. tax resident individuals involved in fund management was substantially rewritten between 2015 and 2017. This area is now very complex, and the U.K. effective tax rate in almost all cases has increased as a result of the changes to the rules.

---

[3] The United Kingdom interprets the scope of the exemption for fund management services more narrowly that certain other European jurisdictions, particularly Luxembourg.

[4] The technical position here as to whether the partnership or the GP is the recipient of the management services, and which entity is registrable for U.K. VAT, is complex and is still somewhat dependent on HMRC's pending consultation on VAT grouping and the impact of the ECJ cases *Larentia + Minerva* and *Marenave* (C-108/14 and C-109/14).

The rules apply to any individual who carries on "investment management services"[5] for a fund that is either a collective investment scheme or an investment trust. The starting point is that, unless any income, gain, or other return arising to such an individual is an "arm's length" return on an investment or "carried interest" (as defined in the legislation), it will be considered to be a "disguised investment management fee" (DIMF) and taxed as the profits of a deemed U.K. trade at a current rate of 47% (assuming the highest income tax rate and national insurance contributions). These rules apply to all U.K. resident investment managers, subject to the new rules on how those not domiciled in the United Kingdom are treated. The rules also apply to non-U.K. resident managers to the extent that they are carrying on their management trade in the United Kingdom through a permanent establishment, although in many cases, the expectation is that DTA protection will be available based on the manager not personally having a U.K. permanent establishment.

Proceeds that are carried interest are taxed at the capital gains tax rate applicable—currently 28%. In addition, if the form of the carried interest is income in nature (e.g., interest or dividends), there is a separate charge to income tax at the applicable (higher) rates, with double tax relief against the chargeable gains on a just and reasonable basis.

Investment managers who are U.K. resident but non-U.K. domiciled may be able to claim the remittance basis of taxation, where foreign chargeable gains are taxed in the United Kingdom only when they are remitted to the United Kingdom, in certain circumstances in relation to carried interest. Gains accruing in respect of carried interest will be treated as foreign chargeable gains capable of benefiting from the remittance basis of taxation only to the extent that the relevant investment management services to which the carried interest relates were undertaken outside the United Kingdom. This rule will require executives to apportion their carried interest, and carry out a complex analysis of their working time spent in the United Kingdom and elsewhere on the relevant investment fund.

The final piece of the revised legislation is the "income-based carried interest" (IBCI) rules. At present, these apply only to individuals who are self-employed (normally as a member of a U.K. limited liability partnership) but not to those who are employees. This legislation can operate to switch off the favorable carried interest treatment of sums arising to an investment manager, and instead move those sums back into the DIMF regime. Again, the rules are complex but essentially test, at the time the carried interest arises to the individual, the weighted average holding period of investments in the fund from which the carried interest has arisen. If the average holding period is 40 months or more, then the IBCI rules will not apply and the favorable carried interest treatment is not jeopardized. If the average holding period is less than 36 months, then all of the carried interest will be IBCI and subject to full income tax as DIMF. There is a sliding scale of relief where the average holding period of investments is between 36 and 40 months. Special rules apply for more complex arrangements (e.g., funds of funds, secondary funds, and debt funds).

Taxation issues at the holding company level

U.K. companies are often used as holding companies for the acquisition of portfolio investment companies by private equity funds because this arrangement frequently represents an efficient structuring option.

A U.K. resident holding company offers the following principal tax advantages:

---

[5] Defined broadly to include fundraising, researching potential investments, and acquiring, managing, or disposing of property on behalf of the fund.

- No withholding tax on dividends paid by the U.K. company.[6]

- Broad exemptions from U.K. tax on dividends received.

- Exemption from taxation of gains realized on disposal of share investments in trading companies under the "substantial shareholding exemption" (SSE), subject to conditions which including a 10% minimum shareholding and one-year holding period.

- Corporation tax rate of 19%, currently scheduled to fall to 17% in April 2020.

- Generous interest deductibility rules, but these have become significantly more restrictive following the United Kingdom's enactment of certain of the OECD "Base Erosion and Profit Shifting" (BEPS) action items.

Shareholder and other related party debt will be subject to the U.K. transfer pricing regime, which will only allow deductions against corporation tax for the amount of interest that would be payable on arm's length terms. The transfer pricing rules should not apply to interest costs on third-party financing.

All debt of a U.K. company is subject to a variety of other restrictions on interest deductibility:

- A cap on net financing costs for a U.K. group equal to (1) 30% of taxable EBITDA, or (2) the net external interest to earnings ratio for the worldwide group, whichever is higher.

- The disallowance of U.K. tax deductions for payments on certain hybrid instruments or hybrid payments where there is a mismatch of treatment in the payee jurisdiction. These rules are particularly broad and also require the U.K. company to examine any hybrid features in related upstream non-U.K. financing arrangements.

- Late paid interest rules can defer deductions for accrued interest until it is paid by the U.K. borrowing company (where it is not paid until 12 months after the end of the accounting period in which it accrues). These rules will be in point in relatively limited circumstances—principally, where a loan is made to a U.K. company that is a close company (companies under the ultimate control of a partnership such as a standard private equity limited partnership will generally be close) by one of the participants in the company and certain other conditions are met.

The United Kingdom imposes withholding tax on interest paid by a U.K. company at the rate of 20%. This amount can be reduced or eliminated under the terms of any applicable DTA between the United Kingdom and the lender's jurisdiction of residence. Advance clearance from HMRC is required in order to pay the interest subject to a DTA rate of withholding tax. Foreign lenders who benefit from a DTA with a favorable withholding tax rate with the U.K. can apply for a "Double Taxation Treaty Passport" (DTTP) from HMRC, which can significantly speed up the process for obtaining a clearance for the U.K. borrower to pay interest subject to the relevant DTA withholding tax rate. In addition, various other domestic law exemptions apply to the withholding tax charge on interest. These include payments to a bank or company that is resident in the United Kingdom and brings the interest into the charge to U.K. corporation tax. There are also exemptions for interest payable on a "quoted Eurobond," which is a loan note listed on a recognized stock exchange, and also for interest payable on a "qualifying private placement" (QPP). A QPP is an arm's

---

[6] Assuming it is not a REIT.

length loan that (1) is not entered into for tax avoidance purposes, (2) is unlisted, and (3) has a term no longer than 50 years. It cannot form part of a single placement with an initial aggregate minimum value of £10 million. The lender must satisfy various conditions, including that it is a resident of a "qualifying territory" (i.e., a state with which the U.K. has a DTA containing a non-discrimination article).

APPENDIX A: U.S. INCOME TAX FRAMEWORK

General

In the United States, "U.S. persons" (generally, individuals who are citizens of the United States or are otherwise present in the United States for a statutory period of time, certain entities organized under the laws of the United States and certain trusts and estates) are subject to tax in the United States on their worldwide income. In contrast, non-U.S. persons are subject to the tax in the United States only on income from sources within the United States (so-called "U.S. source income").

U.S. federal income tax is collected through (1) the filing of a return by the applicable person, possibly together with a payment of taxes by such person, and/or (2) the imposition of a withholding tax on the person making the payment giving rise to taxation. If tax is required to be collected by withholding, the person required to make the withholding may be personally liable for the tax if withholding is not made. Taxes withheld from payments to a person are treated as an advance against amounts otherwise due from such person.

In the United States, tax is determined on an annual accounting convention, where tax is typically imposed on gross income, less applicable deductions, for the taxpayer's tax year. A significant part of the tax rules is devoted to determining what items are taken into account in calculating taxable income and deductions, and when those items are to be taken into account.

Once taxable income is determined, an additional set of rules governs the applicable tax rate, with tax rates varying based on the type of income (e.g., "ordinary" versus "capital") and the type of taxpayer (e.g., individuals versus corporations).

Numerous statutory provisions govern the timing of recognition of tax items, including provisions relating to the deferral of recognition (e.g., certain exchanges of stock of a corporation for stock of another corporation, and certain contributions of property to a partnership or a corporation) and the disallowance of losses (e.g., a sale of property between related parties).

Tax rates

Gains from the disposition of a capital asset such as stock of a corporation are characterized as either long-term capital gain or loss (if the holding period of the asset is more than one year) or short-term capital gain or loss (if the holding period of the asset is one year or less). Other types of income are referred to as "ordinary income." The highest marginal tax rate for ordinary income and short-term capital gains is currently 35% for corporations and 39.6% for individuals. Corporations are similarly subject to a maximum marginal tax rate of 35% for long-term capital gains. Individuals, however, are eligible for a preferential maximum marginal tax rate of 20% for long-term capital gains as well as dividends (but with respect to dividends paid by a non-U.S.

corporation, this preferential rate does not apply in all cases). Individuals are also potentially subject to a 3.8% tax on "net investment income."

Basis

The "basis" of an asset is generally the cost of an asset, as otherwise adjusted. A taxpayer's basis in an asset will impact many of the tax consequences resulting from the asset. For example, gain (or loss) from the sale of an asset is measured by the difference between proceeds from the sale of the asset and its tax basis. In addition, the amount of depreciation (i.e., the amount of deductions available per year from the ownership of the asset) is a function of tax basis, where the period of time over which basis is depreciated varies based on the type of asset. The basis of an asset is generally reduced by the amount of depreciation available for the asset in any particular year.

A partner's basis in a partnership is the partner's cost of the partnership interest (1) increased by the partner's share of any income or gains, the amount of money contributed, and, with respect to contributions of property, the basis of the property so contributed, and (2) decreased by the partner's share of any items of loss, expense, or credit of the partnership, the amount of money distributed, and, with respect to distributions of property, the basis of the property so distributed. Finally, a partner's share of debt at the partnership level will increase the partner's basis in the partnership, and any reduction in a partner's share of debt at the partnership level will be treated as a distribution by the partnership to the partner. Note that a partner's basis in property distributed generally will be a carryover basis (i.e., the partnership's basis in the distributed property), but in no event more than the partner's basis in the partnership.

Character of an instrument as debt versus equity

The tax consequences of a security issued by an entity vary depending on whether the security is debt or equity for U.S. federal income tax purposes. The income from debt is interest income to the debt holder and generally deductible by the borrower, and the payment of principal on the debt is generally tax free to the debt holder and not deductible by the borrower. As with most tax regulations, there are numerous exceptions to these general rules. For example, debt issued for a price that is less than the redemption price—e.g., lender loans $9.9 million to a borrower for a debt instrument with a face amount of $10 million—will give rise to $100,000 of "original issue discount" that is generally treated as interest income over the period during which the note is outstanding. Similarly, special rules apply where a debt instrument is purchased by a third party at a discount (or premium) to the amount owed on the debt.

The determination of whether an instrument is treated as debt rather than equity is based on facts and circumstances. For purposes of this chapter, an instrument referred to as debt or equity is presumed to have that treatment for applicable tax purposes. Things get more complicated when an instrument is treated as debt (or equity) for U.S. federal income tax purposes, but is treated differently for relevant non-U.S. tax purposes.

Entity classification and the double tax system

For U.S. federal income tax purposes, an entity is generally characterized as a corporation or a partnership. The determination of whether an entity is a corporation or a partnership for U.S. federal income tax purposes is made pursuant to the "check the box" rules. Under these rules, certain entities are "per se" corporations and cannot make an election to be treated as a partnership, whereas all other entities can elect their desired tax status, with a set of default rules applicable to an entity that does not make any election. Under a separate set of rules, an entity otherwise taxable as a partnership will be treated as a corporation if the entity is a "publicly traded partnership." To avoid these publicly traded partnership rules, as well as for other commercial reasons, most private investment funds have strict limitations on the ability of investors to transfer fund interests.

C corporations and S corporations

A C corporation is taxable at the entity level. Distributions by the corporation are taxable as dividends (to the extent of the corporation's "earnings and profits"—a tax concept similar to taxable income—where a corporation will have "current earnings and profits" based on the operations of the corporation for the year in which a distribution is made, or "accumulated earnings and profits" based on the cumulative operations of the corporation for all years prior to the year of a distribution), then tax free to the extent of basis (where distributions that are tax free for this reason reduce a shareholder's basis in the stock of the corporation), and then taxed as gain from the sale of the stock of the corporation. A shareholder of a C corporation will further recognize gain (or loss) upon a disposition of the stock of the corporation. The imposition of a tax on the corporation and an additional tax on the shareholder from distributions by the corporation or disposition of the stock of the corporation is the so-called "two levels of tax" created by a C corporation. Unless specifically stated otherwise, all references herein to a "corporation" refer to a C corporation.

An S corporation, in contrast, generally is not taxed on its income. Instead, the shareholders of the S corporation are subject to tax on the tax items realized by the S corporation as well as gains from the sale of stock of the S corporation, but distributions are generally tax free. In addition, basis in stock of an S corporation is increased (or decreased) by the shareholder's pro rata share of tax items realized by the S corporation, and is also decreased by distributions by the S corporation (and distributions in excess of basis result in gain to the S corporation shareholder). These basis adjustments effectively eliminate the two levels of tax typically associated with a C corporation. Because eligibility for S corporation status is limited, private equity funds typically do not own stock of an S corporation. Note that a somewhat obvious tax planning opportunity of causing a corporation to elect S corporation status and then selling its assets (thereby avoiding the corporate-level tax imposed on C corporations) is not available, because "built in gains" at the time of conversion from C corporation to S corporation are subject to an entity-level tax if realized within five years following the conversion.

Similar to an S corporation, partners of a partnership are subject to tax on their pro rata share of the partnership's tax items, with basis adjustments similar to those applicable to an S corporation. As a result, ownership of a business through an entity treated as a partnership for U.S. federal income tax purposes eliminates the two levels of tax associated with a C corporation. There is a detailed and complex set of rules that apply in determining a partner's share of tax items realized by the partnership. These rules are beyond the scope of this chapter.

Exceptions to the double tax system of corporations

Although a corporation is generally subject to tax on its income with no deduction for dividends paid, in some cases, a deduction for dividends may be allowed (thereby substantially eliminating tax at the corporation level) for a C corporation that has elected to be a REIT or a RIC.

Non-U.S. governmental entities

Non-U.S. governmental entities enjoy special tax status for U.S. federal income tax purposes. These types of investors—so-called "Section 892 investors" (because the applicable rules are set forth in Section 892 of the U.S. Internal Revenue Code of 1986, as amended—are generally exempt from U.S. tax. The exemption does not apply to income from a "commercial activity." Distilled down, these rules effectively exempt Section 892 investors from tax on any interest, dividends, and capital gains from the stock of a corporation (including a corporation that is a USRPHC), as long as (1) the Section 892 investor does not own (by vote or value) 50% or more of the entity paying such interest, dividends, or capital gains, and (2) in the case of interest income, the interest is not from a lending trade or business. If the Section 892 investor is not eligible for Section 892 status, then the investor would be subject to U.S. tax in the same manner as any other non-U.S. investor.

An important distinction to note is that there are two types of Section 892 investors. Although both types are subject to the same immediate tax liability noted above, one type will always retain its Section 892 status regardless of the activities of the investor, and the other type will potentially lose its exempt status if it is engaged in any "commercial activity" which could include being a partner in a partnership that is engaged in a commercial activity. Although the potential for loss of exemption has been narrowed in recent years, most Section 892 investors will create subsidiaries to hold interests in partnership entities in order to ring-fence the commercial activity risk due to the potential significant adverse tax consequences of losing exempt status.

APPENDIX B: GLOSSARY OF ABBREVIATIONS

U.S. Taxation

AIV	Alternative Investment Vehicle
CFC	Controlled Foreign Corporation
ECI	Effectively Connected Income
FATCA	Foreign Account Tax Compliance Act
FIRPTA	Foreign Investment in Real Property Tax Act
PFIC	Passive Foreign Investment Company
REIT	Real Estate Investment Trust
RIC	Regulated Investment Company
UBTI	Unrelated Business Taxable Income
UDFI	Unrelated Debt Financed Income
USRPHC	United States Real Property Holding Company

U.K. Taxation

DIMF	Disguised Investment Management Fee
DTA	Double Tax Agreement
DTTP	Double Taxation Treaty Passport
HMRC	The U.K. tax authority: Her Majesty's Revenue and Customs
IBCI	Income-Based Carried Interest
QPP	Qualifying Private Placement
SSE	Substantial Shareholding Exemption
VAT	Value-Added Tax

11 Risk Management in Private Equity

Risk is like fire: If controlled it will help you; if uncontrolled it will rise up and destroy you.
Theodore Roosevelt

INTRODUCTION

The recent financial crisis has undoubtedly increased awareness among limited partners (LPs) about risk management practices employed by general partners (GPs). Anecdotal evidence suggests that many LPs conduct risk analyses not just of the fund but also of the private equity firm as a whole. Risk management is a particularly important area for large GPs that follow multiple investment strategies. Private equity managers are also becoming much more proactive in terms of risk management. Increased competition has made it more difficult to raise, borrow, invest, and return capital, while legal and regulatory risks have increased as new regulations—such as the Dodd-Frank Act, Basel III, Solvency II, the Alternative Investment Fund Managers Directive in Europe, and the Foreign Account Tax Compliance Act in the United States—came into effect. The stiffening regulatory environment of the private equity industry has been highlighted by former European Commission president Jose-Manuel Barroso, who stated that "no financial player should be exempt from regulation and oversight." This commitment covers both hedge funds and private equity funds.

Like many other asset classes, private equity involves significant risk. In fact, lacking continuous marking-to-market makes this asset class more difficult to measure and manage in terms of risk. From a GP's standpoint, risk management primarily involves mitigating risks associated with the GP's investments and the management of these investments. In addition to these risks, which GPs are compensated for managing, there are many other types of risk, ranging from market and operational risks to regulatory, legal, accounting, and tax risks. Clearly, GPs have different risk management needs depending on the type of private equity assets they invest in and the length of time for which they are holding them. The more thorough their approach to risk management, the higher the probability of delivering better returns to LPs. On the other hand, from an LP's standpoint, risk management involves implementing procedures and activities that minimize the probability of losing capital and the uncertainty of private equity funds' returns.

Risk management in a private equity firm can be a core activity, a cost center, or a critical differentiator in the market. While some GPs view it as a core operational activity, others may roll their eyes and view it simply

This chapter has benefited from feedback provided by senior partners at Validus Risk Management.

as a tedious requirement brought about by increased regulation and LPs' demands for greater transparency of GPs' activities. However, in the case of many fund managers, risk management strategies provide differentiation in the fundraising market and are a source of competitive advantage. For instance, a risk management program could potentially add value to investors by lowering the volatility of a private equity fund's performance.

On the investment side, private equity fund managers engage in substantial risk mitigation activities:

- First, GPs carry out extensive financial, legal, and commercial due diligence on companies and the sustainability of their projections before investing. This due diligence process performs a critical risk management function.

- Second, GPs draw down capital from investors only when needed to invest or cover management fees, and do not hold investors' cash for any significant period. This universal practice among private equity funds acts to limit liquidity risk.

- Third, GPs that use debt when making investments do not take debt at the private equity fund level (except for short-term bridge financing in some circumstances)[1]. They typically hold the leverage at the portfolio company level, thus insulating the private equity fund from default risk.

- Fourth, GPs often mitigate risks through portfolio diversification. Within a single private equity fund, this approach is usually achieved through limits on a fund's maximum exposure to any single investment. Investments are also made across industries and by deploying the capital over an investment period of three to five years. However, while these features of private equity investing fulfill a risk management role, they do not fully eliminate all investment risks.

Beyond investment activities, effective market risk management is a crucial area for GPs to address in light of the currency, commodity price, and interest rate fluctuations that have become commonplace since the global financial crisis. In addition, operational risk—that is, the risk of losses stemming from inadequate or failed internal processes, people, and systems—is also at the top of GPs' agendas as managers seek to meet the above-mentioned raft of new regulatory requirements.

Finally, LPs view illiquidity and a lack of precise valuation of the assets under management as major risks. The measurement risk is partially offset by GPs applying conservative valuations for their portfolios, in part because reputation is critical for raising the next fund.

TOPOLOGY OF RISK CATEGORIES

Regardless of whether a formal or an informal risk management policy exists, most GPs assign the responsibility of implementing this policy to senior professionals in the firm, highlighting the importance of risk management in the governance of the fund's day-to-day activities. Very often, a chief risk officer, a managing partner, the board, or an executive risk management committee is responsible for implementing the risk management strategy. Depending on the size of the firm and the assets under management, these responsibilities may be further allocated to other lower-level committees, including investment and portfolio review committees or regional committees. Frequently, GPs implement risk management policies because they are concerned about capital losses in the portfolio in worst-case outcomes, because they want to improve the fund's risk-adjusted performance, or simply because LPs request risk management policies during and after fundraising (see survey by Talmor and Vasvari, 2014).

Before discussing the measurement and management of risks by both GPs and LPs, it is worth classifying the various types of risks; one way to do so is to distinguish between *qualitative* and *quantifiable* risks.

---

[1] Nevertheless, some GPs started to use fund level leverage. This could be a significant (and controversial) trend in the industry.

Qualitative risks

Qualitative risks cannot be accurately and easily measured using objective data, and must therefore be considered through relative measures which inherently involve subjective assessments. For example, these risks are captured through rankings (e.g., first, second, etc.), descriptive categories (e.g., high, medium, and low), or scales (e.g., 1–10). Such assessments require deep knowledge and experience of the market in which the fund operates.

From the perspective of GPs, qualitative risks cover many aspects related to their investments (e.g., quality and commitment of the portfolio company's management, likelihood that the transaction can be executed, likelihood that the operational strategy can succeed, regulatory effects on the portfolio company, quality of information about the portfolio company, etc.) or the performance of the portfolio company (e.g., achievability of business and profitability targets, market environment, demand for company's products, strength of competitors, expansion strategy, management performance, or quality of environmental, social, and governance criteria).

From the perspective of an LP, qualitative risks are likely to include assessments of the quality of the fund managers (e.g., experience, team size, deal sourcing capability, execution capability, incentive structures, ability to recruit and retain talent, ability to obtain subsequent funding, etc.), quality of the information about the environment in which the fund operates (e.g., macroeconomic indicators, regulatory changes, competitive pressures, etc.), or quality of other investors in the fund (e.g., likelihood that they fail to meet capital calls, likelihood that they will exert undue influence over the manager, etc.).

Quantifiable risks

Quantifiable risks are those that can be measured and benchmarked using objective and verifiable data obtained at a relatively low cost. In the case of GPs, quantifiable risks may include market risks (e.g., commodity and currency risks) or portfolio company metrics (e.g., sales and EBITDA growth rates, valuation multiples, leverage multiples, etc.). Some of the quantifiable risks that LPs care about are private equity portfolio diversification (i.e., across industries, years, managers, funds, and investment strategies, given that in private equity it is not possible to rebalance portfolios easily) and market risks (e.g., foreign exchange fluctuations, commodity price changes, etc.). Because private equity is an illiquid, long-term asset class and provides irregular cash flows, LPs find it difficult to adopt a standard risk measurement framework.

Another way to classify risks is from the perspective of whether the risks are under the control or beyond the control of the LPs and GPs. *Intrinsic risk* factors can be defined as factors that are specific to the investment process followed by GPs and LPs, while *extrinsic risk* factors are specific to the external environment in which the private equity funds operate. We discuss each set of risks separately in the sections below.

Intrinsic risks

Intrinsic risks are those that are intrinsic to the nature of running a private equity fund, which involves the selection, structuring, monitoring, and exiting of the investments. A typical private equity fund takes investors' capital and invests it into companies, expecting that their valuation will improve by the time they are sold. Naturally, this expectation is subject to uncertainty, as there is no guarantee that the managers have selected the right companies or that the business strategies that they will implement while holding the investment will be successful. In addition, managers' abilities to create value and extract cash from investee companies vary greatly across industries. Intrinsic risks can be further sub-classified into investment risks, operational risks, and legal risks.

- **Investment** risks are commonly defined as positive or negative deviations from an expected return outcome. In the case of an LP, it is the risk that the private equity fund might underperform its peers; in the case of a GP, it is the risk that the investment in the portfolio company fails to provide the expected return. Private equity fund managers and their investors are ultimately paid to mitigate and control these risks, which they typically do via careful due diligence of investments (for GPs) or of managers and funds (for LPs). Investment risks also arise due to the potential negative impact of misjudged strategic decisions on returns, a lack of responsiveness to industry changes, or a lack of expertise necessary for the investment.

- **Operational** risks capture the potential loss resulting from inadequate or failed internal processes, people, or systems. Operational mishaps often damage private equity firms' reputations, and can lead to negative publicity, costly litigation, a decline in investors' interest for follow-up funds, or the departure of key employees. An example of failed processes could involve failing to file accounting statements according to the appropriate accounting standards (e.g., US GAAP/IFRS) or with due care and attention to auditing standards. In the case of failed monitoring procedures for people, there is a risk of loss when employees or affiliated persons act in an inappropriate or dishonest manner that causes a financial loss to the firm (e.g., funds stolen). Alternatively, there might be a risk that a portfolio company mistreats its customers or employees, causing them damage. In terms of systems, both GPs and LPs must handle uncertainties associated with the implementation of new technologies, including systems, software, or networks. Such implementation can lead to hardware and software failures, security breaches, data theft, data loss, and so on.

- **Legal risk** is the risk that clients, employees, regulators, or counterparties may take legal action against the GP, the fund's portfolio companies, or the LPs, resulting in protracted litigation, financial loss, and reputational damage. In particular, regulatory and compliance risk has become a significant part of the decision-making process for private equity investments. In the aftermath of the recent financial crisis, regulators have adopted tight regulations that are often unclear and require substantial effort to implement. Compliance with these regulations requires more attention and resources than ever. As a result, some fund managers have appointed separate chief compliance officers rather than expecting the CFO or general counsel to do this compliance work. In parallel, LPs are paying more attention to the extent to which fund managers comply with rules and regulations. Although economic performance remains the key criterion in selecting managers, LPs now assess more carefully the extent to which managers' transparency, governance, and information access meets the standards set by existing regulations.

Extrinsic risks

Extrinsic risk factors are specific to the external environment in which the private equity fund operates. We identify four main types of extrinsic risks that are faced by funds and their managers: market risks, liquidity risks, capital/funding risks, and credit/counterparty risks.

- **Market** risks reflect the uncertainty that *market events* might affect the values of private equity investments.[2] We discuss these risks in detail below.

  Limited partnership and investment management agreements between GPs and LPs are often quite flexible about market-related risk management activities. For instance, the manager may—but is not obliged to—enter into currency or interest rate hedging transactions on behalf of the partnership. The manager may also have the authority to enter into hedging arrangements to mitigate interest rate or currency risk for an investment's realization proceeds once a sale decision has been made. However, lenders may push GPs to look at hedging these risks at the portfolio company level.

  With volatility across asset classes rising, hedging various market risks, such as currency, interest rate, or commodity risks, could help private equity firms improve their return on equity. Obtaining consistently good returns is becoming much more difficult and, as market volatility increases, managing these risks poorly can drastically reduce the return on equity. There has been very little consensus in terms of what constitutes best practice with respect to market risk hedging at the private equity fund level. Academic survey evidence has shown that private equity managers undertake some currency and interest rate hedging to protect against "macro risks" (see Talmor and Vasvari, 2014). To date, the focus has been on currency hedging within larger leveraged buyout funds, listed funds, and funds of funds, as well as funds with return characteristics which are more stable (e.g., mezzanine and debt funds). Natural hedges can also mitigate against market risk volatility via a diversified portfolio over various geographies, vintages, and industries.

  From the perspective of LPs, there is a long-term risk of not recovering the value of their invested capital. This long-term capital risk can be affected by a number of market factors, such as low equity valuations that make it difficult for managers to exit at high prices,[3] substantial changes in interest rates (which can affect the value of investee companies purchased with significant leverage), or foreign exchange exposure. The latter can occur when there is a mismatch between the LP's reporting currency and the functional currency of the private equity fund.

- **Liquidity risks** occur when a GP is unable to redeem an investment at its preferred exit time. Private equity investments are structurally illiquid, in contrast to asset classes that are cyclically illiquid during periods of financial stress (e.g., high-yield bonds), but for which sufficiently liquid markets exist during "normal" cycles. A significant liquidity risk persists with private equity investments as the secondary market has not fundamentally altered the illiquid characteristics of private equity investing. Even though the secondary market has broadened substantially over the last two decades, it is still relatively small when compared to the total primary private equity fund market. Liquidity risk is generally difficult to measure and can be quite high in the private equity market relative to that in the public equity market.

- **Capital/funding risk** is one of the most important types of risk faced by a fund. It reflects the possibility that LPs might not be able to meet capital calls that follow their commitments to the fund.

---

[2] Market risk can also be viewed as the change in net asset value of the private equity fund which is driven by the portfolio company performance or capital structure (e.g. Revenue and EBITDA change). It is, however, important to note that this risk is also dependent on decisions made by fund managers and their auditors (e.g., the use of fair value accounting to measure the fund's net asset value). One way to measure the risk of a change in the fund's net asset value is to implement the Discounted Cash Flow methodology which can derive the value of the investments under different scenarios. The cash flows are discounted using appropriate risk-adjusted rates that quantify the risk inherent to the future cash flows.

[3] Managers have full discretion as to the timing of divestments from investee companies within the life time of the fund and can wait for better or acceptable market conditions to exit their investments. However, sometimes the fund needs to liquidate and the market conditions are unfavorable for long periods.

Capital risk needs to be diligently managed as investors can lose their full investment in the fund if they cannot follow up on capital calls in accordance with the limited partnership agreement rules.

– LPs have few liquidity sources to meet capital calls—namely, (1) distributions from other private equity funds, (2) external liquidity (e.g., borrowing from banks), (3) fund interest sales in the secondary market, and (4) sales of public equity positions or other assets in the portfolio. LPs can develop internal stress tests, including assumptions about accelerated drawdowns, delayed repayments, and lower investment returns compared to historically observed patterns. These stress tests can help in developing effective contingency plans.

– In buoyant economies, distribution proceeds are more than enough to cover LPs' open commitments. However, market downturns can pose challenges, forcing LPs to find alternative ways to finance open commitments. During the financial crisis in 2008, distributions from private equity funds dried up and LPs encountered difficulties in finding additional capital.[4] When the post-financial crisis recovery commenced, funds started investing again, creating potentially significant risks for LPs, especially for those that pursued "over-commitment" strategies that relied on an assumed ratio of distributions to drawdowns. While LPs can sell their stakes in private equity funds to fund their open commitments, the secondary market for private equity investments might be relatively small and highly inefficient exactly during those periods with high liquidity needs. Moreover, secondary market prices are often influenced by factors beyond the fair value of the partnership, which usually translate to heavily discounted prices. As a result, investors selling during periods of high liquidity are frequently forced to accept steep discounts to reported net asset values (NAVs).

– GPs should try to minimize capital risk by accepting commitments from large numbers of investors that have different sizes and cover many geographies.

• Apart from the portfolio companies and LPs which can default, a private equity fund faces a whole range of other counterparties, such as banks, brokers, and service providers. Thus, **credit/counterparty risks** involve an amount owed to the fund and the parameters, such as the exposure's duration or the creditworthiness of the counterparty, that determine the level of these risks.

STEPS IN A HEDGING PROGRAM

When GPs or LPs decide to pursue a hedging program, they need to go through several steps that ensure a dynamic hedging program. These steps include (1) identifying and measuring risk, (2) designing the hedging strategy, (3) establishing infrastructure, (4) executing and managing the hedging strategy (e.g., regularly adjusting the risk management parameters), and (5) monitoring and reporting to the investor base. We discuss each of these activities in detail below.

• **Risk identification and measurement:** At this stage, the risks must be identified and quantified. GPs/LPs should try to assess the magnitude of the risk exposure and its impact on the return profile of their investment vehicle and the proportion of risks that could be mitigated with hedges.

---

[4] A prominent example was from the university endowment of Harvard University which, in the last financial crisis, issued a $ 1 Bn bond to fund future capital calls and considered selling a private equity portfolio of $ 1.5 Bn at a 50% discount to its recorded net asset value to solve the funding issue.

- **Design of the hedging strategy:** The second step in the implementation of a hedging program involves defining the hedging guidelines/strategy. The GP/LP must design an optimal way to balance the risk reduction with hedging costs and liquidity requirements. This process involves defining the eligible hedging instruments, the net risk exposure to be hedged, the hedge ratio, and the hedge duration. The GP/LP must also decide on the frequency of monitoring the hedging strategy (i.e., daily, monthly, or quarterly). If these guidelines are not adequately established, the hedging program may not deliver the expected outcome due to poor implementation and/or may prove costly.

- **Infrastructure set-up:** The GP/LP must select eligible counterparties to implement the hedging program with, the terms to be negotiated, the document governing the hedging program, and the communication strategy toward stakeholders.

- **Hedging strategy execution and management:** At this stage, the GP/LP needs to decide how to manage the hedging program on an ongoing basis, as hedging contracts usually require calibration. More specifically, the GP/LP must determine the risk budget for the purpose of covering liquidity needs due to hedging (e.g., credit lines, expected cash flows, and commitments), the trigger levels (e.g., utilized cash flow thresholds) and the trigger actions (e.g., a temporary adjustment of the hedge ratio or closing an open hedging position).

- **Monitoring and reporting:** At this final stage, the hedging positions in correspondence to fluctuations in market variables (e.g., currencies, interest rates, or commodities) need to be regularly monitored, with any resulting hedging performance reported regularly. Most importantly, procedures need to be put in place to comply with regulatory reporting requirements.

The main challenge of any hedging strategy for a private equity investment is to avoid a situation where liquidating parts of the investment are required in order to generate proceeds to cover hedging losses. In this way, cash flow management is the central task of risk management, especially given that hedging risks in illiquid private equity investments are more complex than the risks associated with more liquid assets that have discrete cash flows and relatively objective valuations.

The reality is that many funds do not hedge their risk exposure to critical market risks that affect their performance. Market participants often cite low currency or interest rate volatility, forecasting uncertainty, difficulty in managing the liquidity impacts of hedging, large hedging costs, potential accounting volatility (created if the hedge and underlying exposure do not perfectly offset), or an overall lack of investor concern toward hedging. However, despite some complexity, hedging has proven advantages in terms of reducing the return dilution due to, for instance, adverse currency or interest rate fluctuations.

In the sections that follow, we discuss strategies to hedge market risks, which are extrinsic and can be quantified with relatively better accuracy. We start with a discussion on hedging currency risk, from both the LP and GP perspective, followed by an exploration of hedging interest rate and commodity risks.

HEDGING CURRENCY RISK

Introduction and key risks

The 2008 global financial crisis created a growing interest in currency risk management within the private equity sector. Consequently, an increasing number of private equity and debt funds are now implementing hedging strategies, often with a partial hedge ratio (e.g., 50% or lower for private equity funds, and a higher hedge ratio for fixed-income portfolios). Fund managers and their investors also started to use customized derivatives structures to overcome traditional hedging issues such as liquidity constraints. In fact, many GPs look at currency risk management as a potential source of competitive advantage. Reasons for this focus on currency risk within private equity include, among others:

- the recognition that currency volatility has a material impact on fund returns (e.g., the gap between the first and the fourth quartile return performance is about 15%, a level which is frequently matched by the annualized currency volatility);

- the increasing focus among LPs on risk management, including currency risk management; and

- a desire to capture and monetize large currency swings in favor of the fund.

From an LP's point of view, there are three options available in the case of currency risks: (1) hedging at the fund level, (2) hedging at the portfolio level, and (3) remaining unhedged. Currency risk may be mitigated through the construction of a well-diversified portfolio of investments (either within the fund or the overall portfolio) in order to establish a natural hedge; this implies that currency exposures need to be actively managed when selecting investments, suggesting that potentially attractive opportunities might be passed to avoid overexposure to certain currencies.

An alternative is to mitigate currency risks by hedging with derivatives (e.g., forward contracts, futures, options, and swaps). While these hedging methods can be effective in providing protection from the financial impact of exchange rate movements, as well as relatively easy to execute, they do have some disadvantages. The main two disadvantages are the cost (especially with options), which increases in periods of high volatility and market uncertainty, and the portfolio impact that arises when imprecise hedging methods are applied (e.g., with forwards and futures). As cash flow timing and size are unpredictable with private equity investments, these hedging instruments provide only imperfect solutions.

As noted, the most important drawback to creating a perfect hedging strategy is the sheer inability to estimate with any accuracy the *timing* and *size* of the cash distributions from private equity funds, as fund managers have their own agendas when deciding on distribution timing. When the exact foreign exchange exposure within the portfolio is ascertained, LPs need to make practical projections about the timing of cash inflows and outflows from their private equity investments. The margin of error could be very low or very high, leading to significant over- and under-hedging of the currency risk. The inability to forecast the timing and amount of cash flows and the resulting variation of the currency hedging program could lead to higher unnecessary risk in the portfolio. Thus, for many LPs, the optimal strategy for dealing with currency risk is simply to take no action, especially given the hedging costs involved.

An LP can decide whether to hedge the currency risk arising from private equity investment by assessing (1) the level and effectiveness of protection achieved, (2) the hedging costs, and (3) the currency volatility direction/magnitude and its impact on liquidity.

- **Level and effectiveness of protection:** LPs must determine the currency exposure at risk and how this can negatively impact the returns achieved from private equity fund investments relative to investments in other asset classes. They must also assess whether the currency hedging program is adequately tailored to cover currency risks in accordance with the desired level of protection against/tolerance of currency volatility.

- **Hedging costs:** LPs need to consider the large amount of hedging costs involved. These can be broken down into explicit costs (option premiums) and implicit costs (forward curve/credit charges). In addition, there are also ancillary/running costs such as reporting requirements, legal fees, and hedging adviser fees.

- **Liquidity impact:** Hedging currency risk can create a liquidity risk if the hedge (e.g., forward contract) requires the LP to monetize losses or post collateral before the underlying (illiquid) exposure generates losses. This process can be managed by selecting the right hedging strategy (i.e., options versus forwards) or by obtaining credit (trading lines) to fund negative mark-to-market hedging positions.

Many of the currency hedging considerations for LPs described above are similar for GPs. However, currency risk hedging for GPs can only occur at either the portfolio company level or the fund level. Although GPs can hedge currency risk at the company level, the process is cumbersome and requires significant resources, given the replication requirement for all of the portfolio companies in the fund. Therefore, currency hedging at the fund level sometimes is more efficient.

One way of dealing with currency risk at the fund level is to build a well diversified portfolio of underlying companies, in terms of relevant currencies. In this way, the correlation structure of the respective currencies may cancel out any unwanted currency volatility effects, effectively smoothing out the fund's cash flows. Managing currency risk exposure at the fund level can also allow the GP to create a *fund net currency balance*, which can then be more effectively hedged using derivatives.

Given that currency risk hedging has very different implications and dynamics at different private equity stages (from fundraising to exit), we provide a more detailed discussion of the subject in the following paragraphs.

Fundraising (GP currency risk mitigation)

A significant issue which often arises during the fundraising process is that certain LPs prefer not to be exposed to the denomination currency of the fund although they are eager to invest in the fund for diversification purposes. For instance, because pension funds' assets and liabilities are in the same currency, investments abroad require the conversion of the assets into a new currency whose value is uncertain at the time of receiving the financial return. To eliminate the currency risk, these LPs can attempt to hedge the currency exposure themselves. However, the GPs raising the fund can structure the fund in such a way to facilitate the hedging of the currency risk on the investors' behalf.

The GP can implement a currency feeder fund structure to attract investors who are concerned about the currency risk in order to provide a return profile that is protected from currency movements.[5] As an example, a manager of a euro-denominated fund may create a US$ feeder so that the investors in the fund can invest and receive dollars, without being directly exposed to the euro. This option may appeal to investors who are restricted from investing in other currencies, do not have the capability to manage currency exposures inherent in their investments, or want to avoid the additional effort and resources required to manage the currency exposures.

---

[5] Feeder funds are used extensively by private equity fund managers to cater to investors that are (or are not) subject to onshore taxation, to bundle together a large volume of smaller investors, to cater to a single investor (i.e., a single managed account) or to provide regulatory solutions.

There are important advantages to providing LPs with multiple investment options into the same fund. The key advantage is that the fund manager is immediately able to approach a much larger audience during fundraising, making LP diversification more likely, as well as increasing the chances of meeting (or exceeding) fundraising targets (especially if cornerstone investors are only able to commit if they can invest without having direct currency exposure). A hedged currency feeder fund structure can solve this issue and ensure that the fund closes are achieved in time. Feeder funds may also make the investment case more attractive to existing LPs. At the same time, of course, there are disadvantages to this approach, such as setup costs and the requirement to manage the currency risk that arises from these feeder structures.

The following example, illustrated in Exhibit 1, shows how the currency risk can shift effectively from the LPs to the GP as the GP is responsible for managing the feeder fund:

- A U.S. pension fund (LP) makes a commitment to a Continental European GP, which in turn draws the funds to acquire a company based in the United Kingdom. That company has operations worldwide, and while some revenues and costs offset each other, the company ends up with a complicated net currency exposure.

- The portfolio company provides the European GP with proceeds in the form of dividends, other distributions, or an outright sale. Those returns get distributed to the U.S. pension fund (net of fund manager's fees).

Exhibit 1: The sequence of multi-currency fund streams (from LP to portfolio company)

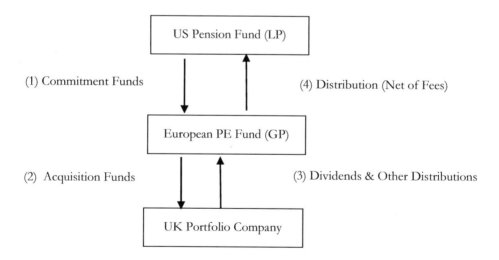

The exhibit illustrates a myriad of different currency exposures can affect the different parties in both direct and indirect ways. When taking into account the complex timing of cash flows at each level, the picture becomes even more obscure. The fund streams with varying currency exposures affect various stakeholders. The currency risk exposures may also impact the competitiveness of the U.K. portfolio company, or they may cause large financial losses to LPs.

The indirect currency exposure impacts the investment case for the GP in that the internal rate of return (IRR) of the deal may be reduced in GBP terms. However, as the GP needs to convert the investment proceeds to EUR, the master fund's IRR may also be directly impacted by the GBP/EUR rate. Both of these factors will impact the fund manager's carry and track record. When distributing returns to the U.S.-based LP, these factors indirectly impact the LP's investment as well, and, on top of that, the US$/EUR exchange rate will have a direct effect. In reality, the currency exposures of LPs are even more complicated to assess, given that most LPs tend to invest in a multitude of funds, and those funds tend to have diversified portfolios themselves.

Some LPs try to "look through" the funds that they invest in to get a clear view of the currency risk, in both direct and indirect terms, so that they can hedge out their net exposure. However, this is a daunting task if one considers the complexities of currency exchange rates mixed with different notionals, timing, and distribution profiles. In addition, many GPs will not disclose the full details of their investments on a timely basis. Even if the LP was able to effectively hedge out its currency exposure, this would still leave the GP and portfolio company exposed.

Best practice dictates that *the entity closest to the risk is best placed to manage it*—in this case, that entity is the GP. Therefore, it is widely accepted that LPs, GPs, and portfolio companies only manage their direct risk (i.e., the portfolio company is responsible for managing the currency risk arising from its operations, the GP is responsible for managing the currency risk that arises from its investment, and the LP is responsible for managing the currency risk that arises from its commitments).

Though there are many exceptions, in most cases, the LP is a passive investor who does not have the same insight as the GP. For this reason, some GPs offer to provide a hedged return profile for their LPs, typically in the form of a currency feeder fund (discussed in greater detail later in this chapter). Yet, as previously illustrated, this arrangement does shift ownership of the risk from the LP to the GP, so that the GP must manage currency risk at both the asset level and the investee level.

Although the LPs capital commitment is known, currency risk arises when capital calls are made, at which point both the IRR of the fund and the funding can be impacted. Once capital has been drawn and deployed, funding risk no longer exists, but the risk to the fund's IRR remains until the proportionate amounts of principal and return have been distributed to the LPs.

Capital drawdowns or funding risk (LP and GP currency risk)

As most LPs in the alternative investment space know, the unpredictable timing of capital drawdowns poses funding risks. Committed capital must be made available within a short period of time when capital calls are requested. In addition, even though the committed amount is capped, it is rarely drawn down entirely (in many cases limited to 90–95%).

While LPs are typically well aware of this dynamic, and have measures in place to either monitor, project, or mitigate funding risk, the implications of currency exposures must also be taken into account. Currency exposures can exacerbate funding risk for either the LP or the GP, as illustrated in the two examples below:

- **The committed capital is unknown in the LP's currency:** For example, a U.S. LP commits to invest a certain EUR amount, which will fluctuate versus US$ over time. Thus, the LP does not know how much total capital was committed in US$. Moreover, the LP is exposed to currency volatility over the funding period from the capital call request to the fund transfer (typically 10 days). In these scenarios, the *LP owns the funding risk*.

- **The committed capital is unknown in the GP's currency:** For instance, a U.S. LP commits to invest a certain US$ amount into a EUR fund. In this scenario, the LP knows exactly how much capital has been committed in US$, but the GP does not know what amount has been committed in EUR. The GP may therefore find that, depending on the prevailing spot rate, a disproportionate amount of the US$ capital gets called relative to the capital that has been committed in EUR. In addition, the GP is exposed to currency volatility over the funding period. In these scenarios, the *GP owns the funding risk.*

The scenario where the LP owns the funding risk (i.e., where the U.S. LP commits a certain EUR amount) is the most realistic scenario because very few GPs will allow a foreign currency LP commitment unless it is part of a hedged feeder fund offering. It is also worth mentioning that due to the different timing aspects of various capital calls, it is the average foreign exchange rate across all the capital calls that determines how the commitments are being depleted; this may have a mitigating effect on extreme currency volatility.

Fund performance can be viewed both on a *relative basis* (i.e., the money multiple of an individual investment) or on an *absolute basis* (i.e., the performance of an investment on a dollar or euro basis). Viewing performance on a relative basis means that currency risk exposure does not commence until the entry rate of the investment is fixed. In practice, this means that a EUR GP does not face any currency exposure while capital has not yet been called from investors because, up until this point, any depreciation of the investment currency which erodes absolute EUR returns will be irrelevant in terms of the investment multiple. For example, if an investment has an expected multiple of 2.0x, and the investment currency depreciates by 10% against the EUR before the capital is called, the expected multiple will remain at 2.0x. However, the ultimate absolute cash return will be 10% lower in EUR terms.

If the sole objective is to hedge relative returns (i.e., multiples generated by the fund), then the GP is not at risk while the investment is still held in the local currency. But if the objective is also to minimize/eliminate the absolute risk (i.e., the ultimate absolute EUR return), then the EUR GP would be at risk from the point at which the deal closes, irrespective of whether the entry rate is fixed or not.

Capital distributions (LP and GP currency risks)

Having covered the impact of funding risk (from both the LP and GP standpoints), we look further along the J-curve to currency risk in distributions. Once capital is returned to investors, the magnitude of the currency impact becomes evident. However, from the outset, there is no certainty regarding how spot rates will move over time, as well as limited certainty of timing and volume of distributions. While empirical evidence supports theories that currencies are mean-reverting over time, the timing and size of the cash flows (for both capital calls and distributions) make it very difficult to reliably benefit from any mean-reverting trait in spot prices.

Exhibits 2 summarizes a cash flows simulation for a typical private equity fund in terms of capital calls and distributions. We can determine the currency effect on the investment performance from an LP's point of view by looking at the best and worst exchange rates (i.e., EUR/US$). More specifically, when taking into account the timing of both capital calls and distributions, and assuming that the investment period is 3 years and the life of the fund is 5.5 years, we get the following scenario (for a €30 million investment and a €90 million return):

This example demonstrates that the currency impacts could have resulted in a US$ LP underperforming a EUR LP by 0.76x, or outperforming a EUR LP by 0.45x, representing an uncertainty range of 1.21x (approx. 40% of the target multiple). Such variation in the multiple is quite substantial, and underlines the significant currency risk between capital calls and distributions.

Exhibit 2: Currency risk example from the LP perspective

EUR/USD Exposure	Time Period	EUR mm Amount	Worst FX Rate	Best FX Rate	Worst LP Exposure	Best LP Exposure
Capital Call	2007-2008	30	1.5990	1.2932	48.0	38.8
Distribution	2010-2011	90	1.4874	1.1953	107.6	133.9
Multiple		3.00x			2.24x	3.45x
Δ					(0.76x)	0.45x

Using the numbers from the above table, we can see that the foreign exchange ranges could have had a significant impact:

- The multiple in EUR is 3.00x (i.e., €90 million divided by €30 million)

- The best multiple in US$ is 3.45x (i.e., US$133.9 million divided by US$38.8 million)

- The worst multiple in US$ is 2.24x (i.e., US$107.6 million divided by US$48.0 million)

Hedging with feeder funds

Given the impact of currency exposures on both capital calls and distributions discussed above, LPs can face serious risks when investing in funds that are denominated in a foreign currency. If GPs are considering a currency feeder fund offering, then they can assume some, if not all, of this risk (depending on the terms of the feeder fund). Thus, having a hedging program in place is an essential component of the feeder fund offering. However, there are a few important issues associated with currency feeder fund structures that GPs should be aware of:

- **Protection:** Foreign exchange rates can negatively impact the returns of the feeder fund versus the master fund as spot rate volatility represents a significant risk and is typically not part of the investment case. Most GPs and LPs prefer a very high level of protection against currency moves, so that the feeder fund return profile mirrors that of the master fund as closely as possible.

- **Costs:** Although LPs understand that hedging may come at a cost, they are often reluctant to invest in a feeder fund that projects a substantial reduction in the IRR versus the master fund due to hedging costs. It is therefore paramount that a maximum hedging budget is agreed upon and that the hedging program stays within that limit. In the case of some foreign exchange rates, there could actually be a possibility to hedge with little or no cost due to favorable interest rate differentials.

- **Liquidity:** Neither GPs nor their LPs have much appetite for allocating cash to fund negative mark-to-market differentials of a hedging program (i.e., margin calls). While this consideration does not represent a direct cost, it can create a cash drag on the fund, reducing the IRR. This risk can be mitigated by optimizing the hedging strategy, either in the form of instrument selections (e.g., embedding optionality), negotiating special terms with banking counterparties, establishing/utilizing credit lines, or a combination of these strategies.

In order to effectively manage the currency risk in a currency feeder fund, one must first establish exactly what that risk is. As with any investment, there is an entry point and an exit point, but the details of these events may be unclear. Uncertainties will also make it harder to quantify and mitigate the risk. What is certain is the size of the committed capital and the maximum duration. Uncertainties are due to the size and timing of the capital drawn down, the size of the distributions, the timing of the distributions, and the IRR of the fund.

Derivative instruments can prove to be very useful in the context of currency hedging. In terms of hedging the currency risk of private equity investments, the two main instruments used are *currency forward contracts* and *currency options*. Option contracts can be prohibitively expensive when used in a stand-alone capacity. As a result, most strategies solely utilize forward contracts ("forwards"), or use option contracts ("options") in conjunction with a forward contract.

- **Forward contracts:** Forwards lock in the exchange rate at some date in the future by allowing a currency to be bought or sold versus another currency at a predetermined time and rate (set by the forward curve). A forward is a financial contract between two parties and is separate from any underlying asset, but if structured correctly, it is a very efficient instrument to hedge the currency risk to which an underlying asset is subject. Critically, a forward contract locks in the exchange rate, thus offering protection at the expense of not being able to participate in favorable spot rate moves. In contrast to futures contracts, (which are standardized forward contracts), the terms of forwards can be tailored to the specific needs of the situation. In this way, currency forwards offer the flexibility (in terms of size and timing) that is essential for private equity funds.

- **Option contracts**: Options give the purchaser the right—but not the obligation—to buy or sell a currency at a predetermined rate (determined by the buyer) at any time before a set expiry date. The option is a financial contract between two parties, but the buyer does not have any obligations apart from paying the option premium (normally at the outset, although this can be deferred in some instances). The price of the premium is determined by the strike rate, the forward curve, the duration of the contract, and current levels of volatility and liquidity in the market. Therefore, in addition to offering protection, an option allows participation if the spot rate moves favorably. Options are similar to insurance contracts since the buyer pays a premium to receive protection against unwanted currency exchange movements. Compared to currency forwards, currency options are perhaps a better hedging solution, but they are also costlier.

Derivatives can prove to be very useful for GPs wanting to hedge currency fluctuations as they can impact the funds' achieved IRR levels considerably. However, GPs must consider the cost of hedging as well and realize that the overall hedging impact is contingent upon the cash flow timing and the corresponding currency developments.

In the following paragraphs, we outline the dynamics of hedging with a forward contract, the instrument of choice for most funds. The duration may vary, with some funds favoring a *rolling strategy*, whereby short-term forward contracts are bought and then "rolled over" to extend the protection. Other funds choose to buy longer-term forwards to more accurately match the expected distributions, and to mitigate interest rate differential risk. For some foreign exchange rates, there is also a financial benefit to buying longer-term forwards.

Exhibit 3 illustrates the use of forwards in the context of hedging currency feeder funds. In the case of a US$ investor making an investment in a EUR master fund, that investor would be exposed to fluctuations in the EUR/US$ spot rate over time. In order to mitigate this risk on behalf of the investor, the US$ feeder fund enters into a forward contract at the time of the investor's initial US$ investment. The contract locks in the future exchange rate at which the feeder fund is able to sell EUR and buy US$ (i.e., at the anticipated investment exit date). Assume that this date is approximately four years ahead for purposes of this illustration. This "locked in" future spot rate is known as the *forward rate*, and is usually different from the current *spot rate*. The difference between today's EUR/US$ spot rate and the four-year forward rate is driven by interest rate differentials between the two jurisdictions, and may be favorable for a US$ investor hedging expected future inflows in EUR. This favorable dynamic (i.e., the *forward pickup*) could, for example, yield approximately 175 basis points (1.75%) per annum for four years. It is important to note that the implementation of a hedging strategy using only forward contracts exposes the investor to other risks, such as changing interest rate differentials (when adjusting the hedge) and liquidity risk (i.e., margin calls if the hedge is negatively marked-to-market).

Exhibit 3: Illustration of using a forward contract in the context of hedging feeder funds

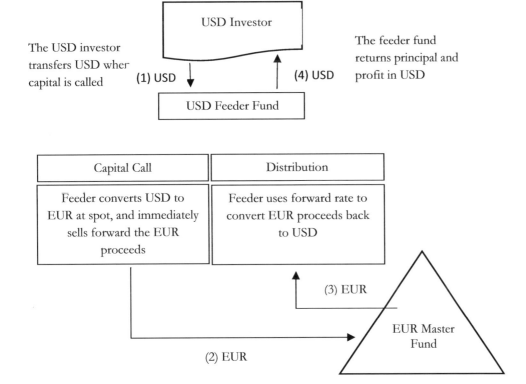

In a typical scenario, all costs associated with a feeder fund are deducted before cash is distributed back to LPs. Therefore, costs and other impacts will change the IRR profile of the feeder fund, and this is normally communicated as part of the initial feeder fund offering. The main components of the IRR impact of feeder funds are as follows:

- **Hedging costs:** These costs are mainly determined by the chosen strategy and market dynamics (typically interest rate differentials and/or options pricing). The initial risk quantification is crucial to allow for changing market conditions when determining maximum hedging costs over the life of the fund (bearing in mind that interest rate differentials and options participation could also result in a gain). Transaction costs and credit charges with counterparties will also have an impact on the hedging costs.

- **Cash drag:** A cash drag manifests itself primarily as a result of liquidity impacts (i.e., cash margin applied to outstanding trades). The initial risk quantification is key to estimate the maximum liquidity impact, and thus, the cash drag effect. However, a cash drag can also be a result of funding risk (e.g., if more capital is called than what is needed). Liquidity impacts can be mitigated so that any cash drag effect is reduced.

- **Setup and running costs:** These costs can consist of (1) costs related to fund administration and accounting, (2) legal fees, and (3) fees of the hedging adviser.

The manager needs to quantify the maximum negative deviation between the master fund IRR and the feeder fund IRR so that LPs can consider the cost-benefit analysis of such an investment alternative. The maximum negative impact on IRR does not mean that the IRR is guaranteed to be lower than that of the master fund. In fact, the feeder fund's IRR can exceed that of the master fund under certain favorable hedging environments.

Investing and valuation (GP currency risk)

Buying a portfolio company can take 3–12 months to complete, during which time, any number of things can change. If the acquirer is a European private equity fund and the target a U.K. company, a transaction will likely be priced in GBP. If the pound appreciates significantly against the euro during the period before completion, the deal will become more expensive, and the IRR of the deal will be lower. To hedge this risk, a GP could simply use a foreign exchange forward contract to lock in the investment size. But if the deal fails (e.g., because the seller changes his/her mind at the last minute or the deal is rejected by anti-trust authorities) the hedge must be unwound. Further, if the market moves against the hedge, the GP will incur costs (in addition to the disruption caused by the failure of the deal itself). Such costs could prove problematic, given that GPs rely on their LPs to fund the acquisitions.

A more effective solution is to hedge the currency risk associated with the transaction on a deal-contingent basis. A *deal-contingent hedge* combines the best aspects of a standard foreign exchange forward and a foreign exchange option: it requires no payment upfront and allows the GP to lock in a forward rate. A small spread is added to pay for the solution, which is only applied if the deal is successful and the hedge is used. If the deal fails, the deal-contingent hedge disappears without the GP incurring a fee.

When investing in a foreign company, the GP faces other currency risks as well. For example, consider again the euro-denominated fund investing in the U.K. company. Assume that the company is a GBP functional entity and its revenues are denominated in currencies other than GBP (mainly EUR), given a diverse client portfolio. In this case, there is a potential material currency risk facing the company and its financial performance (i.e., EBITDA).

The GP should undertake a currency risk analysis on the portfolio company according to its current risk exposure and risk management processes. This analysis will allow the GP to contextualize the potential negative impact of currency risk on the value of the investment in the company. If, for example, approximately 50% of the company's revenue is denominated in EUR, then a weaker euro could reduce the company's revenue and EBITDA in GBP terms.

GPs could also introduce a "pass-through" pricing mechanism so that a proportion of the currency risk exposure is covered by the customers of that portfolio company via long-term contracts. The impact of this currency risk on the company's future financial performance can be estimated by looking at the 12-month currency exposure (contrasting high versus low foreign exchange rates), adding (or subtracting) customer contract pass-through adjustments related to foreign exchange rates as well as any other cash impacts.

When a GP has investments in foreign companies, the fund will face direct currency risk to its NAV on all foreign currency-denominated investments. Should the foreign currency weaken against the fund's reference currency, it will negatively impact the fund's NAV, and this exposure can have a material impact on the fund's NAV returns leading to uncertainty in valuations. As such, the GP could consider hedging this exposure via foreign exchange derivatives, as described earlier in this chapter.

Fund administration (LP and GP currency risk)

Designing currency hedging strategies to hedge the management fees is a straightforward process, as the amount being paid out to the GP is fixed and the transactions are distributed over a specified timeline. A long-term forward strategy (adjusted for management fee pay-out dates, typically six months) can be used to minimize the future currency risk, allowing the GP to receive predictable fees. The liquidity and cost impact of this currency hedging strategy can be managed by adjusting the hedge ratio (e.g., hedging only 80% of the fees) and/or negotiating sufficient credit facilities with the banks.

GPs can also employ hedging strategies for carried interest, although the amounts hedged are uncertain as they are dependent on the performance of the portfolio investments. Therefore, the main risk related to carried interest is the uncertainty regarding the amount that will be paid out to the fund's partners. In addition, predicting exactly when the asset will reach maturity is difficult, which means that cash distributions are uncertain.

Hedging carried interest has long been challenging, given the high uncertainty involved. Thus, it is vital that GPs introduce flexibility into the hedging strategy. A potential route would be to use an option (e.g., a *participating forward*), whereby the GP locks in a fixed protection while still maintaining some ability to participate in a favorable market move.[6] The key advantage of a participating forward is that the GP is only obliged on a portion of the hedged notional (this needs to be negotiated); this helps GPs avoid becoming "over-hedged" if the carry does not materialize as originally anticipated. However, one of the key

---

[6] A participating forward contract provides a secured protected currency rate, while still allowing beneficial moves on a predetermined portion of the amount hedged. If the spot rate at expiry is more favorable than the protected rate then the holder of the participating forward is only obligated to transact a predetermined proportion of the hedged amount at the protected rate and is free to transact the remainder at the spot rate. Participating forwards are generally structured as zero-cost premium products.

disadvantages of the participating forward is that it can create a liquidity impact that needs to be managed on an ongoing basis.

HEDGING INTEREST RATE RISKS

Interest rate risk should be managed where interest rate fluctuations impact the performance of the private equity fund or its investments. Private equity buyout investments flourish when interest rates are low, given the potential to lever up target companies significantly, which in turn is a response to higher valuations due to these lower interest rates. When a private equity fund manages its interest rate exposure appropriately, the returns will be purely driven by operational improvements and deleveraging at the portfolio company level without exposing the fund performance to interest rate fluctuations.

In order to maximize the returns to equity holders, private equity funds often leverage the capital they raise by taking on large amounts of debt. However, when interest rates are rising, the cash flows will be more constrained as a result of the higher debt service requirements. Thus, an increase in interest rates could cause many negative effects such as (1) declining profit margins due to increasing borrowing costs for portfolio companies; (2) potential financial distress of portfolio companies that have loans with variable rates; (3) a slowdown in acquisition activity because the GP needs to pay more to acquire a company, given the increased cost of borrowing; (4) a decrease in exit options as valuations decrease when interest rates go up; (5) fundraising difficulties as the funds' NAVs decrease and potential investors switch to fixed income securities that provide better yields; and (7) a reduction in returns for both the GPs and LPs as the higher cost of debt impacts the return on equity or IRR. These effects explain why GPs are looking for target companies with steady cash flows and low capital requirements.

Interest rate risk can arise from a number of important sources, including the following:

- Performance-linked pricing provisions, where interest rates vary depending on the performance of the portfolio company in response to its debt covenants.[7]

- Interest rate resets on loans.

- A change in forward foreign exchange rates, affected by the differential between domestic interest rates and foreign rates.[8]

Given the reasons outlined above, private equity funds would be wise to measure and manage interest rate risk adequately on their debt payments in anticipation of interest rate hikes; otherwise, cash flow constraints might arise, which in turn would lead to costly debt restructurings and even insolvency.

---

[7] Interest rates might change, for example, depending on whether the company satisfies varying levels of debt service coverage ratios (i.e. cash flow available for debt service divided by interest and principal payments).

[8] For example, if European interest rates increase relative to rates in the US, then the cost of hedging imports from the US will increase and the cost of hedging exports will fall.

Measuring interest rate risks

Although the many ways to measure interest rate risk at the portfolio company level range from very simple to more sophisticated and mathematically complex measures, there are two measures that GPs typically employ:

- **The interest coverage ratio:** This ratio is defined as EBITDA scaled by interest expenses. There is a significant risk of an interest payment default if the interest equals or exceeds EBITDA. This debt service level basically implies that the firm will have no cash for working capital fluctuations, to make capital investments, or to pay taxes. Interest coverage ratio is a key ratio for determining whether a performance shortfall could lead to a default on interest payments.

- **The debt service coverage ratio:** This ratio is usually defined as cash flow available for debt service scaled by principal and interest payments. When the cash flow available for debt service (i.e., cash flow left after operational and investing cash flow outgoings) is less than the principal and interest payments, a breach of a debt covenant will most likely occur. Violations of debt coverage ratios prohibit the GP from incurring additional debt.

The GP can also measure the impact of changes in interest rates on the EBITDA of the portfolio company or its valuation. For example, if interest rates increase by 1%, what will the impact be on the company's EBITDA and valuation (i.e., as a result of a change in free cash flows and discount rate)? Alternatively, the GP can measure the impact of multiple changes in interest rates and other related variables on the portfolio company's financial performance. For instance, if the company is 50% hedged, interest rates increase by 1%, and EBITDA falls by 10%, what will the impact be on the company's interest coverage and debt service coverage covenants used in the debt documentation? The GP can model the impact of a substantial change in interest rates on the borrowings of the portfolio company or the fund investments in accounting terms (e.g., EBITDA) or risk outcomes.

Managing interest rate risks

Before using financial instruments to manage interest rate risk, the GP should first develop a strategy to determine the interest rate risk appetite of key investors in the fund. Based on this risk appetite, the GP can manage the interest rate risk in a few ways:

- Employ only fixed rate (as opposed to floating rate) debt to acquire or finance portfolio companies in order to mitigate any potential interest rate risk exposure.

- When fixed rate loans are not feasible, GPs can turn to financial derivatives to hedge the interest rate risk exposure. Before using derivatives, GPs need to be conscious that, although interest rate risk is reduced or even eliminated, liquidity risk might be created (related to the margin requirements associated with the financial hedging program). The GP can obtain protection from rising interest rates through an *interest rate cap* or *option*, which is essentially an insurance against rising rates. If interest rates rise, the portfolio company manager (or the GP) will exercise the option, and if interest rates fall, the option will not be exercised to retain the benefit of the lower interest rates. Interest rate options are quite expensive as the portfolio company (or the fund) will need to pay a premium for this protection from rising interest rates. Therefore, an alternative product, the *interest rate swap*, might be considered.

In an *interest rate swap*, no upfront fee is required. This derivative allows the GP to lock in an interest rate for one to five years and a payment is required to the counterparty for the fixed vs floating difference when the rate falls below the fixed swap rate.

Given that an investment in a portfolio company takes a couple of months to complete, many financing conditions can change in that time. If interest rates rise during the due diligence and acquisition period, the cost of finance to pay for the investment will be higher and the IRR of the deal will fall. Thus, a GP could consider deal-contingent interest rate hedging, which removes the interest rate risk when the GP expects interest rate rises. Possible solutions include a *forward-starting swap*, which locks in current rates for an acquisition loan on a deal-contingent basis as there is no cost if the deal fails. Forward-starting swaps are often used for large private equity deals or infrastructure transactions, which are typically financed with long-dated debt and are therefore more susceptible to interest rate changes.

HEDGING COMMODITY RISKS

Introduction

Commodity risk entails the risk that the performance of a fund's investment portfolio could be adversely affected by fluctuations in commodity prices. The portfolio of a private equity fund can be impacted by commodity prices in two ways:

- **Falling commodity prices** can directly decrease the revenue of portfolio companies that are commodity producers (e.g., companies that are active in mineral extraction, agriculture, and energy), and can indirectly reduce the production viability of certain companies in response to lower prices. The fund manager can encourage portfolio company managers to undertake specific price risk management activities to manage this risk, such as (1) writing sales contracts that lock in the quantity delivered and price received, (2) engaging in collective pricing arrangements with other producers, and (3) storing products when increased production leads to reduced selling prices.

- **Rising commodity prices** can increase the cost base and reduce profitability for portfolio companies that are commodity consumers (e.g., firms in transportation, manufacturing, retail, construction, etc.), assuming there are no cost pass-through mechanisms to their customers. Commodity-consuming portfolio companies can manage the rising commodity prices by (1) negotiating fixed prices with suppliers, (2) using alternative sourcing channels, and (3) conducting production process reviews in order to find a less costly input mix.

Hedging price *rises* will be the more prevalent concern in the private equity industry as portfolio companies are more likely to be commodity consumers than commodity producers. Companies are often squeezed by rising and volatile commodity input prices that cannot be passed along to customers. Fund managers should consider hedging or managing the commodity risks when commodity price fluctuations have a direct impact on the profitability of a portfolio company. Most companies, particularly those at the end or in the middle of the value chain, can improve their commodity risk exposure via measurement and management of those commodity risks (as explained later in this section).

Although commodity pricing is widely regarded as the top commodity risk in private equity, there are actually three main commodity risks, where each of these risks should be carefully considered:

- **Price risk** arises from adverse movements in commodity prices, which in turn impact business revenue and/or costs.

- **Quantity risk** arises from changes in the availability of commodities.

- **Political risk** arises from regulation requirements and their impact on commodity prices or supply.

Measuring commodity risks

Measuring commodity risk requires a structured approach that includes an analysis of the potential exposure and a thorough understanding of how commodity price fluctuations affect both the financial and operational drivers of the organization. Three methods are usually applied in the context of measuring commodity risk:

- **Sensitivity analysis**, which involves measuring the potential impact of adverse movements in commodity prices or volumes on the financials of the portfolio company. This analysis is mostly conducted by selecting arbitrary movements in commodity prices or volumes and then assessing their impact on a company's EBITDA.

- **Portfolio analysis**, which encompasses the full suite of commodity risk sources to the portfolio company or the overall fund portfolio (i.e., adverse movements in commodity prices, availability of commodities, and political policies). Such comprehensive analysis allows for deeper insights into the impact of one or a combination of the risk variables on the portfolio companies' EBITDA and their operations.

- **Value at risk (VaR)**, which is a probability approach when undertaking sensitivity analysis. While the above-mentioned methods measure the potential impact of commodity fluctuations, VaR measures the probability of the adverse movement occurring (by using commodity history and applying it to current exposure levels). For example, based on a VaR analysis, a fund manager may conclude that, given a certain confidence interval, the fund (or the portfolio company) will not experience a loss of more than a particular amount.

The above methods of measurement assist in determining the extent of the commodity exposure and its impact on key financial metrics that affect the ultimate success of an investment in a portfolio company (e.g., earnings, cash flows, debt covenants, etc.).

Managing commodity risks

Once commodity risks are measured and their impact is deemed significant, it is paramount that the fund manager deals with these risks adequately. In the context of portfolio companies that are commodity consumers, which is the most likely scenario, the manager has various risk management options at its disposal:

- **Product pricing pass-through:** The manager can use the portfolio companies' market pricing power to recover a change in input costs from the companies' customers, leading to stabilized margins and earnings certainty. However, customers could potentially move to a lower-priced competitor in response to the pricing pass-through.

- **Procurement contract clauses:** The manager can encourage the portfolio company to use contract mechanisms with suppliers that effectively mitigate commodity price risks (e.g., price ceilings). These contract provisions would transition the commodity risk back to suppliers. While the suppliers might demand a premium for risk sharing, the manager has certainty about input costs, and can plan the investment and exit processes accordingly.

- **Value chain integration:** The manger can pursue a strategy of upstream vertical integration by acquiring an upstream company to ensure sufficient supply of raw materials and diversify commodity risk exposure. Such transactions could generate significant value for a portfolio company and be part of the manager's operational toolkit. The manager would need to be able to deal with integration strategies that require an effective approach to costs and margins management as well as appropriate capital and expertise in acquisitions. The manager should also be able to manage the organizational complexities inherent to integration exercises.

- **Financial hedging:** The fund manager could manage commodity risk via financial instruments in which the price exposure is hedged through either forwards, futures, or options. This downside limitation exercise has no impact on supplier contracts and provides price volatility protection. With financial hedging, the manager has three instruments at its disposal to manage commodity risk:

  - **Forward contracts:** Agreements to purchase or sell a specific commodity amount on a future date at a predetermined price with expected physical delivery and payment at maturity. A forward contract effectively locks in the price and provides protection for both the seller and purchaser against adverse movements in the commodity price. A forward contract can be tailored to specific delivery dates and quantities, but may lead to losses when current prices deviate unfavorably from future prices.

  - **Futures contracts:** These contracts are very similar to forward contracts but settlement does not require a physical delivery, unlike with forward contracts. Futures contracts are traded on commodity exchanges and are subject to margin calls when there is an adverse movement between the contract and current price, impacting the cash flows of the portfolio company or the fund. Moreover, unlike forwards, futures contracts are standardized and cannot be tailored.

  - **Commodity options:** These instruments provide the right, but not the obligation, to undertake a commodity transaction at an agreed future date. An option requires a premium payment in order to unlock this flexibility, and is essentially insurance against adverse movements in the commodity price. This instrument is a more effective hedging product when there is significant uncertainty but the premiums can be very expensive.

It should be noted that private equity fund managers that are able to anticipate and manage commodity risks can create a strong competitive advantage. They should therefore attract LPs' attention when they evaluate the holistic risk management framework within the portfolio of a private equity fund.

RISK MANAGEMENT ISSUES FOR OTHER TYPES OF FUNDS

The initial part of this chapter focused mainly on the standard type of private equity funds (i.e., buyout funds). It is important to realize, however, that many other fund types exist and they are subject to various specific risks. This section discusses the idiosyncratic risks inherent to each fund type that require diligent risk management procedures.

Funds of funds

Funds of funds (FoFs) aggregate capital from multiple investors in private equity and invest a sizable amount of their capital into the private equity asset class.[9] In general, the FoF risk profile is not well understood due to the relatively opaque and illiquid market dynamics involved. FoFs typically attempt to achieve a significant risk reduction by diversifying into multiple fund investments on a global basis, given the imperfect correlation between funds' returns. Even though this approach results in a lower overall risk level, FoF managers still need to manage and measure certain risks.

For instance, many FoFs deliberately run so-called "*over-commitment strategies*" by using cash proceeds from one fund's distributions to help finance the future drawdowns from other funds.[10] When projecting the "recycling" of these cash distributions, FoFs might over-commit on certain capital allocation promises, leading to the potential inability to finance some capital calls. *Over-commitment risk* is therefore defined as the failure to honor future capital calls, and can be heavily penalized (depending on the limitations defined in the limited partnership agreements). Given the upstreaming of capital distributions, this risk factor is often a direct result of the risk that private equity fund managers do not distribute capital as per the FoF's initial expectations.

Another relevant risk for FoFs is the currency risk of their commitments. As covered earlier in this chapter, if FoFs commit an investment in a different currency from their own reference currency, then they are exposed to currency risk during the investment period until the final cash distribution from the private equity fund manager. This foreign exchange commitment risk is a real possibility since many fund managers will not accept commitments in a different currency than the reference currency of the funds they manage. Hence, feeder funds are often used to mitigate this currency risk. Feeder funds allow FoFs to invest in their reference currency, effectively transferring the currency risk from the FoF to the private equity fund manager, who, in turn, will need to hedge the currency risk.

When determining their asset allocation, FoFs must select across the public and private investment spectrum, with both sides carrying idiosyncratic risks depending on economic cycles, capital markets, and industry sectors. FoFs need to ensure they diversify adequately across investment styles, fund managers, investment stages, sectors, geographies, and vintages in order to realize an optimal diversification while reducing the *asset allocation risk* associated with these risk dimensions. The *allocation risk* is critical for FoFs in the private equity class as the return differential between top-quartile fund managers and average-performing managers is more significant than for public equity or public bond managers—mainly because the private equity market is less efficient than public markets due to the information asymmetry and lack of information

---

[9] One can also think of pension funds, banks, insurance companies, and other corporate investors who invest in many private equity funds as facing the same issues as the funds of funds.

[10] Over-commitment is defined as the NAV from underlying funds plus Undrawn Commitments from underlying funds divided by the NAV from underlying funds and the Undrawn Commitments from investors.

that exists between investors and fund managers. In addition, allocation risk is driven by the fact that some preferred managers are oversubscribed, and thus cannot accept additional capital, or are simply not raising funds during the relevant investment period for the FoF.

In light of how important the manager selection is, FoFs must be highly effective at developing relationships with managers who demonstrate attributes such as portfolio fit, investment strategy, industry focus, reputation, track record, sound operating strategy, and deal flow. When FoFs allocate funds to the private equity asset class, they often retain the flexibility to make commitments into various private equity funds in addition to direct co-investments in private firms alongside private equity funds to enhance returns and reduce fees.

Secondaries funds

The risk-return balance in secondaries funds is different from that of traditional buyout funds, as illustrated by Exhibit 4.

Exhibit 4: The spectrum of secondaries private equity risk-return position

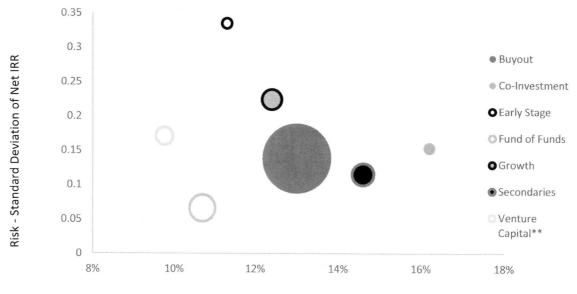

Source: Preqin

The generic risks specific to the secondary private equity market cover two types of investments: (1) LP positions in other private equity funds and (2) direct portfolios of private companies. Each type of investment has a different return profile and distinct risk implications as well. Typically, followers of the LP position model are scale players that continuously deploy capital in order to justify their fee base. Given that many GPs report on a quarterly basis (i.e., 30 to 60 days after the financial quarter end), there is an inherent valuation lag effect between the release of the portfolio company accounts and the date when the LP position is revalued, generating an increased volatility of returns. Whereas secondary investing in LP positions is relatively light work, a "direct model" secondary investor has to work on time-consuming transactions and extensive post-investment monitoring. In this way, the direct model risk profile is very similar to a fully invested primary private equity fund (i.e., buyout fund) from a portfolio-level risk management perspective, as described. Consequently, this subsection focuses on risk management in the context of LP position acquisitions by secondary funds.

Generally, secondary investors in LP positions occupy an attractive position on the risk-return curve with below-average volatility of returns. Because secondary funds acquire fund interests at a later stage of the investment period, they have a better visibility on the financial and operating performance of the underlying asset, and therefore undertake a smaller "blind pool" risk.

Secondary funds mainly consider four qualitative risks when they prospect a stake acquisition in a fund from another LP:

- **GP/manager quality:** When considering a fund interest, secondary fund managers analyze the team's qualities (e.g., experience, track record, size, coherence, motivation, key man risks), deal capabilities (sourcing, screening, and execution), likelihood of future fundraising success, and so on. The ability of managers to create value and extract cash from portfolio companies varies greatly, which makes good manager selection paramount for secondary fund managers.

- **Information availability:** The availability of information is highly variable since the information quantity and quality that fund managers are willing to share with their institutional investors varies significantly.[11] Thus, a secondary investor has limited information when considering the risk profile of a potential LP position investment (i.e., Is there sufficient level of detail to identify key risks? What is the overall information quality and transparency?). Not surprisingly, secondary investors review fund reporting, limited partnership agreements, and capital accounts in their due diligence efforts.

- **Alignment risk:** Manager alignment is typically not an issue when a secondary investor is buying into a fund that is in, or goes into, carry. However, issues will most likely arise when buying into a private equity fund that fails to generate carry, potentially causing the GP to either lose interest in the fund (thereby not maximizing returns) or attempt to maximize fee income (thereby delaying returns).

- **Other investor base:** Secondary investors will take a view on the probability of LP investors defaulting on capital calls and the investor base concentration and their ability to exert influence on GP managers.

Apart from the above-mentioned qualitative risk assessments, secondary fund managers also measure and benchmark five most relevant quantitative risks:

- **Portfolio diversification:** Secondaries funds prefer to invest in fund interests that are diversified across vintage/investment years, sectors, geographies, strategies, and currencies. This diversification exercise might be limited by restrictions on allocations to specific individual GPs or non-secondary strategies (e.g., primary fund commitments or single company co-investments).

- **Company metrics:** The financial performance, valuations, and debt levels of the underlying portfolio companies are key metrics when analyzing potential volatility within fund interests. The price that secondary investors pay is typically quoted at a discount or premium to the NAV which makes portfolio valuations a key due diligence area.

- **Investment structure:** Secondaries funds prefer a priority on distributions (e.g., via a mezzanine or a preferred equity structure), given the lower return volatility. However, certain secondary investors might prefer levered equity structures more, partly due to higher rent-seeking behavior or simply due

---

[11] There are no minimum informational standards in existence as in the public markets.

to the return thresholds promised to their respective investors. Secondaries investor prefer discounts to NAV which can be established via DCF-based models (i.e., a "bottom-up" approach) or via multiples/benchmarking exercises with other fund portfolios (i.e., a "top-down" approach).

- **Credit risk:** Credit risk in secondaries funds is not materially different from that experienced by FoFs or other institutional investors in primary funds. The only fundamental difference is that since acquired secondaries assets are usually more mature, many leveraged portfolio companies would have significantly reduced their risk position by rigorously progressing in their deleveraging strategy.

- **Tax risk:** The assets acquired by secondary funds are often tax-efficiently structured for the seller, and hence, may not be tax efficient for the secondary fund. Therefore, a key requirement is that the secondary fund manager can assess and adequately price the tax aspect of an LP position.

Given the risks identified above, it is critical that secondary fund managers have suitable risk management processes embedded in their investment procedures; this ensures that avoidable risks are mitigated and unavoidable risks are identified and adequately priced in.

Co-investment funds

Co-investment funds could make investments in an existing private equity portfolio (usually on preferred equity terms) or they could make a minority investment directly into a portfolio company alongside a private equity fund. Co-investment opportunities are typically offered to LPs already participating in the private equity fund, and are passive in nature as the fund managers maintain full discretion in managing the portfolio company.

When comparing co-investments to direct buyout investments, co-investments are not that different. However, when comparing co-investments to secondary investments, co-investments seem to offer better visibility at the underlying asset level, including better financial disclosure regarding the business plan and valuation drivers. Thus, co-investments can be used by secondaries funds to improve the risk-return profile.

In line with the risks outlined earlier, the risks in co-investments can be described as follows:

- **Minimal funding risk:** There is typically no legal obligation to fulfil subsequent capital calls with co-investments following the initial investment, in contrast to regular buyout funds, which are often involved in follow-on expansion programs after the initial investment. Nevertheless, there is a degree of funding risk associated with follow-on equity injections when there is a strict requirement to comply with debt covenants or when the solvency of the underlying company is limited.

- **Large liquidity risk:** Co-investments are more illiquid than buyout fund investments as their secondary market is very limited and could be impacted by legal constraints imposed by the GPs that run private equity funds and also own a stage in the investment. Consequently, co-investments are usually classified as "buy-and-hold" investment exposures, and are arguably more illiquid than secondary fund investments.

- **Large credit/counterparty risk:** The risk of losing capital because of counterparty risk is a realistic threat in single co-investments given the idiosyncratic and direct exposure to financial factors (e.g., cash flow stability, leverage levels, and debt covenant thresholds) and operational factors (e.g, management quality, business plan achievability, etc.).

In summary, co-investment funds have due diligence and risk considerations that are very similar to those of secondary funds. Since they are passive investors that rely on fund managers to create sufficient value from the underlying assets to repay the investments, co-investment funds also regard manager quality and information availability as key criteria for assessing risk.

Credit/Direct lending funds

It is important to understand the risk exposure of private debt funds vis-à-vis other fund types. Given the limited upside potential of private debt funds, managers of these funds will not be able to rely on high-performance assets to dilute the negative impact from a specific risk factor. Contrastingly, in private equity, deals with large exit multiples (e.g., 3x or 4x) can compensate for potential write-offs. Therefore, private debt funds need to assess the risk profile accurately and employ an adequate risk management strategy to deal with the various risks involved. The risk topology of private debt funds can be described as follows:

- **Lower liquidity risk:** While private debt fund investments are illiquid by nature (similar to those of private equity funds), they are characterized by less liquidity risks because interest income and principal payments can be predicted with a high level of certainty. Conversely, the payoffs of private equity investments are uncertain as exit events are less clearly defined.

- **High credit risk:** This risk primarily refers to the probability of default by a borrower on any given fund investment. In this respect, a covenant design that can be tailored to idiosyncratic borrowing requirements is crucial as standardized covenants are often insufficient. In addition, many private debt funds require the posting of collateral as a security measure against intrinsic credit risk, as well as tailoring the debt maturity profile to the cash flow profile of the borrower.

- **High market risk:** This risk usually entails currency risk and interest rate risk. Foreign exchange risk arises when the investment currency is different from the fund's reference currency and can be significant; hence, forward contracts are frequently used in order to mitigate this risk factor. Interest rate risk, on the other hand, can often be mitigated by negotiating floating rate private debt transactions, which represent a natural hedge against rising interest rate environments. Falling interest rates, in turn, are hedged by stating a LIBOR or EURIBOR floor (of 0%) in the debt documentation.

In summary, private debt fund managers can remove volatility and risk factors as much as practically feasible as lenders do not profit from favorable market movements, unlike in a private equity fund. Thus, the awareness of sensitivity to various risk drivers (i.e., liquidity, credit, and market risk) is more acute in a private debt fund context. Consequently, these funds are highly focused on downside protection.

Emerging market funds

The main risk factors in an emerging market fund context are currency risk and political/regulatory risk. Many emerging market fund managers recognize the importance of currency risk, but political risk should not be overlooked due to its potential large detrimental impact on the value of the investments.

Currency risk is regarded as one of the principal risks when investing in emerging market funds as fund managers often invest in companies that operate in emerging market currencies that are different from the reference currency of the fund. As a result, fund performance is highly dependent on the evolution of the local investment currency against the fund reference currency, given the uncertainty of the cash flows' timing and the illiquidity of the private equity investments in those markets. More specifically, currency risk manifests itself when the investment currency depreciates against the fund reference currency, eroding the IRR of the emerging market fund. Therefore, emerging market fund managers have the delicate task of managing their foreign exchange exposure adequately, which is challenging since the investment duration is unknown (due to the illiquid nature of private equity). Moreover, because investments could potentially span a number of years, the cost of hedging the currency exposure to an emerging market currency is significantly higher.

One approach to deal with the currency risk is to aggregate assets in the reference currency to establish the net exposure and consequently hedge it. The main impediment to this approach is that investments made by the fund have different durations, so the net exposure would need to be established by vintage. Another approach would be to focus on the long-term deviations of currencies and to determine thresholds for intervention, given the costs involved when managing foreign exchange exposure. In addition, emerging market currencies face many tail risks. When market turmoil occurs, most emerging markets experience a sell-off and subsequent currency depreciation. Thus, a fund portfolio protection mechanism against sell-offs could consist of a basket hedge (of selected local currencies).

The main challenge of currency hedging for emerging market private equity is to avoid any situation that would require liquidating investments in order to cover hedging losses (given the illiquidity constraints in private equity). These adverse scenarios could be avoided by having different liquidity sources available (e.g., access to a credit bridge facility). However, despite the many complexities involved, emerging market funds should consider currency hedging as essential in terms of reducing the return dilution due to adverse currency fluctuations.

Political risk is another important risk factor to be considered within emerging market funds. Historically, in immature or volatile political systems, political risk was synonymous with expropriation risk in that host governments would seize foreign-owned assets. Political risk also reflects the danger that government actions might negatively affect the cash flows that investors expect from their investments, or that a government entity might one-sidedly change the laws, regulations, or even the contracts governing an investment, decreasing the fund's returns. This specific risk could be caused by economic mismanagement by the government (e.g., allowing inflation to accelerate too rapidly (thereby reducing the value of investments) or triggering a recession, which could cause corporate bankruptcy within the underlying assets of the fund). In many instances, political risk refers to government actions designed to penalize investors or companies (e.g., increasing corporate taxes, more regulation, potential nationalization, or trade barriers). For example, a 2004 World Bank study discovered that approximately 15–30% of private infrastructure investments in the 1990s were subject to government-initiated disagreements.

Both political and regulatory risk could be insured via either credit default swaps (CDS) or "export credit agencies" (ECAs)—public agencies that offer insurance to companies from their home country that seek to engage in business activities in emerging markets. However, given that companies with the greatest risk exposure are often the most likely to seek insurance, underwriters will price their coverage very high and only offer relatively short-term coverage. In addition, the insurance coverage is often imperfect as it is frequently based on retrospective country risk ratings (i.e., reflecting past country policy outcomes) which might be different from the country's present policy shaping factors.

In summary, some emerging market jurisdictions might represent an element of risk that is too high to justify an investment. But where funds can recognize these dynamics and implement appropriate strategies to address any currency and political risks, then emerging market funds should find these risks manageable.

Real estate funds

Real estate funds entail a number of risks that are very specific to this asset class due to the idiosyncratic nature of real estate. The main risks involved when investing in real estate are as follows:

- **Large liquidity risk:** Real estate assets can be very illiquid, with prices subject to specific negotiation positions, the speed at which a buyer can execute, and the marketing associated with the asset. In terms of risk mitigation, many real estate funds will therefore focus on well-located prime real estate assets which provide more liquidity in the event of a sale, although they may generate a lower yield and lower cash flows.

- **High leverage risk:** Real estate investments attract high loan-to-value ratios given the relatively stable and predictable cash flows coupled with the existence of tangible underlying assets. However, more debt also implies higher risk in the overall investment. Leverage risk manifests itself when the investments are performing poorly and the resulting high debt levels diminish the equity value on what might be an inherently good property. Real estate funds can mitigate this risk by managing the debt structure in several ways: choosing fixed versus floating interest rates; choosing a diversified group of lenders; negotiating a loan maturity profile that fits the asset's cash flows; negotiating away covenants on loans; and so on. Since leverage is a key risk in real estate investing, the top-performing real estate funds tend to have a strong grip on their leverage risk.

- **High tenant risk:** Real estate investments produce a steady cash flow in the form of rental income or net operating income, paid by tenants based on their trading results. When tenants default, the real estate fund manager may have to actively repossess the asset and, if necessary, undertake any capital expenditure works and re-let the asset. This risk is mitigated by diligently assessing each tenant's covenant strengths and using adequate credit rating scores.

- **High development risk:** Real estate development strategies (either greenfield or brownfield) involve investing significant amounts of capital into constructing or repositioning an asset. This is an inherently risky strategy that can deliver high returns or, conversely, substantial capital losses.

There are many risks associated with real estate investing that are not present in other asset classes, largely because real estate is not a purely financial asset class. Therefore, real estate funds face idiosyncratic risks that require specialist risk mitigation knowledge.

Venture capital funds

Although venture capital (VC) funds can realize high returns, there are many risks as well, given the high risk-return trade-off inherent to early stage investing. The main risks are the following:

- **Entrepreneur risk:** Entrepreneurs are the primary catalysts behind companies' growth; many early-stage companies succeed or fail based on their founders' business acumen. In light of the entrepreneur's profound influence on the future success of the venture—often combined with a limited prior track record—VC funds consider entrepreneur risk to be a major risk factor, which is intrinsically difficult to assess given the limited potential for due diligence efforts. Yet, this risk can be mitigated by value-add services from VC fund managers as they work to professionalize young firms and offer admission to networks which were previously inaccessible. The spill-over reputational and operational improvement effects from VC fund managers cannot be underestimated, and can counterbalance the risk posed by the entrepreneur.

- **Technology risk:** Technology is perceived as a main risk factor within VC since it is hard to assess a new and unproven technology. Patents can reduce the technology risk to some extent as they intrinsically award the exclusive use of the technology and hinder competitors from imitating it. However, patent costs can be very high if firms want to ensure patent protection in multiple countries. Further, technologies can become obsolete due to the rapid pace of innovation, thereby effectively increasing the technology risk.

- **Asset risk:** In line with technology risk, VC funds face a relatively high asset risk as well, given the prevalence of assets facing potential obsolescence. Along with a heavy reliance on human capital, there is an overall lack of collateralizable assets (e.g., patents) in VC, leading to elevated risk levels as the intangibility of a young firm's assets is a common proxy for low residual value. Yet, unlike with traditional investments, collateral is only part of the story within VC; the early stage company needs to be able to raise subsequent equity rounds or even realize an exit event (e.g., an IPO or sale). Nevertheless, the presence of collateral does not completely remove the risk as asset liquidation can be more value destructive in the event of bankruptcy or default of a relatively young company.

RISK GOVERNANCE MECHANISMS

An effective risk governance mechanism at the fund level is one of the most important routes for value creation. In addition, major regulatory changes such as the Dodd-Frank Act in the United States and the European Directive for Alternative Investment Fund Managers (AIFMD) in Europe require fund managers to follow more stringent guidelines for risk governance. Risk governance requires continuous monitoring of the fund managers and fund progress so that investors can maintain control over their private equity portfolios and undertake strategic decisions accordingly.

Sound risk management involves the application of four basic elements in the management of the funds' assets and liabilities:

- Appropriate board and senior management oversight;
- Adequate risk management policies and procedures;
- Appropriate risk measurement, monitoring, and control functions; and
- Comprehensive internal controls and independent audits.

The specific manner in which private equity fund managers apply these elements in managing various risks will depend on the complexity and nature of the fund's holdings and activities, as well as on the level of risk exposure. For example, more complex currency or interest rate risk management processes require adequate internal controls that include audits or other appropriate oversight mechanisms to ensure the integrity of the information used by senior professionals in the private equity firm in overseeing compliance with policies and limits.

The duties of the individuals involved in risk measurement, monitoring, and control functions should be sufficiently separate, relevant, and independent from the deal or operational partners to ensure the avoidance of conflicts of interests.

Fund managers should monitor risks at the fund level but also at the firm level if they manage multiple funds. While a view at the fund level may provide a comprehensive measure with respect to critical market risks, it may also underestimate risk when, for example, positions in one portfolio company are used to offset positions in another portfolio company. Therefore, managers should monitor portfolio companies that are exposed to significant market risks separately.

To achieve effective risk governance, fund managers should establish risk committees, perform risk audits, and provide detailed risk disclosures to their investors. In the paragraphs below, we briefly outline the basic functions of these governance elements.

Risk committees

The risk committee is an independent committee within the private equity fund organization which undertakes the responsibility of the risk management policies regarding the fund's operations. This function is both a challenging and an important one, given that private equity funds invest in securities that are illiquid and difficult to price due to a lack of publicly available prices. Depending on the risk appetite of the fund manager, the responsibilities of a risk committee may include: (1) risk management policies oversight, (2) establishment of a risk management strategy, (3) process approval for risk identification, (4) risk tolerance assessment, and (5) risk monitoring.

The risk committee should have the ultimate responsibility for understanding the nature and level of market risks taken by the private equity fund. It should approve investment strategies that establish or influence the risks, the risk appetite, and the risk management policy. At least once a year, the board of the fund manager or its risk management committee, as appropriate, should re-evaluate the fund's risk management policies, the business strategies that influence exposures to various risks, the key assumptions used in risk management, and the results of sensitivity tests.

The committee should also define the lines of responsibility and authority for managing risk exposure. In particular, the committee may ensure that the management of portfolio companies takes the necessary steps to identify, measure, monitor, and control market risks at the company level. The management of the portfolio companies should also be reviewed regularly to understand and assess its performance in terms of monitoring and controlling market risks. In some circumstances, the committee should ensure that the portfolio companies' management teams understand the risks they are exposed to and that they have personnel with the necessary technical skills to evaluate and control these risks or engage with advisers if necessary.

Risk audits

Financial regulation reforms have brought a new level of audit supervision to private equity funds. One important aspect of this process pertains to the fair value measurements of assets and liabilities, which are sitting on private equity funds' balance sheets. Since valuations require significant judgment and assumptions, risk auditors have a major role in foreseeing risk associated with any mispricing or misstatement.

Regardless of which audit approach is pursued, auditors need to understand how fund managers and portfolio company managers identify and control relevant risks. Key factors that risk auditors should consider (as they evaluate private equity funds) include analyses of valuation methodologies and approaches, and investigations of reported losses and gains by the fund and its investments.

Risk disclosure

All alternative funds should meet certain minimum disclosure requirements in terms of the annual report contents. The annual report of a fund should include a balance sheet, an income and expenditure account, a report on the fund's activities during the financial year, detailed information regarding the remuneration of professionals advising the fund, and the overall risk profile of the fund. If the manager ever exceeds a specific risk limit—with respect to market, credit, liquidity, counterparty or operational risk—the manager must notify investors immediately, explaining the circumstances together with any remedial actions taken.

The risk disclosures should provide accurate, informative, and timely information on the various risks discussed above, and describe how fund managers manage specific risk exposures. Best practice disclosures involve the following actions:

- Reporting risk measures regularly.

- Clearly comparing current exposures to policy limits. In addition, past forecasts or risk estimates should be compared with actual results to identify any modeling shortcomings (back testing).

- Detailing risk exposures of the fund in reports submitted to the fund manager's board and investors.

- Reporting aggregate information together with sufficient supporting details so that management can evaluate the fund's sensitivity to changes in market conditions and to other important risk factors.

CONCLUSION

Due to the unique characteristics of private equity investments, the standard risk management tools used in other asset classes are difficult to implement. Risks specific to private equity, which an institutional investor should be aware of, require the application of non-conventional risk management procedures and techniques.

Risk management in the private equity industry does not solely concern the funds' portfolio investments, but also concerns risks that are inherent to the structure of the fund and the constraints of the fund's investors. It is therefore important that fund managers carefully assess the quality of their risk management processes and understand the risk appetite of their investors. A best practice risk management process involves a detailed analysis of risk exposures to determine the key risk indicators that must be regularly monitored, implementation of risk management standards, stress testing, creation of reporting dashboards, and so on. Most importantly, managers need to set up risk management functions that are compliant with current regulations in the jurisdictions where they operate.

In his own words: Kevin Lester, Founder and CEO, Validus Risk Management

The history of currency risk management for private capital managers can be divided into three cycles. The first, corresponding to the emergence of private equity in the second half of the last century, involved a focus on the management of currency risks <u>within</u> portfolio companies; fund level hedging, involving the risks associated with investing in foreign currency assets, was rarely considered and almost never hedged.

The second cycle, beginning in the early 2000's, saw managers begin to consider the implications of currency risk on investment decisions; this involved the innovation of new hedging instruments, such as deal-contingent forward contracts, but the scope of FX hedging remained narrow, typically limited to hedging 'known' transactions such as investments and divestments.

The 'third wave' of currency risk management began to gain momentum in the second half of this decade (circa 2015 onwards). This phase involved the development of sophisticated net investment hedging programs, designed to protect private capital fund performance from the uncompensated currency risks created by investing in overseas assets.

There are a number of factors behind this evolution: 1) an increasing awareness of the potential catastrophic impact of currency risk following the volatility spikes of the 2008 financial crisis and subsequent financial crises; 2) a trend towards more internationally diverse investment portfolios; 3) investor and regulatory pressure to prioritize best practice risk management strategies; 4) a migration of best practice from certain spheres of the private capital world (e.g. credit, infrastructure) to others (private equity, fund of funds); 5) macroeconomic factors which incentivize hedging as a means to capture favorable interest rate differentials, and boost returns; and 6) the evolution of fund structures (e.g., feeder funds) to cater for international investors as private capital has become more mainstream, attracting an increasingly diverse pool of investors.

This increased demand for sophisticated hedging solutions has led directly to the growth of turnkey risk management products, such as those pioneered and offered by Validus since 2010. Our 'currency hedging as a service' approach enables private capital managers to deploy customized hedging strategies across their platforms, and meet the operational demands of managing a hedging program (trading, back office, reporting), without having to incur the financial costs and operational risks of establishing in-house capabilities in non-core areas.

12 Fund Finance

The only man who sticks closer to you in adversity than a friend is a creditor.
Unknown

INTRODUCTION

Over the last few years, the private capital industry has added a new level of complexity for investors. It started to use fund finance, a broad range of financing structures at the fund level, to support funds' liquidity and help boost their reported returns. The fund finance market has experienced substantial growth over recent years, with private capital funds often seeking to obtain credit from lenders in various forms and structures. The rapid growth has been helped by the low interest rate environment.

Many banks are still entering this market bringing substantial price pressure due to increasing competition. The low interest rate environment has led many of these creditors to revert to fund finance products with yields that are more attractive than alternative short-term uses of their capital. In addition, banks get the opportunity to work with experienced managers who may purchase other products or services that the bank offers. The low cost of fund financing instruments has been offset by the benefits they bring to fund managers and their investors. However, if the interest rates rise, investors are likely to question seriously these facilities and may put pressure on managers to discontinue their use.

In this chapter we discuss four main categories of fund finance facilities:

- **Subscription lines** which are short-term lines backed by LPs' capital commitments.

- **Net Asset Value facilities** which are short or long term lines backed by the cash flows or distributions generated by the underlying portfolio of the borrowing fund.

- **Hybrid facilities** are a hybrid of subscription lines and net asset value facilities and are backed by a combination of both LPs' undrawn commitments as well as the underlying portfolio of the fund.

- **GP-level facilities** which are technically not provided to the fund but to the manager of the fund, the GP, and are tailored to specific circumstances of the GP.

It is important to note that as of the end of 2019 there were no regulatory requirements for GPs to submit information on fund facility usage, besides the pressure received from LPs or their willingness to comply with ILPA guidance voluntarily. As a result, we currently know very little about the usage of fund facilities. Using a sample of over 8000 funds with vintages after 2000, Preqin (2019) documents that only 29% of the funds have disclosed the extent to which they use fund facilities. Although the fund finance market is not public, the U.S. law firm Cadwalader, estimates that it is has reached over $500 billion with lender commitments increasing by over 20% in 2018. The Economist (2019) arrives at a similar figure of over $400 billion. According to Cadwalader, subscription line facilities together with hybrid facilities are getting close to 65% to 90% of the transaction volume depending on the year and geographical location (Europe versus U.S.). The main users of fund finance facilities are secondaries funds and private equity funds followed by the larger venture/growth funds (see Hutchinson and Cross, 2019).

While most LPs have generally been willing to accept the use of fund finance instruments some worries still remain. First, LPs are uneasy about the costs of obtaining and servicing some fund finance instruments such as subscription lines which are classified as fund expenses (thus payable by LPs). These costs are likely to increase if a significant dislocation in the financial sector occurs. Second, some LPs worry that if they wish to exit the fund via a secondaries transaction, they might not be able to do so if the transfer is blocked by the GP because it triggers a default on a fund finance instrument. Finally, long-duration fund financing facilities significantly postpone capital calls and/or allow for a return of the capital much sooner than expected, causing the LPs to be underweight in their strategic allocations to the private equity asset class.

In the future, it is likely that increasing investor sophistication, improved reporting standards set by industry bodies (e.g., the Institutional Limited Partners Association) and more transparency from fund managers will alleviate some of the concerns levelled against the use of fund finance instruments. Already some investors require fund managers to report both unlevered and levered returns achieved by their funds.

SUBSCRIPTION (OR CAPITAL CALL) FACILITIES

Private equity funds have been increasingly seeking more subscription lines (or capital call facilities) from lenders. These lines are senior revolving or term credit facilities secured by the unfunded capital commitments of the fund's investors. The main aim of these facilities is to bridge the investors' commitments to the fund. Similar to other forms of debt financing, banks may sometimes syndicate subscription lines of credit, especially when they are very large.

Subscription lines have interest rates typically based on EURIBOR/LIBOR plus a spread and often include additional upfront fees (e.g., arrangement and commitment fees, letter of credit fees).[1] The maturity of a subscription line ranges from few months to several years and at maturity, there might be an opportunity for the lending contract to be renewed. Finally, the typical subscription line includes a covenant that relates to the ratio of total unfunded commitments to the fund's total debt. Exhibit 1 illustrates the typical structure of a subscription line:

It is important to note that subscription lines cannot be used to increase the fund's investable capital; this capital remains capped at the original total amount of investor commitments plus recycled distributable proceeds (to the extent that capital recycling is permitted by the fund's Limited Partnership Agreement). Therefore, a subscription line does not magnify the returns on invested capital from the underlying fund investments, making this type of facility quite different from fund leverage facilities that are used to increase the capital of the fund.

Whether a subscription line is classified as leverage or not has significant regulatory implications in UK and Continental Europe, because a manager of leveraged funds is required to obtain full-scope permission under European regulations once it has total assets under management (i.e., committed capital of all the funds managed) of €100m. For unleveraged funds the assets under management threshold is much higher at €500m. The European Securities and Markets Authority issued regulatory guidance in August 2018 confirming that borrowing arrangements such as subscription lines are not considered leverage if they are "temporary" and "fully covered by contractual capital commitments from investors". Nevertheless, GPs should still take care

---

[1] If by any chance, the EURIBOR / LIBOR rates are less than zero, then contracts usually specify that these rates are deemed to be zero.

about the structuring of these facilities: the longer the duration of a subscription facility, and the less frequently it is payed down, the more likely will be that regulators will classify it as not "temporary".

Exhibit 1: Subscription lines

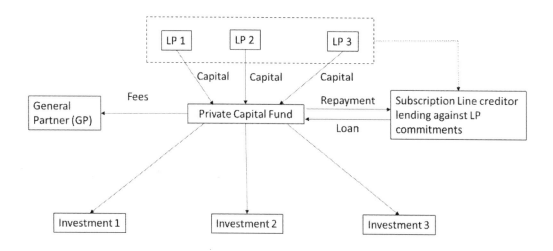

Given that lenders have recourse to the uncalled investor commitments to the fund, they need to assess the creditworthiness of the investors to make sure that the subscription line is appropriately priced. However, over the last few years, the use and maturities of such funding instruments have increased significantly. Approximately, 93% of Hamilton Lane GPs were using fund level subscription lines in 2018 whereas the same proportion was only 61% in 2009-2011 (Tikkanen, 2018). According to Preqin (2018), 31% of GPs surveyed were using subscription credit while another 14% declared that they would start using such lines at a later date. The duration of subscription lines has also been increasing recently. Based on a data sample from Nordic Capital, although only 15% of subscription lines had a duration of more than 1 year, almost 41% had a longer than expected duration of more than 3 months. Historically, almost all subscription lines, if used at all, were for less than 90 days.

The data suggests that banks seem to have embraced subscription financing as a relatively safe form of lending. The creditworthiness of the fund's investors, most of whom are investment-grade institutions, is very high. Moreover, while subscription lines are large loans they have relatively short maturities. Banks' confidence in the robustness of fund finance as a business line is arguably backed by a rarity of defaults. The only large default so far has been that of Abraaj Group in 2018, which acquired a business in Turkey with a subscription line from Société Générale just prior to its default. Many players in the market would argue that Abraaj's default, caused by the manager's deceit of investors and misuse of funds, is a very rare and unusual event.

Benefits and costs

Subscription lines bring some important advantages that can enhance a fund manager's competitive advantage in the market:

- **Fast access to liquidity:** A subscription line supplies liquidity to the fund faster than calling investors' capital contributions, thus being especially beneficial for time-sensitive fund investments. Under the subscription line, borrowed funds usually can be made available within a day while under the limited partnership agreement, capital calls may take at least ten to fifteen working days. Subscription lines are also useful for unexpected ad-hoc working capital needs.

- **Bridge financing:** A subscription line can provide a bridge to permanent asset-level debt financing when the fund is unable to secure that financing before the consummation of an investment. Therefore, the fund can show the seller of an asset that it has quick access to liquidity to finalize the transaction. For example, a private equity fund could use a subscription facility to bridge the period between the acquisition of the property and the incurrence of a more permanent mortgage. In addition, subscription lines can give the fund a stronger bargaining power when negotiating for asset-level financing with other lenders.

- **Cheaper financing:** Incurring debt under the subscription facility is usually cheaper than alternative asset-level financing. As a result, many fund may be incentivized to leave the subscription facility outstanding for a more extended period. For instance, subscription lines with tenors of one to three years are priced at around 160bp while five-year loans at the portfolio company level can be priced at more than 300bp.[2]

- **Lower transaction costs:** Since GPs can consolidate various credit requirements at the level of the asset or underlying portfolio companies under one financing (and potentially from a single creditor), the use of subscription lines can lead to lower associated transaction costs.

- **Easy access to alternative currencies:** For funds operating or expanding globally, subscription lines can offer ready access to alternative currencies, eliminating the need to call capital in one currency and convert it to another. This improves the speed of capital access, lessening the impact of exchange rate exposure and reducing the administrative burden.

- **Smooth capital calls:** A subscription line can provide smooth capital calls to investors by avoiding avoids frequent and small capital drawdowns for working capital or management fees, relieving the fund and its investors from an excessive administrative burden associated with the processing of the drawdowns. The subscription facility also helps with capital contributions made by investors that join the fund later during the fundraising period and who need to provide true-up capital contributions.[3] With a subscription line facility available for the fund's capital needs before the final fund closing, the fund may be able to eliminate or reduce needs for true-up requirements thus avoiding significant back office costs.

- **Improve the fund's reported internal rate of return (IRR):** The use of subscription facilities means that the fund delays capital drawdowns from investors, shortening the holding period of investors' money and thus increasing the fund's reported IRR.[4] In fact, if the subscription line is used to make investments and is repaid twelve to fifteen months after making the investments, the capital drawdowns

---

[2] As per a banking team procurement survey conducted by the team at Nordic Capital, the interest rate cost for a fund subscription line can be below 1.5%, a big reduction from the interest rate costs of above 3% in 2012 (see Tikkanen, 2018).

[3] The true-up process ensures that capital contributions made by the first set of investors are rebalanced so that new investors have their pro-rata interest in the fund.

[4] It is worth highlighting that the delay in calling investors' capital dominates the decrease in net cash flows due to the interest expense and fees paid by the fund for the subscription line in the computation of the IRR. The impact of a subscription line on fund performance measured using IRR is significantly larger when the line is used earlier in a fund's life.

from investors might even experience a positive IRR on the first day of the capital call thus eliminating the well-known J-curve effect that is specific to private equity funds at the beginning of their life. The subscription line can also increase reported IRRs if it can be used to post collateral on hedging agreements during the fund's life. The funds can thus avoid the drag on IRRs caused by keeping investor's capital as collateral on hand to settle hedging agreements.

While it is clear that subscription line facilities do bring some clear benefits such as better cash flow management and a reduced administrative burden, investors should pay attention to their use for several reasons:

- The costs of obtaining and servicing the subscription line are often classified as fund expenses, thus payable by investors.

- As the maturity of these facilities increases, capital calls are postponed for longer periods to the extent that an institutional investor may end up with a lower allocation to the private equity asset than initially planned.

- The use of subscription lines (and other facilities discussed below) leads to a lack of comparability of fund performance across GPs. Some GPs may have an unfair competitive advantage arising from the use of subscription facilities to which other GPs may not have access or may not want to use.[5]

- The use of a subscription line might contribute to an increase in the fees from carried interest by making it more likely that the fund's reported IRR reaches the fund's hurdle rate. GPs have also been accused in the past of using these lines to manage carried interest pay-out timings. To partly mitigate these issues, some investors require that the hurdle rate starts to kick in when the subscription line is drawn down not when the capital is called.

Investors' concerns are reflected in a new set of principles published by the Institutional Limited Partners Association (ILPA) in June 2019. ILPA recommends that subscription lines should be used primarily to benefit the fund partnership as a whole rather than chiefly for the purpose of enhancing the reported IRR to accelerate the accrual and distribution of carried interest. For carried interest calculations where a credit facility is in place, the preferred fund return should accrue from the date that capital is at risk (i.e., when the credit facility is drawn) instead of when the capital is ultimately called from investors. Further, ILPA recommends that subscription lines should not facilitate the provision of fund distributions from divestments and have limited use. For example, the lines should be outstanding for a maximum of 180 days (a special permission from investors should be required if the maturity is above one year) and should not be greater than 20% of all uncalled capital. With these limitations, more transparency is also strongly advised. LPs should be notified when subscription lines are used to learn that a certain amount of capital commitment has been allocated. Specific information on fund credit facilities should be disclosed to investors in annual and quarterly reports including a disclosure on the unlevered net IRR (i.e. the net IRR that would have resulted without the use of any subscription lines). The LPAC (Limited Partners Advisory Committee) of a fund should have oversight of all subscription credit facilities and all LPs should consider detailed information on the use of subscription credit facilities when conducting due diligence on fund managers.

---

[5] In the highly competitive world of private equity investing, a few percentage points in the net reported IRR figure can mean a different decile or quartile with serious fund raising repercussions.

Terms and structuring of a subscription facility

Before providing subscription lines, lenders demand significant information from the fund manager such as the limited partnership agreement of the borrowing fund, the private placement memorandum of the fund, any side letters entered into by investors in the fund and all subscription agreements for each investor. After receiving the subscription line for a fund, the fund managers must continue to provide information to lenders such as audited financial statements of the fund, compliance certificates that confirm that there is no breach of the lending agreement, investor drawdown and distribution notices, details of material litigation events, notices if the investment period of the fund is suspended, amendments to the fund's documentation, etc.

Typically, the documents for a subscription facility contain provisions securing the rights of the lender, including a pledge of the capital commitments of investors, the requirement that the fund's GP calls capital from investors in the event of default and the right to enforce a payment from the account into which investors made capital contributions. Therefore, the collateral and expected source of repayment in the subscription line facility is the capital commitments of the investors. In the UK, subscription facility lenders usually insist that the uncalled commitments of the LPs be more than or equal to the aggregate loans outstanding at the fund level. In the US, creditors typically require letters from LPs which confirm that they (1) have committed a certain amount of capital to the borrowing fund, (2) give permission to grant security over the uncalled capital commitments and (3) provide representations and warranties to the creditor. Often banks negotiate the power of attorney to make capital calls to LPs or obtain security over the bank accounts of the fund. In most cases, the bank providing the facility is the only secured creditor of the fund.

If an LP defaults on the capital call, the fund manager can sell the interest to another LP in the fund or to a third party at a significant discount while distributions entitled to the defaulting LP may be used to offset outstanding capital call amounts. In the case of last resort, the bank can secure the senior right to any future distributions before it is paid out to LPs to settle outstanding credit with the ultimate recourse being the winding up the fund by liquidating all of its assets.

Most subscription lines provide so called accordion options which basically allow the borrower to request an increase to the facility principal by a certain amount. Lenders are generally not obliged to accept such requests. Subscription lines are typically repayable at the end of their interest period (i.e., in a "bullet" payment) unless the borrower uses an option to roll over the loan's principal and interest at the end of the loan's maturity. Subscription lines are of course repayable in full upon occurrence of an event of default or if the fund manager ceases to by the general partner of the fund.[6]

ASSET-BACKED FACILITIES OR NET ASSET VALUE (NAV) FACILITIES

The fund finance market has been evolving recently with the growth of a newer product: the net asset value (NAV) or the asset-backed facility. These types of fund finance facilities are provided to the fund (or to a special purpose vehicle owned by the fund or fund manager) and are secured against the distributions and cash flows that are coming from the underlying portfolio of investments. Therefore, in contrast to

---

[6] The definition of the event of default varies from one subscription line to another but generally include non-payments, breach of covenants stated in the loan documentation, default by investors with aggregate commitments exceeding a certain threshold of total commitments to the fund (e.g., 10-15%), misrepresentations, default on other junior debt taken by the fund, material litigation, etc.

subscription lines, there is no recourse available with the LPs of the fund. The proceeds from these facilities are often used to:

- Pay investors a fund distribution during the mid to later stages of the fund's lifetime (in advance of a full exit of the underlying portfolio). Sometimes NAV facilities whose main purpose is to accelerate the payment of proceeds to investors in the fund are called *exit facilities*. These facilities simply provide bridge financing to a fund looking to sell individual investments (typically a portfolio company) soon. Because the facility this enables the fund to repay investors early, it will also boost the fund's IRR. These facilities are typically secured over the sub-portfolio of assets earmarked for disposal.[7]

- Make additional acquisitions and support portfolio companies. These type of facilities provide long term funding to funds that are fully invested. These NAV facilities are typically more flexible and better priced than taking leverage at the investment level and are constructed through borrowing base mechanics. They could also be used to add capital infusions in distressed investments that are in the portfolio thus protecting the value for the fund.

Exhibit 2 presents a typical structure of an NAV facility:

Exhibit 2: NAV facilities

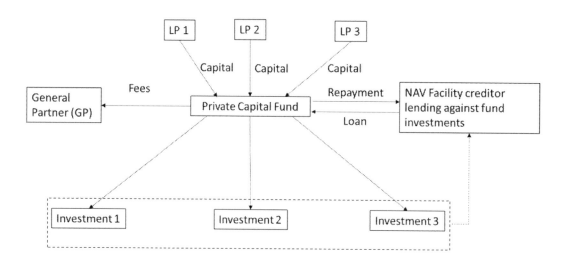

Supplying NAV facilities can allow lenders to continue to provide liquidity lines to their clients, even when the investment period of a fund has terminated, and no uncalled capital commitments are remaining. Not surprisingly, NAV facilities are given to the same fund managers who also use subscription line facilities, providing an opportunity for lenders to widen the products they currently offer and to strengthen the relationships they have with their fund clients.

It is important to note that NAV facilities used to make acquisitions and support portfolio companies could be very helpful for many private equity funds that invest in emerging markets (such as Africa or Central

---

[7] Sometimes the lender simply provides the agreed purchase price of the portfolio company between the fund and the buyer with the loan being repaid upon settlement of the sale between the fund and the buyer.

and Eastern Europe). These funds often struggle to obtain competitive financing locally against the assets of each portfolio company. Therefore, emerging markets fund managers might find it much more attractive to seek financing from lenders who are able to offer NAV facilities at the fund level, secured against cash-flows of the portfolio companies, with the benefits that portfolio diversification can provide.[8]

Due to the nature of the NAV facilities and lack of recourse from LPs (who tend to be more credit worthy), generally, NAV facilities are priced materially higher than subscription lines (typically LIBOR plus 300 to 700 basis points depending on the use of the funds). These facilities also charge arrangement and commitment fees. From a lender's perspective, the risk is higher since the eventual distributions from the underlying portfolio still carry some degree of uncertainty. As a result of the potential for higher returns, an increasing number of new lenders are entering the NAV facility market. These new entrants to the market are not only the existing banks that provide subscription lines, but also credit and special situations funds that are searching for higher yields.

The credit analysis that is required to be undertaken by creditors for NAV type facilities is very different from that needed for subscription lines. For pure NAV facilities, the creditworthiness of the investors of the fund is much less important than the value of the underlying assets. The main factors influencing the amount of leverage that can be deployed via a NAV facility would include the reputation of the fund manager, the diversity and maturity of the portfolio, the existing leverage at the investment level, and the projected cash flows or distributions from the underlying investments in the fund's portfolio. Lenders often insist on a cash sweep on the distributions from the portfolio such that they have seniority.

With the increasing adoption of fund finance facilities, a lot of lenders have also begun to venture in providing GPs with so-called "*hybrid facilities*" where the exact facility structure and terms are somewhere in the middle between those of a subscription line and a NAV line. These structures are often negotiated on a case-by-case basis given specific circumstances. From the perspective of the creditors, these hybrid facilities may provide recourse to both kinds of collateral: (1) LP capital commitments and (2) the fund's underlying portfolio assets. To maintain sufficient collateral at all times of the fund's lifetime, creditors providing these facilities put in place certain covenants to ensure that the level of undrawn investor commitments together with the net asset value of the fund remain above a minimum threshold.

Hybrid facilities provide the flexibility to not have to refinance the debt as the fund calls down committed capital over the investment period of the fund. These hybrid facilities are a great way for creditors to build strong relationships with GPs such that the creditors can offer several other products tailored to different stages of the fund life to the GP and become a one-stop shop for all sorts of financing needs. These facilities are preferred by funds that are looking for long-term financing that is available from the first close until the end of the fund's life, when the fund is fully invested.

Sometimes hybrid facilities are used when there is some sort of issue obtaining security over all of the relevant LP undrawn commitments. For instance, a group of investors, may invest in a fund through a separate feeder fund vehicle for tax or other reasons. If the feeder fund vehicle has not been set up by the manager of the fund then the fund is not able to provide security over the rights of the feeder fund to draw down from the LPS. To mitigate this imperfect collateral, lenders will then take security over the rights of the fund to draw down from the feeder fund but also over any company shares that the fund has invested in. Exhibit 3 presents a typical structure of a hybrid facility:

[8] This is often facilitated by the fact that holding vehicles that sit between the fund and the companies in the portfolio that are located in emerging markets are based in off-shore jurisdictions that have tested legal systems and allow NAV facility lenders to enforce their rights if needed.

Exhibit 3: Hybrid facilities

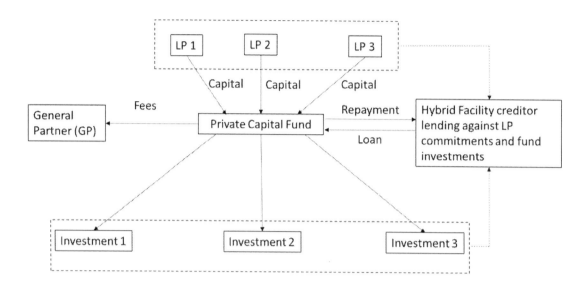

The use of NAV facilities by different types of funds

There is a wide variety of various private capital funds focusing on different types of investments that could benefit from using asset-backed facilities.[9] Buyout funds can borrow funds by using shares of the portfolio companies in which they have invested as collateral such that lenders have recourse to these shares in case of default. Since buyout funds usually invest in more stable and mature companies, the shares are often a source of comfort to the creditors. However, most lenders providing such facilities to buyout GPs are structurally junior to other lenders that may have provided debt secured directly against the underlying portfolio companies at the portfolio company level.

Funds of funds or secondary funds holding limited partnerships and other equity interests in private equity funds obtain credit facilities by providing the limited partnership interests they hold as collateral. Creditors secure direct rights to any distributions made to the borrowing fund from these limited partnership interests. Due to commercial and legal issues, this borrowing may be structured via a special purpose vehicle (SPV) that is placed in the middle to hold all of the limited partnership interests provided as collateral. The creditors usually directly fund the SPV while taking over shares of the SPV as collateral and getting access to any bank accounts of the SPV into which distributions are paid. Upon enforcement, the creditor can take control of the SPV and its bank accounts such that it would be the sole beneficiary of any and all distributions that are paid up to the SPV.

Direct lending funds and credit funds can borrow funds against their underlying loan portfolios. The creditors analyze the underlying loan portfolio to determine the level of loan-to-value (LTV) ratio that can be provided. Only the underlying loans that meet certain eligibility criteria such as senior secured, not subject to any default, and provided to a borrower located in a particular jurisdiction or geography may qualify as

---

[9] Asset-backed facilities to hedge funds are structured very differently from those assets backed funds facilities provided to closed-ended funds such as secondary, direct lending and private equity funds. The hedge fund often segregates the investments it wishes to use as collateral into separate securities accounts with a bank (see Stephenson, 2019).

collateral. It is also likely that certain borrower concentration limits are applied to the collateral assets such that no one group of loans to the same borrower or its affiliates may exceed a certain percentage of the whole portfolio of collateral assets. The level of diversification of the underlying loan portfolio is also an important factor. A more thorough due diligence analysis may be required by the creditor when lending against individual loans and the collateral needs to be include the security on the underlying loan if there is a default. Facilities provided to credit and direct lending funds generally carry less risk than those provided against a portfolio of companies which are usually less diversified. Direct lending funds' portfolios have more assets from different borrowers and industries and are thus better diversified.

Although NAV and asset-backed facilities are typically put in place during the later stages of the life of a fund, due to the fact that these facilities generally lend themselves more to funds that have been fully or nearly fully invested and have assets to lend against, some fund managers are looking to put in place these facilities at the start of the fund. The idea is to use these facilities when investments are brought into the portfolio. This is particularly the case of credit fund (especially direct lending funds), given that leverage by way of NAV or asset-backed facilities ensures that the fund is producing the rates of return promised to its investors.

Structure and terms

In contrast to subscription lines that typically have a revolving loan structure, NAV or asset-backed facilities are mostly structured with a fixed term (anywhere between 1 and 5 years) and amount. If the loan is being used for a certain liquidity event or to bridge a specific exit of a portfolio company, then the term may be short: from six to eighteen months. However, if the GP intends to use the loan as part of a leverage strategy (this is more typical for credit funds), then the facility will have a longer tenure, perhaps five years or more.

The most important covenant in structuring such credit facilities is the loan-to-value ratio (LTV), a very common measure in credit terms. In the context of a NAV facility, it is defined as the ratio of the value of the loan taken up by the borrowing fund to the net asset value of the fund's portfolio that will be used as collateral to secure the facility. For credit funds and secondary funds, LTV ratios can range from 10% to as high as 60%, varying according to the level of the diversification of the underlying assets. Likewise, the interest rate charged on the facility typically decreases for a well-diversified portfolio. The eligibility criteria for the fund's portfolio to qualify as collateral would be often listed in a schedule to the loan agreement. The creditor may also require a veto right on the acquisition of assets but there is usually strong push-back from the borrowing fund manager on this demand. Negotiating the collateral package between the creditor and borrower can be a lengthy process as the underlying assets are likely to be located in different geographies or subject to different legal systems. The creditor usually insists on an overriding security document, often governed by English or New York/Delaware law which seeks to take security over all of the underlying assets. In addition, the creditor may then require local security to be granted.[10]

NAV facilities often have covenant triggers linked to LTV ratios. These are designed to capture material fund NAV declines or a credit weakening in the underlying asset portfolio. The triggers may be in the form of pricing step-ups, agreed disposal programs and/or principal repayments or a stepped framework that incorporating all these triggers.

The fund manager will often be expected to provide to the lenders monthly collateral reports (accompanied by an excel spreadsheet with portfolio data) and quarterly financial statements for companies in the portfolio.

---

[10] See Stephenson (2019) for a more detailed discussion.

Sometimes, lenders require that a third party is named as a collateral administrator and provides detailed portfolio information on a weekly/monthly basis in order to assist the lenders with their internal monitoring requirements. Lenders also ask for the right to inspect businesses covered in the fund's portfolio (on-site, if requested).

NAV facilities often have cash-sweep and amortization features such that all or some part of any distributions paid up to the borrower from the underlying investments go first, in preference, to repay outstanding amounts under the credit facility. The amount of such cash-sweep can vary depending on the LTV when the distribution is paid out.

There would be a cost-benefit analysis at the start of the transaction to determine whether a full collateral package can be provided, and also a discussion about whether there are any legal restrictions on providing such security.

- **Private equity funds:** For facilities provided to private equity funds, if security was granted over shares in a holding company that owns the underlying assets, no change of control provisions must be triggered in senior facilities agreements or under material contracts entered by the portfolio companies. The lender will want to make sure there is tight security over the bank accounts into which the distributions from the underlying assets flow. Often, the lender (usually a bank) will require a new account to be opened with itself and require the borrower to direct that all distributions paid into the account. In some instances, lenders that are lending to a special purpose vehicle owned by the fund will require a guarantee or other shareholder support to be provided by the fund to further enhance the security for the asset-backed facility. However, lenders need to be careful and ensure that if this is the proposed structure, no borrowing limits of the fund are exceeded.

- **Secondary funds:** For facilities provided to secondary funds against their limited partnership interests, taking security over the underlying limited partnership interests usually requires the general partner of the underlying fund to give its consent. Therefore, the lender and the borrowing fund may need to devise structures to avoid seeking the consent, or to make it more likely that general partners of the underlying funds will give permission.

- **Credit funds:** For facilities provided to direct lending and other credit funds, the terms of the underlying loan agreements will need to be reviewed carefully. The provisions relating to transfers and assignments of the loans (typically entitled "Changes to the Lenders" in loan agreements) must also be examined to see whether the underlying borrower has any consent or consultation rights before the fund can transfer its loan to the lender in an enforcement event.

If the fund has a subscription line facility, the terms of the subscription line finance documents must be reviewed to ensure there are no restrictions on other financial indebtedness and that there are no negative pledges included. NAV facility lenders might even require a second-ranking security recourse to the undrawn commitments of investors. This can give rise to detailed discussions on inter-creditor arrangements, with the subscription line provider and the NAV facility lender negotiating to get the strongest position concerning the fund's assets. Inter-creditor discussions focus on essential issues like cross-defaults between the NAV facility and the subscription line facility, restrictions on payments going to and from the fund when there is a default under the NAV facility or the subscription line facility, and standstill periods during which one lender must wait until the other lender has decided whether to enforce.

Monitoring

NAV facility lenders typically require significant information rights in the facility agreement to become aware at any time of potential issues connected with the value of the underlying assets. The borrowing fund is also required to provide regular certificates confirming that financial covenants such as loan-to-value (LTV) ratios, leverage ratios and portfolio interest coverage ratios are met. NAV facility lenders might also schedule quarterly portfolio telephone calls with the managers of the fund to discuss the performance of the collateral assets. Some lenders go further and require copies of management presentations, rating agency reports, and detailed financial information concerning the underlying assets.

Lenders also insert detailed provisions about the valuation of the underlying assets. The valuation methodology is set out in a schedule to the facility agreement so that the borrower and the lender agree to the principles and terms on which the underlying assets are valued. While a valuation agent is appointed by the manager of the borrowing fund, this agent needs to be agreed by lenders. The lender would usually want to make sure that the valuation agent owes a contractual duty to the lender, and this may be documented through a specific engagement letter with the valuation agent that is addressed to both the borrower and the lender, or through a separate reliance letter. The valuation agent is required to provide periodic valuations to the lender. This is particularly important because, sometimes, the latest valuation is needed to determine a particular course of action under the facility agreement. For example, an LTV ratio may need to be determined before any acquisition or sale of an asset. Only if the LTV exceeds a given threshold will the relevant acquisition or sale of the collateral asset be permitted.

NAV facilities often include provisions that allow the lender to seek an alternative valuation if the lender does not agree with the valuation provided by the valuation agent. The amount of deviation between the lender's calculation of the value of the portfolio and that of the valuation agent may be negotiated between the borrower and the lender before the lender has the right to instruct a separate valuation. The cost of this additional separate valuation is covered by the borrowing fund.

GP-LEVEL FACILITIES (BORROWING AT THE FUND MANAGER LEVEL)

GP-level facilities include any credit lines provided directly to the GP or fund manager. These can either be used to finance GP commitments to the fund managed or be used to fund operating financing needs such as working capital. GPs managing private capital funds have been increasing their personal commitments to the funds over time. As the size of funds has been growing along with proportionate commitments of GPs, the absolute size of these commitments has become increasingly large relative to the liquidity that GPs have available. Therefore, many GPs started to rely on carry from previous funds. Preqin (2018) calculates that more than a third, 36 per cent, of GPs rely on carry to finance commitments to future funds, while one in five (19%) use external debt. With average fund commitments at over 3%, banks can step in and provide valuable services to such GPs to better manage their funding needs. Exhibit 4 portrays a typical structure of a GP-level facility:

Exhibit 4: GP-level facilities

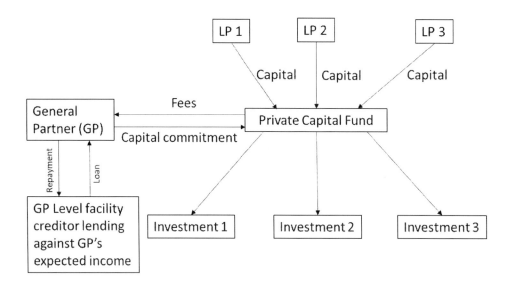

There is a risk that GPs who excessively rely on reinvesting carry from previous or current funds could fall short of their funding commitments should their exits not deliver the expected returns, potentially decreasing the capital they expect to receive. This is one of the main reasons why such credit tends to be materially more expensive when compared to subscription line facilities or NAV facilities where the portfolio is already in place and returns can be better estimated.

Credit facilities at the fund management company level are fairly non-standard and so customized to every single situation on a case-by-case basis. The cost of the facility would typically depend on factors such as the quality of the collateral or security pledge by the GP, the performance record of the borrowing GP, and the particular context of the circumstances under which the loans are made. The kinds of collateral that may be used to secure GP-level financing could potentially include carried interest, excess operating cash flows or management fees expected to come in from the funds managed. With such collateral, the borrowing costs would be lower as compared to a financing where the only security provided is the return generated from the sponsor commitment paid in to the fund where eventual returns are still not certain.

GP level facilities often might have attached to them certain financial covenants depending on the circumstances. For instance, lenders might ask for a management fee income test which requires that the aggregate amount of management fees that are subject to collateral requirements and are paid into the bank account of the GP shall be equal to or greater than a certain absolute amount. Similarly an LTV test might be required. For instance, the ratio of GP's total financial indebtedness to the net asset value of the GP's interest in the Fund shall be not greater than a certain threshold.

A case study that received a lot of attention from the industry and media was the downfall in 2018 of one of the largest emerging market private equity firms globally, Abraaj Capital. Its founder and CEO, Arif Naqvi, was embroiled in lawsuits both from creditors as well as LPs. This was a scenario where GP credit facilities were used to plug operating cash flows at a regular and unsustainable level.[11]

CONCLUSION

A large amount of capital is locked up in the fund finance market and recently, fund-level debt is opportunistically and increasingly being used by GPs as an alternative or complement to secured senior financing at the level of portfolio companies. Nowadays, GPs require flexible, responsive and creative financing from their debt providers to react quickly to market opportunities and maximize investments returns in the ever-competitive private equity industry.

The fund finance market has also experienced some syndication of these facilities. Pension funds and other non-bank investors who would typically invest in a fund as a limited partner, are also considering providing capital by way of fixed income by participating in these fund level facilities. Therefore an investment bank can arrange the transaction, then go out to these non-bank lenders to sell down its participation in the loan to reduce its exposure. At the same time, the bank is often keen to continue to hold a majority portion of the loan and run the facility agency and security agency functions. This facilitates the development of a relationship with the underlying fund manager.

The different processes and features of fund debt facilities are likely to continue to grow. The subscription facility market is already quite sophisticated and robust for both borrowers and lenders, helping borrowers to reach an effective and efficient access to capital. As more and more private equity funds begin to understand the benefits associated with fund level facilities, one would expect a higher utilization of these instruments.

REFERENCES

Hutchinson, S. and Cross, J. (2019). Fund Finance 2019, Market presentation Cadwalader.

Economist. (2019). *After Abraaj*.

Sharif, A. (2018). *What's Left of Abraaj and How It Collapsed So Quickly*. Bloomberg.

Stephenson, L (2019). *Hybrid and asset backed fund finance facilities*. Reed Smith LLP

Tikkanen, K. (2018). Lines of credit and track record. *SuperReturn CFO/COO Conference*, (p. 2).

---

[11] As per reports from Bloomberg (Sharif, 2018), PwC reported in its liquidation report dated 11 July 2018 that the fund manager at Abraaj, Abraaj Investment Management Ltd, had been borrowing regularly to meet the financing needs of running the firm day to day. The management fees being earned by the fund manager were less than the operating expenses (mostly salary, marketing expenses, and administration expenses) for several years beginning 2014 right up until its demise in 2018.

In her own words: Sarah Lobbardi, Partner and Head of Finance Advisory, Validus Risk Management

Fund finance has been continuously increasing over the last few years with more sophisticated and complex structures and increased competition between lenders. Our group's expertise comes from real market experience gained on both sides of a transaction: as an adviser of financial sponsors on acquisitions and exits and as an originator of fund finance.

For the last few years we have seen a material growth in the non-subscription line facility space with a higher volume of asset backed lending and hybrid facilities. This growth has been mainly driven by credit and secondaries funds. Added to this, transactions are becoming more sophisticated and complex with bigger loans requiring more than one lender to form a club deal. At Validus we provide an independent advisory service to support and assist sponsors to determine the appropriate fund finance product for their fund, get the best offers available and navigate them through all lenders in the market. Appropriately filtering the lender market is key. At the moment, the global fund finance market counts many lenders but not all of them have appetite for large exposures, different types of private equity funds or types of facilities.

Identifying lenders and sourcing the best offer is the first step but structuring the facilities is one of the key parts of the process. Challenges are often encountered with term sheet negotiations that can lead to high legal costs. We advise on the optimal structuring, best terms and mitigating refinancing risk while lending our experience with the structuring and modelling of bespoke solutions.

The most important reasons why managers want independent non-bank advice on fund finance is because they want to reduce their workload and costs. These can be very high when managers run many funds. However, smaller managers also benefit from independent advice given their limited knowledge of the market and inability to attract the right lenders. A fund finance advisor like us is seen by managers as a trusted partner that provides an extension of their business and team. As a result, managers are able to focus on maximizing growth and returns within their funds while letting us concentrate on the structuring and the negotiation of the right fund finance facilities.

13 Environmental, Social, and Governance (ESG) Criteria in Private Equity

Problems cannot be solved at the same level of awareness that created them.
Albert Einstein

INTRODUCTION

Environmental, social, and governance (ESG) refers to the range of non-financial investment considerations embedded in the concept of responsible investing. Common objectives of ESG management include energy savings, waste diversion, improved labor practices in the supply chain, employee health and safety, and ethical transactions. Many private equity stakeholders, including investors in the private equity funds, expect fund managers to integrate social, environmental, and ethical considerations into their investment decision making.

ESG private equity investing differs from conventional investments in two ways. First, socially responsible private equity fund managers (i.e., general partners, managers) apply a set of investment screens to select or exclude assets based on non-financial criteria, in addition to financial criteria. These non-financial aspects can be as important and sometimes more important than the financial ones. Second, the fund managers often engage in shareholder activism to foster ESG strategies in the firms they own. As a result, private equity funds that embed ESG in their investment process face a larger set of risks and opportunities given the need to manage ESG factors.

Interest in ESG issues in relation to private equity funds has grown exponentially over the last two decades. Investors in private equity funds have played a leading role in the initial push for ESG. Although it is hard to identify the beginning of responsible investing to a specific point in time, the South African apartheid divestment movement in the 1980s is widely considered to be the first large-scale ethically driven investment. Since then, ESG investing has continued to attract the interest of more investors and asset managers, mainly due to higher levels of scrutiny by a wide range of stakeholders in society over the activity of the financial industry. The accelerated pace at which interest has grown, is reflected by the fact that by the end of 2018, most of the S&P 500 publicly listed companies reported on ESG factors and that, globally, there were close to $90 trillion of assets being professionally managed under responsible investment strategies.[1] Currently, a greater number and a larger variety of private equity investors are increasing their ESG expectations of fund managers. Europe has led the adoption of ESG investment practices by asset managers: 58% of pension fund investors already see ESG as an important consideration, compared to just 21% of the same group in the United States.[2] Adoption of ESG criteria in private equity is also on the rise in emerging markets where it has been driven by development finance institutions (DFIs). In addition, DFIs, whose main scope is to promote sustainable development, have themselves evolved over time, becoming more sophisticated in their ESG requirements.

---

[1] See the website of Principles for Responsible Investments (www.unpri.org).
[2] See Schroders (2016).

Despite this increased interest over the last decade, the level of integration of ESG factors in the private equity industry has been significantly lower vis-à-vis the listed equities market. The relative lack of interest in ESG investing has traditionally been attributed to the lower disclosure requirements and public scrutiny faced by the private equity market, and the comparatively high cost of incorporating in-house capacity for ESG due diligence or reporting requirements. An additional challenge is the perceived notion that engaging in responsible investing practices may undermine private equity fund managers' fulfillment of their fiduciary duties.

However, a growing number of managers believe that integrating ESG factors is not only an efficient risk management practice, but also an essential source of competitive advantage in achieving optimal financial returns.[3] Given its business model, the private equity industry is well positioned to lead on ESG investing for several reasons:

- **Active investing:** Private equity firms often acquire significant or controlling equity positions in portfolio companies, allowing them to take an active approach to corporate governance and ensure that ESG integration takes place.

- **Time frame:** Most private equity funds hold onto their investments for at least five years, providing enough time to obtain the upside potential from ESG activities. In contrast, the market short-termism that characterizes investors in publicly listed companies is one of the main reasons public companies struggle with ESG integration.

- **Innovation:** Private equity funds are naturally drawn to innovative sectors, such as cleantech or personal services, that place ESG at the center of their business model.

ESG integration offers managers the possibility of overcoming the traditional criticism attached to private equity (such as restructuring portfolio companies without much consideration for labor issues or the local community) by introducing changes in portfolio companies aimed at obtaining investment returns that are consistent with the principles of responsible investing.

WHAT IS ESG?

ESG investing represents the main investment practice under the category of "responsible investing." Investors' growing interest in responsible investing has facilitated the emergence of other practices, which, despite being used interchangeably with ESG, respond to different focuses:

- **Socially responsible investing:** focusing on the screening of companies using ethical criteria. Such screening can be either positive (selecting companies with positive performance on specific metrics), or negative (excluding companies based on specific performance or overall industry considerations). The majority of investors show a clear concern for ethical principles when investing. Exhibit 1 shows the results from a 2016 survey by Schroders (covering the views of over 20,000 investors in 28 countries) on the ethical principles followed.

---

[3] A report from Morgan Stanley Institute of Sustainable Investing (2015) found that the performance of the MSCI KLD 400 Social Index, including firms meeting high ESG standards, outperformed the S&P 500 on an annualized basis by 45 basis points since its inception.

Exhibit 1: Negative ESG effect on investments

	Definitely would move it	Would consider moving it	Would not move it
Links to repressive regimes	40%	40%	20%
Associated with pornography/sex industry	39%	33%	28%
Associated with arms or weapons…	38%	36%	26%
Companies that have a poor record of social…	33%	47%	20%
Use animal testing	32%	40%	28%
Associated with gambling activities	30%	38%	32%
Ongoing activities negatively contribute to…	29%	48%	23%
Reportedly using legal tax minimization schemes	26%	42%	32%
Companies in the news for the wrong reasons	27%	48%	25%
Associated with tobacco or alcohol products	20%	38%	42%

Source: Schroders

- **Impact investing:** focusing on companies that deliver specific and measurable social and/or environmental benefits, or that positively impact traditionally underserved communities. Examples of impact investing include companies in education, healthcare, or renewable resources that are based in developing countries.

- **Sustainability investing:** focusing on companies with business models that are sustainable in the way resources are utilized in a particular economic activity, or that avoid negative externalities. Such companies deal effectively with recycling or foster a more efficient use of resources (e.g., water efficient manufacturing).

ESG investing considers a number of areas of action and/or risk. For example, Exhibit 2 depicts the ESG framework used by Morgan Stanley Capital International, an equity index provider, for the construction of its MSCI ESG Index. ESG activities are identified across three pillars (environment, social, and governance) and 10 themes totaling 37 key issues.

Integrating the above ESG factors when managing private equity funds can help managers identify, control, and report ESG-related risks and opportunities in their investment decisions and monitoring activities. Although there are still no formal ESG standards in the industry, several initiatives provide guidance on how private equity funds could invest responsibly and report these activities:

- **The United Nations-supported Principles for Responsible Investment (PRI):** The PRI initiative defines several voluntary and aspirational investment principles for incorporating ESG factors into investment practice such as:

  - Integration of ESG issues into the investment analysis and decision-making process

  - Being an active owner and incorporating ESG issues into ownership policies

Exhibit 2: ESG key issues hierarchy

3 Pillars	10 Themes	ESG Key Issues	
Environment	Climate Change	Carbon Emissions	Financing Environmental Impact
		Energy Efficiency	Climate Change Vulnerability
		Product Carbon Footprint	
	Natural Resources	Water Stress	Raw Material Sourcing
		Biodiversity & Land Use	
	Pollution & Waste	Toxic Emissions & Waste	Electronic Waste
		Packaging Material & Waste	
	Environmental Opportunities	Opportunities in Clean Tech	Opportunities in Renewable Energy
		Opportunities in Green Building	
Social	Human Capital	Labor Management	Human Capital Development
			Supply Chain Labor Standards
	Product Liability	Product Safety & Quality	Privacy & Data Security
		Chemical Safety	Responsible Investment
		Financial Product Safety	Health & Demographic Risk
	Stakeholder Opposition	Controversial Sourcing	
	Social Opportunities	Access to Communications	Access to Health Care
		Access to Finance	Opp's in Nutrition & Health
Governance	Corporate Governance	Board	Ownership
		Pay	Accounting
	Corporate Behavior	Business Ethics	Corruption & Instability
		Anti-Competitive Practices	Financial System Instability

- Seeking appropriate disclosure on ESG issues

- Promoting the acceptance and implementation of the principles above

- Collaborating to enhance the effectiveness the principles' implementation.

From a group of only six institutional investor signatories in 2006, when the principles were first put forward, supporters for PRI increased to over 1,900 signatories by the end of 2018, including many private equity fund managers. Investor signatories to PRI are now required to publish a set of mandatory indicators that are considered core to responsible investment.

- **U.S. Private Equity Growth Capital Guidelines for Responsible Investments (PEGCC):** An alternative to PRI, PEGCC includes several ESG guidelines, some of which were adopted from PRI. PEGCC does not monitor the implementation of its guidelines and the signatories are not required to follow the standard; adherence is essentially voluntary.

- **Invest Europe's (IE) Handbook of Professional Standards for Responsible Investments:** IE is the European private equity industry's representative body who is charge of developing professional standards. One of its mandates is to shape the principles of ethical behavior and trust that govern the relationships between private equity managers, their investors and portfolio companies. All IE members must adhere to a Code of Conduct and are strongly encouraged to act according to the standards when they join the organization. IE has developed a ESG due diligence guidelines and is regularly involved in training managers on responsible investment practices.

- **The Sustainability Accounting Standards Board (SASB):** The standards issued by the SASB can also be used to identify the relevant ESG issues for a company by industry. Related to these standards, the Global Reporting Initiative Sustainability Reporting framework includes additional sector guidance to identify ESG issues. A private equity manager can review the issues highlighted in these frameworks and incorporate them into its due diligence process.

In addition to the guidelines and standards above, several development finance institutions provide publicly available toolkits that assist private equity firms operating in emerging markets with ESG integration:

- **International Finance Corporation's Environmental and Social Management System:** this system offers managers an extensive overview of templates and tools that private equity fund managers can deploy during the due diligence phase of the investment process. For example, the toolkit includes an overview of the eco-labels available in a particular industry, which helps managers develop a better understanding of existing initiatives and a general sense of where a specific industry is heading with regard to environmental trends.

- **FMO:** this Dutch development bank offers a tool, which provides managers with an initial assessment of environmental and social risks against the performance standards set by the International Finance Corporation. The assessment is based on the sector and geography where the portfolio company is being active. The tool also provides value-added environmental and social opportunities for managers to look into.

- **CDC Group:** wholly owned by the UK government, this development institution provides a comprehensive overview of issues related to geography, sector, industry, and supplies frameworks for managers to integrate ESG into the due diligence process and their operations.

ESG INTEGRATION IN THE PRIVATE EQUITY LIFE CYCLE

ESG integration in the private equity industry has increased due to some specific drivers exclusive to the industry, which include the following:

- **Investor mandates**: investors are increasingly demanding higher standards of environmental and social responsibility attached to fund managers' activities and their investments.

- **Risk management**: Traditionally the main driver for ESG integration, this approach focuses on identifying and mitigating ESG risks via regulatory scrutiny, fines, and litigation over potential ESG management issues.

- **Value creation**: A rapidly growing driver related to financially material aspects of ESG, value creation focuses on reducing the consumption of resources such as water or power, capturing a higher market share as a result of improved reputation, or simply enhancing valuations and exit opportunities.

At the organizational level, to ensure the success of ESG integration, private equity firms should cultivate a corporate culture that embeds ESG considerations at all levels, and demonstrate the necessary commitment in terms of motivation and resources to these activities. Specifically, private equity firms can:

1. become PRI signatories;

2. adopt internal ESG policies and metrics;

3. hire in-house ESG dedicated professionals and empower them to work closely with the investment team and the portfolio companies;

4. engage proactively with stakeholders about ESG issues and participate in industry forums that discusses them;

5. create an ESG platform that disseminates best practices across portfolio companies;

6. integrate the ESG program into the fundraising process.

At the investment level, the integration of ESG factors is about having the right processes in place to help fund managers identify and assess ESG-related risks and opportunities when making investment decisions or when monitoring their investments. This integration often involves developing ESG criteria for each stage of the investment process:

Due diligence phase

During the due diligence (or screening) phase the fund manager is expected to screen for ESG risks and opportunities, establishing an exclusion list for high-level risks. The ESG risk assessment may start by evaluating a target company's compliance with local laws and regulations with a view to mitigating reputational risk. A high ESG risk assessment often precludes investment. Based on the risks identified, the manager should consider how to allocate resources for ESG due diligence, and how to use due diligence questions in industry toolkits. Specific actions could include:

- assessing legal compliance;

- adopting industry-specific ESG due diligence criteria;

- creating ESG policies that go beyond industry standards;

- creating standardized procedures to integrate ESG in the due diligence process;

- involving ESG teams in the due diligence process; and

- integrating ESG factors in the 100-day plan.

Investment phase

ESG findings from due diligence should be carefully discussed in the investment memorandum. The private equity firm should include ESG considerations in the investment committee discussions and allow an in-house ESG team to advise the investment committee. Private equity professionals could also use templates from existing industry toolkits to integrate ESG clauses into the investment agreement. During this stage, the private equity managers should share ESG objectives, policies, and practices with the portfolio company's management and owners as well. Specific actions could include

- adopting ESG guidelines for the investment committee;

- adopting and formulating processes for measuring ESG performance;

- seeking a formal commitment from the portfolio company's management to incorporate ESG issues into the deal documents and the 100-day plan;

- collaborating with the management of the portfolio company to formulate a roadmap with clear ESG objectives to be achieved over the ownership period; and

- incorporating regional differences when setting ESG objectives.

Ownership phase

During this phase, the private equity fund managers should proactively engage with the portfolio company to implement the ESG program, leveraging the ESG experience and expertise obtained from other portfolio companies. Most importantly, the managers should define company-specific or portfolio-wide ESG indicators and prioritize ESG issues in the short/medium term. As part of this monitoring process, the manager could

- provide the portfolio company's management with the tools to monitor and measure ESG practices;

- train employees of the portfolio companies on ESG factors;

- measure ESG performance regularly to assess progress;

- conduct periodic visits to the portfolio company to ensure implementation of ESG objectives;

- include information on ESG developments in the annual review of both the portfolio company and its management;

- continuously improve ESG objectives;

- hire an experienced ESG specialist that understands the portfolio company's needs and can help with the execution;

- benchmark ESG objectives across portfolio companies;

- share best practices across portfolio companies; and

- report ESG performance regularly.

Despite consistent progress in the development of frameworks for the identification, integration, and measurement of ESG-related issues, private equity fund managers sometimes struggle to integrate ESG criteria into their investment process successfully. Several factors contribute to this challenge:

- **Diversity in portfolio companies:** The diversity of companies owned by private equity funds—in terms of their industry, geography, and development stage—gives rise to a variety of ESG-related issues and constraints. For instance, small and mid-sized companies are less willing to allocate resources to structure sustainable development approaches or regulatory differences create different demands for ESG factors.

- **Diversity in priorities:** Different private equity fund investors give different weights to different ESG aspects and/or related issues, undermining specific methodologies.

- **Poor data quality:** It is difficult to measure and compare ESG performance in certain areas (e.g., biodiversity protection, waste management, business ethics, etc.) as relevant data is not compiled in a systematized manner by portfolio companies.

- **Inefficient manager-investor communication:** Increased demand for ESG-labeled funds during fundraising phases, together with the lack of a generally accepted framework, have facilitated the emergence of vague ESG integration claims by managers.

ESG measurements and reporting to investors

Fund managers, investors, and the private equity industry at large have an aligned interest in communicating how the management of ESG factors contributes positively to risk-adjusted returns. However, the private equity industry faces significant challenges with respect to reporting, evaluating, and monitoring ESG initiatives. The industry does not have a standardized and practical methodology that can allow a rigorous assessment of the managers' ESG performance. The first consequence of this situation is a growing difficulty in comparing ESG performance among different private equity funds or portfolio companies, especially if they operate in different industries and geographies. The second consequence is that this difficulty may ultimately translate into an inefficient capital allocation by investors interested in ESG, as they may not reward the best ESG-performing managers.

In response to this challenge, the PRI initiative, in collaboration with more than 40 investors from 11 countries, 20 private equity associations, and 10 leading private equity fund managers, drafted the ESG Disclosure Framework for Private Equity in 2014. This framework is intended to provide guidance on the rationale behind ESG, facilitate an informed discussion between managers and their investors, and offer a practical tool. It is divided into two sections: "Due Diligence" (on the fund manager's fundraising phase) and

"Disclosure Questions" (on monitoring investors' investments). The framework is a guidance tool that can be adapted to different situations and implemented progressively over time or in response to changing practices. As with any disclosure, a variety of practical and legal considerations may restrict what can be disclosed on ESG-related practices and outcomes. Where this is the case, investors may benefit from understanding the nature of these considerations. The original ESG Disclosure Framework was continued and integrated by Invest Europe into its Professional Standards Handbook and Investor Reporting Guidelines. The work has also recently been continued by the PRI with input from private equity industry participants.

In total, eight objectives are devised to assist investors in adopting ESG considerations in a more standard and comparable manner:

- **During fundraising**, a fund manager should seek to disclose information sufficient to enable an investor that has expressed an interest in ESG management to:

    - assess if the fund manager is aligned with the investor's ESG-related policy and investment beliefs;

    - assess the manager's policies, processes, and systems for identifying ESG-related value drivers and dealing with material ESG-related risks, as well as identify possible areas for future development;

    - understand if and how the manager influences and supports the mitigation of ESG-related risks and pursuit of ESG-related opportunities in the running of portfolio companies;

    - assess how the manager will help the investor to monitor and, where necessary, ensure that the manager is acting in accordance with the agreed-upon ESG-related policies and practices as set forth at fund formation; and

    - assess the manager's approach to managing and disclosing material incidents at the private equity firm and portfolio companies.

- **During the life of a fund**, a manager should seek to disclose information sufficient to enable an investor that has expressed an interest in ESG management to:

    - establish if a manager is acting in a manner consistent with the manager's investment policies, processes, and agreed-upon fund terms regarding ESG management;

    - understand positive and negative ESG-related developments that may impact portfolio companies in the fund; and

    - determine if responses to manager and portfolio company incidents and incident reporting are consistent with relevant investment terms, the fund's policies, and the investor-stated objectives regarding incident disclosure.

Ensuring proper ESG management and reporting in accordance with investors' needs requires that private equity firms have a system in place to assess the importance of ESG aspects, as well as a systematic process to generate accurate ESG data. A high-quality systematic reporting process demands that the manager clearly define roles and responsibilities concerning the quality of financial systems and accounting, and identify the steps for data collection and validation. Some investors might require control measures for the ESG reporting process to ensure proper implementation of the overall ESG reporting process; for instance, they might expect that an independent third party regularly audits this reporting.

To properly evaluate ESG factors materiality is important. When evaluating materiality, private equity firms should consider impacts to external stakeholders and ecosystems in addition to those directly affecting the portfolio companies. This process allows fund investors to better assess the systemic and longer-term risks that inevitably arise through these impacts. Direct reporting of ESG performance data provides just one important part of the overall performance of the private equity fund; understanding external impacts better highlights the fund's overall value proposition and long-term risk profile.

While ESG-related data can be disseminated in annual reports or the private equity firm's website, many fund managers prefer to present it via specific yearly (or quarterly) ESG reports. These reports could discuss the amount of renewable energy deployed across the portfolio companies, amounts spent on research and development, philanthropic initiatives to support social causes or communities where portfolio companies operate, and so on. Investors find it useful if the ESG report presents a series of key performance indicators (KPIs) which are consistent with the PRI framework and the progress achieved with respect to these indicators over time. Effective KPIs for ESG need to meet several criteria. Namely, they must be (1) correlated with the risk and success of the investments in the private equity fund's portfolio; (2) significant and relevant for investment decisions; (3) available in the private equity firm's management system; (4) easy to measure and benchmark; and (5) manageable (i.e., not too many indicators). The private equity fund managers should publish regularly these KPIs and ensure that they are trustworthy by requiring external independent validations and assurance.

Defining KPIs for private equity funds is inherently difficult since funds invest in companies that cover many industries. Given the wide variety of available topical areas and performance indicators for a specific sector, managers should attempt to establish the validity of the KPIs selected. In light of the objectives and challenges discussed, we present a potential list of KPIs that can cover various aspects of ESG management at the portfolio company level (these can also be aggregated at the fund level):

- **Environmental KPIs**

  – Presence of environmental policies and frequency of reporting on these policies.

  – Energy efficiency (e.g., total energy consumption per unit of revenue/volume or employee, energy certifications, list of primary energy sources, etc.)

  – Environmental consumption (e.g., total greenhouse gas emissions per unit of revenue/volume or employee, energy usage, water usage, carbon emissions per service or sales, etc.)

  – Use of renewable energy resources (e.g., percentage of energy from renewable sources in total energy consumed, renewable energy generated, etc.)

  – Waste and water management (e.g., waste per units produced, percentage of waste recycled, water consumed and recycled, etc.).

- **Social KPIs**

  – Staff turnover (e.g., percentage of employees leaving every year, new hire 90 day failure rate, etc.)

  – Staff absenteeism (e.g., number of days lost per employee)

  – Staff engagement (e.g., percentage of employees that feel valued, percentage of employees happy with their career progression, employee net promoter score, etc.)

- Staff training and education (e.g., percentage of employees leaving, expenses with employee training, etc.)

- Staff diversity (e.g., structure/distribution of employees across criteria such as sex, level of education, cultural background, temporary worker ratios, etc.)

- Staff relocations/restructurings (e.g., total cost of relocation per employee, total cost of indemnities paid to restructured staff, etc).

- Pay issues (e.g., CEO pay to median full time employee pay, gender pay ratios, links of pay packages to ESG objectives, etc).

- Presence of non-discriminatory policies

- Health, wellness and safety (e.g., presence of policies that cover occupational and global health issues, total spending on safety and health issues per employee, injury rates, support to female employees with children, vacation days used, etc.)

- Investments in accordance with ESG criteria (e.g., percentage of investments in accordance with ESG criteria in total investments)

- Supplier/Customer agreements (e.g., presence of codes of conduct for suppliers/customers, percentage of suppliers/customers that meet ESG criteria)

- **Governance KPIs**

  - Existence of internal controls (e.g., board-level oversight of portfolio companies, quality of audit systems, IT security, accounting quality, etc.)

  - Governance factors (e.g., level of board independence and diversity at both portfolio company and private equity firm levels, remuneration incentives, and implications for risk taking, existence of board transparent practices, etc.)

  - Litigation risks (e.g., level of fines paid, number of lawsuits, litigation payments, tax transparency, number of tax issues, etc.)

  - Corruption risks (e.g., presence of policies related to anti-bribery and anti-corruption, percentage of assets or companies in regions with high corruption levels, percentage of revenues from government contracts, etc.)

  - Contributions to political parties (e.g., contributions to local political parties as a percentage of revenues)

Managers of private equity funds that are majority shareholders in portfolio companies are better positioned to influence portfolio company management compared with managers whose funds are minority shareholders. Additionally, managers are likely to experience varying levels of support from portfolio companies on ESG initiatives depending on the company's culture or region of operations. To ensure a successful implementation of an ESG strategy managers should aim to help senior portfolio company executives and management better understand the potential impact of ESG risks and opportunities on the value of their business. It may also be the case that the manager can learn from a portfolio company's practices and share these practices with other companies in their portfolio.

As soon as a fund invests in a portfolio company, private equity fund managers should work to set up an ESG program (i.e., draft a policy, assign responsibility for ESG operations and set up processes to manage ESG activities). The managers could also engage external technical consultants to achieve operational ESG improvements. Ultimately, the company should be responsible for day-to-day management and reporting of ESG issues and its board should be explicitly accountable for ESG initiatives.

According to PRI, it is good practice to leverage expertise and experience on ESG matters across the private equity firm's portfolio by encouraging sharing of knowledge and good practices between different companies. This could be achieved by scheduling periodic meetings with representatives from portfolio companies or dedicated sessions for certain portfolio companies around particular relevant ESG topics. Most importantly, the private equity fund managers should conduct periodic site visits that can help verify the portfolio company's reported information and reveal the full extent of the company's ESG activities. Such visits will also prove that the fund manager is fully committed to working with the portfolio companies on ESG activities.

While investors may value managers' reporting of ESG-related KPIs, knowing how to use this information presents particular difficulties. First, managers may choose different periods in which to report (annually, biannually, or at irregular intervals). Second, unsurprisingly, managers report different indicators even for companies in the same industry. Finally, managers report in various formats, use different units of measurement and choose different benchmarks against which to measure performance (e.g., historical, peers, industry, etc.). These issues do not allow investors to make apples-to-apples comparisons of the relative ESG performance of various managers and their funds.

CONCLUSION

Managers' consideration of ESG issues has moved beyond simply satisfying demanding investors. No longer an "add-on" to the private equity investment process, ESG is now a critical part of the investment process for many private equity firms. These firms recognize that ESG integration can enhance and protect the value of their portfolio companies and reputation. While not all managers exhibit this changed mindset, it is clear that in today's market, many view ESG policies very differently.

It is however worth highlighting that, because of its business model (active management, mid-/long-term investment period), the private equity industry has the opportunity to capture emerging trends in the field of responsible investing and ESG integration. However, to capture such trends, some challenges must be overcome. The primary challenge is the lack of a generally accepted methodology for the identification, integration, and measurement of ESG investments. If this challenge can be met, private-equity-specific ESG metrics can be developed, triggering a more efficient competition for investors' investments among managers.

REFERENCES

Global Sustainable Investment Alliance (GSIA) (2016) "2016 Global Sustainable Investment Review".

KKR (2015) "ESG and Citizenship Report".

Malk Sustainability Partners (2015) "ESG in Private Equity – 2015".

Morgan Stanley Institute for Sustainable Investing (2015) "Sustainable Reality: Understanding the Performance of Sustainable Investment Strategies".

MSCI ESG Research (2017) "ESG Ratings Methodology, Executive Summary".

PricewaterhouseCoopers (2015) "Bridging the gap: Aligning the Responsible Investment Interest of Limited Partners and General Partners".

PricewaterhouseCoopers (2015) "ESG Considerations for Private Equity Firms".

Principles for Responsible Investment (2011) "Responsible Investment in Private Equity - A guide for limited partners".

Principles for Responsible Investment (2014) "Integrating ESG in Private Equity - A guide for general partners".

Principles for Responsible Investment "Limited Partners' Responsible Investment Due Diligence Questionnaire".

Principles for Responsible Investment (2016) "Report on Progress – Private Equity"

Schroders (2016) "Global Investor Study – What investors think about responsible investing".

In her own words: Therése Lennehag, Head of Sustainability, EQT

It starts with mindset. At EQT, we want to make a positive impact with everything we do. Having a long-term, responsible and sustainable approach to investment and ownership is EQT's way of creating value for investors, in portfolio companies and to society at large. The key lies in having a thematic approach and a focus on ESG throughout the entire investment cycle - from deal sourcing to exit - and making sustainability an integral part of the business model. This mindset enables EQT to identify and capture opportunities as well as mitigate relevant risks, allowing both EQT and EQT portfolio companies to remain relevant, successful and be part of the regenerative solutions needed for the future.

Every investment, every fund has an impact, positive or negative, whether intended or not. In EQT's case there has always been a positive intention. Since inception in 1994, a large emphasis has been on tracking KPIs beyond the financial. To begin with, this included metrics such as job creation (please refer to "Five years post exit study"). Today, it covers all aspects of ESG, such as greenhouse gas emissions and diversity. And "what gets measured gets done, what gets done well gets rewarded, and what gets rewarded gets repeated". EQT portfolio companies are also asked to identify more specific KPIs that are significant to their businesses in a philosophy to focus on what matters. EQT is convinced that strong ESG performance and strategic business alignment with the Sustainable Development Goals (SDGs) provide a temperature check of investments' and companies' overall resilience and long-term profitability, hence how well they are set to continue to grow and prosper.

EQT as a firm is no exception in this regard. For EQT to succeed in the long-term, as well as to be a source of inspiration for portfolio companies, we need to lead by example. This includes being concrete and setting ambitious goals in areas with systemic relevance to make a positive impact at an accelerated pace and scale. Because focus, pace and scale are more important than ever. Only by walking the talk, EQT can with credibility ask and expect portfolio companies and other stakeholders to do the same.

The private equity model is a favorable ownership type for driving transformational, sustainable change given its strong alignment of interest, long-term view coupled with a sense of urgency to make things happen. With that said, the private equity industry, along with other market participants, today know that the current system lacks conformity for how to price a number of externalities, which we all need to consider and optimize for if we want our society to continue to prosper. With countries moving beyond GDP to understand the true state and wealth of their nation, people and resources, it is not hard to imagine our industry moving beyond IRR (internal rate of return). For this to happen, we cannot treat ESG investing as a niche, as an addition on the side. We need to scale the investment and ownership art of optimizing for risk, return and impact. An example is the UNDP SDG Impact initiative, which EQT along with other stakeholders have engaged in so that we together can accelerate the entire ecosystem's contribution, not only a single organization's. The private equity industry has an important role to play in transforming the financial markets into the next generation of responsible and sustainable investing and owning. As highlighted above, good progress has already been made and EQT is now excited about jointly taking it to the next level.

14 Secondary Fund Transactions

Every man lives by exchanging.
Adam Smith

INTRODUCTION

The private equity secondary market refers to the buying and selling of pre-existing investor commitments (i.e., limited partnership interests) to buyout, venture capital (VC), and other alternative investment funds. Interests sold not only include the current investments in private equity funds, but also the remaining unfunded capital commitments into these funds. Typically, a secondary transaction involves the sale of a limited partner (LP) interest in a fund or a portfolio of funds, although it may involve the sale of an investment portfolio of operating companies.[1]

Many investors initially target private capital funds to gain exposure to potentially higher returns and diversify their portfolios. While the main approach is to invest directly with private capital fund managers, the task of building a robust and high-quality direct portfolio of funds can be very challenging. It is not easy to map and evaluate the thousands of fund managers that are out there. As a result, many investors prefer to start their exposure to private markets by allocating capital to funds of funds or secondary funds, which are the main buyers of fund interests in the secondary market. In particular, secondary funds offer diversified fund portfolios with typically earlier distributions that mitigate the J-curve effect specific to a new private capital investment program.[2] Secondary funds also allow new investors to build initial exposure to private investments with limited resources and in-house knowledge.

Over the past 20 years, the secondary private equity market has experienced rapid and unprecedented growth. Fueled by the development of the primary market, the private equity secondary market, or simply secondaries, exists to provide liquidity to an intrinsically illiquid asset class. As private capital fund investors have become increasingly sophisticated and the economic environment has become increasingly volatile, there has been a growing need for investors to re-evaluate their portfolios over shorter time frames and adapt to changing circumstances. The secondary market has flourished by allowing investors far greater flexibility and liquidity in their investment decisions and encouraging new participants to enter the private market.

Transaction volume in the secondary market has increased, from approximately $3 billion in 2000, to a record of about $72 billion in 2018 (Coller Capital, 2018). While the global secondary transaction volume has reached a new peak by the end of 2018, it remains low relative to the level of fundraising in the primary market experienced by private equity and private debt funds, which raised approximately $650 billion in 2018 alone. As another benchmark, the secondary market's volume has been below 3% of total private equity funds' reported net asset value since its inception (e.g., Coller Capital 2018). The significant increase in secondary transactions can be attributed to certain regulatory changes that require investors to meet liquidity standards (e.g., Basel II & III, the Volcker Rule, and Solvency II), a broadening of the assets available for sale in the

---

[1] The sale of interest in an individual company from one fund to another is not considered a private equity secondary transaction. Instead, it is often labeled as a secondary buyout transaction.

[2] The J-curve effect illustrates the tendency of private equity funds to deliver negative returns and cash flows in the early years and investment gains and positive cash flows in later years as companies owned by the funds mature and are gradually exited.

secondary market (e.g., multi-asset portfolios, new asset classes such as infrastructure, natural resources, or real estate), an increase in general partner (GP)[3] -led transactions , investors' desire to rebalance their portfolios and manage their relations with fund managers more actively or the merger and acquisition activities experienced by LPs. Ultimately, the recent growth of the market reflects the large volume and variety of commitments made to private capital funds in recent years.

SECONDARY MARKET

Secondary private equity began to emerge after the equity market crash in October 1987 and the world economic crises of the early 1990s. These challenging economic conditions produced an intense need for liquidity among many financial institutions and corporations, which forced some to sell their investments in private equity funds. The interest from these sellers attracted a small number of buyers, thus creating a new market for secondary interests in private equity funds or in companies in which these sellers had invested (e.g., Meyer and Mathonet, 2005).

During these early days of the industry, sellers generally sold assets to generate liquidity. Many also wished to reduce their funding obligations on committed capital, rebalance their private equity portfolios relative to public equity, or divest interests in underperforming private equity funds. Given the illiquidity of private equity investments and the novelty of the market, these transactions were considered as distressed; therefore, the prices paid reflected a significant discount to the net asset value (NAV) of these interests.

The number of secondary deals was relatively low until the mid-1990s, after which the market expanded dramatically. Secondary transactions had previously been viewed as an admission of failure, but this stigma faded. Selling assets in the secondary market is no longer an option of last resort for distressed sellers; the market has evolved into an attractive portfolio optimization tool for long-term private capital fund investors. The secondary market is a place where investors can mitigate the J-curve effect by investing in more mature funds, thereby obtaining returns over a shorter time horizon.

An increasing inflow of capital into private equity after 1995 also contributed to the rapid rise in secondary transactions. In contrast to the late 1990s, when a small group of specialists had been the main buy-side participants, by the early 2000s, numerous specialist firms, funds of funds, and leading institutional investors such as endowments, foundations, and pension funds had started to enter the secondary market. The additional demand from institutional investors improved pricing, as these new investors had a lower cost of capital than dedicated secondary and traditional fund-of-funds firms that charge fees and carried interest. With these lower underwriting rates, these new buyers could significantly outbid specialists in competitive situations. Moreover, these non-traditional secondary buyers began to participate in transactions that involved not only single funds, but also interests in large portfolios of funds.

In addition to the increasing number of non-traditional buyers, secondary specialist buyers bolstered their continued presence in the market with ever-growing pools of capital. As this trend continued, GPs became more accustomed to seeing stakes in their funds trade on secondary markets and no longer viewed such deals with suspicion. With the growth of competition in the secondary market, what had once been known as a "buyer's market" became more evenly balanced. While transactions in which sellers negotiated directly with buyers continued, the market entered a new phase in which auctions, often administered by qualified sell-side

[3] GP-led transactions are transactions initiated by GPs that involve the sale of interests in the assets (or investor commitments) of the mature private equity funds these GPs manage.

advisory firms, became more prevalent. Over 60% of the transactions in the market take place through auctions organized by these intermediaries (Campbell Lutyens, 2018).

While the trade of LP fund positions still dominates secondary sales, GP-led transactions have expanded dramatically, growing at a rate of over 66% per year since 2015 and comprising 33% of the total volume by the end of 2018 (Coller Capital, 2018). The secondary market continues to be highly concentrated, with buyers that manage at least $2 billion accounting for over 70% of transaction volume (Campbell Lutyens, 2018). Most of the transactions in the market (69%) involve assets related to buyout funds (Evercore, 2018). Exhibit 1 provides the evolution of the transaction volume in the market.

Exhibit 1: Transactions volume in the secondary market (US$ billions)

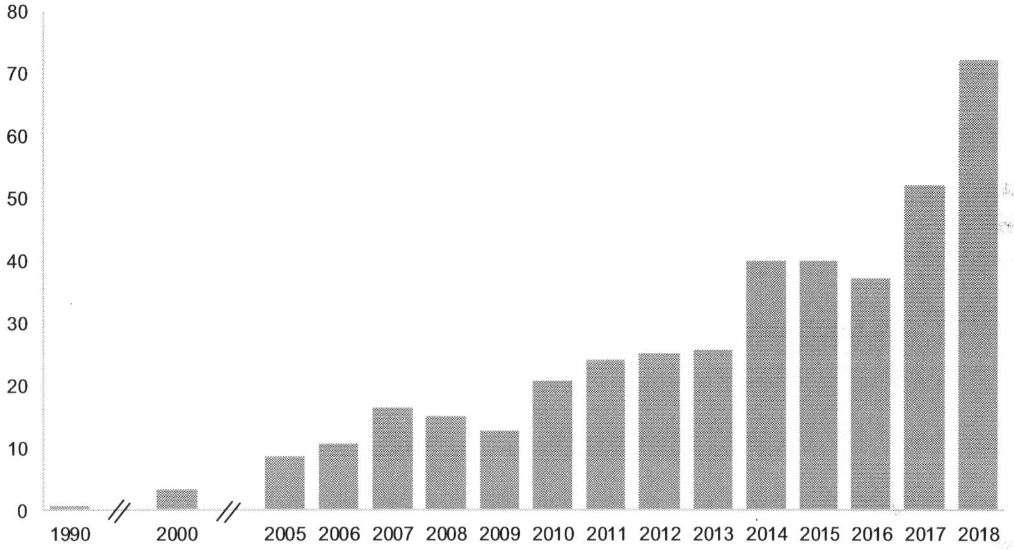

Source: Coller Capital, based on market consensus derived from reports from Greenhill, Evercore, Campbell Lutyens, Setter Capital, Credit Suisse and Lazard.

The price of secondary deals remains competitive given sustained buy-side demand. The growth in the volume of transactions contributed to significant increases in the pricing levels of secondary transactions which have been trading, on average, at discounts of 7-11% of the funds' net asset value (NAV) over the last few years (Greenhill, 2018). These averages hide significant variation across different types of funds, with buyout funds trading at discounts of 1-6% of NAVs and venture funds trading at discounts of 17-25% of NAV. In fact, it is not uncommon to see the highest quality buyout funds trading at a premium of 10% of NAV. When public equity markets experienced dramatic volatility and deep lows in 2008 and 2009, private equity positions on the secondary market were less liquid and traded at discounts of close to 40% of the funds' NAV. Exhibit 1 shows that volumes were down by approximately 15% in 2009 due to increased market uncertainty, substantial risk premiums, the pace of capital calls, and the risk in public markets. This risk heightened the impact of the "denominator effect" on private equity allocations during that period.[4] The growth of the market in both favorable and adverse conditions highlights its resilience and important role going forward.

The financial performance of dedicated secondary funds is one of the best indicators of the profitability of secondary purchases.[5] According to Preqin (2019), median net IRRs for secondary funds from 1999 to 2014 vintages have been mostly in the range of 9% to 21%, with a short dip for fund vintages in 2005 and 2006 when the net IRRs were about 6%. The aggregate median performance of secondary funds has been above that of the median private capital fund (which include private equity, credit, infrastructure and natural resources funds) since 2009. This performance has supported increased fundraising by secondary funds.

Overall, there are several strong signs that the secondary market is maturing. First, large fund portfolio transactions over $1 billion continue to be common in the market. Second, the market has experienced an increase in "tail-end" portfolios of funds of funds and secondary funds, both increasingly looking to the secondary market to wind down their mature investment vehicles. Third, an increasing number of well-known GPs take advantage of the secondary market with GP-led deals. These deals include total fund liquidity options, secondary-primary transactions, restructurings, asset sales and strip sales (we discuss these types of transactions later in the chapter). Fourth, the secondary market also expanded in emerging markets and Asia recently. Finally, there is also an upsurge in infrastructure and real estate fund interest transactions. These types of transactions indicate the increasing diversity and complexity in the market.

PARTIES INVOLVED IN SECONDARY TRANSACTIONS

There are at least three, and sometimes four, parties involved in secondary transactions: buyers, sellers, intermediaries, and GPs. Each party is driven by its own motives and goals.

Sellers

Typical sellers in the secondary market are LPs invested in buyout, venture capital, or other investment strategies, such as natural resources, infrastructure, real estate, or credit. These LPs include pension and endowment funds, sovereign wealth funds, banks, hedge funds, insurance companies, foundations, family offices, funds of funds, and other institutional investors. There are also secondary funds that subsequently decide to sell a portfolio of fund interests purchased earlier, perhaps because of a change in strategy caused by fund liquidations.

Because the typical private equity fund has a nominal life of 10 years (with an even longer actual life of 14-15 years), LPs' whose priorities and strategies change need access to liquidity; the secondary market provides the perfect solution. LPs sell private equity interests for a variety of reasons. Beyond providing simple access to liquidity, the secondary market has become an important management tool for the increasingly active

---

[4] The denominator effect arises due to the way large LPs allocate their portfolios across different asset classes. Assume that a large LP allocates 5% of its portfolio to private equity investments while the remaining 95% is allocated to public markets. If a significant decline in public share valuations occurs, the portfolio will experience a severe drop in the public market allocation. As a result, the LP will be over-allocated in private equity. This imbalance can be resolved by increasing the denominator (i.e., investing more money in the public markets) or reducing the denominator (i.e., selling a percentage of the private equity holdings).

[5] Some of the main players in the secondary market are Coller Capital, Lexington Partners, Ardian, HarbourVest, Strategic Partners and Goldman Sachs.

approach investors have taken to managing their alternative asset portfolios. Factors that contribute to the decision to sell include:

- poor actual or expected fund performance;

- reallocation of capital across asset classes;

- changes in management or investment strategy;

- regulatory changes[6];

- fund liquidity requirements; and

- MA activities.

There can be two types of sellers in the market. *Tactical sellers* constantly adjust their asset allocations in response to changing market conditions, taking a pro-active approach. For instance, after the financial crisis, these investors found themselves with portfolios created for a pre-crisis world. As a result, they took advantage of good liquidity and attractive pricing to readjust their portfolios. *Strategic sellers* are typically those LPs who experience significant unexpected changes in their investment strategies because of the appointment of a new chief investment officer, a change in their investment mandate or business model, new regulatory requirements or mergers and acquisitions. The secondary market transactions resulting from these strategic changes are usually significantly more complex.

During the global financial crisis, difficult economic conditions seemed to trigger asset reallocation decisions that affected private equity holdings. For example, although the market value of various publicly quoted asset classes fell in 2009, the value of allocations to private assets, including private equity, rose above allocation targets. In some cases, this led to sales of private equity commitments to reinstate these targets. Reduced distributions from prior investments in private equity have also meant that LPs could no longer rely on recycling distributions to support their commitments to new funds. Thus, investors were forced either to sell fund investments earlier or to surrender these commitments.

In the recent years however, the secondary market evolved to include transactions of interests in private companies not held within independent private capital funds. These transactions are known as *direct secondaries* (or sometimes simply as 'directs'). In addition, GP-led (as opposed to investor-led) secondaries have become an increasingly important part of the market. Financial institutions, also started to use the secondary market to dispose assets that share certain similar characteristics with private equity such as collateralized loan obligations and nonperforming loans. Finally, the proportion of sellers from outside the United States and Europe is growing, as the primary private equity market matures in other areas of the world.

Buyers

Most buyers in the secondary market were traditionally interested in acquiring stakes in buyout and venture funds. However, buyers are increasingly interested in acquiring assets across a wider variety of investment

[6] Regulatory bodies have issued higher capital requirements for private capital fund investments. Therefore, these investments have become more expensive for banks, insurance companies and pension funds.

strategies such as infrastructure, real estate or credit. Buyers differ in their approaches: some are completely opportunistic, while others have a dedicated investment strategy.

The universe of potential buyers for secondary transactions has been expanding steadily. These potential buyers have varying levels of experience and different reputations and objectives. On the one hand, there are dedicated secondary funds and other funds of funds whose main or partial investment objective is to buy private equity interests on the secondary market. On the other hand, there are the so-called "non-traditional" buyers, such as pension funds, endowment funds, hedge funds, insurance companies, sovereign wealth funds, banks, family offices, foundations, and even GPs. Many of these non-traditional investors view secondaries as a significant component of their overall investment strategy. About 74% of investors seeking fund opportunities on the secondary market are traditional secondary market buyers, consisting of primary and secondary fund-of-funds managers while non-traditional investors make up the remaining 26% of investors (Evercore, 2018). Exhibit 2 illustrates the distinct preferences buyers have and their varying target rates of return.

Most institutional investors seeking exposure to the secondary market invest in dedicated secondary funds, which allows them to counteract the J-curve effect. By investing in the interests of more mature funds, they potentially avoid paying early management fees and portfolio losses. With dedicated secondary funds, they can obtain immediate exposure to a diverse range of managers, underlying companies, and vintage years; such broad diversification can provide valuable insights into the strengths and weaknesses of various GPs in the primary market. Also, since secondary funds typically return cash faster than buyout funds or funds of funds, investors in these funds significantly reduce the capital at risk. More importantly, because secondary funds typically target mature, substantially invested portfolios, they may be able to generate attractive returns with a significantly lower risk than primary funds.

Exhibit 2: Segmentation of the buyer universe

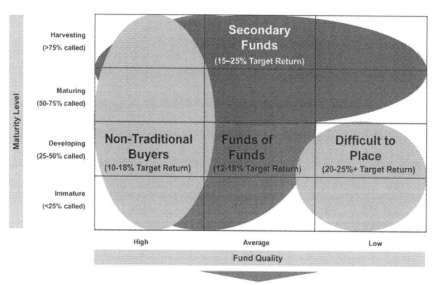

Different types of buyers have distinct asset preferences and varying target rates of return that drive unique transaction opportunities

Source: Greenhill.

Investors in the secondary market can minimize, or even eliminate, the risk of investing in a *blind pool*. Whereas investors in the primary market make commitments to funds to finance future investments in portfolio companies that are not yet known, investors in the secondary market purchase an existing pool of assets. Thus, these transactions offer greater transparency of the underlying investments, which can allow buyers to create downside protection based on the identifiable value.

Intermediaries

In the past, the only option available to LPs to manage a secondary sale process was to do so themselves. However, managing such a process can be a daunting prospect, given the limited resources and expertise of most LPs. Secondary transactions occur infrequently, and the requisite up-to-date knowledge of market conditions and potential buyers is not always available in-house. The secondary sale process is also time consuming. It involves contacting the GPs; collecting, organizing, and distributing information about the fund interests to be sold; identifying and contacting a shortlist of prospective buyers; and, most importantly, understanding how to price a portfolio of fund interests.

As a result, several advisory firms have identified the opportunity to offer these services (including valuation and market research) to sellers. They are used mainly by sellers that want to dispose of large private equity portfolios and need assistance in the sale process. More than 60% of secondary transactions were completed through intermediaries (Campbell Lutyens, 2018). Greenhill, Campbell Lutyens, Park Hill, Lazard, Credit Suisse, Evercore and UBS are the main secondary advisors; other advisors are mainly firms that are normally active as placement agents, such as Probitas Partners and Triago. Intermediaries generally charge a transaction fee of 1–2% of the value of the transaction, depending on the services they offer.

These intermediaries play an important role in the structuring of fund interest offerings. Confidentiality remains a critical concern for many GPs and, since a sale process may include the disclosure of fund documents, there are natural obstacles to executing a transaction. Intermediaries can help to alleviate these concerns by standardizing practices and demanding execution of non-disclosure agreements with potential secondary buyers before sharing sensitive information. Intermediaries also provide consistency in transaction management, which addresses the market's need for a more formal and systematic mechanism for the exchange of limited partnership interests.

Secondary advisors take fund offerings to a large number of target buyers to maximize the possibility of achieving a good price. To maintain a competitive process, the marketing of secondary fund sales might involve calling on many potential buyers with varying profiles, sizes, and primary lines of business. At the start of the sales process, advisors frequently inform the GP of the interest being sold, which helps to obtain their consent and identify up front any concerns they may have. If a large portfolio of fund interests is up for sale, intermediaries might divide the portfolio into multiple subsets involving multiple buyers. They assign groups of prospective bidders to specific assets, and these parties receive confidential information only on the relevant funds, thereby allowing intermediaries and sellers to limit the distribution of sensitive information.

Buyers seeking to purchase stakes in private equity funds also benefit from the services that intermediaries offer. Advisors can help buyers identify and acquire stakes in funds that fit with their existing portfolios and strategy. They offer help in negotiations and guidance regarding appropriate pricing as well.

General partners

In the past, GPs have been the "silent partner" in secondary transactions or have used the secondary market for *'tail-end' sales* – the wholesale disposal of remaining assets in ageing, largely liquidated funds. Thus, GPs traditionally did not initiate many deals; they only facilitated them by:

- controlling of data sharing on the fund(s);

- reviewing and approving potential purchasers;

- responding to due diligence enquiries during the later stages of the sale process; and

- completing transfer documentation to move ownership of the interest(s) from sellers to buyers.

Most fund managers treated secondary sales in a thoroughly non-emotional, professional manner. Indeed, the most astute GPs viewed secondary sales solely as an investor relations opportunity and worked with the seller or the intermediary to find a replacement LP of equal or greater quality.

However, in recent years a new segment of the secondary market has appeared as private equity fund managers have begun to take a more proactive approach to managing liquidity for their investors. GP-led secondaries, as these secondary solutions are known, involve a private equity manager working with a secondary specialist to offer liquidity options to a fund's existing LPs and to secure additional time and capital for the fund's unrealized portfolio.

SECONDARY TRANSACTIONS

Types of transactions

The traditional secondaries

Traditional secondaries involve the transfer of LP interests in a private equity fund to a new investor. For an agreed price, this investor assumes ownership of the selling LP's capital account value and any remaining unfunded obligations. In any given year, traditional secondaries represent the vast majority of transaction volume.

Occasionally, these transactions are linked to the raising of a new fund by a GP: these types of secondary deals are often referred to as *stapled transactions*. A secondary buyer purchases an interest in an existing fund from a current investor and, simultaneously, makes a commitment to a new fund being raised by the GP.

Synthetic secondaries

Synthetic secondaries (also called *secondary directs*) involve creating a new partnership to purchase a portfolio of direct investments. The transaction involves the participation of an incumbent or a new GP, contracted to oversee and ultimately sell the assets in the partnership. In this transaction, there is a transfer of ownership of interests held in a portfolio of private companies. The crucial difference from the traditional secondary market is that in secondary directs, interests transferred are held directly in underlying portfolio companies, whereas in the traditional secondary market, the interests are generally in limited partnerships, which themselves hold interests in the underlying portfolio companies. Synthetic secondaries typically represent a much smaller portion of transaction volume.

Structured secondaries

Structured secondary transactions involve creating a new special purpose vehicle that establishes a unique legal framework or structure to accomplish a particular seller's goals in closing a transaction. For example, the seller may keep some or all of the fund interests on its balance sheet, but the buyer agrees to fund all future capital calls of the seller's portfolio in exchange for a preferred return secured against future distributions of the seller's portfolio. These types of secondary transactions were explored from mid-2008 and throughout 2009, as many sellers did not want to take a loss through a straight sale of their portfolio at a steep discount, but were instead ready to abandon some of the future upside in exchange for a bridge of the uncalled capital commitments.

Structured secondary transactions tend to be discussed, and occasionally completed, at either the end or the beginning of a macroeconomic cycle (e.g., during 2002–2003 and 2008–2009). As they do not feature regularly, it is impractical to estimate their overall share of transaction volume.

GP-led secondaries

GP-led secondaries involve a private equity manager working with a secondary specialist to offer liquidity options to a fund's existing LPs and secure additional time and capital for the fund's unrealized portfolio from new LPs. These transactions are often complex and challenging, especially because they need to align the interests of both the new and remaining investors with those of the sponsoring GP. As a result, they tend to be highly bespoke and require a sophisticated buyer, typically a dedicated secondary fund.

GP-led transactions (as opposed to investor-led) began in the wake of the global financial crisis when managers needed to restructure their funds. As a result of the crisis, many private equity portfolio companies were impaired and, consequently, were subject to prolonged holding periods. Since 2012, these transactions have been evolving and becoming an increasingly important segment of the private equity secondary market. Preqin (2018) reports that the average holding period for private equity funds has increased from 4 years in 2008 to almost 6 years over the period 2014-017. This means that these funds may not earn carried interest for their managers, creating a misalignment of interests between GPs and LPs.

Although every situation is unique, GP-led transactions seek to accomplish a number of objectives, including:

- Provide a liquidity option to funds' existing investors through the sale of their fund interests or the sale of portfolio assets

- Diversify or replace a fund's LP base

- Amend the terms of a Limited Partnership Agreement (LPA), to strengthen alignment between a fund's LPs and GP or to allow the GP more time to execute a successful exit of the assets

- Raise additional capital to support a fund's existing portfolio, or primary capital for a new fund

The number of GP-led transactions has increased over the last few years, reaching 33% of the overall secondary market (Coller Capital, 2018). Not only the level of transactions has increased, but also the quality of the GPs sponsoring these transactions. In addition, institutional investors have become more comfortable in assessing and analyzing GP-led transactions. Therefore, the volume of GP-led transactions is likely to continue to grow and become increasingly important in the future.

GP-led transactions can take many forms, but usually they fall into three main categories:

- **Tender offer:** A tender offer gives existing LPs the option to sell their interests in a fund to a new investor; the new investor will fill-in with no change to the fund's LPA. In a tender offer, the buyer makes a formal offer to purchase a fund's LP interest at a fixed price. In these transactions, it is important to consider the requirements of applicable laws, which can include maintaining an offering period for a minimum amount of time, producing a detailed offering circular that describes the transaction, and ensuring that there is parity of information between the buyer and the selling LPs. Tender offers can be very complex, especially from an execution perspective.

- **Asset sale:** This involves the sale of fund's existing assets to a newly created vehicle to be managed by the GP of the original fund and capitalized by the buyers. The LPs in the original fund are given the option to take the cash from the sale or an equivalent ownership in the new vehicle. The new vehicle is likely to have new terms and conditions, which are negotiated with the new buyers. Aggregate fees and carry rates will typically be lower than for a standard primary fund investment. It is however crucial to ensure alignment of interests with the fund's original LPs through a transparent process.

- **Portfolio strip sale:** In this type of transaction, a new buyer purchases a "pro rata" strip of a fund's unrealized portfolio companies. Strip transactions are usually structured as the sale of a strip to a new vehicle managed by the sponsoring GP and capitalized by the buyers. Portfolio strip sales are becoming a common form of GP-led transactions because they allow a significant amount of cash to be returned to the fund's original investors earlier, enabling them to de-risk their portfolios. In strip sales, it is important to ensure a strong alignment with the sponsoring GP, which can be accomplished by designing terms that incentivize GPs to maximize the value of the unrealized portfolio, or by mandating the sponsoring GP to make a new financial commitment at the buyer's entry cost.

The secondary transaction process

Some transactions—typically for individual funds or small portfolios of around $25 million)—continue to be negotiated bilaterally, or with only a small number of buyers involved. However, intermediated auctions have become increasingly common. Most of the large transactions, and more than 60% of overall secondary transactions, go through an intermediary process and a bidding process. The number of buyers per fund in auctions varies, but for multi-hundred million dollar deals there are usually many buy-side participants.

Intermediaries generally manage all aspects of the sale. Transaction management is typically divided into three distinct phases: transaction origination, structuring, and execution (e.g., Penn and Welsch-Lehmann, 2004).

Transaction origination

During this first phase, secondary advisors evaluate the seller's situation and motivation and determine the transaction's feasibility. They also provide up-to-date information on current market conditions and pricing guidance for the specific funds or relevant segments of the private capital industry.

Transaction structuring

In the structuring phase, intermediaries determine the most efficient transaction structure with respect to tax, legal, and regulatory considerations, and set specific milestones and targets. Transaction structuring is particularly important when sellers are rebalancing their portfolios. The structure of such a transaction is usually driven by the seller, and depends on the seller's objectives and needs. Intermediaries will design a package for sale based on the vintage year, sub-asset class, geography, or quality of a GP according to the seller's preferences (Penn and Welsch-Lehmann, 2004). For example, a portfolio manager might want to reduce its overall private equity exposure while optimizing price in a sale. However, the institution might not be as concerned about when it receives sales proceeds. Thus, a transaction could be structured in such a way that the portfolio manager receives deferred payments to obtain a higher purchase price.

In a different scenario, a portfolio manager might want to reduce its overall private equity exposure, but maintain its relationships with the GPs. In this case, a portfolio manager might offer to sell a strip of its entire portfolio (e.g., a 25% interest in a basket of fund interests instead of the whole fund or portfolio), allowing it to maintain relationships and subclass weightings while reducing overall exposure.

In yet another scenario, a portfolio manager might want to sell down its portfolio, but be worried about the headline risk of a subsequent large winner that the manager might not be familiar with. The transaction could be structured so that the buyer will share a portion of all proceeds after it receives back twice its invested capital.

As these examples show, there are many ways to structure a transaction to meet individual objectives.

Transaction management and execution

The management and execution of the transaction are as critical as the transaction structuring phase. Advisors guide the sale process through the creation of the relevant legal agreements (e.g., purchase and sale agreements and transfer agreements). In addition, advisors often provide guidance on transfer conditions, consents, and other closing matters.

Intermediaries typically organize a managed auction to ensure the best value for the selling client. They reach out to a number of buyers, which are chosen jointly with, or approved by, the seller, usually from a database of active purchasers around the world. Intermediaries may also maintain an in-house proprietary database of such potential buyers. The intermediary selects participants before the first round of bidding, and these potential buyers undergo the required due diligence. The intermediary will provide all buyers with the same set of information with which to make their valuation decisions, such as financial statements, capital account statements, and (in most cases) fund performance guidance.

Although bids provided by buyers are collected in an openly competitive process, and all buyers have access to standard information and asset insights from the intermediary representing the sell-side, the range of bids presented for the same portfolio of fund interests can still vary widely.

After the first round of bidding, the client and intermediary decide on whom to invite to the second round. The intermediary then informs the parties as to whether or not they have been successful, and the bidding proceeds to the second round. It is common for bidders to revise their valuations in the second round because they are better informed at that stage when the imbalance of information between the seller and buyer evens out. The bidding process typically takes three to six weeks, depending on whether the auction takes place in one or two rounds.

SECONDARY PRIVATE EQUITY FUNDS

In the secondary private equity firm space, there are many investors with secondary asset acquisition programs. Most belong to one of the following categories:

- **Funds of funds:** These are funds that invest in other funds to diversify their portfolio, accelerate their returns, and achieve access to top-tier GPs (as they are often oversubscribed). Funds of funds tend to invest only a fraction (approximately 20%) of their funds in the secondary asset class, as they also entertain primary and co-investment capabilities. A fund-of-funds is often referred to as an "integrated" fund investor.

- **Non-traditional investors:** Some investors revert opportunistically to the secondary market to act on specific opportunities through straight and opportunistic sales of LP interests. Examples of non-traditional investors include pension funds, insurance companies, family offices, endowments, and foundations.

- **Dedicated secondary funds:** Dedicated secondary funds mainly prospect investments in LP interests (preferably managed by top-tier GPs) or direct company holdings (either single company holdings or larger portfolios). The majority of dedicated secondary fund managers are from the United States and Europe.

Traditionally, the secondary fund universe was mostly comprised of dedicated secondary funds but, in more recent times, it has grown to include all of the types of investors mentioned above who are attracted to this asset class. GPs regard secondary funds as an opportunity to develop new LP relationships and to expand their investor universe in the hope of facilitating future fundraising. GPs typically need to consent to a change in their LP base, and therefore tend to favor integrated funds with primary, secondary, and co-investment capabilities, as these are widely perceived as potential future sources of capital.

Secondary private equity funds can differ widely across various dimensions and investment strategies:

- **Transaction size:** The secondary market is dominated by very large funds. These large secondary funds have highly diversified portfolios, whereas the smaller end of the secondary market is characterized by inherent inefficiencies and informational asymmetries (as they are less frequently intermediated by brokers).

- **Geographic reach:** Some secondary funds focus on specific geographies with respect to geopolitical opportunities and risks, such as deregulation and taxation. Other funds prefer to have a wide geographic coverage to maintain flexible capital allocations.

- **Strategic flexibility:** Secondary funds that can address various levels of transaction complexities have more opportunities and are able to create value throughout different market cycles. For example, some secondary funds prefer to invest in plain vanilla, simple secondary transactions whereas more sophisticated secondary funds tend to invest in highly complex fund restructurings, where assets have value creation potential that has not been crystallized yet. Structural complexities (e.g., unusual holding structures) can potentially hide value implications and therefore incentivize certain investors to cut through these complexities in order to find these undervalued opportunities.

Some secondary funds aim to focus on areas that are underserved by the wider secondary investor community (e.g., cleaning up orphaned or tail-end portfolios that require substantial resources), but the overwhelming majority of funds prefer plain vanilla investments. Secondary funds' financial returns tend to be lower than the financial returns that GPs are targeting. This is because they are driven by a lower risk perception, as secondary funds offer lower loss rates than primary market funds as well as lower return variability.

According to Preqin (2019), secondary funds' returns (15% median IRR) outperform buyout and venture funds' returns by 2% and 6% respectively. The same study also argues that secondary funds' annual return volatility (10%) is lower than that of buyout and venture funds (14% and 18% respectively). Nevertheless, net multiples delivered by secondary funds have declined for vintages 2012–2016 in comparison with previous vintage years; for instance, secondary funds with a 2009 vintage year report a median net multiple of 1.61x, compared with 1.42x for a 2015-vintage secondary fund.

The relatively good economic performance of secondary funds is generally explained by several factors:

- **Enhanced visibility:** Secondary funds offer better visibility of the underlying asset base and a smaller "blind pool" risk, as they come in when there is usually good visibility on the underlying portfolio companies.

- **Shorter J-curve effect:** Secondary funds acquire fund interests at a later stage of their life after much of the fee load has already been paid, allowing for a partial or entire mitigation of the J-curve effect. The J-curve reflects negative returns in the initial years of a fund investment due to the front-loaded nature of the fund's fee structure.

- **Better access to certain GPs:** Secondary funds can gain access to oversubscribed funds, obtaining GP relationships that were not previously available.

- **Lower loss rates:** Secondary funds offer lower "loss rates" vis-à-vis primary and/or buyout funds due to diversification, and therefore have a lower overall risk. Secondary funds tend to achieve a very broad diversification along many dimensions (e.g., geography, sector, investment strategy, managers, and vintage years)

- **Smoother cash flow profile:** Mixing secondary funds into a fund portfolio smooths out the cash flow profile, especially when the secondary fund's underlying funds are quite mature and have relatively short remaining holding periods. Therefore, secondary funds generally return cash to investors rather early in their fund life, and can report a relatively high distributed versus committed capital comparison relative to buyout and venture funds.

PRICING OF SECONDARY TRANSACTIONS

Pricing in the secondary market for fund interests is usually expressed as a percentage of the valuation that is being reported by the fund managers. In a typical secondary transaction, the seller and the buyer agree on a valuation date, or a reference date, at the start of the transaction, and the reported valuation for the fund interest as of the reference date forms the basis which prices are based on.

In all markets, buyers and sellers must agree on the value of an asset to trigger a transaction. The secondary market for alternative assets is no different. However, the lack of transparency in the secondary market mean there is often a notable discrepancy between the valuations of a given asset by buyers and sellers. Sellers are concerned with what the asset is worth today, and their view is typically some distillation of the current NAV ascribed by the GP. In contrast, buyers are much more focused on what the asset will be worth in the future.

As with other transactions, there are many ways to value the asset(s) being offered. The sell-side bankers or buy-side analyst can use a macro, top-down approach to value the asset. Most commonly, a bottom-up approach is used by determining the future cash flows of the fund's investments and costs of running the fund to formulate an appropriate bid. This process requires a significant amount of detail regarding portfolio company performance and projections, timing of capital commitments and disbursements, and the fund's strategy of deploying uncommitted capital. A *top-down valuation* is similar to performing a precedent transaction or comparable company analysis of a private company. With limited information—such as type of fund, current funding ratio, vintage year, and previous fund returns—the value of the fund is determined by applying a discount of a comparable fund or transaction to the fund.

There is a strong correlation between the average highest bid compared to NAV on the secondary market and the trading premium or discount on publicly listed private equity funds. However, the use of listed private equity to provide an approximate value of funds listed on the secondary market is not a completely reliable method. The public market distorts the true value of the funds given that it incorporates market sentiment and conditions in the credit market. There might also be significant differences between the portfolio companies targeted by listed and unlisted private equity funds.

Buyers' valuation of secondary assets

Most often, buyers use the bottom-up valuation approach in order to determine the value of an asset and the price they are willing to pay for an asset today. To do so, they usually conduct a discounted cash flow (DCF) analysis. This analysis uses several factors to arrive at the cash flow stream: expected exit value and exit timing for current portfolio investments, projected future capital calls and the return on future investments made using these capital calls, the legal structure of the fund, and the return the buyer would like to earn on the transaction (the target return or discount rate).

Current portfolio valuation

With the implementation of FAS 157[7] and IAS 39[8] (which was replaced in 2014 by IFRS 9,[9] which became effective in 2018), GPs face increased pressure to value their underlying portfolio companies at what they believe they could sell the companies for in the current market. However, a secondary buyer is not concerned with the GP's estimated value of a given company today, as it is unlikely that the manager will be selling the

[7] The Financial Standards and Accounting Board (FASB) of the United States issued Financials Accounting Standards 157 (FAS 157) in September of 2006 to define fund's fair value, establish the framework for measuring fair value by GAAP methods and expand the disclosure of fair value measurements.

[8] The International Accounting Standards Board (IASB) issued International Accounting Standard 39 (IAS 39) in December 1998 (made effective January 2001) to define the requirements for recognition and measurement of financial assets, financial liabilities, and some contracts to buy or sell non-financial items.

[9] IASB issued International Financial Reporting Standard 9 (IFRS 9) in July 2014, to be effective in January 2018, to further expand IAS to include additional recognition and measurement requirements, with new impairment, derecognition, and general hedge accounting requirements.

company today. Rather, a buyer is interested in a portfolio company's future value at the time of realization, as a portion of the proceeds from that realization will be payable to the buyer.

What is the appropriate method for determining portfolio companies' exit value? The answer depends on the type of investment. To determine the value of a privately held buyout company at the time of sale, or of any company generating significant revenue or earnings before EBITDA, the buyer will probably calculate the expected enterprise value of the company at exit. If the company is generating significant revenue or EBITDA, this calculation should be relatively straightforward. Exhibit 3 shows a simple example of pricing for a mini-LBO in a secondary transaction.

Exhibit 3: Example of a mini-LBO to compute an enterprise's value

Date of financials	Dec 31, 2018
EBITDA	$100,000,000
Growth rate per year	10%
Years to exit	3.00
Expected exit date	Dec 31, 2021
Calculated EBITDA at exit	*$133,100,000*
EBITDA multiple	7.5x
Calculated enterprise value at exit	*$998,250,000*
Net debt as of Dec 31, 2018	$500,000,000
Net debt annualized paydown	10%
Calculated net debt at exit	*$364,500,000*
Equity value at exit	$633,750,000
% Ownership as of Dec 31, 2018	50.0%
Fund exit proceeds	*$316,875,000*
Current cost	$200,000,000
Current value	$150,000,000
Implied current equity value to fund	$125,000,000

Projected multiple to cost	1.58x
Projected multiple to value	2.11x

To perform this calculation, buyers need basic data on the company, such as EBITDA (or another metric for which enterprise value multiples are available) and the company's debt load, net of excess cash on the balance sheet. The fund's ownership in the company is also a necessary input. Further, the buyer must estimate the remaining length of time the manager will hold the company, the EBITDA growth rate, the rate of debt pay down, and the future EBITDA multiple.

The number of years until exit can be estimated by looking at the GP's historical holding periods, tempered with a view of the current and future exit environment. The EBITDA growth rate can be based on several things, including the company's historical growth rate and the analyst consensus industry growth rate, or possibly the company's projections. Applying the expected growth before exit to the current EBITDA provides the estimate of EBITDA at the time of sale.

Possibly the most unpredictable variable is net debt at exit. Often, a company's net debt does not change significantly over time. However, sometimes a company will be expected to have sufficient free cash flow for the net debt to be paid down (to some extent) before exit. Likewise, for companies that have the option of payment in kind, net debt may increase before exit. This issue is best dealt with on a case-by-case basis. For instance, LBO funds with vintage years of 2006 or 2007 experienced significant discounting in the secondary market due to the relatively high purchase prices of portfolio companies.

Given the number of highly levered companies that have large debt principal payments coming due over the next few years, buyers need to project whether that debt can be refinanced and, if so, when. Some companies may be unable to simply pay off the principal and may be forced to refinance at more punitive terms than those of the current debt, which will have a strong impact on equity value.

An estimate of the exit EBITDA multiple should begin with an analysis of comparable public companies. The EBITDA multiple at which these companies are currently trading can provide a starting point. This multiple can be adjusted, using the historical trading ranges for the companies, to indicate multiple expansion or contraction. A liquidity discount may need to be applied to this multiple if the company is not a likely IPO candidate.

These steps provide an estimated exit value for this set of assumptions. However, buyers may perform multiple calculations—perhaps assuming lower or higher growth rates, shorter or longer holding periods, EBITDA multiple contraction or expansion, and varying levels of net debt—and then assign probabilities to each case. For companies that are highly levered, the buyer may consider a scenario in which the company is unable to refinance or service its debt and is forced into bankruptcy. Buyers are typically conservative in their assumptions, assigning higher weights to the more negative scenarios and, quite possibly, arriving at a lower future exit value than if a seller were to perform the same exercise.

Venture valuation is much more difficult since it is quite a complex assignment to supply a value for a venture-backed company, even for a venture capitalist. Buyers will be far more reliant upon receiving information from the manager, and may base their valuations largely on that manager's reputation. As venture investments have a notoriously wide range of potential outcomes, from a write-off to a Google-sized exit, buyers may attempt to assign probabilities to different outcomes. History suggests that the largest probability weights should be assigned to outcomes that result in a loss.

Venture investments that have suffered may need to raise more equity capital than previously expected. Buyers must thus examine whether a fund has sufficient capital to participate in these future funding rounds for its investments. If it does not, the buyer must assume that the fund's equity stakes in its companies will be significantly diluted because of the participants' liquidity preferences in future rounds.

The valuation of portfolio companies that are public is also relevant. GPs are required to mark these companies to market. However, a buyer is unlikely to pay market price for a public stock that is potentially restricted, and over which the buyer has no control. As a result, buyers are likely to apply a substantial discount to the current market value of the holding.

Value of unfunded capital

One major component of value that the GP's NAV does not consider is a fund investor's legal obligation to contribute unfunded capital to the fund in the future. Depending on the buyer's opinions of the fund manager's quality and of the current investment environment, this can be considered either a liability (which will subtract from value) or an asset (which will add value).

The first step in valuing the unfunded capital is estimating how much of it will be used for investments (either follow-on/add-on investments to current portfolio companies or new investments) and how much will be used for fund fees and expenses. The rate at which this investment capital will be called can be estimated by looking at historical data on how much capital funds have called at various points in their life cycles. This information can be tempered with a current macroeconomic viewpoint to project future capital calls.

The next step is to estimate what value these capital calls will generate. A buyer may assume that the estimated capital calls will generate a certain multiple or IRR; this can be based on the GP's quality and historical returns. If the manager is of high quality, then the unfunded capital may add value to the fund, as the buyer will pay for the manager's investment selection skills. However, if the manager is of inadequate quality, the buyer may assume that it will lose a portion of every dollar it contributes, which will have an obvious drag on the valuation.

In funds whose investment periods have ended, the buyer's expected return on capital called will be much lower, given that the GP will be making only follow-on investments going forward. As these investments typically support portfolio companies only for working capital needs or to preserve a liquidity position, they often generate a much lower return than new investments.

Fund Structure

Another factor that the GP's current NAV does not take into account is the fund structure. Estimating the exit value and timing for current portfolio holdings and future capital calls and distributions related to these capital calls provides the buyer with a gross cash flow stream. The buyer will then create a financial model of the fund that considers key fund terms, such as management fees, preferred returns, and carry.

The method the GP uses to account for carry may substantially depress secondary market pricing. In some cases, the GP may have accrued carried interest but not yet have taken it. If the accrued carried interest has not been deducted from the LP's capital account, then the nominal price of the fund will be much lower (the absolute price will be divided by a larger NAV).

Discounting estimated net cash flows

After the buyer has taken the fund structure into account, the only remaining input required is the buyer's target rate of return or the discount rate. This rate will vary depending on the type of fund in question and the current state of the market. All other things being equal, a mezzanine fund will have a lower required return than a buyout fund, and a buyout fund will have a lower discount rate than a venture fund. Greenhill Cogent's data indicates that buyers' target rates of return dipped below 15% at the peak of the private equity boom in 2006–2007. Conversely, target returns may have been as high as 30% in late 2008 and early 2009 (Greenhill Cogent, 2006, 2008, 2009).

Buyers will sometimes underwrite to a multiple, rather than to a rate of return. This approach is typical for very mature funds, for which the buyer may use a target multiple to ensure that it receives a sufficient cash-on-cash return from the short duration of the investment.

Other buyer valuation considerations

Other factors to consider that might lead a buyer to pay either a premium or a discount to a fund's modeled value include the supply of and demand for a given fund interest, the blind pool risk, and a GP's reputation.

Many mega-buyout funds with 2007 or 2008 vintage years have seen investors looking to sell. Given the large amount of supply, buyers are unwilling to bid aggressively, as they can simply wait for the next interest to hit the market. In addition, a buyer may have purchased a large amount of the fund already and have reached a diversification limit. As with any other market, a large number of investors attempting to sell the same interest will cause a decrease in pricing.

The liquidity squeeze of 2008–2009 highlighted a difficulty associated with highly unfunded assets. Secondary buyers always prefer the highest possible visibility into a potential purchase. However, increasingly, sellers have been attempting to shed funds that may be only 10% funded and have just a handful of investments. There are some secondary buyers that will not bid on these assets because of the blind pool risk and the similarity to investing on a primary basis. Those who do bid will typically assign a large risk premium to the unfunded position—in some cases, taking on the liability of the unfunded position without paying anything for the current NAV or even asking the seller for payment to take on the liability. In practice, highly unfunded positions will be valued at a large additional discount by potential buyers.

Sometimes, a fund may be given additional value over the modeled value. This most often occurs in VC funds, when the fund's manager has a top-tier reputation. Some investors will pay an "access premium" to invest with these managers, particularly if they have not invested with the manager before. By purchasing a fund interest on the secondary market, they hope to be invited to invest in the manager's future funds, and the value of the potential future commitments filters into the secondary price for the asset. Such opportunities are rarely on the market unless a seller wants to exit a position only partially, or is exiting the asset class in general.

How sellers view valuation

Sellers typically approach valuation from a very different perspective than buyers. Whereas buyers are concerned mainly with the price they should pay to achieve their target returns, sellers are more concerned with the buyer's valuation relative to the fund's NAV as provided by the manager, particularly when a buyer is offering to purchase a fund at a discount to the fund's most recently reported NAV, thereby creating a loss on the seller's books. No seller ever looks favorably on a loss, but alternative asset investors might be particularly unwilling to accept losses because of compensation issues (i.e., personal compensation tied to performance) or political concerns (i.e., investors that must report publicly).

Few sellers are equipped to perform a typical buyer-style valuation. Sellers will often use more aggressive assumptions than buyers; this is partly due to comfort with the assets and partly due to psychology. The seller has probably been in constant contact with the fund manager for the life of the fund and may be more familiar than a buyer with a given portfolio company's prospects, allowing more confidence in an aggressive assumption. The seller may also have made the initial recommendation to make the fund investment, and may be anchored to a positive outlook for the investment.

Another major difference in a seller valuation can be the discount rate used. Sellers, like buyers, typically have a target rate of return for a given asset, but a seller's targets are often lower than a buyer's targets, which will cause the seller's valuation to be higher. Even larger discrepancies can be seen when an organization uses its cost of capital, which should always be lower than the target rate of return, or when pension funds use target rates of return that must be quite low for actuarial reasons. However, the reasons for selling would generally increase the required rate of return for the seller. If a sale is planned for liquidity reasons, the target rate of return for the asset is no longer particularly relevant, and the discount rate should be increased in proportion to the size of the liquidity problem. If the seller wants to redeploy the capital from the sale into another asset with a higher expected return, the discount rate should also be increased for the asset being sold, in line with the desired return in redeployment. Seller discount rates can normally be moved in line with buyer targets when the circumstances of the sale are fully considered.

Exhibit 5 shows bid dispersion across multiple buyers bidding for the same fund vintage. As can be seen from the chart, the bid dispersion is higher in newer vintage funds and have achieved more "premium" pricing, as these funds are perceived by buyers to have more future appreciation potential. In vintages newer than 2012, 34% of the bids received a "premium" pricing and 59% received a pricing of over 90% NAV. Older vintage funds achieve a lower pricing, where only 9% of 2009 vintage funds or older were able to achieve premium pricing and 23% received pricing above 90% NAV.

Exhibit 5: Bid dispersion as percentage of NAV, by vintage

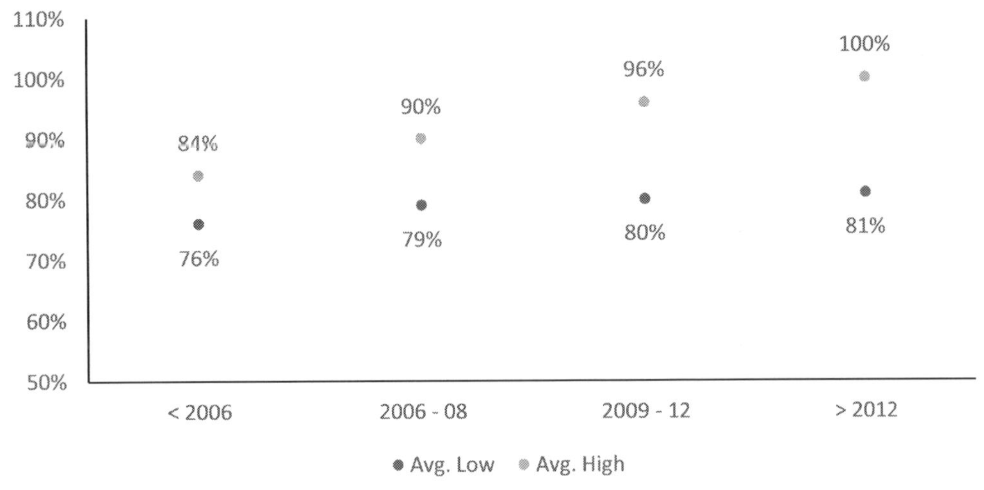

Note: Includes only funds for which multiple bids were received.
Source: Greenhill, 2018.

Pricing in the secondary market for fund interests is typically expressed as a percentage of the valuation that is being reported by the fund managers. In the average secondary transaction, the seller and the buyer agree on a valuation date (i.e., the reference date) and the reported valuation for the fund interest as of the reference date forms the foundation which prices are based on. This reference date price is then adjusted for subsequent cash flows. It is important to note that, unless they are agreed upon up front, changes to the valuations of the underlying funds usually accrue to the benefit or detriment of the buyer. Note that these numbers do not represent closing prices for transactions, which can be substantially higher, and that pricing levels can vary greatly depending on fund age, perceived GP quality, fund strategy, and size of the fund interest for sale.

DRIVERS OF RISK FOR INVESTORS IN SECONDARY FUNDS

The market in which secondary funds operate is characterized by price and information asymmetries, which means that secondary funds must endeavor to control their level of risk by influencing the following risk parameters:

- **Fund age:** It is worth noting that because early secondary funds target primary funds that are typically still in their investment period, they can exhibit features like primary funds.

- **Acquisition price:** A lower acquisition price on the secondary market leads to a more advantageous risk profile, all things being equal. Co-investing in an existing private equity portfolio with a senior preferred position, contractual return, and priority on portfolio distributions also lowers the risk profile.

- **Underlying fund quality:** Secondary fund managers can reduce the blind pool risk by investing in identifiable underlying assets that satisfy certain investment criteria regarding cash flow profile and earnings growth. In this regard, the due diligence process is paramount to assess the quality of the fund's underlying assets as the secondary manager can do a comprehensive analysis of the embedded performance and future value potential of these underlying companies.

- **Economic cycle:** Depending on the specific economic cycle, the secondary fund might invest at high or low company valuations which directly affect future returns.

- **Investment conditions:** Whenever a secondary fund buys an LP stake, it has bargaining power (to some extent) in terms of investment conditions and seniority protection. The most important items are downside protection in terms of fixed assets or when investing in debt securities, deal-by-deal or whole fund carried interest, preferred IRR hurdles, and key man clauses.

- **Portfolio diversification:** The secondary private equity funds market allows secondary fund managers to diversify their portfolio with specific GP fund holdings across various vintage years, geographies, sectors, investment strategies, and asset classes. Achieving sufficient diversification can optimize the risk-return trade-off.

CONCLUSION

The past two decades have seen explosive growth in the secondary market, fueled by LPs' needs for liquidity, increased interest from non-traditional investors (e.g., pension funds, family offices), changes in the regulatory framework, and other structural changes. The global financial crisis spurred further growth with investors facing pressure to exit their primary investments early because of liquidity needs, thus increasing the supply of funds available for sale in the secondary market.

Increased activity in the primary private equity market means that the secondary private equity market is expected to keep growing as investors continue to rebalance their portfolios and use secondary to mitigate the effects of the J-curve. The growth of the market has also given rise to specialist advisory firms that assist with structuring and managing secondary transactions. Most potential secondary market buyers now consider relying on the services of such intermediaries. Finally, pricing in the secondary market is of significant importance to both buyers and sellers, who typically have different motives and considerations when estimating prices for funds. As a result, bidding processes through managed auctions have gained prominence, as they optimize the outcome for both buyers and sellers.

REFERENCES

Borel, P., A. Janis and J. Gull (2009), Active Portfolio Management in Private Equity, Private Equity International.

Campbell Lutyens (2018), Second Market Overview.

Coller Capital (2018), White Paper – The Private Equity Secondary Market.

Coller Capital (2018), White Paper – GP-led secondary.

Evercore (2018), Secondary Market Survey Results.

Greenhill Cogent (2006), Secondary Pricing Level Eclipses NAV for the First Time.

Greenhill Cogent (2008), Secondary Pricing Declines with Public Market Drop.

Greenhill Cogent (2009), Greenhill Cogent Closes Over $2.5B in Transactions—Less than 20% Purchased by Secondary Funds.

Greenhill (2018,) Secondary Market Trends Outlook, January.

Greenhill (2018), Secondary Market Trends Outlook, July 2018.

Gordon, B.A., and J. M. Toomey Jr. (2004), "The secondary market: Sellers challenge buyers to be more creative," The Private Equity Analyst Guide to the Secondary Market, Dow Jones..

Johnson, S. (2009), "Investors facing private equity trap," Financial Times, May 10.

Konkel, T. (2004), "Secondary prices: A rising tide," Private Equity Analyst Guide to the Secondary Market, Dow Jones.

McGrady, C. (2007), "2006 secondary pricing analysis and outlook," Private Equity Analyst Guide to the Secondary Market, Dow Jones.

Meyer, T., and P-Y Mathonet (2005), Beyond the J Curve: Managing a Portfolio of Venture Capital and Private Equity Funds, John Wiley & Sons.

Penn, L. and A. O. Welsch-Lehmann (2004,) The Private Equity Analyst Guide to the Secondary Market.

Permal Capital Management (2009), Private Equity Observations: Golden Age of Secondary?, August.

VCFA (2002), Secondary Sales of Private Equity Interests: The Advent of Secondary Private Equity Fund Interest Transactions, Venture Capital Fund of America, February.

In his own words: Michael Schad, Partner, Head of Investment Management at Coller Capital. London Business School alumnus

From its early days as a forum for the exchange of fund interests, the secondary market evolved to embrace interests in private companies not held within independent private equity funds. These transactions are known as direct secondaries (or sometimes simply as 'directs').

In recent years, GP-led (as opposed to investor-led) secondaries have become an increasingly important part of the market. While limited partners (LPs) have used the secondary market for portfolio management purposes for nearly three decades, it is only in recent years that general partners have recognized the full value of the secondary market as a fund management tool.

Whatever their form, GP-led secondaries are usually large and complex transactions. They make certain demands of would-be buyers: access to significant capital; an in-depth understanding of a transaction's sponsoring GP and its assets; and an ability to align the interests of multiple stakeholders.

GP-led secondaries have increased rapidly in importance as a market dynamic. They represented a third of secondary transactions by value in 2018,and are expected to comprise an increasing share of total transaction value in the years ahead.

Not only has the number (and often size) of GP-led transactions increased, there has been a corresponding increase in the quality of the general partners sponsoring transactions and of the fund assets in question. Several well-regarded and high-performing GPs have recently opted to initiate liquidity solutions in this way – including Nordic Capital, which recently completed a transaction with Coller Capital.

Nordic Capital's GP-led secondary transaction:

On its close in April 2018, the restructuring of Nordic Capital VII became the world's largest GP-led secondary transaction. Nordic Capital VII was nearing the end of its life, and its manager wished for more time, and additional capital, with which to maximize the value of its remaining assets.

Coller Capital led the secondary transaction, in which nine private companies were sold to a newly created continuation vehicle managed by Nordic Capital.

Investors that did not want to commit to a longer holding period were able to achieve liquidity through the transaction. A tiered carry structure, plus investment by Nordic Capital into the new continuation vehicle, ensured strong alignment between Coller Capital's investors and the Nordic team.

15 Private Debt Funds and Distressed Investing

Creditors have better memories than debtors.
Benjamin Franklin

INTRODUCTION

The private debt fund market has evolved remarkably over the last few years, moving from a niche asset class into one that is more mainstream. Two principal drivers are contributing to this development: a decline in the availability of capital from traditional bank lenders (corresponding to a need to refinance existing debt) and an increasing demand for capital from businesses to finance growth. With ongoing bank disintermediation, the size of private debt funds and the size of the loans that they can offer to markets has grown.

The lending environment is undergoing a structural change as private debt lenders are becoming key capital providers while banks continue to deleverage their balance sheets. Since 2008, banks have deleveraged significantly due to the financial crisis and increased regulatory pressure under Basel III, the Volcker Rule (which also reduced liquidity in bond markets by banning proprietary trading), and other regulatory changes. Thus, banks have been forced to reduce the size of their loan books while increasing capital, reducing both their exposure to the debt of leveraged companies (compared to pre-2008) and their lending to small and mid-sized companies by selling non-core loan portfolios. Private debt funds are some of the largest buyers of these loan portfolios.

Traditionally, private debt was considered too illiquid when compared to debt capital markets alternatives, and too low-yielding when compared to private equity funds. However, with the private lending market growing since the global financial crisis, new players are raising debt funds for the following reasons:

- **Size of the financing gap**, particularly for senior debt where historically banks used to be the main lending group.

- **Attractive risk-adjusted returns**, especially for private equity-owned (or "sponsored") companies, which have lower default rates, on average, than those of non-sponsored leveraged companies.

- **Liquidity** as a result of a larger secondary loan market and more participants.

- **Historically low interest rates**, which have resulted in extremely low returns in traditional fixed income assets, and high volatility in equity markets.

Private debt funds offer a viable option because the debt securities they invest in are mostly based on floating rates that link the interest rate to market benchmarks, such as the federal funds rate or the LIBOR rate. In addition, private debt funds can offer superior risk-adjusted returns, especially when the funds are managed by a private debt manager with an established credit platform and with privileged access to deal flow that facilitates superior credit selection capabilities. Institutional investors like the relatively predictable yields, the downside protection due to the collateralization provided by real assets, and the low correlation to equities (compared to the traditional fixed income) that come with private debt funds.

The rise of private debt funds has been accompanied by ever higher levels of "dry powder" in the asset class and fierce competition among general partners (GPs—ranging from private equity houses to alternative asset managers) in fundraising. Exhibit 1 illustrates the relevant segments of the private debt markets. We discuss direct lending, mezzanine debt, and distressed debt funds in this chapter. The characteristics of venture debt funds are discussed in a separate chapter, "Venture Lending."

Exhibit 1: Segments of private debt markets

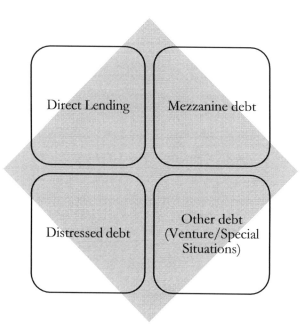

As the private debt market continues to grow and offer attractive risk-adjusted returns, interest from institutional investors has increased. As of 2018, some 30% of institutional investors globally are investing in private debt and 91% of surveyed investors in private debt felt the asset class either met or exceeded performance expectations. These investors are accessing the opportunity through dedicated funds or managed accounts offered by leading private debt managers. In particular, insurance groups are increasingly attracted to private debt funds—mainly due to the limited fixed income alternatives in the market, the fit of the cash flow profile with their asset allocation strategies, the limited volatility due to the private nature of the instruments (no mark-to-market), and the Solvency II efficiency.[1] In addition, public pension funds have become more familiar with private debt funds as they fit with their overall asset allocation. In the long term, private debt funds can match pension funds' liabilities and offer very attractive regular returns with a yearly coupon.

---

[1] The regulatory capital charge is often less than 20% for private debt fund investments and even lower for large insurance groups that develop their own internal ratings models; this compares to 39% for equity. Many other OECD regulators use a similar approach favoring credit over equity investments.

MARKET STATISTICS ON FUNDS

With declining yields elsewhere in fixed income, the private debt asset class has become the single fastest-growing sector in the alternative investments asset class. There were over 1,604 active private debt fund managers globally at the end of 2018, with total private debt AUM at $769 billion, $307 billion in dry powder and the rest in unrealized portfolio investments as at June 2018.[2] This surge is attributed to the fact that for the last two decades, private debt as an asset class has outperformed global high yield and U.S. investment grade indices, and has been relatively stable through market cycles. The performance of the individual categories of private debt frequently delivers double-digit returns. Direct lending achieved double-digit returns in 5 out of 11 years, with a median average net IRR across all funds of 11.40%. Mezzanine funds achieved double-digit returns in 17 out of 27 years with a median net IRR of 10%. Meanwhile, distressed debt delivered a significantly higher average return of 14.44%.

In 2018, fundraising stood at $110 billion in capital commitments, down from the all-time high of $129 billion in 2017. Fundraising statistics by strategy show that direct lending, mezzanine, and distressed debt have been the primary drivers of private debt's growth as an asset class over the last decade; these strategies accounted for 41%, 28%, and 19% (respectively) of all aggregate capital raised in 2018. Special situations accounted for 10% of the total and the rest was fund of funds and venture lending.

In terms of world regions, North America remains the epicenter of the private debt market with 62% of the market share. Europe accounted for 33% of total private debt fundraising globally. Private debt in the rest of the world lags behind, only accounting for the remaining 4% of market share. Accumulation of dry power implies that North America and Europe will continue to dominate the private debt landscape for several years to come. Expansion into other regions is still slow, largely because North American and European regulatory and legal environments are currently the most conducive for lending on a large scale.

Regarding the locations and types of investors, 25% of private debt investors are based in Europe, while 56% are based in North America, the region which continues to be the main hub for private debt activity. Private sector and public pension funds account for the largest proportion (28%) of the investor universe, followed by foundations (13%).

OVERVIEW OF INVESTING STYLES

Private debt funds source investments through primary and secondary markets. Primary market investments are typically undertaken by *direct lending* and *mezzanine* funds. Primary market opportunities include provision of (1) *first-lien* debt, (2) subordinated debt in the form of *second-lien* secured loans or mezzanine debt, and sometimes (3) third-lien debt such as *payment-in-kind (PIK) instruments* or *unitranche* loans in scenarios where traditional senior debt is not (or only partially) available from bank lenders. These scenarios include financing growth opportunities, refinancings (where existing debt is repriced down, or its quantum increased with or without the support of incumbent lenders), or rescue financings during periods of stress, financial restructuring, and/or operational turnaround. Primary market investments are often in private equity-owned borrowers (i.e., sponsored borrowers), although funds are increasingly exploring the non-sponsored market. Primary market lending can also be undertaken in the form of specialty finance structures, such as *asset-backed*

---

[2] Data in this section is cited from 2019 Preqin Global Private Debt Report

loans and/or lending that requires sector-specific knowledge (e.g., about real estate, maritime assets, financial institutions, healthcare, etc.).

Secondary market investments involve the purchase of companies' existing debt and can be implemented across a borrower's capital structure (from senior loans to subordinated debt, as well as, in some cases, accompanying equity positions). Secondary market investments may involve portfolios of performing highly liquid senior loans and high-yield bonds, or less liquid subordinated debt. In the distressed funds' context, secondary market opportunities include debt instruments

- that are deemed undervalued (value investment), including single assets or portfolios being sold by motivated sellers (such as European banks disposing of non-performing loans);

- where the investment professionals expect a near-to-medium term event (such as a restructuring, merger or divestment) to generate returns (known as special situations); and

- that would entitle the debt holder to lead, or play a lead role in, the financial restructuring of the borrower, thereby providing increased opportunities for returns. This approach sometimes takes the form of "loan-to-own," where the secondary buyer of the debt plans to force an equitization of the debt in order to take control of the borrower.

Hence, private debt funds can each specialize in a different type of debt, with corresponding variance in target returns and fee structures. Each fund's performance depends on its individual circumstances. Generally, loss rate—which is a significant (but not the only) factor in the performance of direct and mezzanine lending—is correlated with economic trends. In contrast, distressed funds' strategies are countercyclical and tend to exploit improved opportunities during downturns, provided an economic upturn occurs during the holding period of course.

TYPES OF DEBT INSTRUMENTS

Most of the private debt funds target debt instruments in the leveraged debt market. The leveraged debt market broadly covers senior and junior private debt investments (i.e., senior and subordinated loans as well as unitranche) and public debt investments (i.e., bonds) used for the acquisition, refinancing, and development of companies. By market convention, the classification of "leveraged debt" entails that

- the borrower has a rating below investment grade (i.e., below "BBB-" or "Baa3"), and/or

- the borrower is a sponsored company (i.e., a company owned by a private equity sponsor).

The private debt market has been characterized as both filling the financing gap left by banks following the 2008 credit crisis, and providing more flexible and tailor-made financing solutions, frequently with faster execution than that available from banks. Unitranche transactions (discussed in further detail below) are a notable example of these abilities, as banks generally do not offer this type of product. Because the offerings are unique, the terms of debt instruments offered by these funds may depart from those offered by banks under similar market conditions; for this reason, debt originated at a fund is typically considered highly illiquid. However, as discussed below, funds may also acquire more liquid assets—leveraged loans (with conventional bank or institutional lender terms) and high-yield bonds, for example—depending on the investment strategy. From the borrower's perspective, the illiquid nature of private debt may be viewed as beneficial because the borrower does not bear the risk of (a) "market flex" terms or the additional administrative burden associated with bank syndication and the book building process, and (b) changes in its lending group to loan-to-own investors.

We provide an example of a leveraged debt structure and key characteristics in the private market below (see Exhibit 2). This figure shows that first-lien debt is typically the largest piece of the debt structure, sitting at the top of the capital structure; for this reason, it is sometimes referred to as "senior debt." This top position in the "waterfall" illustrates the most important feature of first-lien debt—namely, that it is secured with a priority ranking against all other pieces in the capital structure (including all debt and equity). Although we offer a brief overview of these instruments below, a more detailed discussion may be found in the chapter "Acquisition Finance."

Exhibit 2: Overview of a typical debt structure in a private firm

Type of debt	Proportion of Total Capital Structure	Pricing Structure	Asset Returns p.a.	Estimated Market Loss Rate
First Lien	35-50% (1st Priority Ranking)	EURIBOR/LIBOR E+3.5% - 8.0% p.a. + Fees	4.5% - 9.0%	0.4% p.a.
Second Lien		E+7.0% - 8.0% + Fees	8.0% - 9.0%	
Mezzanine	+15% - 20%	E+10.0% - 11.0% + Fees	12.0% - 14.0%	1.5% - 2.5% p.a.
PIK		E+11.0% - 13.0% + Fees	13.0% - 15.0%%	

First lien includes unitranche. Returns are estimated based on a three-year hold.
Source: S&P, LCD European Leveraged Buyout Review 2014, Q3 2015

Introduction to first-lien debt

First-lien debt consists of both private and public debt instruments. Direct lending funds usually target private first lien debt securities. These securities provide better information to investors and can offer greater legal protection than public bonds. Another benefit of private debt instruments is better relative pricing. The main types of private first-lien debt are as follows:

- **Loans**
    - Revolvers: These facilities allow borrowers the flexibility to drawdown, repay, and redraw the capital over the duration of the agreement. These types of loans offer repayment and reborrowing flexibility and are usually provided by banks.

– Term Loan A (TLA): A TLA is the senior loan instrument with the shortest maturity (five to six years), with an amortizing repayment structure. This form of debt is usually provided by banks and also carries the lowest margin among the senior term loan instruments.

– Term Loan B, C (TLB, TLC): These are the senior loan instruments with the second-shortest maturity (usually six to seven years), with a non-amortizing repayment structure (also called "bullet" loans). TLBs and TLCs pay a higher margin than TLAs from the same borrowers. This form of debt is provided by institutional investors, including private debt funds.

- **Unitranche debt**: This debt is typically provided to a private company as the only debt instrument in the capital structure, and is sometimes used as a substitute for the more traditional first-lien and subordinated debt structures.

Characteristics of first-lien loans

Below is a summary of the chief contractual characteristics of first-lien loans:

- **Interest:** Interest is structured as a floating base rate (e.g., EURIBOR, LIBOR) plus a cash margin. The floating rate nature provides investors with a hedge against rising inflation and interest rates. Cash interest is typically paid every three to six months, giving rise to regular cash distributions, which reduces the risk profile of the instrument for the private debt fund.

- **Other fees:** The loan might have a contractual EURIBOR or LIBOR floor (usually 0.0–1%) and front-end underwriting fees (1–3%).

- **Legal maturity:** Most first-lien loans must be repaid between five and seven years, depending on the nature of the instrument (TLA, TLB, or TLC) and the individual characteristics of the transaction that it is financing. Instruments tend to be repaid earlier than their legal maturities either via (a) voluntary or mandatory prepayments (e.g., due to financial covenants), (b) a refinancing, or (c) a sale of the underlying business (private debt typically has a "change of control" covenant requiring a mandatory prepayment should 51% ownership of the borrower change). Hence, the average life of first-lien debt is three to five years. It is also worth noting that floating rate first-lien notes do not charge fees payable for early prepayments.

- **First secured ranking and security package:** First-lien debt benefits from having collateral such as a first ranking pledge over the shares of the borrower and a first ranking security interest over its assets. In capital structures that include first-lien loans and senior secured bonds, first-lien loans typically rank above senior secured bonds.

- **Financial covenants:** Depending on the size of the transaction and the market conditions, loans are often protected by a number of maintenance covenants. These include up to four types of financial covenants (i.e., leverage ratios, interest coverage ratios, cash flow cover ratios, and restrictions on capex levels), which are typically tested on a quarterly basis. A breach of one or more of these financial covenants allows the lenders to renegotiate the terms, and in some situations, to request an accelerated repayment through enforcement of the security package. Loans without maintenance covenants are often referred to as "covenant-lite" (this term also refers to loans with limited restrictions on collateral, payment terms, and level of income).

Banks provided a substantial portion of the first-lien debt before the credit crisis. Today, however, they are increasingly focusing on the provision of ancillary facilities like revolving credit, working capital, and capex facilities. Nevertheless, investment banks continue to arrange and underwrite first-lien debt instruments before syndicating them to institutional investors such as debt funds. Debt funds or managed accounts (operated by private debt managers on behalf of their clients, i.e., pension funds and insurance companies among others) are playing a more significant role in this market. In addition, collateralized loan obligations (CLOs) invest in first-lien debt instruments (with a small allocation to subordinated debt), forming diversified portfolios (we discuss these entities later in the chapter).

Due to the generally stronger protection features of first-lien loans compared to bonds (including senior secured bonds), the loss expectation for these loans has historically been lower—mainly because of the higher recovery rates (i.e., the percentage of the original investment that the investor recovers when there is a borrower default) for loans compared to bonds. According to Moody's, the recovery rates on loans over the period from 1987 to 2015 averaged around 80%, while the recovery rates for senior secured (unsecured) bonds averaged 63% (48%).

Besides the generally low average loss rates and lender-protective contractual characteristics of first-lien debt, another attractive feature is its higher liquidity compared to subordinated debt, particularly in the context of private equity-owned companies. That liquidity comes from

- the larger size of the first-lien debt tranches per transaction, which can accommodate and therefore attract more investors;

- the larger volume of total investment vehicles with appetite to invest in first-lien debt; and

- the large group of private debt funds and other institutional investors—facilitated by the more tailor-made investment vehicles, such as managed accounts, which provide a greater platform of potential counterparties to trade with.

The benefit of greater liquidity of institutional first-lien debt is that it is less critical to "time" trades strategically, as compared with other bonds (especially since bonds are fixed rate while loans are floating rate), or to buy-to-hold across vintages, as compared with subordinated debt. Consequently, investments and disinvestments can be executed more flexibly, and hold periods can be shorter than they are for other asset classes. Moreover, higher liquidity enables better trading through bids wanted in competition where the investors in a managed account offer their loan portfolio through a listing to various securities dealers, and then sell to the dealer with the highest bid.

Characteristics of unitranche debt

As its name suggests, unitranche debt operates as (1) a single facility in place of the sometimes complex tranching senior and subordinated loans, and (2) senior debt partially stretching into the space that is traditionally seen as the preserve of mezzanine debt funds. Because it is a single facility (supplemented by any necessary revolving and capex/acquisition facilities), the finance agreements presented to the borrower are less voluminous. Unitranche debt structures can be compelling because they have low (or often zero) amortization. Such structures also provide higher leverage than senior debt (though generally lower than senior plus mezzanine structures), but often with less complex intercreditor issues to deal with. Another advantage of unitranche lending for smaller borrowers is that the direct lending funds that provide this financing are able to offer and hold much larger amounts than the banks, thereby reducing the complexity and time needed to execute buyout deals.

Unitranche debt is a tailor-made instrument, primarily used for smaller borrowers, and has either just one or a very small group of debt investors, which are usually direct lending funds. Some borrowers find the simplicity and flexibility offered by unitranche debt attractive. The interest rate is a "blended" rate that is often higher than, or about the same as, the interest rate of first-lien loans, but lower than the interest rate for traditional second-lien or mezzanine debt. Unitranche debt is typically priced at 6.5–8% above a benchmark rate such as EURIBOR or LIBOR (plus underwriting fees and non-call features) depending on (1) the size of the transaction, (2) the flexibility requested by the borrower (e.g., financial covenants), and (3) the track record of the underlying borrower. Due to the instrument's less standardized nature and the usually smaller size of the transaction (typically below €250 million total unitranche size, with larger transactions being rather exceptional), it is generally a less liquid instrument.

Introduction to second-lien debt and mezzanine debt

Mezzanine funds typically invest in second-lien debt and mezzanine debt, as well as the occasional third-lien PIK instrument (hence, some of these funds have rebranded themselves as "subordinated debt" funds). Before we discuss the operation of these funds, it is worth providing a brief introduction to these securities.

Characteristics of second-lien debt

Second-lien debt refers to loans that are reimbursed only after loan balances on first-lien debts are repaid in full following a default. Due to the subordinated claim on assets, if a borrower defaults on a secured loan, the first-lien holder may receive 100% on the loan balance from the sale of the underlying collateral or of the borrower itself, while the second-lien holder might receive only a fraction of the loan amount.[3] Due to the subordinated call on pledged collateral, second-lien loans carry more risk for private debt funds than senior first-lien loans. As a result of the elevated risk, these loans usually have higher borrowing rates and more stringent processes for approval than first-lien debt. In addition, second-lien loans have longer maturities than first-lien loans.

The primary risk to lenders posed by second-lien loans is insufficient collateral in the event of a default or a bankruptcy filing. In the investment process, managers of debt funds usually assess many of the same factors as first-lien lenders, including borrowers' debt-to-income ratios, credit scores, and senior management experience. Generally speaking, borrowers perceived as posing a low risk of default can be approved for larger loans that may exceed the value of the underlying 'real' asset. To mitigate risk with less creditworthy borrowers, managers of debt funds must also determine the amount of equity in excess of the balance owed on senior debt. This calculation usually includes variables such as the cost of liquidation and the potential for the underlying business to lose value. In these circumstances, they may restrict the size of second-lien loans to ensure that the balance of cumulative loans is significantly less than the value of the underlying borrower.

In the United States, the second-lien facility may be used as a substitute for high-yield bonds (e.g., in smaller transactions where a bond would not be sufficiently liquid). Very recently, the second-lien loan has

---

[3] For example, in a real estate loan where a borrower in default also has a second mortgage, creditors can foreclose and sell the home, followed by full payment on the balance of the first mortgage and the distribution of any remaining proceeds to the lender on the second mortgage.

morphed into an all-cash-pay mezzanine loan; this lowers its cost as it lowers the lender's risk more rapidly, but at the cost of less cash flow retention.

Characteristics of mezzanine debt

Mezzanine debt is placed between the first and second-lien debt and the equity in a borrower's capital structure. This type of debt can decrease overall capital costs by providing additional debt financing that can enhance equity returns. Mezzanine debt usually finances leveraged transactions, recapitalizations or corporate acquisitions. Mezzanine debt is junior in the capital structure and takes the form of senior unsecured debt for middle market companies.[4] By creating a capital structure with a "right-sized" combination of mezzanine debt and first-lien borrowings, private middle-market companies can leverage their equity capital to generate attractive returns for their owners. In the case of larger companies, mezzanine debt is structured as high-yield bonds. The minimum issuance size for a company to access the high-yield bond market is generally over $200-300 million thus most middle-market firms do not have the ability to access the bond market.

Due to their subordinated or junior position in an issuer's capital structure, mezzanine debt investors generally demand higher prospective returns compared to senior secured debt investors. The total returns on mezzanine debt typically come from

- **high rates** that can average 11–12%, paid quarterly, part in cash, part in PIK (in Europe the proportion tends to be 50/50);

- **front-end commitment or arrangement fees**, often paid in the form of original issue discounts;

- **call protection** (i.e., premium payments if the mezzanine debt is repaid early); and

- **equity kickers** (i.e., options to purchase equity in the underlying borrower), which result in the potential for additional returns beyond those contracted for by the junior debt investment by itself.

From the mezzanine debt fund investor's perspective, the mezzanine debt allocation in a portfolio may be considered as part of the "alternatives" (rather than fixed income) bucket, given the double-digit return. Mezzanine funds have historically targeted blended gross annualized returns in the mid-teens. Certainly, the avoidance of borrower defaults and subsequent losses is the most important aspect for mezzanine investors striving to achieve attractive total returns. In addition, since mezzanine debt is provided through privately negotiated transactions, it is far less liquid than public securities if it needs to be sold. Exhibit 3 provides a sample set of terms for a mezzanine loan.

PIK securities are a type of mezzanine financing, and have characteristics indicative of debt and equities. They tend to pay a relatively high rate of interest but are considered risky. Investors who can afford to take above-average risks, such as private debt mezzanine funds and hedge funds, are most likely to invest in PIK securities.

---

[4] Sometimes market participants classify second-lien debt as mezzanine debt.

Exhibit 3: Sample mezzanine debt term

Current fixed coupon	Ranking	Maturity	Equity participation	Commitment fees	Call Protection
• 11–12.5 (e.g., 11% cash, 0–1.5% PIK)	• Subordinated unsecured	• 7–8 years (typically one year after 1st Lien Debt)	• Purchased Equity	• 2–3 basis points upfront	• 1–2 years non-call; premium prepayment schedule thereafter

PIK notes give the issuer a chance to delay making interest payments in cash, and in return for the delay, the issuing company typically agrees to offer a higher rate of return on the note. To illustrate how PIK notes work, imagine that a mezzanine fund offers a struggling company PIK notes worth €2 million. The notes have a 10% interest rate, and they mature at the end of a 10-year period. Each year, the note incurs €200,000 in interest. However, instead of being required to repay that amount or any principal payments, the interest is added to the debt in kind, meaning more debt. Hence, by the end of the first year, the company owes €2.2 million, and that amount continues to grow until the loan matures, at which time the cash is due. In this way, PIK securities are attractive to companies preferring not to make cash outlays, and they are often used in LBOs.

The interest of many mezzanine instruments is frequently structured as a combination of cash interest (i.e., spread over EURIBOR/LIBOR as a cash margin) and PIK margin. More often than not, mezzanine debt is structured to include quarterly interest payments (mostly in cash). These payments compensate lenders for subordinating their position in the capital structure. A typical contractual interest of a mezzanine instrument might be EURIBOR/LIBOR (1% floor) plus a 10%–11% cash/PIK margin. The proportion of PIK margin (+/- 50% of the total margin) is usually negotiated on a case-by-case basis depending on the cash flow characteristics of the borrower.

OPERATIONS OF PRIVATE DEBT FUNDS

The essence of the success of a debt fund lies in the risk management and investment selection process followed by the manager. Accordingly, for many debt funds, accounting, administration, reporting, corporate secretary services, tax services, and transfer agent and loan servicing functions are outsourced (we discuss these functions separately in the chapter "Fund Administration"). The investment selection process and sourcing activities, and the corresponding compensation for the GP, follow various models, some of which are described below.

Private debt fund terms and structures

Private debt funds may be structured (1) in a fashion similar to private equity funds or (2) in a way that is more akin to hedge funds (which have more relaxed capital withdrawal regimes). Additionally, some asset managers are offering single investor managed account structures where investors can have access to co-lending deals on larger transactions and more flexibility via customization. There are also floating rate funds such as CLOs, which provide liquid exposure to performing leveraged loans purchased in the institutional investor market.

Exhibit 4 highlights key structural considerations relevant to private debt funds' private equity model and the hedge fund model. As highlighted in the table, following the private equity model, private debt funds use a closed-end fund structure with a finite life, an investment period, and a harvest period (which may be extended by the GP if needed).[5] The limited partners (LPs) of debt funds commit capital for an extended period (e.g., 7–10 years) to allow for the deployment of the funds and harvesting of the returns. Returns in private debt fund platforms may be achieved through a few means:

- Fee and coupon payments.

- Debt redemptions.

- Debt buybacks.

- Sales of debt instruments to third parties.

These debt funds may or may not employ fund-level leverage (i.e., leverage backed by the underlying assets which may therefore exceed the fund's equity commitments) as part of their investment strategy. In most cases, they tend to borrow funds for bridging and liquidity purposes (i.e., revolvers backed by uncalled capital commitments).

Exhibit 4: Comparison of private debt funds with hedge funds

	Private debt funds	**Hedge funds**
Redemption Options	No redemption	Lock-up period of 1 year with quarterly withdrawals thereafter. Manager may have the ability to suspend redemptions in crisis.
Management Fees	1–2% on committed capital, step down to a lower percentage determined based on invested capital after commitment period.	1.5–2% of NAV
Fees from Borrowers Shared with LPs	50–100% of fees shared with LPs	Typically not addressed in documentation
Carried Interest	5–20%, with preferred return of 6–10%; sometimes graduated carry percentages after achievement of IRR thresholds.	Typically 20%

---

[5] In contrast, hedge fund capital can usually be withdrawn on shorter notice (e.g., three months).

Clawback/High Watermark	Clawback; periodic and/or after the end of the fund's term	High watermark and loss carryforward
Commitment Period	Typically 5 or 6 years	N/A
Fund Term	10-year term, potentially with a 1–3 year extension option	35 years
Open End/Closed End	Closed end	Open end
Termination Events	Key person triggers; no-fault termination; removal of GP provisions	No-fault termination or no ability to terminate before the end of the term
Recycling	Limited recycling may be permitted, subject to a cap based upon committed capital (i.e., 120%) and/or subject to the types of proceeds that can be recycled	All capital constantly invested
GP Commitment	1–5% of committed capital	Below 1% of NAV
Distributions	Interest payable quarterly Net proceeds payable quarterly tied to available cash	Only upon request, periodically after lock-up period
Formation of Successor Funds	Typically restricted until 75% of capital is invested, reserved, or used for investments or expenses	No limitation
Closings	Open for a period of 6–18 months	Continuous offering
Fund Expenses	Charged to fund (except placement fees)	Charged to fund (except placement fees)

Source: Mayer Brown

Fees and carry

The fee structure of debt funds can also vary greatly. Public information on fees is extremely limited, and terms may sometimes be subject to intense negotiations with LPs. Nevertheless, we discuss some recent general trends. While earlier debt funds were based on the traditional private equity fund "2-and-20" fee structure (2% management fee and 20% of returns), this approach has come under increasing pressure as investors have expanded their due diligence efforts in performance attribution and manager selection. Fee structures for private debt funds tend to vary depending on the fund's investment style, with fee amounts corresponding to target returns. For example, a distressed fund with a target return of above 20% may feature a 2-and-20 fee structure (or, more frequently, a 1.75% management fee). The management fee for mezzanine and direct lending funds (including unitranche) could be lower, 1.5% or 1.25%. A more conservative (and relatively passively managed) senior loan fund may have an even lower fee structure (e.g., 1 and 10).

Additionally, due to LP pressure for preferential terms—especially when the LPs are large or come in early—there is further variation in fees across investors.

Another variable is whether management fees are paid on committed capital (irrespective of actual investments) or invested capital only (calculated on capital actually deployed). LPs naturally prefer the latter approach, and support this position in private debt funds on the basis that funds should be able to be deployed faster than they would be in conventional private equity funds. This approach has become increasingly common in recent years. In response, some funds have adopted a hybrid approach (e.g., 0.25% on committed capital and 1.25% on invested capital).

Distressed debt investment, which requires the most hands-on investment analysis and targets higher returns, has been relatively resilient to downward fee pressure. Private debt funds lending to non-sponsored borrowers (i.e., those non-investment grade private companies outside the context of private equity-led LBOs) with higher target returns may enjoy similar status, on the basis that the credit analysis is more intense: the fund cannot ride on the coattails of the underwriting/analysis of other creditors, nor can it rely on a private equity sponsor to inject more equity in adverse circumstances. Fees may also remain higher at more established GPs or in cases where the manager has specialized skills. The same applies to some mezzanine funds.

The carry portion (a percentage of returns) is triggered as returns rise over an agreed hurdle rate (such as 8%). Catch-up terms may also vary between funds. The "catch-up" phase in a distribution waterfall refers to the period after the LPs have received their hurdle return, where the GP receives 80–100% of subsequent distributions, until the GP has received its entitlement to carried interest (20% traditionally) for investments harvested thus far (see the chapter on the economics of private equity funds). For senior debt funds, the "catch-up" may be significantly lower (e.g., 50%) or there may be no catch-up mechanism at all. In sum, management fees and carry are crucial aspects of fund structuring because they focus the minds of managers, advisers, and prospective investors.

Structural issues

A key theme in relation to private debt fund structures has been the prominence of single investor managed accounts. As capital commitment levels to the asset class increase, managed accounts allow investors to negotiate attractive economics while making very large investments. Furthermore, as the private debt market continues to grow, in terms of capital commitments by investors and the number of fund managers, the spectrum of investment strategies is likely to broaden further to accommodate the risk-return preferences of different investors.

Another key structural component for a private debt fund is its domicile, which is the jurisdiction of the main fund vehicle represented by the entity in which the investors commit their funds. Usually, a private debt fund consists of an investment company and a carry entity. Additional entities may be included for funding mechanisms and other requirements. Investors prefer a familiar fund domicile that mitigates any issues arising from local legislation and regulation. Many large investors have found that separately managed account structures (discussed above) provide the most advantageous and flexible solution by offering bespoke operational and economic terms that meet unique needs. Generally speaking, U.S. private debt funds tend to have domiciles in Delaware and the Cayman Islands, and European private debt funds tend to have domiciles in Luxembourg (given the country's double tax treaty arrangement with numerous nations), the Channel Islands, the Cayman Islands, and the United Kingdom.

Tax transparency is another important consideration of the fund structure and, relatedly, the mechanism by which income flows are able to pass from underlying special purpose vehicles used as booking or holding vehicles to the top of the fund and ultimately the investors. All private debt fund structures are constructed with the goal of maximizing tax efficiency for the specific type of investor. For example, taxable U.S. investors prefer to invest in a pass-through investment vehicle (i.e., partnerships), while foreign U.S. investors prefer to organize the fund as an entity that is treated as a corporation for U.S. tax purposes. (We discuss the structuring of private equity and debt funds in greater detail in the chapter "Fund Structuring.")

As the private debt market continues to evolve, many funds try to combine a number of jurisdictions within the same fund to offer potential investors flexible fundraising solutions that cater to specific strategies. Additionally, private debt funds have started to provide innovative fund liquidity solutions to accommodate an increasingly broader investor base. A small number of open-ended structures may be privately held or publicly listed on an exchange. While the open-ended structure appeals to a wider investor base, the underlying investments within the private debt spectrum are illiquid and very difficult to value. Therefore, many open-ended funds need to have restrictions placed on redemptions in terms of amount and timing.

Direct lending funds

Direct lending funds mainly emerged after the credit crisis as a viable alternative investment to conventional credit and debt-based investment fund strategies. These funds pursue a traditional strategy for lending money to businesses and projects that require it. Direct lending funds typically control one or more finance companies that carry out the day-to-day lending and credit analysis activities that are key to a successful strategy. The successful direct lending funds have deep market knowledge (i.e., many funds focus on a particular sector or geography) and employ personnel with strong commercial lending backgrounds and sector-specific expertise; this brings essential ground-level knowledge that is required for good loan risk management. In addition, fund managers are in constant contact with their underlying customers and carry out detailed and ongoing due diligence of the borrowers to assess credit risks.

Direct lending funds often rely on a predictable portfolio of loans that provides a regular income stream to the fund. The managers must ensure that this portfolio is diversified across a range of risks within the sector they invest in. Direct lending funds follow three different main investment models. Note that the first lending model is resource intensive, as the fund manager must develop the respective infrastructure in-house (origination, IT, risk management, back office, etc.); hence, this model requires high volumes in order to be profitable. The second and third models are typical cases for debt funds.

1. In the first model, **bilateral lending** or **private placement**, the fund manager develops dedicated expertise to invest directly in loans (i.e., in screening and selecting suitable borrowers or projects). In some jurisdictions (e.g., the United States), these activities are not new and have been in place for quite some time.[6] In other jurisdictions (e.g., especially in parts of Europe), non-bank lending and private placements are in the process of being developed. Large European insurance companies also started to set up dedicated debt teams to invest in corporate loans, commercial real estate, and infrastructure projects.

2. In the second model, **specialized loan funds**, the fund manager pools a number of loans together and non-bank investors buy equity in the funds. The launch of loan funds has accelerated markedly since mid-2012, not only in Europe where banks are still deleveraging, but also in the United States. In recent

---

[6] For instance, the U.S. "private placement" market has enabled insurance companies to finance corporates for decades, also benefiting from a specific credit assessment infrastructure.

launches, the fund manager has generally been part of a hedge fund or a private equity fund, but there are also specialized credit managers. In particular, private equity funds leverage on their expertise of identifying target companies for acquisition purposes, and extend it to debt financing. Investors in loan funds are usually non-banks that cannot develop an in-house credit selection and assessment capacity and/or that want to diversify exposures.

3. The third model, **co-origination with a bank**, relies on the "originate-to-distribute" model that was common before the credit crisis. A debt fund and a bank enter into a partnership whereby the bank screens the borrowers, originates the loans, and distributes them to the debt fund, which provides the capital. "Skin-in-the-game" arrangements are generally in place to facilitate the alignment of incentives between the bank and the fund.

In the United States, publicly traded investment vehicles are more common, including business development corporations (BDCs) and floating rate funds (open-end mutual funds ("prime" funds) and exchange-traded funds that buy senior leveraged loans). BDCs are American closed-end investment companies that are typically publicly traded. To be eligible for status as a BDC, the investment company must be operated for the purpose of making investments in securities issued by small and medium-sized businesses, make available significant managerial assistance to such businesses, and fulfill other tax and regulatory conditions. BDCs are eligible for exemption from corporate income tax (similar to a real estate investment trust) as long as certain income, diversity, and distribution requirements are met.[7] In contrast, floating rate funds and CLOs (see below) invest in institutional leveraged loans (i.e., TLBs) in the secondary market.

The CLO is another distinct investment vehicle, which provides for exposure to a broad pool of high-yield debt. A CLO is generally considered a "public" strategy, investing (as secondary market purchasers) in a pool of traded leveraged loans (and in some cases, high-yield bonds) which are structured and distributed by banks. Additionally, unlike with other fund types, investors gain exposure through securities of various tranches with different ratings, depending on the rank of their claims on the pool. CLOs are subject to U.S. banking regulations and need to follow credit risk retention rules (under which the CLO sponsors must retain 5% of the credit risk of the loan assets in the CLO). It is not clear whether this regulatory requirement will reduce the volume of new CLO issuance, given the higher compliance costs on the CLO industry. Because the European CLO market has been especially slow to recover from the crisis, investors that previously obtained exposure to leveraged loans through CLOs must find alternative vehicles (i.e., other asset management platforms or direct lending) in Europe. Hence, private debt vehicles are becoming more dominant players in the European private debt market.

Overall, the CLO is distinct from other fund vehicles discussed here and would not ordinarily be associated with privately originated loans or distressed loans. While a complete discussion of CLOs is beyond the scope of this chapter, many asset managers and GPs with expertise in private lending and distressed debt also participate in the leveraged finance market as CLO managers.

The market for direct lending funds, however, has expanded further in recent years. The demand for credit from small and medium-sized companies has increased due to the contraction in loan supply from banks since the credit crisis. As a result, direct lending funds have found significant opportunities in the middle market direct lending (MMDL) segment. Smaller companies that can no longer rely on banks for financing are starting to look for direct lending funds as a source of financing. Typically, these companies include private equity-

---

[7] Apollo Investment Corp. and Ares Capital Corp. are examples of BDCs operated by major players in the debt space which engage in primary lending.

sponsored or unsponsored companies that seek capital to finance LBOs, acquisitions, growth through capital expenditures, or a dividend recapitalization. Further, direct lending can be a source of capital for highly levered companies. Direct lending loans, especially in the MMDL segment, have higher interest rates and are structured to have unique lender-friendly protections and covenants to compensate for their added risk and low liquidity. They are usually senior secured loans that sit on top of the company's capital structure, but they can also be structured as first-lien, unitranche, second-lien, or even mezzanine loans.

Even though historically senior secured loans have predominated in the direct lending sector, unitranche loans have gained increasing popularity due to their simplicity and because they allow higher leverage. A unitranche structure combines a senior and a junior tranche in one blended loan with one set of legal documentation and one blended rate that incorporates both the senior and junior risk, with a single lien that is often senior, first lien. Borrowers frequently prefer this structure as it offers a "one-stop" source of financing and limited syndication risk. Unitranche debt has usually higher leverage levels than traditional first-lien debt because it mixes a subordinated component that allows it to go deeper into the capital structure, thus allowing more leverage.

The MMDL segment has struggled to find a place in institutional investors' asset allocation among direct lending managers. However, more funds are being carved out from their allocations and into MMDL due to recent yield compressions in traded products. Institutional investors find this segment attractive because of the floating nature of the loans, high current yields, and lack of correlation with traded assets. The stronger covenant packages, more frequent and transparent financial reporting, and higher amortization payments have contributed to capital preservation and lower default rates among borrowers. As a result, the amount of capital that has been raised to meet this emerging non-bank lending opportunity has increased over the past few years. Recent studies show that while the supply of institutional capital has increased in the middle market, there are still significant opportunities to lend in this segment of the economy. Preqin reports that as of December 2017, U.S. private equity dry powder totaled $530 billion, reflecting considerable opportunities in sponsored buyouts, which could be larger depending on the leverage strategy defined by each sponsor. Private equity dry powder in Europe is also at historical high levels, rising from €90 million in 2012 to €150 million in 2017. There is a large amount of dry powder and strong middle market company performance that will drive growth in MMDL credit demand.

Thanks to the growing acceptance of direct lending among institutional investors and the significant amount of credit demand, the number of MMDL fund managers has also increased in recent years. Managers focus on certain segments where they have competitive advantages in sourcing, underwriting, or managing loans. Few managers focus solely on one market, given that deal flow can be sporadic, and most managers seek to build a diversified portfolio. Investors will seek to invest in managers that have scale, origination advantages, and significant credit expertise. There are three main origination channels for middle-market loans:

1. **Sponsored:** Deals are sourced from financial sponsors such as private equity funds that look to secure credit for a portfolio company or for an LBO. The sponsored channel provides advantages for the lender, by investing alongside financial sponsors that are control oriented, take an active role in managing portfolio companies, and have specific insights into industry trends. Additionally, sponsors usually support their portfolio companies by providing additional equity for growth, acquisitions, or even for liquidity if necessary. While building relationships with private equity sponsors can take considerable time and resources, it will often lead to further opportunities in the future.

2. **Direct-to-company:** Unsponsored transactions or direct to company transactions require continuous communication and relationship building with management teams, law firms, business brokers, and

accounting firms. These transactions require more involvement from the lender in the due diligence process and the portfolio monitoring, given that the lender is likely to represent the only institutional capital within the company. Despite being more labor-intensive transactions, direct to company loans offer attractive returns, and in some cases, higher risk-adjusted returns.

3. **Capital markets:** This channel typically involves participation in a third-party distributed investment that is usually efficiently priced. However, given that these transactions are intermediated, terms have often already been negotiated.

Due to the increased competition in the MMDL segment, managers now seek to differentiate their investment strategies in an effort to boost returns. The recent success of unitranche loans is an example of this approach. For managers, unitranche loans have provided a way to boost returns without adding to the proportion of subordinated loans in portfolios. Other lenders are now introducing a component of PIK as a strategy to enhance returns, but simultaneously create a more back-ended structure. PIK increases the duration risk of the loan but it also increases overall returns at the end of the loan if the PIK is fully delivered. Investors should keep a careful eye on the structures and terms of new loans, as a range of increasingly complex structures have emerged, effectively replicating a variety of conventional financing options. Loans are now incorporating second-lien and even mezzanine debt into the portfolio. However, almost 80% of all loans still use simpler term-loan or term-loan-plus-revolver structures.

U.S. senior debt funds tend to produce higher returns than European funds, largely due to the higher leverage used at the fund level, which averages between 1.0x and 2.5x on senior debt. European institutional investors are not prepared to tolerate this amount of leverage; the average tolerable leverage in Europe is between 0.0x and 1.0x. To compensate for this lower tolerance, European funds have historically involved more PIK and less cash-pay structures than their U.S. equivalents (a 50/50 structure is a reasonable standard in Europe). Another difference is the key contribution of origination fees, which forms a greater portion of the overall return in European funds. Origination fees are approximately 2.5–4.0% in Europe, compared to 1.0–2.0% in the United States, and are also split in different ways. In addition, the majority of the direct lending transactions in Europe involve only one lender, who not only retains the origination fee but also puts together the covenant and holds more influence in an event of default, increasing the likelihood of recovering the loan. The process of workout and bankruptcy also differs between the United States and Europe. In the former country, the process is driven by Chapter 11 of the U.S. Bankruptcy Code, while in Europe these processes tend to be more consensual and amicable. Other dissimilarities emerge from the manager fee, which can follow two different structures: carry and catch-up (used with over 90% of managers) and carry-only (used with less than 10% of managers). The carry-only structure is preferred by investors due to lower fee leakage. However, hurdle rates tend to be smaller, contributing to higher-than-ideal fee leakage. Management fees of 1.0% plus carry of 15% tend to be the industry norm for unlevered senior debt funds, with averages noticeably higher in the United States than in Europe.

Mezzanine debt funds

Private limited partnerships under the form of mezzanine funds are the most common way for investors to access the mezzanine debt market. This access is typically achieved through capital commitments that are aggregated with the express purpose of investing in mezzanine debt. Asset management firms usually organize these funds and act as the GP. The GP seeks attractive risk-adjusted returns for the partnership, while maintaining a diversified portfolio of investments.

In the middle market, mezzanine debt is generally issued through privately negotiated transactions. A mezzanine fund manager's decision to extend credit to a borrower is usually based on the issuer's ability to generate free cash flow (as opposed to being based on asset backing), and on the growth prospects for the business and industry. Before investing, mezzanine fund managers typically perform extensive private-side due diligence over a four- to six-week period. As part of this due diligence, mezzanine lenders receive greater access to company information, such as historical financial statements, earnings and audit reports, and environmental or other expert analyses; this gives mezzanine fund managers the ability to better understand the borrower, negotiate terms, and structure loans in ways that are appropriate for the underlying business. In addition, fund managers also have the opportunity to interact with the company's management several times before an investment is made.

After making an investment, mezzanine funds usually receive monthly or quarterly financial statements. Furthermore, many mezzanine fund managers negotiate board observation rights as part of the terms of their investment. Receiving board of director materials and attending the meetings, alongside (often frequent) dialogue with company owners and management, enables mezzanine fund managers to closely monitor their investments and stay ahead of potential business issues. It also helps to stay up to date with company performance should amendments to the credit documents be necessary.

Although debt financing to large corporate issuers has increasingly become covenant-lite with no-maintenance financial covenants (e.g., a maximum leverage ratio), mezzanine fund managers continue to demand both incurrence and maintenance covenants. These covenants provide additional risk management and enforcement tools should the business underperform. Fund managers often work with borrowers to take proactive steps to upgrade operating performance and maximize liquidity. These proactive steps may include cost reductions, divestitures of less productive assets, and changes to operations or management. Further steps to address underperformance may even include voluntarily deferring the cash portion of interest due on the mezzanine debt in order to help the company avoid defaulting on its senior secured debt. Senior secured debt for larger issuers is more likely to be syndicated and may include lenders who are less willing to work through cyclical downturns.

Distressed debt funds

Distressed investment funds refer to either (1) funds that follow a private equity style of distressed investing (further described below), or (2) hedge funds investing in distressed securities.[8] Three types of investment strategies can be classified as "distressed private equity":

1. **Loan-to-own investment (or control investing)** is a medium- to long-term investment strategy whereby the fund manager purchases undervalued distressed debt securities to gain control of the issuing company (or a blocking position vis-à-vis other creditors) and turn it around. The manager often intends to facilitate a recapitalization of the company that may include the fund's injection of new equity capital, together with the arrangement of rescue financing. Most distressed funds follow this type of strategy.

2. **Turnaround investment** see the fund manager focus on purchasing equity in companies that are in distress, aiming to subsequently restore the company to profitability.

---

[8] Hedge funds typically invest over a short to medium term, do not require control, and trade only on public information. In this respect, hedge funds take a relatively passive approach to distressed investing.

3. **Special situations investment** focuses on event-driven or complex situations, where a fund manager may be able to exploit pricing inefficiencies due to an expected or actual significant event.

The focus of this section is on the first type of strategy. In contrast to the investment strategies of direct lending and mezzanine funds, which follow passive investments, loan-to-own investing involves a more active approach and constitutes a medium- to long-term strategy that is consistent with the life of the typical private equity fund.[9] Given the complexity involved, we allocate more space to the discussion of this investment strategy in a separate section below.

LOAN-TO-OWN INVESTING

In a loan-to-own strategy, the fund manager acquires distressed debt securities of a company with the intention of acquiring a controlling position through financial restructuring which can take place in court.[10] Subsequent to the financial restructuring of the company, distressed fund managers implement an operational turnaround and sell the company. There is no standard definition of a distressed debt instrument; however, the "distressed" designation is usually based on a significantly high yield over government debt (1,000 basis points or more) and/or a significant discount to par (80% or more, although by some measures, a discount of 30–40% could be considered distressed). Therefore, high-yield bonds (rated below BBB/Baa) and leveraged loans make up the bulk of the pool of potential distressed securities. Distressed investments may also include investments in other parts of a distressed company's capital structure, including investment in more subordinated debt tranches, convertible debt, preferred shares, warrants, and common stock (both public and privately traded), as well as acquisitions of trade claims (claims of suppliers, vendors, landlords, etc.) against the distressed company.

A typical first step in a distressed investment strategy is to implement a debt-for-equity exchange which involves a reduction of the company's debt burden and diluting or eliminating the incumbent equity owners. In many situations, the distressed fund manager often facilitates a further re-capitalization of the company with "new money," which may include the injection of new equity capital and the arrangement of new debt financing—sometimes based on super-senior basis such as debt-in-possession (DIP) in the United States. As a result of these factors, the execution of this type of investment is often time intensive and, in some cases, may involve a structured non-public due diligence process.

An alternative to the strategy described above is to pursue directly the acquisition of assets or subsidiaries of the bankrupt company through an asset sale or divestiture. For example, the U.S. Bankruptcy Code allows for an asset sale procedure known as a "Section 363 Sale." In this procedure, a distressed fund manager can acquire the assets of a bankrupt company without its liabilities.

---

[9] Occasionally, a passive investment may be a stepping stone to a control implementation approach, with the discovery of new information. Non-control strategies derive returns from passively holding securities—where the value of securities is enhanced through negotiations during the bankruptcy process.

[10] It is important to note that historically there were generally no reporting requirements for the transfer of debt. Therefore, such a strategy to control a corporation can often pass unnoticed during the secondary market trading of securities; this has been noted by private equity sponsors who now frequently impose various forms of transfer restrictions.

Distressed companies

Companies whose debt instruments become distressed often have one or more of the following characteristics: (i) high leverage, (ii) poor cash management, (iii) poor or declining margins, (iv) a poor competitive position, or (v) poor capital allocation (overexpansion or over-diversification). Additionally, the distressed companies may have been negatively impacted by economic disruption, business cycles, or market shifts, or become subject to major legal liabilities or regulatory concerns. These indicative conditions may, however, be present in companies that never become truly distressed.

When a firm reaches distress, it usually has to decide between two courses of action: *liquidate* or *restructure*. This decision is made based on the value of the reorganized firm compared to the liquidation value. Reorganization may be achieved through financial reorganization, aimed at reducing the value of outstanding claims on the company, or through operational reorganization, aimed at increasing the value of the firm's assets. If the valuation for the restructured firm is greater than the liquidation value, then the firm should restructure so that the claimholders recover more out of their claims on the firm. If the "ongoing concern value" is less than the liquidation value, the firm should be liquidated, as it is this course of action that will provide the greatest coverage to the claims of the claimholders; the liquidation or restructuring can be done inside or outside of bankruptcy court. Increasingly, in modern economies based on soft rather than hard assets (whether trademarks, knowhow, the installed base, or a book of subscription paying customers), "liquidation" takes the form of selling the going concern parts of the business.[11]

A distressed company's prospects are in danger of getting worse as time passes, with the company's value declining further until the sources of distress are alleviated. From an operational perspective, more accounts payable become due. Upon learning of the distress, suppliers may tighten credit terms or demand payment up front. In addition, customers may be lost and those that remain may delay or suspend payments, increasing delinquencies. All of these developments put increased stress on cash management. From a financial perspective, debt service may become past due (payment default) and financial covenants may be breached (technical default). The company may also face a looming debt maturity. As the situation worsens, opportunities for out-of-court debt restructuring with relationship banks and original syndicate members may be lost, as banks seek to reduce their exposure by selling their positions in the secondary market. If the distressed company enters into court-supervised restructuring procedures (e.g., Chapter 11 in the United States or a Scheme of Administration in the United Kingdom), the operational and financial strains increase, and the recovery rates of creditors typically decrease. Consequently, court-supervised procedures often reduce the company's value. A prepackaged restructuring, where the parties have agreed to terms before going to court, can mitigate or avoid this outcome.

The financial position of a distressed company is characterized by face value (par) debt claims that exceed the value of the company as a going concern. Thus, distressed debt funds only purchase the debt at a discount to par. In contrast, the original lenders and debt purchasers in the secondary market (before the company became distressed) hope to avoid or minimize write-downs. Furthermore, any secured creditors may be more willing to see the company liquidate collateral assets to repay them, thereby disrupting the business and leaving minimal recovery for unsecured creditors and equity owners. Finally, equity owners often hope to salvage value and, in the case of private companies (including sponsor- or family-controlled companies), retain

---

[11] If the value of the ongoing concern is greater than the liquidation value, the difference between the two is negotiated among the different claimholders. The law is rarely clear on how this difference in value is distributed. The only rule is that each claimholder cannot receive less than it would have if the firm were liquidated. This invariably gives rise to lengthy negotiations and "games" that claimholders play, whether they are in court or out of court.

control. The asymmetry of rights and interests among these various claimants drives negotiations in the restructuring process.

The fulcrum security and valuation of a distressed company

Valuation is used to determine what is available for distribution among the competing claimants on the company, with reference to the priority of claims. In a hypothetical liquidation, the majority (if not all) of the company's value could be distributed to the secured creditors and those preferred by law (e.g., employees, taxes, and pension funds). In this scenario, equity would be worthless in the strict sense, and the same may be said for unsecured debt, depending on the valuation range. In such a situation, the distressed company valuation identifies the *fulcrum security*. The fulcrum security is the last class of securities where the distressed company's value can provide any recovery, and is therefore the security most likely to be exchanged for equity in a restructuring. Securities junior to the fulcrum security would be entitled to nothing under strict priorities. Hence, distressed funds following a controlling strategy attempt to build a significant position in the fulcrum security via acquisitions in the secondary debt market.

The perceived fulcrum security may change depending on the valuation thesis. A higher valuation would indicate that the fulcrum security lies lower in the capital structure; this is because there is more value to be distributed, implying that the senior claimants can be paid in full, with the remaining value being distributed to more junior claimants. Accordingly, as a rule of thumb, the most senior debt claimants will prefer the lowest (or the most conservative) valuation of the company, because this will imply that most (or all) available value should be distributed to them. Any valuation of a distressed company by distressed fund managers must consider

- **the company's going concern value** under a range of outcomes under financial restructuring, including sensitivities for various assumptions; and

- **the company's liquidation value**, an estimate of how much the distressed company's entire assets could be sold for if restructuring fails.

The purpose of the valuation exercise is to identify a defensible range of values of the distressed company in order to determine the fulcrum security and the appropriate price range for purchasing it. Relative (multiples-based) valuation and discounted cash flow (DCF) valuation are typically employed to consider the company as a going concern. The distressed company's going concern value must then be reduced by the expected costs of financial distress, which are calculated by multiplying the estimated costs of financial distress by the estimated probability of distress. The estimated probability of distress is based on statistical data (Altman Z-score, credit rating information, and other sources):

$$Distressed\ company\ value = Going\ Concern\ Value - P_{distress}(Going\ Concern\ Value - Liquidation\ Value)$$
$$= Going\ Concern\ Value - Expected\ Financial\ Distress$$

The costs of financial distress include direct costs (e.g., the fees of lawyers, accountants, and advisers called in to assist the distressed company) and indirect costs (e.g., the costs of lost customers and employees and reduced productivity), as well as increased financing costs. Indirect costs are especially difficult to estimate accurately. Because of this difficulty, the costs of financial distress are often estimated by calculating the difference between the company's going concern value and its liquidation value (since this is the value lost if the company is liquidated).

For multiples-based valuation, care must be taken in selecting the peer group. Some peers may be more instructive than others due to their similarities with the company (including being under distress). Peers composed of only healthy firms may distort the analysis. Rather than a trailing twelve-month EBITDA, EV/EBITDA multiples used by distressed fund managers often employ trough EBITDA (the lowest EBITDA expected from the company, based on the economic cycle) to provide a conservative valuation.[12]

For DCF valuations, the impact of loss carryforwards (from losses accumulated during the period of distress) and proposed changes to the company's capital structure (as a result of restructuring) must be considered in calculating free cash flows. From the point of view of a distressed fund manager seeking control, this type of fundamental valuation should also consider the free cash flow generated from improvements that could be implemented under an investor-influenced restructuring plan and/or assumption of post-restructuring management control.

In light of the different approaches available and the wide range of defensible assumptions, highly disparate views of the distressed company's true value may develop among the competing claimants.

In most cases, the value of the distressed company as a going concern will exceed liquidation value. Claimants will therefore have a collective tendency to prefer restructuring over liquidation (subject to the threats of holdouts: claimants who attempt to extract value in exchange for their agreement with a proposed restructuring plan). In cases where the distressed company cannot reasonably be expected to generate positive cash flow in the future, however, value would usually be maximized under liquidation.

Liquidation value may be estimated with reference to the carrying value of the distressed company's assets, subject to agreed recovery discounts. These discounts may vary depending on the sector and company. For example, land and buildings and capital equipment may be expected to yield a high recovery rate, whereas accounts receivable may be subject to a significant discount due to expected collection issues. In all cases, however, liquidation is at least a hypothetical outcome, which will become a reality if the claimants cannot agree to a restructuring plan. Therefore, negotiations occur against the backdrop of the claimant priorities in liquidation.

Legal considerations

Laws and practices regarding bankruptcy and reorganizations vary considerably from country to country. Consequently, a sophisticated understanding of varied proceedings is important in navigating distressed investment opportunities, especially in cases involving multinational corporations (where multiple proceedings in different countries may be required). U.S. bankruptcy law is considered relatively debtor friendly, with Chapter 11 providing a well-known regime for court-supervised restructuring while the debtor continues to operate its business. Chapter 11 has been internationally influential, as countries modernize their laws.

The precise priorities of claimants on the distressed company vary depending on the jurisdictions to which the company is subject. In this respect, the rule of *absolute priority* (in the United States), or a similar principle

---

[12] Revenue multiples may need to be used if the distressed company's EBITDA is negative.

in other countries, plays an important role. According to this rule, all claims have different priorities, and each claim must be made complete *before* the claims with the next highest priority (seniority) can receive anything. Capital structure outside of distress generally provides that secured creditors rank ahead of unsecured creditors and equity ranks last. This simplistic description may be subject to considerable complexity, including multiple classes of debt, different types of security being given to different types of lenders, and debt being issued at different levels in the corporate structure. In distress, the company must also deal with claims from trade creditors, employees, pensions, and the government (unpaid taxes and other charges), among others.

Insolvency laws typically provide a detailed priority for application of proceeds if a company is liquidated, and these laws can supplement or (in some cases) supersede the expressed contractual and security arrangements put in place. The United Kingdom, for example, generally supports the following priority: [13]

1. Secured creditors benefiting from "fixed charges" (security over specifically identified assets of the company).

2. Liquidation fees and expenses.

3. Preferred creditors (which include claims by employees for unpaid wages and benefits, and contributions to pensions and state benefit schemes).

4. Ordinary unsecured creditors in relation to a "prescribed part" of up to £600,000 from the proceeds of assets subject to a "floating charge" (a general security interest over present and future assets).

5. Secured creditors benefiting from a floating charge.

6. Ordinary unsecured creditors.

7. Subordinated creditors.

8. Interest on debts accrued after the company went into liquidation.

9. Equity.

Alternatively, the U.S. Bankruptcy Code Chapter 11 procedure, which is considered a model for restructuring procedures, makes no distinction between "fixed" and "floating" securities, and secured creditors generally rank first, followed by administrative expenses and claims with statutory preference, general unsecured creditors, subordinated claims, and equity.

Cross-border insolvency proceedings have been rationalized to some extent by the adoption of *The UNCITRAL Model Law on Cross-Border Insolvency* by the United Nations Commission on International Trade Law (1997). This model law is intended to address scenarios where an insolvent company has assets or creditors in more than one country and facilitates cooperation between courts. To date, 23 countries have adopted this law (in the United States, it appears in Chapter 15 of the Bankruptcy Code). This regime provides a basis for some consistency across jurisdictions.

In addition to priorities, the types of issues that should be considered by a distressed fund manager when evaluating a jurisdiction's insolvency laws with regard to a distressed investment opportunity include:

---

[13] Other English Commonwealth countries have adopted similar approaches, although there may be considerable variation in the details.

- whether there is an automatic stay or moratorium on enforcement/remedies, the duration of this, and any exceptions available (e.g., for particular types of collateral or contracts);

- the extent to which contracts can be rejected or disclaimed by the company;

- whether the court has authority to consolidate entities and affect structural subordination;

- the types of courts and types of judges that handle insolvency cases (local or national, generalists or specialists);

- the typical duration of an insolvency case (including any particular mandatory deadlines or timelines);

- the types of security interests available and the remedies associated with those interests; and

- whether incumbent management can remain in control of the company during the proceedings (i.e., debtor-in-possession proceedings).

Distressed fund return drivers and exits

The investment returns of distressed funds that follow control strategies are realized through exchanging the fulcrum security for a controlling equity stake in the distressed company and subsequently selling this stake at a higher valuation. These returns are possible, in part, because the nature of distressed securities encourages the market to undervalue the fulcrum security before the restructuring. Relevant factors include

- the lack of equal access to up-to-date information (with companies often suspending or delaying public filings and releasing material non-public information only to incumbent lenders);

- price pressure on debt securities that have recently been downgraded, due to their sale by asset managers that are only authorized to hold investment grade securities or "performing debt";

- banks selling distressed loans at prices below intrinsic value to manage non-performing asset ratios and to shrink their balance sheets;

- complexities in accurately valuing a distressed company and its debt securities;

- the need for specialist knowledge regarding insolvency regimes and legal issues;

- other investors' unwillingness or inability to be interventionist by participating in restructuring discussions and taking control;

- general illiquidity with respect to distressed securities; and

- in a downturn, the inability of hedge fund investors to maintain long-term positions in debt securities when fund investors are withdrawing capital from the hedge fund.

The distressed fund manager can exploit these market inefficiencies to buy distressed securities below their intrinsic value. Accordingly, distressed fund managers generally require capital markets' trading capabilities for executing bond and loan trades, as well as a sourcing network that includes institutions that may need to dispose of non-performing loans and other troubled assets from time to time.

It is essential that distressed fund managers gain control of the distressed company. This control is achieved by accumulating a sufficient interest in the fulcrum security (to be converted to equity) and, if necessary, by contributing new money in the restructuring. Gaining control gives the investor the benefit of the upside of post-restructuring improvements in value. The investor may also continue to participate in the debt, for downside protection and yield returns.

The post-restructuring capital structure is based on the consensual agreement of claimants in an out-of-court restructuring, or a court-mandated outcome, which may include a *cram down*, (i.e., the imposition of a plan without the consent of some claimants, typically those junior to the fulcrum security). The distressed fund manager would propose a view of the distressed company's appropriate capital structure in line with its valuation assumptions. The proposed capital structure will usually be based on

- estimated sustainable cash flow and cash flow available to service debt;

- estimated stability of cash flows and any cyclicality;

- leverage levels within the distressed company's peer group; and

- leverage levels in relation to the company's enterprise value.

Distressed fund managers typically improve the distressed company's prospects by originating, or contributing to, the *turnaround plan*—that is, participating in the restructuring process and gaining control post-restructuring. During the investment holding period, the manager aims to improve the value of the company in ways consistent with the approaches used in conventional buyouts, as well as undertaking more extensive operational turnaround efforts, as necessary. Incumbent management may have already begun an operational turnaround effort prior to the financial restructuring. The process can involve significant cost cutting, changes in strategy, divestments, acquisitions ("add-on" transactions), capital expenditures, and organizational restructuring, among other initiatives. Operational restructuring steps may necessarily involve departures from the pre-investment thesis because some challenges may not become apparent or materialize until after the investor has taken the reins as the controlling shareholder.

The distressed funds ultimately exit the investments through one of the same routes available in conventional buyouts: an IPO or a sale to a strategic or financial investor. If selling the entire company is not possible, the fund manager may break up the enterprise into separate functional entities (disposing of some and retaining the balance), or leverage the company and distribute the cash. Additionally, where a loan-to-own strategy has not been fully realized with a control position, debt positions that have been accumulated in earlier phases can be sold, hopefully providing an appropriate return. Naturally, the timing of the transaction and the cyclical nature of the companies are important considerations when selecting an exit plan.

RISK MANAGEMENT ISSUES SPECIFIC TO PRIVATE DEBTS FUNDS

The risks that debt funds face are unusually difficult to predict. Debt securities' returns are a combination of credit risk premium and the illiquidity premium from holding less liquid securities that are issued by private companies. Credit risks are mainly driven by the possibility that borrowers will default. If they end up in a bankruptcy court, the recovery of capital is often beyond the control of the debt fund managers. Thus, typical risks of private debt funds include:

- borrower-specific recovery risks,

- risks from a general widening of credit spreads, and

- illiquidity.

In the case of distressed funds that follow control investing strategies, other risks include plan risk execution risks, court negotiation risks that can affect the ultimate recovery, and escalating legal costs during the bankruptcy process, including those from litigation with subordinated creditors.

Many of these fund managers are forced to devote substantial resources toward managing their reputations, media coverage, and relationships with the stakeholders of distressed companies. Therefore, they favor negotiated outcomes and often avoid taking adversarial positions during deals.

Below, we discuss the main risks faced by debt funds as well as their mitigation strategies.

Borrower-specific recovery risks

Debt investments can lose significant value if borrower-specific, event-driven situations lead to default. In such a situation, fund managers need to deal with the reorganization of the borrower, which is a complex legal and financial process. Hence, it is important to identify and act on credit issues as early as possible. Some risk mitigation strategies that relate to borrower-specific default risk may involve

- carefully screening borrowers,

- requiring extensive protection (via covenants, pricing, collateral, etc.) in the debt contract or investing only in debt securities that have strong security features,

- employing financial advisers, legal experts, or industry experts to conduct in-depth valuation analyses (or developing these skills in house),

- developing a good understanding of the bankruptcy laws that apply to the debt security purchased.

Widening of credit spreads

The difference between the yield on a debt security and a government bond is called the "credit spread" (or sometimes, the "yield spread"). As such, the credit spread reflects the extra compensation that debt funds receive for bearing credit risk. Therefore, the total yield on a debt security is a function of both the yield on the government debt and the credit spread, which is greater for lower-rated debt securities. Predicting changes in a credit spread is difficult for a fund manager because it depends on both the specific borrower and the overall debt market conditions.

After purchasing a debt security with a fixed rate, a debt fund benefits from declining interest rates and from a narrowing of the credit spread, which contributes to a lessening yield to maturity of newly issued debt securities; this in turn drives up the price of the debt security initially purchased. On the other hand, rising interest rates and a widening of the credit spread works against the fund by causing a higher yield to maturity and a lower price for the security. A slowing economy tends to widen credit spreads, as companies are more likely to default. Conversely, an economy emerging from a recession tends to narrow the spread, as companies are (theoretically) less likely to default in a growing economy.

Fund managers have a couple of options at their disposal to help mitigate the interest rate risks, particularly an increasing interest rate on government debt. The most popular strategies include the following:[14]

- Buying interest rate futures on government bonds. These trades enable managers to lock in a certain interest rate and hedge their portfolios. Other interest rate derivatives can be also employed (e.g., interest rate options, interest rate swaps, etc.)

- Investing in floating rate debt securities.

Illiquidity

Debt funds tend to invest in securities, loans, or other assets for which only a limited liquid market exists. Interest rates, the price of securities, and participation by other investors in the financial market often affect the value of these securities. In addition, some securities may be subject to legal or other restrictions on transfers. Accordingly, market prices for such assets tend to be volatile, and fund managers may be unable to sell the debt securities at what they perceive to be fair value. Moreover, the sale of illiquid assets and restricted securities often requires more time, and results in higher charges from market intermediaries in the secondary market; this is why most debt funds tend to have long lock-up structures. Fund managers can mitigate illiquidity risks by:

- investing in debt securities with a robust over-the-counter market,

- investing in debt securities issued by companies that are not controlled by an external single majority holder, and

- diversifying the fund's portfolio across many types of securities, geographies, and industries.

CONCLUSION

The confluence of bank regulations, low yields on traditional fixed income, and a strong demand for capital from U.S. and European corporate borrowers has convinced many alternative fund managers to enter the private debt fund space. The conditions that brought opportunity and growth to this market are likely to remain in place for some time.

Historically, European debt markets had a strictly national focus. However, this focus has shifted as the markets become more integrated to serve the full European Union. Further, demand for direct financing in Europe has been outpacing supply, as demonstrated by the significant increase in the number of European direct lending managers. A similar integration trend has been in place for over a decade in the United States, where it has provided much-needed fuel for growth. It is therefore logical to assume that the EU model is likely to follow the American banking system toward smaller, more sustainable balance sheets, thus opening up a mid-market lending opportunity for alternative players.

Additional factors are likely to reinforce the growth in private lending, such as the provision of flexible loan terms by private debt fund managers, the increased familiarity of corporate borrowers with private debt fund lenders, and the validation provided by the AIFMD and the Dodd-Frank Act, which have increased

---

[14] The inverse of these strategies can also be used to protect against falling interest rates.

investors' confidence in the alternative debt funds market; the latter factor will probably lead to rising investor allocations to private debt over the long term.

REFERENCES

Ares (2018), "Opportunities in Global Direct Lending," Ares Management L.P.

Atkinson, T. (2017), "Direct Lending," Meketa Investment Group

Bfinance (2017), "Direct Lending: What's different now?" Bfinance White Paper

In his own words: Lemy Gresh, Managing Partner and Founder, MV Credit Partners LLP

The most critical activity in the management of a private debt fund is the daily monitoring of the various loans in the portfolio and insuring that the vast majority continue to perform. Credit losses are by far the biggest risk factor in the business. From time to time, and more so during economic downturns, borrowers face financial difficulties, which brings us to the "black art" of workouts. Financial difficulties arise because of technological changes, fraud, poor capex implementation, and of course poor management.

This aspect of investing is where extensive experience (i.e., "gray hair") has a competitive advantage: the ability to appraise the quality of management. Appraisal may involve reviewing management's prior experience, referencing the managers with their former colleagues, and attending management presentations to ask questions.

What should creditors do when confronted with a borrower in distress? In the case of borrowers who require a substantial amount of effort to turn a 5% recovery into a 10% recovery, my advice is to collaborate with a distressed fund and let this fund take over the company. In the case of a fundamentally sound business where time—and sometimes new management—can re-establish the business on a sound track to turn a 50% recovery into a 100% recovery, the strategy is to design a recovery plan with the private equity sponsor.

I am aware that some people believe that restructuring 101 dictates that equity should collaborate with the senior debt in order to strike out the mezzanine debt. However, I have yet to see an example of this approach actually work, given that most senior lenders know that they are unable to own and manage their borrowers. Therefore, for a mezzanine lender, the strategy is to cajole the private equity sponsor into injecting new money in the business. This approach requires designing all kinds of waterfalls upon an eventual exit in order to convince the private equity sponsor that it is not throwing good money after bad, and to demonstrate that the mezzanine lenders are a force of stability by fending off loan-to-own funds, designing a new management incentive plan, changing management (as some individuals are terrific growth facilitators but bad cost cutters and vice versa), and presenting the senior lenders with a sound new financial structure. Like most unpleasant things, if they don't kill you, workouts make you a better and wiser investor, with just a bit more gray hair.

Finally, some lenders (particularly banks) transfer distressed loans to a specialist workout group. While this choice is understandable, it is not necessarily good practice given that such specialists are incentivized to outperform the loan's internal transfer price. We believe that whoever provided the initial loan should also be responsible for monitoring and, if required, restructuring.

16 Real Estate Private Equity

Buy land, they're not making it anymore.
Mark Twain

INTRODUCTION

From an investment perspective, real estate is considered an alternative asset class along with hedge funds, private equity, and infrastructure. The sub-segment of the real estate asset class that allows investors to pool their capital through funds is commonly referred to as "real estate private equity" (REPE) or "private equity real estate" (PERE). Both terms refer to equity and debt investments in real estate via private equity-type funds. These funds are characterized by a medium-term investment horizon, an active management strategy implemented by the fund manager, and a significant upfront capital commitment over several years. The strategy of such funds may cover anything from a moderate market repositioning of properties to extensive property developments and redevelopments.

Real estate is by far the most significant store of wealth. The total value of all developed real estate globally (i.e., commercial and residential property, forestry and agricultural real estate) was estimated to be over $280 trillion by Savills Word Research (2018). To put this number into perspective, it represents about 3.5 times the total global GDP. Approximately 78% of the total real estate value is residential, followed by commercial real estate at 12%, and agricultural real estate at 10%. Although real estate is a vast asset class, even when considering only the investable portion, it has been traditionally considered an alternative investment.[1]

Historically, large institutional investors have allocated only 5–10% of their portfolios to real estate. This lower allocation to real estate is mainly due to real estate's fundamental characteristics—tangibility, illiquidity, information asymmetry, and hybrid returns of income and capital growth—which we discuss later in this chapter. The debate on real estate allocations in investment portfolios has been very active for the past decade. While some investors argue that real estate allocations should reflect their market weight, others believe that real estate should mainly be held through listed entities. Nevertheless, major investors have been steadily increasing their allocation to real estate. According to Preqin, US (European) investors' target allocations to real estate have been climbing over the past several years, rising from an average of 6% of total assets under management to a level of about 8% (10%) by the end of 2018. While real estate investments have allowed these investors to diversify their portfolios, they have also performed well in terms of delivering good risk-adjusted returns.

REPE funds are typically closed-ended funds and have a lock-up period of up to 10 years, similar to private equity funds. They raise a fixed amount of capital during an initial fundraising phase which could take from six months to two years depending on the manager. As with most private equity funds, capital commitments cannot be made once the fund is closed, meaning investors can only enter the fund during the capital-raising period, before any investing has occurred. Immediately after the fundraising period, the investment phase of the fund begins. During this phase (which is usually predetermined for five years), the fund makes

---

[1] A large portion of the global real estate stock is held by private individuals or owner-occupiers and thus it is not investable.

investments, although some fund managers choose to leave the investment period open-ended. During the remaining five years, investments are exited to provide fund investors with their pro rata share of the proceeds, after paying management fees. As in the case of the typical private equity fund, these fees include both a fixed management fee as well as carried interest.

PERE funds experienced strong growth over the last few years. The total assets under management (AUM) surpassed $900 billion for the first time at the end of 2018 from only $391 billion at the end of 2009. In terms of fundraising, North America is the dominant geographic area with the largest number of PERE funds raised and aggregate capital secured (over 65% of the global total). PERE funds focused on Asia are growing the fastest, merely reflecting the fact that Asia dominates the global real estate stock. The market is relatively concentrated with the largest 50 funds in the market consistently getting about 60% of the capital raised annually.

One factor that has contributed to the significant increase in the capital managed by PERE funds is the level of capital distributions back to investors. From 2009 to 2016, the level of capital returned to investors increased year on year, with net cash flows turning positive in 2013 and continuing to be positive until 2018. This means that, despite increasing their target allocations to real estate, LPs continued to receive more capital back from PERE funds than the capital drawn down. As a result, many investors continued to reallocate the capital received back to real estate, helping to maintain strong fundraising levels over the recent years. Exhibit 1 shows annual fundraising levels over the last 15 years.

Exhibit 1: Annual global private real estate fundraising, 2004 - 2018

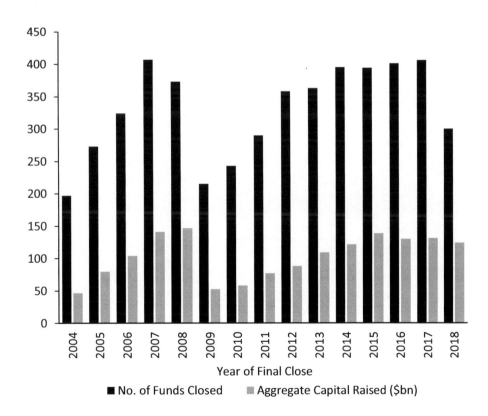

Source: Preqin

INVESTING IN REAL ESTATE

Characteristics of real estate investments

Before discussing the characteristics of REPE funds, it is necessary to provide an overview of real estate investing. In general, real estate is often thought of as office buildings, high-street retail, warehouses, and residential structures. Fundamentally, however, real estate is nothing more than land. In developed economies, real estate is heavily regulated through zoning regulations which dictate what buildings can be used for, their physical appearance, and whether a building can be developed at all. Regardless of the type of property involved, real estate investments display several key characteristics, outlined below.

Physicality/Tangibility

Real estate is tangible, immovable, and has an inherent physicality. This physicality means that, unlike many other financial asset classes, each asset is unique. Even if two buildings are identical and are erected next to each other, they are still unique because of their separate locations. Anyone who has followed the real estate industry has probably heard the response "location, location, location" to the common question of what is the most important feature in real estate.[2] However, the technology of physical assets has also started to become increasingly important. Sustainable (or "green") real estate has the potential to offer financial benefits to tenants and landlords in addition to its benefits for the environment. While an environmental objective can be met with investor skepticism, effective energy efficiency efforts can be viewed as a proxy for operational excellence. Under this premise, it is easy to connect energy efficiency to an overall improvement in property maintenance and operations, which ultimately benefits investment performance.

Liquidity

Real estate can be very illiquid, and investors generally require compensation for the inherent liquidity risk involved. In addition, real estate markets are cyclical. Due to this cyclicality, and to the herd behavior of investors, many real estate investors take defensive positions in a downturn and are unwilling to transact, causing further price declines and illiquidity. Another reason real estate is not considered a liquid asset is that there are no marketplaces where real estate assets, or portfolios, are traded continuously. There are, of course, platforms where real estate is listed for sale, but these are for marketing purposes rather than for trading. While such marketplaces bring sellers and buyers together, they still cannot overcome the relative illiquidity of the asset.[3]

Transparency and information asymmetry

Due to the unique qualities of real estate, extensive knowledge of both assets and markets is vital. The specificity of a property means that information about that property is unavailable, or at least severely limited, to anyone other than the current owner. This situation creates an information asymmetry between sellers and

---

[2] It is unclear when this phrase originated, but there is written evidence of its use in Chicago as early as 1926, suggesting that it was a familiar expression in the city at that time.

[3] One way to reduce the relative illiquidity of the asset class is to invest in real estate through a dedicated vehicle (e.g., a fund, trust, limited company, or special purpose vehicle (SPV)). The vehicle owns the real estate directly and the investors are free to trade its shares.

buyers of real estate, as well as between investors who regularly transact in a market and those who do not. The due diligence process is one method that real estate investors use to overcome information asymmetry, but even so, the fundamental information asymmetry holds. Transparency can be another issue in certain real estate markets. As there is no marketplace to transact real estate, real estate transactions are instead settled between parties on a discretionary basis. The parties involved hold all the pertinent information about the transaction and can choose not to disclose it.

Transaction costs

Investing in real estate is associated with high costs. The value of real estate is often used in various jurisdictions as a tax base when real estate changes hands. Moreover, real estate transactions typically include additional legal fees, agency fees, and due diligence costs. Real estate also requires active management, which increases operational costs. Those considering investing in real estate, whether directly or indirectly, should consider all costs associated with this type of investment.

The characteristics of real estate investments outlined above bring several attractive benefits to investors in this asset class:

- a local monopoly of space since real estate owners compete—mainly on quality, location, and price—in a limited geographical space.

- stable and predictable returns in the form of rent by commercial, retail, or residential tenants, in addition to capital appreciation.

- an imperfect correlation with other traditional asset classes, such as bonds, equities, and commodities such as gold. Thus, real estate can improve the mean-variance efficiency of investors' portfolio.

- low volatility of intrinsic values due to the tangibility of the underlying assets.

- inflation hedges; cash flows from real estate are usually protected from inflation through indexation or the possibility of rental contract renegotiations.

Types of real estate investment vehicles

Investing in real estate does not necessarily mean acquiring property directly from a seller. There are many ways of financially investing in, or otherwise increasing exposure to, real estate. One way to view the many ways of investing in real estate is to think about exposure to real estate in terms of public versus private investments, or equity versus debt investments (see Exhibit 2). REPE funds usually invest on the private side via both debt and equity instruments.

- **Private equity:** Traditionally, the private equity funds involved in buying a real estate asset uses equity and leverage with bank loans. This kind of real estate exposure is also called a "direct equity investment." Another investment avenue is to gain indirect exposure to the equity side of a real estate investment by investing in a vehicle that owns real estate assets, thus achieving one level (or more) of separation from the assets. The main vehicles in the private market are open-ended and closed-ended real estate funds. *Open-ended* real estate funds enable investors to access unitized real estate

Exhibit 2: Investments in real estate

	Private	Public
Equity	Private equity: • Direct • Indirect	Public equity: • Investment in listed real estate (e.g., Real estate investment trusts, Exchange traded funds)
Debt	Private debt: • Direct (e.g., mortgages, mezzanine) • Indirect (e.g., private equity real estate funds)	Public debt • Investment in public real estate and mortgages (e.g., ABS, MBS, CMBS)

vehicles tailored in many shapes, sizes, and risk profiles. Liquidity is provided through redemptions, usually after a lock-up period, and the redemption price is based on the latest valuations of the properties in the fund. In contrast, *closed-ended* real estate funds, which are really REPE funds, have a 10-year lock-up period. As a result, REPE funds do not provide liquidity through redemptions and are considered riskier investment vehicles than open-ended funds. The larger REPE funds might pursue a combination of investment strategies and are often agnostic about the opportunities they pursue, whereas smaller REPE funds often implement more focused investment strategies. We discuss these strategies in more detail in the section below.

- **Public equity:** Investing in public equity involves buying the listed stock of entities that have real estate exposure. The main two examples of investing in real estate via public markets are (a) real estate investment trusts (REITs), which invest directly in property or mortgages on properties, and (b) real estate mutual funds, which buy equity or debt securities issued by real estate companies. These vehicles offer investors a diversified exposure to real estate at a low cost and with an increased level of liquidity and transparency. Further, since there is no need to pay legal fees, agency fees, or due diligence costs, investors have control and receive undiluted income. However, the market share price of REITs may not always reflect the NAV of its underlying property assets. The share price might have similar volatility to that of the stock market, thus creating a discrepancy about the underlying value of the properties. It is important to note that, in contrast to funds in the private equity market, publicly traded REITs and mutual funds must comply with regulations set forth by the exchange they trade on or by government financial regulators, which typically impose strict liquidity requirements.

- **Private debt:** Private debt involves investing in instruments that have a higher claim on cash flows than the equity holders; this is achieved by either lending directly to real estate investors or committing capital to mezzanine funds that lend to real estate investors. This type of investment usually involves a passive ownership role and the relationships with equity real estate investors are regulated by loan agreements, with stipulated covenants. It is also possible to invest in private real estate debt that is in breach of covenants (i.e., non-performing loans), especially when the original lenders want or need to remove bad debts from their balance sheets. The most common private debt strategies include investing in:

  - structured senior loans - preferred by investors who target a diversified portfolio of senior, first mortgage loans that are secured by high-quality properties;

- mezzanine debt - preferred by investors who want higher yields, the collateral being properties with more volatile income; and

- high-leveraged debt - preferred by investors who want high yields and are willing to finance the acquisition of distressed properties, non-performing loan portfolios, or unrated securitized debt instruments.

- **Public debt:** Investments in publicly traded debt can take many forms, with one example being investments in publicly traded bonds—asset-backed or not—issued by real estate firms. The most common public debt investment vehicles in real estate are asset-backed securities (ABSs), mortgage-backed securities (MBSs), residential mortgage-backed securities (RMBSs), and commercial mortgage-backed securities (CMBSs). Another public debt investment vehicle commonly used in Europe, especially in Germany and Denmark, is a covered bond; the key difference between covered bonds and MBSs is that the banks that make loans and package them into covered bonds keep those loans on their books. CMBSs are securities collateralized by a pool of mortgages in commercial real estate, in which all principal and interest from the mortgages flow to certificate holders in a defined sequence. There are other public debt investments, similar to collateralized mortgage obligations, that are special purpose vehicles used for pooling mortgage loans and issuance of MBS. All these investment vehicles provide hedging opportunities and could be used for addressing the distinctive features and risks of the real estate assets (i.e., separating financial and real rent for property appreciation).

CHARACTERISTICS OF REPE FUNDS

Historical developments

Although leveraged buyout private equity funds existed in the United States since the late 1970s, and real estate seemed to be well suited to this investment model given its capital intensity, no meaningful REPE investments were made until the late 1980s. Until this period, lenders were happy to supply debt equivalent to 100%, or even higher, of the real estate asset values to create tax shields for buyers. However, the U.S. Tax Reform Act of 1986 changed the real estate industry significantly by targeting the tax shields used in real estate investing. This legislation resulted in a downward spiral in real estate values, forcing many borrowers to default and reducing the availability of debt financing. In light of the increased restrictions on lending, REPE funds started to emerge about 10 years after the inception of the private equity buyout industry.

It is not clear which firm first ventured into REPE, but the Zell-Merrill I Real Estate Opportunity Fund raised $409 million in equity commitments in 1988. As with most innovations, this fund arose as an opportunistic solution to pursue distressed real estate investments in the United States. Given that it was no longer possible to invest in real estate without meaningful equity commitments, the late 1980s offered abundant opportunities for investors with access to equity to acquire high-quality real estate at fire-sale prices. Soon after, others also recognized the opportunity. Goldman Sachs launched its first real estate dedicated fund in 1991, the $166 million Whitehall I Fund, which was followed by its $790 million successor, the Whitehall II Fund. Many other investment firms followed, such as the Blackstone Group, Apollo Global Management, Soros Fund Management, and Cerberus Capital Management. Numerous private equity fund managers that focused exclusively on real estate (e.g., Lone Star Funds, Starwood Capital Group, Colony Capital, and Westbrook Partners) also emerged.

Strategies of REPE funds

Like many other asset classes, real estate has its own terminology. When discussing investment strategies, REPE practitioners mainly refer to "core," "core-plus," "value-add," and "opportunistic" strategies. These strategies can be applied to any geography, and there are numerous funds targeting specific countries or regions. Larger funds, however, are usually either global or focused on North America, Europe, or Asia-Pacific.

Core and core-plus strategies

A core strategy fund pursues investments in assets with low to moderate risk, stable cash flows, and no or only a small element of potential active value creation. The assets are of high quality, and have tenants with strong credit ratings and long lease durations. The distinction between core and core-plus is gradual, and difficult to establish firmly. An investment is viewed as core-plus if there is an element of moderate-risk value creation during the expected holding period. The target annual returns for core and core-plus funds are about 8-10%.

Core investments are the least risky, as the properties are generally stabilized and fully leased, particularly to high-quality tenants with low credit risk on long-term leases. Core properties often include Class A buildings located in central business districts of major cities or other highly desirable locations. These properties are well maintained and require little to no renovation work. Therefore, while the assets·do not experience a significant appreciation in value, they provide stable and predictable cash flows, with relatively low risk.

Core-plus real estate funds invest in moderate-risk real estate with moderate return expectations. Investments are predominantly core but with an emphasis on a modest value-add approach. These funds typically focus on Class A or lower-quality buildings that require some minor enhancements. As a result, core-plus investments generally require some additional capital investments.

Value-add strategies

Value-add funds pursue investments with significant opportunities for active value creation, and take moderate levels of risk to achieve their target returns. Assets that fit this strategy frequently exhibit some type of operational or financial problems. It could be that the asset requires physical improvement and/or suffers from capital constraints but can be repositioned in the market by refurbishing or extending it. Value-add strategies could also involve re-gearing of leases (i.e., active management of tenant agreements). There are no locational attributes that characterize where such real estate assets are typically found. The identification of these assets depends on their operational and financial characteristics in the local market. The target annual returns for value-add funds are approximately 12%-15%.

Opportunistic strategies

Opportunistic funds seek opportunities with high-return prospects and are willing to take on considerable risk to realize their desired return. It is not uncommon for opportunistic investors to acquire land or development projects with significant zoning, project, and/or development risk, and to assume market risk during the development period. Often, opportunistic investments also include holdings in distressed portfolios or vehicles, where the fund can invest at a discount to the NAV and pursue workable solutions.

Within this sub-segment of opportunistic REPE funds, there are targeted distressed strategy funds that focus solely on distressed opportunities. The target annual returns for opportunistic funds are about 15%-20%. The opportunistic strategy, together with the value-add strategy, is what is most commonly associated with the REPE industry.

Other strategies

In addition to those outlined above, there are other types of strategies that can be applied to REPE. Distressed strategies, which have been on the rise since the 2008 global financial crisis and the European sovereign debt crisis, are considered a sub-segment of opportunistic strategies. Another recent trend is the rise of dedicated debt strategies—senior stretch, mezzanine, and bridge financing—especially for real estate development. Typically, senior lenders are not active in development financing and require secured cash flows for acquisition financing. Such strategies are targeting the financing void created by new regulations on capital requirements (Basel III) regulating banks to more conservative lending practices.

In reality, many funds pursue a combination of these strategies when underwriting individual deals, which are assessed on a discretionary basis. As with portfolio management in general, REPE funds need to manage their overall exposure and risks. A fund's overall investment strategy is an indication of how it attempts to achieve the returns promised to investors, but that does not necessarily mean each investment is in line with this overarching strategy.

Non-discretionary managers taking a deal-by-deal approach may also focus on individual property types and pursue one of the aforementioned strategies in various geographies, usually targeting investments in retail, logistics, or offices. For example, there are specific funds that focus on the hotel and leisure sectors. Europe has experienced recent growth in funds focused on student housing, aparthotels, and other alternative property segments. Such specialization, of course, is not only true for REPE funds but applies to any type of real estate vehicle.

Structuring of REPE funds

REPE funds are investment vehicles with typical LP-GP structures that have pooled investments from investors who want exposure to the real estate asset class. A REPE fund is set up by a sponsor and the GP who advises and manages the fund. The GP identifies opportunities in the real estate markets and designs a strategy to capitalize on these opportunities. If the investors are interested in the strategy of the fund and believe that the GP can successfully implement the strategy, they provide a designated amount of capital and become LPs in the fund.

REPE funds can be set up in many ways, such as using the trust system, corporation system, or limited partnership or limited liability corporation (LLC) model. The most common type of structure is the LLC model (shown in Exhibit 3).

GPs raise capital from a large set of investors that may include sovereign wealth funds, endowments, foundations, financial institutions, corporations, and pension funds, as well as high-net-worth individuals. The minimum equity commitments are usually substantial (i.e., at least $500,000–1 million). As alternative investment managers, managers of REPE funds fall under the Alternative Investment Fund Managers Directive (AIFMD) introduced by the European Union in 2011. The "passport" required by AIFMD allows managers to market the shares of an alternative investment fund to professional investors.

Exhibit 3: Characteristics and structure of a limited partnership

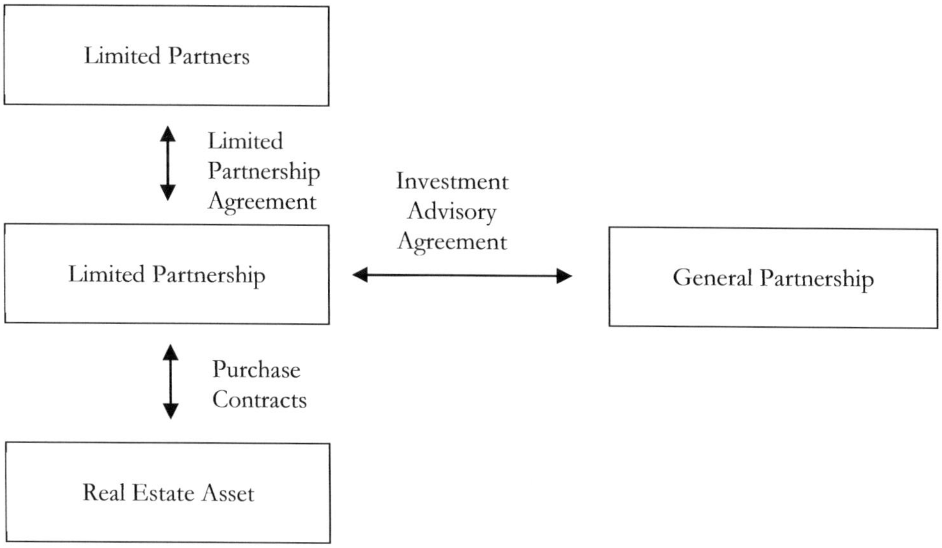

GPs raising capital for a fund have a target size for the equity commitments they seek. LPs who commit early in the fundraising process generally have a stronger position of negotiation and are able to achieve better terms for their investments. A fund will not launch if it has not achieved a minimum level of capital commitments. As in the case of regular private equity funds, it is common for the GP to divide the fundraising into several stages; the first closings occur when a certain threshold of committed equity is reached or when cornerstone investors are confirmed. As REPE funds are usually closed-ended funds, they do not accept new capital after the last closing.

REPE funds target average IRRs of 10–20%, with varying hurdle rates depending on the fund strategy. Most value-add and opportunistic funds have hurdle rates of between 7% and 10%. The managers of these funds have significant flexibility to develop various business plans depending on the real estate asset pursued and investor preferences. As mentioned, the funds can invest in both equity and debt instruments related to real estate.

Investing in REPE funds

LPs must invest their capital in order to generate returns, but they usually have considerable discretion in deciding how to allocate the capital between asset classes, and, even more so, within asset classes. Therefore, it is important to understand how LPs search for new opportunities in the real estate asset class.

A REPE fund is only one type of real estate investment available to LPs. The choice between equity, bonds, or an alternative exposure usually comes down to the portfolio allocation functions for large investment managers. Most LPs rely quite heavily on investment consultants, who are specialists in their respective fields, when making investment decisions. In fact, 45% of institutional investors prefer to use an investment consultant when sourcing new REPE funds, and many of those are mandated to employ such consultants in order to perform an objective screening. Preqin (2015) reports that 26% of LPs mention direct approaches from fund managers as one of the main methods in sourcing new investments, indicating that direct marketing does impact fundraising. Additionally, 34% mention their internal investment teams as one of the main methods of sourcing new investments; these LPs tend to be larger entities, and thus represent more placement power.

When it comes to what institutional investors want to see in a potential investment, about 40% of LPs rate past performance as the principal consideration when choosing to invest with a GP. While, arguably, there is a correlation between the performance of a previous fund and that of its successor, there is also a great deal of variability between different funds. Other factors that LPs consider when investing include the fund's management team (including members' personal incentives, track record, and networks—it is not uncommon for the fund terms to stipulate key people that need to remain with the fund); staff turnover, average tenure, and other similar metrics that help to determine the stability and performance of the fund; the logic and feasibility of the fund's strategy; fees; structure; tax considerations; and other general fund terms.

The role of the GP

In addition to raising external capital, the GP manages the fund throughout its lifetime, which is typically 10 years, although extensions are not uncommon. The GP's role during the life of the fund includes investor relations, reporting, administration, sourcing investments, executing acquisitions, asset management, and value creation, as well as divesting and distributing returns to the investors (see Exhibit 4).

Exhibit 4: GP value creation at various levels

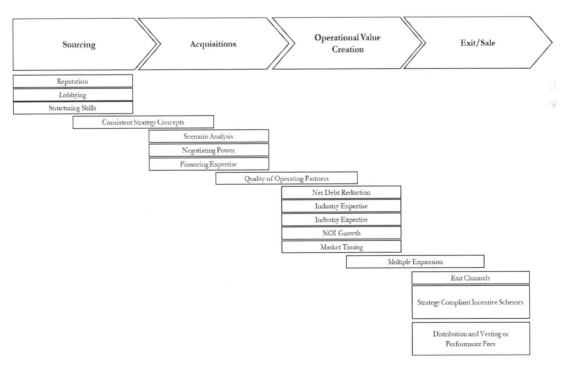

The first step that GPs take is sourcing the market. They are constantly looking for investment opportunities based on the location and condition of properties. Once a property has been identified, the GPs prepare a case for it; to do so, they may analyze the property's market returns and compare them to other investment vehicles, such as equities and bonds or inflation-linked bonds. GPs also look at property performance indices which track retail, office, and industrial spaces in a particular geographical area.[4] Once they gather information from these sources, GPs examine further details of the specific market where the property is located and focus on information such as (a) supply/demand imbalance, (b) recent transactions, (c) capitalization (i.a., cap) rates, (d) vacancy rates, (e) rents, and most importantly, (f) the local economy.

As it is costly for LPs to have capital committed but undeployed (i.e., not "at work" or sitting as "dry powder"), the GP is under pressure to find investment opportunities quickly. Hence, there is usually an overlap between the fundraising and the investment period when the GP is seeking opportunities to deploy the committed capital. If GPs find a property that fits the fund's investment criteria and the market conditions allow them to buy it, then an investment proposal is prepared. Typically, GPs want to acquire a property at the highest cap rate possible, while the seller would prefer to sell at the lowest cap rate possible.

When a transaction has been completed, the GP makes a capital call (i.e., a drawdown). The LPs transfer the appropriate amount to the GP based on their pro rata share of the total capital commitments. If an LP fails to meet a commitment, it might lose its share in the fund, which is then distributed to the rest of the investors.

Since real estate typically generates rental income, distributions are made throughout the life cycle of the REPE fund. However, distributions could be strategy dependent: core/core-plus strategies will generally involve cash distributions, while value-add or opportunistic strategies may not distribute until the end of the fund or deal life. GPs aim to match the capital requirements for the individual assets with the operational cash flows to avoid having to make unnecessary capital calls or distributions. After the initial investment period, most funds will generate a positive cash flow throughout the holding period, which GPs distribute to the LPs on a quarterly basis. Closer to the end of the fund's life, the GP will start divesting the remaining real estate assets and repaying all debts related to these assets. If the fund is successful, there is a significant positive distribution to the LPs which will depend on the carry structure of the fund (i.e., deal by deal or fund carry).

Terms and alignment of interests

LPs often require GPs to invest alongside them in an attempt to ensure that all parties' interests are aligned. While this requirement may seem surprising, there are unique agency issues in REPE investing. GPs commonly charge LPs a management fee of 1.0–2.5% on the fund's committed capital. Further, direct REPE funds usually charge asset management fees, development management fees, and acquisitions/structuring fees. The exact levels vary between funds and strategies, but core funds generally have lower management fees than opportunistic funds; this level is relevant for the vast majority of funds. Yet, management fees have come under pressure in recent years as LPs are increasingly considering alternative ways of investing in real estate besides the REPE model. In cases where the GP is actively managing a fund or advising the portfolio companies, the GP might charge property management fees and portfolio company advisory fees in addition to the management fees. This situation creates a potential conflict of interest, so GPs should disclose such fees to the LPs.

When LPs require a GP to invest in the fund, such investments are typically 0.5%–1.0% of the aggregate equity commitments in larger funds, but can often reach 5% for medium-sized or smaller funds of up to $750

---

[4] In the United Kingdom, the Investment Property Databank index is the standard benchmark for investors to analyze the performance of property in the U.K. market.

million. Some larger fund GPs have been known to commit up to 10% (or even higher) of the aggregate nominal committed equity.

In addition to earning fees, GPs also have a financial interest in the performance of the fund. A problem arises, however, when returns are low, which entitles the GP to a disproportionate compensation. In order to resolve this disparity, fund proceeds are often disbursed in a so-called "return waterfall." After the debt has been paid, the residual proceeds are split between the LPs and the GP according to their seniority and the fund terms. The mean absolute return requirement (or hurdle rate) when LPs commit capital is an IRR of 8–9% depending on the investment strategy, and the fund is set up so that the LPs have a preferred claim on the proceeds to meet the return terms.

Assuming that a fund's performance has met the hurdle rate, the GP splits the residual proceeds with the equity investors. Historically, a 20/80 split between the GP and "the money" has been common. As the GP (typically) invests in the fund alongside the LPs, the GP also receives a share of the 80% portion of the proceeds. In addition, the fund terms sometimes include a catch-up provision, which stipulates that the GP is entitled to—for example, in a 20/80 split—50% of all proceeds above the hurdle of 9%, until the GP has reached 20% of the total profits and the remaining profits are the 20/80 split. More complex structures with multiple hurdles are also possible. For instance, during the development phase of the project, the hurdles could first be set at 14% with a 20/80 split, and then above 18%, the split could be amended to 40/60.

Institutional investors have criticized the broader private equity industry for having poor alignment of interests; this is also true for the REPE industry. GPs have attempted to resolve these issues by investing alongside their LPs, as well as changing the fee structure and profit-sharing agreements.

THE INVESTMENT PROCESS

Underwriting

Sourcing and investing in real estate assets is a fundamental requirement for funds to generate returns, and GPs are usually under pressure to deploy committed capital shortly after raising it. With many central banks engaged in long-lasting quantitative easing, bond yields have plummeted and equities are trading at higher multiples, making real estate increasingly attractive to long-term investors. Many institutional asset managers have therefore increased their strategic allocation to real estate. A consequence of the increased amount of capital to be invested in real estate is that fund managers are experiencing a "wall of capital" when seeking placement. Unlike other asset classes, when demand for real estate surges, supply does not move in the short term. Thus, the ability to secure assets has become even more of a differentiator for REPE GPs. GPs must have strong deal-sourcing and execution capabilities to attract and retain LPs.

Investment opportunities might arise when listed real estate companies trade at a discount to the NAV. These opportunities present strong financial motivations to take them private in structured divestments with brokers or investment banks managing the process. Divestment may also arise from strategic or financial investors looking to divest a current real estate holding. Further, there are "off-market" investment opportunities that are pursued and negotiated under exclusivity and/or with very limited direct competition. Regardless of the opportunity, the investment process always follows the same procedure, referred to as the "underwriting" process.

Underwriting begins with the identification of an opportunity. Usually, the GP and the seller sign a non-disclosure agreement, and the GP is then given access to limited financial information about the asset. After reviewing this information, the GP submits an indicative bid, or indication of interest (IOI), in a term sheet. If the two parties agree that the indicative price is in an acceptable range, the next step is for the seller to provide the GP with additional material and the due diligence process commences. The due diligence process reduces the information asymmetry that may exist between the owner and the GP, providing the GP with a sound basis upon which to make a binding offer. Due diligence can be a fairly extensive process. Most commonly, the process encompasses commercial, technical, legal, financial, and environmental surveys and feasibility studies, but it can also be extended to examine taxes, labor laws, or any number of detailed areas. The underwriting process is usually tightly coordinated internally with the investment committee of the GP, which needs to approve the investment at multiple stages.

The findings from the due diligence process are then consolidated into a financial model to reflect the prospects of the potential investment. The financial model encompasses the sources and uses of funds, forecasted cash flows, financing costs, taxes, potential hedging costs and forward FX curves, asset-specific management fees, and waterfall structure. The latter two figures are usually only calculated at an aggregated fund level. The GP runs different scenarios and sensitivities to determine the most important value drivers and risks; this is not only a quantitative exercise, but also an experiential knowledge and qualitative assessment which relies on an iterative due diligence process.

After the due diligence process is completed, the GP's acquisitions team presents the investment case to the fund's investment committee for final approval. If the investment is approved and the seller and GP agree on the price and terms of the transaction, they will sign a sale and purchase agreement (SPA) detailing the transfer of the asset from one party to the other. This event is later followed by a closing meeting in which the transaction is finalized, and both the asset and the payment change hands.

The underwriting process is finalized when the asset has been acquired and the transaction has been completed. In the case of an REPE fund, underwriting also typically refers to the base case that was modeled and reflected in the final bid offer. This underwriting scenario forms the basis against which the asset is evaluated throughout the holding period in order to evaluate incremental performance up to divestment.

Due diligence on real estate assets

The GP's due diligence process begins once the parties to a potential transaction have agreed on high-level terms through a letter of intent, a term sheet, or a similar non-binding legal document. While each transaction is different, a core due diligence process applies to most acquisitions. The due diligence process covers a range of topics (e.g., commercial, legal, financial, tax, technical, etc.—with the most common discussed below). The main objective of a detailed due diligence process is for the GP of the REPE fund to assess an investment's attractiveness across a wide range of factors. A significant difference between direct and indirect investments is that direct REPE fund managers conduct asset-level due diligence, in addition to the due diligence on the asset operator. First and foremost, the accuracy of the information provided by vendors must be verified. Second, potential risks must be identified and mitigated to the greatest extent possible. Financial analyses will frequently be reviewed throughout the process, with adjustments to the potential acquisition's business plan and strategy, in light of any issues identified. Material issues can be used to negotiate with the vendor(s) and incorporated into pricing expectations or representations and warranties in the transaction documents.

Commercial due diligence

Commercial due diligence is performed by advisory firms hired by the GP during the due diligence process. This process includes local market analysis, rental and investment transaction comparables, the outlook for values, and so on. Furthermore, sustainability analyses may be conducted to assess the commercial attractiveness of different post-acquisition business plans. Large brokerage houses such as CBRE, Jones Lang LaSalle, and Cushman & Wakefield offer deep market knowledge across sectors and geographies. These firms can rely on extensive networks of owners, developers, investors, and other parties to ensure maximum market penetration and up-to-date information.

Legal due diligence

GPs may seek legal counsel during the due diligence process in order to identify key issues or unique considerations pertaining to an acquisition target. They may even provide advice on negotiating, signing, and closing the transaction. Indeed, legal counsel is first retained to review leases in place, legal titles and chain of ownership, zoning laws, and so on. The objectives of legal due diligence include establishing a tenant credit analysis, ensuring that the property's title can be transferred and will not be subject to unidentified liens or claims, and ascertaining that commercial and other activities performed on site abide by zoning regulations. The legal counsel may review and negotiate SPAs, management agreement contracts, and other documentation specific to the transaction. Legal counsel is instrumental in assisting with the signing and closing of a transaction, as well as making sure that all required licenses and permits are in place.

Financial review, taxes, and structuring

Large international accounting firms are typically hired by GPs during the due diligence process to perform a financial review of the target (i.e., confirm the financial performance of the target), and to examine the tax and structuring aspects, as acquisitions may take several forms (e.g., asset versus share deals). The quality of earnings generated by the target property is conducted relative to historical financial statements, with a view to analyze revenue and cost structures, non-recurring items, assets by type, working capital composition and variation, the target's net financial position, off-balance sheet items, and more. The tax review will cover topics such as income and capital taxes, deferred taxes, implications of real estate capital gains taxes upon entry or exit, and so on. Tax structuring is performed in an effort to maximize tax efficiency across entities and legal jurisdictions, since acquisitions often involve dealing with complex cross-border tax and accounting compliance considerations.

Technical and environmental

The aim of the technical and environmental review during the due diligence process is to assess the condition of the property and identify major issues, defects, or risks. The property is inspected in great detail by a technical team through an on-site physical visit, as well as a documentation review. Conformity is assessed against local country standards and construction norms, relative to the structure(s), installations, and other fixed assets. Technical matters related to residential configuration and floor layouts are also reviewed. The property's condition is assessed and compared to the local market, and often, a 5- to 10-year capital expenditure assessment is performed to identify defects or required remedial works; this includes a review of maintenance records and service contracts. Urban planning documentation and licenses are assessed together with any insurance claims and contractor warranties. The property is also examined from an environmental perspective to determine whether there are any significant environmental concerns that could result in liabilities.

Valuation

The two main elements of property valuation are *cash flows* (pro forma analysis) and *discount rates* (or *cap rates* if cash flows are growing in perpetuity). The cap rate is similar to the current yield of an investment and can vary across property types, countries, and investor classes. The two main determinants of cap rates are (1) the cost of capital for the property, and (2) the growth rate of future property cash flows.

The GP may hire property surveyors to produce a formal valuation of the property's fair market value. Property surveyors are typically required to abide by professional standards within their home country and to provide market knowledge, skills, and understanding when conducting valuations. These requirements may apply for several purposes, especially for third-party lending. The property valuation can serve to confirm terms and criteria of a potential loan (e.g., when lending is provided on a loan-to-value percentage basis). We discuss common valuation approaches and methodologies in the next section.

The formal valuation report usually begins with an executive summary where the property's suitability for a loan is analyzed based on key issues such as location, condition of the property, and characteristics of the tenant(s). The report also includes the terms of the lease, initial rent payment per annum, details of increases/decreases in rent over the course of the lease, and a description on how rents will be linked to inflation.[5] The property surveyor then evaluates the rental agreements outlined in the terms of the lease and compares them to its own estimated rental value to arrive at a recommendation on whether the property offers suitable security for a mortgage.

The property valuation report is divided into several sections, including the following:

- **Property details**, such as location, communication technology, description of the property, accommodation (available leasable area per floor), state of repair, environmental considerations, property rating, town planning, and value-added tax.

- **Legal considerations**, including tenure, tenancies, terms of the lease to be granted, insurance, tenant options to review, and break clauses.

- **Market commentary**, which includes information about the market surrounding the property, supply/demand, occupancy rates, rental levels, rental growth forecasts, comparable properties, past transactions, yield applicable to the subject property, and so on.

- **Valuation considerations**, such as income summary and analysis of passing rents, tenant covenant strength, void periods, relettability, key valuation factors, marketability, potential purchasers, and valuation methodology.

- **Opinion of value**, which represents the property surveyor's ultimate opinion regarding the market value of the property, as well as a market value on the special assumption that the property is vacant.

Property management team

---

[5] In the United Kingdom, rents are usually linked to the retail price index, while in the United States, rents are linked to the consumer price index.

If the GP is looking to keep the existing property management team, the due diligence process may include an evaluation of the team's track record and management capabilities. A common approach to this evaluation is to use detailed question-and-answer sessions, as well as a review of management reports and other documentation covering business strategy implementation and initiatives, day-to-day operational management actions, and so on. Qualifications and experience are crucial.

Other due diligence issues

Some acquisitions will be contemplated from a redevelopment angle, which may require discussions with local planning authorities and councils during the due diligence process to assess the need for special planning permissions, permits, licenses to operate, and other such materials. The feasibility, cost, and timeline for a redevelopment project are all important considerations.

Throughout the due diligence process, the GP's acquisition team will act as the main contact for all third-party advisers. The primary objective of the process is to understand and quantify potential issues and incorporate them into the financial review of the property. Conducting detailed due diligence can be a very costly process (typically, 1–3% of the asset purchase price), but it serves to lower the overall risk of the investment.

While GPs' due diligence is vital to carrying out the investment strategy, the investing LPs should also evaluate the GPs' strategy in the following key areas:

- Fund manager profiles (e.g., organizational structure; real estate fund management business; environmental, social, and governance (ESG) criteria; staff; risk management and compliance; regulations and external auditors; and performance record).

- Investment vehicle information (e.g., vehicle snapshot, investment strategy, ESG criteria, existing portfolio or seed assets, track record and financial information of the existing vehicle, bank leverage and management strategy, investment process, reporting and valuation, other investors, etc.).

- Tax specifics (e.g., general questions, details of the existing vehicle, details of the investment structure, etc.).

Pertinent due diligence questions are listed in Appendix A.

Real estate valuation methods

A property's market value is usually the estimated amount for which the property can exchange on the date of valuation between a willing buyer and a willing seller in an arm's length transaction after proper marketing wherein the parties are knowledgeable, and prudent. Market value may differ from investment value in the sense that buyers may derive a different value based on a market context that is unique to them. Other definitions of "value" exist, such as value-in-use (value to one particular user), insurable value, and liquidation value. In the context of real estate assets, three main valuation approaches are used to arrive at the market value: (1) the sales comparison approach, (2) the income approach, and (3) the cost approach.

1. In the *sales comparison approach*, pricing multiples from recent transactions of similar properties used for the same purpose are utilized to determine the fair market value of a target property. This approach is

very similar to a comparable multiples analysis for public or private companies. However, instead of relying on metrics such as EBITDA multiples or P/E ratios, real estate investors will typically look at purchase price per square foot or square meter, purchase price to net operating income (NOI), all revenue from the property minus all reasonably necessary operating expenses, or in-place income. Usually, the data can be obtained from a variety of sources (e.g., public records, specialized industry publications, real estate brokers and agents, professional services firms, etc.). Comparables are often restricted to a specific geography in order to best capture and reflect local conditions. For even better accuracy, adjustments can be made for the site's size, age, quality of construction, other physical features and amenities, and so on.

2. The *income approach* to private real estate valuation consists of calculating the present value of expected cash flows derived from the ownership of the property. Cash flows produced by a property usually take the form of rental income and other lease payments. Most often, the individual lease contracts will be bundled to calculate an overall gross rental income, from which a vacancy rate will be applied to determine a net rental income figure. Indeed, most properties will not be completely occupied at all times; therefore, there is a need for a vacancy rate provision for less than 100% utilization. Calculations can also include a provision for potential collection losses. Real estate expenses will include items like property taxes, building maintenance and repair costs, and insurance premiums. The contractual agreements between the lessor and lessee will specify which costs are borne by which party. A common type of agreement is the "triple net lease," which designates the lessee as the sole party responsible for the costs mentioned above. Once costs are netted out, the property's NOI can be determined by totaling all revenue from the property minus all reasonably necessary operating expenses.

The most often used method to derive a property's value is to rely on the capitalization rate: *Value = NOI/Cap Rate*. In its simplest form, a capitalization rate is a way to express a property value per dollar of current net income. The capitalization rate is the rate of return on a real estate investment property based on the income that the property is expected to generate. The property value determined by the capitalization rate method is a key determinant in evaluating the leverage potential of the asset (see Appendix B).

The property's NOI should be stabilized before being capitalized, in order to avoid putting too much weight on a recent event, which will have a major impact on the NOI. A variation of the income approach is the discounted cash flow (DCF) analysis (see Appendix C). Using this method, multiple years of operations can be modeled. A terminal value is calculated using an estimated market yield (or capitalization rate) or income multiple. The typical valuation model would include investment assumptions (e.g., acquisitions costs and fees, structuring fees, and sales price assumptions), operational assumptions (i.e., development costs, rent levels, and macro indicators), financing assumptions (i.e., leverage—amount and cost, equity, and hybrid facilities), cash flow forecasts (based on operational assumptions, used to construct the DCF valuation), and returns calculations (i.e., the waterfall structure).

3. The least common valuation method, the *cost approach*, is used to evaluate what it would cost to buy the bare land and build a new property on the site, assuming such a property could fulfill the same operating purpose as the previous structure. The cost will then be reduced by accumulated depreciation to reflect the property's age. There are two main types of cost approach appraisals: (1) the reproduction method, which considers that a replica of the property is built and gives attention to duplication of original materials, and (2) the replacement method, which assumes the new structure has the same function with newer materials, using current construction methods and an updated design.

FINANCING FOR REAL ESTATE TRANSACTIONS

Leverage, or debt financing, is an important and even necessary part of most real estate deals. Leverage refers to the total amount of debt financing on a property relative to its current market value, and includes all the different layers of debt in the capital stack, such as first and second mortgages and mezzanine financing. Leverage is common in real estate investments for two reasons: (1) real estate is a physical asset which retains some value, and which can be used as collateral when taking a loan; and (2) as real estate assets generate fixed cash flow streams from rents, banks are usually willing to lend at a lower cost.

While leverage can result in enhanced returns for REPE funds, it carries a certain level of risk. From a theoretical perspective, leverage is preferable as long as the marginal increase in expected return per unit of extra risk from leverage exceeds that obtained from buying riskier assets. A fundamental difference between non-sponsored real estate financing and real estate financing backed by an REPE fund is the backing, or guarantee, that the REPE provides, which usually results in more favorable financing terms.

The typical capital structure of a real estate property is comprised of senior debt (A-note), mezzanine capital (B-note, mezzanine loan, and preferred equity), and equity (preferred and common). The senior debt is provided by banks or other commercial lenders and is the amount used to calculate the loan-to-value ratio of a property (discussed in greater detail below), while mezzanine capital is provided by mezzanine funds.

Features of commercial real estate financing

Commercial real estate, the primary target of REPE funds, is income-producing real estate. Financing for the acquisition, development, and construction of these properties is typically accomplished through commercial real estate loans—that is, mortgage loans secured by liens on commercial property. As with residential loans, banks and independent lenders are actively involved in making loans on commercial real estate. However, insurance companies, pension funds, private investors, and other capital sources can also provide loans for commercial real estate.

An entity or fund may not have a financial track record or any credit history, in which case the lender may require the principals, owners, or GP(s) of the entity to guarantee the loan. This guarantee provides lenders with a credit history and/or financial track record, as well as an accountable party from whom they can recover funds in the event of loan default. If this type of guarantee is not required by the lender, and the property is the only means of recovery in the event of loan default, the loan is called a "non-recourse loan," meaning that the lender has no recourse against anyone or anything other than the property.

Once a bank or independent lender approves a loan, it distributes the term loan facility agreement, a legal document that encompasses all the terms and conditions of the loan. Some key loan features include the following:

- **Purpose of the proceeds:** This item states that proceeds should be applied to assist in the purchase of the specific property or toward capitalization of interest during the interest roll-up period (i.e., the period indicated in the amortization schedule).

- **Drawdown dates:** The borrower may borrow the loans during the commitment period after making a request, which is irrevocable.

- **Rate of interest:** The rate of interest on the loan for each of its interest periods is the per annum rate determined to be the aggregate of (1) a credit margin, (2) the LIBOR rate, and (3) mandatory costs.

- **Maturity:** The maturity of commercial loans typically ranges from five years (or less) to 20 years, and the amortization period is often longer than the term of the loan.[6] The length of the loan term and the amortization period affects the rate that the lender charges. In general, the longer the loan repayment schedule, the higher the interest rate.

- **Amortization schedule:** The borrower should repay the loans on the dates and in the amounts specified in the amortization schedule. If the borrower fails to pay on its due date, it must pay interest on the overdue amount at a "default" rate specified in the term loan agreement.

- **Hedging arrangements:** On or before the drawdown date, the borrower may have the option to enter into and maintain hedging arrangements with the original holding counterparty, in aggregate for the notional principal amount equal to the loan, for the period from the drawdown date to the repayment date.

- **Negative pledge:** A negative pledge clause is a covenant stating that the borrower will not pledge, create, or permit to subsist any security interests over any of its assets, as doing so gives the lender less security.

- **Prepayment fees:** For any voluntary prepayment, there will be fixed fees or fees charged in an amount equal to the margin loss. The margin loss is calculated as a fraction of the relevant annual interest and varies depending on the date when the prepayment was made (e.g., within one year of the drawdown, more than two years after the drawdown, etc.), and will decrease over the life of the loan. The relevant annual interest is the aggregate total amount paid or payable to the hedging counterparties in respect of the amount prepaid for the year in which the prepayment occurs. In addition to prepayment fees, there are two other common types of "exit" penalties for paying off a loan early: (1) a lockout, in which the borrower cannot pay off the loan before a specified period (e.g., a five-year lockout), and (2) a defeasance, where instead of paying cash to the lender, the borrower exchanges new collateral (usually treasury securities) for the original loan collateral.

Key leverage metrics

As debt plays such an important role in real estate financing, there are certain leverage metrics that are widely used by lenders. The most common one is the *loan-to-value* (LTV) ratio, which measures the amount of money that a bank lends in relation to the property value. In hand with the LTV ratio, banks also focus on another relevant leverage ratio, the *debt-service coverage ratio* (DCR). The DCR measures the property's ability to pay down its debt. Banks also use the *break-even ratio* (BER) when considering underwriting a loan. In general, all of these metrics are useful for both investors and banks in determining their projections and capabilities toward an investment or loan.

---

[6] For example, a lender might provide a commercial loan for a term of seven years with an amortization period of 30 years. In this situation, the investor would make payments for seven years at an amount based on the loan being paid off over 30 years, followed by one final "balloon" payment of the entire remaining balance on the loan at the end of year 7.

LTV ratio

A lender calculates LTV by dividing the amount of the loan by the lesser of (1) the property's appraised value, or (2) the purchase price. For example, the LTV for a $90,000 loan on a $100,000 property would be 90% ($90,000 / $100,000 = 0.9, or 90%). Borrowers with lower LTVs will qualify for more favorable financing rates than those with higher LTVs because they have more equity (or stake) in the property, which equals less risk in the eyes of the lender.

Commercial loan LTVs generally fall into the 65–80% range. While some loans may be made at higher LTVs, they are less common. The specific LTV often depends on the loan category. For instance, a maximum LTV of 65% may be allowed for raw land, while an LTV of up to 80% might be acceptable for a very high-quality building.

DCR

Commercial lenders also consider DCR, which compares a property's annual NOI to its annual debt service (including principal and interest), measuring the property's ability to service its debt. DCR is calculated by dividing the NOI by the annual debt service. For example, a property with $140,000 in NOI and $100,000 in annual mortgage debt service would have a DCR of 1.40 ($140,000 / $100,000 = 1.4). The ratio helps lenders determine the maximum loan size based on the cash flow generated by the property.

A DCR of less than 1 indicates a negative cash flow (e.g., a DCR of 0.92 means that there is only enough NOI to cover 92% of annual debt service). In general, commercial lenders look for DCRs of at least 1.25 to ensure adequate cash flow. A lower DCR may be acceptable for loans with shorter amortization periods and/or properties with stable cash flows. Conversely, higher ratios may be required for properties with volatile cash flows (e.g., hotels, which lack the long-term—and therefore, more predictable—tenant leases common to other types of commercial real estate).

BER

Many lenders use BER when considering underwriting a loan, as it allows them to determine the vulnerability of a property toward a default on its debt in the event of a decline in the rental income stream. The formula used to measure BER is (Debt Service + Operating Expenses)/Gross Operating Income. Lenders usually target a BER equal to 85% or less.

EXIT POSSIBILITIES

An exit from REPE investments can occur at two levels: the asset level and the fund level. The former pertains to an asset exiting a fund, whereas the latter refers to investors exiting a fund. The total return of an asset is often highly sensitive to the pricing at exit, particularly when highly leveraged. Although the exit is not usually considered part of the value creation process, when it is executed appropriately, it can add significant value. However, certain risks and circumstances greatly impact exit opportunities, including their flexibility and pricing. Moreover, the dynamics of the exit can be very different depending on the type of REPE fund.

Asset-level divestments

When funds move closer to the end of their life cycle, management's focus shifts naturally from active value creation to seeking the best divestment opportunities. Opportunistic and value-add funds divest assets when those assets have reached a steady state (i.e., the business plan has been executed and the majority of the value creation has been realized), assuming that the market is favorable for an exit, as determined by the GP's rigorous divestment analysis. This analysis typically involves an appraisal of key return metrics (e.g., IRR and whole profit from underwriting to exit), and then comparing them to the underwriting assumptions. Even if the expected returns look favorable for an exit, the GP might conduct an incremental returns analysis for holding the asset (also called a "next buyer analysis") to see if those returns are accretive or dilutive to underwritten returns. If the exit opportunity arises early compared to underwriting, there may be further costs involved—usually financing and/or hedging-related costs.

During exit, the lenders providing the leverage used in a particular asset must be considered as well. Lenders often have a clause for early sale in debt facility agreements in order to protect them against early repayments; this is called "release pricing," and means that the fund must repay a multiple (usually 100–120%) of the nominal loan amount after amortization when concluding the divestment. This payment is then settled against the total property repayment at the end of the financing period, and acts as a negative cash release component in the sale proceeds. There might also be implications from interest rate and foreign exchange swap agreements that dampen the incentives for—or even prevent—an early sale.

GPs may divest real estate assets individually or in portfolios, or even divest the entire fund's holdings. The GP usually has different exit strategies in the business plan but will act opportunistically to seek the best opportunities when an exit is favorable according to the analyses mentioned above. If an asset is worth more as a separate entity than what it contributes to a portfolio, that asset is likely to be sold separately. Alternatively, if there is market demand for volume and real estate product is scarce, it might make sense to divest assets in aggregate and receive premium pricing. While it is possible to gauge the current market sentiment to make such assessments, it is very difficult to make accurate long-term forecasts. Therefore, GPs tend to take an opportunistic approach to divestments and assess them on a discretionary basis.

In most cases, there are several exit options available to REPE funds. These include sales to strategic buyers in the direct real estate market, as well as divestments to financial buyers in the capital markets. A divestment to a strategic buyer in the real estate market (typically a real estate company with an overlapping focus on segments and geographies) is relatively straightforward, but there are other, less obvious ways to divest assets. Financial buyers can be entities (listed or non-listed), but it is also possible to syndicate the asset or to pursue an IPO. It is rare for funds to pursue IPOs for individual assets, as this is costly and usually only allows a partial exit; however, this approach might make sense for portfolios of real estate assets. REPE funds can also divest to syndicators, who match real estate assets with institutional investors and high-net-worth individuals or pursue syndication themselves. The problem with such a divestment—specifically for a closed-ended fund with a finite life—is that it might not allow for a complete exit in the given time frame, because of a lock-up period. If it is unfavorable to wind down a fund at the end of its life cycle, the investors can agree to extend the fund's life via a so-called "rollover." Typically, a rollover requires the approval of 75% of the LPs.

Fund-level divestments

A fund's agreement terms specify how LPs can exit a fund. The main difference between open-ended and closed-ended funds is the redemption rights. In some cases, a GP may not operate to its designated full term—for instance, because the fund has reached its return requirements quite soon after its launch. In this situation, it might be optimal for both the GP and LPs to divest early and take their distributions of the proceeds. The opposite may also occur, where the fund does not (and is unlikely to ever) meet its return requirements, so LPs prefer to receive the proceeds from liquidation early rather than wait and take a greater risk. In either scenario, it would be common for the GP to make a recommendation and for the LPs to have a vote. For opportunistic funds, the GP typically has more control, or sometimes total discretion. GP-LP agreements represent one way to exit a fund early, although there are a few other general mechanisms that could trigger an early exit (e.g., refinancing opportunities in the market). LPs can also exit by selling their interests in the fund to another LP or a secondary private equity GP. It is common for these sales take place at a discount.

In cases of negligence, fraud, and/or failure to fulfill the fiduciary responsibilities, it is usually possible to remove the fund's GP; however, since it is often difficult and time consuming to do so, many LPs now demand that a no-fault removal clause be included in the fund agreement. Enforcing such a clause typically requires the approval of at least 75% of the investors in the fund. The fund can then be unwound (i.e., in the case of liquidity pressure on the LPs), or the GP can be replaced.

Finally, if there are material legal changes, such as changes to the taxation of the profits, it may no longer be economically favorable to keep the fund going. Given that many funds are structured using offshore jurisdictions, fund dissolution is a standard clause in the LP-GP agreements of most cross-border funds. Yet, in practice, this clause is rarely used.

CONCLUSION

Real estate has become a relevant asset class for investors who want to diversify their portfolios in an effort to increase their risk-adjusted returns. Real estate has many positive qualities: it generates stable returns in the form of rents and capital appreciation, it has a negative correlation with traditional asset classes such as equities and bonds, it has low volatility of intrinsic value due to the tangibility of the underlying asset, and it can act as an inflation hedge.

Private equity funds have created commingled investment vehicles defined as REPE funds with the purpose of pooling investments from investors who want exposure to this asset class. REPE funds consist of equity and debt instruments in real estate. They are generally closed-ended funds that target an IRR of 15–20%, with a life cycle of 8–10 years. Further, REPE funds offer investors active management strategies ranging from moderate reposition or releasing of properties to extensive redevelopment.

Generally PERE fund managers and their investors perceive two major challenges in the market: rising interest rates which affect financing costs and inflated asset values. Asset valuations have been growing in recent years due to increases in competition, investor demand for real estate and the level of capital available to PERE funds. However, while these factors may make it more difficult to generate good PERE fund returns, the demand for real estate is likely to stay strong in line with economic growth.

APPENDIX A

Due diligence questionnaire (a basic example)

1) Describe the diversification of the properties the manager targets for this fund:
   a) By geography (which part of the country, and which economic zones?)
   b) By value of the properties (e.g., less than $10 million, over $100 million)
   c) By number of properties
   d) By type of properties (e.g., downtown office, suburban office, retail malls, strip centers, warehouses, light industrial, apartments, single-family residential, hotels, raw land)
2) If the fund will invest internationally, which countries will the fund invest in, and what experiences does the manager have investing in those countries?
   a) How does the manager gain local expertise in real estate value and the future desirability of specific locations?
   b) How does the manager handle local financing?
   c) What country diversification does the manager target?
3) How does this sector and geographic diversification differ from manager's prior funds?
4) What portion of the total returns is likely to come from rents and capital gains?
5) What part of the real estate cycle is the fund in now? How does the manager expect to take advantage of this position?
6) How effective has the manager been in adapting prior funds as markets have changed?
7) With respect to prior funds, what insight has the manager demonstrated at the macro level?
8) What insight, creativity, and management expertise has the manager demonstrated at the micro level?
9) How effective has the manager been in both buying and selling properties opportunistically?
10) In prior funds, with respect to strategy, acquisition, asset management, project management, and financing, which team members were most responsible, and do they remain fully dedicated to the fund?
11) Relative to existing properties and those anticipated for the fund,
    a) Is there any litigation outstanding or expected?
    b) Are there any rights or easements on land held by the fund, including water or mineral rights?
    c) Are there any restrictions or requirements relative to zoning?
    d) What environmental surveys are available, particularly regarding prior and subsequent use of the land?
12) Does the fund use local operating partners?
13) What use of leverage does the manager anticipate?
    a) Why?
    b) How will the fund finance the leverage?
    c) How great is the risk that the fund will run out of cash at a time when property values fall and credit dries up, as they did in 2008?
14) What risks does the manager consider most important? What is the manager's plan to protect against those risks?

APPENDIX B

Example of maximum property debt calculation using the capitalization rate method

Pro Forma Net Operating Income (NOI) and Value	
Pro Forma NOI	$523,942
Capitalization Rate	6.00%
Value of Income Property Only (NOI/Cap Rate)	$8,732,373
Loan Terms	
Interest Rate	5.75%
Amortization (years)	30
Debt Based on Loan to Value (LTV)	
Maximum LTV Percentage	75.00%
Maximum Loan Based on LTV for Income Property	$6,549,280
Using Debt Coverage Ratio (DCR)	
Monthly NOI	43,662
Maximum DCR	1.20
Maximum Monthly Payment (NOI/DCR/12)	$36,385
Maximum Loan Based on DCR for Income Property	$6,234,849
Maximum Loan (Lesser of LTV or DCR Result)	
Maximum Loan for Income Property	$6,234,849
Add: Loan for For-Sale Property	*$682,500*
Total Initial Project Debt	**$6,917,349**

APPENDIX C

Sample DCF Valuation

Discounted Cash Flow (DCF) Analysis   SAMPLE

As discussed in the text, an internal rate of return (IRR) is the discount rate that will exactly equate the present value of a projected stream of cash flows with an initial equity investment. Alternatively, subtracting a initial equity investment from the present value of projected cash flows (discounted at a given discount rate) yields net present value (NPV). **No inputs on this worksheet.**

Anticipated holding period: 6

Initial Investment Basis	
Purchase price	11,444,500
Transaction costs	150,000
Initial Investment Basis:	11,594,500
Mortgage:	8,000,000
Initial Equity:	3,594,500

After-Tax Equity Reversion	
Selling Price	17,800,000
- Selling Costs:	890,000
Net Sales Proceeds:	16,910,000
- Mortgage Balance:	6,750,100
Before-tax Equity Reversion:	10,159,900
- Taxes due on sale:	1,563,400
After-Tax Equity Reversion:	8,596,500

	0	1	2	3	4	5	6	7	8	9	10
BTCF:		462,700	635,700	731,800	667,900	732,500	799,300	0	0	0	0
BTER:		0	0	0	0	0	10,159,900	0	0	0	0
Total:	(3,594,500)	462,700	635,700	731,800	667,900	732,500	10,959,200	0	0	0	0

Before-tax IRR: 31.31%

	0	1	2	3	4	5	6	7	8	9	10
ATCF:		339,600	443,500	495,000	450,100	481,700	508,500	0	0	0	0
ATER:		0	0	0	0	0	8,596,500	0	0	0	0
Total:	(3,594,500)	339,600	443,500	495,000	450,100	481,700	9,105,000	0	0	0	0

After-tax IRR: 24.60%

In their own words: Ira Shaw, Partner and Avi Turetsky, Managing Director, Landmark Partners

Institutional investors incorporate real estate in their portfolio for a variety of reasons, two of the most common of which are income and capital appreciation. With several exceptions (such as the purchase of raw land), real estate is an income generating asset class. Property owners generate income by charging tenants rent. Rental payments are often inflation indexed, and through income growth and favorable market dynamics, investors are hopeful to see long term value appreciation. The prospect for income growth and capital appreciation is driven by a property's location. For that reason, real estate investors focus their diligence on local market dynamics, such as supply constraints, local employment drivers, access to transit, retail amenities, and neighboring competition.

Investors have traditionally accessed real estate through (1) the direct acquisition of property, (2) purchase of shares of publicly listed real estate investment trusts, and (3) open-ended private equity funds, a type of vehicle that was launched in the late 1970s that seeks stable cash flow dividends and capital preservation. The late 1990s and early 2000s saw the emergence of another private equity format: value-add and opportunity funds. These vehicles seek to generate excess return by developing, redeveloping, repurposing, re-tenanting, and rehabilitating impaired or obsolescing property. "Buy it, fix it, sell it," is a mantra pursued by many real estate fund sponsors.

Increasing investor allocations to value add and opportunistic real estate funds from 2004 through 2007 coincided with wide availability of leverage to finance real estate acquisitions. These factors, among others, drove increases in commercial real estate prices until the Global Financial Crisis in 2009.

Lessons learned from the prior crisis might benefit investors looking to build durable portfolios. In our experience, successful real estate investors are often those that exhibit both strong local knowledge as well as capital markets sophistication. Effective management of a commercial real estate property requires on-the-ground expertise to maintain operating efficiency, while driving rents and maximizing occupancy. However, managing a real estate investment requires awareness of capital markets conditions, access to capital, and prudent use of leverage. What we found during the prior crisis was that even some of the strongest operators experienced distress when problems related to income shortfalls and value declines were magnified by debt maturity defaults and the inability to access capital. Ultimately, managers that combine operational and capital markets strengths with strong local investment intelligence are those that position their portfolios for success in the long run.

17 Infrastructure and Natural Resources Funds

If you don't know where you are going, any road will get you there.
Lewis Carroll

INTRODUCTION

Infrastructure and natural resources have attracted private capital for decades if not centuries, but has received remarkably increased attention from institutional investors over the last decade or so. Despite their trendiness, the two groups of assets (often considered together) have established themselves as a permanent and independent asset class within the broader set of private capital.

Infrastructure assets are the facilities essential for the orderly operation of an economy, such as transportation networks, healthcare, social care, waste management, and telecommunications towers. Investment in infrastructure and its continuous maintenance is principally the role of the government as part of its fiscal policy. Indeed, globally, the vast majority of infrastructure assets are owned by the public sector. However, the private sector is increasingly involved in both financing and operating such projects. Private funding allows risk-shifting to the private sector and provides off-balance-sheet financing to infrastructure projects—it does not require government borrowing and it alleviates the budgetary burden. In addition, with government budgets being slashed, infrastructure spending is particularly vulnerable. Cutting infrastructure budgets does not tend to attract strong taxpayer opposition, and scarce government resources are focused on higher political priorities than long-term investment infrastructure projects. In recognizing the importance of infrastructure investment, several governments have significantly increased their reliance on private sector funding. In essence, private sector funding provides off-balance-sheet financing to government infrastructure projects[1].

The important underlying economic characteristic of most infrastructure and natural resources investments is the ability to deliver, within acceptable level of predictability, long-term streams of stable revenues. In some cases, these revenues are regulated, in other cases contracted, and in other cases (especially natural resources) subject to pure market forces of supply and demand. We briefly detail these three cases below.

First, utilities that have been privatized (most notably in the water, electricity and gas sectors) are most often regulated (because of their monopoly nature), which dictates much of their financial return profile.[2] These companies are operating businesses that can benefit from the financial and operational improvements

---

We are grateful to Alan Synnott, Managing Director and Global Head of Product Strategy for Real Assets, BlackRock and to Marine Richard (LBS MIFPT 2019 and Investment Manager at John Laing Group) for their contribution to this chapter.

[1] However, in some countries there has been public backlash over the cost of early Public Private Partnerships (PPPs) and waning political support for private financing of infrastructure projects.

[2] Under government ownership, the focus is on public services, which have been historically cost-inefficient. Conversely, under private ownership, the focus is on profitability and quality of service is often dictated by regulation and a costing base such as cost plus or incentive based.

that private equity firms offer. While the revenues of these businesses are reliant on customers and not guaranteed per se, they are still highly predictable.

Second, governments can procure new infrastructure by providing guaranteed, contracted revenues for some or all of the life of the project. Traditionally this has been done through the well-established PPP model pioneered in the UK, where the private sector bids a certain return for delivering and operating an individual asset (e.g., a road, school or hospital). These structures place the risk of completing infrastructure projects on time, on budget and to high standards on the private sector. The private sector also faces penalties if the asset does not meet pre-defined operational standards. It must not be forgotten however while governments do not pay for these projects upfront, the public purse has historically paid for these assets through long-term fixed charges (called unitary fees) through the life of the project, providing a guaranteed revenue stream for the private sector. Likewise, feed-in-tariffs and contracts for difference have provided long-term contracted revenues to fund renewable energy projects. However, as we will cover later in the chapter, these government payments are decreasing and in some cases disappearing altogether for certain assets (e.g. merchant toll roads and subsidy-free renewable energy projects).

Third, natural resources include sectors such as agriculture, energy, and mines, which have a shared characteristic that even if governments do not own the assets or have a principal responsibility, investments still most often require licensing and regulation. In comparison to infrastructure, the proportion of private sector ownership is far larger than in infrastructure, and the risk-return investment profile is also different due to the exposure to commodity prices fluctuations.

Regulated assets and natural resources closely resemble the private equity model. As with private equity, these real assets require fund managers to proactively engage in a full spectrum of activities in diverse areas: finance, operations, project management, government, privatization, regulation, and corporate development. These assets also require disciplined corporate governance in setting strategy, key management appointments and succession planning, and risk oversight, as well as an emphasis on orchestrating debt finance (often from a syndicate of financial institutions). As the infrastructure sector has matured, it has become an intensified competitive environment.

While real assets are grouped together as one class, they vary widely in their return patterns. Understanding, structuring, and allocating risk is key to the successful financing of an infrastructure project. The risk profile depends on the following non-exhaustive factors: (i) stage of development of the project; (ii) level of regulated or contracted revenues compared to merchant revenues; (iii) country risk, including legal, political and macroeconomic risks; (iv) technical and technology risks.

Risk profiles change significantly as the project moves both within and between planning, construction, and operational phases. For example, a power generation project may be a greenfield, and thus subject to licensing, permitting and development challenges. At the other end of the investment spectrum, there is a purchase of an existing power plant with an offtake agreement with a rate structure that is set in advance. Whereas a mine development is entrepreneurial in nature, maintenance and service concessions of infrastructure facilities like airports and prisons resemble a fixed income security. In this sense, infrastructure and natural resources share the characteristics of real estate, the third sibling of the real assets family, where projects diverge all across the spectrum from pure developments to hotels and commercial real estate management to ownership of the assets. Each of these types has a cash flow profile with its own pattern, time horizon, and predictability—all of which must be factored into its risk assessment and pricing.

Private funds

Infrastructure has only recently surged to be a more widely accepted and understood asset class by institutional investors. From just a handful of funds raising in aggregate a single digit billions in the early 2000s, infrastructure has grown to reach astounding figures. An estimated aggregate value of $645 billion was invested in 1,774 infrastructure fund deals completed globally in 2016. The number of unlisted infrastructure funds that successfully raised money (i.e., reached a first close) during that year was 52, with a record high average fund size of $1.3 billion. Average deal size in 2016 also reached an all-time high of $364 million.[3]

For natural resources, there were $455 billion in assets under management of unlisted funds in 2016, and a record of $162 billion capital commitment ("dry powder"); the vast majority of this amount was in the energy sector. Seventy-four unlisted natural resources funds raised $60 billion of aggregated capital during 2016, with an average fund size of $900 million.

In the United States, the watershed event for the growth in the real assets market turned out to be the global financial crisis, which greatly accelerated the development of the infrastructure sector. The crisis reduced the supply of infrastructure capital from traditional sources, as governments practiced fiscal restraint and banks were forced to deleverage. Globally, the last decade has witness a strong desire by institutional investors to seek prudent and less correlated alternatives to stocks and bonds and new sources of return in a climate of near-zero interest rates. Given the increasing awareness of institutional investors in the sector, and the push by governments and other entities around the world to advance infrastructure investment, reliance on the private sector to help fund infrastructure appears to be a permanent phenomenon.[4]

From an investor point of view, infrastructure offers an appealing risk-reward combination. As discussed later, there are a wide variety of subsectors and asset types as well as investment strategies that further define the type of risk exposure. Exhibit 1 shows the net internal rate of return (IRR) to investors across the 2004–2014 vintage years.

While their exponential expansion is recent, private sector infrastructure vehicles have existed in some countries for many years—most notably, in Australia and Canada. The relatively long operational lives of assets that provide essential services appeal to institutional investors. Regulation usually brings some form of inflation protection, which enables to structure investments that offer reliable long-term cash flows and also leverage infrastructure projects. In addition to sector diversification, institutional investors can use infrastructure to help meet their long-term liabilities with a distribution stream that is predictable, and often correlated with inflation.

As noted, there is great variety not only in the types of physical assets but also in the cash flow patterns of infrastructure investments. They share therefore characteristics with fixed income, real estate, leverage buyout, and venture capital.

Individual PPP and renewable energy assets with contracted revenues for the majority of the project life involve construction and operational risks, which must be actively managed by infrastructure funds. These risks are mitigated through the guarantees and warranties provided by contractors and by hiring technical

---

[3] The number of institutional investors in the infrastructure asset class more than doubled from 2013 to 2017 (Preqin Investor Outlook Alternative Assets H1 2017 and Real Asset Spotlight August 2017).

[4] Certain initiatives such as the G20 organization Global Infrastructure Hub Project Pipeline and the European Investment Project Portal seek to match pipelines of deals with investors.

specialists to manage the assets. When properly managed, these assets have relatively little upside or downside from the base case used in the investment thesis.

Exhibit 1: Unlisted infrastructure: Median net IRRs by vintage year

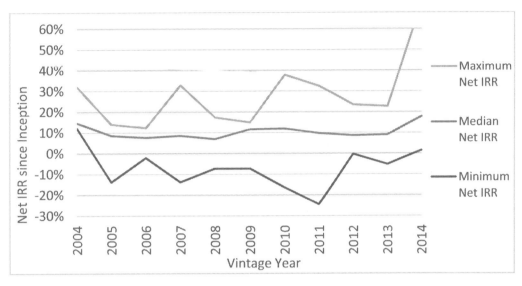

Source: Preqin, Infrastructure Q3 2017

For regulated utilities and natural resources, the general partners structure the vehicle, manage the investment more actively, and package it with other assets, as in private equity. For managers of finite life funds, they must seek an outright exit after a period of a few years. In this case, the investment thesis is to build or enhance the value during the holding period of the asset. However, unlike buyout transactions, infrastructure assets have substantial barriers to entry and often supply essential and monopolistic services, so they tend to be less exposed to the macro economy. Cash flows are more stable and there is a strong yield component. Infrastructure assets also resemble buyouts in that the projects are typically large and gravitate to platform investments such as cellular towers, wind farms, and healthcare facilities.

Infrastructure and natural resources share traits with venture capital in cases where the investment is staggered in stages with a strong dependency on early milestones before further and more significant capital is committed; example includes oil drilling, mining, and permitting renewable energy projects. Another similarity to venture investment is the preference for scalable projects or platforms.

Similarities to real estate were already discussed above, particularly the importance of cash yield. In addition, like in real estate, location is critical in both infrastructure and natural resources projects. Unlike real estate, there are high barriers to entry in infrastructure, which results in a different risk profile due to more stringent regulation but less exposure to valuation cycles.

In terms of fund operation, infrastructure and natural resources funds are largely similar to the other forms of private capital. General partners are responsible for sourcing and screening deal opportunities, as well as executing the transaction directly or by backing portfolio companies that specialize in building or acquiring assets in a particular sector and geography.

SECTORS

Three sectors have seen the most investment in recent years: transportation, energy, and power generation, including renewable power. From 2006 to 2016, power and energy accounted for 82% of the North American market, and 49% of Europe's volume of deal flow.[5] Rounding out the roster of major sectors are social infrastructure and transportation, the latter accounting for one-third of the total volume of deal flow in Europe, Latin America, and Asia Pacific (see Exhibit 2). Although infrastructure investment is ultimately a highly local activity, requiring bottom-up analysis, developing a top-down view of what is happening in the main sectors is an essential part of the process.

Exhibit 2: Deal volume by sector over time and by geography

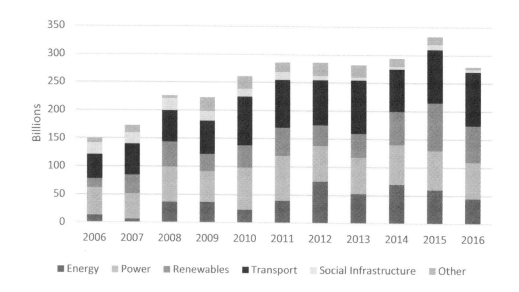

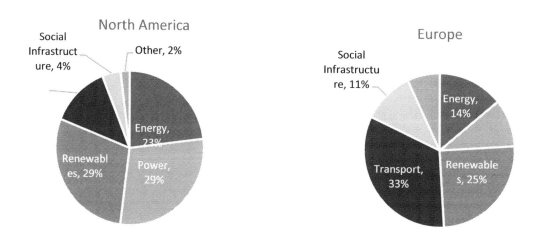

[5] Data from Dealogic as of March 2017, for the years 2006–2016. Excluding project financing in sectors such as mining, oil and gas exploration, and manufacturing.

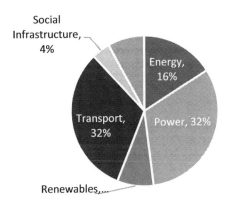

Asia Pacific

- Social Infrastructure, 4%
- Energy, 16%
- Power, 32%
- Transport, 32%
- Renewables,...

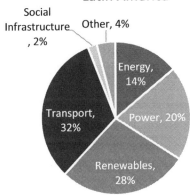

Latin America

- Social Infrastructure, 2%
- Other, 4%
- Energy, 14%
- Power, 20%
- Transport, 32%
- Renewables, 28%

Power generation

This category includes infrastructure for the generation and transmission of electrical power from both conventional and renewable sources. Conventional and renewable power account for 40–50% of total new infrastructure investment, depending on the specific continent.[6] Overall, the split between conventional and renewable sources is roughly equal across the world.

In the United States, deal flow in recent years was coming from the closing of aging coal plants, the growth of renewable power, and the move to natural gas (now abundant thanks to the fracking revolution). It is not just that gas has gotten cheaper; gas plants are also more efficient and flexible for generating electricity. In Europe, the restructuring of the power sector has multiple facets. The EU is seeking to improve energy security by boosting electricity interconnectors between countries. Large utilities are unbundling, selling stable, income-generating assets and recycling their capital into growth opportunities, namely renewables. It has been more difficult to finance gas-fired power plants in Europe, as equity and debt investors are no longer willing to take full merchant risk. As such, new European gas-fired power plants now usually require some form of government financial support to get off the ground.

6 Ibid.

In both North America and Europe, renewable power (mainly wind and solar) enjoys strong government backing. Wind and solar accounted for over 60% of new U.S. power capacity in 2016, followed by 33% from natural gas, according to the US Energy Information Administration. In Europe, the EU has set a renewables target of 20% of total energy consumption by 2020, and proposed a target of 27% by 2030. Concerning the infrastructure fund industry, renewable energy represented 27% of the dollar value of deals closed in Europe and the Americas during 2011–2016, and 56% of the total number of infrastructure deals.[7]

While renewable energy has historically been supported by government subsidies in the form of feed-in-tariffs in Europe or tax credits in the US, the industry is moving towards a subsidy-free future. Governments are moving to renewable energy auctions, which have awarded long-term offtake contracts at or below current wholesale power prices. Some auctions have resulted in zero subsidy bids, notably for solar in Spain and offshore wind in Germany and the Netherlands, meaning that future projects will be completely unsubsidized. This has been made possible through drastic reductions in equipment costs, efficient supply chains and low-cost debt financing. While some projects will operate on a fully merchant basis (taking full risk on wholesale power prices), most projects are looking to sign utility or corporate Power Purchase Agreements (PPAs) with utilities or large industrial players. Contracting part of the power in this way gives investors comfort on the security of the revenue streams, but also introduces a new counterparty risk.

Notably, renewable energy demands new means to negotiate supply and carry power to the grid. For example, wind power growth in Texas requires an additional $12 billion in transmission capital that private investors are funding, attracted by long-term offtake contracts. While the renewable energy sector is now mature, new technologies have the potential to disrupt the power market. This includes battery storage, which has been hailed as the solution to smooth the intermittent output from renewables. As of 2018, the technology costs are still quite high and the revenue streams largely merchant. Battery storage is likely to become a more important part of the market as costs come down further and new contracts and business models are developed to finance this type of infrastructure.

Energy

The energy sector consists of gas pipelines and storage, including upstream and midstream infrastructure, as well as consumer-facing gas distribution networks.

The U.S. shale gas revolution has created considerable need for supporting infrastructure, and while the decline in global energy prices calls for heightened due diligence in evaluating investments, it has done little to change the bigger picture. In Mexico, plans to end the state oil monopoly are drawing interest from private capital. Activity in the EU has been accelerated by efforts to lessen dependence on Russian gas. Separately, there has been a push by countries such as Spain to link its substantial gas infrastructure with that of its neighbors, and also by utility restructuring.

Pipeline construction in the United States has not kept up with the boom in shale gas production. Large "gathering" networks are required to link shale sites and for long-range transport. Moreover, although the country is becoming a gas exporter, many U.S. pipelines were designed to carry gas inland from coastal plants—not outward from the shale production sites in the middle of the country. Since many of the major oil and gas infrastructure investments in the past 30 years were premised on falling domestic production, the

---

[7] Data from Dealogic as of March 2017, for the years 2006–2016. Excluding project financing in sectors such as mining, oil and gas exploration, and manufacturing.

overall need for further infrastructure is huge. A recent forecast of oil and gas infrastructure investment over the upcoming decade by IHS Global estimated cumulative spending of $900 billion, with crude oil and natural gas gathering systems and direct production support facilities accounting for the largest share of the investment, at 60%.

Considering the risk profile, energy assets are exposed to commodity prices, a lower degree of revenue certainty, and a higher degree of construction complexity. Counterparty risk varies from project to project and is a particularly critical consideration given the current climate of low energy prices.

Transportation

This sector includes roads, railways, bridges, and tunnels, often structured as PPPs—as well as seaports and airports. Many OECD countries now have large refurbishment requirements to replace their existing transportation infrastructure built directly after World War II. Meanwhile, emerging markets like China and India are experiencing an enormous demand for appropriate infrastructure for their fast-growing economies. Traditionally, these types of projects have been a public sector initiative, but stretched budgets and pressing needs are changing the equation. A growing portion of the roughly $80 billion invested annually in transportation deals globally is through PPPs.

Europe has a track record of private investment in transportation with many brownfield opportunities through secondary sales and privatizations. Public-private partnerships are less common in North America but some local governments are exploring new partnership structures for airport renovations, light rail projects, and toll road syndications. The will to attract and accommodate private capital varies by region. Some U.S. cities favor municipal bonds for transportation projects because tax incentives for investors make them economical for issuers.

When executing a transportation investment, project structure is key. Facilities with an established or predictable traffic pattern—or where a state or a third party, such as the European Investment Bank, has guaranteed a portion of the debt—can offer investors some protection. Further, contracts with revenue based on asset availability rather than traffic flows are much more attractive as they offer greater certainty of long-term revenue.

Social and healthcare infrastructure

Social and healthcare infrastructure refers to schools, healthcare facilities, waste management, student housing, recreation, prisons, and more.

Around the world, governments and other entities look to private capital to help finance social infrastructure, usually through various types of PPPs. A dearth of government funds was a major driver behind this choice, but so is the belief that non-public financing can increase efficiency and speed to market through risk-shifting to the private sector. Concessions are generally granted by established public entities such as a school board, healthcare provider, or government office, and are usually stand-alone projects. Charges are typically paid by a central authority rather than the end user, and revenues tend to be linked to inflation rather than growth.

As in other infrastructure sectors, Australia has an advanced market, having used PPPs extensively for hospitals, among other assets. Europe also has a tradition of social deals, with a strong pipeline of education and municipal projects on the continent. The United States has much less experience, but that may be changing as PPP markets become more established.

Other types of healthcare facilities include private hospitals, care home operations, laboratories, and companies that provide technical or administrative services to public healthcare systems. In most of these cases, however, investments in such facilities are made by buyout funds. An example is the $33 billion acquisition of HCA (the largest private hospital in the United States) by the consortium of KKR, Bain Capital, and Merrill Lynch. Another case is the Apax and Nordic Capital takeover of Capio, which owns hospitals, specialist clinics, and primary care units in five European countries. The 2013 privatization of U.K. blood plasma supplier Plasma Resources offers yet another example; in that case, an 80% stake was sold by the government to Bain Capital for £230 million.

Other sectors

There are other significant sectors of the economy not outlined above that fall within the category of infrastructure and natural resources. Infrastructure can include communication and broadcasting towers, and privatizations of defense research agencies such as Carlyle's acquisition of the defense contractor Qinetiq from the U.K. government (it has since been listed). Natural resources, in addition to energy, also include agriculture (farmland and marine), timber, and more.

INVESTMENT INSTRUMENTS

The origin of infrastructure investment consisted of a so-called core equity exposure to an operating asset in a well understood and mature market. Structuring has markedly expanded over time with the growing sophistication and experience of the investors.

Today, the structured investment categories range from senior debt through junior debt and a quartet of progressively more appreciation-oriented equity strategies: core, core plus, value-add, and opportunistic (see Exhibit 3). The structured investment strategies cut across sectors and geographies, where each category is characterized by its own economic life cycle, likely financial outcomes, and the specific bundle of risks it presents.

Exhibit 3: Infrastructure strategies and comparative risk and return positioning

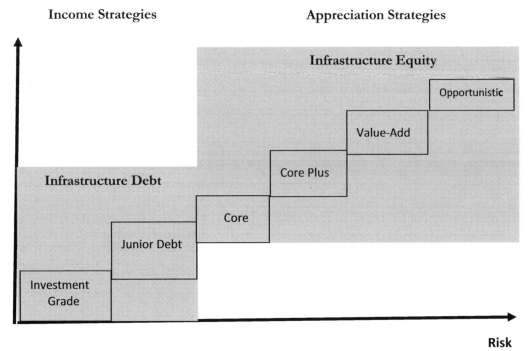

Source: BlackRock.

Consider the case of a toll road. One could invest in the senior debt of an established road, seeking a predictable flow of income. If the road has a long-term government contract and an operating history, it could be a core equity investment. With a contract but no operating history, the investment may be core plus. If the road is in a turnaround situation, it could be a value-add investment. If it is not yet built, in an unfamiliar geography or has an element of merchant risk, it fits the label "opportunistic." Exhibit 4 summarizes the characteristics of the different categories.

Exhibit 4: Infrastructure strategies: Key characteristics

	Investment Grade Debt	Junior Debt	Core	Core Plus	Value-Add	Opportunistic
Current segment return range	3.5 – 6%	5.5 – 12%	5 – 9%	8 – 12%	11 – 15%	15 – 18%
Key risks	Operating assumptions, investment structure	Market risk, operating assumptions, strategy implementation	Operating assumptions, leverage levels, regulatory	Construction	Strategy Implementation	Market risk, political risk and currency risk
Contracted revenue	Yes	In some cases	Yes	Yes	In some cases	In some cases
Already revenue generating?	In some cases	In some cases	Yes	No	In some cases	In some cases
Income or appreciation	Income	Income	Income	Income/ Appreciation	Appreciation	Appreciation
GDP sensitivity	Low	High	Low	Low	High	High
Greenfield or Brownfield	Both	Both	Brownfield	'Dark Green'	Both	Both
Development risk	None	None	None	None	In some cases	In some cases
Return driven by exit	No	No	No	No	Yes	Yes
Operating complexity	Low	Low	Medium	Medium	Medium/High	High

Source: BlackRock.

Infrastructure debt

This category includes senior and junior debt, both investment grade and below, issued by infrastructure entities at fixed, floating, or index-linked rates with maturities ranging from five to 30 years. It offers its holders a private-market premium over comparably rated public credit, and allows a credit diversification. Risk of infrastructure debt, like that of other debt, can be rated or scored with external or internal models. Investment grade debt is generally issued by entities with good revenue security. A 10-year study by Moody's found default rates below 5% for investment grade debt.

Traditionally, an ability to match funding to the long-term profiles of infrastructure projects, together with staff expertise in project finance credit evaluation and skills to make appropriate decisions when a borrower's circumstances change, meant that banks were the first port of call for the financing (including the hedging of interest rate and inflation risk) of many infrastructure projects. For the equity sponsors of infrastructure deals, bank relationships could be leveraged to ensure the maximum flexibility offered by loans—in terms of pre-determined drawdown schedules, pre-payment options, and a simple process for amendments and waivers to the financing terms.

Yet, post-crisis banks face stricter capital and liquidity requirements. Banks loans are in shorter supply and they are less attractive for infrastructure projects due to increasing restrictions in the tenor of the loans they were able to offer. As a result, commercial banks have been forced to scale back lending and investment banks pursue originate-to-distribute deals. European deal flow includes both primary and refinancing issuance in multiple sectors. In the United States, power, energy, and renewables offer debt, with potential new flows from PPPs in the transport and social sectors. While the market is still fairly new, it continues to grow and the competition for investments can be stiff.

Core equity

Core equity refers to equity investments in operating assets with established cash flows and good revenue security from contracts or a regulated position, situated in developed markets. Risks to consider in core equity infrastructure investment include underestimating the operating costs as well as unanticipated future capital expenditure needs (called lifecycle costs). For some PPPs, penalties are payable if minimum availability is not met. Inappropriate leverage and regulatory change can also hamper performance.

As can be seen all across the private equity spectrum, strong capital inflows have pushed valuations up and returns down. Returns in the United Kingdom's regulated water sector have recently been set as low as a 3.75% weighted average cost of capital. Other recent transactions displayed multiples of 20 times EBITDA paid for U.K. airports, and above 25 times EBITDA for Australian toll roads and ports.

Core plus equity

This category includes assets with the same revenue security as core assets, but typically added construction (though not development) risk. When successful, core plus equity migrates over time to the core bucket. Investing in construction has historically offered a return uplift, and with carefully structured investments and the right technical oversight, construction can be well managed. Risks in this category are related to construction schedules, diligence on equipment, contracts, engineering, and early operational matters.

There is a growing appetite in the market for construction assets and associated return premiums. Investors able to fund construction or analyze more complex transactions have an advantage in sourcing deals. Examples include tunnels, light rail and thermal power plants (e.g. gas-fired and biomass).

While complex infrastructure projects with long construction times can still command a premium compared to operational assets, this margin has decreased in recent years. In particular it is slim for some renewable energy assets (namely onshore wind and solar), whose construction risk is perceived to be low and can be managed through EPC wraps.

Value-add equity

Investments in this class of strategies can use a variety of methods to increase the value of an asset, with capital appreciation usually crystallized in an exit. Examples include buy-and-develop, platform roll-ups, turnarounds, and work-outs. Value-add equity fits investors seeking capital appreciation who are comfortable with the risks of managing complex businesses. In the United States, a number of companies are trying to roll up midstream energy assets in a fragmented market. In Europe, investors are seeking to build portfolios of port assets.

Opportunistic or international equity

In developed markets, this category includes assets with development risk or less predictable revenues, such as uncontracted pipelines, service companies, some telecommunications investments or large greenfield projects. In growing or emerging markets, this category includes assets where the investment case relies heavily on growth of the domestic economy.

THE GEOGRAPHICAL VIEW

As mentioned earlier, infrastructure is inherently a local activity. A power or transport investment in Europe may well have different characteristics than one in the same sector in the United States or a developing country. Conditions in the relevant local industries play a role, as does the depth and experience of the local infrastructure financial market. Australia, an infrastructure trailblazer, has much in common with Europe, historically the largest arena for deals; it has less in common with the United States, where so much infrastructure is financed via municipal bonds, or with emerging markets.

Most important, of course, are the local political and regulatory regimes. The choice of region or country can be the single greatest determinant of the viability of an infrastructure investment. But regulatory regimes are evolving, and the geographic dimension of infrastructure investing is changing fast. Governments across the globe see infrastructure investment as a fiscal tool, and are faced with the same question: How can governments, mostly non-OECD markets, attract more private capital to help fund infrastructure development? In an attempt to respond to this question, countries that do not have PPP programs are evaluating them. Many countries have put together ambitious long-term plans to expand and maintain infrastructure.

In fast-growing markets such as Mexico and India, national plans include sweeping reforms intended to encourage international investors in nearly every sector—efforts that may create opportunities to benefit from the fundamental growth of these economies. Yet, not all national plans carry open invitations. In China, the world's biggest infrastructure market, projects are almost exclusively financed domestically.

Selecting desirable geographies for infrastructure investment starts from a country or regional analysis of the domestic policy, regulatory, economic and other forces, in order to identify territories that are on course to boost the flow of potentially attractive deals.

United States

The United States is really two infrastructure markets, with the power and energy sectors drawing deep private funding while there is scope for much more private investment in the transport sector. In 2016, renewables represented over 60% of total new built power generation based on installed capacity.[8] Still, the overall trend was toward a lower energy deal flow, as low oil and gas prices reduced the number of large energy projects reaching a financial close.

U.S. transport need is huge—deferred maintenance has left the U.S. infrastructure in desperate need of repair and renewal. The American Society of Civil Engineers (ASCE) assigned a D+ grade to the national infrastructure and estimates that nearly $4.6 trillion will be required to maintain it. According to the ASCE report card, one in 11 of the country's 600,000+ bridges was considered "structurally deficient." Approximately 20% of U.S. highways were considered to have "poor pavement conditions," and aging delivery systems have led to water main breaks, resulting in 2 trillion gallons of waste water.

Beyond power, energy, and transport, the number of PPPs in 2016 doubled compared to the previous year, including campus housing, broadband, water, waste, courthouses, and street lighting. But the PPP model that could meet the spectrum of infrastructure needs has yet to reach critical mass compared to Canada, although there have been major transactions in the last few years. The bonds issued for the $2 billion I66 toll road were 2-3 times oversubscribed. Many believe that incentivizing private capital is the most feasible path to achieve large-scale infrastructure upgrades. Tax policies, grant programs, and state education are considered as key incentives to facilitate such a solution.[9]

Looking forward, President Trump pledged to stimulate $1 trillion in investment over 10 years with the American Energy and Infrastructure Act. The administration aims to facilitate capital investment in addition to providing government capital and enacting federal legislation (e.g., by forming an infrastructure bank). The increased use of the PPP model will drive private investment across transportation., e.g., in roads and bridges, and into social infrastructure. Infrastructure in the US is primarily driven at the local and state level. While there are federal incentives, initiatives are not usually reliant on federal support.

The new energy policy is to increase supply and potentially lower production costs helped by expanded permitting for offshore drilling, drilling on federal lands, and opening of shale deposits. In the midstream, the new path is for approval of controversial interstate pipelines and related midstream infrastructure. Downstream is expected to benefit from a continued build-up of processing facilities as part of the re-industrialization plans. To boost private sector participation, the new policy aims to expand the definition of assets that can qualify for master limited partnership (MLP) treatment to include renewable power and electric transmission.

Latin America

[8] Data from EIA as of March 2017.
[9] American Investment Council, Private Capital, and Public Good: Revitalizing Infrastructure with Private Capital, May 2017.

About 90% of 2016 deal volume in Latin America was from Brazil, Mexico, Chile, Peru, and Colombia.[10]

The OECD recently described the pace of reform underway in Mexico as "breathtaking." President Peña Nieto has enacted sweeping reforms and introduced an extensive program aimed at increasing infrastructure investment. Major plans were unveiled calling for $590 billion in public and private spending throughout 2018, identifying over 700 specific projects. In 2016, Mexico witnessed a significant volume of activity from the country's highway PPP projects. Ambitious goals were set to increase production of oil and lower electricity prices for companies and consumers, as well as to attract tens of billions of dollars in foreign investment in the energy, power, renewables, and transport sectors. A series of reform plans have been designed to address regulatory weakness and attract private capital. Congress took the first big step with a historic bill to end the monopoly of state-run electricity and oil companies.

Notable trends in other countries include "Chile 2020," a $28 billion program including 25 PPP-based projects. In Colombia, the deal flow has quadrupled in 2016 compared to the previous year. The outlook is further growth in the country with the "4G" program, a road concession program to grow the national highway system by over 400%.

United Kingdom

Historically among the busiest markets, the United Kingdom has been a rich source for core assets, and maintained its leading share of deals in 2016 despite uncertainty surrounding Brexit. On one hand, the road network is at capacity, and 20% of the country's conventional electricity generation is scheduled for retirement in the next five years. The government's remedy to these issues is the National Infrastructure Delivery Plan 2016–2021, which outlines more than £460 billion of planned investment, In the transport sector there is more of a focus on specific upgrades to relieve bottlenecks, rather than greenfield motorways. The infrastructure pipeline is composed of a smaller number of larger schemes such as HS2. On the other hand, there has been weak public and political support for new PPPs in recent years due to the perceived high cost of earlier projects.[11]

Continental Europe

The EU is a diverse set of markets offering investments from gas distribution to transport PPPs to refinancing deals. From an investor point of view, there is intense competition for both greenfield brownfield projects in the north and west which is pushing prices up. With such opportunities dwindling, countries in the south and the east, are gaining appeal.

The EU plans to use infrastructure investment to spur growth, and approved €37 billion in EU funding in 2017 to advance a total of nearly €200 billion in public and private investment. As part of this initiative, the European Fund for Strategic Investments (EFSI) was created to mobilize private financing for infrastructure. The European Investment Advisory Hub was formed to remove sector regulations that hamper investment.

---

[10] Calculated from Dealogic data as of March 2017, for the years 2006–2016. Excluding project financing in sectors such as mining, oil and gas exploration, and manufacturing.

[11] www.gov.uk/government/uploads/system/uploads/attachment_data/file/520086/2904569_nidp_ deliveryplan.pdf

Asia-Pacific

In 2016, Asia-Pacific was the most active infrastructure region both in terms of number of deals and deal flow (43% of global infrastructure deal volume). Nearly 60% of the deal volume in Asia was in the transportation sector, particularly driven by China.[12] A desire for cleaner air in major cities has driven demand for renewable energy capacity, which dominated the number of deals in the region (43% of the total number of deals in Asia). In May 2017, China pledged to spend over $120 billion in support of its large-scale development plan centered on building trade and connectivity infrastructure across Asia, Africa, and Europe. The Belt and Road initiative is an effort to revive the ancient Silk Road that connected the three continents, and will require heavy investments in ports, railways, and roads to boost trade and economic growth.[13]

India, long seen as one of the less mature infrastructure markets, has drawn new interest from international investors because of reforms enacted by Prime Minister Modi, who has an infrastructure investment plan that calls for significant growth in private sector participation. India's 12th Five Year Plan, currently underway, already aims to achieve infrastructure spending of 10% of GDP. To stimulate investment and attract new capital, Prime Minister Modi is changing the way road development contracts are awarded, streamlining land acquisition policies around infrastructure projects, and identifying a pipeline of projects in almost every area of infrastructure (power, energy, renewables, rails, and roads).

In Japan, Prime Minister Shinzo Abe's program of monetary easing, fiscal stimulus, and structural reform—widely known as Abenomics—envisions opening up part of Japan's huge stock of infrastructure to private investment. To date, however, the flow of projects remains on the low side, with Japanese domestic consortia leading the buyer lists for those assets that have come to market. In fact, international investors find greater Japanese competition for the best assets in Asia and the rest of the world following reforms to Japan's Government Pension Investment Fund. The fund, which represents the largest pension investment pool in the world with over $1 trillion in assets, created a 5% allocation to alternative investments in 2014 and, following that, started to making infrastructure investments.

Australia was an early adopter of private capital for infrastructure projects, starting with the privatization of regulated assets in the 1980s and 1990s. A PPP program was launched which delivered projects across a wide range of sectors including social infrastructure and transport. In the last few years, there has been another push for the privatization of large assets driven by federal incentives through bonuses available to return capital in new infrastructure, e.g. energy distribution businesses in New South Wales and major ports in Melbourne, Sydney and Brisbane. Australia also has a booming renewable energy industry driven by exceptional natural resources and the potential for large scale, low cost wind farms and solar parks. There is a reasonable bipartisan support for PPPs in most states, and the long-term outlook for infrastructure investments in Australia is positive, with a strong pipeline of deals in transport, education, health, corrections and renewable energy on the horizon.

---

[12] Data from Dealogic as of March 2017, for the years 2006–2016. Excluding project financing in sectors such as mining, oil and gas exploration, and manufacturing.

[13] Dubbed as the "project of the century," funding includes a commitment of $14.5 billion to China's state-owned investment fund dedicated to the project, and lending schemes worth $55 billion from China's development and export-import bank.

OUTLOOK

The headline numbers in infrastructure are compelling, but no more so than the goals of the institutions investing in it. A 2016 McKinsey report estimates that the world needs to invest about 3.8% of GDP annually until 2030—or an average of $3.3 trillion a year—in economic infrastructure just to support expected rates of growth.[14] Emerging economies account for some 60% of that need. This is a substantial increase over current investment levels of $2.5 trillion per year. The magnitude of the need increases further once one considers the additional investment required to meet the new United Nations Sustainable Development Goals.

In a 2014 report, Standard & Poor's explored how much of this total need institutional investors might supply. Projecting average government infrastructure spending at 3% of GDP, S&P calculated that the global gap between investment needs and available public funds could be around $500 billion per year. Projecting bank lending at $300 billion per year, S&P then put the infrastructure financing need addressable by institutional investors at $200 billion per year.[15] That figure is a significantly larger sum than the $60 billion which all unlisted infrastructure funds raised in 2016. In a survey reported by Preqin in June 2017, 90% of institutional investors plan to increase or maintain their allocation to the infrastructure asset class.[16] In theory, at least, investors targeting higher allocations should be able to achieve them over time.

Investors incorporate infrastructure in their portfolios in several different ways, about 40% use a dedicated infrastructure bucket, though the percentage has fallen in recent years as new investors have come to the asset class. Use of a real assets bucket is becoming more common, while use of a private equity bucket has declined. Questions of sizing and categorizing tie into two other key decisions that investors must make: how many internal resources to add, and what is the best way to get exposure. With respect to the resource question, surveys show that staffing for real assets, including infrastructure, is increasing at many institutions, and the emerging trend is to have a dedicated real assets team (or be planning to create one in the near future).

Other trends include the increasing appetite for co-investments among the limited partners and the rise in direct investing. It remains to be seen how many institutions will find it worthwhile to add the substantial sector-specific and geographic expertise as well as project management capabilities required to make direct investments; there may be only a few dozen institutions actually doing it, with most of them among the world's largest investors (e.g., sovereign wealth funds).

For investors that do not wish to build the teams needed to go direct, closed end equity funds are likely to remain the vehicle of choice. Fund structures have experienced an important evolution in recent years. Prior to the global financial crisis, private-equity style funds—exit-oriented, with relatively high levels of leverage— were the norm. In today's market, there is more attention to matching time horizons, fee structures, and leverage levels to investment objectives, with a clear distinction between buy-to-hold and buy-to-sell investments.

There are current efforts to improve the perspective of stakeholders in infrastructure financing, with a particular focus on encouraging private sector finance for infrastructure projects. A 2017 white paper by the Association for Financial Markets in Europe and the International Capital Market Association outlines

---

[14] McKinsey Global Institute, Bridging the Global Infrastructure Gaps, 2016.

[15] With the more recent McKinsey 2016 estimates, the World Economic Forum refers to a $800 billion gap per year (www.weforum.org/agenda/2016/06/the-world-has-an-800bn-annual-infrastructure-gap-heres-how-to-close-it).

[16] Preqin Investor Outlook: Alternative Assets H1 2017.

initiatives to advance stability, develop standardization practices, and harness expertise in this highly complex field. The paper also discusses charges for infrastructure for Solvency II and Basel III capital requirements.

Finally, one must consider the classification of infrastructure for purposes of Solvency II and Basel III capital requirements. Generally, there are higher capital charges for infrastructure as compared to other asset classes. Advocacy working groups provided evidence to the European Insurance and Occupational Pensions Authority (EIOPA) to assist with the latter's analysis of the identification and analysis of infrastructure investment risk categories. As a result, the European Commission established an infrastructure project asset class for which insurers benefit from reduced capital charges. Ongoing efforts to review the calibration of risk charges for infrastructure corporates are currently being considered by the European Commission in relation to the Solvency II Delegated Regulation.

In his own words: Alan Synnott, MD and Global Head of Product Strategy & Research for Real Assets, BlackRock

Infrastructure investment has emerged as one of the fastest growing alternatives asset classes of the last decade, driven in large part by investor desire for sources of long-term income in the prevailing low-yield environment.

This is an asset class that is in the process of maturing. In the first phase, we have seen strong growth driven by investor demand for positive outcomes such as yield and absolute returns. We are also seeing the growing use of infrastructure investment as a tool for duration and liability matching. However, without a growing supply of new investment opportunities, this fresh capital can create an uneven world of opportunity for investors as demand for appropriate investments can exceed the supply of available deal flow. In the second phase, we are now seeing a move to outcome-based allocation in which investors globally focus on strategy outcomes (e.g., income, growth, balanced, and liquid outcomes). We are also seeing signs of a third phase of maturity, in which the asset class creates its own structure and terms and a more developed conversation about risk develops.

Phase 1: Particularly since the global financial crisis, we have seen an acceleration of allocations to infrastructure investment. Institutional investors have embraced the space and we have seen it grow from $40 billion in assets under management to $400 billion in little more than a decade. This trend looks set to continue in the short term: in BlackRock's annual institutional rebalancing survey, published in January 2017 and covering 200 of the largest global institutional investors, 61% of respondents said they would further increase their allocations to real assets investment in 2017. At the same time, governments across the world are focused on promoting private investment in public infrastructure as both a fiscal stimulant and a way to fill national infrastructure financing gaps; in emerging markets this is viewed as a tool to create the essential building blocks for economic and social growth, and in developed Markets private capital can play a role in sustaining and maintaining critical national infrastructure.

Phase 2: We are seeing a growing realization that the infrastructure investment opportunity is neither static nor homogenous. Infrastructure investments are generally long term in nature and investors need to have a view of key long-term trends such as the impact of technology, the importance of sustainability, the demographic implications of an increasingly urban world, and the prominent role of governments and policymakers. At the same time, the short-term investment opportunity can move quickly. Distinct markets can operate in unique cycles with some sectors offering differing degrees of demand for and supply of investment capital; this can manifest in changing returns and is perhaps best illustrated by the high growth of renewable power infrastructure, which has moved from the fringes of the infrastructure investment universe into the mainstream, driven by technology-led advancements that have dramatically reduced the cost-competitiveness of wind and solar power. Renewables infrastructure initially offered investors the potential for excess return when compared to other sectors, principally driven by high rates of government tariffs and support, leading to investment decisions that become focused on counterparty credit rather than project fundamentals. With the rapid pace of technological development, we are now seeing renewable power projects that can compete on cost with other forms of power generation, and in some markets, compete free of support; this means that your investment underwriting becomes less about credit quality and instead requires deeper and more specific asset class knowledge. In addition, as investor comfort with the sector matures, we are seeing assets that now trade at comparable, and sometimes lower, multiples to those in other sectors.

Phase 3: In the face of increased competition for investment deal flow and a varied global investment opportunity, we have seen the asset class respond with relatively substantial innovation in a short period of time. We have seen the emergence of long-term buy & hold structures which seek to invest on an unlevered basis and provide certain investors with long-term income streams that are often inflation linked. We have seen rapid changes in terms and fees to reflect the underlying management styles in respective funds, and also the emergence of new approaches to the asset class such as the growth in infrastructure debt funds or a variety of approaches develop more liquid strategies. Perhaps most interesting is the developing language around risk in infrastructure investing and investor desires for increased transparency about the risks they take in order to achieve the returns they seek.

INDEX

www.privatecapitalbook.com

Private Capital
Volume I: Funds
Copyright © 2020 by Eli Talmor and Florin Vasvari
Edited by Kontent360
Printed in the United Kingdom

ISBN 978-1-9162110-4-9

Printed in Great Britain
by Amazon